WileyPLUS

W9-BKT-300

WileyPLUS is a research-based online environment for effective teaching and learning.

WileyPLUS builds students' confidence because it takes the guesswork out of studying by providing students with a clear roadmap:

- what to do
- how to do it
- if they did it right

It offers interactive resources along with a complete digital textbook that help students learn more. With *WileyPLUS*, students take more initiative so you'll have greater impact on their achievement in the classroom and beyond.

Now available for

Bb

Blackboard

WileyPLUS

ALL THE HELP, **RESOURCES,** AND PERSONAL **SUPPORT** YOU AND YOUR STUDENTS NEED!
www.wileyplus.com/resources

1st DAY OF CLASS ...AND BEYOND!

2-Minute Tutorials and all of the resources you and your students need to get started

WileyPLUS
Student Partner Program

Student support from an experienced student user

Wiley Faculty Network

Collaborate with your colleagues, find a mentor, attend virtual and live events, and view resources
www.WhereFacultyConnect.com

WileyPLUS
Quick Start

Pre-loaded, ready-to-use assignments and presentations created by subject matter experts

Technical Support 24/7
FAQs, online chat, and phone support
www.wileyplus.com/support

© Courtney Keating/ iStockphoto

Your *WileyPLUS* Account Manager, providing personal training and support

Introduction to Information Systems

Supporting and Transforming Business

Fifth Edition

R. Kelly Rainer Jr.
Brad Prince
Casey Cegielski

With contributions by
Alina M. Chircu, Bentley University
Marco Marabelli, Bentley University

WILEY

Vice President & Executive Publisher	Don Fowley
Executive Editor	Beth Lang Golub
Senior Content Manager	Kevin Holm
Senior Marketing Manager	Margaret Barrett
Design Director	Harry Nolan
Senior Designer	Maureen Eide
Senior Photo Editor	Lisa Gee
Editorial Program Assistant	Katherine Willis
Senior Content Editor	Wendy Ashenberg
Senior Product Designer	Jennifer Welter
Editorial Operations Manager	Melissa Edwards
Production Editor	Tim Lindner
Production Management Services	Thomson Digital
Front Cover Image	A-Digit/Getty Images
Icons	Chad Zuber/Shutterstock, VladimirCetinski/iStockphoto, iQoncept/Shutterstock, William Schultz/iStockphoto, ©chudo-yudo/Shutterstock, ©Constantine Pankin/Shutterstock, ©urfin/Shutterstock

This book was set in 9.5/11.5 Electra LT Std by Thomson Digital, and printed and bound by RR Donnelley. The cover was printed by RR Donnelley. This book is printed on acid free paper.

Founded in 1807, John Wiley & Sons, Inc. has been a valued source of knowledge and understanding for more than 200 years, helping people around the world meet their needs and fulfill their aspirations. Our company is built on a foundation of principles that include responsibility to the communities we serve and where we live and work. In 2008, we launched a Corporate Citizenship Initiative, a global effort to address the environmental, social, economic, and ethical challenges we face in our business. Among the issues we are addressing are carbon impact, paper specifications and procurement, ethical conduct within our business and among our vendors, and community and charitable support. For more information, please visit our website: *www.wiley.com/go/citizenship*.

ISBN   978-1-118-67436-9 (Main Book)
ISBN   978-1-118-77964-4 (Binder-Ready Version)

Preface

What Do Information Systems Have to Do with Business?

This edition of Rainer, Prince, and Cegielski's *Introduction to Information Systems* will answer this question for you. In every chapter, you will see how real global businesses use technology and information systems to increase their profitability, gain market share, improve their customer service, and manage their daily operations. In other words, you will learn how information systems provide the foundation for modern business enterprises.

Our goal is to teach all business majors, especially undergraduates, how to use IT to master their current or future jobs and to help ensure the success of their organization. Our focus is not on merely *learning* the concepts of information technology but rather on *applying* those concepts to perform business processes more effi ciently and effectively. We concentrate on placing information systems in the context of business, so that you will more readily grasp the concepts presented in the text.

The theme of this book, *What's in IT for Me?*, is a question asked by most students who take this course. Our book will show you that IT is the backbone of any business, whether you're majoring in Accounting, Finance, Marketing, Human Resources, Operations Management, or MIS.

New to This Edition

The fifth edition contains many exciting additions and changes. These elements make the text more interesting and readable for students of all majors, while still providing the most current information possible in the rapidly changing field of information systems.

Overall

- A new chapter on Social Computing (Chapter 9).
- A new Technology Guide on Cloud Computing (Technology Guide 3).
- A new section on Big Data in Chapter 5 (Data and Knowledge Management).
- A new section on Enterprise Resource Planning in Chapter 10 (Information Systems Within Organizations.)
- An expanded section on Business Processes in Chapter 2 (Organizational Strategy, Competitive Advantage, and Information Systems).

- All new or updated chapter-opening and closing cases.
- All new or updated *IT's About Business* boxes in every chapter.
- New "Internship Activities" replace the Ruby's Club activities from previous editions. Students act as interns to solve problems by applying decision-making skills to the chapter content.

Specifically

- Chapter 2
  - Chapter 2, Section 2.1, contains an expanded, rewritten discussion on Business Processes, focusing on cross-functional business processes.
  - Chapter 2, Section 2.2, contains an expanded, rewritten discussion on Business Process Reengineering, Business Process Improvement, and Business Process Management.
- Chapter 10
  - Chapter 10 has a completely rewritten, expanded section on Enterprise Resource Planning systems (Section 10.3).
  - Chapter 10 has a new section on Enterprise Resource Planning systems support for business processes (Section 10.4).

Key Features

We have been guided by the following goals that we believe will enhance the teaching and learning experience.

"What's in IT for Me?" theme

- We show why IT is important by calling attention in each chapter to how that chapter's IT topic relates to students in each major.
  - A new feature of this edition is chapter-opening "teasers" that list specific tasks for each major that the chapter will help prepare students to do.
  - Throughout each chapter, icons guide the reader to relevant issues for their specific functional area—Accounting (ACC), Finance (FIN), Marketing (MKT), Operations Management (POM), Management Information Systems (MIS), and Human Resources Management (HRM).
  - Every chapter concludes with a summary of how the concepts relate to each functional area ("What's in IT for Me?").

Active Learning

We recognize the need to actively involve students in problem solving, creative thinking, and capitalizing on opportunities. Therefore, we have included in every chapter a variety of hands-on exercises, activities, and mini-cases, including exercises that require students to use software application tools. Through these activities and an interactive Web site, we enable students to apply the concepts they learn.

Diversified and Unique Examples from Different Industries

Extensive use of vivid examples from large corporations, small businesses, and government and not-for-profit organizations helps to enliven concepts by demonstrating the capabilities of IT, its cost and justification, and innovative ways in which real corporations are using IT in their operations. Each chapter constantly highlights the integral connection between IT and business. This is especially evident in the "IT's About Business" boxes and a new "IT's about *Small* Business" box in each chapter.

Misuse of IS

Like other textbooks, this text presents many examples of IS success. But we also provide numerous examples of IS failures, in the context of lessons that can be learned from such failures. Misuse of IS can be very expensive, as we illustrate.

Innovation and Creativity

In today's rapidly changing environment, creativity and innovation are essential for a business to operate effectively and profitably. Throughout the text we demonstrate how IT facilitates these concepts.

Global Focus

Because an understanding of global competition, partnerships, and trading is essential to success in business, we provide a broad selection of international cases and examples. We discuss how IT facilitates export and import, the management of multinational companies, and electronic trading around the globe. These global examples are highlighted with the global icon.

Focus on Ethics

With corporate scandals appearing daily in the news, ethics and ethical questions have come to the forefront of business people's minds. In addition to a chapter that concentrates on ethics and privacy (Chapter 3), we have included examples and cases that focus on business ethics throughout the chapters. These examples are highlighted with the ethics icon.

Pedagogical Structure

Other pedagogical features provide a structured learning system that reinforces the concepts through features such as chapter-opening organizers, section reviews, frequent applications, and hands-on exercises and activities.

Chapter-opening organizers include the following pedagogical features:

- The *Learning Objectives* provide an overview of the key concepts students should come away with after reading the chapter.
- *Web Resources* highlight ancillary materials available on the book companion site and within *WileyPLUS* for both instructors and students.
- The *Chapter Outline* lists the major chapter headings.
- An opening *case* identifies a business problem faced by an actual company, describes the IT solution applied to the business problem, presents the results of the IT solution, and summarizes what students can learn from the case.
- New "What's in IT for Me?" "teasers" give students a quick hint about skills in their majors for which this chapter will help prepare them.

Study aids are provided throughout each chapter. These include the following:

- *IT's About Business* cases provide real-world applications, with questions that relate to concepts covered in the text. Icons relate these sections to the specific functional areas.
- New *IT's About Small Business* cases show examples of small businesses to which students may relate more closely than to large corporations.
- Highlighted *Examples* interspersed throughout the text illustrate the use (and misuse) of IT by real-world organizations, thus making the conceptual discussion more concrete.
- *Tables* list key points or summarize different concepts.
- End-of-section reviews (*Before You Go On . . .*) prompt students to pause and test their understanding of basic concepts before moving on to the next section.

End-of-chapter study aids provide extensive opportunity for the reader to review and actually "do something" with the concepts they have just studied:

- *What's in IT for Me?* is a unique chapter summary section that demonstrates the relevance of topics for different functional areas (accounting, finance, marketing, production/operations management, and human resources management).
- The *Chapter Summary*, keyed to learning objectives listed at the beginning of the chapter, enables students to review the major concepts covered in the chapter.
- The end-of-chapter *Glossary* facilitates studying by listing and defining all of the key terms introduced in the chapter.
- *Discussion Questions, Problem-Solving Activities*, and *Team Assignments* provide practice through active learning. These exercises are hands-on opportunities to use the concepts discussed in the chapter.
- A *Case* presents a brief case study organized around a business problem and explains how IT helped to solve it. Questions at the end of the case relate it to concepts discussed in the chapter.
- "Internship Activities" present problems found in four recurring businesses (in the areas of healthcare, banking, manufacturing, and retail.) Students are asked to act as interns to solve the problems by applying decision-making skills to the chapter content.

Online Resources

www.wiley.com/college/rainer

This text also facilitates the teaching of an introductory IS course by providing extensive support materials for instructors and students. Go to *www.wiley.com/college/rainer* to access the Student and Instructor Web Sites.

Instructor's Manual

The *Instructor's Manual*, created by Bob Gehling of Auburn University at Montgomery, includes a chapter overview, teaching tips and strategies, answers to all end-of-chapter questions, supplemental mini-cases with essay questions and answers, and experiential exercises that relate to particular topics.

Test Bank

The *Test Bank*, written by Aditi Mukherjee of University of Florida is a comprehensive resource for test questions. It contains multiple-choice, true/false, short answer, and essay questions for each chapter. The multiple-choice and true/false questions are labeled according to difficulty: easy, medium, or hard. New to this edition are "Apply the Concept" questions that require the students to use critical thinking to solve a problem.

The test bank is available for use in Respondus' easy-to-use software. Respondus is a powerful tool for creating and managing exams that can be printed to paper or published directly to Blackboard, WebCT, Desire2Learn, eCollege, ANGEL, and other eLearning systems. For more information on Respondus and the Respondus Test Bank Network, please visit *www.respondus.com*.

PowerPoint Presentations

The *PowerPoint Presentations* created by Ken Corley of Appalachian State University consist of a series of slides for each chapter of the text that are designed around the text content, incorporating key points from the text and all text illustrations as appropriate.

Wiley Information Systems Hub

http://wileyiscommunity.ning.com/

This is a new online, interactive community designed to support the teaching of the Intro IS course. The Hub will allow IS faculty to explore a centralized and constantly updated set of current articles for use in class, connect with IS colleagues for help and advice about upcoming course topics, and share course materials with other IS faculty. The Community Manager is David Firth of University of Montana

Weekly Updates

Weekly updates, harvested from around the web by David Firth of the University of Montana, provide you with the latest IT news and issues. These are posted every Monday morning throughout the year at *http://wileyinformationsystemsupdates.com/* and include links to articles and videos as well as discussion questions to assign or use in class.

Image Library

All textbook figures are available for download from the Web site. These figures can easily be added to PowerPoint presentations.

OfficeGrader

OfficeGrader™ is an Access-based VBA macro that enables automatic grading of Office assignments. The macros compare Office files and grade them against a master file. OfficeGrader™ is available for Word, Access, Excel, and PowerPoint for Office 2010 and Office 2013. For more information, contact your Wiley sales representative or visit www.wiley.com/college/microsoft and click on "OfficeGrader."

WileyPLUS

This online teaching and learning environment integrates the **entire digital textbook** with the most effective instructor and student resources to fit every learning style.

With *WileyPLUS*:

- Students achieve concept mastery in a rich, structured environment that's available 24/7.
- Instructors personalize and manage their course more effectively with assessment, assignments, grade tracking, and more.

WileyPLUS can complement the textbook or replace the printed textbook altogether for about half the price of a new textbook.

For Students

Different learning styles, different levels of proficiency, different levels of preparation—each of your students is unique. *WileyPLUS* empowers them to take advantage of their individual strengths.

- **Integrated, multi-media resources** provide multiple study-paths to fit each student's learning preferences and encourage more active learning. Resources include:
  - Author podcasts, several for each chapter, to use for review,
  - Manager Videos,
  - Internship Activities,
  - Student lecture slides (PowerPoint) for note-taking,
  - Microsoft Office lab manual
- *WileyPLUS* includes **many opportunities for self-assessment** linked to the relevant portions of the text. Students can take control of their own learning and practice until they master the material. Resources include:
  - Automatically-graded practice questions from the Test Bank
  - Pre- and post-lecture quizzes,
  - Vocabulary flash cards and quizzes

For Instructors:

WileyPLUS empowers you with the tools and resources you need to make your teaching even more effective.

- You can customize your classroom presentation with a wealth of resources and functionality. You can even add your own materials to your *WileyPLUS* course. Resources include:
  - PowerPoint presentations
  - Completely revised Testbank with a wide range of levels and new "Apply the Concepts" questions.
- With *WileyPLUS* you can identify those students who are falling behind and intervene accordingly, without having to wait for them to come to office hours.
- *WileyPLUS* simplifies and automates such tasks as student performance assessment, making assignments, scoring student work, keeping grades, and more.

For more information on *WileyPLUS* or for a demo, contact your Wiley sales representative or visit *www.wileyplus.com*.

Wiley Flex

Wiley provides a wide variety of printed and electronic formats that provide many choices to your students at a range of price points. Contact your Wiley sales representative for more details on any of the below.

Wiley E-Textbook

E-Textbooks are complete digital versions of the text that help students study more efficiently as they:

- Access content online and offline on your desktop, laptop and mobile device
- Search across the entire book content
- Take notes and highlight
- Copy and paste or print key sections

Wiley E-Text: Powered by VitalSource and CourseSmart (available for all titles) Ask your sales representative about other available formats.

Wiley Binder Version

A three-hole punched, loose-leaf format allows students to:

- Carry only the content they need
- Insert class notes and hand-outs
- Keep all your materials in one place

Wiley Custom

This group's services allow you to:

- Adapt existing Wiley content and combine texts
- Incorporate and publish your own materials
- Collaborate with our team to ensure your satisfaction

Wiley Custom Select

Wiley Custom Select allows you to build your own course materials using selected chapters of any Wiley text and your own material if desired. For more information, contact your Wiley sales representative or visit http://customselect.wiley.com/.

Acknowledgments

Creating, developing, and producing a text for an introduction to information technology course is a formidable undertaking. Along the way, we were fortunate to receive continuous evaluation, criticism, and direction from many colleagues who regularly teach this course. We would like to acknowledge the contributions made by the following individuals.

We would like thank the Wiley team: Beth Lang Golub, Executive Editor; Wendy Ashenberg, Senior Content Editor; Jennifer Welter, Senior Product Designer, Margaret Barrett, Senior Marketing Manager; and Katherine Willis, Editorial Program Assistant. We also thank the production team, including Kevin Holm, Senior Content Manager; Tim Lindner, Production Editor; and Namit Grover of Thomson Digital. And thanks to Harry Nolan, Design Director; Maureen Eide, Senior Designer; and Lisa Gee, Senior Photo Editor. We also would like to thank Robert Weiss for his skillful and thorough editing of the manuscript.

We also acknowledge and appreciate Bob Gehling, Aditi Mukherjee, and Ken Corley for their work on the supplements, and David Firth for his work on the Weekly Updates and the new Faculty Hub. Many thanks also to Alina M. Chircu and Marco Marabelli of Bentley University for developing new material that enhances our coverage of business processes and ERP. Finally, we thank all the faculty listed below who have generously shared their varied opinions by reviewing the manuscript and/or completing our user surveys.

KELLY RAINER
BRAD PRINCE
CASEY CEGIELSKI

Reviewers

Gaya P. Agrawal, *Rutgers University*
Ihssan Alkadi, *South Louisiana Community College*
Mary Baldwin-Grimes, *Gateway Technical College*
Mary Barnard, *IUPUI*
Nicholas Barnes, *Nichols College*
Lisa Reeves Bertin, *Penn State University Shenango Campus*
Mark Best, *The University of Kansas*
Neelima Bhatnagar, *University of Pittsburgh at Johnson*
Dan Brandon, *Christian Brothers University*
Fredrick Bsharah, *Cape Cod Community College*
Jessie Brown, *Macquarie City Campus*
Patrick Browning, *The University of Southern Mississippi*
Trini Callava, *University of Miami*
Pam Carter, *North Carolina A&T State University*
Antoinette Cevenini, *Macquarie City Campus*
Lewis Chasalow, *The University of Findlay*
H. Michael Chung, *California State University Long Beach*
Ken Corley, *Appalachian State University*
Jose Cruz, *University of Puerto Rico - Mayaguez*
Barry Cumbie, *University of Southern Mississippi*
Subhasish Dasgupta, *George Washington University*
Lauren Eder, *Rider University*
Greg Foudray, *Salem State University*
Bob Gehling, *Auburn University Montgomery*
Cody Gray, *Portland Community College*
Eileen Griffin, *Canisius College*
Heather Griffo, *Portland Community College*
Joseph Harder, *Indiana State University*
Jeff Harper, *Indiana State University*
Jim Howatt, *Luther College*

Chang-tseh Hsieh, *University of Southern Mississippi*
Scott Hunsinger, *Appalachian State University*
Micki Hyde, *Indiana University of Pennsylvania*
Jinman Kim, *University of Sydney*
Richard Klein, *Florida International University*
Dana Ladd, *University of Findlay*
Faith Lamprey, *Rhode Island College*
Christine Lazaro, *Gateway Technical College*
Mark Lewis, *Alfred University*
Susan Li, *Adelphi University*
Thomas Long, *DePaul University*
James Scott Magruder, *The University of Southern Mississippi*
Kalana Malimage, *Mississippi State University*
Efrem Mallach, *Rhode Island College*
Steven Mandelbaum, *George Washington University*
Nichelle Manuel, *IADT*
Stanley Marcinczyk, *Central Connecticut State University*
Robert Marmelstein, *East Stroudsburg University*
Tom Mattson, *University of Hawaii*
Lee McClain, *Western Washington University*
Rodger Morrison, *Troy University*
Mahdi Nasereddin, *Penn State University*
Bill Neumann, *University of Arizona*
Cynthia Nitsch, *University of San Diego*
Anthony Offor, *Sanford-Brown College*
Jim Ott, *Fontbonne University*
Neal Parker, *Appalachian State University*
Sheila Pearson, *Southern Arkansas University*
Jennifer Percival, *University of Ontario Institute of Technology*
Olga Petkova, *Central Connecticut State University*

Brief Contents

Contents

Chapter 1

Introduction to Information Systems

[LEARNING OBJECTIVES]

1. Identify the reasons why being an informed user of information systems is important in today's world.

2. Describe the various types of computer-based information systems in an organization.

3. Discuss ways in which information technology can affect managers and nonmanagerial workers.

4. Identify positive and negative societal effects of the increased use of information technology.

[CHAPTER OUTLINE]

1.1 Why Should I Study Information Systems?

1.2 Overview of Computer-Based Information Systems

1.3 How Does IT Impact Organizations?

1.4 Importance of Information Systems to Society

[WEB RESOURCES]

- Student PowerPoints for note taking

WileyPLUS

- E-book
- Author video lecture for each chapter section
- Practice quizzes
- Flash Cards for vocabulary review
- Additional "IT's About Business" cases
- Video interviews with managers
- Lab Manuals for Microsoft Office 2010 and 2013

What's In IT For Me?

This Chapter Will Help Prepare You To...

ACCT	FIN	MKT	POM	HRM	MIS
ACCOUNTING	FINANCE	MARKETING	PRODUCTION OPERATIONS MANAGEMENT	HUMAN RESOURCES MANAGEMENT	MIS
Forecast revenues	Determine best sources for funds	Develop new goods and services	Process customer orders	Hire new employees	Directly support all functional areas

The Business Problem

S ixty years into the computer revolution, 40 years into the age of the microprocessor, and 20 years into the rise of the modern Internet, all of the technology required to transform industries through software has been developed and integrated and can be delivered globally. Billions of people now access the Internet via broadband connections. Worldwide, more than 5 billion people use cell phones. Of those users, 1 billion have smartphones that provide them with instant access to the Internet at all times from multiple locations.

In addition, software programming tools and Internet-based services allow companies in many industries to launch new software-powered startups without investing in new infrastructure or training new employees. For example, in 2000, operating a basic Internet application cost businesses approximately $150,000 per month. Today, operating that same application in Amazon's cloud (we discuss cloud computing in detail in Technology Guide 3) costs about $1,000 per month.

In essence, software is disrupting every industry, and every organization must prepare for this disruption. Numerous companies have attempted to meet the disruption challenge: Some have succeeded and some have failed.

Software Disruptions

Let's look at examples of software disruption across several industries. Many of these examples focus on two scenarios: (1) industries where software disrupted the previous market-leading companies and (2) industries where a new company (or companies) used software to achieve a competitive advantage.

- *The book industry*: A dramatic example of software disruption is the fate of Borders bookstore. In 2001, Borders agreed to hand over its online business to Amazon because the bookstore was convinced that online book sales were nonstrategic and unimportant. Ten years later, Borders filed for bankruptcy. That same year, the www.borders.com Web site was replaced with a redirect link to the Barnes & Noble Web site (www.bn.com).

[Today, Every Company Is a Technology Company]

Then, in January 2012, Barnes & Noble warned analysts that it would lose twice as much money in 2012 as it had previously predicted. On April 30, 2012, the bookstore entered into a partnership with Microsoft that will spin off the Nook and college businesses into a subsidiary.

Today, the world's largest bookseller, Amazon, is a software company. Its core capability is its software engine, which can sell virtually anything online without building or maintaining any retail stores. Amazon has even reorganized its Web site to promote its Kindle digital books over physical books. (In August 2012, Amazon announced that it sold more electronic books than hardback books and paperback books combined.) Now, even the books themselves are software products.

- *The music industry*: As with publishing, today's dominant music companies are software companies: Apple's iTunes (www.apple.com/itunes), Spotify (www.spotify.com), and Pandora (www.pandora.com). Traditional record labels now exist largely to provide those software companies with content. In mid-2013, the Recording Industry Association of America (RIAA) continues to fight battles over copyright infringement and the illegal download and sharing of digital music files.

- *The video industry*: Blockbuster—which rented and sold videos and ancillary products through its chain of stores—was the industry leader until it was disrupted by a software company, Netflix (www.netflix.com). In mid-2013, Netflix has the largest subscriber base of any video service with some 33 million subscribers. Meanwhile, Blockbuster declared bankruptcy in February 2011 and was acquired by satellite television provider Dish Networks in March 2011.

- *The software industry*: Incumbent software companies such as Oracle and Microsoft are increasingly threatened by software-as-a-service products (e.g., Salesforce.com) and Android, an open-source operating system developed by the Open Handset Alliance (www.openhandsetalliance.com). (We discuss operating systems in Technology Guide 2 and software-as-a-service in Technology Guide 3.)

- *The videogame industry*: Today, the fastest-growing entertainment companies are videogame makers—again, software. Examples are

   ○ Zynga (www.zynga.com), which makes FarmVille, delivers its games entirely online.

   ○ Rovio (www.rovio.com), the maker of Angry Birds, made almost $195 million in 2012. The company was nearly bankrupt when it launched Angry Birds on the iPhone in late 2009.

   ○ Minecraft (www.minecraft.net), another video game delivered exclusively over the Internet, was first released in 2009. By January 2013, more than 20 million people had downloaded it. Interestingly, the creator of Minecraft, Markus Persson, has never spent any money to market his game. Instead, sales resulted entirely from word of mouth.

- *The photography industry*: This industry was disrupted by software years ago. Today it is virtually impossible to buy a mobile phone that does not include a software-powered camera. In addition, people can upload photos automatically to the Internet for permanent archiving and global sharing. The leading photography companies include Shutterfly (www.shutterfly.com), Snapfish (www.snapfish.com), Flickr (www.flickr.com), and Instagram (www.instagram.com). Meanwhile, the long-time market leader, Kodak—whose name was almost synonymous with cameras—declared bankruptcy in January 2012.

   ○ Each day people upload more than 350 million digital photos just to Facebook. Snapchat (www.snapchat.com) is a smartphone app that enables users to send a photo (or video) to someone and have it "self-destruct" within seconds. Snapchat users are now sharing more than 100 million "snaps" daily.

- *The marketing industry*: Today's largest direct marketing companies include Facebook (www.facebook.com), Google (www.google.com), Groupon (www.groupon.com), Living Social (www.livingsocial.com), and Foursquare (www.foursquare.com). All of these companies are using software to disrupt the retail marketing industry.

- *The recruiting industry*: LinkedIn (www.linkedin.com) is a fast-growing company that is disrupting the traditional job recruiting industry. For the first time, employees and job searchers can maintain their own resumes on LinkedIn for recruiters to search in real time.

- *The financial services industry*: Software has transformed the financial services industry. Practically every financial transaction is now performed by software. Also, many of the leading innovators in financial services are software companies. For example, Square (https://squareup.com) allows anyone to accept credit card payments with a mobile phone.

- *Fundraising*: In early 2013, Joel Silver and Rob Thomas, the producers of *Veronica Mars*, a feature film, used Kickstarter (www.kickstarter.com) to raise money to produce the film. They achieved their goal of $2 million in just 10 hours. Kickstarter takes a 5 percent cut of every transaction.

- *Genomics*: Illumina (www.illumina.com) has reduced the cost of sequencing a human genome from more $1 million in 2007 to $4,000 in 2013. Illumina's technology has helped medical researchers develop cancer drugs that target specific genetic mutations that can cause cancer.

- *The motion picture industry*: Making feature-length computer-generated films has become incredibly IT intensive. Studios require state-of-the-art information technologies, including massive numbers of servers (described in Technology Guide 1), sophisticated software (described in Technology Guide 2), and an enormous amount of storage (described in Technology Guide 1).

  Consider DreamWorks Animation (www.dreamworksanimation.com), a motion picture studio that creates animated feature films, television programs, and online virtual worlds. The studio has released 26 feature films, including the franchises of *Shrek*, *Madagascar*, *Kung Fu Panda*, and *How to Train Your Dragon*. By late 2012, its feature films had grossed more than $10 billion globally.

  For a single motion picture such as *The Croods*, the studio manages more than 500,000 files and 300 terabytes (a terabyte is 1 trillion bytes) of data, and it uses about 80 million central processing unit (CPU; described in Technology Guide 1) hours. As DreamWorks executives state, "In reality, our product is data that looks like a movie. We are a digital manufacturing company."

Software is also disrupting industries that operate primarily in the physical world. Consider the following examples:

- *The automobile industry*: In modern cars, software is responsible for running the engines, controlling safety features, entertaining passengers, guiding drivers to their destinations, and connecting the car to mobile, satellite, and GPS networks. Other software functions in modern cars include Wi-Fi receivers, which turn your car into a mobile hot spot; software, which helps maximize fuel efficiency; and ultrasonic sensors, which enable some models to parallel-park automatically.

  The next step is to network all vehicles together, a necessary step toward driverless cars. The creation of software-powered driverless cars is already being undertaken at Google as well as several major car companies.

- *The logistics industry*: Today's leading real-world retailer, Walmart, uses software to power its logistics and distribution capabilities. This technology has enabled Walmart to become dominant in its industry.

- *The postal industry*: FedEx, which early in its history adopted the view that "the information about the package is as important as the package itself," now employs hundreds of developers who build and deploy software products for 350,000 customer sites to help customers with their mailing and shipping needs.

- *The oil and gas industry*: Companies in this industry were early innovators in supercomputing and data visualization and analysis, which are critically important to oil and gas exploration efforts.

- *The agriculture industry*: Agriculture is increasingly powered by software, including satellite analysis of soils linked to per-acre seed selection software algorithms. In addition, precision agriculture makes use of automated, driverless tractors controlled by global positioning systems and software.

- *National defense*: Even national defense is increasingly software based. The modern combat soldier is embedded in a web of software that provides intelligence, communications, logistics, and weapons guidance. Software-powered drone aircraft launch airstrikes without placing human pilots at risk. (We discuss drone technology later in the chapter.) Intelligence agencies perform large-scale data mining with software to uncover and track potential terrorist plots.

- *The retail industry*: Women have long "borrowed" special-occasion dresses from department stores, buying them and then returning them after one night wearing them. Now, Rent the Runway (www.renttherunway.com) has redefined the fashion business, making expensive clothing available to more women than ever before. The firm is also disrupting traditional physical retailers. After all, why buy a dress when you can rent one for a very low price? Some department stores feel so threatened by Rent the Runway that they have reportedly told vendors that they will pull floor merchandise if it ever shows up on that company's Web site.

  Rent the Runway employs 200 people, including one of the nation's largest dry-cleaning operations. Their Web site has more than 3 million members, and it features 35,000 dresses and 7,000 accessories created by 170 designers.

- *Education*: College graduates owe approximately $1 trillion in student debt, a crippling burden for many recent graduates. UniversityNow (www.unow.com) was founded to make college more accessible to working adults by offering online, self-paced degrees. Two key characteristics distinguish UniversityNow from an increasing number of rivals: (1) very low fees (as little as $2,600, which includes tuition and books for as many courses students can complete in one year) and (2) fully accredited degrees, from an associate's degree to an M.B.A.

- *The legal profession*: Today, electronic discovery (e-discovery) software applications can analyze documents in a fraction of the time that human lawyers would take, at a fraction of the cost. For example, Blackstone Discovery (www.blackstonediscovery.com) helped one company analyze 1.5 million documents for less than $100,000. That company estimated that the process would have cost $1.5 million if performed by lawyers.

  E-discovery applications go beyond simply finding documents rapidly using relevant terms. They can also extract relevant concepts, even in the absence of specific terms, and they can deduce peoples' patterns of behavior that would have eluded lawyers examining millions of documents. These applications can also analyze documents for information pertaining to the activities and interactions of people—who did what and when, and who talked to whom.

The Results

Clearly, then, an increasing number of major businesses and industries are being run on software and delivered as online services—from motion pictures to agriculture to national defense. Regardless of the industry, companies face constant competitive threats from both established rivals and entrepreneurial technology companies that are developing disruptive software. These threats will force companies to become more agile and to respond to competitive threats more quickly, efficiently, and effectively.

Sources: Compiled from C. Howard, M. Noer, and T. Post, "Disruptors," *Forbes*, April 15, 2013; S. Mendelson, "Can Fox and DreamWorks Combined Challenge Disney's Animation Empire?" *Forbes*, April 10, 2013; S. Greengard, "DreamWorks Takes a Picture-Perfect Approach to IT," *Baseline Magazine*, April 1, 2013; M. K. Rodriguez, "Traditional vs. Disruptive Tech: What's Best for Your Business?" *Amadeus Consulting White Paper*, February 28, 2013; S. Noonoo, "How Disruptive Technologies Are Leading the Next Great Education Revolution," *T.H.E. Journal*, January 16, 2013; De La Merced, "Eastman Kodak

Files for Bankruptcy," *The Wall Street Journal*, January 19, 2012; J. Trachtenberg and M. Peers, "Barnes & Noble Seeks Next Chapter," *The Wall Street Journal*, January 6, 2012; "Driverless Car: Google Awarded U.S. Patent for Technology," *BBC News*, December 15, 2011; J. McKendrick, "Five Non-IT Companies That Are Now Indistinguishable from Software Companies," *ZDNet*, December 7, 2011; A. Bleicher, "Five Reasons Every Company Should Act Like a Software Startup," *Forbes*, November 14, 2011; B. Austen, "The End of Borders and the Future of Books," *Bloomberg BusinessWeek*, November 10, 2011; M. Andreessen, "Why Software Is Eating the World," *The Wall Street Journal*, August 20, 2011; J. Knee, "Why Content Isn't King," *The Atlantic*, July/August, 2011; J. Checkler and J. Trachtenberg, "Bookseller Borders Begins a New Chapter...11," *The Wall Street Journal*, February 17, 2011.

Questions

1. If every company is now a technology company, then what does this mean for the company's employees? Provide specific examples to support your answer.
2. If every company is now a technology company, then what does this mean for every student attending a business college? Provide specific examples to support your answer.

What We Learned from This Case

The chapter-opening case illustrates that the impacts of information technology are wide-ranging, global, and disruptive. You will encounter many other examples of the societal and environmental effects of information technology throughout this text. The opening case underscores how important it is for you to have an understanding of information technology, regardless of your career choice.

Before we proceed, we need to define information technology and information systems. **Information technology (IT)** refers to any computer-based tool that people use to work with information and to support the information and information-processing needs of an organization. An **information system (IS)** collects, processes, stores, analyzes, and disseminates information for a specific purpose.

The opening case is a dramatic example of the far-reaching effects of IT on individuals, organizations, and our planet. Although this text is largely devoted to the many ways in which IT has transformed modern organizations, you will also learn about the significant impacts of IT on individuals and societies, the global economy, and our physical environment. In addition, IT is making our world smaller, enabling more and more people to communicate, collaborate, and compete, thereby leveling the digital playing field.

When you graduate, you either will start your own business or you will work for an organization, whether it is public sector, private sector, for-profit, or not-for-profit. Your organization will have to survive and compete in an environment that has been radically transformed by information technology. This environment is global, massively interconnected, intensely competitive, 24/7/365, real-time, rapidly changing, and information-intensive. To compete successfully, your organization must use IT effectively.

As you read this chapter and this text, keep in mind that the information technologies you will learn about are important to businesses of all sizes. No matter what area of business you major in, what industry you work for, or the size of your company, you will benefit from learning about IT. Who knows? Maybe you will use the tools you learn about in this class to make your great idea a reality!

The modern environment is intensely competitive not only for your organization, but for you as well. You must compete with human talent from around the world. Therefore, you will also have to make effective use of IT.

Accordingly, this chapter begins with a discussion of why you should become knowledgeable about IT. It also distinguishes among data, information, and knowledge, and it differentiates computer-based information systems from application programs. Finally, it considers the impacts of information systems on organizations and on society in general.

As you see in IT's About [Small] Business 1.1, small business owners do not need to be experts in information technology to be successful. The core competency of Warby Parker's business is not technology. Rather, the company's business model is its core competency. However, the firm is effectively using IT to support its business model and, thus, to create a successful business.

IT's about [small] business

1.1 Warby Parker

Warby Parker (www.warbyparker.com) is an online eyewear retailer that was founded in 2010. The idea for the company was conceived when the firm's founders (MBA students at the time) observed that glasses—uncomplicated, easily breakable, and mass-produced—were typically quite expensive ($500 or more, for example). Significantly, the founders were convinced they knew the reason why glasses cost so much. They perceived the optical industry as an *oligopoly*, meaning that a small number of companies dominate the business and are making large margins.

Consider, for example, Luxottica (www.luxottica.com), based in Milan, Italy. This company owns LensCrafters, Pearle Vision, Sunglass Hut, Ray-Ban, Oakley, and Oliver Peoples, in addition to the optical shops in Target and Sears. In addition, as a result of a series of license agreements, Luxottica manufactures eyewear for more than 20 top brands, including Chanel, Burberry, Prada, and Stella McCartney. Warby Parker's founders realized that Luxottica had "created the illusion of choice," when in fact they practically monopolized the industry.

Warby Parker devised a strategy to compete with Luxottica. The company uses the same materials and the same Chinese factories as Luxottica. It then sells its glasses at a lower price because it does not have to pay licensing fees, which can amount to as much as 15 percent of the $100 wholesale cost of a pair of glasses. In addition, because Warby Parker markets and sells its products directly to its customers, it does not have to deal with retailers, whose markups can double prices.

Warby Parker's business model allows customers to test the company's retro-style glasses via a mail-order, try-it-at-home program. The glasses (including prescription lenses) cost a mere $95, and customers may test up to five frames at a time. In addition, the Warby Parker Web site enables shoppers to upload photos and "try on" frames virtually. Such large-scale individualized shopping experiences have attracted a devoted following among young, trendy professionals. This business model has made the firm a commercial success.

By mid-2013, Warby Parker had sold more than 100,000 pairs of glasses. The company raised $1.5 million from investors in May 2011, and in 2012 it raised an additional $37 million. It has 113 employees, and it opened a 2,500-square-foot store in New York City.

In addition to enjoying great commercial success, Warby Parker has a social mission. For every pair of glasses it sells, it provides subsidies to help someone in need to buy a pair—although not one of Warby's creations.

The company's success is inspiring competition from more established eyeglass retailers. For example, discount fashion site Bluefly (www.bluefly.com) has introduced Eyefly (www.eyefly.com), which sells custom, vintage-looking glasses for $99.

Another competitor is Ditto (www.ditto.com), where shoppers use a computer webcam to record a video of their faces and create a virtual, three-dimensional "you." Then, shoppers can virtually try on different frames, look side to side, and blink. They can also solicit feedback from friends on Facebook by sharing shots of their virtual selves wearing different frames.

Google wants to avoid making users of its Google Glass product look like an actor in a science fiction movie. As a result, the company is working with Warby Parker to design more fashionable frames for Google Glass.

Sources: Compiled from S. Rodriguez, "Google in Talks with Warby Parker for Its Glasses," *The Los Angeles Times*, February 21, 2013; D. Primack, "Warby Parker Raises $37 Million," *CNN Money*, September 9, 2012; A. Pack, "Warby Parker's Vision for Growth," *CNBC*, June 11, 2012; L. Sanders, "Ditto Lets You Try on Glasses via Webcam," *San Francisco Chronicle*, April 27, 2012; D. Muse, "The New Startup Scene: From Silicon Strip to Silicon Mitten," *Forbes*, December 19, 2011; S. Berfield, "A Startup's New Prescription for Eyewear," *Bloomberg BusinessWeek*, July 4–10, 2011; D. Mau, "Warby Parker vs. Eyefly," *Fashionista*, June 6, 2011; H. Elliot, "The New Model for Retail: Buying Glasses Online," *Forbes*, January 17, 2011; N. Perlroth, "Name You Need to Know in 2011: Warby Parker," *Forbes*, November 22, 2010; www.warbyparker.com, www.eyefly.com, accessed February 18, 2013.

Questions

1. Provide two examples of how Warby Parker uses information technology to support its business model.
2. How might Warby Parker further use information technology to counter large competitors who want to copy their business model? Be specific.

1.1 Why Should I Study Information Systems?

You are part of the most connected generation in history: You have grown up online; you are, quite literally, never out of touch; you use more information technologies (in the form of digital devices), for more tasks, and are bombarded with more information, than any generation in history. The MIT Technology Review refers to you as *Homo conexus*. Information technologies are so deeply embedded in your lives that your daily routines would be almost unrecognizable to a college student just 20 years ago.

Essentially, you practice continuous computing, surrounded by a movable information network. This network is created by constant cooperation between the digital devices you carry (e.g., laptops, media players, and smartphones); the wired and wireless networks that you access as you move about; and Web-based tools for finding information and communicating and collaborating with other people. Your network enables you to pull information about virtually anything from anywhere, at any time, and to push your own ideas back to the Web, from wherever you are, via a mobile device. Think of everything you do online, often with your smart phone: register for classes; take classes (and not just at your university); access class syllabi, information, PowerPoints, and lectures; research class papers and presentations; conduct banking; pay your bills; research, shop, and buy products from companies or other people; sell your "stuff"; search for, and apply for, jobs; make your travel reservations (hotel, airline, rental car); create your own blog and post your own podcasts and videocasts to it; design your own page on Facebook; make and upload videos to YouTube; take, edit, and print your own digital photographs; "burn" your own custom-music CDs and DVDs; use RSS feeds to create your personal electronic newspaper; text and tweet your friends and family throughout your day; and many other activities. (Note: If any of these terms are unfamiliar to you, don't worry. You will learn about everything mentioned here in detail later in this text.)

The Informed User—You!

So, the question is: Why you should learn about information systems and information technologies? After all, you can comfortably use a computer (or other electronic devices) to perform many activities, you have been surfing the Web for years, and you feel confident that you can manage any IT application that your organization's MIS department installs.

The answer lies in your becoming an **informed user**; that is, a person knowledgeable about information systems and information technology. There are several reasons why you should be an informed user.

In general, informed users tend to get more value from whatever technologies they use. You will enjoy many benefits from being an informed user of IT.

- First, you will benefit more from your organization's IT applications because you will understand what is "behind" those applications (see Figure 1.1). That is, what you see on your computer screen is brought to you by your MIS department, who are operating "behind" your screen.
- Second, you will be in a position to enhance the quality of your organization's IT applications with your input.
- Third, even as a new graduate, you will quickly be in a position to recommend—and perhaps help select—the IT applications that your organization will use.
- Fourth, being an informed user will keep you abreast of both new information technologies and rapid developments in existing technologies. Remaining "on top of things" will help you to anticipate the impacts that "new and improved" technologies will have on your organization and to make recommendations on the adoption and use of these technologies.
- Fifth, you will understand how using IT can improve your organization's performance and teamwork as well as your own productivity.
- Finally, if you have ideas of becoming an entrepreneur, then being an informed user will help you use IT when you start your own business.

Going further, managing the IS function within an organization is no longer the exclusive responsibility of the IS department. Rather, users now play key roles in every step of this process. The overall objective in this text is to provide you with the necessary information to contribute immediately to managing the IS function in your organization. In short, the goal is to help you become a very informed user!

IT Offers Career Opportunities

Because information technology is vital to the operation of modern businesses, it offers many employment opportunities. The demand for traditional IT staff—programmers, business

FIGURE 1.1 IT skills open many doors because IT is so widely used. What do you think is this woman's job?

@ Slaomir Fajer/iStockphoto

analysts, systems analysts, and designers—is substantial. In addition, many well-paid jobs exist in areas such as the Internet and electronic commerce (e-commerce), mobile commerce (m-commerce), network security, telecommunications, and multimedia design.

The information systems field includes the people in various organizations who design and build information systems, the people who use those systems, and the people responsible for managing those systems. At the top of the list is the chief information officer (CIO).

The CIO is the executive who is in charge of the IS function. In most modern organizations, the CIO works with the chief executive officer (CEO), the chief financial officer (CFO), and other senior executives. Therefore, he or she actively participates in the organization's strategic planning process. In today's digital environment, the IS function has become increasingly strategic within organizations. As a result, although most CIOs still rise from the IS department, a growing number are coming up through the ranks in the business units (e.g., marketing, finance, etc.). So, regardless of your major, you could become the CIO of your organization one day. This is another reason to be an informed user of information systems!

Table 1.1 provides a list of IT jobs, along with a description of each one. For further details about careers in IT, see www.computerworld.com/careertopics/careers and www.monster.com.

Career opportunities in IS are strong and are projected to remain strong over the next ten years. In fact, the *U.S. News & World Report* and *Money* magazines listed their "100 top jobs" for 2012, and *Forbes* magazine listed its "10 top jobs" for 2013. Let's take a look at these rankings. (Note that the rankings differ because the magazines used different criteria in their research.) As you can see, jobs suited for MIS majors rank extremely high in all three lists. The magazines with their job rankings are:

Forbes
#1 Software developer
#4 Systems analyst
#6 Network and systems administrator

U.S. News & World Report
#4 Computer systems analyst
#6 Database administrator

#7 Software developer
#9 Web developer
#20 IT manager

Money
#3 Software architect
#5 Database administrator
#9 Software developer
#13 IT consultant
#21 Systems administrator
#28 IT business analyst

Table 1.1
Information Technology Jobs

Position	Job Description
Chief Information Officer	Highest-ranking IS manager; is responsible for all strategic planning in the organization
IS Director	Manages all systems throughout the organization and the day-to-day operations of the entire IS organization
Information Center Manager	Manages IS services such as help desks, hot lines, training, and consulting
Applications Development Manager	Coordinates and manages new systems development projects
Project Manager	Manages a particular new systems development project
Systems Manager	Manages a particular existing system
Operations Manager	Supervises the day-to-day operations of the data and/or computer center
Programming Manager	Coordinates all applications programming efforts
Systems Analyst	Interfaces between users and programmers; determines information requirements and technical specifications for new applications
Business Analyst	Focuses on designing solutions for business problems; interfaces closely with users to demonstrate how IT can be used innovatively
Systems Programmer	Creates the computer code for developing new systems software or maintaining existing systems software
Applications Programmer	Creates the computer code for developing new applications or maintaining existing applications
Emerging Technologies Manager	Forecasts technology trends; evaluates and experiments with new technologies
Network Manager	Coordinates and manages the organization's voice and data networks
Database Administrator	Manages the organization's databases and oversees the use of database-management software
Auditing or Computer Security Manager	Oversees the ethical and legal use of information systems
Webmaster	Manages the organization's World Wide Web site
Web Designer	Creates World Wide Web sites and pages

Not only do IS careers offer strong job growth, but the pay is excellent as well. The Bureau of Labor Statistics, an agency within the Department of Labor that is responsible for tracking and analyzing trends relating to the labor market, notes that the median salary in 2013 for "computer and information systems managers" is approximately $115,000.

Managing Information Resources

Managing information systems in modern organizations is a difficult, complex task. Several factors contribute to this complexity. First, information systems have enormous strategic value to organizations. Firms rely on them so heavily that, in some cases, when these systems are not working (even for a short time), the firm cannot function. (This situation is called "being hostage to information systems.") Second, information systems are very expensive to acquire, operate, and maintain.

A third factor contributing to the difficulty in managing information systems is the evolution of the management information systems (MIS) function within the organization. When businesses first began to use computers in the early 1950s, the MIS department "owned" the only computing resource in the organization, the mainframe. At that time, end users did not interact directly with the mainframe.

In contrast, in the modern organization, computers are located in all departments, and almost all employees use computers in their work. This situation, known as *end user computing*, has led to a partnership between the MIS department and the end users. The MIS department now acts as more of a consultant to end users, viewing them as customers. In fact, the main function of the MIS department is to use IT to solve end users' business problems.

As a result of these developments, the responsibility for managing information resources is now divided between the MIS department and the end users. This arrangement raises several important questions: Which resources are managed by whom? What is the role of the MIS department, its structure, and its place within the organization? What is the appropriate relationship between the MIS department and the end users? Regardless of who is doing what, it is essential that the MIS department and the end users work in close cooperation.

There is no standard way to divide responsibility for developing and maintaining information resources between the MIS department and the end users. Instead, that division depends on several factors: the size and nature of the organization, the amount and type of IT resources, the organization's attitudes toward computing, the attitudes of top management toward computing, the maturity level of the technology, the amount and nature of outsourced IT work, and even the countries in which the company operates. Generally speaking, the MIS department is responsible for corporate-level and shared resources, and the end users are responsible for departmental resources. Table 1.2 identifies both the traditional functions and various new, consultative functions of the MIS department.

So, where do the end users come in? Take a close look at Table 1.2. Under the traditional MIS functions, you will see two functions for which you provide vital input: managing systems development, and infrastructure planning. Under the consultative MIS functions, in contrast, you exercise the primary responsibility for each function, while the MIS department acts as your advisor.

before you go on...

1. Rate yourself as an informed user. (Be honest; this isn't a test!)
2. Explain the benefits of being an informed user of information systems.
3. Discuss the various career opportunities offered in the IT field.

Table **1.2**
The Changing Role of the Information Systems Department

Traditional Functions of the MIS Department

- Managing systems development and systems project management
  - As an end user, you will have critical input into the systems development process. You will learn about systems development in Chapter 13.
- Managing computer operations, including the computer center
- Staffing, training, and developing IS skills
- Providing technical services
- Infrastructure planning, development, and control
  - As an end user, you will provide critical input about the IS infrastructure needs of your department.

New (Consultative) Functions of the MIS Department

- Initiating and designing specific strategic information systems
  - As an end user, your information needs will often mandate the development of new strategic information systems.
  - You will decide which strategic systems you need (because you know your business needs better than the MIS department does), and you will provide input into developing these systems.
- Incorporating the Internet and electronic commerce into the business
  - As an end user, you will be primarily responsible for effectively using the Internet and electronic commerce in your business. You will work with the MIS department to accomplish this task.
- Managing system integration including the Internet, intranets, and extranets
  - As an end user, your business needs will determine how you want to use the Internet, your corporate intranets, and extranets to accomplish your goals. You will be primarily responsible for advising the MIS department on the most effective use of the Internet, your corporate intranets, and extranets.
- Educating the non-MIS managers about IT
  - Your department will be primarily responsible for advising the MIS department on how best to educate and train your employees about IT.
- Educating the MIS staff about the business
  - Communication between the MIS department and the business units is a two-way street. You will be responsible for educating the MIS staff on your business, its needs, and its goals.
- Partnering with business-unit executives
  - Essentially, you will be in a partnership with the MIS department. You will be responsible for seeing that this partnership is one "between equals" and ensuring its success.
- Managing outsourcing
  - Outsourcing is driven by business needs. Therefore, the outsourcing decision resides largely with the business units (i.e., with you). The MIS department, working closely with you, will advise you on technical issues such as communications bandwidth, security, etc.
- Proactively using business and technical knowledge to seed innovative ideas about IT
  - Your business needs often will drive innovative ideas about how to effectively use information systems to accomplish your goals. The best way to bring these innovative uses of IS to life is to partner closely with your MIS department. Such close partnerships have amazing synergies!
- Creating business alliances with business partners
  - The needs of your business unit will drive these alliances, typically along your supply chain. Again, your MIS department will act as your advisor on various issues, including hardware and software compatibility, implementing extranets, communications, and security.

1.2 Overview of Computer-Based Information Systems

Organizations refer to their management information systems functional area by several names, including the MIS Department, the Information Systems (IS) Department, the Information Technology Department, and the Information Services Department. Regardless of the name, however, this functional area deals with the planning for—and the development, management, and use of—information technology tools to help people perform all the tasks related to information processing and management. Recall that information technology relates to any computer-based tool that people use to work with information and to support the information and information processing needs of an organization.

As previously stated, an information system collects, processes, stores, analyzes, and disseminates information for a specific purpose. The purpose of information systems has been defined as getting the right information to the right people, at the right time, in the right amount, and in the right format. Because information systems are intended to supply useful information, we need to differentiate between information and two closely related terms: data and knowledge (see Figure 1.2).

Data items refer to an elementary description of things, events, activities, and transactions that are recorded, classified, and stored but are not organized to convey any specific meaning. Data items can be numbers, letters, figures, sounds, and images. Examples of data items are collections of numbers (e.g., 3.11, 2.96, 3.95, 1.99, 2.08) and characters (e.g., B, A, C, A, B, D, F, C).

Information refers to data that have been organized so that they have meaning and value to the recipient. For example, a grade point average (GPA) by itself is data, but a student's name

FIGURE 1.2 Binary Code, the foundation of information and knowledge, is the key to making complex decisions.

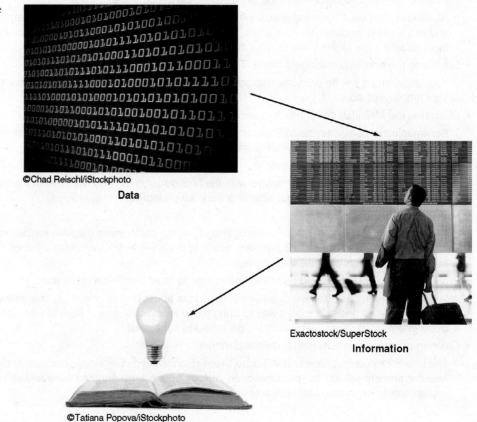

©Chad Reischl/iStockphoto
Data

Exactostock/SuperStock
Information

©Tatiana Popova/iStockphoto
Knowledge

coupled with his or her GPA is information. The recipient interprets the meaning and draws conclusions and implications from the information. Consider the examples of data provided in the preceding paragraph. Within the context of a university, the numbers could be grade point averages, and the letters could be grades in an Introduction to MIS class.

Knowledge consists of data and/or information that have been organized and processed to convey understanding, experience, accumulated learning, and expertise as they apply to a current business problem. For example, suppose that a company recruiting at your school has found over time that students with grade point averages over 3.0 have experienced the greatest success in its management program. Based on this accumulated knowledge, that company may decide to interview only those students with GPAs over 3.0. This example presents an example of knowledge because the company utilizes information—GPAs—to address a business problem—hiring successful employees. As you can see from this example, organizational knowledge, which reflects the experience and expertise of many people, has great value to all employees.

Consider this example:

Data	Information	Knowledge
[No context]	**[University context]**	
3.16	3.16 + John Jones = GPA	* Job prospects
2.92	2.92 + Sue Smith = GPA	* Graduate school prospects
1.39	1.39 + Kyle Owens = GPA	* Scholarship prospects
3.95	3.95 + Tom Elias = GPA	
[No context]	**[Professional baseball pitcher context]**	
3.16	3.16 + Ken Rice = ERA	
2.92	2.92 + Ed Dyas = ERA	* Keep pitcher, trade pitcher, or send pitcher to minor leagues
1.39	1.39 + Hugh Carr = ERA	* Salary/contract negotiations
3.95	3.95 + Nick Ford = ERA	

GPA = grade point average (higher is better)
ERA = earned run average (lower is better); ERA is the number of runs per nine innings that a pitcher surrenders

You see that the same data items, with no context, can mean entirely different things in different contexts.

Now that you have a clearer understanding of data, information, and knowledge, let's shift our focus to computer-based information systems. As you have seen, these systems process data into information and knowledge that you can use.

A **computer-based information system (CBIS)** is an information system that uses computer technology to perform some or all of its intended tasks. Although not all information systems are computerized, today most are. For this reason the term "information system" is typically used synonymously with "computer-based information system." The basic components of computer-based information systems are listed below. The first four are called **information technology components**. Figure 1.3 illustrates how these four components interact to form a CBIS.

- **Hardware** consists of devices such as the processor, monitor, keyboard, and printer. Together, these devices accept, process, and display data and information.
- **Software** is a program or collection of programs that enable the hardware to process data.
- A **database** is a collection of related files or tables containing data.
- A **network** is a connecting system (wireline or wireless) that permits different computers to share resources.

FIGURE 1.3 It takes technology (hardware, software, databases, and networks) with appropriate procedures to make a CBIS useful for people.

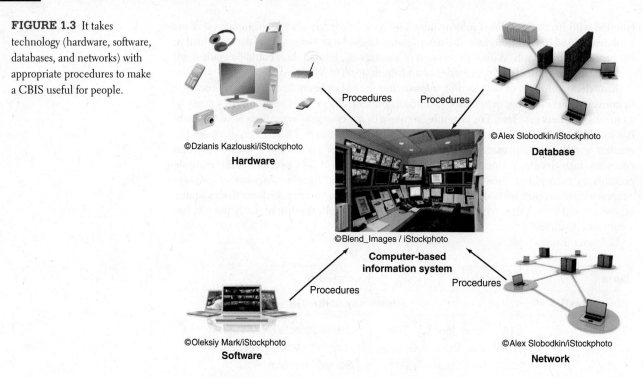

©Dzianis Kazlouski/iStockphoto
Hardware

©Alex Slobodkin/iStockphoto
Database

©Blend_Images / iStockphoto
Computer-based information system

Procedures   Procedures

Procedures

Procedures   Procedures

©Oleksiy Mark/iStockphoto
Software

©Alex Slobodkin/iStockphoto
Network

- **Procedures** are the instructions for combining the above components to process information and generate the desired output.
- *People* are those individuals who use the hardware and software, interface with it, or utilize its output.

Figure 1.4 illustrates how these components are integrated to form the wide variety of information systems found within an organization. Starting at the bottom of the figure, you see

FIGURE 1.4 Information technology inside your organization.

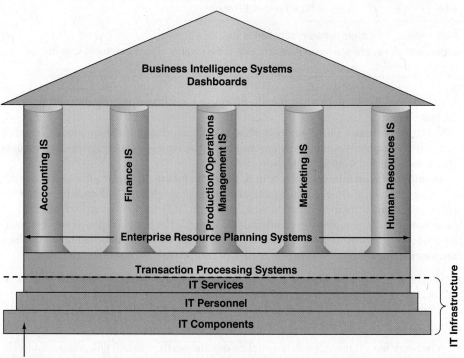

Business Intelligence Systems
Dashboards

Accounting IS

Finance IS

Production/Operations
Management IS

Marketing IS

Human Resources IS

Enterprise Resource Planning Systems

Transaction Processing Systems

IT Services

IT Personnel

IT Components

IT Infrastructure

IT Platform

that the IT components of hardware, software, networks (wireline and wireless), and databases form the **information technology platform**. IT personnel use these components to develop information systems, oversee security and risk, and manage data. These activities cumulatively are called **information technology services**. The IT components plus IT services comprise the organization's **information technology infrastructure**. At the top of the pyramid are the various organizational information systems.

Computer-based information systems have many capabilities. Table 1.3 summarizes the most important ones.

Information systems perform these various tasks via a wide spectrum of applications. An **application** (or **app**) is a computer program designed to support a specific task or business process. (A synonymous term is *application program*.) Each functional area or department within a business organization uses dozens of application programs. For instance, the human resources department sometimes uses one application for screening job applicants and another for monitoring employee turnover. The collection of application programs in a single department is usually referred to as a *departmental information system* (also known as a *functional area information system*). For example, the collection of application programs in the human resources area is called the *human resources information system (HRIS)*. There are collections of application programs—that is, departmental information systems—in the other functional areas as well, such as accounting, finance, marketing, and production/operations.

Types of Computer-Based Information Systems

Modern organizations employ many different types of information systems. Figure 1.4 illustrates the different types of information systems that function *within* a single organization, and Figure 1.5 shows the different types of information systems that function *among* multiple organizations. You will study transaction processing systems, management information systems, and enterprise resource planning systems in Chapter 10. You will learn about customer relationship management (CRM) systems and supply chain management (SCM) systems in Chapter 11.

In the next section, you will learn about the numerous and diverse types of information systems employed by modern organizations. You will also read about the types of support these systems provide.

Breadth of Support of Information Systems.   Certain information systems support parts of organizations, others support entire organizations, and still others support groups of organizations. This section addresses all of these systems.

Recall that each department or functional area within an organization has its own collection of application programs, or information systems. These **functional area information systems (FAISs)** are supporting pillars for the information systems located at the top of Figure 1.4, namely, business intelligence systems and dashboards. As the name suggests, each FAIS supports a particular functional area within the organization. Examples are accounting IS, finance IS, production/operations management (POM) IS, marketing IS, and human resources IS.

Perform high-speed, high-volume numerical computations.
Provide fast, accurate communication and collaboration within and among organizations.
Store huge amounts of information in an easy-to-access, yet small space.
Allow quick and inexpensive access to vast amounts of information, worldwide.
Interpret vast amounts of data quickly and efficiently.
Automate both semiautomatic business processes and manual tasks.

Table
1.3
**Major Capabilities of
Information Systems**

FIGURE 1.5 Information systems that function among multiple organizations.

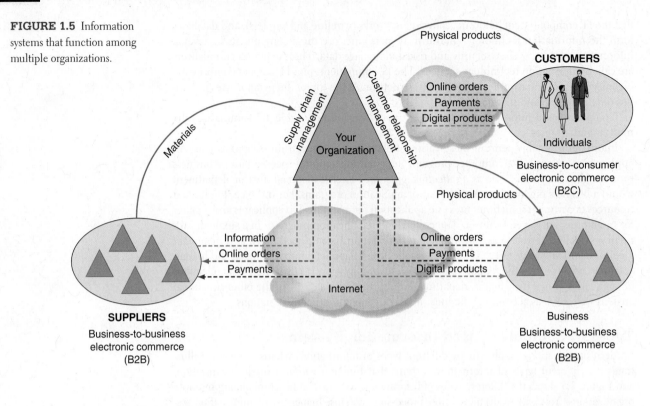

 Consider these examples of IT systems in the various functional areas of an organization. In finance and accounting, managers use IT systems to forecast revenues and business activity, to determine the best sources and uses of funds, and to perform audits to ensure that the organization is fundamentally sound and that all financial reports and documents are accurate.

In sales and marketing, managers use information technology to perform the following functions:

- *Product analysis*: developing new goods and services
- *Site analysis*: determining the best location for production and distribution facilities
- *Promotion analysis*: identifying the best advertising channels
- *Price analysis*: setting product prices to obtain the highest total revenues

 Marketing managers also use IT to manage their relationships with their customers. In *manufacturing*, managers use IT to process customer orders, develop production schedules, control inventory levels, and monitor product quality. They also use IT to design and manufacture products. These processes are called *computer-assisted design* (CAD) and *computer-assisted manufacturing* (CAM).

Managers in *human resources* use IT to manage the recruiting process, analyze and screen job applicants, and hire new employees. They also employ IT to help employees manage their careers, to administer performance tests to employees, and to monitor employee productivity. Finally, they rely on IT to manage compensation and benefits packages.

Two information systems support the entire organization: enterprise resource planning systems and transaction processing systems. **Enterprise resource planning (ERP) systems** are designed to correct a lack of communication among the functional area ISs. For this reason Figure 1.4 shows ERP systems spanning the FAISs. ERP systems were an important innovation because the various functional area ISs were often developed as standalone systems and did not communicate effectively (if at all) with one another. ERP systems resolve this problem by tightly integrating the functional area ISs via a common database. In doing so, they enhance communications among the functional areas of an organization. For this reason, experts credit ERP systems with greatly increasing organizational productivity.

A transaction processing system (TPS) supports the monitoring, collection, storage, and processing of data from the organization's basic business transactions, each of which generates data. When you are checking out at Walmart, for example, a transaction occurs each time the cashier swipes an item across the bar code reader. Significantly, within an organization, different functions or departments can define a transaction differently. In accounting, for example, a transaction is anything that changes a firm's chart of accounts. The information system definition of a transaction is broader: A transaction is anything that changes the firm's database. The chart of accounts is only part of the firm's database. Consider a scenario in which a student transfers from one section of an Introduction to MIS course to another section. This move would be a transaction to the university's information system, but not to the university's accounting department (the tuition would not change).

The TPS collects data continuously, typically in *real time*—that is, as soon as the data are generated—and it provides the input data for the corporate databases. TPSs are considered critical to the success of any enterprise because they support core operations. Significantly, nearly all ERP systems are also TPSs, but not all TPSs are ERP systems. In fact, modern ERP systems incorporate many functions that previously were handled by the organization's functional area information systems. You study both TPSs and ERP systems in detail in Chapter 10.

ERP systems and TPSs function primarily within a single organization. Information systems that connect two or more organizations are referred to as **interorganizational information systems (IOSs)**. IOSs support many interorganizational operations, of which *supply chain management* is the best known. An organization's **supply chain** is the flow of materials, information, money, and services from suppliers of raw materials through factories and warehouses to the end customers.

Note that the supply chain in Figure 1.5 shows physical flows, information flows, and financial flows. Digitizable products are those that can be represented in electronic form, such as music and software. Information flows, financial flows, and digitizable products go through the Internet, whereas physical products are shipped. For example, when you order a computer from *www.dell.com*, your information goes to Dell via the Internet. When your transaction is completed (i.e., your credit card is approved and your order is processed), Dell ships your computer to you. (We discuss supply chains in more detail in Chapter 11.)

Electronic commerce (e-commerce) systems are another type of interorganizational information system. These systems enable organizations to conduct transactions, called business-to-business (B2B) electronic commerce, and customers to conduct transactions with businesses, called business-to-consumer (B2C) electronic commerce. E-commerce systems typically are Internet-based. Figure 1.5 illustrates B2B and B2C electronic commerce. Electronic commerce systems are so important that we discuss them in detail in Chapter 7, with additional examples interspersed throughout the text.

Support for Organizational Employees.   So far, you have concentrated on information systems that support specific functional areas and operations. Now you will learn about information systems that typically support particular employees within the organization.

Clerical workers, who support managers at all levels of the organization, include bookkeepers, secretaries, electronic file clerks, and insurance claim processors. *Lower-level managers* handle the day-to-day operations of the organization, making routine decisions such as assigning tasks to employees and placing purchase orders. *Middle managers* make tactical decisions, which deal with activities such as short-term planning, organizing, and control.

Knowledge workers are professional employees such as financial and marketing analysts, engineers, lawyers, and accountants. All knowledge workers are experts in a particular subject area. They create information and knowledge, which they integrate into the business. Knowledge workers, in turn, act as advisors to middle managers and executives. Finally, *executives* make decisions that deal with situations that can significantly change the manner in which business is done. Examples of executive decisions are introducing a new product line, acquiring other businesses, and relocating operations to a foreign country.

Office automation systems (OASs) typically support the clerical staff, lower and middle managers, and knowledge workers. These employees use OASs to develop documents (word processing and desktop publishing software), schedule resources (electronic calendars), and communicate (e-mail, voice mail, videoconferencing, and groupware).

Functional area information systems summarize data and prepare reports, primarily for middle managers, but sometimes for lower-level managers as well. Because these reports typically concern a specific functional area, report generators (RPGs) are an important type of functional area IS.

Business intelligence (BI) systems provide computer-based support for complex, nonroutine decisions, primarily for middle managers and knowledge workers. (They also support lower-level managers, but to a lesser extent.) These systems are typically used with a data warehouse, and they enable users to perform their own data analysis. You learn about BI systems in Chapter 12.

Expert systems (ESs) attempt to duplicate the work of human experts by applying reasoning capabilities, knowledge, and expertise within a specific domain. They have become valuable in many application areas, primarily but not exclusively areas involving decision making. For example, navigation systems use rules to select routes, but we do not typically think of these systems as expert systems. Significantly, expert systems can operate as standalone systems or be embedded in other applications. We examine ESs in greater detail in Technology Guide 4.

Dashboards (also called **digital dashboards**) are a special form of IS that support all managers of the organization. They provide rapid access to timely information and direct access to structured information in the form of reports. Dashboards that are tailored to the information needs of executives are called *executive dashboards*. Chapter 12 provides a thorough discussion of dashboards.

Table 1.4 provides an overview of the different types of information systems used by organizations.

Table **1.4**
Types of Organizational Information Systems

Type of System	Function	Example
Functional area IS	Supports the activities within specific functional area.	System for processing payroll
Transaction processing system	Processes transaction data from business events.	Walmart checkout point-of-sale terminal
Enterprise resource planning	Integrates all functional areas of the organization.	Oracle, SAP system
Office automation system	Supports daily work activities of individuals and groups.	Microsoft® Office
Management information system	Produces reports summarized from transaction data, usually in one functional area.	Report on total sales for each customer
Decision support system	Provides access to data and analysis tools.	"What-if" analysis of changes in budget
Expert system	Mimics human expert in a particular area and makes decisions.	Credit card approval analysis
Executive dashboard	Presents structured, summarized information about aspects of business important to executives.	Status of sales by product
Supply chain management system	Manages flows of products, services, and information among organizations.	Walmart Retail Link system connecting suppliers to Walmart
Electronic commerce system	Enables transactions among organizations and between organizations and customers.	www.dell.com

before you go on...

1. What is a computer-based information system?
2. Describe the components of computer-based information systems.
3. What is an application program?
4. Explain how information systems provide support for knowledge workers.
5. As we move up the organization's hierarchy from clerical workers to executives, how does the type of support provided by information systems change?

How Does IT Impact Organizations?

1.3

Throughout this text you will encounter numerous examples of how IT affects various types of organizations. This section provides an overview of the impact of IT on modern organizations. As you read this section you will learn how IT will affect you as well.

IT Reduces the Number of Middle Managers

IT makes managers more productive, and it increases the number of employees who can report to a single manager. Thus, IT ultimately decreases the number of managers and experts. It is reasonable to assume, therefore, that in coming years organizations will have fewer managerial levels and fewer staff and line managers. If this trend materializes, promotional opportunities will decrease, making promotions much more competitive. Bottom line: Pay attention in school!

IT Changes the Manager's Job

One of the most important tasks of managers is making decisions. A major consequence of IT has been to change the manner in which managers make their decisions. In this way, IT ultimately has changed managers' jobs.

IT often provides managers with near-real-time information, meaning that managers have less time to make decisions, making their jobs even more stressful. Fortunately, IT also provides many tools—for example, business analytics applications such as dashboards, search engines, and intranets—to help managers handle the volumes of information they must deal with on an ongoing basis.

So far in this section, we have been focusing on managers in general. Now, let's focus on you. Due to advances in IT, you will increasingly supervise employees and teams who are geographically dispersed. Employees can work from anywhere at any time, and teams can consist of employees who are literally dispersed throughout the world. Information technologies such as telepresence systems (discussed in Chapter 6) can help you manage these employees even though you do not often see them face-to-face. For these employees, electronic or "remote" supervision will become the norm. Remote supervision places greater emphasis on completed work and less emphasis on personal contacts and office politics. You will have to reassure your employees that they are valued members of the organization, thereby diminishing any feelings they might have of being isolated and "out of the loop."

Will IT Eliminate Jobs?

One major concern of every employee, part-time or full-time, is job security. Relentless cost-cutting measures in modern organizations often lead to large-scale layoffs. Put simply, organizations are responding to today's highly competitive environment by doing more with less. Regardless of your position, then, you consistently will have to add value to your organization and to make certain that your superiors are aware of this value.

Many companies have responded to difficult economic times, increased global competition, demands for customization, and increased consumer sophistication by increasing their investments in IT. In fact, as computers continue to advance in terms of intelligence and capabilities, the competitive advantage of replacing people with machines is increasing rapidly. This process frequently leads to layoffs. At the same time, however, IT creates entirely new categories of jobs, such as electronic medical record keeping and nanotechnology.

IT Impacts Employees at Work

Many people have experienced a loss of identity because of computerization. They feel like "just another number" because computers reduce or eliminate the human element present in noncomputerized systems.

The Internet threatens to exert an even more isolating influence than have computers and television. Encouraging people to work and shop from their living rooms could produce some unfortunate psychological effects, such as depression and loneliness.

IT Impacts Employees' Health and Safety. Although computers and information systems are generally regarded as agents of "progress," they can adversely affect individuals' health and safety. To illustrate this point, we consider two issues associated with IT: job stress and long-term use of the keyboard.

An increase in an employee's workload and/or responsibilities can trigger *job stress*. Although computerization has benefited organizations by increasing productivity, it also has created an ever-expanding workload for some employees. Some workers feel overwhelmed and have become increasingly anxious about their job performance. These feelings of stress and anxiety can actually diminish rather than improve workers' productivity while jeopardizing their physical and mental health. Management can help alleviate these problems by providing training, redistributing the workload among workers, and hiring more workers.

On a more specific level, the long-term use of keyboards can lead to *repetitive strain injuries* such as backaches and muscle tension in the wrists and fingers. *Carpal tunnel syndrome* is a particularly painful form of repetitive strain injury that affects the wrists and hands.

Designers are aware of the potential problems associated with the prolonged use of computers. To address these problems, they continually attempt to design a better computing environment. The science of designing machines and work settings that minimize injury and illness is called **ergonomics**. The goal of ergonomics is to create an environment that is safe, well lit, and comfortable. Examples of ergonomically designed products are antiglare screens that alleviate problems of fatigued or damaged eyesight and chairs that contour the human body to decrease backaches. Figure 1.6 displays some sample ergonomic products.

IT Provides Opportunities for People with Disabilities. Computers can create new employment opportunities for people with disabilities by integrating speech-recognition and vision-recognition capabilities. For example, individuals who cannot type can use a voice-operated keyboard, and individuals who cannot travel can work at home.

Going further, adaptive equipment for computers enables people with disabilities to perform tasks they normally would not be able to do. For example, the Web and graphical user interfaces (GUIs; e.g., Windows) can be difficult for people with impaired vision to use. To address this problem, manufacturers have added audible screen tips and voice interfaces, which essentially restore the functionality of computers to the way it was before GUIs become standard.

Other devices help improve the quality of life in more mundane, but useful, ways for people with disabilities. Examples are a two-way writing telephone, a robotic page turner, a hair brusher, and a hospital-bedside video trip to the zoo or the museum. Several organizations specialize in IT designed for people with disabilities.

before you go on... ∧⅄⅄∧

1. Why should employees in all functional areas become knowledgeable about IT?

2. Describe how IT might change the manager's job.

3. Discuss several ways in which IT impacts employees at work.

Media Bakery

a

Media Bakery

b

Media Bakery

c

Media Bakery

d

FIGURE 1.6 Ergonomic products protect computer users.
(a) Wrist support.
(b) Back support.
(c) Eye-protection filter (optically coated glass).
(d) Adjustable foot rest.

Importance of Information Systems to Society 1.4

This section explains in greater detail why IT is important to society as a whole. Other examples of the impact of IT on society appear throughout the text.

IT Affects Our Quality of Life

IT has significant implications for our quality of life. The workplace can be expanded from the traditional 9-to-5 job at a central location to 24 hours a day at any location. IT can provide employees with flexibility that can significantly improve the quality of leisure time, even if it doesn't increase the total amount of leisure time.

From the opposite perspective, however, IT also can place employees on "constant call," which means they are never truly away from the office, even when they are on vacation. In fact, surveys reveal that the majority of respondents take their laptops and smartphones on their vacations, and 100 percent took their cell phones. Going further, the majority of respondents did some work while vacationing, and almost all of them checked their e-mail regularly.

Information technology clearly affects our quality of life. Interestingly, IT can also impact the quality of life of an entire country, as you see in IT's About Business 1.2.

IT's [about business]

1.2 Internet Registry Enhances Island Nation's Economy

Tokelau is a four-square-mile island nation in the Pacific Ocean that is home to only 1,500 people. Tokelau has the smallest economy of any country in the world, with an annual per capita purchasing power of $1,000 U.S. Tokelau's government is almost entirely dependent on subsidies from New Zealand. However, is generating income through its country code top-level domain, .tk.

As we discuss in detail in Chapter 6, a top-level domain is the highest level in the hierarchical Domain Name System of the Internet. A generic top-level domain (gTLD) is one of the categories of top-level domains maintained by the Internet Assigned Numbers Authority for use in the Domain Name System of the Internet. gTLDs are visible to users as the suffix at the end of a domain name.

If you are among the companies trying to obtain one of the nearly 2,000 new gTLDs, the application will cost you about $185,000, plus a $25,000 annual fee. Fortunately, there are cheaper options. One of the most popular domains is .tk, a country code top-level domain (a country code top-level domain is a type of gTLD) similar to .ca for Canada and .fr for France.

Tokelau's prominence on the Internet is a result of the efforts of Joost Zuurbier of Amsterdam. Zuurbier wanted to use Hotmail's business model. He reasoned that if Hotmail could make money by providing free e-mail, then he could make money by offering free domains. He found Tokelau, whose citizens were unaware that they are entitled to their country code domain. In fact, no one on the island had ever seen a Web page before.

Zuurbier traveled to Tokelau with the satellite equipment needed for Internet access. After years of effort and many meetings with Tokelau's citizens, Zuurbier's company, Freedom Registry (www.freedomregistry.com), launched its .tk domain in 2006. By mid-2013, more than 9 million Web sites had .tk domains. Freedom Registry continues to expand, particularly by conducting business with emerging economies such as China, Brazil, Russia, Peru, and Vietnam. These countries have local country code top-level domains: .cn, .br, .ru, .pe, and .vn, respectively. However, registering Web sites in those domains can be expensive, so individuals and companies turn to .tk.

If Freedom Registry provides domain names for free, then how does it make money? The answer is that the company generates revenue through ads on expired domains. Essentially, when users abandon their Web site or do not meet the minimum requirements of 25 unique visitors every 90 days, the domain is "parked." In other words, the URL still exists, but the content is replaced with ads tailored to the original Web site. For instance, if the original Web site involved travel to Europe, then the ads on that parked site would pertain to European travel. Freedom Registry can target these ads to specific audiences because it has software tools that examine the content of all Web sites on the .tk domain.

In return for the use of the .tk domain, Freedom Registry pays part of the money it earns to the people of Tokelau. In fact, one-sixth of the country's economy comes from the .tk domain. In addition, Zuurbier has brought connectivity to the nation. Prior to his arrival, the country had four phone lines that provided only low-bandwidth, dial-up connections to the Internet. Today, citizens have Internet access via the satellite connection provided by Zuurbier. There are now 120 computers on the island, although the power still goes off at 10 PM.

Tokelau has increased its gross domestic product (GDP) by more than 10 percent through registrations of domain names. In fact, a report from Verisign, the global registry operator for .com and .net, revealed that .tk is the third-most popular country code top-level domain in the world, behind only Germany (.de) and the United Kingdom (.uk).

On an unfortunate note, in 2011 the Anti-Phishing Working Group (www.antiphishing.org) claimed that the .tk domain was favored by spammers and scammers. The group rated the .tk domain as one of the most widely used in the world for sheltering criminal Web sites. In response, in 2012, Freedom Registry expanded its anti-abuse strategy by enabling trusted partners to electronically report any active Web sites that are used in spam, phishing, or other abuse. Freedom Registry allows its partners, such as Facebook, Kaspersky Labs, and Twitter, to connect their anti-abuse systems with Freedom Registry's domain name database. When Freedom Registry receives an electronic report of abuse, it immediately blocks the Web site.

Sources: Compiled from "Tokelau Profile," *BBC News*, November 7, 2012; T. Khalid, "How Tiny Tokelau Built a Huge Internet Domain," *Internet Evolution*, June 11, 2012; T. Andres, "The Tiny Island with a Huge Web Presence," *CNN*, June 13, 2012; D. Pauli, "Pacific Atoll a Phishing Haven," *ZDNet*, April 27, 2011; "Biggest Expansion in gTLDs Approved for Implementation," *ICANN.org*, June 26, 2008; www.tokelau.org.nz, www.freedomregistry.com, accessed April 5, 2013.

Questions

1. Describe several benefits that Zuurbier brought to the citizens of Tokelau.
2. Now that the citizens of Tokelau have Internet access, what other strategies can they use to generate income for themselves?

The Robot Revolution Is Here Now

Once restricted largely to science fiction movies, robots that can perform practical tasks are becoming more common. In fact, "cyberpooches," "nursebots," and other mechanical beings may be our companions before we know it. Around the world, quasi-autonomous devices have become increasingly common on factory floors, in hospital corridors, and in farm fields.

For home use, iRobot (www.irobot.com) produces the Roomba to vacuum our floors, the Scooba to wash our floors, the Dirt Dog to sweep our garages, the Verro to clean our pools, and the Looj to clean our gutters. The chapter closing case takes a look at Baxter, a new, more human-like robot.

Robots are becoming widely used in a variety of areas. IT's About Business 1.3 discusses three additional types of robots: telepresence robots, autonomous cars, and drones.

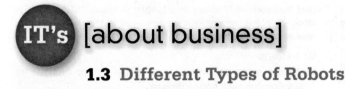

1.3 Different Types of Robots

Telepresence robots. Telepresence robots are designed to help companies save money on travel and on expensive teleconferencing technology. They enable people in remote offices or locations to have a rich communications experience without using a complicated video conference system.

A telepresence robot has both a video camera and a video screen embedded in its "head." It also has wheels so it can be moved around remotely by computer. It is designed to steer its way clear of obstacles and people.

These robots enable an individual to maintain a consistent connection with co-workers, customers, or clients. The user places the robot at a remote location and directs it to move around, for example, a conference room during a meeting, broadcasting what is going on to the human controlling it from afar. Interestingly, the robots actually break down barriers of awkwardness that people sometimes feel in person-to-person meetings.

Telepresence robots are used for purposes other than conducting business. For example, they let homebuyers virtually tour distant properties, they enable doctors to conduct bedside consultations from a distance (telemedicine), they provide an inexpensive method to patrol workplaces at night, and they allow parents who are out to dinner to stay in touch with their children at home. Other examples are

- Business managers are using telepresence robots to virtually walk factory floors.
- Healthcare organizations are employing robots for home care.
- In the retail environment, a robot could wander the floor with a customer who asks it purchasing or support questions. The person controlling the robot could answer the questions, essentially making the robot a mechanical sales clerk.

Many start-up companies are developing telepresence robots. Let's take a look at some of them.

- Oculus, made by Xaxxon Technologies (www.xaxxon.com), is utilized primarily for security patrols. The robot is essentially a set of wheels for a laptop that runs Skype videoconferencing software. Oculus can be controlled with a smartphone.
- In December 2012, a start-up called Robotics Valley (www .roboticsvalley.com), began manufacturing a $300 three-wheeled telepresence robot called Botiful. Botiful is remotely piloted, it carries an Android-based smartphone, and streams video via Skype.

Autonomous Cars. *Autonomy* is commonly defined as the ability of a machine to make decisions without human intervention. The best-known example of an autonomous, or self-driving, car is the Google driverless car. In August 2012, Google announced that its autonomous car team had completed more than 300,000 accident-free, self-driving miles. As of September 2012, four states had passed laws permitting driverless cars: Nevada, Florida, Texas, and California.

As of mid-2013, Google had not announced any plans to commercially develop the system. An attorney for the California Department of Motor Vehicles raised concerns that Google's technology is "ahead of the law in many areas," citing state laws that "all presume to have a human being operating the vehicle."

Audi, Toyota, and Cadillac, among other car brands, are developing autonomous cars as well. It is worth noting that each of Google's driverless test cars contains about $150,000 in equipment. With so many automobile manufacturers developing autonomous cars, the price will undoubtedly drop quickly.

Drones. An unmanned aerial vehicle (UAV), commonly known as a drone, is an aircraft that does not have a human pilot on board. Its flight is controlled either autonomously by computers contained in the vehicle or via remote control by a pilot located either on the ground or in another vehicle. UAVs are deployed predominately for military applications, but they are also employed in a growing number of civil applications including police work, firefighting, and nonmilitary security work such as surveillance of pipelines and border control.

The ultimate goal in the development of autonomous technology in UAVs is to replace the human pilot. To this end, artificial intelligence has advanced to the point where UAVs are capable of taking off, landing, and flying by themselves. It remains to be seen, however, whether the perception of autonomous technology, and, most importantly, the political climate surrounding the use of such technology, will limit the development and utility of autonomous UAVs.

There is a great deal of controversy concerning the use of UAVs within the United States. These drones are powerful surveillance tools, capable of carrying facial recognition systems, license plate scanners, thermal imaging cameras, open Wi-Fi scanners, and many other types of sensors. On January 10, 2012, the Electronic Frontier Foundation (EFF), an advocacy group for free speech and privacy rights in technology-related areas, filed a Freedom of Information Act lawsuit against the Federal Aviation Administration.

In response, the FAA, for the first time, released a list of the names of all public and private entities that have applied for authorization to fly drones domestically. Among these organizations is the U.S. Customs and Border Protection Agency (CBP), located within the Department of Homeland Security (DHS). The CBP has used UAVs to patrol U.S. borders since 2005. Other organizations on the list include the FBI, the Department of Defense, and local law enforcement agencies.

Significantly, U.S. citizens currently have few legal privacy protections from aerial surveillance conducted with UAVs. In one case, the U.S. Supreme Court held that individuals do not have the right to privacy from police observation from public airspace, even on their private property. The weakness of legal protection from UAV surveillance has led civil liberties advocacy groups to pressure the U.S. government to issue laws and regulations that establish both privacy protections and greater transparency regarding the use of UAVs to gather information about individuals.

Sources: Compiled from A. Vance, "Google Self-Driving Robot Cars Are Ruining My Commute," *Bloomberg BusinessWeek*, March 28, 2013; J. Horgen, "Unmanned Flight," *National Geographic*, March 2013; W. Knight,

"The Perfect Parking Garage: No Drivers Required," *MIT Technology Review*, March 27, 2013; "Your Alter Ego on Wheels," *The Economist*, March 9, 2013; M. Whittington, "Law Proposed in Texas to Require Licensed Driver in Self-Driving Vehicles," *Yahoo! News*, March 8, 2013; M. Stewart, "Drones Patrolling U.S. Borders Spark Controversy Over Privacy," *TheDenverChannel.com*, February 24, 2013; J. Oram, "Governor Brown Signs California Driverless Car Law at Google HQ," *WebProNews*, September 27, 2012; M. Slosson, "Google Gets First Self-Driven Car License in Nevada," *Reuters*, May 8, 2012; D. Bennett, "I'll Have My Robots Talk to Your Robots," *Bloomberg BusinessWeek*, February 21–27, 2011; A. Diana, "12 Advances in Medical Robotics," *InformationWeek*, January 29, 2011; www.xaxxon.com, www.roboticsvalley.com, accessed March 23, 2013.

Questions

1. Discuss some disadvantages of (a) telepresence robots; (b) autonomous cars; and (c) drones.
2. Would you be willing to ride in an autonomous car? Why or why not?
3. Which occupations are most at risk from a widespread adoption of autonomous cars? Support your answer.
4. Debate the privacy issues associated with domestic use of drones by police forces.

It probably will be a long time before we see robots making decisions by themselves, handling unfamiliar situations, and interacting with people. Nevertheless, robots are extremely helpful in various environments, particularly those that are repetitive, harsh, or dangerous to humans.

Improvements in Healthcare

IT has brought about major improvements in healthcare delivery. Medical personnel use IT to make better and faster diagnoses and to monitor critically ill patients more accurately. IT also has streamlined the process of researching and developing new drugs. Expert systems now help doctors diagnose diseases, and machine vision is enhancing the work of radiologists. Surgeons use virtual reality to plan complex surgeries. They also employ surgical robots to perform long-distance surgery. Finally, doctors discuss complex medical cases via videoconferencing. New computer simulations recreate the sense of touch, allowing doctors-in-training to perform virtual procedures without risking harm to an actual patient.

Not all uses of information technology to improve health are expensive and sophisticated. IT's About Business 1.4 illustrates how Zamzee is using gamification to help young people lose weight.

 IT's [about business]

1.4 Getting Kids in Shape

Jerry never paid much attention to how much physical activity he engaged in. However, one day he played basketball while wearing a small activity tracker called a Zamzee on his waist. Later, he plugged the device into his computer's USB port and uploaded the data captured by the device's accelerometers (devices to help determine the speed and distance of the person wearing the device). Unlike a FitBit (www.fitbit.com), a popular pedometer geared to adults, his Zamzee did not tell

Jerry how many steps he took or how many calories he burned. Instead, it gave him points for the movement he had made: a total of 758 points. These points are the currency that he can spend in the virtual world of Zamzee.com, where he created an avatar representing himself. If Jerry continues to exercise, he can eventually collect enough "Zamz" to be able to purchase real items like an iPod Nano (16,000 Zamz) or a Wii console (18,000 Zamz).

Jerry's experience illustrates the goals of Zamzee (www .zamzee.com), a company that is testing the idea that the addictiveness of games can be harnessed to solve a difficult social problem—in this case, childhood obesity. The concept is called *gamification*, which is the use of game thinking and game mechanics in a non-game context to engage users and solve problems.

Rather than focusing on weight loss or diet, Zamzee hopes to reward movement of any kind in children ages 11 to 14. Zamzee has targeted this demographic because research indicates that these are the ages when physical activity drops precipitously. Significantly, this is also the period when children adopt lifelong habits.

Zamzee is a for-profit venture started by HopeLab, the non-profit foundation funded by eBay founder Pierre Omidyar and his wife, Pam. Zamzee will formally launch in the fall of 2013. By mid-2013, however, pilot programs were already underway in schools and community centers in Atlanta, Chicago, Honolulu, and San Francisco.

Jerry is one of the middle-school boys who have been trying Zamzee at a Boys & Girls Club in Atlanta. Georgia ranks second in the nation for childhood obesity, and more than half of its middle-school students fail to meet the Center for Disease Control's recommendations for daily activity. The situation is so serious that Children's Healthcare of Atlanta, a system of pediatric centers, recently launched an ad campaign aimed at overweight children.

Zamzee concentrates on carrots rather than sticks. Parents put money into an account to fund the rewards that their children can try to earn with their Zamz (though some donors, such as the Mayo Clinic, are providing funding during the pilot tests).

Neuroscientist Sandra Aamodt, the author of *Welcome to Your Child's Brain*, praises Zamzee's focus on physical activity instead of weight. She cautions, however, that research has revealed that intrinsic motivation outlasts extrinsic rewards. (Intrinsic motivation comes from inside an individual rather than from external rewards, such as money or grades.) With that in mind, Zamzee's developers have been testing multiple methods for motivating children. They have found that combining virtual (electronic) and monetary rewards can be successful.

And the bottom line? According to Zamzee, studies confirm that kids who use Zamzee move almost 60 percent more on average than kids who do not.

Sources: Compiled from "Zamzee Improves Kids' Health Using Gamification Tools from Bunchball," *Yahoo! Finance*, March 8, 2013; N. Mott, "Zamzee Cracks Gamified Fitness....For the Children," *Pandodaily .com*, October 5, 2012; M. Frazier, "Virtual World Takes on Childhood Obesity," *MIT Technology Review*, May 16, 2012; J. Temple, "Jury Out on Zamzee, Other Forms of 'Gamification'," *San Francisco Chronicle*, February 26, 2012; H. Shaughnessy, "The Day I Knew Gamification Would be a Winner," *Forbes*, February 8, 2012; www.zamzee.com, accessed April 5, 2013.

Questions

1. Why is Zamzee using games to help kids lose weight?
2. In your opinion, would Zamzee be as successful for adult weight loss? Why or why not?

Among the thousands of other healthcare applications, administrative systems are critically important. These systems perform functions ranging from detecting insurance fraud, to creating nursing schedules, to financial and marketing management.

The Internet contains vast amounts of useful medical information (see www.webmd.com, for example). In an interesting study, researchers at the Princess Alexandra Hospital in Brisbane, Australia, identified 26 difficult diagnostic cases published in the *New England Journal of Medicine*. They selected three to five search terms from each case and then conducted a Google search. Next, they recorded the three diagnoses that Google ranked most prominently and that appeared to fit the symptoms and signs. Finally, they compared these results with the correct diagnoses as published in the journal. The researchers discovered that their Google searches had found the correct diagnosis in 15 of the 26 cases, a success rate of 57 percent. Despite these results, the research team cautions against self-diagnosis. They maintain that people should use diagnostic information gained from Google and medical Web sites such as WebMD (www.webmd.com) only to ask questions of their physicians. In the closing case of Chapter 2, you will see the medical applications of IBM's Watson system.

before you go on...

1. What are some of the quality-of-life improvements made possible by IT? Has IT had any negative effects on our quality of life? If so, explain, and provide examples.
2. Describe the robotic revolution, and consider its implications for humans.
3. Explain how IT has improved healthcare practices.

What's In IT For Me?

In Section 1.2, we discussed how IT supports each of the functional areas of the organization. Here we examine the MIS function.

MIS

For the **MIS Major**

The MIS function directly supports all other functional areas in an organization. That is, the MIS function is responsible for providing the information that each functional area needs in order to make decisions. The overall objective of MIS personnel is to help users improve performance and solve business problems using IT. To accomplish this objective, MIS personnel must understand both the information requirements and the technology associated with each functional area. Given their position, however, they must think "business needs" first and "technology" second.

[Summary]

1. **Identify the reasons why being an informed user of information systems is important in today's world.**

   The benefits of being an informed user of IT include:

   - You will benefit more from your organization's IT applications because you will understand what is "behind" those applications.
   - You will be able to provide input into your organization's IT applications, thus improving the quality of those applications.
   - You will quickly be in a position to recommend, or participate in the selection of IT applications that your organization will use.
   - You will be able to keep up with rapid developments in existing information technologies, as well as the introduction of new technologies.
   - You will understand the potential impacts that "new and improved" technologies will have on your organization and therefore will be qualified to make recommendations concerning their adoption and use.
   - You will play a key role in managing the information systems in your organization.
   - You will be in a position to use IT if you decide to start your own business.

2. **Describe the various types of computer-based information systems in an organization.**

   - Transaction processing systems (TPS) support the monitoring, collection, storage, and processing of data from the organization's basic business transactions, each of which generates data.
   - Functional area information systems (FAISs) support a particular functional area within the organization.
   - Interorganizational information systems (IOSs) support many interorganizational operations, of which supply chain management is the best known.
   - Enterprise resource planning (ERP) systems correct a lack of communication among the FAISs by tightly integrating the functional area ISs via a common database.
   - Electronic commerce (e-commerce) systems enable organizations to conduct transactions with other organizations (called business-to-business (B2B) electronic commerce), and with customers (called business-to-consumer (B2C) electronic commerce).
   - Office automation systems (OASs) typically support the clerical staff, lower and middle managers, and knowledge workers, by enabling them to develop documents (word processing and desktop publishing software), schedule resources (electronic calendars), and communicate (e-mail, voice mail, videoconferencing, and groupware).

- Business intelligence (BI) systems provide computer-based support for complex, nonroutine decisions, primarily for middle managers and knowledge workers.
- Expert systems (ESs) attempt to duplicate the work of human experts by applying reasoning capabilities, knowledge, and expertise within a specific domain.

3. Discuss ways in which information technology can affect managers and nonmanagerial workers.

Potential IT impacts on managers:

- IT may reduce the number of middle managers;
- IT will provide managers with real-time or near-real-time information, meaning that managers will have less time to make decisions;
- IT will increase the likelihood that managers will have to supervise geographically dispersed employees and teams.

Potential IT impacts on nonmanagerial workers:

- IT may eliminate jobs;
- IT may cause employees to experience a loss of identity;
- IT can cause job stress and physical problems, such as repetitive stress injury.

4. List positive and negative societal effects of the increased use of information technology.

Positive societal effects:

- IT can provide opportunities for people with disabilities;
- IT can provide people with flexibility in their work (e.g., work from anywhere, anytime);
- Robots will take over mundane chores;
- IT will enable improvements in healthcare.

Negative societal effects:

- IT can cause health problems for individuals;
- IT can place employees on constant call;
- IT can potentially misinform patients about their health problems.

[Chapter Glossary]

application (or app) A computer program designed to support a specific task or business process.

business intelligence (BI) systems Provide computer-based support for complex, nonroutine decisions, primarily for middle managers and knowledge workers.

computer-based information system (CBIS) An information system that uses computer technology to perform some or all of its intended tasks.

dashboards A special form of IS that support all managers of the organization by providing rapid access to timely information and direct access to structured information in the form of reports.

data items An elementary description of things, events, activities, and transactions that are recorded, classified, and stored but are not organized to convey any specific meaning.

database A collection of related files or tables containing data.

electronic commerce (e-commerce) systems A type of inter-organizational information system that enables organizations to conduct transactions, called business-to-business electronic commerce, and customers to conduct transactions with businesses, called business-to-consumer electronic commerce.

enterprise resource planning (ERP) systems Information systems that correct a lack of communication among the functional area ISs by tightly integrating the functional area ISs via a common database.

ergonomics The science of adapting machines and work environments to people; focuses on creating an environment that is safe, well lit, and comfortable.

expert systems (ESs) Attempt to duplicate the work of human experts by applying reasoning capabilities, knowledge, and expertise within a specific domain.

functional area information systems (FAISs) ISs that support a particular functional area within the organization.

hardware A device such as a processor, monitor, keyboard, or printer. Together, these devices accept, process, and display data and information.

information Data that have been organized so that they have meaning and value to the recipient.

information system (IS) Collects, processes, stores, analyzes, and disseminates information for a specific purpose.

information technology (IT) Relates to any computer-based tool that people use to work with information and support the information and information-processing needs of an organization.

information technology components Hardware, software, databases, and networks.

information technology infrastructure IT components plus IT services.

information technology platform Formed by the IT components of hardware, software, networks (wireline and wireless), and databases.

information technology services IT personnel use IT components to perform these IT services: develop information systems, oversee security and risk, and manage data.

informed user A person knowledgeable about information systems and information technology.

interorganizational information systems (IOSs) Information systems that connect two or more organizations.

knowledge Data and/or information that have been organized and processed to convey understanding, experience, accumulated learning, and expertise as they apply to a current problem or activity.

knowledge workers Professional employees such as financial and marketing analysts, engineers, lawyers, and accountants, who are experts in a particular subject area and create information and knowledge, which they integrate into the business.

network A connecting system (wireline or wireless) that permits different computers to share resources.

procedures The set of instructions for combining hardware, software, database, and network components in order to process information and generate the desired output.

software A program or collection of programs that enable the hardware to process data.

supply chain The flow of materials, information, money, and services from suppliers of raw materials through factories and warehouses to the end customers.

transaction processing system (TPS) Supports the monitoring, collection, storage, and processing of data from the organization's basic business transactions, each of which generates data.

[Discussion Questions]

1. Describe a business that you would like to start. Discuss how you would use global outsourcing to accomplish your goals.

2. Your university wants to recruit high-quality high school students from your state. Provide examples of (1) the data that your recruiters would gather in this process, (2) the information that your recruiters would process from these data, and (3) the types of knowledge that your recruiters would infer from this information.

3. Can the terms data, information, and knowledge have different meanings for different people? Support your answer with examples.

4. Information technology makes it possible to "never be out of touch." Discuss the pros and cons of always being available to your employers and clients (regardless of where you are or what you are doing).

5. Robots have the positive impact of being able to relieve humans from working in dangerous conditions. What are some negative impacts of robots in the workplace?

6. Is it possible to endanger yourself by accessing too much medical information on the Web? Why or why not? Support your answer.

7. Is the vast amount of medical information on the Web a good thing? Answer from the standpoint of a patient and from the standpoint of a physician.

8. Describe other potential impacts of IT on societies as a whole.

9. What are the major reasons why it is important for employees in all functional areas to become familiar with IT?

10. Refer to the study at Princess Alexandra Hospital (in the "Improvements in Healthcare" section). How do you feel about Google searches finding the correct diagnosis in 57 percent of the cases? Are you impressed with these results? Why or why not? What are the implications of this study for self-diagnosis?

[Problem-Solving Activities]

1. Visit some Web sites that offer employment opportunities in IT. Prominent examples are: www.dice .com, www.monster.com, www.collegerecruiter.com, www.careerbuilder.com, www.jobcentral.com, www.job .com, www.career.com, www.simplyhired.com, and www.truecareers.com. Compare the IT salaries to salaries offered to accountants, marketing personnel, financial personnel, operations personnel, and human resources personnel. For other information on IT salaries, check *Computerworld*'s annual salary survey.

2. Enter the Web site of UPS (www.ups.com).

   a. Find out what information is available to customers before they send a package.

   b. Find out about the "package tracking" system.

   c. Compute the cost of delivering a 10″ × 20″ × 15″ box, weighing 40 pounds, from your hometown to Long Beach, California (or to Lansing, Michigan, if you live in or near Long Beach). Compare the fastest delivery against the least cost.

3. Surf the Internet for information about the Department of Homeland Security (DHS). Examine the available information, and comment on the role of information technologies in the department.

4. Access www.irobot.com, and investigate the company's Education and Research Robots. Surf the Web for other companies that manufacture robots, and compare their products with those of iRobot.

[Team Assignments]

1. (a) Create an online group for studying IT or an aspect of IT that you are interested in. Each member of the group must establish a Yahoo! e-mail account (free). Go to *http://groups.yahoo.com*.

   Step 1: Click on "Start Your Group."

   Step 2: Select a category that best describes your group (use Search Group Categories, or use the Browse Group Categories tool). Yahoo! will force you to be very specific in categorizing your group. Continue until you see the button: "Place My Group Here."

   Step 3: Name your group.

   Step 4: Enter your group e-mail address.

   Step 5: Describe your group.

   Step 6: Select your Yahoo! Profile and e-mail addresses for your group.

   Step 7: Now you can customize your group and invite people to join.

   Step 8: Conduct a discussion online of at least two topics of interest to the group.

   Step 9: Find a similar group (use Yahoo!'s "find a group" and make a connection).

   Write a report for your instructor.

   (b) Now, follow the same steps for Google Groups.

   (c) Compare Yahoo! Groups and Google Groups.

2. Review the *Wall Street Journal*, *Fortune*, *Business Week*, and local newspapers for the last three months to find stories about the use of computer-based information systems in organizations. Each group will prepare a report describing five applications. The reports should emphasize the role of each application and its benefit to the organization. Pre-sent and discuss your work.

[Closing Case **Baxter: Coming to Work Right Next to You**]

The **Problem**

Manufacturing constitutes a $2 trillion sector of the U.S. economy. For the past 60 years, worker productivity in the manufacturing sector has increased by about 3.7 percent per year.

In the past, the United States has retained higher-value-added manufacturing jobs while allowing lower-value-added jobs go elsewhere. Interestingly, the definition of "elsewhere" has changed over time. The manufacture of simple goods (e.g., toys) is constantly moving to the location with the lowest wages. After the end of World War II, there was an abundance of low-cost labor in Japan, so manufacturing moved there. As the Japanese economy recovered, however, the standard of living rose, and with it the costs of producing goods. As a result, low-cost manufacturing moved to South Korea, where a scenario similar to Japan took place. Manufacturing simple goods then moved to Taiwan, to mainland China, and, most recently, to Vietnam.

From the perspective of a manufacturing company, a more highly educated and skilled workforce typically has less interest in low-skilled jobs designed to manufacture simple goods.

As a result, the world will eventually run out of places where low-cost labor is available. Therefore, the question is: What will it take to break out of the cycle of making inexpensive goods by hand with unskilled, inexpensive labor? Perhaps robots are the answer.

The **Initial Solution:** **Industrial Robots**

The first industrial robot developed in the United State was put to work in 1961 in the Unimate, a General Motors factory located in Ewing, New Jersey. The Unimate placed hot, forged car parts into a liquid bath to cool them. At the time, companies could not place a computer on an industrial robot, because computers cost millions of dollars and were room-sized. Sensors were also extremely expensive. As a result, early industrial robots were effectively blind and very dumb, and they performed repeated actions only by following a closely defined physical path dictated by a computer program.

Today's industrial robots still perform well on very narrowly defined, repeatable tasks. However, they are not adaptable, flexible, or easy to use. In addition, most industrial robots are not safe for people to be around. Moreover, it typically takes 18 months to integrate an industrial robot into a factory operation.

As of mid-2013, 70 percent of all industrial robots were being utilized in automobile factories. These machines are often thought of as money savers for companies. However, the cost to integrate one of today's industrial robots into a factory operation is often 3 to 5 times the cost of the robot itself. Such integration requires the services of computer programmers and machine specialists. In addition, companies must place safety cages around the robots so that they do not strike people while they are operating. Further, most industrial robots have no sensors or means to detect what is happening in their environment.

There are some 300,000 small manufacturing companies in the United States that have fewer than 500 employees. Almost none of these firms have an industrial robot, for the reasons we have just discussed. In addition, almost all of these firms have relatively small production runs, meaning that they are constantly changing the design and manufacturing procedures for what they produce. Some of these companies, called job shops, produce a wide variety of goods for other companies. They specialize in manufacturing a type of product that can be highly customized to an individual client's needs. In a typical factory that uses an industrial robot, a production run is rarely less than four months long. For a job shop, a production run can be as short as one hour. Clearly, then, small manufacturing firms need a different kind of robot.

A Next-Generation Solution: Baxter

Rethink Robotics (www.rethinkrobotics.com) may have an answer with Baxter, a new kind of industrial robot that sells for $22,000. Baxter is very different from existing industrial robots. It does not need an expensive or elaborate safety cage, and factory operators do not need to segregate it from human workers. In fact, humans can actually share a workspace with Baxter.

Unlike other industrial robots, Baxter works right out of the box. It can be integrated into a factory's work flow in about an hour. Baxter also requires no special programming. In addition, engineers can go deeper into Baxter's menu system to adjust and optimize settings for different tasks.

Interacting with Baxter is more like working with a person than operating a traditional industrial robot. If Baxter picks up something it shouldn't on the assembly line, for instance, workers can take its arm and move the robot to put the object down.

Baxter also contains a variety of sensors, including depth sensors as well as cameras in its wrists, so it "sees" with its hands. It is constantly building and adjusting a mathematical model of the world in front of it, enabling it to recognize different objects.

Another benefit of Baxter is that other factory workers can train it. In fact, a factory worker who has never seen a robot before can learn to train Baxter to do simple tasks in five minutes. For example, a worker can show Baxter a part of the task she is asking the robot to perform, and Baxter can infer the rest of the task. Also, if a human is interacting with Baxter or doing part of the task, the robot can figure out how to perform the rest of the task.

The Results

Rethink Robotics launched Baxter on September 18, 2012. It is therefore too early to evaluate this technology. It is worth noting, however, that by mid-2013 Baxter had been "hired" by one company and was being tested by several others.

Specifically, Baxter was working at a K'Nex (www.knex.com) plant outside Philadelphia, helping to stack Super Mario toys and ship them to China. Later in 2013, Baxter is scheduled to begin working at three plastics companies: Rodon (www.rodongroup.com), Nypro (www.nypro.com), and Vanguard Plastics Corporation (www.vanguardplastics.com).

Let's take a closer look at Vanguard Plastics, a small company with $6 million in annual revenue. Vanguard operates state-of-the-art automated electric presses that crush plastic pellets into different shapes under 1,000 atmospheres of pressure. Custom-built industrial robots—running on overhead tracks—swing down to collect the finished parts and place them on a conveyor.

Vanguard's key statistic is sales divided by man-hours. Vanguard executives claim that for the company to stay in business, this statistic must improve by 1 percent or more every year. The only way to accomplish this goal is to increase productivity.

One routine job that is still performed by hand is packing parts. Coming off one of the presses are small, textured, plastic cups, which Vanguard sells for 2 cents each to a medical company that uses them to package liquid medicines. A worker from a temporary agency, earning $9 per hour, stacks the cups and then flicks a plastic bag over the stacks.

This is the job for which Vanguard is testing Baxter. Vanguard claims that if Baxter can eliminate one temporary worker—a move that would earn back the company's investment in a single year—then the company will buy Baxter. However, for the cup-stacking job, Baxter will need a specially designed gripper, which Rethink Robotics is developing. The company is also developing software that will enable Baxter to communicate with other machines. For example, Baxter would be able to tell the conveyor when to move forward or stop.

Sources: Compiled from R. Brooks, "Robots at Work: Toward a Smarter Factory," *The Futurist,* May–June, 2013; G. Anderson, "Help Wanted: Robots to Fill Service Jobs," *Retail Wire,* April 10, 2013; J. Young, "The New Industrial Revolution," *The Chronicle of Higher Education,* March 25, 2013; L. Kratochwill, "Rethink's Baxter Robot Got a Job Packaging Toys and Sending Them to China," *Fast Company,* February 26, 2013; A. Regalado, "Small Factories Give Baxter the Robot a Cautious Once-Over," *MIT Technology Review,* January 16, 2013; T. Geron, "The Robots Are Coming," *Forbes,* November 12, 2012; W. Knight, "This Robot Could Transform Manufacturing," *MIT Technology Review,* September 18, 2012; F. Harrop, "Buckle Up for the Robot Revolution," *Rasmussen Reports,* September 18, 2012; K. Alspach, "Rethink Robotics Unveils 'Human-Like' Robot," *Boston Business Journal,* September 18, 2012; J. Markoff, "Skilled Work, Without the Worker," *The New York Times,* August 19, 2012; J. Leber, "The Next Wave of Factory Robots," *MIT Technology Review,* July 23, 2012; www.rethinkrobotics.com, accessed April 4, 2013.

Questions

1. Rethink Robotics claims that Baxter will not necessarily replace workers; rather, it will enable workers to transition into higher-paying jobs. Will Baxter replace workers in small manufacturing companies? Why or why not? Support your answer.

2. Discuss the possible reactions of labor unions to Baxter.

3. Discuss additional potential applications for Baxter.

[Internship Activity]

Banking Industry

Information Systems impact every facet of an organization. This is especially true in the banking industry. Information Systems have revolutionized the way customers interact with banks, pay bills, manage accounts, and more. Information Systems now make it easier to communicate with customers via e-statements, use databases make loan decisions, monitor account status, and much, much more.

For this Internship Activity, you will work for Jeremy Farr, Associate Vice President and IT Officer of Noble Bank & Trust in Anniston, AL. Jeremy is working hard to bring Noble Bank into the "21st Century" in regards to technology. In some cases, this requires a complete overhaul of hardware, software, and user training. Jeremy would like for you to do some research on the web to see if you can find examples of how other banks have implemented Information Systems to their advantage.

Please visit the Book Companion Site to receive the full set of instructions.

Chapter 2

Organizational Strategy, Competitive Advantage, and Information Systems

[LEARNING OBJECTIVES]	[CHAPTER OUTLINE]	[WEB RESOURCES]

[LEARNING OBJECTIVES]

1. Discuss ways in which information systems enable cross-functional business processes and business processes for a single functional area.

2. Become familiar with business process definition, measurement, and analysis.

3. Compare and contrast *business process improvement*, *business process reengineering*, and *business process management* to identify the advantages and disadvantages of each one.

4. Identify effective IT responses to different kinds of business pressures.

5. Describe the strategies that organizations typically adopt to counter Porter's five competitive forces.

6. Describe the characteristics of effective business–information technology alignment.

[CHAPTER OUTLINE]

2.1 Business Processes

2.2 Business Process Reengineering, Business Process Improvement, and Business Process Management

2.3 Business Pressures, Organizational Responses, and Information Technology Support

2.4 Competitive Advantage and Strategic Information Systems

2.5 Business–Information Technology Alignment

[WEB RESOURCES]

- Student PowerPoints for note taking

WileyPLUS

- E-book

- Author video lecture for each chapter section

- Practice quizzes

- Flash Cards for vocabulary review

- Additional "IT's About Business" cases

- Video interviews with managers

- Lab Manuals for Microsoft Office 2010 and 2013

What's In IT For Me?

This Chapter Will Help Prepare You To...

ACCT
ACCOUNTING
Perform audits

FIN
FINANCE
Determine best uses for funds

MKT
MARKETING
Conduct price analyses

POM
PRODUCTION OPERATIONS MANAGEMENT
Monitor product quality

HRM
HUMAN RESOURCES MANAGEMENT
Help employees manage their careers

MIS
MIS
Develop systems to support firm's strategy

The Problem

In the months leading up to the terrorist attacks of September 11, 2001, the U.S. government had all the necessary clues to stop the al Qaeda perpetrators. The attackers were from countries known to harbor terrorists, they entered the United States on temporary visas, they had trained to fly civilian airliners, and they purchased one-way airplane tickets on September 11.

Unfortunately for thousands of workers in the World Trade Center, those clues were located in different databases scattered across many government agencies. Organizations like the CIA and the FBI maintain thousands of databases, each with its own data: financial records, DNA samples, voice and other sound samples, video clips, maps, floor plans, human intelligence reports from all over the world, and many other types of data. Integrating all of those data into a coherent whole is potentially overwhelming. In 2001 there was no tool available that would have enabled government analysts to integrate all of these different types of data that were dispersed across so many locations.

A Potential IT Solution

Today, more than a decade after the terrorist attacks, the government has an important new tool at its disposal, known as Palantir. The origins of Palantir go back to PayPal. Because PayPal was so successful, it attracted criminals who used it to carry out money laundering and fraud. By 2000, PayPal was in financial trouble because the existing antifraud software tools could not keep up with the criminal activity. Each time PayPal analysts caught onto one ploy, the perpetrators simply changed tactics.

To deal with these issues, PayPal's analysts created software that could view each transaction as a part of a pattern, rather than as just a single database entry. This process enabled analysts to spot networks of suspicious accounts and to discover patterns that PayPal's computers had missed. PayPal utilized this software to freeze suspicious payments before they were processed. The software saved the company hundreds of millions of dollars.

Several PayPal engineers who had worked on the software and Stanford computer scientists formed a startup company to develop PayPal's fraud-detection tool into a data-analysis system that integrated pattern recognition, artificial intelligence software, and human cognitive

[A Tool to Combat Terrorism and Fight Crime]

skills. They named the tool Palantir (www.palantir.com) for the "Seeing Stones" in the *Lord of the Rings*.

In an early deployment of Palantir, the U.S. intelligence community used the software tool in the war on terrorism. Palantir technology essentially solves the types of intelligence problems that allowed September 11 to occur. That is, it helps law enforcement agencies spot patterns in the vast amounts of data they analyze every day. Palantir software combs through all of the available databases, identifies related pieces of information, and integrates everything into a unified picture.

The Results

Palantir's customer list currently includes the U.S. Department of Defense, the CIA, the FBI, the Army, the Marines, the Air Force, the police departments of New York and Los Angeles, and an increasing number of financial institutions that have an interest in detecting bank fraud. Most of Palantir's government work remains classified, but information on some cases has leaked out.

In April 2010, for example, security researchers in Canada used Palantir software to crack a spy operation called the Shadow Network that had, among other things, broken into the Indian Defense Ministry and infiltrated the Dalai Lama's e-mail account. Palantir has also been used to unravel child abuse and abduction cases, to locate suspects in the murder of a U.S. Immigration and Customs Enforcement special agent, and to uncover bombing networks in Syria, Afghanistan, and Pakistan.

In Afghanistan, the U.S. Special Operations Forces use Palantir to plan assaults. They type a village's name into the system, and it generates a map of the village that details the locations of all reported shooting skirmishes and improvised explosive device (IED) incidents. The soldiers then utilize the timeline function to discover where the most recent attacks occurred, and they plot their mission in the village accordingly.

Another scenario that illustrates Palantir's usefulness involves the U.S. Marines. The Marines used to spend years gathering fingerprint and DNA evidence from IEDs and trying to match those data against a database of similar information collected from villagers. Usually, by the time they obtained any results, the bombers had disappeared. In contrast, field operatives can now upload fingerprint/DNA evidence from villagers into Palantir and instantly find matches from past attacks.

Wall Street banks are also utilizing Palantir to search their transaction databases for criminal fraud, trading insights, and even new ways to price mortgages. One of the world's largest banks employs Palantir software to break up a popular scam called BustOut. In this scam, criminals steal or purchase access to thousands of people's online identities and then break into their bank and credit card accounts. Rather than act immediately, however, they spend weeks biding their time until someone on their radar purchases a plane ticket or leaves on a holiday. They then siphon money out of the accounts as quickly as they can while the victim is in transit. The criminals hide their trails by anonymizing their computing activity and disabling alert systems in the bank and credit card accounts. When the bank identifies a small number of compromised accounts, it uses Palantir to discern the characteristics of those accounts. Palantir then helps the bank discover thousands of other accounts with those characteristics that have not yet been tapped.

Another organization, the FBI, utilizes Palantir technology to instantly compile thorough dossiers on U.S. citizens. For example, agents can integrate surveillance videos with credit card transactions, cell phone records, e-mails, air itineraries, and Web search information. Privacy advocates worry that Palantir will make the FBI and other government agencies even more intrusive consumers of personal data. One specific event that raised concerns among privacy advocates concerned a Palantir engineer who was placed on leave after being exposed by the hacker collective Anonymous for participating in a plot to break into the personal computers of WikiLeaks supporters, but later was quietly rehired.

Palantir responds to these concerns by asserting that it has developed very sophisticated privacy-protection technology. Its software creates audit trails that detail who is privy to certain pieces of information and what they have done with the information. Palantir also has a permission system that ensures that agency workers using their software can access only the data allowed by their clearance level.

Palantir is also generating controversy within the U.S. Army. In late 2012, the Pentagon's top weapons tester assigned a failing grade to the Army's premier battlefield intelligence system, which troops in Afghanistan have criticized as being too slow and unreliable in analyzing data to locate enemy combatants. A memo from the testing agency called the updated version of the $2.5 billion Defense Common Ground System "not operationally effective, not operationally suitable, and not operationally survivable against cyber threats." The negative report was a blow to the Army's analysis system. Further, the system faces competition from Palantir.

At first, the Army resisted Palantir, but overseas troops were clamoring for access to the system. One U.S. congressman accused the Army of protecting its own system, to the detriment of U.S. troops. Finally, in early 2013 the Army announced that it will attempt to integrate Palantir into its existing intelligence system. The results remain to be seen.

Sources: Compiled from J. Gould, "Army May Work With Palantir on Intel Software," *The Army Times*, January 3, 2013; M. Hoffman, "Army Considers Palantir to Boost Intelligence Architecture," *Defense.org*, December 20, 2012; J. Lonsdale, "How Did Palantir Build Such a Strong Brand?" *Forbes*, December 12, 2012; R. Scarborough, "Army's Own Data Mining System Fails Test," *The Washington Times*, December 2, 2012; R. Scarborough, "Military Leaders Urgently Push for New Counterterrorism Software," *The Washington Times*, August 27, 2012; A. Good, "Who Actually Uses Palantir Finance?" *Forbes*, August 15, 2012; W. Hickey, "This Peter Thiel Company Is Ripping the Army Intelligence Community Apart," *Business Insider*, August 3, 2012; A. Vance and B. Stone, "Palantir, the War on Terror's Secret Weapon," *Bloomberg BusinessWeek*, November 22, 2011; "Husky Names Palantir as Software and Consulting Partner," *Oil & Gas Financial Journal*, November 4, 2011; P. Gobry, "Secretive Spy Tech Company Palantir Technologies Raises Another $50 Million," *Business Insider*, May 11, 2011; D. Primack, "Analyze This: Palantir Worth More than $2 Billion," *CNN Money*, May 6, 2011; A. Greenberg, "Palantir Apologizes for WikiLeaks Attack Proposal, Cuts Ties with HBGary," *Forbes*, February 11, 2011; D. Storm, "Bank of America Using Three Intelligence Firms to Attack WikiLeaks," *Computerworld*, February 9, 2011; S. Gorman, "How Team of Geeks Cracked the Spy Trade," *Wall Street Journal*, September 4, 2009; www.palantir.com, accessed February 16, 2013.

What We Learned from This Case

The chapter-opening case illustrates the importance of the Palantir system in helping organizations respond to business pressures (in this instance, national security and bank fraud) and providing support for their strategy. In particular, the system helps organizations collate and analyze vast amounts of data stored in different places and different organizations. The case also highlights the incredible complexity of the modern high-tech world, and it shows how organizations are using Palantir to make sense of a rapidly changing environment. Finally, it demonstrates that any information system can be *strategic*, meaning that it can provide a competitive advantage if it is used properly.

Competitive advantage refers to any assets that provide an organization with an edge against its competitors in some measure such as cost, quality, or speed. A competitive advantage helps an organization to control a market and to accrue larger-than-average profits. Significantly, both strategy and competitive advantage take many forms.

Although there are many companies that use technology in more expensive ways, Alta Bicycle Share, which is discussed in IT's About [Small] Business 2.1, demonstrates that an entrepreneurial spirit coupled with a solid understanding of what IT can do for you will provide competitive advantages to entrepreneurs just as it does for Wall Street CIOs. As you study this chapter, think of the small businesses in your area that are utilizing popular technologies in interesting and novel ways. Have any of them found an innovative use for Twitter? Facebook? Amazon? PayPal? If not, then can you think of any businesses that would benefit from employing these technologies?

This chapter is important for you for several reasons. First, the business pressures we address in the chapter will affect your organization. Just as important, however, they also will affect *you*. Therefore, you must understand how information systems can help you—and eventually your organization—respond to these pressures.

In addition, acquiring competitive advantage is essential for your organization's survival. Many organizations achieve competitive advantage through the efforts of their employees. Therefore, becoming knowledgeable about strategy and how information systems affect strategy and competitive position will help you throughout your career.

This chapter encourages you to become familiar with your organization's strategy, mission, and goals and to understand its business problems and how it makes (or loses) money. It will help you understand how information technology contributes to organizational strategy. Further, you likely will become a member of business/IT committees that decide (among many other things) how to use existing technologies more effectively and whether to adopt new ones. After studying this chapter, you will be able to make immediate contributions in these committees when you join your organizations.

Information systems can be just as strategic to a small- or medium-sized company as they are to a large firm. IT's About [Small] Business 2.1 illustrates how information systems are strategically important to bicycle-sharing companies.

IT's about [small] business

2.1 Sharing Bicycles POM

A bicycle-sharing system, as the name suggests, is a service that makes bicycles available for individuals to use on a very short-term basis. The overall goal of these systems is to provide free or affordable access to bicycles for short-distance trips in urban areas to reduce traffic congestion, noise, and air pollution.

Bike-sharing systems have progressed through three generations: the first generation, called white bikes (or free bikes); the second generation of coin-deposited systems; and the third generation, or information technology-based systems. An emerging fourth generation includes all of the components of third-generation systems, but with one major difference: Fourth-generation systems are linked with public transit. The goal is seamless integration of bike sharing with public transportation and other modes of transit, such as taxis and carpooling. Fourth-generation systems will locate bike-sharing stations and parking conveniently near transit stations. In addition, they will coordinate transportation schedules, such as bus and train arrivals and departures. Finally, they will provide customers with a single payment smartcard that allows access to all of the available transportation options. Let's take a closer look at one fourth-generation system, Alta Bicycle Share.

On a Washington, DC, morning, Alison Cohen rides her bicycle to work. She makes the 2 mile trip in 10 minutes—a trip that would otherwise entail a 20 minute subway ride, a 40 minute walk, or a $7 cab ride. Cohen is president of Alta Bicycle Share (www.altabicycleshare.com), the company behind Washington's bicycle-sharing program. Formed in 2010, Alta combines three companies: (1) Alta Planning & Design, based in Portland, Oregon, which designs bike lanes and parks; (2) Montreal's Public Bike System Company, which owns the credit card processing technology; and (3) Alta itself, which bids for government contracts and runs operations in cities across the United States, as well as in Melbourne, Australia. In mid-2013, Alta had

bicycle-sharing services in Washington, DC, Chicago, Boston, and Chattanooga, Tennessee, with New York City, Portland, Oregon, and Columbus, Ohio, soon to be added.

How does this system operate? Basically, the participating cities buy the bikes and install docking stations where users can rent them with a credit card. Alta maintains the bikes and collects payment. In return, it receives either part of the revenue generated by the rentals or a flat annual management fee.

Significantly, Alta is reportedly turning a profit. However, the company faces competition from B-Cycle (www.bcycle.com), which operates 1,500 bicycles in 16 cities, including Chicago and Denver.

Interestingly, the rent-a-bike phenomenon is also being adopted by the Beijing municipal government. To ease the city's notorious traffic jams, the Beijing China Municipal Commission of Development and Reform is setting up 500 rental kiosks around the city to offer residents the choice of more than 20,000 rental bikes.

Sources: Compiled from C. Lyon, "Portland Bike Share Moves Forward," *Alta Bicycle Share Press Release*, December 12, 2012; "Why the Latest Delay to the Bike Share Program May Not Be the Last," *The Gotham Gazette*, December 2012; "Emanuel's Bike-Share Program Hits Speed Bump," *Fox News*, August 15, 2012; M. Pamer, "California Gets Its First City Bike-Sharing Program in Anaheim," *NBC News*, August 9, 2012; G. Hesselberg, "B-Cyclists Log Thousands of Trips in Madison," *Wisconsin State Journal*, February 3, 2012; "More Rental Bikes, Subway Lines to Ease Beijing Traffic Congestion," *English.xinhuanet.cn*, January 6, 2012; S. Shaheen and S. Guzman, "Worldwide Bikesharing," *Access Magazine*, Fall, 2011; H. Coster, "New Commute," *Forbes*, June 27, 2011; www.altabicycleshare.com, www.bcycle.com, accessed February 21, 2013.

Questions

1. Describe the problems involved with setting up a bicycle-sharing program in a new city.
2. Describe how information technology can help address these problems.

In many cases, organizations achieve competitive advantage by managing their business processes more profitably than their competitors do. Therefore, you begin this chapter with an introduction to business processes and business process management. You will then see how information systems enable organizations to respond to business pressures. Next, you will learn how information systems help organizations gain competitive advantages in the marketplace. The chapter concludes by discussing business–IT alignment; in other words, how an organization's IT function supports the organization's strategy.

Business Processes

2.1

A **business process** is an ongoing collection of related activities that create a product or a service of value to the organization, its business partners, and/or its customers. A process is comprised of three fundamental elements:

- *Inputs*: Materials, services, and information that flow through and are transformed as a result of process activities
- *Resources*: People and equipment that perform process activities
- *Outputs*: The product or a service created by the process

If the process involves a customer, then that customer can be either internal or external to the organization. A manager who is the recipient of an internal reporting process is an example of an internal customer. In contrast, an individual or a business that purchases the organization's products is the external customer of the fulfillment process.

Successful organizations measure their process activities to evaluate how well they are executing these processes. Two fundamental metrics that organizations employ in assessing their processes are efficiency and effectiveness. *Efficiency* focuses on doing things well in the process; for example, progressing from one process activity to another without delay or without wasting money or resources. *Effectiveness* focuses on doing the things that matter; that is, creating outputs of value to the process customer—for example, high-quality products.

Many processes cross functional areas in an organization. For example, product development involves research, design, engineering, manufacturing, marketing, and distribution. Other processes involve only a single functional area. Table 2.1 identifies the fundamental business processes performed in an organization's functional areas.

Cross-Functional Processes

All of the business processes in Table 2.1 fall within a single functional area of the company. However, many other business processes, such as procurement and fulfillment, cut across multiple functional areas; that is, they are **cross-functional business processes**, meaning that no single functional area is responsible for their execution. Rather, multiple functional areas collaborate to perform the process. For a cross-functional process to be successfully completed, each functional area must execute its specific process steps in a coordinated, collaborative way. To clarify this point, let's take a look at the procurement and fulfillment cross-functional processes. We discuss these processes in greater detail in Chapter 10.

The procurement process includes all of the tasks involved in acquiring needed materials externally from a vendor. Procurement comprises five steps that are completed in three different functional areas of the firm: warehouse, purchasing, and accounting.

The process begins when the warehouse recognizes the need to procure materials, perhaps due to low inventory levels. The warehouse documents this need with a purchase requisition, which it sends to the purchasing department (Step 1). In turn, the purchasing department identifies a suitable vendor, creates a purchase order based on the purchase requisition, and sends the order to the vendor (Step 2). When the vendor receives the purchase order, it ships the materials, which are received in the warehouse (Step 3). The vendor then sends an invoice, which is received by the accounting department (Step 4). Accounting sends payment to the vendor, thereby completing the procurement process (Step 5).

The fulfillment process is concerned with processing customer orders. Fulfillment is triggered by a customer purchase order that is received by the sales department. Sales then validates the purchase order and creates a sales order. The sales order communicates data related to the order to other functional areas within the organization, and it tracks the progress of the

Table **2.1**
Examples of Business Processes

Accounting Business Processes
- Managing accounts payable
- Managing accounts receivable
- Reconciling bank accounts
- Managing cash receipts
- Managing invoice billings
- Managing petty cash
- Producing month-end close
- Producing virtual close

Finance Business Processes
- Managing account collection
- Managing bank loan applications
- Producing business forecasts
- Applying customer credit approval and credit terms
- Producing property tax assessments
- Managing stock transactions
- Generating financial cash flow reports

Marketing Business Processes
- Managing post-sale customer follow-up
- Collecting sales taxes
- Applying copyrights and trademarks
- Using customer satisfaction surveys
- Managing customer service
- Handling customer complaints
- Handling returned goods from customers
- Producing sales leads
- Entering sales orders
- Training sales personnel

Production/Operations Management Business Processes
- Processing bills of materials
- Processing manufacturing change orders
- Managing master parts list and files

- Managing packing, storage, and distribution
- Processing physical inventory
- Managing purchasing
- Managing quality control for finished goods
- Auditing for quality assurance
- Receiving, inspecting, and stocking parts and materials
- Handling shipping and freight claims
- Handling vendor selection, files, and inspections

Human Resources Business Processes
- Applying disability policies
- Managing employee hiring
- Handling employee orientation
- Managing files and records
- Applying healthcare benefits
- Managing pay and payroll
- Producing performance appraisals and salary adjustments
- Managing resignations and terminations
- Applying training/tuition reimbursement
- Managing travel and entertainment
- Managing workplace rules and guidelines
- Overseeing workplace safety

Management Information Systems Business Processes
- Antivirus control
- Computer security issues incident reporting
- Training computer users
- Computer user/staff training
- Applying disaster recovery procedures
- Applying electronic mail policy
- Generating Internet use policy
- Managing service agreements and emergency services
- Applying user workstation standards
- Managing the use of personal software

order. The warehouse prepares and sends the shipment to the customer. Once accounting is notified of the shipment, it creates an invoice and sends it to the customer. The customer then makes a payment, which accounting records.

An organization's business processes can create a competitive advantage if they enable the company to innovate or to execute more effectively and efficiently than its competitors. They can also be liabilities, however, if they make the company less responsive and productive. Consider the airline industry. It has become a competitive necessity for all of the airlines to offer electronic ticket purchases via their Web sites. To provide competitive advantage, however, these sites must be highly responsive and they must provide both current and accurate information on

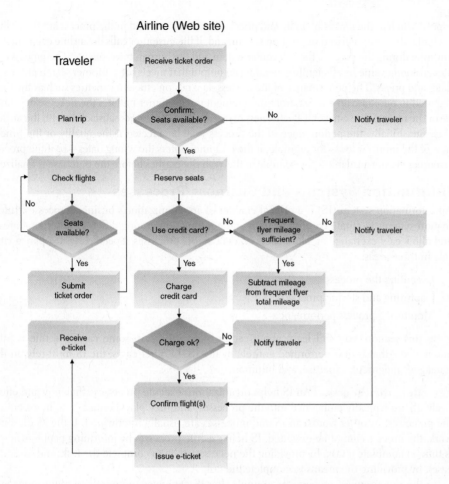

Airline (Web site)

Traveler

FIGURE 2.1 Business process for ordering e-ticket from airline Web site.

flights and prices. An up-to-date, user-friendly site that provides fast answers to user queries will attract customers and increase revenues. In contrast, a site that provides outdated or inaccurate information, or has a slow response time, will hurt rather than improve business.

Clearly, good business processes are vital to organizational success. But, how can organizations determine if their business processes are well designed? The first step is to document the process by describing its steps, its inputs and outputs, and its resources. The organization can then analyze the process and, if necessary, modify it to improve its performance. We examine this procedure in Section 2.2.

To understand this point, let's consider the e-ticketing process. E-ticketing consists of four main process activities: searching for flights, reserving a seat, processing payment, and issuing an e-ticket. These activities can be broken down into more detailed process steps. The result may look like the process map in Figure 2.1. Note that different symbols correspond to different types of process steps. For instance, rectangles (steps) are activities that are performed by process resources (reserve seats, issue e-ticket). Diamond-shaped boxes indicate decisions that need to be made (seats available?). Arrows are used as connectors between steps; they indicate the sequence of activities.

These symbols are important in the process flowchart (which is similar with a programming flowchart). Other symbols may be used to provide additional process details. For example, D-shaped boxes are used instead of rectangles when a waiting period is part of a process; ovals can show start and stop points; and process resources can be attached to activities with resource connector lines, or included as an annotation or property for each activity box.

The customers of the process are travelers planning a trip, and the process output is an e-ticket. Travelers provide inputs to the process: the desired travel parameters to begin the search, the frequent flyer miles number, and their credit card information. In addition, a computerized reservation system that stores information for many airlines also provides some of the process inputs—such as the seat availability and prices. The resources used in the process are the airline Web site, the computerized reservation system, and, if the customer calls the airline call center at any time during the process, the call center system and the human travel agents. The process creates customer value by efficiently generating an output that meets the customer search criteria— dates and prices. The performance of the process depends on efficiency metrics such as the time required to purchase an e-ticket, from the moment the customer initiates the ticket search until he or she receives the e-ticket. Effectiveness metrics include customer satisfaction with the airline Web site. Finally, the performance of the process may be affected if the quality or the timeliness of the inputs is low—for example, if the customer enters the wrong dates—or if the process resources are not available—for example, if the Web site crashes before the purchase is finalized.

Information Systems and Business Processes

An information system (IS) is a critical enabler of an organization's business processes. Information systems facilitate communication and coordination among different functional areas, and allow easy exchange of, and access to, data across processes. Specifically, ISs play a vital role in three areas:

- Executing the process
- Capturing and storing process data
- Monitoring process performance

In this section, you will learn about each of these roles. In some cases the role is fully automated—that is, it is performed entirely by the IS. In other cases, the IS must rely on the manager's judgment, expertise, and intuition.

Executing the Process. An IS helps organizations execute processes efficiently and effectively. IS are typically embedded into the processes, and they play a critical role in executing the processes. In other words, an IS and processes are usually intertwined. If the IS does not work, the process cannot be executed. IS help execute processes by informing people when it is time to complete a task, by providing the necessary data to complete the task, and, in some cases, by providing the means to complete the task.

In the procurement process, for example, the IS generates the purchase requisitions and then informs the purchasing department that action on these requisitions is needed. The accountant will be able to view all shipments received to match an invoice that has been received from a supplier and verify that the invoice is accurate. Without the IS, these steps, and therefore the process, cannot be completed. For example, if the IS is not available, how will the warehouse know which orders are ready to pack and ship?

In the fulfillment process, the IS will inform people in the warehouse that orders are ready for shipment. It also provides them with a listing of what materials must be included in the order and where to find those materials in the warehouse.

Capturing and Storing Process Data. Processes create data such as dates, times, product numbers, quantities, prices, and addresses, as well as who did what, when, and where. IS capture and store these data, commonly referred to as *process data* or *transaction data*. Some of these data are generated and automatically captured by the IS. These are data related to who completes an activity, when, and where. Other data are generated outside the IS and must be entered into it. This data entry can occur in various ways, ranging from manual entry to automated methods involving data in forms such as bar codes and RFID tags that can be read by machines.

In the fulfillment process, for example, when a customer order is received by mail or over the phone, the person taking the order must enter data such as the customer's name, what the customer ordered, and how much he or she ordered. Significantly, when a customer order is received via the firm's Web site, then all customer details are captured by the IS. Data such as the name of the person entering the data (who), at which location the person is completing the task (where), and the date and time (when) are automatically included by the IS when it creates the order. The data are updated as the process steps are executed. When the order is shipped, the warehouse will provide data about which products were shipped and in what quantities, and the IS will automatically include data related to who, when, and where.

An important advantage of using an IS compared to a manual system or multiple functional area information systems is that the data need to be entered into the system only once. Further, once they are entered, other people in the process can easily access them, and there is no need to reenter them in subsequent steps.

The data captured by the IS can provide immediate feedback. For example, the IS can use the data to create a receipt or to make recommendations for additional or alternate products.

Monitoring Process Performance.   A third contribution of IS is to help monitor the state of the various business processes. That is, the IS indicates how well a process is executing. The IS performs this role by evaluating information about a process. This information can be created either at the *instance level* (i.e., a specific task or activity) or the *process level* (i.e., the process as a whole).

For example, a company might be interested in the status of a particular customer order. Where is the order within the fulfillment process? Was the complete order shipped? If so, when? If not, then when can we expect it to be shipped? Or, for the procurement process, when was the purchase order sent to the supplier? What will be the cost of acquiring the material? At the process level, the IS can evaluate how well the procurement process is being executed by calculating the lead time, or the time between sending the purchase order to a vendor and receiving the goods, for each order and each vendor over time.

Not only can the IS help monitor a process, it can also detect problems with the process. The IS performs this role by comparing the information with a standard—that is, what the company expects or desires—to determine if the process is performing within expectations. Management establishes standards based on organizational goals.

If the information provided by the IS indicates that the process is not meeting the standards, then the company assumes that some type of problem exists. Some problems can be routinely and automatically detected by the IS, whereas others require a person to review the information and make judgments. For example, the IS can calculate the expected date that a specific order will be shipped and determine whether this date will meet the established standard. Or, the IS can calculate the average time taken to fill all orders over the last month and compare this information to the standard to determine if the process is working as expected.

Monitoring business processes, then, helps detect problems with these processes. Very often these problems are really symptoms of a more fundamental problem. In such cases, the IS can help diagnose the cause of the symptoms by providing managers with additional, detailed information. For example, if the average time to process a customer order appears to have increased over the previous month, this problem could be a symptom of a more basic problem.

A manager can then drill down into the information to diagnose the underlying problem. To accomplish this task, the manager can request a breakdown of the information by type of product, customer, location, employees, day of the week, time of day, and so on. After reviewing this detailed information, the manager might determine that the warehouse has experienced an exceptionally high employee turnover rate over the last month and that the delays are occurring because new employees are not sufficiently familiar with the process. The manager might conclude that this problem will work itself out over time, in which case there is nothing more to be done. Alternatively, the manager could conclude that the new employees are not being adequately trained and supervised. In this case, the company must take actions to correct the problem. Section 2.2 discusses several methodologies that managers can use to take corrective action when process problems are identified.

before you go on...

1. What is a business process?
2. Describe several business processes carried out at your university.
3. Define a cross-functional business process, and provide several examples of such processes.
4. Pick one of the processes described in questions 2 or 3 given above, and identify its inputs, outputs, customer(s), and resources. How does the process create value for its customer(s)?

2.2 Business Process Improvement, Business Process Reengineering, and Business Process Management

Excellence in executing business processes is widely recognized as the underlying basis for all significant measures of competitive performance in an organization. Consider these measures, for example:

- *Customer satisfaction*: The result of optimizing and aligning business processes to fulfill customers' needs, wants, and desires.
- *Cost reduction*: The result of optimizing operations and supplier processes.
- *Cycle and fulfillment time reduction*: The result of optimizing the manufacturing and logistics processes.
- *Quality*: The result of optimizing the design, development, and production processes.
- *Differentiation*: The result of optimizing the marketing and innovation processes.
- *Productivity*: The result of optimizing each individual's work processes.

The question is: How does an organization ensure business process excellence?

In their book *Reengineering the Corporation*, first published in 1993, Michael Hammer and James Champy argued that to become more competitive, American businesses needed to radically redesign their business processes to reduce costs and increase quality. The authors further asserted that information technology is the key enabler of such change. This radical redesign, called **business process reengineering (BPR)**, is a strategy for making an organization's business processes more productive and profitable. The key to BPR is for enterprises to examine their business processes from a "clean sheet" perspective and then determine how they can best reconstruct those processes to improve their business functions. BPR's popularity was propelled by the unique capabilities of information technology, such as automation and standardization of many process steps and error reduction due to improved communication among organizational information silos.

Although some enterprises have successfully implemented BPR, many organizations found this strategy too difficult, too radical, too lengthy, and too comprehensive. The impact on employees, on facilities, on existing investments in information systems, and even on organizational culture was overwhelming. Despite the many failures in BPR implementation, however, businesses increasingly began to organize work around business processes rather than individual tasks. The result was a less radical, less disruptive, and more incremental approach, called **business process improvement (BPI)**.

BPI focuses on reducing variation in the process outputs by searching for root causes of the variation in the process itself (such as a broken machine on an assembly line) or among the process inputs (such as a decline in the quality of raw materials purchased from a certain supplier). BPI is usually performed by teams of employees that include a process expert—usually the process owner (the individual manager who oversees the process)—as well as other individuals who are involved in the process. These individuals can be involved directly; for example, the workers who actually perform process steps. Alternative, these individuals can be involved indirectly; for example, customers who purchase the outputs from the process.

Six Sigma is a popular methodology for BPI initiatives. Its goal is to ensure that the process has no more than 3.4 defects per million outputs by using statistical methods to analyze the process. (A defect is defined as a faulty product or an unsatisfactory service.) Six Sigma was developed by Motorola in the 1980s, and it is now used by companies worldwide, thanks in part to promotional efforts by early adopters such as GE. Six Sigma is especially appropriate for manufacturing environments, where product defects can be easily defined and measured. Over the years, the methodology has been modified so that it focuses less on defects and more on customer value. As a result, it can now be applied to services as well as products. Today,

Six Sigma tools are widely used in financial services and healthcare institutions as components of process-improvement initiatives.

Regardless of the specific methodology you use, a successful BPI project generally follows five basic phases: define, measure, analyze, improve, and control, or DMAIC.

- In the *define phase*, the BPI team documents the existing "as is" process activities, process resources, and process inputs and outputs, usually as a graphical process map, or diagram. The team also documents the customer and the customer's requirements for the process output, together with a description of the problem that needs to be addressed.

- In the *measure phase*, the BPI team identifies relevant process metrics, such as time and cost to generate one output (product or service), and collects data to understand how the metrics evolve over time. Sometimes the data already exist, in which case they can be extracted from the IS that supports the process, as described in the previous section. Many times, however, the BPI team needs to combine operational process data already stored in the company's IS systems with other data sources, such as customer and employee observations, interviews, and surveys.

- In the *analysis phase*, the BPI team examines the "as is" process map and the collected data to identify problems with the process (such as decreasing efficiency or effectiveness) and their root causes. If possible, the team should also benchmark the process; that is, compare its performance with that of similar processes in other companies, or other areas of the organization. The team can employ IT applications such as statistical analysis software or simulation packages in this phase.

  It is often valuable to use process simulation software during the analysis phase. Utilizing this software provides two benefits. First, it enables a process manager to quickly simulate a real situation (e.g., with a certain number of people undertaking activities) for a specific amount of time (e.g., a working day, a week, or a month). The manager can then estimate the process performance over time without having to observe the process in practice. Second, it allows the manager to create multiple scenarios; for instance, using a different number of resources in the process and/or using a different configuration for the process steps. In addition, process simulation software can provide a number of outputs regarding a process including the time used by all resources to execute specific activities, the overall cycle time of a process, the identification of resources that are infrequently used, and the bottlenecks in the process. Simulating a process is extremely valuable for process managers because it is a risk-free and inexpensive test of an improvement solution that does not need to be conducted with real resources.

- In the *improve phase*, the BPI team identifies possible solutions for addressing the root causes, maps the resulting "to be" process alternatives, and selects and implements the most appropriate solution. Common ways to improve processes are eliminating process activities that do not add value to the output and rearranging activities in a way that reduces delays or improves resource utilization. The organization must be careful, however, not to eliminate internal *process controls*—those activities that safeguard company resources, guarantee the accuracy of its financial reporting, and ensure adherence to rules and regulations.

- In the *control phase*, the team establishes process metrics and monitors the improved process after the solution has been implemented to ensure the process performance remains stable. An IS system can be very useful for this purpose.

Although BPI initiatives do not deliver the huge performance gains promised by BPR, many organizations prefer them because they are less risky and less costly. BPI focuses on delivering quantifiable results—and if a business case cannot be made, the project is not continued. All employees can be trained to apply BPI techniques in their own work to identify opportunities for improvement. Thus, BPI projects tend to be performed more from the bottom-up, in contrast to BPR projects, which involve top-down change mandates. BPI projects take less time overall, and even if they are unsuccessful, they consume fewer organizational resources than BPR projects. However, if incremental improvements through BPI are no longer possible, or if significant changes occur in the firm's business environment, then the firm should consider

BPR projects. One final consideration is that over time, employees can become overstretched or lose interest if the company undertakes too many BPI projects and does not have an effective system to manage and focus the improvement efforts.

To sustain BPI efforts over time, organizations can adopt **business process management (BPM)**, a management system that includes methods and tools to support the design, analysis, implementation, management, and continuous optimization of core business processes throughout the organization. BPM integrates disparate BPI initiatives to ensure consistent strategy execution.

Important components of BPM are process modeling, Web-enabled technologies, and business activity monitoring. BPM begins with *process modeling*, which is a graphical depiction of all of the steps in a process. Process modeling helps employees understand the interactions and dependencies among the people involved in the process, the information systems they rely on, and the information they require to optimally perform their tasks. Process modeling software can support this activity. IT's About Business 2.2 shows how Chevron has employed BPR, BPI, and BPM.

Web-enabled technologies display and retrieve data via a Web browser. They enable an organization to integrate the necessary people and applications into each process, across functional areas and geographical locations.

Finally, *business activity monitoring* (BAM) is a real-time approach for measuring and managing business processes. Companies use BAM to monitor their business processes, identify failures or exceptions, and address these failures in real time. Further, because BAM tracks process operations and indicates whether they succeed or fail, it creates valuable records of process behaviors that organizations can use to improve their processes.

BPM activities are often supported by *business process management suites* (BPMS). A BPMS is an integrated set of applications that includes a repository of process information, such as process maps and business rules; tools for process modeling, simulation, execution, coordination across functions, and re-configuration in response to changing business needs; as well as process-monitoring capabilities.

BPM is growing in business value. In 2012, Capgemini (www.capgemini.com), an international consulting firm, surveyed more than 1,000 senior business executives. The majority of the respondents indicated that BPM would play a more prominent role in their organizations in 2013 and 2014.

Further, Gartner (www.gartner.com), a leading IT research and advisory firm, stated that companies need to focus on developing and mastering BPM skills throughout the organization. Gartner predicts that by 2016, high-performing companies will use BPM technologies such as real-time process monitoring, visualization, analytics, and intelligent automated decision making—all of them integrated in second-generation BPMS—to support intelligent business operations.

Another promising emerging trend is *social BPM*. This technology enables employees to collaborate, using social media tools on wired and mobile platforms, both internally across functions and externally with stakeholders (such as customers or experts), to exchange process knowledge and improve process execution.

BPM initially helps companies improve profitability by decreasing costs and increasing revenues. Over time, BPM can create a competitive advantage by improving organizational flexibility—making it easy to adapt to changing business conditions and to take advantage of new opportunities. For many companies, BPM can reduce costs, increase customer satisfaction, and ensure compliance with rules and regulations. In all cases, the company's strategy should drive the BPM effort. The following example illustrates these benefits.

Example

The State of Alaska Streamlines Its Processes

The Alaska Department of Natural Resources (DNR) manages most state-owned land, water, and natural resources on behalf of Alaska residents. The group's primary mission is to responsibly develop and use Alaska's natural resources for the maximum benefit of the public.

One of the largest divisions of the DNR, the Division of Mining, Land, and Water (DMLW), is responsible for processing authorizations that allow individuals, corporations, or nonprofit organizations to use state resources. The authorization process begins when applicants submit a request. The DMLW then decides whether to allow the activity based on many criteria, such as how the activity will affect the adjoining properties, the neighbors, or current or future land development. It is advantageous for the state to process as many of these permit authorizations as possible because allowing such activity can generate significant revenue and an increase in jobs for the state and its residents. In fact, the state derives approximately 90 percent of its state budget from oil and gas revenue. In addition, these operations can create job opportunities that benefit the state economy.

However, for 20 years the DMLW has experienced a backlog of permit authorizations, resulting in missed revenue and business opportunities. Facing a mandate from the state legislature to fix the problem within three years, the Division needed to identify a solution that would enable it to streamline its processes and to eliminate the backlog (and prevent it from recurring).

In the past, the Division had used Microsoft Visio diagrams to map processes, and, on paper applications, to manage the permit authorization process. These manual, paper-based methods contributed to the backlog. Today, the Division uses IBM Business Process Manager Advanced software to handle the authorization process. Now, authorization requests are scanned and entered into a content management system. The act of entering the request triggers a new business process, which enables staff members to begin processing the application. Employees use the software to complete the adjudication process consistently and appropriately.

In the past, Division managers found it nearly impossible to easily assess the backlog. Managers had no way to effectively track the status of work in progress or work completed, resulting in processing delays. With the IBM software, managers use dashboards (you will learn about dashboards in Chapter 12) to quickly determine how much work is outstanding, the status of all work in process, and the target due dates of work in the queue.

The IBM software also helps the Division establish greater process consistency. Under the old system, where three regional offices employed manual and generally undocumented processes, enforcing consistency was a sometimes overwhelming challenge. An application that was approved by one office, for example, might be denied by another. Today, the new system guides employees through the application processes, and it coaches them on the next steps to take. By mid-2013, the backlog was decreasing, and all stakeholders were benefiting from the Division's improved authorization process management.

Sources: Compiled from "State of Alaska Streamlines Processes with Agile BPM Platform," *IBM Case Study*, March 4, 2013; S. Sweet, "Don't Even Start a BPM Project Without 5 Critical Pieces," *bpm.com*, December 5, 2012; J. vom Brocke and M. Rosemann, "Handbook on Business Process Management," *International Handbooks on Information Systems* (v. 1), Berlin: Springer, 2010; www.ibm.com, http://dnr.alaska.gov/mlw/, accessed April 12, 2013.

 IT's [about business]

2.2 BPR, BPI, and BPM at Chevron

Chevron, one of the world's largest oil and gas companies, and its subsidiaries are involved in exploration and production of oil and natural gas, as well as in manufacturing, transporting, and distributing petrochemical products, including gasoline and refined products. In 2013, Chevron employed more than 60,000 people worldwide, produced the equivalent of more than 2.6 million barrels of oil every day, and reported more than $230 billion in sales. Chevron has been involved in several process-reengineering and improvement efforts over the years, evolving from BPR to BPI and eventually to BPM, as described below.

In 1995, Chevron was less than half of its current size today, producing roughly 1 million barrels of oil per day across six plants. The company was divided into three major departments: Refining, Marketing, and Supply and Distribution (S&D). Management decided that they needed to improve their supply chain (see Chapter 11) to better integrate their multiple internal processes. A key figure in decision making concerning process management was Vice

President Peter McCrea. McCrea was convinced that the best strategy to dramatically improve performance at Chevron was to reengineer its end-to-end core processes, from the acquisition of crude oil crude through distribution of final products to Chevron customers.

To accomplish this task, the Chevron team collaborated with a consultant company to create a model of the existing processes. The objective was to radically improve the existing processes to reflect Chevron's business goals. In other words, Chevron's strategy was not to analyze the existing processes to identify specific areas to improve. Rather, the project identified the desired outputs and then examined the supporting processes, utilizing BPR. As an added benefit, this holistic approach led the company to examine the interdependencies between processes executed in different business units. Adopting this holistic perspective ultimately improved the company's overall performance. In a 1996 report, Chevron claimed that the BPR project saved the company $50 million.

This complex BPR effort was initially followed by several smaller, employee-driven BPI initiatives. For example, in 1998, six Chevron employees initiated a project to improve water treatment processes at a company plant in California. Their efforts generated a 30 percent reduction in operating costs. Their success inspired other employees to initiate BPI projects in Indonesia, Angola, and other locations around the globe by employing Six Sigma improvement techniques. Although some managers were able to demonstrate benefits of BPI at the local level, BPI did not achieve companywide recognition and corporate backing until 2006, when Lean Six Sigma, a methodology that combines statistical process analysis with techniques to eliminate waste and improve process flow, became the preferred improvement methodology at Chevron. Since then, hundreds of BPI projects have been executed worldwide, resulting in significant financial benefits. For example, from 2008 to 2010 Chevron reported more than $1 billion in BPI benefits. To support these internal improvement efforts, Chevron engaged its suppliers in BPI initiatives as well.

To coordinate these various BPI efforts, Chevron has adopted a unified BPM approach that involves standardizing processes across the entire company and consolidating process information within a central repository. Chevron estimates that only 20 percent of its processes can be fully automated—the rest involve a combination of manual and automated steps. Thus, process standardization involves not only supporting processes through integrated information systems, but also ensuring that relevant employees are familiar with the standards for manual activities. To facilitate this task, Chevron implemented Nimbus (nimbus.tibco.com), a BPMS that acts as an intelligent repository of standard, companywide business rules and procedures. In addition, Nimbus can provide employees with detailed work instructions.

Consider, for example, Chevron's shipping process, which experienced efficiency and risk problems due to its different execution in locations throughout Asia, Europe, and the United States. To establish uniform company standards, Chevron employed a BPI approach. The company analyzed "as is" operations across different geographical locations, identified best practices, and combined them into a common "to be" process. It then created documents that detailed these policies and procedures and distributed them to managers through the Web-based BPMS.

Chevron's BPM strategy is part of a larger companywide management system that focuses on operational excellence. The program requires all Chevron operating companies and business units to adopt a continuous improvement perspective, directed by guidelines, metrics, and targets that are reviewed and adapted every year. Apart from process efficiency, Chevron focuses on metrics related to safety, risk, and the environment. All employees participate in operational excellence activities, and managers receive specific operational excellence training to support the continuous improvement culture.

Sources: Compiled from "Operational Excellence," *chevron.com*, March, 2012; "Chevron—using Nimbus Control software to manage processes," Finding FindingPetroleum.com, September 23, 2010; "Chevron Wins Boston Strategies International's 2010 Award for Lean Six Sigma Implementation in Oil and Gas Operations," www.bostonstrategies.com, September 22, 2010; "From the Bottom Up: Grassroots Effort Finds Footing at Chevron," *isixsigma.com*, March 1, 2010; "Business Process Improvement: A Talk With Chevron's Jim Boots," *Ebizq.net*, August 26, 2009; P. Harmon, *Business Process Management*, Elsevier, Burlington, MA, 2007; www.chevron.com, accessed May 14, 2013.

Questions
1. What was one of the main advantages of BPR at Chevron?
2. Why did Chevron adopt BPI?
3. How does Chevron apply BPM in its operations today?

---

before you go on...

1. What is business process reengineering?
2. What is business process improvement?
3. What is business process management?

2.3   Business Pressures, Organizational Responses, and Information Technology Support

Modern organizations compete in a challenging environment. To remain competitive they must react rapidly to problems and opportunities that arise from extremely dynamic conditions. In this section you examine some of the major pressures confronting modern organizations and the strategies that organizations employ to respond to these pressures.

Business Pressures

The **business environment** is the combination of social, legal, economic, physical, and political factors in which businesses conduct their operations. Significant changes in any of these

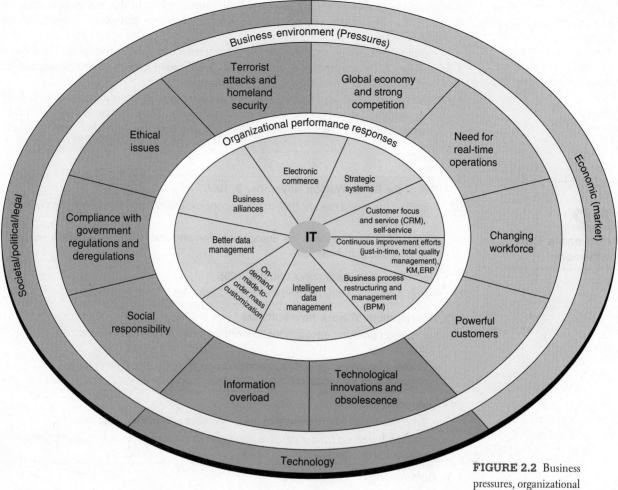

FIGURE 2.2 Business pressures, organizational performance and responses, and IT support.

factors are likely to create business pressures on organizations. Organizations typically respond to these pressures with activities supported by IT. Figure 2.2 illustrates the relationships among business pressures, organizational performance and responses, and IT support. You will learn about three major types of business pressures: market, technology, and societal pressures.

Market Pressures.   Market pressures are generated by the global economy, intense competition, the changing nature of the workforce, and powerful customers. Let's look more closely at each of these factors.

Globalization.   **Globalization** is the integration and interdependence of economic, social, cultural, and ecological facets of life, made possible by rapid advances in information technology. In his book *The World Is Flat*, Pulitzer Prize-winning author Thomas Friedman argues that technology is leveling the global competitive playing field, thereby making it "flat."

Friedman identifies three eras of globalization. The first era, Globalization 1.0, lasted from 1492 to 1800. During this era, the force behind globalization was how much muscle, horsepower, wind power, or steam power a country could deploy.

The second era, Globalization 2.0, lasted from 1800 to 2000. In this era, the force behind globalization was the emergence of multinational companies; that is, companies that had their headquarters in one country but operated in several countries. In the first half of this era, globalization was driven by falling transportation costs, generated by the development of the steam engine and the railroads. In the second half, the driving force was falling telecommunications costs resulting from the telegraph, telephones, computers, satellites, fiber-optic cable, and the Internet and World Wide Web. The modern global economy began to evolve during this era.

Around the year 2000, the world entered Globalization 3.0. In this era, globalization has been driven by the convergence of ten forces that Friedman calls "flatteners." Table 2.2 identifies these forces.

According to Friedman, each era has been characterized by a distinctive focus. The focus of Globalization 1.0 was on countries, the focus of Globalization 2.0 was on companies, and the focus of Globalization 3.0 is on groups and individuals.

As you look at Table 2.2, note that nine of Friedman's ten flatteners directly relate to information technology (all except the fall of the Berlin Wall). These flatteners enable individuals to connect, compute, communicate, collaborate, and compete everywhere and anywhere,

Table

2.2

Friedman's Ten Flatteners

- **Fall of the Berlin Wall on November 9, 1989**
  - Shifted the world toward free-market economies and away from centrally planned economies.
  - Led to the emergence of the European Union and early thinking about the world as a single, global market.

- **Netscape goes public on August 9, 1995**
  - Popularized the Internet and the World Wide Web.

- **Development of work-flow software**
  - Enabled computer applications to work with one another without human intervention.
  - Enabled faster, closer collaboration and coordination among employees, regardless of their location.

- **Uploading**
  - Empowered all Internet users to create content and put it on the Web.
  - Led the transition from a passive approach to content to an active, participatory, collaborative approach.

- **Outsourcing**
  - Contracting with an outside company to perform a specific function that your company was doing itself and then integrating their work back into your operation; for example, moving customer call centers to India.

- **Offshoring**
  - Relocating an entire operation, or certain tasks, to another country; for example, moving an entire manufacturing operation to China.

- **Supply chaining**
  - Technological revolution led to the creation of networks composed of companies, their suppliers, and their customers, all of which could collaborate and share information for increased efficiency.

- **Insourcing**
  - Delegating operations or jobs within a business to another company that specializes in those operations; for example, Dell hires FedEx to "take over" Dell's logistics process.

- **Informing**
  - The ability to search for information, best illustrated by search engines.

- **The Steroids** (computing, instant messaging and file sharing, wireless technologies, Voice over Internet Protocol, videoconferencing, and computer graphics)
  - Technologies that amplify the other flatteners.
  - Enable all forms of computing and collaboration to be digital, mobile, and personal.

anytime and all the time; to access limitless amounts of information, services, and entertainment; to exchange knowledge; and to produce and sell goods and services. People and organizations can now operate without regard to geography, time, distance, or even language barriers. The bottom line? Globalization is markedly increasing competition.

These observations highlight the importance of market pressures for you. Simply put, you and the organizations you join will be competing with people and organizations from all over a flat world.

Let's consider some examples of globalization. Regional agreements such as the North American Free Trade Agreement (NAFTA), which includes the United States, Canada, and Mexico, have contributed to increased world trade and increased competition. Further, the rise of India and China as economic powerhouses has increased global competition.

One important pressure that businesses in a global market must contend with is the cost of labor, which varies widely among countries. In general, labor costs are higher in developed countries like the United States and Japan than in developing countries such as China and El Salvador. Also, developed countries usually offer greater benefits, such as healthcare, to employees, driving the cost of doing business even higher. Therefore, many labor-intensive industries have moved their operations to countries with low labor costs. IT has made such moves much easier to implement.

However, manufacturing overseas is no longer the bargain it once was, and manufacturing in the United States is no longer as expensive. For example, manufacturing wages in China have more than doubled between 2002 and 2013, and they continue to rise. Meanwhile, the value of China's currency has steadily risen.

The Changing Nature of the Workforce.   The workforce, particularly in developed countries, is becoming more diversified. Increasing numbers of women, single parents, minorities, and persons with disabilities are now employed in all types of positions. IT is easing the integration of these employees into the traditional workforce. IT is also enabling people to work from home, which can be a major benefit for parents with young children and for people confronted with mobility and/or transportation issues.

Powerful Customers.   Consumer sophistication and expectations increase as customers become more knowledgeable about the products and services they acquire. Customers can use the Internet to find detailed information about products and services, to compare prices, and to purchase items at electronic auctions.

Organizations recognize the importance of customers and they have increased their efforts to acquire and retain them. Modern firms strive to learn as much as possible about their customers to better anticipate and address their needs. This process, called *customer intimacy*, is an important component of *customer relationship management* (CRM), an organization-wide effort toward maximizing the customer experience. You will learn about CRM in Chapter 11.

Technology Pressures.   The second category of business pressures consists of those pressures related to technology. Two major technology-related pressures are technological innovation and information overload.

Technological Innovation and Obsolescence.   Few and improved technologies rapidly create or support substitutes for products, alternative service options, and superb quality. As a result, today's state-of-the-art products may be obsolete tomorrow. For example, how fast are new versions of your smartphone being released? How quickly are electronic versions of books, magazines, and newspapers replacing traditional hard copy versions? These changes force businesses to keep up with consumer demands.

Consider the Apple iPad (www.apple.com/ipad). Apple released the first iPad in April 2010 and sold 3 million of the devices in 80 days. Rather than taking time to enjoy its success, Apple made its iPad2 available for sale on March 11, 2011, only 11 months later. Apple released the iPad 3 on March 7, 2012, and the company released the iPad 4 on November 2, 2012.

An interesting aspect of technological innovation is "bring your own device (BYOD)." BYOD refers to the policy of permitting employees to bring personally owned mobile devices (laptops, tablet computers, and smartphones) to the workplace, and use those devices to connect to the corporate network. BYOD also describes this same practice applied to students using personally owned devices in educational settings to connect to their school's network. BYOD is causing concern to organizational IT departments, as you see in IT's About Business 2.3.

 # IT's [about business]

2.3 "Bring Your Own Device" Can Cause Problems

Hamilton Fraser (www.hamiltonfraser.co.uk), located in North London, is an insurance company that specializes in home insurance. The firm is one of Great Britain's major contractors for its deposit protection system, which assigns an independent arbitrator to both tenants and landlords to resolve any disputes when a tenant moves from a rented property.

The company's IT manager, Pete Agathangelou, claims that information security is his highest priority because credibility is critical to his company's success. He began to focus specifically on security threats from "bring your own device (BYOD)" in 2012 when he observed basic changes in his office environment. For example, he noticed that at lunchtime younger employees utilized their mobile devices to play games and contact their friends on social networks. He also observed that many senior executives were accessing their e-mail on mobile devices when they were out of the office.

Hamilton Fraser had already embraced mobile computing by allowing its employees to have iPhones and iPads. However, employees were using other devices—particularly Android devices—on the company network. Agathangelou concluded that he needed a system to manage all of the mobile devices that the employees were utilizing.

The first step in creating this system was to find a vendor who could manage the issue of employees accessing the corporate network with their own mobile devices. The company ultimately selected MobileIron (www.mobileiron.com), a firm that provides mobile device management and security to large enterprises.

MobileIron allowed Hamilton Fraser to identify which mobile devices the company would support. The MobileIron software enabled Hamilton Fraser to keep track of how many employees were accessing the firm's network for business purposes (as opposed to, e.g., playing games or shopping) and whether they were using an approved device. The company's human resources department developed an acceptable use policy, and it began to conduct short training sessions to raise awareness of this policy among employees. The policy dictates that employees who use mobile devices must download an application to their smartphone or tablet that will enable the IT department to erase any corporate data from the device if it is lost or stolen, or to erase all data from the device if the employee so wishes.

Sources: Compiled from J. Gold, "Has BYOD Peaked?" *Computerworld*, March 21, 2013; J. Scott, "Case Study: Hamilton Fraser Embraces BYOD with MobileIron," *Computer Weekly*, March 20, 2013; G. Marks, "Do You Really Need a BYOD Policy?" *Forbes*, February 25, 2013; M. Endler, "4 Big BYOD Trends for 2013," *InformationWeek*, February 21, 2013; T. Kaneshige, "BYOD to Change the Face of IT in 2013," *CIO*, February 7, 2013; T. Kemp, "Beyond BYOD: The Shift to People-Centric IT," *Forbes*, January 14, 2013; L. Mearian, "Nearly Half of IT Shops Ignore BYOD," *Computerworld*, November 29, 2012; E. Lai, "Infographic: The Ten Things We Fear (and Love) About BYOD," *Forbes*, July 16, 2012; www.hamiltonfraser.co.uk, www.mobileiron.com, accessed April 14, 2013.

Questions

1. What are the advantages of allowing employees to use any mobile device to connect to the corporate network? The disadvantages?

2. Why is it necessary to be able to erase corporate data if a mobile device is lost or stolen?

Information Overload. The amount of information available on the Internet doubles approximately every year, and much of it is free. The Internet and other telecommunications networks are bringing a flood of information to managers. To make decisions effectively and efficiently, managers must be able to access, navigate, and utilize these vast stores of data, information, and knowledge. Information technologies, such as search engines (discussed in Chapter 6) and data mining (Chapter 12) provide valuable support in these efforts.

Societal/Political/Legal Pressures. The third category of business pressures includes social responsibility, government regulation/deregulation, spending for social programs, spending to protect against terrorism, and ethics. This section will explain how all of these elements affect modern businesses. We start with social responsibility.

Social Responsibility. Social issues that affect businesses and individuals range from the state of the physical environment, to company and individual philanthropy, to education. Some corporations and individuals are willing to spend time and/or money to address various social problems. These efforts are known as **organizational social responsibility** or **individual social responsibility**.

One critical social problem is the state of the physical environment. A growing IT initiative, called *green IT*, is addressing some of the most pressing environmental concerns. IT is instrumental in organizational efforts to "go green" in at least four areas.

- *Facilities design and management*: Organizations are creating more sustainable work environments. Many organizations are pursuing Leadership in Energy and Environmental Design (LEED) certification from the U.S. Green Building Council, a nonprofit group that promotes the construction of environmentally friendly buildings. One impact of this development is that IT professionals are expected to help create green facilities. Consequently, IT personnel have to consider how their computing decisions influences sustainable design and, in turn, how the building's design influences the IT infrastructure. Green design influences the type of IT devices a company uses and the locations where IT clusters personal computers, people, and servers. IT must become familiar with the metering and monitoring systems employed in green buildings and the requirements of buildings' computerized infrastructure.

- *Carbon management*: As companies try to reduce their carbon footprints, they are turning to IT executives to develop the systems needed to monitor carbon throughout the organization and its supply chain, which can be global in scope. Therefore, IT employees need to become knowledgeable about embedded carbon and how to measure it in the company's products and processes.

    Consider, for example, application development. IT managers will have to ask whether an application will require new hardware to test and run, or how much additional server space (and thus energy) it will require—and how these issues translate into carbon output.

- *International and U.S. state environmental laws*: IT executives must deal with federal and state laws and international regulations that impact everything from the IT products they buy, to how they dispose of them, to their company's carbon footprint. IT managers must understand environmental compliance issues so they can ask their vendors the right questions regarding specific state, national, and international environmental standards before they purchase, deploy, and dispose of equipment.

- *Energy management*: IT executives must understand their entire organization's energy needs for several reasons. First, energy management systems are becoming increasingly sophisticated. To employ these systems effectively and to make intelligent consumption decisions, IT personnel must understand the system's complex monitors and sensors. Second, utilities are offering incentives to commercial customers who take certain energy conservation steps, such as enabling computer power management across their networks and designing energy-efficient data centers. Finally, utilities are offering variable rate incentives depending on when companies use electricity and how much they use. Addressing these issues requires IT systems that can regulate electricity use.

Continuing our discussion of social responsibility, social problems all over the world may be addressed through corporate and individual philanthropy. In some cases, questions arise as to what percentage of contributions actually goes to the intended causes and recipients and what percentage goes to the charity's overhead. Another problem that concerns contributors is that they often exert little influence over the selection of projects their contributions will support. The Internet can help address these concerns and facilitate generosity and connection. Consider the following examples:

- PatientsLikeMe (www.patientslikeme.com), or any of the thousands of message boards dedicated to infertility, cancer, and various other ailments. People use these sites and message boards to obtain information about life-and-death decisions based on volunteered information, while also receiving much-needed emotional support from strangers.

- *GiftFlow* (www.giftflow.org): GiftFlow is a virtual community where you can obtain things you need for free and find people who need the "stuff" you have to give away. GiftFlow connects community organizations, businesses, governments, and neighbors in a network of reciprocity.

- *OurGoods* (www.ourgoods.org): OurGoods enables creative people to help one another produce independent projects. More work is accomplished in networks of shared respect and shared resources than in competitive isolation.
- *Sparked* (www.sparked.com): Sparked is an online "microvolunteering" Web site where large and small organizations list opportunities for people looking to volunteer.
- *Thredup* (www.thredup.com): Thredup is a Web site where parents trade children's clothing and toys.
- *Collaborative Consumption* (www.collaborativeconsumption.com): This Web site is an online hub for discussions about the growing business of sharing, resale, reuse, and barter (with many links to Web sites engaged in these practices).
- *Kiva* (www.kiva.org): Kiva is a nonprofit enterprise that provides a link between lenders in developed countries and entrepreneurs in developing countries. Users pledge interest-free loans rather than tax-deductible donations. Kiva directs 100 percent of the loans to borrowers.
- *DonorsChoose* (www.donorschoose.org): DonorsChoose is an education-oriented Web site that functions entirely within the United States. Users make donations rather than loans. The Web site addresses the huge problem of underfunded public schools.

Still another social problem that affects modern business is the digital divide. The **digital divide** refers to the wide gap between those individuals who have access to information and communications technology and those who do not. This gap exists both within and among countries. IT's About Business 2.4 provides an example of how modern information technologies are enabling the Surui people of the Amazon region in Brazil to bridge the digital divide.

IT's [about business]

2.4 The Surui Tribe of the Amazon

Chief Almir of the Surui tribe of the Brazilian Amazon is using Google to help his tribe maintain its traditional way of life. In 1969, the Surui experienced their first contact with outsiders, who brought with them disease, violence, and death. Then, loggers arrived and laid waste to the Surui's homeland.

Chief Almir assumed a leadership role in his tribe at age 17, and he became the tribe's first member to attend college. In 2006, he fled briefly to the United States when loggers put a bounty on his head. The following year he stumbled upon Google Earth in an Internet café.

During this time Chief Almir came to believe that his tribe's survival depended on outreach. To realize this goal, he partnered with Google to create an online "cultural map" of the Surui with stories provided by the tribe's elders, which are uploaded onto YouTube, as well as a geographical map of their territory created with GPS-equipped smartphones provided by Google. In 2009, Google employees taught the Surui to use cell phones to record illegal logging on their land. Tribal members can now take photos and videos that are geo-tagged and then immediately upload the images to Google Earth. Law enforcement officials can no longer claim ignorance of the problem when evidence of the deforestation is publicly available online. Satellite pictures indicate that the Surui territory is the only remaining intact piece of rainforest in the area. This fact confirms that the Surui use of technology has been highly effective.

Chief Almir views his partnership with Google not only as a way to sustain his traditions and his land, but also as an opportunity to teach other peoples about the Surui. Furthermore, the tribe has mounted an ambitious reforestation plan to combat the aggressive logging that is destroying the Surui's 600,000 acres of land. The tribe now uses smartphones to document cleared areas in the forest and to create planting strategies. The Surui intend to plant 100 million saplings in the next decade. They hope to raise millions of dollars through a United Nations program that awards carbon credits, which recipients can trade for cash, to countries and tribes that maintain their forests. The money would fund new homes, a hospital, and a school. The Surui have created a word for Google in their language: *ragogmakann*, meaning "the messenger."

In the summer of 2012, Google unveiled a cultural map of the Surui. This map serves as a digital tool to help the tribe share their vast knowledge of the rainforest while fighting illegal logging. The map, which is the result of a five-year partnership between Chief Almir and Google, is a collection of picture and videos mapping historical sites and offering three-dimensional visualization of Surui territory. The map is available on the Web site www.paiter .org, as well as on Google Earth.

A Google spokesperson stated that the company hoped that the methodology used to develop the Surui cultural map would be employed to help other indigenous peoples around the world. By late 2012, similar projects were planned for two tribes who are neighbors of the Surui. The Surui themselves are the trainers for the new cultural maps. In addition, Google has been contacted by tribes from all over the world, including the aboriginal First Nations in Canada, the Maoris in New Zealand, and many other Amazon tribes.

Sources: Compiled from J. Forero, "From the Stone Age to the Digital Age in One Big Leap," *NPR.org*, March 28, 2013; "How Mapping Technology Is Helping Chief Almir and the Surui Tribe Protect Their Culture and Environment," *Google Nonprofits Blog*, January 23, 2013; "It's Amazon View! Google Shows Off New Map of Brazilian Rainforests (Put Together by an Indigenous Tribe)," *The Daily Mail*, June 17, 2012; "The Most Creative People in Business 2011," *FastCompany,* June, 2011; S. Zwick, "Brazil's Surui

Establish First Indigenous Carbon Fund," *Ecosystem Marketplace*, December 3, 2010; R. Butler, "Brazilian Tribe Owns Carbon Rights to Amazon Rainforest Land," *Mongabay.com*, December 9, 2009; R. Butler, "Big REDD," *Washington Monthly*, September 7, 2009; R. Butler, "Amazon Conservation Team Puts Indians on Google Earth to Save the Amazon," *Mongabay.com*, November 14, 2006.

Questions

1. Describe the benefits that all of us gain from the Surui's use of IT.
2. Provide specific examples of how the Surui could make further use of IT to improve their lives.

Many government and international organizations are trying to close the digital divide. As technologies develop and become less expensive, the speed at which the gap can be closed will accelerate. On the other hand, the rapid pace of technological development can make it more difficult for groups with few resources to keep up with more affluent groups.

One well-known project to narrow the divide is the One Laptop per Child (OLPC) project (*http://one.laptop.org*). OLPC is a nonprofit association dedicated to developing a very inexpensive laptop—a technology that aims to revolutionize how the world can educate its children.

The first generation of inexpensive laptops appeared in 2007 with a price of $188, which was too high for individuals and groups with limited resources. The second generation was scrapped because the price remained too high. The next generation, a touchscreen tablet computer for schoolchildren in the developing world, uses less power than a light bulb and is unbreakable, waterproof, and half as thick as an iPhone. This computer will be a single sheet of plastic, and will have a projected price of $75.

Compliance with Government Regulations. Another major source of business pressures is government regulations regarding health, safety, environmental protection, and equal opportunity. Businesses tend to view government regulations as expensive constraints on their activities. In general, government deregulation intensifies competition.

In the wake of 9/11 and numerous corporate scandals, the U.S. government passed many new laws, including the Sarbanes-Oxley Act, the USA PATRIOT Act, the Gramm-Leach-Bliley Act, and the Health Insurance Portability and Accountability Act (HIPAA). Organizations must be in compliance with the regulations contained in these statutes. The process of becoming and remaining compliant is expensive and time consuming. In almost all cases, organizations rely on IT support to provide the necessary controls and information for compliance.

Protection against Terrorist Attacks. Since September 11, 2001, organizations have been under increased pressure to protect themselves against terrorist attacks. In addition, employees who are in the military reserves have been called up for active duty, creating personnel problems. Information technology can help protect businesses by providing security systems and possibly identifying patterns of behavior associated with terrorist activities, including cyberattacks (discussed in Chapter 4).

An example of protection against terrorism is the Department of Homeland Security's (DHS) US-VISIT program. US-VISIT is a network of biometric-screening systems, such as fingerprint and ocular (eye) scanners, that ties into government databases and watch lists to check the identities of millions of people entering the United States. The system is now operational in more than 300 locations, including major international ports of entry by air, sea, and land. As another example, refer to the chapter opening case on the Palantir system.

Ethical Issues. Ethics relates to general standards of right and wrong. Information ethics relates specifically to standards of right and wrong in information-processing practices. Ethical issues are very important because, if handled poorly, they can damage an organization's image and destroy its employees' morale. The use of IT raises many ethical issues, ranging from monitoring e-mail to invading the privacy of millions of customers whose data are stored in private and public databases. Chapter 3 covers ethical issues in detail.

Clearly, then, the pressures on organizations are increasing, and organizations must be prepared to take responsive actions if they are to succeed. You will learn about these organizational responses in the next section.

Organizational Responses

Organizations are responding to the various pressures just discussed by implementing IT such as strategic systems, customer focus, make-to-order and mass customization, and e-business. This section explores each of these responses.

Strategic Systems. Strategic systems provide organizations with advantages that enable them to increase their market share and/or profits, to better negotiate with suppliers, and to prevent competitors from entering their markets. As an example, the IT department at P&G (www.pg.com) developed a virtualized environment that the company uses for product design work, product placement research, and consumer feedback studies. P&G utilizes virtual reality models to test design ideas for the next breakthroughs in products such as diapers and cosmetics. Within these "cyberworlds," P&G can rapidly test product performance as well as consumer responses to various kinds of ingredient and packaging choices. IT's About Business 2.5 provides another example of how strategically important information systems can be, by examining the Massachusetts Mutual Life Insurance Company.

IT's [about business]

2.5 Massachusetts Mutual Transforms Its Information Systems   MIS

Founded in 1851, Massachusetts Mutual Life Insurance Company (MassMutual; www.massmutual.com) is a leading mutual life insurance company with 1,800 offices and 13 million clients located throughout the world. Although MassMutual does not guarantee dividends, it has paid them to eligible participating policyholders every year since the 1860s. The company provides products to help meet its clients' financial needs, including life insurance, disability income insurance, long-term care insurance, retirement/401(k) plan services, and annuities.

In 2008, MassMutual undertook a complete transformation of its 1,200-person information technology department. At that time, the firm's IT infrastructure consisted of 60 years of legacy information systems (old systems that had been in use for many years). The company realized that these outdated systems seriously jeopardized its ability to successfully compete, much less gain competitive advantage, in an increasingly dynamic marketplace. As a result, MassMutual initiated the massive project to change IT into a more innovative, flexible organization that focused on company growth, market agility, seizing opportunities, and enabling innovation in the company as a whole. The project required the right people, the right processes, and the right technology—in that order. The mandate was that the project was a business initiative, and anything it accomplished had to benefit the entire company, not just the IT group. To emphasize this point, the project included MassMutual business units as partners.

In the project's first phase, the IT organization, along with PricewaterhouseCoopers (www.pwc.com) as consultants, conducted a comprehensive assessment of itself against its peers in the insurance industry and against best-in-class organizations in other industries. It then shared its findings with the entire organization.

As a result of this assessment, MassMutual redefined every job in the IT organization, and it reduced more than 100 existing job descriptions to 35 industry-standard roles. This reclassification also created new career opportunities in IT. Extensive training helped make the reclassification successful. The firm also used virtual reality training, as well as off-site "boot camps" that featured interactive activities.

MassMutual has created a culture in its IT group that values sharing ideas and making those ideas better. The company began rewarding people for sharing information rather than hoarding it. IT personnel were encouraged to take risks and make mistakes, as long as they learned from those mistakes and shared the lessons they learned with the entire organization.

To make sharing information an ongoing process, MassMutual developed a knowledge management system. The system is a collaborative effort, and employees from IT and the business units continually add information to it. This knowledge base has enabled the firm to capture knowledge and to share ideas throughout the organization.

The IT organization also implemented standard processes. As part of this standardization process, IT created "Communities of Practice." These are teams that share stories and ideas and determine whether the existing processes are working. If they are not, then the teams devise strategies to improve them. The teams also institutionalize those processes that are working effectively. Interestingly, all Communities of Practice include people from the company's business units.

And the end results? In 2013, MassMutual was in the final year of the transformation project, and the IT organization had made significant improvements. For instance, it had achieved an 18 percent reduction in IT costs and a 9 percent improvement in the ability to deliver projects on time and within budget, while giving internal customers (other MassMutual employees) exactly what they require. The IT department had also achieved a 10 percent reduction in legacy applications. For the company's core Universal Life Products, IT was able to reduce the product development life cycle by 9 months while reducing costs by an impressive 84 percent.

Sources: Compiled from E. Feretic, "MassMutual Reinvents Its IT Organization," *Baseline Magazine*, March 21, 2013; L. Malone, "Highly Regulated Companies Tiptoe into Social Media," *Computerworld,* February 11, 2013;

"MassMutual: Improved Customer Service Experience by 50% While Consolidating 17 Systems Down to 1," *Pega.com case study*, 2013; J. Rooney, "How MassMutual Is Breathing New Life into Life Insurance," *Forbes*, January 9, 2012; www.massmutual.com, accessed April 10, 2013.

Questions

1. Explain why the MassMutual IT transformation project requires the right people, the right processes, and the right technology, *in that particular order.*
2. Describe the benefits of the knowledge management system implemented at MassMutual.
3. Why are people from the business units included in IT Communities of Practice?
4. What should MassMutual's IT organization do next?

Customer Focus.   Organizational attempts to provide superb customer service can make the difference between attracting and retaining customers versus losing them to competitors. Numerous IT tools and business processes have been designed to keep customers happy. Consider Amazon, for example. When you visit Amazon's Web site anytime after your first visit, the site welcomes you back by name and it presents you with information about items that you might like, based on your previous purchases. In another example, Dell guides you through the process of purchasing a computer by providing information and choices that help you make an informed buying decision.

Make-to-Order and Mass Customization.   **Make-to-order** is a strategy of producing customized (made to individual specifications) products and services. The business problem is how to manufacture customized goods efficiently and at a reasonably low cost. Part of the solution is to change manufacturing processes from mass production to mass customization. In mass production, a company produces a large quantity of identical items. In **mass customization**, it also produces a large quantity of items, but it customizes them to fit the needs and preferences of individual customers. Mass customization is simply an attempt to perform make-to-order on a large scale. Bodymetrics (www.bodymetrics.com) is an excellent example of mass customization involving men's and women's jeans.

Example

Well-fitting jeans are notoriously difficult to find. To address this problem, Bodymetrics developed a "body scanner" that scans the customer's body, captures more than 150 measurements, and produces a digital replica of the customer's size and shape. This scan is then used to provide three services: made-to-measure jeans, body-shape jeans, and online virtual try-on.

With made-to-measure jeans, the scan is used to create a pattern for the jeans, which are hand-tailored to the exact lines and contours of the customer's body. The jeans are ready in three to six weeks, at which time the customer has a final fitting with a Bodymetrics tailor.

Based on its experience with made-to-measure jeans, Bodymetrics has identified three body shapes: straight, semicurvy, and curvy. Body-shape jeans are specifically designed to fit these different body shapes. After customers are scanned, a Bodymetrics jeans expert helps them determine their body shapes. Customers can then instantly purchase jeans matching their body shapes off the rack in the store.

The online virtual try-on allows customers who have been scanned to try on jeans virtually on their own bodies without physically trying on jeans in a dressing room. The service creates an *avatar* (a three-dimensional graphical representation of the customer), which has an amazing resemblance to her or him. Then, the customer can pick various styles of jeans and "virtually see" what the jeans look like on her or his avatar.

Sources: Compiled from C. Taylor, "Testing Out Bodymetrics, the Startup That Wants to Be a Denim Shopper's Best Friend," *TechCrunch*, September 30, 2012; E. Kim, "Can't Zip Those Jeans? Bodymetrics Can Help," *CNN Money*, July 25, 2012; "The First Time I Had a Bodymetrics Scan," http://howfayeseesit.wordpress.com, March 23, 2011; L. Talbot, "Bodymetrics: What's Your Jean Shape?" http://lisatalbot.blogspot.com, February 2, 2011; Asmita, "Custom-Fit Jeans with Bodymetrics," *www.styleguru.com*, January 18, 2007 (Note: StyleGuru is a promotional blog); R. Young, "Turning Tailoring Over to a Computer," *International Herald Tribune*, January 15, 2007; www.bodymetrics.com, accessed March 1, 2013.

E-Business and E-Commerce.   Conducting business electronically is an essential strategy for companies that are competing in today's business environment. *Electronic commerce* (EC or e-commerce) describes the process of buying, selling, transferring, or exchanging products, services, or information via computer networks, including the Internet. *E-business* is a somewhat broader concept. In addition to the buying and selling of goods and services, e-business also refers to servicing customers, collaborating with business partners, and performing electronic transactions within an organization. Chapter 7 focuses extensively on this topic. In addition, e-commerce applications appear throughout the text.

You now have a general overview of the pressures that affect companies in today's business environment and the responses that they choose to manage these pressures. To plan for the most effective responses, companies formulate strategies. In the new digital economy, these strategies rely heavily on information technology, especially strategic information systems. You examine these topics in the next section.

before you go on...

1. What are the characteristics of the modern business environment?

2. Discuss some of the pressures that characterize the modern global business environment.

3. Identify some of the organizational responses to these pressures. Are any of these responses specific to a particular pressure? If so, which ones?

2.4 Competitive Advantage and Strategic Information Systems

A *competitive strategy* is a statement that identifies a business's approach to compete, its goals, and the plans and policies that will be required to carry out those goals (Porter, 1985). A strategy, in general, can apply to a desired outcome, such as gaining market share. A competitive strategy focuses on achieving a desired outcome when competitors want to prevent you from reaching your goal. Therefore, when you create a competitive strategy, you must plan your own moves, but you must also anticipate and counter your competitors' moves.

Through its competitive strategy, an organization seeks a competitive advantage in an industry. That is, it seeks to outperform its competitors in a critical measure such as cost, quality, and time-to-market. Competitive advantage helps a company function profitably with a market and generate larger-than-average profits.

Competitive advantage is increasingly important in today's business environment, as you will note throughout the text. In general, the *core business* of companies has remained the same. That is, information technologies simply offer tools that can enhance an organization's success through its traditional sources of competitive advantage, such as low cost, excellent customer service, and superior supply chain management. **Strategic information systems (SISs)** provide a competitive advantage by helping an organization implement its strategic goals and improve its performance and productivity. Any information system that helps an organization either achieve a competitive advantage or reduce a competitive disadvantage, qualifies as a strategic information system.

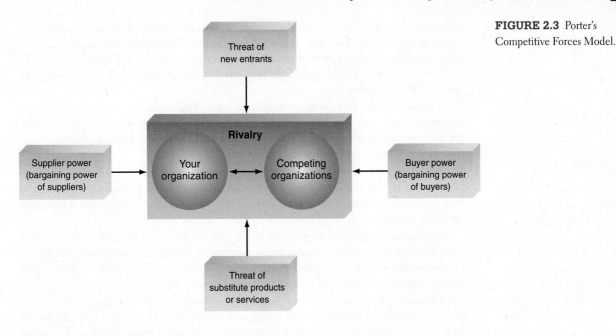

FIGURE 2.3 Porter's Competitive Forces Model.

Porter's Competitive Forces Model

The best-known framework for analyzing competitiveness is Michael Porter's **competitive forces model** (Porter, 1985). Companies use Porter's model to develop strategies to increase their competitive edge. Porter's model also demonstrates how IT can make a company more competitive.

Porter's model identifies five major forces that can endanger or enhance a company's position in a given industry. Figure 2.3 highlights these forces. Although the Web has changed the nature of competition, it has not changed Porter's five fundamental forces. In fact, what makes these forces so valuable as analytical tools is that they have not changed for centuries. Every competitive organization, no matter how large or small, or what business it is in, is driven by these forces. This observation applies even to organizations that you might not consider competitive, such as local governments. Although local governments are not for-profit enterprises, they compete for businesses to locate in their districts, for funding from higher levels of government, for employees, and for many other things.

Significantly, Porter (2001) concludes that the *overall* impact of the Web is to increase competition, which generally diminishes a firm's profitability. Let's examine Porter's five forces and the ways that the Web influences them.

1. *The threat of entry of new competitors.* The threat that new competitors will enter your market is high when entry is easy and low when there are significant barriers to entry. An **entry barrier** is a product or service feature that customers have learned to expect from organizations in a certain industry. A competing organization must offer this feature in order to survive in the marketplace. There are many types of entry barriers. Consider, for example, legal requirements such as admission to the bar to practice law or a license to serve liquor, where only a certain number of licenses are available.

Suppose you want to open a gasoline station. In order to compete in that industry, you would have to offer pay-at-the-pump service to your customers. Pay-at-the-pump is an IT-based barrier to entering this market because you must offer it for free. The first gas station that offered this service gained first-move advantage and established barriers to entry. This advantage did not last, however, because competitors quickly offered the same service and thus overcame the entry barrier.

For most firms, the Web *increases* the threat that new competitors will enter the market because it sharply reduces traditional barriers to entry, such as the need for a sales force or a physical storefront. Today, competitors frequently need only to set up a Web site. This threat of increased competition is particularly acute in industries that perform an *intermediation role*, which is a link between buyers and sellers (e.g., stock brokers and travel agents), as well as in industries where the primary product or service is digital (e.g., the music industry). In addition, the geographical reach of the Web enables distant competitors to compete more directly with an existing firm.

In some cases the Web increases barriers to entry. This scenario occurs primarily when customers have come to expect a nontrivial capability from their suppliers. For example, the first company to offer Web-based package tracking gained a competitive advantage from that service. Competitors were forced to follow.

2. *The bargaining power of suppliers.* Supplier power is high when buyers have few choices from whom to buy and low when buyers have many choices. Therefore, organizations would rather have more potential suppliers so they will be in a stronger position to negotiate price, quality, and delivery terms.

The Internet's impact on suppliers is mixed. On the one hand, it enables buyers to find alternative suppliers and to compare prices more easily, thereby reducing the supplier's bargaining power. On the other hand, as companies use the Internet to integrate their supply chains, participating suppliers prosper by locking in customers.

3. *The bargaining power of customers (buyers).* Buyer power is high when buyers have many choices from whom to buy and low when buyers have few choices. For example, in the past, there were few locations where students could purchase textbooks (typically, one or two campus bookstores). In this situation, students had low buyer power. Today, the Web provides students with access to a multitude of potential suppliers as well as detailed information about textbooks. As a result, student buyer power has increased dramatically.

In contrast, *loyalty programs* reduce buyer power. As their name suggests, loyalty programs reward customers based on the amount of business they conduct with a particular organization (e.g., airlines, hotels, and rental car companies). Information technology enables companies to track the activities and accounts of millions of customers, thereby reducing buyer power. That is, customers who receive "perks" from loyalty programs are less likely to do business with competitors. (Loyalty programs are associated with customer relationship management, which you will study in Chapter 11.)

4. *The threat of substitute products or services.* If there are many alternatives to an organization's products or services, then the threat of substitutes is high. If there are few alternatives, then the threat is low. Today, new technologies create substitute products very rapidly. For example, customers today can purchase wireless telephones instead of land-line telephones, Internet music services instead of traditional CDs, and ethanol instead of gasoline in cars.

Information-based industries experience the greatest threat from substitutes. Any industry in which digitized information can replace material goods (e.g., music, books, and software) must view the Internet as a threat because the Internet can convey this information efficiently and at low cost and high quality.

Even when there are many substitutes for their products, however, companies can create a competitive advantage by increasing switching costs. *Switching costs* are the costs, in money and time, imposed by a decision to buy elsewhere. For example, contracts with smartphone providers typically include a substantial penalty for switching to another provider until the term of the contract expires (quite often, two years). This switching cost is monetary.

As another example, when you buy products from Amazon, the company develops a profile of your shopping habits and recommends products targeted to your preferences. If you switch to another online vendor, that company will need time to develop a profile of your wants and needs. In this case, the switching cost involves time rather than money.

5. *The rivalry among existing firms in the industry.* The threat from rivalry is high when there is intense competition among many firms in an industry. The threat is low when the competition is among fewer firms and is not as intense.

In the past, proprietary information systems—systems that belong exclusively to a single organization—have provided strategic advantage to firms in highly competitive industries.

Today, however, the visibility of Internet applications on the Web makes proprietary systems more difficult to keep secret. In simple terms, when I see my competitor's new system online, I will rapidly match its features to remain competitive. The result is fewer differences among competitors, which leads to more intense competition in an industry.

To understand this concept, consider the highly competitive grocery industry, where Walmart, Kroger, Safeway, and other companies compete essentially on price. Some of these companies have IT-enabled loyalty programs in which customers receive discounts and the store gains valuable business intelligence on customers' buying preferences. Stores use this business intelligence in their marketing and promotional campaigns. (You will learn about business intelligence in Chapter 12.)

Grocery stores are also experimenting with wireless technologies such as *radio-frequency identification* (RFID, discussed in Chapter 8) to speed up the checkout process, track customers through the store, and notify customers of discounts as they pass by certain products. Grocery companies also use IT to tightly integrate their supply chains for maximum efficiency and thus reduce prices for shoppers.

Competition also is being affected by the extremely low variable cost of digital products. That is, once a digital product has been developed, the cost of producing additional "units" approaches zero. Consider the music industry as an example. When artists record music, their songs are captured in digital format. Physical products, such as CDs or DVDs of the songs for sale in music stores, involve costs. The costs of a physical distribution channel are much higher than those involved in delivering the songs digitally over the Internet.

In fact, in the future companies might give away some products for free. For example, some analysts predict that commissions for online stock trading will approach zero because investors can search the Internet for information to make their own decisions regarding buying and selling stocks. At that point, consumers will no longer need brokers to give them information that they can obtain themselves, virtually for free.

Porter's Value Chain Model

Organizations use the Porter competitive forces model to design general strategies. To identify specific activities where they can use competitive strategies for greatest impact, they use his value chain model (1985). A **value chain** is a sequence of activities through which the organization's inputs, whatever they are, are transformed into more valuable outputs, whatever they are. The **value chain model** identifies points where an organization can use information technology to achieve competitive advantage (see Figure 2.4).

According to Porter's value chain model, the activities conducted in any organization can be divided into two categories: primary activities and support activities. **Primary activities** relate to the production and distribution of the firm's products and services. These activities create value for which customers are willing to pay. The primary activities are buttressed by **support activities**. Unlike primary activities, support activities do not add value directly to the firm's products or services. Rather, as their name suggests, they contribute to the firm's competitive advantage by supporting the primary activities.

Next, you will see examples of primary and support activities in the value chain of a manufacturing company. Keep in mind that other types of firms, such as transportation, healthcare, education, retail, and others, have different value chains. The key point is that *every* organization has a value chain.

In a manufacturing company, primary activities involve purchasing materials, processing the materials into products, and delivering the products to customers. Manufacturing companies typically perform five primary activities in the following sequence:

1. Inbound logistics (inputs)
2. Operations (manufacturing and testing)
3. Outbound logistics (storage and distribution)
4. Marketing and sales
5. Services

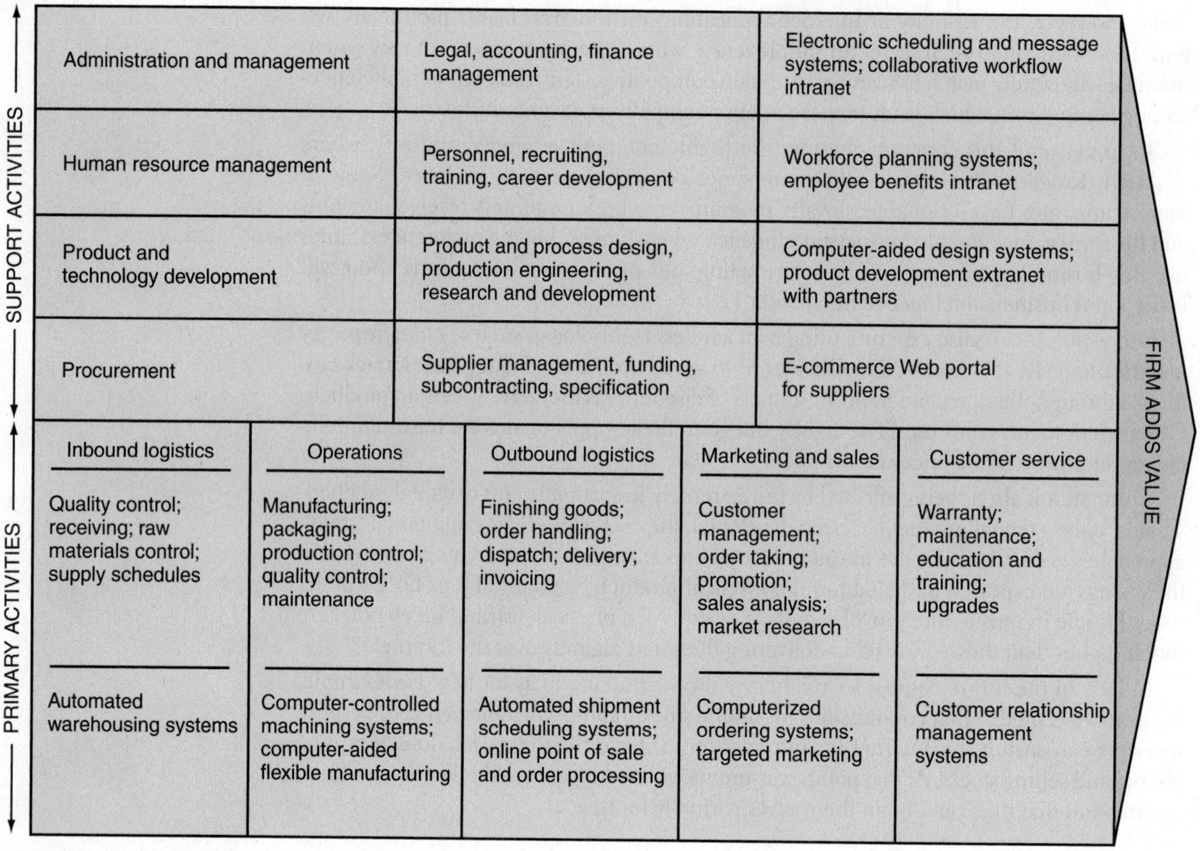

SUPPORT ACTIVITIES			
Administration and management	Legal, accounting, finance management	Electronic scheduling and message systems; collaborative workflow intranet	
Human resource management	Personnel, recruiting, training, career development	Workforce planning systems; employee benefits intranet	
Product and technology development	Product and process design, production engineering, research and development	Computer-aided design systems; product development extranet with partners	
Procurement	Supplier management, funding, subcontracting, specification	E-commerce Web portal for suppliers	

Inbound logistics	Operations	Outbound logistics	Marketing and sales	Customer service
Quality control; receiving; raw materials control; supply schedules	Manufacturing; packaging; production control; quality control; maintenance	Finishing goods; order handling; dispatch; delivery; invoicing	Customer management; order taking; promotion; sales analysis; market research	Warranty; maintenance; education and training; upgrades
Automated warehousing systems	Computer-controlled machining systems; computer-aided flexible manufacturing	Automated shipment scheduling systems; online point of sale and order processing	Computerized ordering systems; targeted marketing	Customer relationship management systems

(PRIMARY ACTIVITIES — FIRM ADDS VALUE)

FIGURE 2.4 Porter's Value Chain Model.

As work progresses in this sequence, value is added to the product in each activity. Specifically, the following steps occur:

1. The incoming materials are processed (in receiving, storage, and so on) in activities called *inbound logistics.*
2. The materials are used in operations, where value is added by turning raw materials into products.
3. These products are prepared for delivery (packaging, storing, and shipping) in the outbound logistics activities.
4. Marketing and sales sell the products to customers, increasing product value by creating demand for the company's products.
5. Finally, the company performs after-sales service for the customer, such as warranty service or upgrade notification, adding further value.

As noted above, the primary activities are buttressed by support activities. Support activities consist of:

1. The firm's infrastructure (accounting, finance, management)
2. Human resources management
3. Product and technology development (R&D)
4. Procurement

Each support activity can be applied to any or all of the primary activities. In addition, the support activities can also support one another.

A firm's value chain is part of a larger stream of activities, which Porter calls a **value system**. A value system, or an *industry value chain*, includes the suppliers that provide the inputs necessary to the firm along with their value chains. After the firm creates products, these products pass through the value chains of distributors (which also have their own value chains), all the way to the customers. All parts of these chains are included in the value system. To achieve and sustain a competitive advantage, and to support that advantage with information technologies, a firm must understand every component of this value system.

Strategies for Competitive Advantage

Organizations continually try to develop strategies to counter the five competitive forces identified by Porter. You will learn about five of those strategies here. Before we go into specifics, however, it is important to note that an organization's choice of strategy involves trade-offs. For example, a firm that concentrates only on cost leadership might not have the resources available for research and development, leaving the firm unable to innovate. As another example, a company that invests in customer happiness (customer-orientation strategy) will experience increased costs.

Companies must select a strategy and then stay with it, because a confused strategy cannot succeed. This selection, in turn, decides how a company will utilize its information systems. A new information system that can improve customer service but will increase costs slightly will be welcomed at a high-end retailer such as Nordstrom's, but not at a discount store like Walmart. The following list presents the most commonly used strategies. Figure 2.5 provides an overview of these strategies.

1. *Cost leadership strategy.* Produce products and/or services at the lowest cost in the industry. An example is Walmart's automatic inventory replenishment system, which enables Walmart to reduce inventory storage requirements. As a result, Walmart stores use floor space only to sell products, and not to store them, thereby reducing inventory costs.

2. *Differentiation strategy.* Offer different products, services, or product features than your competitors. Southwest Airlines, for example, has differentiated itself as a low-cost, short-haul, express airline. This has proved to be a winning strategy for competing in the highly competitive airline industry. Also, Dell has differentiated itself in the personal computer market through its mass-customization strategy.

3. *Innovation strategy.* Introduce new products and services, add new features to existing products and services, or develop new ways to produce them. A classic example is the introduction of automated teller machines (ATMs) by Citibank. The convenience and cost-cutting features of this innovation gave Citibank a huge advantage over its competitors. Like

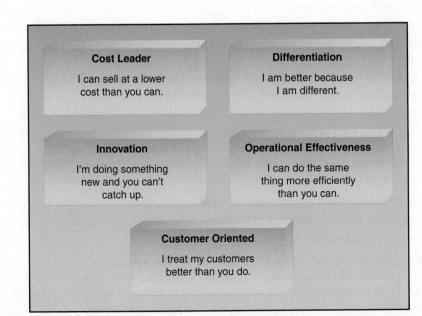

FIGURE 2.5 Strategies for Competitive Advantage.

Cost Leader

I can sell at a lower cost than you can.

Differentiation

I am better because I am different.

Innovation

I'm doing something new and you can't catch up.

Operational Effectiveness

I can do the same thing more efficiently than you can.

Customer Oriented

I treat my customers better than you do.

many innovative products, the ATM changed the nature of competition in the banking industry. Today, an ATM is a competitive *necessity* for any bank.

4. *Operational effectiveness strategy.* Improve the manner in which a firm executes its internal business processes so that it performs these activities more effectively than its rivals. Such improvements increase quality, productivity, and employee and customer satisfaction while decreasing time to market.

5. *Customer-orientation strategy.* Concentrate on making customers happy. Web-based systems are particularly effective in this area because they can create a personalized, one-to-one relationship with each customer.

before you go on...

1. What are strategic information systems?

2. According to Porter, what are the five forces that could endanger a firm's position in its industry or market places?

3. Describe Porter's value chain model. Differentiate between Porter's competitive forces model and his value chain model.

4. What strategies can companies use to gain competitive advantage?

2.5 Business—Information Technology Alignment

The "holy grail" of organizations is business–information technology alignment, or strategic alignment (which we will call simply *alignment*). **Business–information technology alignment** is the tight integration of the IT function with the organization's strategy, mission, and goals. That is, the IT function directly supports the business objectives of the organization. There are six characteristics of excellent alignment:

- Organizations view IT as an engine of innovation that continually transforms the business, often creating new revenue streams.

- Organizations view their internal and external customers and their customer service function as supremely important.

- Organizations rotate business and IT professionals across departments and job functions.

- Organizations provide overarching goals that are completely clear to each IT and business employee.

- Organizations ensure that IT employees understand how the company makes (or loses) money.

- Organizations create a vibrant and inclusive company culture.

Unfortunately, many organizations fail to achieve this type of close alignment. In fact, according to a McKinsey & Company survey on IT strategy and spending, only 16 percent of the IT and business executives who participated agreed that their organization had adequate alignment between IT and the business. Given the importance of business–IT alignment, why do so many organizations fail to implement this policy? The major reasons are:

- Business managers and IT managers have different objectives.

- The business and IT departments are ignorant of the other group's expertise.

- A lack of communication.

Put simply, business executives often know little about information technology, and IT executives understand the technology but may not understand the real needs of the business. One solution to this problem is to adopt a process view, as explained in Sections 2.1 and 2.2, to map and improve business and IT processes to achieve greater alignment.

Businesses can also utilize enterprise architecture to foster alignment. Originally developed as a tool to organize a company's IT initiatives, the enterprise architecture concept has evolved to encompass both a technical specification (the information and communication technologies and the information systems used in an organization) and a business specification (a collection of core business processes and management activities).

before you go on...

1. What is business–IT alignment?

2. Give examples of business–IT alignment at your university, regarding student systems. (Hint: What are the "business" goals of your university with regard to student registration, fee payment, grade posting, etc.?)

For all Majors

All of the functional areas of any organization are literally composed of a variety of business processes. Regardless of your major, you will be involved in a variety of business processes from your first day on the job. Some of these processes you will do by yourself, some will involve only your group or department, and others will involve several (or all) of the organization's functional areas.

It is important for you to be able to visualize processes, understand the inputs and outputs of each process, and identify the "customer" of each process. These capabilities will enable you to make the organization's business processes more efficient and effective, eliminate waste, and safeguard company resources through appropriate controls. This task generally involves incorporating information technology in the process. It is also important for you to appreciate how each process interacts with other processes in the organization and how each process fits into your organization's strategy.

All functional areas in any organization must work together in an integrated fashion in order for the firm to respond adequately to business pressures. These responses typically require each functional area to utilize a variety of information systems to support, document, and manage cross-functional business processes. In today's competitive global marketplace, the timeliness and accuracy of these responses is even more critical.

Closely following this discussion, all functional areas must work together for the organization to gain competitive advantage in its marketplace. Again, the functional areas use a variety of strategic information systems to achieve this goal. BPR and BPI process change efforts contribute to the goal as well.

You have seen why companies must be concerned with strategic advantage. But why is this chapter so important for you? There are several reasons. First, the business pressures you have learned about have an impact on your organization, but they also affect you as an individual. So, it is critical that you understand how information systems can help you, and eventually your organization, respond to these pressures.

In addition, achieving competitive advantage is essential for your organization's survival. In many cases, you, your team, and all your colleagues will be responsible for creating a competitive advantage. Therefore, having general knowledge about strategy and about how information systems affect the organization's strategy and competitive position will help you in your career.

You also need a basic knowledge of your organization's strategy, mission, and goals, as well as its business problems and how it makes (or loses) money. You now know how to analyze your organization's strategy and value chain, as well as the strategies and value chains of your competitors. You also have acquired a general knowledge of how information technology contributes to organizational strategy. This knowledge will help you to do your job better, to be promoted more quickly, and to contribute significantly to the success of your organization.

What's In
IT For
Me?

[Summary]

1. **Discuss ways in which information systems enable cross-functional business processes and business processes for a single functional area.**

A business process is an ongoing collection of related activities that produce a product or a service of value to the organization, its business partners, and/or its customers. Examples of business processes in the functional areas are managing accounts payable, managing accounts receivable, managing post-sale customer follow-up, managing bills of materials, managing manufacturing change orders, applying disability policies, hiring employees, training staff and computer users, and applying Internet use policy.

2. **Compare and contrast business process improvement, business process reengineering, and business process management to determine the different advantages and disadvantages of each.**

Business process reengineering is a radical redesign of an organization's business processes that is intended to improve the efficiency and effectiveness of these processes. The key to BPR is for enterprises to examine their business processes from a "clean sheet" perspective and then determine how they could best reconstruct those processes to improve their business functions. Because BPR proved difficult to implement, organizations have turned to business process improvement.

Business process improvement is an incremental approach to enhancing the efficiency and effectiveness of a process that is less risky and less costly than BPR. BPI relies on a structured approach (define, measure, analyze, improve, and control, or DMAIC), and many methodologies, such as Six Sigma, can be used to support these required steps.

Business process management is a management technique that includes methods and tools to support the documentation, design, analysis, implementation, management, and optimization of business processes. BPM coordinates individual BPI activities and creates a central repository of a company's processes, generally by utilizing software such as BPMS.

3. **Identify effective IT responses to different kinds of business pressures.**

- *Market pressures:* An example of a market pressure is powerful customers. Customer relationship management is an effective IT response that helps companies achieve customer intimacy.

- *Technology pressures:* An example of a technology pressure is information overload. Search engines and business intelligence applications enable managers to access, navigate, and utilize vast amounts of information.

- *Societal/political/legal pressures:* An example of a societal/political/legal pressure is social responsibility, such as the state of the physical environment. Green IT is one response that is intended to improve the environment.

4. **Describe the strategies that organizations typically adopt to counter Porter's five competitive forces.**

Porter's five competitive forces:

- *The threat of entry of new competitors:* For most firms, the Web increases the threat that new competitors will enter the market by reducing traditional barriers to entry. Frequently, competitors need only to set up a Web site to enter a market. The Web can also increase barriers to entry, as when customers come to expect a nontrivial capability from their suppliers

- *The bargaining power of suppliers:* The Web enables buyers to find alternative suppliers and to compare prices more easily, thereby reducing suppliers' bargaining power. From a different perspective, as companies use the Web to integrate their supply chains, participating suppliers can lock in customers, thereby increasing suppliers' bargaining power.

- *The bargaining power of customers (buyers):* The Web provides customers with incredible amounts of choices for products, as well as information about those choices. As a result, the Web increases buyer power. However, companies can implement loyalty programs in which they use the Web to monitor the activities of millions of customers. Such programs reduce buyer power.
- *The threat of substitute products or services:* New technologies create substitute products very rapidly, and the Web makes information about these products available almost instantly. As a result, industries (particularly information-based industries) are in great danger from substitutes (e.g., music, books, newspapers, magazines, software). However, the Web also can enable a company to build in switching costs, so that it will cost customers time and/or money to switch from your company to a competitor.
- *The rivalry among existing firms in the industry:* In the past, proprietary information systems provided strategic advantage for firms in highly competitive industries. The visibility of Internet applications on the Web makes proprietary systems more difficult to keep secret. Therefore, the Web makes strategic advantage more short-lived.

The five strategies are as follows:

- *Cost leadership strategy*—produce products and/or services at the lowest cost in the industry;
- *Differentiation strategy*—offer different products, services, or product features;
- *Innovation strategy*—introduce new products and services, put new features in existing products and services, or develop new ways to produce them;
- *Operational effectiveness strategy*—improve the manner in which internal business processes are executed so that a firm performs similar activities better than its rivals;
- *Customer-orientation strategy*—concentrate on making customers happy.

5. **Describe the characteristics of effective business–information technology alignment.**

   Business–IT alignment is the tight integration of the IT function with the strategy, mission, and goals of the organization. There are six characteristics of effective alignment:

   - Organizations view IT as an engine of innovation that continually transforms the business.
   - Organizations view customers and customer service as supremely important.
   - Organizations rotate business and IT professionals across departments and job functions.
   - Organizations provide clear, overarching goals for all employees.
   - Organizations ensure that IT employees understand how the company makes (or loses) money.
   - Organizations create a vibrant and inclusive company culture.

[Chapter Glossary]

business environment The combination of social, legal, economic, physical, and political factors in which businesses conduct their operations.

business–information technology alignment The tight integration of the IT function with the strategy, mission, and goals of the organization.

business process A collection of related activities that produce a product or a service of value to the organization, its business partners, and/or its customers.

business process improvement (BPI) A methodology for achieving incremental improvements in the effectiveness and efficiency of a process.

business process management (BPM) A management technique that includes methods and tools to support the design, analysis, implementation, management, and optimization of business processes.

business process reengineering (BPR) A radical redesign of a business process that improves its efficiency and effectiveness, often by beginning with a "clean sheet" (from scratch).

competitive advantage An advantage over competitors in some measure such as cost, quality, or speed; leads to control of a market and to larger-than-average profits.

competitive forces model A business framework devised by Michael Porter that analyzes competitiveness by recognizing five major forces that could endanger a company's position.

cross-functional business process A process in which no single functional area is responsible for its completion; multiple functional areas collaborate to perform the function.

digital divide The gap between those who have access to information and communications technology and those who do not.

entry barrier Product or service feature that customers expect from organizations in a certain industry; an organization trying to enter this market must provide this product or service at a minimum to be able to compete.

globalization The integration and interdependence of economic, social, cultural, and ecological facets of life, enabled by rapid advances in information technology.

individual social responsibility See **organizational social responsibility**.

make-to-order The strategy of producing customized products and services.

mass customization A production process in which items are produced in large quantities but are customized to fit the desires of each customer.

organizational social responsibility (also **individual social responsibility**) Efforts by organizations to solve various social problems.

primary activities Those business activities related to the production and distribution of the firm's products and services, thus creating value.

Six Sigma A methodology for continuous BPI focused on reducing defects in process outputs by using statistical methods.

strategic information systems (SISs) Systems that help an organization gain a competitive advantage by supporting its strategic goals and/or increasing performance and productivity.

support activities Business activities that do not add value directly to a firm's product or service under consideration but support the primary activities that do add value.

value chain A sequence of activities through which the organization's inputs, whatever they are, are transformed into more valuable outputs, whatever they are.

value chain model Model that shows the primary activities that sequentially add value to the profit margin; also shows the support activities.

value system Includes the producers, suppliers, distributors, and buyers, all with their value chains.

[Discussion Questions]

1. Consider the student registration business process at your university:
   - Describe the steps necessary for you to register for your classes each semester.
     Who are the customers of the process? What inputs and outputs does the process have? What organizational resources are used in the process?
   - Describe how information technology is used in each step of the process (or is not used).
     Evaluate the process performance. Is it efficient? Is it effective? Why or why not?

2. Explain how an organization may choose between applying business process improvement versus business process reengineering to solving a process performance problem.

3. Why is it so difficult for an organization to actually implement business process reengineering?

4. How can organizations benefit from BPM?

5. Is IT necessary for BPM? Why or why not?

6. Explain why IT is both a business pressure and an enabler of response activities that counter business pressures.

7. What does a flat world mean to you in your choice of a major? In your choice of a career? Will you have to be a "lifelong learner"? Why or why not?

8. What might the impact of a flat world be on your standard of living?

9. Is IT a strategic weapon or a survival tool? Discuss.

10. Why might it be difficult to justify a strategic information system?

11. Describe the five forces in Porter's competitive forces model, and explain how the Internet has affected each one.

12. Describe Porter's value chain model. What is the relationship between the competitive forces model and the value chain model?

13. Describe how IT can be used to support different value chains for different companies.

14. Discuss the idea that an information system by itself can rarely provide a sustainable competitive advantage.

[Problem-Solving Activities]

1. Surf the Internet for information about the Department of Homeland Security. Examine the available information, and comment on the role of information technologies in the department.

2. Compare and contrast the shopping process at a bricks and mortar store such as Macy's or Target and at an Internet retailer such as Amazon.com. How are these processes different? (Hint: Consider the process steps, the inputs, outputs, resources, and customers.) Are there differences in the performance (effectiveness and efficiency) of the two processes? Which process is superior, and why?

3. Experience customization by designing your own shoes at *www.nike.com*, your car at *www.jaguar.com*, your CD at *www.easternrecording.com*, your business card at *www.iprint.com*, and your diamond ring at *www.bluenile.com*. Summarize your experiences.

4. Access *www.go4customer.com*. What does this company do and where is it located? Who are its customers? Which of Friedman's flatteners does this company fit? Provide examples of how a U.S. company would use its services.

5. Enter Walmart China (*www.wal-martchina.com/english/index.htm*). How does Walmart China differ from your local Walmart (consider products, prices, services, etc.)? Describe these differences.

6. Apply Porter's value chain model to Costco (*www.costco.com*). What is Costco's competitive strategy? Who are Costco's major competitors? Describe Costco's business model. Describe the tasks that Costco must accomplish for each primary value chain activity. How would Costco's information systems contribute to Costco's competitive strategy, given the nature of its business?

7. Apply Porter's value chain model to Dell (*www.dell.com*). What is Dell's competitive strategy? Who are Dell's major competitors? Describe Dell's business model. Describe the tasks that Dell must accomplish for each primary value chain activity. How would Dell's information systems contribute to Dell's competitive strategy, given the nature of its business?

8. The market for optical copiers is shrinking rapidly. It is expected that by 2010 as much as 90 percent of all duplicated documents will be done on computer printers. Can a company such as Xerox Corporation survive?

   a. Read about the problems and solutions of Xerox from 2000 to 2010 at *www.fortune.com*, *www.findarticles.com*, and *www.google.com*.

   b. Identify all the business pressures on Xerox.

   c. Find some of Xerox's response strategies (see *www.xerox.com*, *www.yahoo.com*, and *www.google.com*).

   d. Identify the role of IT as a contributor to the business technology pressures (e.g., obsolescence).

   e. Identify the role of IT as a facilitator of Xerox's critical response activities.

[Team Assignments]

1. (a) As a class, describe the business pressures on your university. Each group will then create an online group for studying one of these business pressures, and how your university uses IT to respond to this pressure. Each member of the group must have a Yahoo! e-mail account (free). Form your groups in Google Groups (*http://groups.google.com*).

2. Divide the class into teams. Each team will select a country's government and visit its official Web site (e.g., try the United States, Australia, New Zealand, Singapore, Norway, Canada, the United Kingdom, the Netherlands, Denmark, Germany, and France). For example, the official Web portal for the U.S. government is *www.firstgov.gov*. Review and compare the services offered by each country. How does the United States stack up? Are you surprised at the number of services offered by countries through Web sites? Which country offers the most services? The least?

[Closing Case IBM's Watson] (MKT)

The Problem

Computer scientists have long sought to design computer-based information systems (CBISs) that possess general problem-solving skills. That is, researchers want CBIS to interact in natural human terms across a range of applications and processes, comprehending the questions that humans ask and providing answers that humans can understand. An important step toward this goal is the development of the IBM Watson system.

An Interesting IT Solution

IBM (www.ibm.com) has developed an artificial intelligence (we discuss artificial intelligence in Technology Guide 4) CBIS capable of answering questions posed in natural language. IBM named the system "Watson," after the company's founder, Thomas J. Watson, Sr. IBM describes Watson as an application of advanced natural language processing, information retrieval, knowledge representation and reasoning, and machine learning technologies to the field of open domain (general) question answering.

IBM developed Watson specifically to answer questions on the quiz show *Jeopardy!*. In 2011, Watson competed on Jeopardy against former winners Brad Rutter and Ken Jennings. Watson won the game series and received the first prize of $1 million. (In *Jeopardy!* the host reads the answer, and the contestants must then provide the correct question.)

For *Jeopardy!*, Watson had access to 200 million pages of structured and unstructured content consuming 4 terabytes of disk storage, including the full text of *Wikipedia* (see www.wikipedia.org). Significantly, however, Watson was *not* connected to the Internet during the game. For each clue, Watson's three most probable responses were displayed on the television screen. The probabilities represented Watson's level of confidence in any given answer. Watson consistently outperformed its human opponents, but it did experience problems responding to a few categories, notably those having short clues containing only a few words.

Following the television performance, IBM executives immediately turned their attention to commercializing Watson. They decided to focus on a field in which Watson could have a distinctive social impact while also proving its ability to master a complex body of knowledge. The team chose medicine.

Medicine was a logical choice. Although some health information is structured—for example, blood pressure readings and cholesterol counts—the vast majority is unstructured. This information includes textbooks, medical journals, patient records, and nurse and doctor notes. In fact, modern medicine entails so much unstructured information that its rapid growth has surpassed the ability of practitioners to keep up. Keep in mind that IBM has made it clear that Watson is *not* intended to replace doctors. Rather, its purpose is to assist them in avoiding medical errors and sharpening their medical diagnoses.

Enter Watson. Watson can ingest more data in one day that any human could in a lifetime. It can read all of the world's medical journals in seconds. Simultaneously, it can read patient histories, monitor the latest drug trials, examine the potency of new therapies, and closely follow state-of-the-art guidelines that help doctors choose the best treatments. Watson can also analyze images such as MRIs and EKGs. Watson never goes on vacation; never forgets a fact (in fact, Watson keeps on learning); never gets tired; and works 24/7/365.

The Results: Initial Uses of Watson

Watson at WellPoint. IBM partnered with WellPoint (www.wellpoint.com), the largest managed for-profit healthcare company in the Blue Cross and Blue Shield association, to increase the efficiency of health insurance decisions and claims by utilizing Watson's analytic capabilities. At WellPoint, Watson was trained with more than 25,000 test case scenarios and 1,500 real-life cases. It acquired the ability to analyze queries in the context of complex medical data and human natural language, including doctor's notes, patient records, and medical annotations and clinical feedback. In addition, nurses spent more than 14,700 hours of hands-on training with Watson. Watson continues to learn on the job, while working with the WellPoint nurses who originally conducted its training.

In December 2012, Watson started processing common medical procedure requests by physicians for members in WellPoint-affiliated health plans in five physician offices in the Midwest. The overall goal is for Watson to streamline the review processes between a patient's physician and his or her health plan.

Watson at Memorial Sloan-Kettering. IBM also sent Watson to the Memorial Sloan-Kettering Cancer Center (MSK; www.mskcc.org) in Manhattan to help physicians diagnose and treat lung cancer. Watson's role is to analyze a patient's specific symptoms, medical history, and hereditary history, and then synthesize those data with available unstructured and structured medical information, including published medical books and articles. By February 2013, Watson had ingested more than 600,000 pieces of medical information and 2 million pages of text from 42 medical journals and clinical trials in the area of oncology research. (Oncology is the study and treatment of cancer.) MSK has immersed Watson in the complexities of cancer as well as the explosion of genetic research that has set the stage for changing treatment practices for many cancer patients by basing their treatments on their personal genetic profiles. Starting with 1,500 actual lung cancer cases, MSK clinicians are training Watson to extract and interpret physician notes, lab results, and clinical research, while sharing its expertise with other physicians.

Watson at the Cleveland Clinic. The Cleveland Clinic Lerner College of Medicine of Case Western Reserve University is continuing Watson's medical training by increasing its health expertise. As with other installations of Watson, the goal is for Watson to assist medical professionals in diagnosing and treating patients.

Watson at MCCM and Westmed. In February 2013, IBM announced that oncologists at the Maine Center for Cancer Medicine (www.mccm.org) and Westmed Medical Group (www.westmedgroup.com) in New York had started to use Watson to help diagnose lung cancer and recommend treatment.

Watson at Rensselaer. On January 30, 2013, the Rensselaer Polytechnic Institute (RPI) (www.rpi.edu) received Watson. Watson will be housed at the Institute's technology park and will be available to researchers and students.

Watson at Citigroup. IBM intends to use Watson in other information-intensive fields, such as telecommunications, financial services, and government. At Citigroup (www.citigroup.com), for example, Watson analyzes financial, regulatory, economic, and social data across financial exchanges, currencies, and funds to help simplify and improve the bank's digital interactions with its customers.

One last interesting point: In March 2013, IBM executives noted that Watson's performance had improved by 240 percent since its *Jeopardy!* appearance. Buoyed by this success, IBM is now planning for "Watson 2.0," which will be sufficiently energy efficient to function on smartphones and tablet computers.

Sources: Compiled from "Watson Provides Cancer Treatment Options to Doctors in Seconds," *KurzweilAI.net*, February 11, 2013; N. Leske, "Doctors Seek Help on Cancer Treatment from IBM Supercomputer," *Reuters*, February 8, 2013; B. Upbin, "IBM's Watson Gets Its First Piece of Business in Healthcare," *Forbes*, February 8, 2013; J. Fitzgerald, "Watson Supercomputer Offers Medical Expertise," *USA Today*, February 8, 2013; M. Lev-Ram, "The Supercomputer Will See You Now," *Fortune*, December 3, 2012; "IBM's Watson Goes to Medical School," *KurzeilAI.net*, November 2, 2012; J. Gertner, "Calling Dr. Watson," *Fast Company*, November, 2012; B. Keim, "Paging Dr. Watson: Artificial Intelligence As a Prescription for Health Care," *Wired*, October 16, 2012; J. Gertner, "IBM's Watson Is Learning Its Way to Saving Lives," *Fast Company*, October 15, 2012; D. Zax, "Will Watson Be the New Siri?" *MIT Technology Review*, August 28, 2012; "IBM Creating Pocket-Sized Watson in $16 Billion Sales Push," *KurzweilAI.net*, August 28, 2012; D. Agus, "A Doctor in Your Pocket," *The Wall Street Journal*, January 14, 2012; "Applying Watson Technology for Personalized Cancer Care," *KurzweilAI.net*, March 23, 2012;

B. Jinks, "IBM's Watson Gets Wall Street Job After 'Jeopardy' Win," *Bloomberg BusinessWeek*, March 6, 2012; J. Fitzgerald, "IBM Watson Supercomputer Graduates from 'Jeopardy!' to Medicine," *Huffington Post*, May 21, 2011; M. Lucas, "Can Anyone Afford an IBM Watson Supercomputer? (Yes)," *Computerworld*, February 21, 2011; B. Zimmer, "Is It Time to Welcome Our New Computer Overlords?" *The Atlantic*, February 17, 2011; J. Markoff, "Computer Wins on 'Jeopardy!': Trivial It's Not," *The New York Times*, February 16, 2011; C. Thompson, "What Is I.B.M.'s Watson?" *New York Times*, June 14, 2010; http://www-03.ibm.com/innovation/us/watson/, accessed April 14, 2013.

Questions

1. What applications can you think of for Watson in a university setting?

2. What are potential disadvantages of using Watson in healthcare settings?

3. Would you consider being diagnosed only by Watson? Why or why not?

4. Would you consider being diagnosed by your personal physician, if he or she consulted Watson? Why or why not?

[Internship Activity]

Healthcare Industry

Information Systems have drastically altered the way we conduct business in healthcare. Every day there it seems there is a break through in research, product development, treatments and much of it is made possible by technology. Electronic Health Records have taken the forefront in the last few years because of the strong positives and horrifying negatives it brings to the table. But for those who are in the business of running a healthcare business, the Practice Management side of technology has made more difference.

For this Internship Activity, you will work for Chad Prince, Practice Administrator for Anniston Orthopaedics Associates in Anniston, AL. Chad has recently taken on the role of Practice Administrator and is learning the ins and outs of managing a healthcare organization. His first role is to learn about the market offerings of Practice Management. A quick web search for "Healthcare Practice Management Software" will reveal plenty of information on the relationship between Practice Management and Electronic Health Records.

Please visit the Book Companion Site to receive the full set of instructions on how you can help Chad make a good decision that will be in line with the long-term strategy of Anniston Orthopaedics.

Chapter 3

Ethics and Privacy

[LEARNING OBJECTIVES]	[CHAPTER OUTLINE]	[WEB RESOURCES]
1. Define ethics, list and describe the three fundamental tenets of ethics, and describe the four categories of ethical issues related to information technology.	3.1 Ethical Issues	• Student PowerPoints for note taking
2. Identify three places that store personal data, and for each one, discuss at least one potential threat to the privacy of the data stored there.	3.2 Privacy	**WileyPLUS**

• Student PowerPoints for note taking

WileyPLUS

• E-book
• Author video lecture for each chapter section
• Practice quizzes
• Flash Cards for vocabulary review
• Additional "IT's About Business" cases
• Video interviews with managers
• Lab Manuals for Microsoft Office 2010 and 2013

What's In IT For Me?

This Chapter Will Help Prepare You To...

ACCT	**FIN**	**MKT**	**POM**	**HRM**	**MIS**
ACCOUNTING	FINANCE	MARKETING	PRODUCTION OPERATIONS MANAGEMENT	HUMAN RESOURCES MANAGEMENT	MIS
Ensure correctness of annual reports	Adhere to regulatory environment	Ensure privacy of customers	Monitor labor laws overseas	Monitor appropriate use of IT in workplace	Monitor correct use of sensitive company data

The Problem (?)

O ne of the major controversies generated by the Vietnam War occurred in 1971, when *The New York Times* and other sources publicized excerpts from a secret Defense Department study—quickly labeled *The Pentagon Papers*—that detailed the history of U.S. involvement in Southeast Asia. These documents had been copied by defense analyst Daniel Ellsberg, one of the contributors to the study. Due to the limitations of the existing technologies, Ellsberg had to photocopy thousands of documents by hand. Today, *whistleblowers*—employees with insider knowledge of an organization—can capture huge amounts of incriminating documents on a laptop, memory stick, or portable hard drive. They can then send this information through personal e-mail accounts or online drop sites, or they can simply submit it directly to WikiLeaks (*www.wikileaks.org*).

WikiLeaks (www.wikileaks.org) was officially unveiled in December 2006. Julian Assange, one of the founders, was reportedly inspired by the leak of the Pentagon Papers. Assange intended WikiLeaks to serve as a dropbox for anyone, anywhere, who disagreed with any organization's activities or secrets. According to its Web site, WikiLeaks focuses on material of ethical, political, and historical significance. In its first year, the organization's database expanded to millions of documents. WikiLeaks continues to receive many new documents every day. Since its inception, WikiLeaks has had significant impacts on both businesses and governments. We discuss several examples below.

In January 2008, WikiLeaks posted documents alleging that the Swiss bank Julius Baer (www.juliusbaer.com) hid its clients' profits from even the Swiss government by concealing them in what seemed to be shell companies in the Cayman Islands. The bank filed a lawsuit against WikiLeaks for publishing data that it claimed had been stolen from its clients. Baer later dropped the lawsuit—but only after generating embarrassing publicity for itself.

In October 2008, Iceland's Kaupthing Bank collapsed, saddling the country with $128 billion in debts. Ten months later, Bogi Agustsson, the anchor for Icelandic national broadcaster RUV, appeared on the evening news and explained that a legal injunction had prevented the station from airing an exposé on the bank. Viewers who wanted to view the material, he suggested, should visit WikiLeaks. People who took Agustsson's advice found a summary of Kaupthing's

[**WikiLeaks Marches On**]

loans posted on the Web site, detailing more than $6 billion funneled from the bank to its own-ers and companies they owned, often supported with little or no collateral. WikiLeaks promptly became a household name in Iceland.

The following year, WikiLeaks published documents generated by a pharmaceutical trade group implying that its lobbyists were receiving confidential documents from, and exerting influence over, a World Health Organization (WHO) project to fund drug research in the developing world. The resulting attention helped to terminate the project.

In September 2009, commodities company Trafigura (www.trafigura.com) requested an injunction from the courts to prevent the British media from mentioning a damaging internal report. The report indicated that the company had dumped tons of toxic waste in the Ivory Coast that sickened 100,000 local inhabitants. Although Trafigura could prevent the official media from reporting this story, it could not stop WikiLeaks from publishing the information. The public became aware of the transgression, and Trafigura eventually had to pay out more than $200 million in settlements to Ivory Coast victims of the toxic waste.

As consequential as these business leaks were, probably the most controversial WikiLeaks exposé involved the U.S. government. From November 2009 to April 2010, U.S. Army Private First Class Bradley Manning downloaded hundreds of thousands of diplomatic cables to a CD at an outpost in Iraq. He then passed the information to WikiLeaks. In doing so, Man-ning violated U.S. Code Section 1030(a)(1), which criminalizes unauthorized computer downloads.

Beginning on November 28, 2010, WikiLeaks published the contents of more than 250,000 diplomatic cables, the largest unauthorized release of contemporary classified information in history. Among these cables were 11,000 documents marked "secret." The U.S. govern-ment's definition of a secret document is one that, if released, would cause "serious damage to national security."

Diplomatic flaps quickly ensued. For example, North Korean leader Kim Jong Il learned that China would consider supporting the unification of the peninsula under the leadership of the South Korean government. Similarly, Iranian President Mahmoud Ahmadinejad discov-ered that his Arab neighbors were pleading with the United States to launch an attack against Tehran's nuclear program.

Not surprisingly, the release of the cables also had wide-ranging repercussions within the United States. The government ordered a clampdown on intelligence sharing between agen-cies, and it established new measures to control electronically stored documents. U.S. Secre-tary of State Hilary Clinton charged that the massive cable leak "puts people's lives in danger, threatens national security, and undermines our efforts to work with other countries to solve shared problems." From the opposite perspective, many individuals and groups, including Daniel Ellsberg, supported WikiLeaks' actions.

Wikileaks' activities continue. In July 2010, WikiLeaks released the Afghan War Diary, a compilation of more than 76,000 documents about the War in Afghanistan not previously available to the public. During April 2011, WikiLeaks began publishing secret files relating to prisoners detained in the Guantanamo Bay detention facility. On July 5, 2012, WikiLeaks began publishing the Syria files, more than 2 million e-mails from Syrian political figures, ministries, and associated companies, dating from August 2006 to March 2012. On October 25, 2012, WikiLeaks began publishing The Detainee Policies, which contain classified or other-wise restricted files from the U.S. Department of Defense that discuss the rules and procedures for detainees in U.S. military custody.

The problem, then, boils down to this: How can governments, organizations, and even indi-viduals prevent future disclosures? Is it possible to accomplish this task, given that the sources of WikiLeaks' information appear to be internal?

The Solution (?)

In the initial moments after the State Department cables were released, unknown hackers tried to shut down WikiLeaks by exposing its Web site to denial-of-service attacks (discussed in Chapter 4). It is unclear whether the hackers were working on behalf of the U.S. government, but they seemed to endorse the government's claims that the disclosures threatened national security.

WikiLeaks' supporters retaliated with anonymous "hacktivism," attacking the Web sites of companies such as Amazon, which had thrown WikiLeaks off its servers, and MasterCard and PayPal, which had frozen the organization's accounts and prevented its supporters from donating to the cause.

Ultimately, all attempts to stifle WikiLeaks have proved futile. When the organization is blocked from one host server, it simply jumps to another. Further, the number of mirror Web sites—essentially clones of WikiLeaks' main content pages—had mushroomed to 1,300 by the end of 2010.

Prior to 9/11, the U.S. State Department had operated its own internal cable system and encrypted documents to ensure security. After the attacks, the State Department system was merged into a new digital records system controlled by the Department of Defense. Since the WikiLeaks disclosures, the State Department has temporarily severed its connection to the new system while it takes steps to prevent future unauthorized downloads.

In addition to taking these steps, governments and companies have turned to cyber security to thwart WikiLeaks. Since 2007, every major security software vendor (e.g., McAfee, *www.mcafee.com*; Symantec, www.symantec.com; and Trend Micro, *www.trendmicro.com*) has spent hundreds of millions of dollars to acquire companies in the data leak prevention (DLP) industry. These companies produce software that locates and tags sensitive information and then guards against its being stolen or illegally duplicated. As of mid-2013, DLP software has not been effective.

The failure of DLP software has prompted organizations to turn to *network forensics*, which is the process of constantly collecting every digital "fingerprint" embedded on an organization's servers to trace and identify that an intruder who has broken into the system.

The Results

In February 2013, Private First Class Bradley Manning admitted to sending hundreds of thousands of Iraq and Afghanistan battlefield reports, U.S. State Department diplomatic cables, and other files to WikiLeaks while working as an intelligence analyst in Baghdad. A U.S. Army judge accepted the pleas to 10 charges. Manning could face a maximum of 20 years if convicted.

How can organizations and governments respond to WikiLeaks? Lawsuits will not work, because WikiLeaks, as a mere conduit for documents, is legally protected in the United States. Moreover, even if a company or a government somehow won a judgment against WikiLeaks, that would not shut down the company, because its assets are spread all over the world.

In fact, WikiLeaks has a nation-sized ally—Iceland. Since WikiLeaks discovered the corrupt loans that helped destroy Iceland's biggest bank, the country has set out to become the conduit for a global flood of leaks. Birgitta Jonsdottir, a member of Iceland's parliament, created the Icelandic Modern Media Institute (IMMI). The institute seeks to bring to Iceland all the laws that support protecting anonymous sources, freedom of information, and transparency from around the world. It would then set up a Nobel-style international award for activities supporting free expression. IMMI also would make Iceland the world's most friendly legal base for whistleblowers.

In August 2011, a group of FBI agents traveled to Iceland to request that Icelandic police authorities cooperate with the FBI in investigating WikiLeaks. Significantly, Iceland refused. Instead, the Icelandic Interior Minister ordered police to cease contact with the FBI agents, making it clear that the agents' presence was not "well seen" in Iceland.

In a related development, an Icelandic district court ruled that Valitor, the business partner of Visa and MasterCard, violated contract laws when it imposed a block against credit card donations to WikiLeaks. The court ordered Valitor to remove the block or it would be fined the equivalent of about $6000 per day.

Should WikiLeaks falter, other Web sites around the world are ready to take its place. For example, the Web site OpenLeaks (www.openleaks.org) will not openly publish information sent to it, but it will pass it on to reporters and human rights organizations to disseminate. Perhaps the most controversial group is Anonymous, the hacker collective. Anonymous is a decentralized online community acting anonymously in a coordinated manner, usually toward a self-agreed, hacktivist goal. (Hacktivism is a term that refers to the use of information technology to promote political ends, chiefly free speech, human rights, and information ethics.)

What is the best protection against unauthorized leaks? Icelandic WikiLeaks staffer Kristinn Hrafnsson suggested, rather drily, that companies—and perhaps governments to some extent—reform their practices to avoid being targeted.

And the final word? In December 2012, Julian Assange, one of the founders of WikiLeaks, stated that WikiLeaks was preparing to publish new secret documents. In April 2013, Assange is living in the Ecuadorian embassy in London to avoid extradition to Sweden to face charges of sexual assault.

Sources: Compiled from "Judge Accepts Manning's Guilty Pleas in WikiLeaks Case," *Associated Press*, February 28, 2013; "Iceland Denies Aid to FBI in WikiLeaks Investigation," *Reuters*, February 2, 2013; "FBI Came to Investigate WikiLeaks in Iceland," *Iceland Review*, January 31, 2013; "Julian Assange: Expect More From WikiLeaks," *The Guardian*, December 20, 2012; K. Zetter, "WikiLeaks Wins Icelandic Court Battle Against Visa for Blocking Donations," *Wired Magazine*, July 12, 2012; R. Somaiya, "Former WikiLeaks Colleagues Forming New Web Site, OpenLeaks," *The New York Times*, February 6, 2011; A. Greenberg, "WikiLeaks' StepChildren," *Forbes*, January 17, 2011; M. Calabresi, "Winning the Info War," *Time*, December 20, 2010; A. Greenberg, "WikiLeaks' Julian Assange," *Forbes*, December 20, 2010; J. Dougherty and E. Labott, "The Sweep: WikiLeaks Stirs Anarchy Online," *CNN.com*, December 15, 2010; E. Robinson, "In WikiLeaks Aftermath, An Assault on Free Speech," *The Washington Post*, December 14, 2010; M. Calabresi, "The War on Secrecy," *Time*, December 13, 2010; I. Shapira and J. Warrick, "WikiLeaks' Advocates Are Wreaking 'Hacktivism'," *The Washington Post*, December 12, 2010; F. Rashid, "WikiLeaks, Anonymous Force Change to Federal Government's Security Approach," *eWeek*, December 12, 2010; E. Mills, "Report: Ex-WikiLeakers to Launch New OpenLeaks Site," *CNET.com*, December 10, 2010; G. Keizer, "Pro-WikiLeaks Cyber Army Gains Strength; Thousands Join DDos Attacks," *Computerworld*, December 9, 2010; J. Warrick and R. Pegoraro, "WikiLeaks Avoids Shutdown as Supporters Worldwide Go on the Offensive," *The Washington Post*, December 8, 2010; F. Rashid, "PayPal, PostFinance Hit by DoS Attacks, Counter-Attack in Progress," *eWeek*, December 6, 2010; "Holder: 'Significant' Actions Taken in WikiLeaks Investigation," *CNN.com*, December 6, 2010; "WikiLeaks Back Online After Being Dropped by U.S. Domain Name Provider," *CNN.com*, December 3, 2010; "WikiLeaks Reports Another Electronic Disruption," *CNN.com*, November 30, 2010; "Feds Open Criminal Investigation into WikiLeaks Disclosures," *CNN.com*, November 29, 2010; L. Fadel, "Army Intelligence Analyst Charged in WikiLeaks Case," *The Washington Post*, July 7, 2010; *www.wikileaks.org*, accessed February 11, 2013; G. Goodale, "WikiLeaks Q&A with Daniel Ellsberg, the Man Behind the Pentagon Papers," *The Christian Science Monitor*, July 29, 2010.

What We Learned from This Case

The WikiLeaks case addresses the two major issues you will study in this chapter: ethics and privacy. The two issues are closely related both to each other and to IT and both raise significant questions involving access to information in the digital age. For example, are WikiLeaks' actions ethical? Does WikiLeaks violate the privacy of governments, organizations, and individuals? The answers to these questions are not straightforward. In fact, IT has made finding answers to these questions even more difficult.

You will encounter numerous ethical and privacy issues in your career, many of which will involve IT in some manner. This chapter will give you insights into how to respond to these issues. Further, it will help you to make immediate contributions to your company's code of ethics and its privacy policies. You will also be able to provide meaningful input concerning the potential ethical and privacy impacts of your organization's information systems on people within and outside the organization.

For example, suppose your organization decides to adopt social computing technologies (which you will study in Chapter 9) to include business partners and customers in new product development. You will be able to analyze the potential privacy and ethical implications of implementing these technologies.

All organizations, large and small, must be concerned with ethics. IT's About [Small] Business 3.1 illustrates ethical problems at Pinterest.

Small business (or startup) owners face a very difficult situation when their employees have access to sensitive customer information. There is a delicate balance between access to information and its appropriate use. This balance is best maintained by hiring honest and trustworthy employees who abide by the organization's code of ethics. Ultimately this issue leads to another question: Does the small business, or a startup, even have a code of ethics to fall back on in this type of situation?

IT's about [small] business

3.1 Pinterest

You probably never thought of yourself as a lawbreaker, right? Most likely you would not go into a music store and steal a CD or DVD, or go into a bookstore and steal a book. But, would you download something that you had not purchased? Would you copy a picture from someone else's Web site and claim it for your own? Would you download an article and try to customize it so that it did not appear to be plagiarized?

These issues have become increasingly important as we move further into the 21st century. Social networks are making it very easy to share and reshare information. This reality leads to a fundamental question: Who owns the information that gets posted on the Internet? Consider one social network, Pinterest. Pinterest is a small business with only about 20 employees. It is primarily a technology company that provides infrastructure and software that enable users to "pin" things they like. Realizing that many users would likely try to "pin" pictures or ideas that were not their own, Pinterest pre-empted the problem by incorporating into their user agreement a clause specifying that users could pin only pictures or ideas that they created themselves. Sounds simple enough, right?

Wrong. Many Pinterest users do not adhere to the terms of the user agreement. Rather, they pin ideas that are not theirs. What happens in these cases? The simple answer is that the company will revoke access if it catches users downloading copyrighted third-party material. The issue is more complicated than this, however. Pinterest is a small business, and it does not have the personnel to police every pin that its users make. Given this reality, who is at fault here? Is Pinterest at fault because it does not

adequately police its users? Or, does the fault lie with the users who agree not to steal intellectual property but do so anyway?

Pinterest is just one example of a site that suffers from this dilemma. All social media sites have similar agreements, and they also experience a host of intellectual property issues. Is the main issue here that people do not care about user agreements? Do you think there will eventually be a legal "crackdown" in social media over ethical issues as there was with Napster in 2002? In its first incarnation, Napster was the name of an online, peer-to-peer, file-sharing music service. Napster ran into legal difficulties over copyright infringement, ceased operations, and was acquired by Roxio. In its second incarnation, Napster became an online music store until it was acquired by Rhapsody from Best Buy in December, 2011.

Sources: Compiled from A. Kosner, "Pinterest: Napster for Housewives or Wake Up Call for a Better Copyright Idea," *Forbes*, March 15, 2012; T. Poletti, "Is Pinterest the Next Napster?" *The Wall Street Journal*, March 14, 2012; A. Prakash, "Exploring the Ethics of Pinterest," www.ohmyhandmade.com, accessed March 9, 2012; M. McHugh, "Pinterest Is Blowing Up—With Cries of Copyright Infringement," *Digital Trends*, February 17, 2012; www.pinterest .com, accessed March 5, 2013.

Questions

1. Who is at fault for the third-party copyright infringements enabled by Pinterest? Pinterest, its users, or both? (We discuss copyright infringement in detail in Chapter 4.)

2. Compare the ethics of "pinning" on Pinterest with downloading music files on Napster. Do you think that Pinterest will face the same fate as Napster? Why or why not?

Ethical Issues

3.1

Ethics refers to the principles of right and wrong that individuals use to make choices that guide their behavior. Deciding what is right or wrong is not always easy or clear cut. Fortunately, there are many frameworks that can help us make ethical decisions.

Ethical Frameworks

There are many sources for ethical standards. Here we consider four widely used standards: the utilitarian approach, the rights approach, the fairness approach, and the common good approach. There are many other sources, but these four are representative.

The *utilitarian approach* states that an ethical action is the one that provides the most good or does the least harm. The ethical corporate action would be the one that produces the greatest good and does the least harm for all affected parties—customers, employees, shareholders, the community, and the environment.

The *rights approach* maintains that an ethical action is the one that best protects and respects the moral rights of the affected parties. Moral rights can include the rights to make one's own choices about what kind of life to lead, to be told the truth, not to be injured, and to a degree of privacy. Which of these rights people are actually entitled to—and under what circumstances—is widely debated. Nevertheless, most people acknowledge that individuals are entitled to some moral rights. An ethical organizational action would be one that protects and respects the moral rights of customers, employees, shareholders, business partners, and even competitors.

The *fairness approach* posits that ethical actions treat all human beings equally, or, if unequally, then fairly, based on some defensible standard. For example, most people might believe it is fair to pay people higher salaries if they work harder or if they contribute a greater amount to the firm. However, there is less certainty regarding CEO salaries that are hundreds or thousands of times larger than those of other employees. Many people question whether this huge disparity is based on a defensible standard or whether it is the result of an imbalance of power and hence is unfair.

Finally, the *common good approach* highlights the interlocking relationships that underlie all societies. This approach argues that respect and compassion for all others is the basis for ethical actions. It emphasizes the common conditions that are important to the welfare of everyone. These conditions can include a system of laws, effective police and fire departments, healthcare, a public educational system, and even public recreation areas.

If we combine these four standards, we can develop a general framework for ethics (or ethical decision making). This framework consists of five steps.

- Recognize an ethical issue
  - Could this decision or situation damage someone or some group?
  - Does this decision involve a choice between a good and a bad alternative?
  - Does this issue involve more than legal considerations? If so, in what way?
- Get the facts
  - What are the relevant facts of the situation?
  - Do I have sufficient information to make a decision?
  - Which individuals and/or groups have an important stake in the outcome?
  - Have I consulted all relevant persons and groups?
- Evaluate alternative actions
  - Which option will produce the most good and do the least harm? (the utilitarian approach)
  - Which option best respects the rights of all stakeholders? (the rights approach)
  - Which option treats people equally or proportionately? (the fairness approach)
  - Which option best serves the community as a whole, and not just some members? (the common good approach)
- Make a decision and test it
  - Considering all the approaches, which option best addresses the situation?
- Act and reflect on the outcome of your decision
  - How can I implement my decision with the greatest care and attention to the concerns of all stakeholders?
  - How did my decision turn out, and what did I learn from this specific situation?

Now that we have created a general ethical framework, we will focus specifically on ethics in the corporate environment.

Ethics in the Corporate Environment

Many companies and professional organizations develop their own codes of ethics. A **code of ethics** is a collection of principles intended to guide decision making by members of the organization. For example, the Association for Computing Machinery (*www.acm.org*), an organization of computing professionals, has a thoughtful code of ethics for its members (see *www.acm.org/constitution/code.html*).

Keep in mind that different codes of ethics are not always consistent with one another. Therefore, an individual might be expected to conform to multiple codes. For example, a person who is a member of two large professional computing-related organizations may be simultaneously required by one organization to comply with all applicable laws and by the other organization to refuse to obey unjust laws.

Fundamental tenets of ethics include responsibility, accountability, and liability. **Responsibility** means that you accept the consequences of your decisions and actions. **Accountability** refers to determining who is responsible for actions that were taken. **Liability** is a legal concept that gives individuals the right to recover the damages done to them by other individuals, organizations, or systems.

Before you go any further, it is very important that you realize that what is *unethical* is not necessarily *illegal*. For example, a bank's decision to foreclose on a home can be technically legal, but it can raise many ethical questions. In many instances, then, an individual or organization faced with an ethical decision is not considering whether to break the law. As the foreclosure example illustrates, however, ethical decisions can have serious consequences for individuals, organizations, and society at large.

In recent years we have witnessed a large number of extremely poor ethical decisions, not to mention outright criminal behavior. During 2001 and 2002, three highly publicized fiascos occurred at Enron, WorldCom, and Tyco. At each company, executives were convicted of various types of fraud for using illegal accounting practices. These actions led to the passage of the Sarbanes-Oxley Act in 2002. Sarbanes-Oxley requires publicly held companies to implement financial controls and company executives to personally certify financial reports.

More recently, the subprime mortgage crisis exposed unethical lending practices throughout the mortgage industry. The crisis also highlighted pervasive weaknesses in the regulation of the U.S. financial industry as well as the global financial system. It ultimately contributed to a deep recession in the global economy.

Advancements in information technologies have generated a new set of ethical problems. Computing processing power doubles roughly every two years, meaning that organizations are more dependent than ever on their information systems. Organizations can store increasing amounts of data at decreasing cost. As a result, they can store more data on individuals for longer periods of time. Going further, computer networks, particularly the Internet, enable organizations to collect, integrate, and distribute enormous amounts of information on individuals, groups, and institutions. These developments have created numerous ethical problems concerning the appropriate collection and use of customer information, personal privacy, and the protection of intellectual property, as the chapter-closing case illustrates.

The power of information technology also makes it possible to very quickly implement electronic commerce Web sites that closely resemble successful, existing businesses that practice electronic commerce. This practice is called *cloning* Web sites. IT's About Business 3.2 describes the results of the cloning process.

Ethics and Information Technology

All employees have a responsibility to encourage ethical uses of information and information technology. Many of the business decisions you will face at work will have an ethical dimension. Consider the following decisions that you might have to make:

- Should organizations monitor employees' Web surfing and e-mail?
- Should organizations sell customer information to other companies?
- Should organizations audit employees' computers for unauthorized software or illegally downloaded music or video files?

The diversity and ever-expanding use of IT applications have created a variety of ethical issues. These issues fall into four general categories: privacy, accuracy, property, and accessibility.

1. *Privacy issues* involve collecting, storing, and disseminating information about individuals.
2. *Accuracy issues* involve the authenticity, fidelity, and correctness of information that is collected and processed.
3. *Property issues* involve the ownership and value of information.
4. *Accessibility issues* revolve around who should have access to information and whether a fee should be paid for this access.

Table 3.1 lists representative questions and issues for each of these categories. In addition, Online Ethics Cases presents 14 scenarios that raise ethical issues. These scenarios will provide a context for you to consider situations that involve ethical or unethical behavior.

Many of the issues and scenarios discussed in this chapter, such as photo tagging and geo-tagging, involve privacy as well as ethics. In the next section, you will learn about privacy issues in more detail.

IT's [about business]

3.2 The Dot Clones

Fab (www.fab.com) is a highly successful flash-deal Web site for designer goods. A flash-deal site (also called deal-of-the-day is an electronic commerce business model in which a Web site offers a single product for sale for a period of 24 to 36 hours. Potential customers register as members and receive online offers by e-mail or via social networks.

Launched in June 2011, Fab recorded sales of $20 million in its first six months. The company's CEO attributed Fab's success to the authenticity of its products, product discounts, its refusal to offer knock-offs (a copy or imitation of a popular product), and the fact that its offerings consisted of objects and design products that could not be found elsewhere.

Six months after Fab launched its operations, other sites began to create knock-offs of their products. One prominent example is e-commerce design Web site called Bamarang (www.bamarang.de), which opened for business in Germany, the United Kingdom, France, Australia, and Brazil. Like Fab, Bamarang offers discounts of up to 70 percent on designer goods. Moreover, the layout, color scheme, and typefaces of the Bamarang Web site closely resemble Fab's. Bamarang even has a shot of an Eames chair as the background photo for its sign-in page, just as Fab does.

In an effort to fight Bamarang, on February 21, 2012, Fab acquired a German facsimile of Fab known as Casacanda. The Fab CEO defended this purchase by claiming that Casacanda is less of a copycat and more a group of people who came up with a similar idea to Fab's.

Bamarang is the creation of German brothers Oliver, Marc, and Alexander Samwer. This brotherly trio has hit upon a wildly successful business model: identify promising U.S. Internet businesses and then clone them for the international market. Since starting their first "dot clone" (a German version of eBay) in 1999, they have duplicated Airbnb, eHarmony, Pinterest, and other high-profile businesses. In total, they have launched more than 100 companies. Their Zappos clone, Zalando, now dominates six European markets. *Financial Times Deutschland* estimates the company's total worth at $1 billion.

The Samwers' base of operations is a startup business incubator in Berlin called Rocket Internet (www.rocket-internet.de). Rocket launches companies, hires staff, and provides marketing and design support, search engine optimization, and day-to-day management until startups can take over for themselves.

The Samwers launched their clone of eBay, called Alando, in early 1999. Four months after Alando's launch, eBay bought the company for $53 million—and the Samwers became Germany's first Internet millionaires.

In November 2008, Groupon went live in Chicago, and it quickly became one of the fastest-growing Internet businesses ever. In January 2010, the Samwers launched a Groupon knockoff called CityDeal. Within 5 months it was the top deal-of-the-day Web site in a dozen European nations. Groupon could have fought CityDeal in the marketplace. It also could have filed an intellectual property lawsuit, although the chances of winning such a suit would have been very slim. Companies cannot be patented, and trademarks apply only within the countries where they are registered. Perhaps taking the path of least resistance, in May 2010, Groupon bought its German clone for 14 percent of Groupon's shares.

Wrapp (www.wrapp.com) is a European startup that partners with retailers to enable users to give gifts to their friends through Facebook. Unsurprisingly, the Samwers launched DropGifts, a clone of Wrapp, in February 2012. Unlike Groupon and eBay, however, Wrapp responded aggressively. The company intends to add new territories much faster than originally planned in an attempt to achieve first-mover advantages in important markets. (A first-mover advantage is the edge that a company gains by entering a particular market before any competitors. For instance, the edge might be capturing the majority of a market.) In order to fund its rapid growth, Wrapp is turning back to its investors for additional funding. The Wrapp management team feels that the best defense against copycats is to do a better job. The company is convinced that, compared to the copycats, it has stronger existing relationships with retailer partners and more big partnerships on the way.

Meanwhile, Rocket Internet continues to develop clone businesses. For example, Payleven (https://payleven.com), a spin-off of Square, is a mobile payment service that uses a device attached to a smartphone or tablet computer to make and process card transactions. This service is available in Germany, the Netherlands, Italy, the United Kingdom, Poland, and Brazil. Like its competitors, Payleven takes a 2.75 percent commission on all transactions, with a minimum amount per transaction of 1 euro.

Rocket Internet is also increasing its operations in emerging markets. For example, it has launched Jumia (www.jumia.com), an Amazon clone, in Nigeria, Egypt, and Morocco. Like Amazon, Jumia sells a range of products, including mobile phones, baby and children's products, books, and home electronics.

The Samwers are revered among some young German entrepreneurs for putting Berlin's startup scene on the map. At the same time, however, other entrepreneurs despise them for giving Germany a reputation as the copycat capital of Europe.

There are several indications of the Samwers' image problem. In summer 2011, a Berlin startup called 6Wunderkinder called for an anticopycat revolution in that city. In January 2012, about 20 Rocket employees, some of them close allies of the Samwers, announced that they were leaving to launch a rival startup factory, called Project A Ventures, that would focus on backing original ideas. In February 2012, Russian entrepreneur Yuri Milner, an investor in Facebook, Zynga, and Twitter, pulled out of a plan to invest in Rocket. The German media speculated that his decision was based on the Samwers' reputation.

Despite their questionable image, the Samwers deny that they are copycats. Rather, they claim that they simply take an idea that is already on the Internet and "make it better." Perhaps surprisingly, one individual who came to the Samwer brother's defense was Groupon CEO (at the time) Andrew Mason who stated: "An idea for a company is the easy part, and execution is the hard part." He claimed that the Samwers were the best operators he had ever seen.

Sources: Compiled from I. Lunden, "Summit Partners Puts $26 M into Samwer Brothers' African Amazon Clone Jumia," *TechCrunch.com*, February 25, 2013;

I. Lunden, "Payleven, The Samwer Brothers' Answer to Square, Takes 'High Single-Digit Million Dollar' Round Led by a Mystery Investor," *TechCrunch.com,* January 20, 2013; B. Johnson, "Exclusive: Wrapp CEO Goes Toe-to-Toe with Samwer Bros.," *GigaOM.com*, March 7, 2012; C. Winter, "The German Website Copy Machine," *Bloomberg BusinessWeek*, March 5–11, 2012; M. Cowan, "Inside the Clone Factory: The Story of Germany Samwer Brothers," *Wired*, March 2, 2012; B. Johnson, "Now Samwer Bros Clone Fab and Target European Rollout," *GigaOM.com*, January 25, 2012; "Attack of the Clones," *The Economist*, August 6, 2011; www.rocket-internet.de, accessed March 5, 2013.

Questions

1. Discuss the ethics of the Samwers' business model. Then, discuss the legality of the Samwers' business model. Compare the two discussions.
2. What are some alternative strategies that companies might use to combat dot clones?
3. Discuss the ethical implications of the statement from Groupon's CEO that the Samwers are superb operators, not simply copycats.

Privacy Issues
What information about oneself should an individual be required to reveal to others?
What kind of surveillance can an employer use on its employees?
What types of personal information can people keep to themselves and not be forced to reveal to others?
What information about individuals should be kept in databases, and how secure is the information there?

Accuracy Issues
Who is responsible for the authenticity, fidelity, and accuracy of the information collected?
How can we ensure that the information will be processed properly and presented accurately to users?
How can we ensure that errors in databases, data transmissions, and data processing are accidental and not intentional?
Who is to be held accountable for errors in information, and how should the injured parties be compensated?

Property Issues
Who owns the information?
What are the just and fair prices for its exchange?
How should we handle software piracy (copying copyrighted software)?
Under what circumstances can one use proprietary databases?
Can corporate computers be used for private purposes?
How should experts who contribute their knowledge to create expert systems be compensated?
How should access to information channels be allocated?

Accessibility Issues
Who is allowed to access information?
How much should companies charge for permitting access to information?
How can access to computers be provided for employees with disabilities?
Who will be provided with equipment needed for accessing information?
What information does a person or an organization have a right to obtain, under what conditions, and with what safeguards?

Table 3.1

A Framework for Ethical Issues

before you go on...

1. What does a code of ethics contain?

2. Describe the fundamental tenets of ethics.

3.2 Privacy

In general, **privacy** is the right to be left alone and to be free of unreasonable personal intrusions. **Information privacy** is the right to determine when, and to what extent, information about you can be gathered and/or communicated to others. Privacy rights apply to individuals, groups, and institutions. The right to privacy is recognized today in all U.S. states and by the federal government, either by statute or in common law.

Privacy can be interpreted quite broadly. However, court decisions in many countries have followed two rules fairly closely:

1. The right of privacy is not absolute. Privacy must be balanced against the needs of society.
2. The public's right to know supersedes the individual's right of privacy.

These two rules illustrate why determining and enforcing privacy regulations can be difficult.

As we discussed earlier, rapid advances in information technologies have made it much easier to collect, store, and integrate vast amounts of data on individuals in large databases. On an average day, data about you are generated in many ways: surveillance cameras located on toll roads, on other roadways, in busy intersections, in public places, and at work; credit card transactions; telephone calls (landline and cellular); banking transactions; queries to search engines; and government records (including police records). These data can be integrated to produce a **digital dossier**, which is an electronic profile of you and your habits. The process of forming a digital dossier is called **profiling**.

Data aggregators, such as LexisNexis (*www.lexisnexis.com*), ChoicePoint (*www.choicepoint .com*), and Acxiom (*www.acxiom.com*), are prominent examples of profilers. These companies collect public data such as real estate records and published telephone numbers, in addition to nonpublic information such as Social Security numbers; financial data; and police, criminal, and motor vehicle records. They then integrate these data to form digital dossiers on most adults in the United States. They ultimately sell these dossiers to law enforcement agencies and companies that conduct background checks on potential employees. They also sell them to companies that want to know their customers better, a process called *customer intimacy*.

Data on individuals can also be used in more controversial manners. For example, a controversial map in California identifies the addresses of donors who supported Proposition 8, the referendum approved by California voters in the 2008 election that outlawed same-sex marriage in that state (see *www.eightmaps.com*). Gay activists created the map by combining Google's satellite mapping technology with publicly available campaign records that listed Proposition 8 donors who contributed $100 or more. These donors were outraged, claiming that the map invaded their privacy.

Electronic Surveillance

According to the American Civil Liberties Union (ACLU), tracking people's activities with the aid of information technology has become a major privacy-related problem. The ACLU notes that this monitoring, or **electronic surveillance**, is rapidly increasing, particularly with the emergence of new technologies. Electronic surveillance is conducted by employers, the government, and other institutions.

Americans today live with a degree of surveillance that would have been unimaginable just a few years ago. For example, surveillance cameras track you at airports, subways, banks, and other public venues. In addition, inexpensive digital sensors are now everywhere. They are incorporated into laptop webcams, video-game motion sensors, smartphone cameras, utility meters, passports, and employee ID cards. Step out your front door and you could be captured in a high-resolution photograph taken from the air or from the street by Google or Microsoft, as they update their mapping services. Drive down a city street, cross a toll bridge, or park at a shopping mall, and your license plate will be recorded and time-stamped.

Emerging technologies such as low-cost digital cameras, motion sensors, and biometric readers are helping to increase the monitoring of human activity. In addition, the costs of storing and using digital data are rapidly decreasing. The result is an explosion of sensor data collection and storage.

In fact, your smartphone has become a sensor. The average price of a smartphone has increased 17 percent since 2000. However, the phone's processing capability has increased by 13,000 percent during that time, according to technology market research firm ABI Research (www.abiresearch.com). As you will study in Chapter 8, smartphones can now record video, take pictures, send and receive e-mail, search for information, access the Internet, and locate you on a map, among many other things. Your phone also stores large amounts of information about you that can be collected and analyzed. A special problem arises with smartphones that are equipped with global positioning system (GPS) sensors. These sensors routinely *geotag* photos and videos, embedding images with the longitude and latitude of the location shown in the image. Thus, you could be inadvertently supplying criminals with useful intelligence by posting personal images on social networks or photo-sharing Web sites. These actions would show the criminals exactly where you live.

Another example of how new devices can contribute to electronic surveillance is facial recognition technology. Just a few years ago, this software worked only in very controlled settings such as passport checkpoints. However, this technology can now match faces even in regular snapshots and online images. For example, Intel and Microsoft have introduced in-store digital billboards that can recognize your face. These billboards can keep track of the products you are interested in based on your purchases or browsing behavior. One marketing analyst has predicted that your experience in every store will soon be customized.

Google and Facebook are using facial-recognition software—Google Picasa and Facebook Photo Albums—in their popular online photo-editing and sharing services. Both companies encourage users to assign names to people in photos, a practice referred to as *photo tagging*. Facial-recognition software then indexes facial features. Once an individual in a photo is tagged, the software searches for similar facial features in untagged photos. This process allows the user to quickly group photos in which the tagged person appears. Significantly, the individual is not aware of this process.

Once you are tagged in a photo, that photo can be used to search for matches across the entire Internet or in private databases, including databases fed by surveillance cameras. How could this type of surveillance affect you? As one example, a car dealer can take a picture of you when you step onto the car lot. He or she could then quickly profile you (find out information about where you live, your employment, etc.) on the Web to gain a competitive edge in making a sale. Even worse, a stranger in a restaurant could photograph you with a smartphone and then go online to profile you for reasons of his or her own. One privacy attorney has asserted that losing your right to anonymity would have a chilling effect on where you go, whom you meet, and how you live your life.

The scenarios we just considered deal primarily with your personal life. However, electronic surveillance has become a reality in the workplace as well. In general, employees have very limited legal protection against surveillance by employers. The law supports the right of employers to read their employees' e-mail and other electronic documents and to monitor their employees' Internet use. Today, more than three-fourths of organizations routinely monitor their employees' Internet usage. In addition, two-thirds use software to block connections to inappropriate Web sites, a practice called *URL filtering*. Further, organizations are installing monitoring and filtering software to enhance security by blocking malicious software and to increase productivity by discouraging employees from wasting time.

In one organization, the chief information officer (CIO) monitored about 13,000 employees for three months to determine the type of traffic they engaged in on the network. He then forwarded the data to the chief executive officer (CEO) and the heads of the human resources and legal departments. These executives were shocked at the questionable Web sites the employees were visiting, as well as the amount of time they were spending on those sites. The executives quickly made the decision to implement a URL filtering product.

In general, surveillance is a concern for private individuals regardless of whether it is conducted by corporations, government bodies, or criminals. As a nation the United States is still struggling to define the appropriate balance between personal privacy and electronic surveillance, especially in situations that involve threats to national security.

Personal Information in Databases

Modern institutions store information about individuals in many databases. Perhaps the most visible locations of such records are credit-reporting agencies. Other institutions that store personal information include banks and financial institutions; cable TV, telephone, and utilities companies; employers; mortgage companies; hospitals; schools and universities; retail establishments; government agencies (Internal Revenue Service, your state, your municipality); and many others.

There are several concerns about the information you provide to these record keepers. Some of the major concerns are:

- Do you know where the records are?
- Are the records accurate?
- Can you change inaccurate data?
- How long will it take to make a change?
- Under what circumstances will personal data be released?
- How are the data used?
- To whom are the data given or sold?
- How secure are the data against access by unauthorized people?

Information on Internet Bulletin Boards, Newsgroups, and Social Networking Sites

Every day we see more and more *electronic bulletin boards, newsgroups, electronic discussions* such as chat rooms, and *social networking sites* (discussed in Chapter 9). These sites appear on the Internet, within corporate intranets, and on blogs. A *blog*, short for "Weblog," is an informal, personal journal that is frequently updated and is intended for general public reading. How does society keep owners of bulletin boards from disseminating information that may be offensive to readers or simply untrue? This is a difficult problem because it involves the conflict between freedom of speech on the one hand and privacy on the other. This conflict is a fundamental and continuing ethical issue in the United States and throughout the world.

There is no better illustration of the conflict between free speech and privacy than the Internet. Many Web sites contain anonymous, derogatory information on individuals, who typically have little recourse in the matter. The vast majority of U.S. firms use the Internet in examining job applications, including searching on Google and on social networking sites (see IT's About Business 9.6). Consequently, derogatory information contained on the Internet can harm a person's chances of being hired.

New information technologies can also present serious privacy concerns. IT's About Business 3.3 examines Google Glass and its potential for invading your privacy.

IT's [about business]

3.3 Google Glass: Big Brother Really Is Watching You

We live in a world where the boundaries between what is private and what is public are blurring. New information technologies are largely responsible for this reality. Social media such as Twitter, as well as the widespread use of smartphones with image and video cameras that can upload their content immediately, have caused us to become more comfortable with these technologies. In fact, we are already used to being filmed; for example, closed-circuit television (CCTV) has become a normal part of our lives. (Think of all the CCTV security cameras located on city streets and in your university buildings.) Despite our increasing acceptance of electronic surveillance, however, a new technology known as Google Glass (www.google.com/glass/start) is causing privacy concerns.

Google Glass is an augmented-reality, wearable computer with a head-mounted display. The glasses display information in a hands-free, smartphone-type format, and they can interact with the Internet via natural language voice commands. The device receives data through Wi-Fi, and it contains a GPS chip (global positioning system). (We discuss Wi-Fi and GPS in Chapter 8.) Users issue voice commands by first saying "OK glass" followed by the command. Alternatively, they can use their finger to scroll through the options located along the side of the device. Google Glass can record video, take pictures, start Google+ hangout, perform search, translate, perform facial recognition, provide directions, answer queries, use Google Now, and send a message. Essentially, these glasses can instantly capture and store every movement of every individual around the person wearing them.

Consider these questions relating to the privacy implications of Google Glass. What if someone around you who is wearing Google Glass records you on video or takes your picture and you don't even know he or she is doing it? Or, suppose you are being recorded during a business meeting at lunch? Can a child properly consent to being recorded? Is an adult who happens to be visible in the camera's peripheral vision in a bar consenting? Would you like a stranger to be able to automatically identify you with the glasses' facial recognition feature? These are only a few of the questions regarding the privacy concerns associated with Google Glass.

Perhaps the most fundamental questions are: Who owns the data generated by Google Glass? Who receives these data? What happens to them after they are captured? Presumably the data flow to Google, where they are analyzed to provide more personalized search results as well as more targeted advertising. After all, advertising is a significant source of revenue for Google. Imagine that you are wearing Google Glasses and, whenever you look at something—a shirt, for example—a special offer for that shirt pops up on your glasses. For many people, that would be simply too intrusive.

Some analysts contend that we are too worried over the privacy implications of Google Glass. They note that our courts have outlined a definition of "reasonable expectation of privacy." If we reach a point where our surveillance technology is intrusive to a degree that everyone finds exploitative, then concerned parties will initiate legal challenges to these practices. In response, the government will create new laws or reinterpret exiting ones to address excessive cases.

As of mid-2013, Google Glass was in its initial stages of introduction. It remains to be seen if the functionality offered by this technology will outweigh the privacy concerns it raises. Some individuals and institutions, however, are already addressing these concerns. For example, a Seattle bar known as the 5 Point Café has banned Google Glass. The Café's managers are concerned about their customers' privacy. The bar's policy already prohibits customers from videotaping or photographing inside the bar without the permission of the managers as well as those being videoed or photographed. The managers contend that banning Google Glass is simply an extension of this policy.

Sources: Compiled from L. Moran, "Google Glasses Prompt Ban from Seattle Bar," *New York Daily News*, March 11, 2013; B. Woods, "Google Glass: You'll Kiss Your Privacy Goodbye, and You Won't Mind a Bit," *ZDNet*, March 7, 2013; C. Arthur, "Google Glass: Is It a Threat to Our Privacy?" *The Guardian,* March 6, 2013; S. Bradner, "Privacy as Product Differentiation: Is It Time?" *Computerworld*, March 5, 2013; D. Zax, "Privacy Fears with Google Glass Are Overblown," *MIT Technology Review*, March 4, 2013; G. Marshall, "Google Glass: Say Goodbye to Your Privacy," *TechRadar*, March 1, 2013; A. Keen, "Why Life Through Google Glass Should Be for Our Eyes Only," *CNN News*, February 26, 2013; J. Stern, "Google Glasses: Will You Want Google Tracking Your Eyes?" *ABC News*, April 5, 2012; C. Albanesius, "Google 'Project Glass' Replaces the Smartphone With Glasses," *PC Magazine*, April 4, 2012; N. Bilton, "Behind the Google Goggles, Virtual Reality," *The New York Times*, February 23, 2012; T. Claburn, "7 Potential Problems with Google's Glasses," *InformationWeek*, February 22, 2012; T. Claburn, "Google's Privacy Invasion: It's Your Fault," *InformationWeek*, February 18, 2012; www.google.com/glass/start, accessed March 6, 2013.

Questions

1. Apply the general framework for ethical decision making to Google Glass.
2. Do you feel that the functionality offered by Google Glass outweighs the potential loss of privacy that the technology could create? Why or why not? Support your answer.
3. Would you use Google Glasses? Why or why not? Support your answer.
4. If you were at a party or at a bar, would you be comfortable speaking to someone wearing Google Glasses? Would you be comfortable just being in the room with someone wearing Google Glasses? Why or why not? Support your answer.

Privacy Codes and Policies

Privacy policies or **privacy codes** are an organization's guidelines for protecting the privacy of its customers, clients, and employees. In many corporations, senior management has begun to understand that when they collect vast amounts of personal information, they must protect it. In addition, many organizations give their customers some voice in how their information is used by providing them with opt-out choices. The **opt-out model** of informed consent permits the company to collect personal information until the customer specifically requests that the data not be collected. Privacy advocates prefer the **opt-in model** of informed consent, which prohibits an organization from collecting any personal information unless the customer specifically authorizes it.

Table

3.2

**Privacy Policy
Guidelines: A Sampler**

Data Collection

Data should be collected on individuals only for the purpose of accomplishing a legitimate business objective.

Data should be adequate, relevant, and not excessive in relation to the business objective.

Individuals must give their consent before data pertaining to them can be gathered. Such consent may be implied from the individual's actions (e.g., applications for credit, insurance, or employment).

Data Accuracy

Sensitive data gathered on individuals should be verified before they are entered into the database.

Data should be kept current, where and when necessary.

The file should be made available so that the individual can ensure that the data are correct.

In any disagreement about the accuracy of the data, the individual's version should be noted and included with any disclosure of the file.

Data Confidentiality

Computer security procedures should be implemented to ensure against unauthorized disclosure of data. These procedures should include physical, technical, and administrative security measures.

Third parties should not be given access to data without the individual's knowledge or permission, except as required by law.

Disclosures of data, other than the most routine, should be noted and maintained for as long as the data are maintained.

Data should not be disclosed for reasons incompatible with the business objective for which they are collected.

One privacy tool available to consumers is the *Platform for Privacy Preferences* (P3P), a protocol that automatically communicates privacy policies between an electronic commerce Web site and visitors to that site. P3P enables visitors to determine the types of personal data that can be extracted by the sites they visit. It also allows visitors to compare a site's privacy policy to the visitors' preferences or to other standards, such as the Federal Trade Commission's (FTC) Fair Information Practices Standard or the European Directive on Data Protection.

Table 3.2 provides a sampling of privacy policy guidelines. The last section, "Data Confidentiality," refers to security, which we consider in Chapter 4. All of the good privacy intentions in the world are useless unless they are supported and enforced by effective security measures.

Despite privacy codes and policies, and despite opt-out and opt-in models, guarding whatever is left of your privacy is becoming increasingly difficult. However, several companies are providing help in maintaining your privacy, as illustrated by the following examples.

- Snapchat (www.snapchat.com): This smartphone app is a picture and video viewer, marketed to teenagers, that offers the illusion of security because "snaps" automatically self-destruct. The app also contains a notification feature that lets you know if someone performs a "screen grab" of any photos that you send.

- Wickr (www.wickr.com): This smartphone app allows you to send military-grade encrypted texts, photos, and videos to other Wickr users. (We discuss encryption in Chapter 4.) In addition, it deletes information such as location and type of device from files before sending them. Nothing is stored on Wickr's servers that could be used to track (or subpoena) someone.

- Burn Note (https://burnnote.com): This smartphone app sends encrypted notes that self-destruct after a set amount of time. The notes are deleted from the recipient's computer, and they are not stored on Burn Note servers. Burn Note also displays only a specific spotlit area of a note as the recipient mouses over it. As a result, it is difficult for a screenshot to capture an entire note.

- TigerText (www.tigertext.com): This app is marketed to businesses that need a secure messaging system, especially in healthcare. For example, your physician can use Tiger-Text to securely text X-rays of your knee to a colleague. TigerText also allows you to retrieve messages that you have already sent.

- Facebook Poke (www.facebook.com): Facebook's smartphone app lets you send messages, photos, and videos that expire after a set time limit. It also notifies you if the recipient takes a screenshot of your message.

- Reputation (www.reputation.com): This company manages your online reputation, which is the process of making people and businesses look their best on the Internet. Reputation will search for damaging content online and destroy it. In addition, it helps its clients prevent private information from being made public.

- Silent Circle (https://silentcircle.com): This company produces a smartphone app that allows people to easily make secure, encrypted phone calls and send secure, encrypted texts. In addition, the sender can set a timer so that the file will automatically be deleted from both devices (sending and receiving) after the set time period. This app makes life easier and safer for journalists, dissidents, diplomats, and companies that are trying to evade state surveillance or corporate espionage.

  According to the company, in early 2013, a reporter in South Sudan used the app to record a video of brutality that occurred at a vehicle checkpoint. He then encrypted the video and sent it to Europe. Within a few minutes, the video was automatically deleted from the sender's device. Even if authorities had arrested and searched the sender, they would not have found the footage on his phone. Meanwhile, the film, which included location data showing exactly where it was taken, was already in safe hands, where it can eventually be used to build a case documenting human rights abuse.

  Law enforcement agencies have concerns that criminals will us the Silent Circle app. The FBI, for instance, wants all communications providers to build in backdoors (discussed in Chapter 4) so the agency can secretly spy on suspects. Silent Circle, however, has an explicit policy that it will not comply with law enforcement eavesdropping requests.

International Aspects of Privacy

As the number of online users has increased globally, governments throughout the world have enacted a large number of inconsistent privacy and security laws. This highly complex global legal framework is creating regulatory problems for companies. Approximately 50 countries have some form of data-protection laws. Many of these laws conflict with those of other countries, or they require specific security measures. Other countries have no privacy laws at all.

The absence of consistent or uniform standards for privacy and security obstructs the flow of information among countries, a problem we refer to as *transborder data flows*. The European Union (EU), for one, has taken steps to overcome this problem. In 1998 the European Community Commission (ECC) issued guidelines to all of its member countries regarding the rights of individuals to access information about themselves. The EU data-protection laws are stricter than U.S. laws and therefore could create problems for U.S.-based multinational corporations, which could face lawsuits for privacy violations.

The transfer of data into and out of a nation without the knowledge of either the authorities or the individuals involved raises a number of privacy issues. Whose laws have jurisdiction when records are stored in a different country for reprocessing or retransmission purposes? For example, if data are transmitted by a Polish company through a U.S. satellite to a British corporation, which country's privacy laws control the data, and at what points in the transmission? Questions like these will become more complicated and frequent as time goes on. Governments must make an effort to develop laws and standards to cope with rapidly changing information technologies in order to solve some of these privacy issues.

The United States and the EU share the goal of privacy protection for their citizens, but the United States takes a different approach. To bridge the different privacy approaches, the U.S. Department of Commerce, in consultation with the EU, developed a "safe harbor" framework to regulate the way that U.S. companies export and handle the personal data (such as names and addresses) of European citizens. See *www.export.gov/safeharbor* and *http://ec.europa.eu/justice_home/fsj/privacy/index_en.htm*.

before you go on...

1. Describe the issue of privacy as it is affected by IT.

2. Discuss how privacy issues can impact transborder data flows.

For the Accounting Major

Public companies, their accountants, and their auditors have significant ethical responsibilities. Accountants now are being held professionally and personally responsible for increasing the transparency of transactions and assuring compliance with Generally Accepted Accounting Principles (GAAP). In fact, regulatory agencies such as the SEC and the Public Company Accounting Oversight Board (PCAOB) require accounting departments to adhere to strict ethical principles.

For the Finance Major

As a result of global regulatory requirements and the passage of Sarbanes-Oxley, financial managers must follow strict ethical guidelines. They are responsible for full, fair, accurate, timely, and understandable disclosure in all financial reports and documents that their companies submit to the Securities and Exchange Commission (SEC) and in all other public financial reports. Further, financial managers are responsible for compliance with all applicable governmental laws, rules, and regulations.

For the Marketing Major

Marketing professionals have new opportunities to collect data on their customers, for example, through business-to-consumer electronic commerce (discussed in Chapter 7). Business ethics clearly mandate that these data should be used only within the company and should not be sold to anyone else. Marketers do not want to be sued for invasion of privacy over data collected for the marketing database.

Customers expect their data to be properly secured. However, profit-motivated criminals want that data. Therefore, marketing managers must analyze the risks of their operations. Failure to protect corporate and customer data will cause significant public relations problems and outrage customers. Customer relationship management (discussed in Chapter 11) operations and tracking customers' online buying habits can expose unencrypted data to misuse or result in privacy violations.

For the Production/Operations Management Major

POM professionals decide whether to outsource (or offshore) manufacturing operations. In some cases, these operations are sent overseas to countries that do not have strict labor laws. This situation raises serious ethical questions. For example, is it ethical to hire employees in countries with poor working conditions in order to reduce labor costs?

What's In IT For Me?

HRM

For the Human Resources Management Major

Ethics is critically important to HR managers. HR policies explain the appropriate use of information technologies in the workplace. Questions such as the following can arise: Can employees use the Internet, e-mail, or chat systems for personal purposes while at work? Is it ethical to monitor employees? If so, how? How much? How often? HR managers must formulate and enforce such policies while at the same time maintaining trusting relationships between employees and management.

MIS

For the MIS Major

Ethics might be more important for MIS personnel than for anyone else in the organization, because these individuals have control of the information assets. They also have control over a huge amount of the employees' personal information. As a result, the MIS function must be held to the highest ethical standards.

[Summary]

1. **Define ethics, list and describe the three fundamental tenets of ethics, and describe the four categories of ethical issues related to information technology.**

   Ethics refers to the principles of right and wrong that individuals use to make choices that guide their behavior.

   Fundamental tenets of ethics include responsibility, accountability, and liability. Responsibility means that you accept the consequences of your decisions and actions. Accountability refers to determining who is responsible for actions that were taken. Liability is a legal concept that gives individuals the right to recover the damages done to them by other individuals, organizations, or systems.

   The major ethical issues related to IT are privacy, accuracy, property (including intellectual property), and access to information. Privacy may be violated when data are held in databases or transmitted over networks. Privacy policies that address issues of data collection, data accuracy, and data confidentiality can help organizations avoid legal problems.

2. **Identify three places that store personal data, and for each one, discuss at least one personal threat to the privacy of the data stored there.**

   Privacy is the right to be left alone and to be free of unreasonable personal intrusions. Threats to privacy include advances in information technologies, electronic surveillance, personal information in databases, Internet bulletin boards, newsgroups, and social networking sites. The privacy threat in Internet bulletin boards, newsgroups, and social networking sites is that you might post too much personal information that many unknown people can see.

[Chapter Glossary]

accountability A tenet of ethics that refers to determining who is responsible for actions that were taken.

code of ethics A collection of principles intended to guide decision making by members of an organization.

digital dossier An electronic description of an individual and his or her habits.

electronic surveillance Tracking people's activities with the aid of computers.

ethics The principles of right and wrong that individuals use to make choices to guide their behaviors.

information privacy The right to determine when, and to what extent, personal information can be gathered by and/or communicated to others.

liability A legal concept that gives individuals the right to recover the damages done to them by other individuals, organizations, or systems.

opt-in model A model of informed consent in which a business is prohibited from collecting any personal information unless the customer specifically authorizes it.

opt-out model A model of informed consent that permits a company to collect personal information until the customer specifically requests that the data not be collected.

privacy The right to be left alone and to be free of unreasonable personal intrusions.

privacy codes (see **privacy policies**)

privacy policies (also known as **privacy codes**) An organization's guidelines for protecting the privacy of customers, clients, and employees.

profiling The process of forming a digital dossier.

responsibility A tenet of ethics in which you accept the consequences of your decisions and actions.

[Discussion Questions]

1. In 2008, the Massachusetts Bay Transportation Authority (MBTA) obtained a temporary restraining order barring three Massachusetts Institute of Technology (MIT) students from publicly displaying what they claimed to be a way to get "free subway rides for life." Specifically, the 10-day injunction prohibited the students from revealing vulnerabilities of the MBTA's fare card. The students were scheduled to present their findings in Las Vegas at the DEFCON computer hacking conference. Were the students' actions legal? Were their actions ethical? Discuss your answer from the students' perspective then from the perspective of the MBTA.

2. Frank Abagnale, the criminal played by Leonardo DiCaprio in the motion picture *Catch Me If You Can*, ended up in prison. After he left prison, however, he worked as a consultant to many companies on matters of fraud.

    a. Why do these companies hire the perpetrators (if caught) as consultants? Is this a good idea?

    b. You are the CEO of a company. Discuss the ethical implications of hiring Frank Abagnale as a consultant.

3. Access various search engines to find information relating to the use of drones (unmanned aerial vehicles, or UAVs) for electronic surveillance purposes in the United States.

    a. Take the position favoring the use of drones for electronic surveillance.

    b. Take the position against the use of drones for electronic surveillance.

[Problem-Solving Activities]

1. An information security manager routinely monitored Web surfing among her company's employees. She discovered that many employees were visiting the "sinful six" Web sites. (Note: The "sinful six" are Web sites with material related to pornography, gambling, hate, illegal activities, tastelessness, and violence.) She then prepared a list of the employees and their surfing histories and gave the list to management. Some managers punished their employees. Some employees, in turn, objected to the monitoring, claiming that they should have a right to privacy.

    a. Is monitoring of Web surfing by managers ethical? (It is legal.) Support your answer.

    b. Is employee Web surfing on the "sinful six" ethical? Support your answer.

    c. Is the security manager's submission of the list of abusers to management ethical? Why or why not?

    d. Is punishing the abusers ethical? Why or why not? If yes, then what types of punishment are acceptable?

    e. What should the company do in this situation? (Note: There are a variety of possibilities here.)

2. Access the Computer Ethics Institute's Web site at *www.cpsr.org/issues/ethics/cei*.

    The site offers the "Ten Commandments of Computer Ethics." Study these rules and decide whether any others should be added.

3. Access the Association for Computing Machinery's code of ethics for its members (see *www.acm.org/constitution/code.html*). Discuss the major points of this code. Is this code complete? Why or why not? Support your answer.

4. Access *www.eightmaps.com*. Is the use of data on this Web site illegal? Unethical? Support your answer.

5. The Electronic Frontier Foundation (*www.eff.org*) has a mission of protecting rights and promoting freedom in the "electronic frontier." Review the organization's suggestions about how to protect your online privacy, and summarize what you can do to protect yourself.

6. Access your university's guidelines for ethical computer and Internet use. Are there limitations as to the types of Web sites that you can visit and the types of material you can view? Are you allowed to change the programs on the lab computers? Are you allowed to download software from the lab computers for your personal use? Are there rules governing the personal use of computers and e-mail?

7. Access *http://www.albion.com/netiquette/corerules.html*. What do you think of this code of ethics? Should it be expanded? Is it too general?

8. Access *www.cookiecentral.com* and *www.epubliceye.com*. Do these sites provide information that helps you protect your privacy? If so, then explain how.

[Team Assignments]

1. Access *www.ftc.gov/sentinel* to learn how law enforcement agencies around the world work together to fight consumer fraud. Each team should obtain current statistics on one of the top five consumer complaint categories and prepare a report. Are any categories growing faster than others? Are any categories more prevalent in certain parts of the world?

2. Divide the class into three teams. Each team will access various search engines for information on Terry Childs, who was the network administrator for the City of San Francisco, California. One team will act as the prosecution and will present the case against Childs. The second team will act as the defense and defend Childs. The third team will sit as the jury and will vote on whether Childs is guilty or innocent. (The jury should not feel constrained with the fact that Childs has already been found guilty.)

9. Do you believe that a university should be allowed to monitor e-mail sent and received on university computers? Why or why not? Support your answer.

(a) A single point of failure is a component of a system that, if it fails, will prevent the entire system from functioning. For this reason, a single point of failure is clearly undesirable, whether it is a person, a network, or an application. Is Childs an example of a single point of failure? Why or why not? As he was indeed found guilty, what should the City of San Francisco (or any organization) do to protect itself from this type of problem?

[Closing Case **Target Provides a Surprise**]

The Problem

When you shop, you provide details about your buying habits and about yourself to retailers. The retailers analyze those details to determine what you like, what you need, and how to provide you with incentives so you will buy more of their products. Consider what happened at Target (HYPERLINK "http://www.target.com"www.target.com), for example.

Target sells everything from milk to stuffed animals to lawn furniture to electronics, so the company wants to convince customers that Target is the only store that they really need to visit. Unfortunately, this message is a "tough sell" because once customers form shopping habits, it is extremely difficult to change them.

There are, however, periods of time in a person's life when old routines change, including buying habits. The most important of these periods is the birth of a child. Parents are exhausted and overwhelmed, and their shopping patterns and brand loyalties are up for grabs.

In these cases, timing is everything. Because birth records are usually public, the moment a couple have a new baby, they almost instantaneously receive offers, incentives, and advertisements from all sorts of companies. To be successful, then, a retailer needs to reach them before its competitors are even aware that a baby is soon to arrive. Specifically, Target's marketing managers want to send "targeted" (no pun intended) ads to women in their second trimester, which is when most expectant mothers begin buying all sorts of new items, such as prenatal vitamins and maternity clothing.

The Solution

Target has long collected huge amounts of data on every person who regularly frequents its stores. Target assigns each shopper a unique Guest ID number that collects and maintains data on everything the shopper buys. If you use a credit card or a coupon, fill out a survey, mail in a refund, call the customer help line, open an e-mail message Target has sent you, or visit Target's Web site, then the company records the transaction and links it to your Guest ID.

Target also links demographic information to your Guest ID, such as your age, whether you are married and have children, which part of town you live in, how long it takes you to drive to the store, your estimated salary, whether you have moved recently, which credit cards you carry, and what other Web sites you visit. Further, Target can buy data about your ethnicity, job history, the magazines you read, whether you have declared bankruptcy or been divorced, the year you bought (or lost) your house, where you went to college, what kinds of topics you talk about online, which brand of coffee you prefer, your political leanings, charitable giving, and the number and types of cars you own.

All of that information is meaningless, however, unless someone analyzes and makes sense of it. Using analytics techniques (discussed in Chapter 12), Target analysts discovered about 25 products that, when analyzed together, allowed the retailer to assign a "pregnancy prediction" score to each female customer. In fact, Target could estimate a woman's due date to within a small window, which enabled the store to send coupons timed to very specific stages of her pregnancy. As a result, Target began sending coupons to customers according to their pregnancy scores.

An Unexpected Result

One day, an angry man entered a Target store and demanded to speak with a manager. He claimed that his daughter had received Target coupons for baby clothes and cribs, even though she was still in high school. He bluntly asked the Target store manager, "Are you trying to encourage her to get pregnant?"

The store manager had no idea what the man was talking about. He looked at the mailer and found it was indeed addressed to the man's daughter. Moreover, it contained advertisements for maternity clothing and nursery furniture, as the father had charged. The manager apologized and then called the man a few days later to apologize again. During this conversation, however, the father indicated that he had had a talk with his daughter. He told the manager, "It turns out there's been some activities in my house I haven't been completely aware of. She's due in August. I owe you an apology."

Target discovered that people felt uncomfortable when the retailer knew about their pregnancies in advance. Target emphasizes that the company is very conservative about compliance with all privacy laws. The firm notes, however, that even if they follow the law, their policies can still make people feel uncomfortable.

Target responded to this problem by modifying its marketing policies. Specifically, it began to mix in ads for items the company knew pregnant women would never buy. The purpose was to make these ads appear random. For example, Target would place an ad for a lawn mower next to one for diapers, or a coupon for wineglasses next to one for infant clothes. This strategy created the impression that the company had chosen the advertised products purely by chance. Target discovered that as long as a pregnant woman does not believe she has been spied on, she will use the coupons. She typically assumes that everyone else on her block received the same mailer for diapers and cribs.

Sources: Compiled from M. Wagner, "Target Knows You're Pregnant Before the Stork Does," *The CMO Site*, February 23, 2012; A. Sadauskas, "Target Uses New Technology to Detect Pregnancies," *Smart Company*, February 21, 2012; N. Golgowski, "How Target Knows When Its Shoppers Are Pregnant—And Figured Out a Teen Was Before Her Father Did," *The Daily Mail*, February 18, 2012; G. Lubin, "The Incredible Story of How Target Exposed a Teen Girl's Pregnancy," *Business Insider*, February 16, 2012; K. Hill, "How Target Figured Out a Teen Girl Was Pregnant Before Her Father Did," *Forbes*, February 16, 2012; C. Duhigg, "How Companies Learn Your Secrets," *The New York Times*, February 16, 2012; www.target.com, accessed March 5, 2013.

Questions

1. Are Target's data collection and analysis legal? Why or why not? Support your answer.

2. Are Target's data collection and analysis ethical? Why or why not? Support your answer.

3. Apply the general framework for ethical decision making to Target's data collection and analysis.

4. Do you feel that Target's data collection and analysis invade your privacy? If so, how? If you feel that your privacy is being compromised, what can you do about this problem?

[Internship Activity]

Banking

At the end of the day, banks have to make money to survive. They make their money by charging interest on loans, or by selling CDs (Certificate of Deposit). In both cases, they intend to make money off of your money! Before a bank enters into a legal contract with you as their customer, they want to know all they can about you, your financial history, your current situation, and your financial future so they can make a wise choice. To make these decisions, banks walk very fine lines of ethics and privacy.

For this activity, you will be working with Jeremy Farr of Noble Bank again (you met Jeremy in the Internship Activity for Chapter 1). Jeremy recently heard about a group of loan officers who had met to work through their most recent applications. As the group considered a particular loan, they looked at al the information on the application and thought everything looked positive. Then someone spoke up and shared information that was "off-record" about this individual's personal life, family life, work habits, and general health condition. The new information (even though it was a violation of individual privacy and unethically shared) was now on the table and in everyone's mind.

Since this has NOT happened at Noble Bank, Jeremy wants to put together some information to help people understand how serious of a violation this would be of ethical standards and privacy codes.

Please visit the Book Companion Site to receive the full set of instructions on how you can help Jeremy create something that will help people know how to do the right thing with the information that is so easily found and shared via Information Systems.

Chapter 4

Information Security

[LEARNING OBJECTIVES]

1. Identify the five factors that contribute to the increasing vulnerability of information resources, and provide a specific example of each one.

2. Compare and contrast human mistakes and social engineering, and provide a specific example of each one.

3. Discuss the ten types of deliberate attacks.

4. Define the three risk mitigation strategies, and provide an example of each one in the context of owning a home.

5. Identify the three major types of controls that organizations can use to protect their information resources, and provide an example of each one.

[CHAPTER OUTLINE]

4.1 Introduction to Information Security

4.2 Unintentional Threats to Information Systems

4.3 Deliberate Threats to Information Systems

4.4 What Organizations Are Doing to Protect Information Resources

4.5 Information Security Controls

[WEB RESOURCES]

- Student PowerPoints for note taking

WileyPLUS

- E-book
- Author video lecture for each chapter section
- Practice quizzes
- Flash Cards for vocabulary review
- Additional "IT's About Business" cases
- Video interviews with managers
- Lab Manuals for Microsoft Office 2010 and 2013

What's In IT For Me?

This Chapter Will Help Prepare You To...

ACCT	FIN	MKT	POM	HRM	MIS
ACCOUNTING	**FINANCE**	**MARKETING**	**PRODUCTION OPERATIONS MANAGEMENT**	**HUMAN RESOURCES MANAGEMENT**	**MIS**
Ensure compliance with regulations	Manage investment risk	Secure customer data	Ensure information security with supply chain partners	Secure sensitive employee data	Provide security infrastructure for firm

---

The Problem

C*yberlockers* are third-party file-sharing services that provide password-protected hard drive space online. Prominent examples are Rapidshare (https://www.rapidshare.com), Hotfile (www.hotfile.com), and DropBox (www.dropbox.com). Cyberlockers make money by selling both advertisements and premium subscriptions. Premium subscriptions enable users to download or stream files more quickly than non-subscribing users can.

Cyberlocker users upload files to "lockers." (*Uploading* means copying a file from the user's computer onto the cyberlocker company's Web site, where the file is stored on one of the company's servers.) Many uploaders then publish the name of the file and its locker URL on public blogs or "link farms." Anyone can use a search engine to find the appropriate link and then download or stream the content stored there.

Cyberlockers require their users to sign a click-through agreement in which they agree not to upload content that may infringe on copyright. Despite these agreements, however, many cyberlockers seem to encourage users to upload copyrighted content. Until they began to face civil copyright lawsuits, many cyberlockers offered cash to users based on, for instance, the number of times other people downloaded the content the users uploaded—for example, $15 to $25 for every 1,000 downloads.

Megaupload was one of the most successful cyberlockers. The company was founded by Kim Dotcom (born Kim Schmitz), a German-Finnish Internet entrepreneur who was residing in New Zealand. In 2011–2012, Megaupload claimed more than 82 million unique visitors, and it was responsible for 4 percent of the total traffic on the Internet. Their Web site had 180,000,000 registered members, and hosted 12 billion unique files.

The Solution (?)

In January 2012, a U.S. federal grand jury charged Megaupload and its seven top corporate officers with crimes related to online piracy, including racketeering, conspiracy to commit copyright infringement, and conspiracy to commit money laundering. The U.S. government alleged that the defendants made $175 million (U.S.) from a business that facilitated the illegal distribution of at least $500 million (U.S.) worth of copyrighted movies, music, television shows, books, images, videogames, and software.

[Kim Dotcom: Pirate or Successful Entrepreneur?]

On January 20, 2012, in response to U.S. charges, Kim Dotcom and three other Megaupload executives were arrested in Coatesville, Auckland, New Zealand. Seventy-six police officers staged an armed raid on Dotcom's house. They seized assets worth $17 million (U.S.), including 18 luxury cars and many expensive works of art. In addition, Dotcom's bank accounts were frozen, denying him access to $175 million (U.S.) in cash.

The Law

The law addressing the balance between the rights of copyright holders and Internet service providers (ISPs) is the 1998 Digital Millennium Copyright Act (DMCA). The DMCA provides ISPs with "safe harbor" from liability, so long as the provider (the cyberlocker in this case) (a) does not know for certain which, if any, of its stored materials are copyright-infringing and (b) "expeditiously" removes infringing material following a takedown notice.

When authorities find copyrighted material on a Web site, they issue a takedown notice to the cyberlocker ordering them to remove the infringing material (in essence, to "take it down"). The act was tested in June 2012 when a U.S. district court ruled that YouTube was protected by safe harbor against a $1 billion suit by Viacom. The court maintained that Google employees simply could not be expected to make often impossible decisions as to which clips of, for example, a popular television show, had been uploaded without permission.

The DMCA was intended to clear up gray areas of Internet law. However, by making ignorance of its own business a cyberlocker's only defense, the law has created new problems. The DMCA did not explain how to store data in a manner that is both private and policed. In fact, the DMCA limits copyright holders, even when facing a business built on pervasive infringement (i.e., cyberlockers) to notice-and-takedown remedies in which they must target each offending file, one at a time. Further, nothing in the DMCA prevents each file that is removed from being restored five minutes later by another user.

The DMCA caused so many problems that the U.S. Congress began to work on a new bill. In 2011, the House Judiciary Committee introduced the Stop Online Piracy Act (SOPA). Its most controversial provision would have permitted the Justice Department to ask a federal judge to order ISPs to block their users from reaching foreign copyright-infringing Web sites. SOPA also would have required search engines to stop presenting sites that a court had declared to be dedicated to infringement. Going further, it would have prohibited payment processors, such as PayPal, and ad networks, such as Google's AdSense, from conducting business with such sites.

At this point, technology companies, technology-supported nonprofits, public-access advocates, and many ordinary citizens became alarmed. Critics raised many legitimate questions concerning cybersecurity, the First Amendment, and due process. Bill sponsors found themselves being called "Internet killers" who were going to "break the Internet." The protests culminated in the spectacular SOPA "blackout" protest of January 18, 2012. Confronted with this widespread opposition, many initial SOPA supporters reversed their position. The bill died in Congress.

The Legal Battles

On February 22, 2012, Dotcom won the first round in his legal battle when North Shore District Judge Nevin Dawson overturned previous rulings and ordered Dotcom to be released on bail. On June 28, Dotcom enjoyed another victory—this time in the High Court of New Zealand—when Justice Helen Winkelmann found that the warrants used to seize Dotcom's property were invalid because they were too broad. News emerged later that the police knew they were using the wrong order while the raid was in progress and that Dotcom should have been given the chance to challenge the seizure. The case attracted further notoriety in September 2012 when New Zealand Prime Minister John Key revealed that, at the request of the police, the New Zealand Government Communications Security Bureau (GCSB) had spied on Dotcom, illegally helping police to locate him and monitor his communications in the weeks prior to the raid on his house.

Dotcom maintains that the real issue is a lack of understanding of the Internet. He contends that he was simply operating a hard-disc drive over the Internet. Megaupload, in fact, was a legitimate cyberlocker that stored data for millions of individuals and organizations. Megaupload server logs contain addresses that trace back to U.S. Fortune 100 companies and to governments around the world. It is clear, however, that Megaupload was one of many Internet Web sites that stored, and profited from, copyright-infringing material. The fundamental question is whether Dotcom and his company bear criminal responsibility for those actions.

The U.S. Department of Justice claims that Megaupload knew that its servers contained copyrighted material. The U.S. DOJ is accusing Megaupload of encouraging illegal file sharing with an incentive program that paid cash for popular content. It further charges that the company was slow and selective in complying with takedown notices. Megaupload counters that policing the billions of files on its servers would be both impossible and a violation of their customers' privacy. It maintains that it did its best to comply with takedown notices as the law required, and that it had reasonable expectations of the same DMCA safe harbor afforded to YouTube, as expressed in the 2012 court ruling discussed above.

Significantly, however, the charges against Megaupload are not civil but criminal. The U.S. government case is based on uncertain precedent. Does safe harbor even apply in a criminal case? It is not clear that a criminal statute against second-party copyright violation even exists.

The Results (in March 2013)

Dotcom is fighting his extradition to the United States. In March 2013, a New Zealand appeals court ruled in the U.S. government's favor, ordering Dotcom to be extradited to the United States to stand trial. Dotcom is appealing that decision to the New Zealand Supreme Court.

While the legal battles continue, Dotcom and his co-defendants have developed a new Web site based on the following idea: One click, and a file would be encrypted and uploaded. Only the uploader has the key to unlock the file. If the uploader shares the key, that is his or her business. Because the file is encrypted, other users cannot search it. Even if a government (or a competitor) raided and confiscated the servers, the files would be meaningless without the key. Dotcom calls this service Mega (https://mega.co.nz). It promises to offer users a new level of private data sharing while exempting providers from most legal liabilities.

Sources: Compiled from N. Perry, "U.S. Wins Appeal in Battle to Extradite Kim Dotcom," *Bloomberg BusinessWeek*, March 1, 2013; B. Chappell, "Kim Dotcom Loses Court Battle In Megaupload Extradition Case," *NPR.org*, March 1, 2013; C. Arthur, "Kim Dotcom's Mega to Expand into Encrypted Email," *The Guardian*, February 26, 2013; C. Graeber, "10 Days Inside the Mansion—and the Mind," *Wired*, November 2012; *The Huffington Post*, "New Zealand Prime Minister John Key Apologizes to Kim Dotcom, Says Spying Was Illegal," September 27, 2012; *BBC News*, "Kim Dotcom: Inquiry Ordered into 'Unlawful Spying'," September 24, 2012; R. Parloff, "Megaupload and the Twilight of Copyright," *Fortune*, July 23, 2012; *BBC News*, "Megaupload Extradition Case Delayed Until March 2013," July 10, 2012; J. Hutchison, "Megaupload Founder Goes From Arrest to Cult Hero," *The New York Times*, July 3, 2012; *The New Zealand Herald*, "Dotcom Searches Illegal: Judge," June 28, 2012; *BBC News*, "Megaupload Raid Warrant 'Invalid', New Zealand Judge Says," June 28, 2012; *BBC News*, "Megaupload Founder Extradition Papers Filed by U.S." March 5, 2012; *CNN*, "Megaupload Founder Dotcom Likely to Get Bail," February 22, 2012; *BBC News*, "Megaupload Founder Kim Dotcom Granted Bail," February 22, 2012; *CNN*, "Feds Broaden Piracy Case Against Megaupload.com," February 18, 2012; B. Gruley, D. Fickling, and C. Rahn," Kim Dotcom, Pirate King," *Bloomberg BusinessWeek*, February 15, 2012; M. Foreman, "Kim Dotcom v. United State of America," *Computerworld*, February 3, 2012; M. Barakat and N. Perry, "U.S. Internet Piracy Case Brings New Zealand Arrests," *The Washington Times*, January 20, 2012; G. Sandoval, "FBI Charges Megaupload Operators with Piracy Crimes," *CNET News*, January 20, 2012; G. Fowler, "U.S. Shuts Offshore File-Share 'Locker'," *The Wall Street Journal*, January 20, 2012; C. Albanesius, "Recovering Legitimate Megaupload Files? Good Luck With That," *PC Magazine*, January 20, 2012; C. Kang, "Megaupload Shutdown Raises New Internet-Sharing Fears," *The Washington Post*, January 20, 2012; J. Dvorak, "U.S. Government Kills Megaupload," *PCMag.com*, January 20, 2012; D. Kravets, "Feds Shutter Megaupload, Arrest Executives," *Wired*, January 19, 2012; *BBC News*, "Piracy Websites Attract Billions of Visits," January 11, 2011.

What We Learned from This Case

The lessons that you can learn from the opening case address one aspect of information security, the ownership of information and how to protect that ownership in today's digital age, namely copyright. Copyright is closely related to information technology, and the opening case raises many significant questions. For example, do cyberlocker sites show due diligence in protecting sensitive, classified information? How can cyberlockers address copyright infringement more effectively? Does better protection against copyright infringement on cyberlocker sites involve technology, policy, or both? The most important question raised by the opening case, however, is whether it is possible to secure the Internet. The answer to this question impacts each and every one of us.

The answers to these questions and others are not clear. As you learn about information security in the context of information technology, you will acquire a better understanding of these issues, their importance, their relationships, and their trade-offs. Keep in mind that the issues involved in information security impact individuals and small organizations, as well as large companies. IT's About [Small] Business 4.1 illustrates how information security is critically important to all businesses, particularly small ones.

IT's about [small] business

4.1 Small Businesses in Danger

Picture your graduation day. You have finally completed your undergraduate degree. You initially looked for a job, but you have since decided that you want to start your own business. You pitch your idea to your best friend and ask him/her to join you in a new business venture. Because your degree is in marketing, you would like to start a small promotions business. You and your new business partner develop a solid business strategy, obtain a small business loan from the bank to purchase your computer equipment, and then head over to the courthouse to set up your new Limited Liability Corporation (LLC).

Two years later, things could not have turned out better! Hard work, late nights, and social media exposure have landed your business quite a few clients. The two computers you purchased with your small business loan (one for you and one for your business partner) have turned out to be invaluable. In fact, you now realize more than ever how much you depend on your computers and how lost your business would be without them. You wonder if your antivirus software is up-to-date and if there is anything else you should be doing to protect your critical business data, especially your clients' data. But, you are too busy to research these issues, so you just trust that everything will be OK.

You and your partner have never had such high-quality computers. Fast processors, big monitors, and plenty of memory—all purchased with business intent of course—make these computers superior to the ones you have at home. Naturally you both use your computers for personal work as well. Why not, right?

But then, suddenly, your partner's computer starts to slow down dramatically. Your machine is identical to his, but yours runs much faster. Your partner takes his computer back to Best Buy to have the Geek Squad look it over. The technician determines that **malware** (malicious software) has infected his computer so thoroughly that the hard drive must be replaced. Additionally, the data on his hard drive cannot be recovered, and he has not backed up any of his files—not even the business data.

Now, you have problems. Lost data can result in lost (certainly irritated) customers. In addition, you will have to spend time and money recreating that data.

How could your partner's unprotected Web surfing have resulted in so much lost data? The fact is that even though you both consider yourselves somewhat tech savvy, neither of you ever took steps to protect your computers. You just assumed that a malware infection would never happen to you.

Now, what would you say if you knew that you are not alone? A recent report by GFI Software revealed that more than 40 percent of small- to medium-sized businesses (SMBs) reported a security breach that resulted from an employee visiting a Web site that hosted malware. Amazingly, even though 40 percent of SMBs have experienced this problem, 55 percent reported that preventing this problem from re-occurring was not a priority! Furthermore, 70 percent of the respondents do NOT have any policy about Web use at work, and they claim that Web use is not a problem!

As you can see from this case, installing and maintaining security on computers and information systems is vital to avoid losing business relationships as well as significant amounts of time and money. Fortunately, there are many third-party companies that provide security solutions—see, for example, GFI Software at www.gfi.com. Ultimately, however, you are responsible for seeking out their services and implementing security controls on your own systems and customer data. If you do not prioritize security measures, then you expose your computer and your files to potentially irrevocable damage from thousands of malware systems and viruses.

Sources: Compiled from "GFI Software Survey: 40% of SMBs Have Suffered a Security Breach Due to Unsafe Web Surfing," *Enhanced Online News*, October 12, 2011; "Small Businesses Hacked But Still Not Taking Precautions: Survey Says," *The Huffington Post*, November 7, 2011; www.gfi.com, accessed March 8, 2012.

Questions

1. What security controls should you and your business partner have adopted *at a minimum*?
2. How important are backup plans and file backup procedures to small businesses?
3. Why is it important to protect customer information in businesses of any size?

Information security is especially important to small businesses. Large organizations that experience an information security problem have greater resources to bring to bear on the problem and to enable them to survive. In contrast, small businesses have fewer resources and therefore can be destroyed by a data breach.

Information technologies, when properly used, can have enormous benefits for individuals, organizations, and entire societies. In Chapters 1 and 2, you have seen diverse ways in which IT has made businesses more productive, efficient, and responsive to consumers. You have also explored fields such as medicine and philanthropy in which IT has improved people's health and well-being. Unfortunately, information technologies can also be misused, often with devastating consequences. Consider the following scenarios:

- Individuals can have their identities stolen.
- Organizations can have customer information stolen, leading to financial losses, erosion of customer confidence, and legal action.
- Countries face the threat of *cyberterrorism* and *cyberwarfare*, terms for Internet-based attacks. Cyberwarfare is a critical problem for the U.S. government. In fact, President Obama signed a cyberwarfare directive in October, 2012. In that directive, the White House, for the first time, laid out specific ground rules for how and when the U.S. military can carry out offensive and defensive cyber operations against foreign threats. The directive emphasizes the Obama administration's focus on cybersecurity as a top priority.

Clearly, the misuse of information technologies has come to the forefront of any discussion of IT. Studies have revealed that each security breach costs an organization millions of dollars. For example, after Sony's PlayStation account database was hacked in 2011, the company had to pay $171 million to rebuild its network and protect users from identity theft. The direct costs of a data breach include hiring forensic experts, notifying customers, setting up telephone hotlines to field queries from concerned or affected customers, offering free credit monitoring, and providing discounts for future products and services. The more intangible costs of a breach include the loss of business from increased customer turnover—called *customer churn*—and decreases in customer trust.

Unfortunately, employee negligence caused many of the data breaches, meaning that organizational employees are a weak link in information security. It is therefore very important for you to learn about information security so that you will be better prepared when you enter the workforce.

Introduction to Information Security

4.1

Security can be defined as the degree of protection against criminal activity, danger, damage, and/or loss. Following this broad definition, **information security** refers to all of the processes and policies designed to protect an organization's information and information systems (IS) from unauthorized access, use, disclosure, disruption, modification, or destruction. You have seen that information and information systems can be compromised by deliberate criminal actions and by anything that can impair the proper functioning of an organization's information systems.

Before continuing, let's consider these key concepts. Organizations collect huge amounts of information and employ numerous information systems that are subject to myriad threats. A **threat** to an information resource is any danger to which a system may be exposed. The **exposure** of an information resource is the harm, loss, or damage that can result if a threat compromises that resource. An information resource's **vulnerability** is the possibility that the system will be harmed by a threat.

Today, five key factors are contributing to the increasing vulnerability of organizational information resources, making it much more difficult to secure them:

- Today's interconnected, interdependent, wirelessly networked business environment;
- Smaller, faster, cheaper computers and storage devices;
- Decreasing skills necessary to be a computer hacker;

- International organized crime taking over cybercrime;
- Lack of management support.

The first factor is the evolution of the IT resource from mainframe-only to today's highly complex, interconnected, interdependent, wirelessly networked business environment. The Internet now enables millions of computers and computer networks to communicate freely and seamlessly with one another. Organizations and individuals are exposed to a world of untrusted networks and potential attackers. A *trusted network*, in general, is any network within your organization. An *untrusted network*, in general, is any network external to your organization. In addition, wireless technologies enable employees to compute, communicate, and access the Internet anywhere and anytime. Significantly, wireless is an inherently nonsecure broadcast communications medium.

The second factor reflects the fact that modern computers and storage devices (e.g., thumb drives or flash drives) continue to become smaller, faster, cheaper, and more portable, with greater storage capacity. These characteristics make it much easier to steal or lose a computer or storage device that contains huge amounts of sensitive information. Also, far more people are able to afford powerful computers and connect inexpensively to the Internet, thus raising the potential of an attack on information assets.

The third factor is that the computing skills necessary to be a hacker are *decreasing*. The reason is that the Internet contains information and computer programs called *scripts* that users with few skills can download and use to attack any information system connected to the Internet. (Security experts can also use these scripts for legitimate purposes, such as testing the security of various systems.)

The fourth factor is that international organized crime is taking over cybercrime. **Cybercrime** refers to illegal activities conducted over computer networks, particularly the Internet. iDefense (*http://labs.idefense.com*), a company that specializes in providing security information to governments and Fortune 500 companies, maintains that groups of well-organized criminal organizations have taken control of a global billion-dollar crime network. The network, powered by skillful hackers, targets known software security weaknesses. These crimes are typically nonviolent, but quite lucrative. For example, the losses from armed robberies average hundreds of dollars, and those from white-collar crimes average tens of thousands of dollars. In contrast, losses from computer crimes average hundreds of thousands of dollars. Also, computer crimes can be committed from anywhere in the world, at any time, effectively providing an international safe haven for cybercriminals. Computer-based crimes cause billions of dollars in damages to businesses each year, including the costs to repair information systems and the costs of lost business.

The fifth, and final, factor is lack of management support. For the entire organization to take security policies and procedures seriously, senior managers must set the tone. Ultimately, however, lower-level managers may be even more important. These managers are in close contact with employees every day and thus are in a better position to determine whether employees are following security procedures.

before you go on...

1. Define information security.
2. Differentiate among a threat, an exposure, and a vulnerability.
3. Why are the skills needed to be a hacker decreasing?

4.2 Unintentional Threats to Information Systems

Information systems are vulnerable to many potential hazards and threats, as you can see in Figure 4.1. The two major categories of threats are unintentional threats and deliberate threats. This section discusses unintentional threats, and the next section addresses deliberate threats.

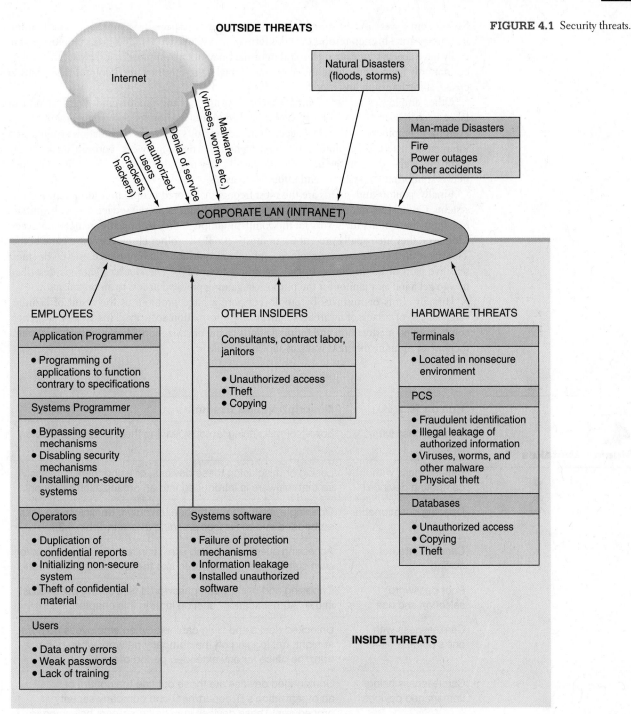

OUTSIDE THREATS

FIGURE 4.1 Security threats.

Unintentional threats are acts performed without malicious intent that nevertheless represent a serious threat to information security. A major category of unintentional threats is human error.

Human Errors

Organizational employees span the breadth and depth of the organization, from mail clerks to the CEO, and across all functional areas. There are two important points to be made about employees. First, the higher the level of employee, the greater the threat he or she poses to information security. This is true because higher-level employees typically have greater access to corporate data, and they enjoy greater privileges on organizational information systems.

Second, employees in two areas of the organization pose especially significant threats to information security: human resources and information systems. Human resources employees generally have access to sensitive personal information about all employees. Likewise, IS employees not only have access to sensitive organizational data, but they often control the means to create, store, transmit, and modify that data.

Other employees include contract labor, consultants, and janitors and guards. Contract labor, such as temporary hires, may be overlooked in information security arrangements. However, these employees often have access to the company's network, information systems, and information assets. Consultants, although technically not employees, perform work for the company. Depending on the nature of their work, they may also have access to the company's network, information systems, and information assets.

Finally, janitors and guards are the most frequently ignored people in information security systems. Companies frequently outsource their security and janitorial services. As with contractors, then, these individuals work for the company although they technically are not employees. Moreover, they are usually present when most — if not all — other employees have gone home. They typically have keys to every office, and nobody questions their presence in even the most sensitive parts of the building. In fact, an article from *2600: The Hacker Quarterly* described how to get a job as a janitor for the purpose of gaining physical access to an organization.

Human errors or mistakes by employees pose a large problem as the result of laziness, carelessness, or a lack of awareness concerning information security. This lack of awareness comes from poor education and training efforts by the organization. Human mistakes manifest themselves in many different ways, as shown in Table 4.1.

Table 4.1
Human Mistakes

Human Mistake	Description and Examples
Carelessness with laptops	Losing or misplacing laptops, leaving them in taxis, and so on.
Carelessness with computing devices	Losing or misplacing these devices, or using them carelessly so that malware is introduced into an organization's network.
Opening questionable e-mails	Opening e-mails from someone unknown, or clicking on links embedded in e-mails (see *phishing attack* in Table 4.2).
Careless Internet surfing	Accessing questionable Web sites; can result in malware and/or alien software being introduced into the organization's network.
Poor password selection and use	Choosing and using weak passwords (see *strong passwords* in the "Authentication" section later in this chapter).
Carelessness with one's office	Unlocked desks and filing cabinets when employees go home at night; not logging off the company network when gone from the office for any extended period of time.
Carelessness using unmanaged devices	Unmanaged devices are those outside the control of an organization's IT department and company security procedures. These devices include computers belonging to customers and business partners, computers in the business centers of hotels, and computers in Starbucks, Panera Bread, and so on.
Carelessness with discarded equipment	Discarding old computer hardware and devices without completely wiping the memory; includes computers, cell phones, BlackBerry® units, and digital copiers and printers.
Careless monitoring of environmental hazards	These hazards, which include dirt, dust, humidity, and static electricity, are harmful to the operation of computing equipment.

The human errors that you have just studied, although unintentional, are committed entirely by employees. However, employees also can make unintentional mistakes as a result of actions by an attacker. Attackers often employ social engineering to induce individuals to make unintentional mistakes and disclose sensitive information.

Social Engineering

Social engineering is an attack in which the perpetrator uses social skills to trick or manipulate legitimate employees into providing confidential company information such as passwords. The most common example of social engineering occurs when the attacker impersonates someone else on the telephone, such as a company manager or an information systems employee. The attacker claims he forgot his password and asks the legitimate employee to give him a password to use. Other common ploys include posing as an exterminator, an air-conditioning technician, or a fire marshal. Examples of social engineering abound.

In one company, a perpetrator entered a company building wearing a company ID card that looked legitimate. He walked around and put up signs on bulletin boards reading "The help desk telephone number has been changed. The new number is 555-1234." He then exited the building and began receiving calls from legitimate employees thinking they were calling the company help desk. Naturally, the first thing the perpetrator asked for was user name and password. He now had the information necessary to access the company's information systems.

Two other social engineering techniques are tailgating and shoulder surfing. *Tailgating* is a technique designed to allow the perpetrator to enter restricted areas that are controlled with locks or card entry. The perpetrator follows closely behind a legitimate employee and, when the employee gains entry, the attacker asks him or her to "hold the door." *Shoulder surfing* occurs when a perpetrator watches an employee's computer screen over the employee's shoulder. This technique is particularly successful in public areas such as in airports and on commuter trains and airplanes.

before you go on...

1. What is an unintentional threat to an information system?

2. Provide examples of social engineering attacks other than the ones just discussed.

Deliberate Threats to Information Systems   4.3

There are many types of deliberate threats to information systems. We provide a list of ten common types for your convenience.

- Espionage or trespass
- Information extortion
- Sabotage or vandalism
- Theft of equipment or information
- Identity theft
- Compromises to intellectual property
- Software attacks
- Alien software
- Supervisory control and data acquisition (SCADA) attacks
- Cyberterrorism and cyberwarfare

Espionage or Trespass

Espionage or trespass occurs when an unauthorized individual attempts to gain illegal access to organizational information. It is important to distinguish between competitive intelligence and industrial espionage. Competitive intelligence consists of legal information-gathering techniques, such as studying a company's Web site and press releases, attending trade shows, and so on. In contrast, industrial espionage crosses the legal boundary.

Information Extortion

Information extortion occurs when an attacker either threatens to steal, or actually steals, information from a company. The perpetrator demands payment for not stealing the information, for returning stolen information, or for agreeing not to disclose the information.

Sabotage or Vandalism

Sabotage and vandalism are deliberate acts that involve defacing an organization's Web site, possibly damaging the organization's image and causing its customers to lose faith. One form of online vandalism is a hacktivist or cyberactivist operation. These are cases of high-tech civil disobedience to protest the operations, policies, or actions of an organization or government agency.

Theft of Equipment or Information

Computing devices and storage devices are becoming smaller yet more powerful with vastly increased storage (e.g., laptops, BlackBerry® units, personal digital assistants, smart phones, digital cameras, thumb drives, and iPods). As a result, these devices are becoming easier to steal and easier for attackers to use to steal information.

Table 4.1 points out that one type of human mistake is carelessness with laptops. In fact, many laptops have been stolen due to such carelessness. The cost of a stolen laptop includes the loss of data, the loss of intellectual property, laptop replacement, legal and regulatory costs, investigation fees, and loss productivity.

One form of theft, known as *dumpster diving*, involves the practice of rummaging through commercial or residential trash to find information that has been discarded. Paper files, letters, memos, photographs, IDs, passwords, credit cards, and other forms of information can be found in dumpsters. Unfortunately, many people never consider that the sensitive items they throw in the trash may be recovered. Such information, when recovered, can be used for fraudulent purposes.

Dumpster diving is not necessarily theft, because the legality of this act varies. Because dumpsters are usually located on private premises, dumpster diving is illegal in some parts of the United States. Even in these cases, however, these laws are enforced with varying degrees of rigor.

Identity Theft

Identity theft is the deliberate assumption of another person's identity, usually to gain access to his or her financial information or to frame him or her for a crime. Techniques for illegally obtaining personal information include:

- stealing mail or dumpster diving;
- stealing personal information in computer databases;
- infiltrating organizations that store large amounts of personal information (e.g., data aggregators such as Acxiom) (*www.acxiom.com*);
- impersonating a trusted organization in an electronic communication (phishing).

Recovering from identity theft is costly, time consuming, and difficult. Victims also report problems in obtaining credit and obtaining or holding a job, as well as adverse effects on insurance or credit rates. In addition, victims state that it is often difficult to remove negative information from their records, such as their credit reports.

Your personal information can be compromised in other ways. For example, your identity can be uncovered just by examining your searches in a search engine. The ability to analyze all searches by a single user can enable a criminal to identify who the user is and what he or she is doing. To demonstrate this fact, *The New York Times* tracked down a particular individual based solely on her AOL searches.

Compromises to Intellectual Property

Protecting intellectual property is a vital issue for people who make their livelihood in knowledge fields. **Intellectual property** is the property created by individuals or corporations that is protected under *trade secret*, *patent*, and *copyright* laws.

A **trade secret** is an intellectual work, such as a business plan, that is a company secret and is not based on public information. An example is the Coca-Cola formula. A **patent** is an official document that grants the holder exclusive rights on an invention or a process for a specified period of time. **Copyright** is a statutory grant that provides the creators or owners of intellectual property with ownership of the property, also for a designated period. Current U.S. laws award patents for 20 years and copyright protection for the life of the creator plus 70 years. Owners are entitled to collect fees from anyone who wants to copy their creations. It is important to note that these are definitions under U.S. law. There is some international standardization of copyrights and patents, but it is far from total. Therefore, there can be discrepancies between U.S. law and other countries' laws.

The most common intellectual property related to IT deals with software. In 1980, the U.S. Congress amended the Copyright Act to include software. The amendment provides protection for the *source code* and *object code* of computer software, but it does not clearly identify what is eligible for protection. For example, copyright law does not protect fundamental concepts, functions, and general features such as pull-down menus, colors, and icons. However, copying a software program without making payment to the owner—including giving a disc to a friend to install on his or her computer—is a copyright violation. Not surprisingly, this practice, called **piracy**, is a major problem for software vendors. The BSA (www.bsa.org) Global Software Piracy Study found that the commercial value of software theft totals billions of dollars per year. The chapter opening case points out the size of this problem.

Software Attacks

Software attacks have evolved from the early years of the computer era, when attackers used malicious software to infect as many computers worldwide as possible, to the profit-driven, Web-based attacks of today. Modern cybercriminals use sophisticated, blended malware attacks, typically via the Web, to make money. Table 4.2 displays a variety of software attacks. These attacks are grouped into three categories: remote attacks requiring user action; remote attacks requiring no user action; and software attacks by programmers during the development of a system. IT's About Business 4.2 provides an example of a software attack.

Table 4.2

Types of Software Attacks	Description
(1) Remote Attacks Requiring User Action	
Virus	Segment of computer code that performs malicious actions by attaching to another computer program.
Worm	Segment of computer code that performs malicious actions and will replicate, or spread, by itself (without requiring another computer program).
Phishing Attack	Phishing attacks use deception to acquire sensitive personal information by masquerading as official-looking e-mails or instant messages.
Spear Phishing Attack	Phishing attacks target large groups of people. In spear phishing attacks, the perpetrators find out as much information about an individual as possible to improve their chances that phishing techniques will be able to obtain sensitive, personal information.

Table **4.2** (continued)	(2) Remote Attacks Needing No User Action	
	Denial-of-Service Attack	Attacker sends so many information requests to a target computer system that the target cannot handle them successfully and typically crashes (ceases to function).
	Distributed Denial-of-Service Attack	An attacker first takes over many computers, typically by using malicious software. These computers are called **zombie**s or **bots**. The attacker uses these bots—which form a **botnet**—to deliver a coordinated stream of information requests to a target computer, causing it to crash.
	(3) Attacks by a Programmer Developing a System	
	Trojan Horse	Software programs that hide in other computer programs and reveal their designed behavior only when they are activated.
	Back Door	Typically a password, known only to the attacker, that allows him or her to access a computer system at will, without having to go through any security procedures (also called a **trap door**).
	Logic Bomb	Segment of computer code that is embedded within an organization's existing computer programs and is designed to activate and perform a destructive action at a certain time or date.

 [about business]

4.2 Can Anonymous Be Stopped?

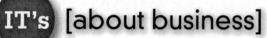

Anonymous, the elusive hacker movement, thinks of itself as a kind of self-appointed immune system for the Internet, striking back at anyone the group perceives as an enemy of freedom, online or offline. Anonymous first gained widespread notoriety when it staged an attack against the Church of Scientology in 2008. In the ensuing years it has carried out hundreds of cyberstrikes. One particularly controversial attack was directed against the Vatican in August 2011.

The campaign against the Vatican involved hundreds of people, some of whom possessed hacking skills and some who did not. A core group of participants openly encouraged support for the attack using YouTube, Twitter, and Facebook. Other activists searched for vulnerabilities on the Vatican Web site. When those efforts failed, Anonymous enlisted amateur recruits to flood the site with traffic, hoping to cause it to crash. The attack, even though it was unsuccessful, provides insight into the recruiting, reconnaissance, and warfare tactics that Anonymous employs.

The Vatican attack was initially organized by hackers in South America and Mexico before it spread to other countries. It was timed to coincide with Pope Benedict XVI's visit to Madrid in August 2011 for World Youth Day. Hackers first tried to take down a Web site that the Catholic Church had set up to promote the pope's visit, handle registrations, and sell merchandise. Anonymous's goal—according to YouTube messages delivered by an Anonymous spokesperson—was to disrupt the event. The YouTube videos that

were posted included a verbal attack on the pope. One video even called on volunteers to "prepare your weapons, my dear brothers for this August 17th to Sunday August 21st, we will drop anger over the Vatican."

The hackers spent weeks spreading their message via their own Web site as well as social media sites such as Twitter and Flickr. Their Facebook page called on volunteers to download free attack software while imploring them to "stop child abuse" by joining the cause. This message featured split-screen images of the pope seated on a gilded throne on one side and starving African children on the other. It also linked to articles about abuse cases and blog posts itemizing the church's assets.

It took 18 days for the hackers to recruit enough people to launch their attack. Then, the reconnaissance phase of the mission began. A core group of approximately 12 skilled hackers spent three days poking around the church's World Youth Day Web site, looking for common security holes that could let them inside. Probing for such loopholes used to be tedious and slow, but the emergence of automated scanning software to locate security weaknesses has made the process much simpler and quicker.

In this case, the scanning software failed to turn up any vulnerabilities. So, the hackers turned to a distributed denial-of-service (DDoS) attack that clogs a Web site with data requests until it crashes. Even unskilled supporters could take part in this attack from their computers or smartphones.

Over the course of the campaign's final two days, Anonymous enlisted as many as a thousand people. In some cases it encouraged them to download attack software. In other instances it directed them to custom-built Web sites that allowed them to participate in the campaign using their smartphones. Visiting a particular Web address caused the phones to instantly start flooding the target Web site with hundreds of data requests each second, without requiring any special software.

On the first day of the DDoS, the Church site experienced 28 times its normal amount of traffic, increasing to 34 times on the following day. Hackers involved in the attack, who did not identify themselves, stated via Twitter that the two-day effort succeeded in slowing down the Web site's performance and making the page unavailable in several countries.

Imperva (www.imperva.com), the firm hired by the Vatican to counter the attack, denied that the site's performance was affected. Imperva asserted that the company's technologies had successfully defended the site against the attack and that the Vatican's defenses held strong because it had invested in the infrastructure needed to repel cyber attacks.

Following this unsuccessful attack, Anonymous moved on to other targets, including an unofficial site about the pope, which the hackers were briefly able to deface. Hacker movements such as Anonymous are now able to attract widespread membership through the Internet. They represent a serious threat to Web sites and organizations.

Unknown to the members of Anonymous, the FBI had arrested one of the group's leaders in 2011. He had continued his hacking activities while being monitored by the agency, which had been gathering information needed to identify members of Anonymous. In a series of arrests in the summer of 2012, authorities around the world arrested more than100 alleged group members.

It is impossible to say if the arrests will shut down, or even seriously inconvenience, Anonymous. The group claims is that it is not organized and it has no leaders. The possibility that Anonymous cannot be shut down by arresting key participants concerns powerful institutions worldwide.

Meanwhile, Anonymous is continuing its activities. In February 2013, the group posted the phone numbers, computer login information, and other personal information of more than 4,000 bank executives on a government Web site. In that same month it threatened a massive WikiLeaks-style exposure of U. S. government secrets. The group announced details of their plan on a hacked government Web site, the U.S. Sentencing Commission (www .ussc.gov). As of March 2013, Anonymous had not yet released that information.

Sources: Compiled from "Anonymous Hackers Leak Personal Information of 4,000 Bank Executives," *Fox News*, February 4, 2013; G. Ferenstein, "Anonymous Threatens Massive WikiLeaks-Style Exposure, Announced on Hacked Gov Site," *TechCrunch*, January 26, 2013; J. Evangelho, "Anonymous Claims Another Sony PSN Breach, Likely a Hoax," *Forbes*, August 15, 2012; Q. Norton, "Inside Anonymous," *Wired*, July, 2012; M. Schwartz, "Anonymous Leaves Clues in Failed Vatican Attack," *InformationWeek*, February 29, 2012; R. Vamosi, "Report: Anonymous Turns to Denial of Service Attacks as a Last Resort," *Forbes*, February 28, 2012; A. Greenberg, "WikiLeaks Tightens Ties to Anonymous in Leak of Stratfor E-Mails," *Forbes*, February 27, 2012; M. Liebowitz, "'Anonymous' Vatican Cyberattack Revealed by Researchers," *MSNBC*, February 27, 2012; N. Perlroth and J. Markoff, "In Attack on Vatican Web Site, a Glimpse of Hackers' Tactics," *The New York Times*, February 26, 2012; P. Olson, "LulzSec Hackers Hit Senate Website 'Just for Kicks'," *Forbes*, June 14, 2011; D. Poeter, "Anonymous BART Protest Shuts Down Several Underground Stations," *PC Magazine*, August 15, 2011; W. Benedetti, "Anonymous Vows War on Sony, Strikes First Blow," *NBC News*, April 4, 2011; www.imperva.com, accessed March 5, 2013.

Questions

1. Describe the various components of Anonymous's attack on the Vatican. Which aspects of the attack are of most concern to security companies?

2. Will the arrest of key members of Anonymous shut down the group? Decrease the effectiveness of the group? Why or why not? Support your answer.

3. Debate the following statement: Anonymous provides necessary oversight of harmful activities by organizations and government agencies.

Alien Software

Many personal computers have alien software, or *pestware*, running on them that the owners do not know about. **Alien software** is clandestine software that is installed on your computer through duplicitous methods. It typically is not as malicious as viruses, worms, or Trojan horses, but it does use up valuable system resources. In addition, it can report on your Web surfing habits and other personal behavior.

The vast majority of pestware is **adware**—software that causes pop-up advertisements to appear on your screen. Adware is common because it works. According to advertising agencies, for every 100 people who close a pop-up ad, 3 click on it. This "hit rate" is extremely high for Internet advertising.

Spyware is software that collects personal information about users without their consent. Two common types of spyware are keystroke loggers and screen scrapers.

Keystroke loggers, also called *keyloggers*, record both your individual keystrokes and your Internet Web browsing history. The purposes range from criminal—for example, theft of passwords and sensitive personal information such as credit card numbers—to annoying—for example, recording your Internet search history for targeted advertising.

Companies have attempted to counter keyloggers by switching to other forms of identifying users. For example, at some point all of us have been forced to look at wavy, distorted letters and type them correctly into a box. That string of letters is called a *CAPTCHA*, and it is a test. The point of CAPTCHA is that computers cannot (yet) accurately read those distorted letters. Therefore, the fact that you can transcribe them means that you are probably not a software program run by an unauthorized person, such as a spammer. As a result, attackers have turned to *screen scrapers*, or *screen grabbers*. This software records a continuous "movie" of a screen's contents rather than simply recording keystrokes.

Spamware is pestware that uses your computer as a launch pad for spammers. **Spam** is unsolicited e-mail, usually advertising for products and services. When your computer is infected with spamware, e-mails from spammers are sent to everyone in your e-mail address book, but they appear to come from you.

Not only is spam a nuisance, but it wastes time and money. Spam costs U.S. companies billions of dollars per year. These costs come from productivity losses, clogged e-mail systems, additional storage, user support, and antispam software. Spam can also carry viruses and worms, making it even more dangerous.

Cookies are small amounts of information that Web sites store on your computer, temporarily or more or less permanently. In many cases, cookies are useful and innocuous. For example, some cookies are passwords and user IDs that you do not want to retype every time you access the Web site that issued the cookie. Cookies are also necessary for online shopping because merchants use them for your shopping carts.

Tracking cookies, however, can be used to track your path through a Web site, the time you spend there, what links you click on, and other details that the company wants to record, usually for marketing purposes. Tracking cookies can also combine this information with your name, purchases, credit card information, and other personal data to develop an intrusive profile of your spending habits.

Most cookies can be read only by the party that created them. However, some companies that manage online banner advertising are, in essence, cookie-sharing rings. These companies can track information such as which pages you load and which ads you click on. They then share this information with their client Web sites, which may number in the thousands. For a cookie demonstration, see *http://privacy.net/track/*.

Supervisory Control and Data Acquisition (SCADA) Attacks

SCADA refers to a large-scale, distributed measurement and control system. SCADA systems are used to monitor or to control chemical, physical, and transport processes such as those used in oil refineries, water and sewage treatment plants, electrical generators, and nuclear power plants. Essentially, SCADA systems provide a link between the physical world and the electronic world.

SCADA systems consist of multiple sensors, a master computer, and communications infrastructure. The sensors connect to physical equipment. They read status data such as the open/closed status of a switch or a valve, as well as measurements such as pressure, flow, voltage, and current. They control the equipment by sending signals to it, such as opening or closing a switch or a valve or setting the speed of a pump.

The sensors are connected in a network, and each sensor typically has an Internet address (Internet Protocol, or IP, address, discussed in Chapter 6). If attackers gain access to the network, they can cause serious damage, such as disrupting the power grid over a large area or upsetting the operations of a large chemical or nuclear plant. Such actions could have catastrophic results, as described in IT's About Business 4.3.

Cyberterrorism and Cyberwarfare

Cyberterrorism and **cyberwarfare** refer to malicious acts in which attackers use a target's computer systems, particularly via the Internet, to cause physical, real-world harm or severe disruption, usually to carry out a political agenda (see IT's About Business 4.3). These actions range from gathering data to attacking critical infrastructure (e.g., via SCADA systems).

We treat the two types of attacks as synonymous here, even though cyberterrorism typically is carried out by individuals or groups, whereas cyberwarfare is carried out by nation states. The following Example examines cyber attacks perpetrated against Estonia and the Republic of Georgia, formerly parts of the Soviet Union.

IT's [about business]

4.3 Cyberwarfare Gains in Sophistication

Stuxnet and more recent types of malicious software, or malware—particularly Duqu, Flame, and Gauss—herald a frightening new era in cyberwarfare. China, Russia, the United States, and other nations have been engaging in cyberwarfare for several years, and these four types of malware represent a major technological escalation. All four types are so sophisticated and complex that they appear to have been developed by nation states for use in ongoing (as of mid-2013) cyberespionage operations.

Stuxnet, first launched in June 2009 and discovered in July 2010, is malware that targets industrial supervisory control and data acquisition systems. In particular, Stuxnet targets Siemens SCADA systems that are configured to control and monitor specific industrial processes. In fact, security experts around the world suspect that the malware's target was the uranium enrichment industrial infrastructure in Iran. On November 29, 2010, Iran confirmed that its nuclear program had been damaged by Stuxnet. The malware may have damaged Iran's nuclear facilities in Natanz and eventually delayed the start-up of the Bushehr nuclear power plant.

Whoever constructed Stuxnet must have possessed an in-depth knowledge of nuclear industrial processes. Stuxnet appears to have impaired Iran's computer-controlled uranium centrifuges, which mysteriously lost 30 percent of their production capacity, thereby delaying any plans to produce a nuclear weapon.

After infecting Iran's nuclear facilities, Stuxnet spread rapidly throughout the country, affecting more than 30,000 Internet Protocol addresses. This problem was compounded by the malware's ability to mutate, meaning that new versions of Stuxnet continued to spread. Stuxnet is believed (but not known) to have been written through a partnership between Israel and the United States.

Duqu is a type of malware discovered in 2011 on computers in Iran, Sudan, and other countries that was designed to steal documents and other data from infected computers. Duqu appeared to gather intelligence specifically about the design of SCADA systems. The malware does not actually cause damage to infected computers; rather, it gathers information required for future attacks. Duqu creates a back door into computer systems that remains open for only 36 days, at which time the malware deletes itself. The reason for this short time period is probably to limit discovery.

Another sophisticated type of malware, called Flame, has been detected infecting systems in Iran, Israel, Palestine, Sudan, Lebanon, Saudi Arabia, and Egypt. Flame was officially discovered by Kaspersky Lab (www.kaspersky.com) in 2012 when the United Nations International Telecommunications Union asked the firm to look into reports that computers belonging to the Iranian Oil Ministry and the Iranian National Oil Company had been infected with malware that was stealing and then deleting information from infected systems. Although Flame has both a different purpose and composition than Stuxnet and it appears to have been written by different programmers, its complexity, the geographic scope of its infections, and its behavior strongly indicate that it is related to Stuxnet.

Flame appears to be designed primarily to spy on the users of infected computers and steal data from them, including documents, recorded conversations, and keystrokes. Flame has several cyberespionage functions. It turns on the internal microphone of an infected computer to secretly record conversations that occur either over Skype or in the computer's vicinity; it scans for Bluetooth-enabled devices in the vicinity of an infected computer to gather names and phone contacts from the contacts folder; it captures and stores frequent screenshots of activity on infected computers, such as instant messaging and e-mail communications; and it opens a backdoor to infected systems.

Flame does not replicate automatically by itself. The spreading mechanisms are turned off by default and must be switched on by the attackers before the malware will spread. This feature is likely intended to control the spread of the malware and to decrease the likelihood that it will be detected.

Another type of malware, called Gauss, is closely related to Flame and Stuxnet. Gauss blends cyber-surveillance with an online banking Trojan horse. It can steal access credentials for various online banking systems and payment methods, as well as browser history, social networking and instant messaging information, and passwords. It can also intercept cookies from PayPal, Citibank, MasterCard, American Express, Visa, eBay, Gmail, Hotmail, Yahoo!, Facebook, Amazon, and some Middle Eastern banks. Gauss appears to target Lebanese banks as well as Citibank and PayPal, according to Kaspersky Lab.

At the time of this writing (mid-2013), Gauss had infected some 2,500 systems in 25 countries, with the majority of infected computers located in Lebanon. Like Flame and Duqu, Gauss is programmed with a built-in time-to-live. Once that time limit is reached, Gauss deletes itself completely from an infected system.

Unfortunately, the techniques used in sophisticated, nation-backed malware are trickling down to less-skilled programmers who target regular Web users and their online accounts or credit card details. As a result, we are all at greater risk from cybercriminals.

Sources: Compiled from "Iranian News Agency Reports Another Cyberattack by Stuxnet Worm Targeting Industries in South," *Associated Press*, December 25, 2012; T. Simonite, "Stuxnet Tricks Copied by Computer Criminals," *MIT Technology Review*, September 19, 2012; "Flame and Stuxnet Cousin Targets Lebanese Bank Customers, Carries Mysterious

Payload," *KurzweilAI.net*, August 11, 2012; E. Nakashima, "U.S., Israel Developed Flame Computer Virus to Slow Iranian Nuclear Efforts, Officials Say," *The Washington Post*, June 19, 2012; "Flame Malware Makers Send 'Suicide' Code," *BBC News*, June 8, 2012; C. Mims, "Stuxnet and Cyber-warfare," *MIT Technology Review*, June 4, 2012; D. Sanger, "Obama Order Sped Up Wave of Cyberattacks Against Iran," *The New York Times*, June 1, 2012; "Meet 'Flame,' the Massive Spy Malware Infiltrating Iranian Com-puters," *KurzweilAI.net*, May 31, 2012; T. Erdbrink, "Iran Confirms Attack That Collects Information," *The New York Times*, May 29, 2012; K. Zetter, "'Flame' Spyware Infiltrating Iranian Computers," *Wired*, May 29, 2012; R. Cohen, "New Massive Cyber-Attack an 'Industrial Vacuum Cleaner for Sensitive Information," *Forbes*, May 28, 2012; C. Albanesius, "Massive 'Flame' Malware Stealing Data Across Middle East," *PC Magazine*, May 28, 2012; D. Lee, "Flame: Massive Cyberattack Discovered, Researchers Say," *BBC News*, May 28, 2012; B. Schneier, "Another Piece of the Stuxnet Puzzle," www.schneier.com, February 23, 2012; "Experts Say Iran Has 'Neutralized' Stuxnet Virus," *Reuters*, February 14, 2012; D. Talbot, "New Malware Brings Cyberwar One Step Closer," *MIT Technology Review*, October 20, 2011; K. Zetter, "Son of Stuxnet Found in the Wild on Systems in Europe," *Wired*, October 18, 2011; R. Vamosi, "Son of Stuxnet," *Forbes*, October 18, 2011; M. Schwartz, "Stuxnet Iran Attack Launched from 10 Machines," *Informa-tionWeek*, February 14, 2011; G. Keizer, "Stuxnet Struck Five Targets in Iran, Say Researcher," *Computerworld*, February 11, 2011.

Questions

1. Discuss the implications of the precisely targeted nature of the Stuxnet, Duqu, Flame, and Gauss attacks.
2. Analyze the statement: "Nations use malware such as Stuxnet, Duqu, Flame, and Gauss when their only alternative is to go to war."
3. Discuss the implications that these four types of malware have for all of us.

Example

Several years ago two former Soviet republics were subjected to severe cyber attacks that appeared to originate in Russia. The first conflict erupted in 2007, when a three-week wave of massive dis-tributed denial-of-service cyber attacks against the Baltic country of Estonia disabled the Web sites of government ministries, political parties, newspapers, banks, and businesses. One of the most wired societies in Europe, Estonia is a pioneer of e-government (discussed in Chapter 7). As a result, the country is highly vulnerable to cyber attack. In the early phase of the attack, Estonian security analysts identified some of the perpetrators by their Internet Protocol addresses. Many of these addresses were Russian, and some of them were from Russian state institutions.

The following year, Russian troops entered the province of South Ossetia in the Republic of Georgia to counter Georgian military efforts to prevent the province from breaking away. DDoS attacks on Georgian Web sites were apparently synchronized with the Russian invasion. The attacks shut down the Web site of the Georgian president, Mikheil Saakashvili, for 24 hours, and they defaced the Web site of the Georgian Parliament with images of Adolf Hitler. Saakashvili blamed Russia for the attacks, but the Russian government denied the charges.

before you go on...

1. Why has the theft of computing devices become more serious over time?
2. What are the three types of software attacks?
3. Define alien software, and explain why it is a serious problem.
4. What is a SCADA system?

4.4 What Organizations Are Doing to Protect Information Resources

Why is it so difficult to stop cybercriminals? Table 4.3 illustrates the many major difficulties involved in protecting information. Because organizing an appropriate defense system is so important to the entire enterprise, it is one of the major responsibilities of any prudent CIO as well as of the functional managers who control information resources. In fact, IT security is the business of *everyone* in an organization.

In addition to the problems listed in Table 4.3, another reason why information resources are difficult to protect is that the online commerce industry is not particularly willing to

Hundreds of potential threats exist.
Computing resources may be situated in many locations.
Many individuals control or have access to information assets.
Computer networks can be located outside the organization, making them difficult to protect.
Rapid technological changes make some controls obsolete as soon as they are installed.
Many computer crimes are undetected for a long period of time, so it is difficult to learn from experience.
People tend to violate security procedures because the procedures are inconvenient.
The amount of computer knowledge necessary to commit computer crimes is usually minimal. As a matter of fact, a potential criminal can learn hacking, for free, on the Internet.
The costs of preventing hazards can be very high. Therefore, most organizations simply cannot afford to protect themselves against all possible hazards.
It is difficult to conduct a cost-benefit justification for controls before an attack occurs because it is difficult to assess the impact of a hypothetical attack.

Table

4.3

The Difficulties in Protecting Information Resources

install safeguards that would make completing transactions more difficult or complicated. As one example, merchants could demand passwords or personal identification numbers for all credit card transactions. However, these requirements might discourage people from shopping online. For credit card companies, it is cheaper to block a stolen credit card and move on than to invest time and money on a prosecution.

Despite these difficulties, the information security industry is battling back against cybercrime. Companies are developing software and services that deliver early warnings of trouble on the Internet. Unlike traditional antivirus software, which is reactive, early-warning systems are proactive, scanning the Web for new viruses and alerting companies to the danger.

Organizations spend a great deal of time and money protecting their information resources. Before doing so, they perform risk management.

A **risk** is the probability that a threat will impact an information resource. The goal of **risk management** is to identify, control, and minimize the impact of threats. In other words, risk management seeks to reduce risk to acceptable levels. Risk management consists of three processes: risk analysis, risk mitigation, and controls evaluation.

Organizations perform risk analyses to ensure that their IS security programs are cost effective. **Risk analysis** involves three steps: (1) assessing the value of each asset being protected, (2) estimating the probability that each asset will be compromised, and (3) comparing the probable costs of the asset's being compromised with the costs of protecting that asset. The organization then considers how to mitigate the risk.

In **risk mitigation**, the organization takes concrete actions against risks. Risk mitigation has two functions: (1) implementing controls to prevent identified threats from occurring, and (2) developing a means of recovery if the threat becomes a reality. There are several risk mitigation strategies that organizations can adopt. The three most common are risk acceptance, risk limitation, and risk transference.

- **Risk acceptance**: Accept the potential risk, continue operating with no controls, and absorb any damages that occur.
- **Risk limitation**: Limit the risk by implementing controls that minimize the impact of the threat.

- **Risk transference**: Transfer the risk by using other means to compensate for the loss, such as by purchasing insurance.

Finally, in controls evaluation, the organization examines the costs of implementing adequate control measures against the value of those control measures. If the costs of implementing a control are greater than the value of the asset being protected, the control is not cost effective. In the next section, you will study the various controls that organizations use to protect their information resources.

before you go on...

1. Describe several reasons why it is difficult to protect information resources.

2. Compare and contrast risk management and risk analysis.

4.5 Information Security Controls

To protect their information assets, organizations implement **controls**, or defense mechanisms (also called *countermeasures*). These controls are designed to protect all of the components of an information system, including data, software, hardware, and networks. Because there are so many diverse threats, organizations utilize layers of controls, or *defense-in-depth*.

Controls are intended to prevent accidental hazards, deter intentional acts, detect problems as early as possible, enhance damage recovery, and correct problems. Before you study controls in more detail, it is important to emphasize that the single most valuable control is user education and training. Effective and ongoing education makes every member of the organization aware of the vital importance of information security.

In the next section, you will learn about three major types of controls: physical controls, access controls, and communications controls. Figure 4.2 illustrates these controls. In addition to applying controls, organizations plan for business continuity in case of a disaster, and they periodically audit their information resources to detect possible threats. You will study these topics in the next section as well.

Physical Controls

Physical controls prevent unauthorized individuals from gaining access to a company's facilities. Common physical controls include walls, doors, fencing, gates, locks, badges, guards, and alarm systems. More sophisticated physical controls include pressure sensors, temperature sensors, and motion detectors. One shortcoming of physical controls is that they can be inconvenient to employees.

Guards deserve special mention because they have very difficult jobs, for at least two reasons. First, their jobs are boring and repetitive and generally do not pay well. Second, if guards perform their jobs thoroughly, the other employees harass them, particularly if they slow up the process of entering the facility.

Organizations also implement physical security measures that limit computer users to acceptable login times and locations. These controls also limit the number of unsuccessful login attempts, and they require all employees to log off their computers when they leave for the day. In addition, they set the employees' computers to automatically log off the user after a certain period of disuse.

Access Controls

Access controls restrict unauthorized individuals from using information resources. These controls involve two major functions: authentication and authorization. **Authentication** confirms the identity of the person requiring access. After the person is authenticated (identified),

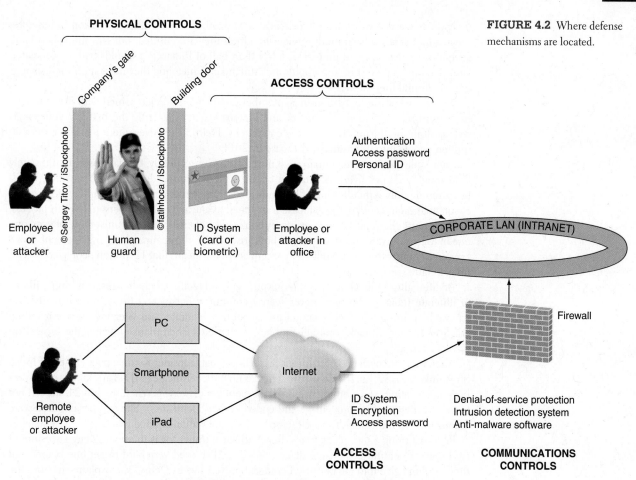

FIGURE 4.2 Where defense mechanisms are located.

the next step is authorization. **Authorization** determines which actions, rights, or privileges the person has, based on his or her verified identity. Let's examine these functions more closely.

Authentication. To authenticate (identify) authorized personnel, an organization can use one or more of the following methods: something the user is, something the user has, something the user does, and/or something the user knows.

Something the user is, also known as **biometrics**, is an authentication method that examines a person's innate physical characteristics. Common biometric applications are fingerprint scans, palm scans, retina scans, iris recognition, and facial recognition. Of these applications, fingerprints, retina scans, and iris recognition provide the most definitive identification. The following example shows how powerful biometrics can be for identification purposes.

Example

The Biometric Identification Project of India

India has vast numbers of anonymous poor citizens. To address this problem, the nation instituted its Unique Identification Project, also known as Aadhaar, which means "the foundation" in several Indian languages. The goal of the Unique Identification Project is to issue identification numbers linked to the fingerprints and iris scans of every single person in India. This process will ultimately encompass some 1.2 billion people who speak more than 300 languages and dialects. The biometrics and the Aadhaar identification number will serve as a verifiable, portable, and unique national ID.

This project seeks to remedy a key problem that relates to poor people. The Indian government does not officially acknowledge the existence of many poor citizens because these individuals do not possess birth certificates and other official documentation. Therefore, they cannot access government services to which they are entitled, nor can they open bank accounts. For example, in mid-2012, fewer than half of Indian households had an associated bank account. The rest of households are "unbanked," meaning they must stash their savings in cash around their homes.

Aadhaar went into operation in September 2010, when officials armed with iris scanners, fingerprint scanners, digital cameras, and laptops began registering the first few villagers as well as slum dwellers in the country's capital city, Delhi. The government plans to enter 600 million people into its biometric database by 2014.

Each individual record contains 4–8 megabytes. Consequently, the database will ultimately hold roughly 20 petabytes. A database of this scale is unprecedented, and managing it will be extraordinarily difficult. One of the most daunting challenges confronting the project is to ensure that each record in the database is matched to one and only one person. For this process, Aadhaar must check all 10 fingerprints and both irises of each person against those of everyone else in the country. Using 10 prints and both irises boosts the accuracy rate to 99 percent. However, in a country the size of India, 99 percent accuracy means that 12 million people could end up with faulty records.

Additionally, Aadhaar faces enormous physical and technical challenges: reaching millions of illiterate Indians who have never seen a computer, persuading them to have their irises scanned, ensuring that their scanned information is accurate, and safeguarding the resulting massive amounts of data. Another problem is that civil libertarians object to the project on privacy grounds.

As an example of the potential impact of this project, consider Kiran, a poor citizen of India. She thinks she is 32, but she is not sure. She has no birth certificate or ID of any kind—no driver's license, no voting card, nothing at all to document her existence. When she was 24, she left her home in a destitute farming village and ended up in a Delhi slum. She and her children were among the first individuals to have their personal information entered into the Aadhaar system.

The first thing Kiran plans to use her Aadhaar number for is to obtain a city government card that will entitle her to subsidized groceries. "I've tried very hard to get one before, but they wouldn't give it to me because I couldn't prove I live in Delhi," she explains. In sum, the Aadhaar project should enable millions of poor Indian citizens to access government services that previously were out of reach to them.

Sources: Compiled from S. Rai, "Why India's Identity Scheme Is Groundbreaking," *BBC News*, June 5, 2012; E. Hannon, "For India's Undocumented Citizens, An ID at Last," *NPR.org*, March 1, 2012; "World's Biggest Biometric ID Scheme Forges Ahead," *BBC News India*, February 12, 2012; M. Magnier, "India's Biometric ID Number Plan Divided by Bureaucracy," *Los Angeles Times*, January 28, 2012; B. Turbeville, "Cashless Society: India Implements First Biometric ID Program for All of Its 1.2 Billion Residents," *Infowars.com*, January 12, 2012; V. Beiser, "Identified," *Wired*, September 2011; www.iaadhaar.com, accessed February 29, 2012.

Questions

1. Describe the problems that India is facing in implementing this biometric identification system.

2. Describe the benefits that India hopes to gain in implementing the biometric identification system.

3. Describe the benefits that the biometric identification system should provide to India's impoverished citizens.

Something the user has is an authentication mechanism that includes regular identification (ID) cards, smart ID cards, and tokens. *Regular ID cards*, or *dumb cards*, typically have the person's picture and often his or her signature. *Smart ID cards* have an embedded chip that stores pertinent information about the user. (Smart ID cards used for identification differ from smart cards used in electronic commerce, which you learn about in Chapter 7. Both types of card have embedded chips, but they are used for different purposes.) *Tokens* have embedded chips and a digital display that presents a login number that the employees use to access the organization's network. The number changes with each login.

Something the user does is an authentication mechanism that includes voice and signature recognition. In *voice recognition*, the user speaks a phrase (e.g., his or her name and department) that has been previously recorded under controlled conditions. The voice recognition system matches the two voice signals. In *signature recognition*, the user signs his or her name, and the system matches this signature with one previously recorded under controlled, monitored conditions. Signature recognition systems also match the speed and the pressure of the signature.

Something the user knows is an authentication mechanism that includes passwords and passphrases. **Passwords** present a huge information security problem in all organizations. Most of us have to remember numerous passwords for different online services, and we typically must choose complicated strings of characters to make them harder to guess. Security experts examined the frequency and usage of passwords belonging to 500,000 computer users. They found that each person had an average of 6.5 passwords that he or she used for 25 different online accounts. Unfortunately, as you see in the chapter's closing case, passwords (even strong passwords) are terribly vulnerable to attack.

All users should use *strong passwords*, which are difficult for hackers to discover. The basic guidelines for creating strong passwords are:

- They should be difficult to guess.
- They should be long rather than short.
- They should have uppercase letters, lowercase letters, numbers, and special characters.
- They should not be recognizable words.
- They should not be the name of anything or anyone familiar, such as family names or names of pets.
- They should not be a recognizable string of numbers, such as a Social Security number or a birthday.

Unfortunately, strong passwords are more difficult to remember than weak ones. Consequently, employees frequently write them down, which defeats their purpose. The ideal solution to this dilemma is to create a strong password that is also easy to remember. To achieve this objective, many people use passphrases.

A *passphrase* is a series of characters that is longer than a password but is still easy to memorize. Examples of passphrases are "maytheforcebewithyoualways" and "goaheadmakemyday." A passphrase can serve as a password itself, or it can help you create a strong password. You can turn a passphrase into a strong password in this manner. Starting with the last passphrase above, take the first letter of each word. You will have "gammd." Then, capitalize every other letter to create "GaMmD". Finally, add special characters and numbers to create "9GaMmD//*". You now have a strong password that you can remember.

To identify authorized users more efficiently and effectively, organizations frequently implement more than one type of authentication, a strategy known as *multifactor authentication*. This system is particularly important when users log in from remote locations.

Single-factor authentication, which is notoriously weak, commonly consists simply of a password. Two-factor authentication consists of a password plus one type of biometric identification (e.g., a fingerprint). Three-factor authentication is any combination of three authentication methods. In most cases, the more factors the system utilizes, the more reliable it is. However, stronger authentication is also more expensive, and, as with strong passwords, it can be irritating to users.

Authorization.   After users have been properly authenticated, the rights and privileges they have on the organization's systems are established in a process called *authorization*. A **privilege** is a collection of related computer system operations that a user is authorized to perform. Companies typically base authorization policies on the principle of **least privilege**, which posits that users be granted the privilege for an activity only if there is a justifiable need for them to perform that activity.

Communications Controls

Communications controls (also called **network controls**) secure the movement of data across networks. Communications controls consist of firewalls, anti-malware systems, whitelisting and blacklisting, encryption, virtual private networks (VPNs), secure socket layer (SSL), and employee monitoring systems.

Firewalls. A **firewall** is a system that prevents a specific type of information from moving between untrusted networks, such as the Internet, and private networks, such as your company's network. Put simply, firewalls prevent unauthorized Internet users from accessing private networks. All messages entering or leaving your company's network pass through a firewall. The firewall examines each message and blocks those that do not meet specified security rules.

Firewalls range from simple, for home use, to very complex for organizational use. Figure 4.3a illustrates a basic firewall for a home computer. In this case, the firewall is implemented as software on the home computer. Figure 4.3b shows an organization that has implemented an external firewall, which faces the Internet, and an internal firewall, which faces the company network. Corporate firewalls typically consist of software running on a computer dedicated to the task. A **demilitarized zone (DMZ)** is located between the two firewalls. Messages from the Internet must first pass through the external firewall. If they conform to the defined security rules, they are then sent to company servers located in the DMZ. These servers typically handle Web page requests and e-mail. Any messages designated for the company's internal network (e.g., its intranet) must pass through the internal firewall, again with its own defined security rules, to gain access to the company's private network.

The danger from viruses and worms is so severe that many organizations are placing firewalls at strategic points *inside* their private networks. In this way, if a virus or worm does get through both the external and internal firewalls, then the internal damage may be contained.

Anti-malware Systems. **Anti-malware systems**, also called *antivirus*, or *AV*, software, are software packages that attempt to identify and eliminate viruses and worms, and other malicious software. AV software is implemented at the organizational level by the information systems department. There are currently hundreds of AV software packages available. Among the best known are Norton AntiVirus (*www.symantec.com*), McAfee VirusScan (*www.mcafee.com*), and Trend Micro PC-cillin (*www.trendmicro.com*). IT's About Business 4.4 provides an example of how a software program known as FireEye helps protect organizations from malware.

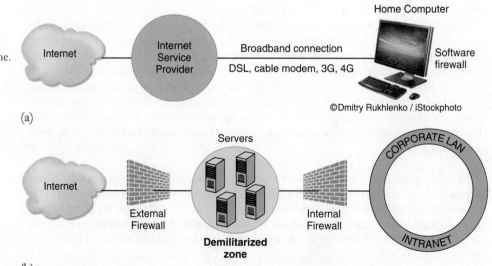

FIGURE 4.3 (a) Basic firewall for home computer. (b) Organization with two firewalls and demilitarized zone.

©Dmitry Rukhlenko / iStockphoto

IT's [about business]

4.4 Fighting Botnets

FireEye (www.fireeye.com) is one of the world's most effective private cybercrime fighters. The company defends corporations and governments against targeted malicious software. FireEye's clients include Fortune 500 companies and members of the U.S. intelligence community.

FireEye's software examines the entire lifecycle of malicious software, how the malware operates in a network, what the malware is looking for, which servers delivered the malware, and which control servers the malware receives its orders from. Since 2005, FireEye has deflected some of the world's most destructive online attacks, including:

- Aurora, the attack originating in China that targeted Google and other technology firms in 2009;
- coreflood, the botnet that had been stealing millions of dollars from global bank accounts since the mid-2000s and possibly earlier;
- Zeus, a program that used personal information to steal hundreds of millions of dollars from financial institutions in 2007.

To understand why FireEye is so effective, consider its confrontation with the Rustock botnet. Rustock was the most advanced botnet ever released onto the Web. It reeled people in by putting out spam that advertised fake drugs, online pharmacies, and Russian stocks. Then, from 2007 to 2011, Rustock quietly and illegally took control of more than a million computers around the world. Symantec, a computer security company, found that Rustock generated as many as 44 billion spam e-mails per day, nearly half of the total number of junk e-mails sent per day worldwide. Profits generated by Rustock were estimated to be in the millions of dollars.

For months, FireEye collaborated with Microsoft and Pfizer to plot a counterattack. Microsoft and Pfizer became involved because Rustock was selling fake Viagra, a Pfizer product, as well as sham lotteries using the Microsoft logo. Working from FireEye's intelligence, in March 2011 U.S. Marshals stormed seven Internet data centers across the United States where Rustock had hidden its 96 command servers. Microsoft lawyers and technicians and computer forensics experts also participated in the raids. A team deployed to the Netherlands confiscated two additional Rustock command servers.

Although the operation was executed flawlessly, Rustock was able to fight back. From an unknown location, the *botmaster* (the person or persons controlling the bots, or zombie computers) remotely sneaked back into its network, locked out Microsoft's technicians, and began to erase files. Clearly, the Rustock masterminds did not want anyone to discover the information contained inside their hard drives. After some difficulty, the Microsoft technicians were able to regain control of the servers. However, the data that were erased in the 30 minutes that the Microsoft technicians required to regain control of their servers may be lost forever.

As FireEye and its partner companies analyzed Rustock's equipment, they discovered that much of it was leased to customers with addresses in the Asian nation of Azerbaijan, which shares a border with Russia. Forensic analysis of the captured servers pointed Rustock's opponents to Moscow and St. Petersburg. Rustock had used the name Cosma2k to conduct business on the Internet, and it maintained a WebMoney account (www.webmoney.com) under the name Vladimir Alexandrovich Shergin. No one knows whether Shergin was a real name or an alias. However, WebMoney was able to inform investigators that "Shergin" had listed an address in a small city outside Moscow.

On April 6, 2011, Microsoft delivered its first status report in its lawsuit against Rustock to the federal court in Seattle (Microsoft headquarters). Then, on June 14, Microsoft published notices in Moscow and St. Petersburg newspapers, detailing its allegations against the botnet spammer. The notices urged the perpetrators of Rustock to respond to the charges or risk being declared guilty. Microsoft also offered (and is still offering) $250,000 for information about the identity of the person or persons operating the botnet. Unfortunately, the Rustock perpetrators have still not been caught, and security experts believe that more than 600,000 computers around the world are still infected with Rustock malware.

Sources: Compiled from "FireEye Testomonials," *FireEye Information Center* (www.fireeye.com), January 8, 2013; S. Ragan, "Dutch Police Takedown C&Cs Used by Grum Botnet," *Security Week*, July 17, 2012; P. Cohan, "FireEye: Silicon Valley's Hottest Security Start-up," *Forbes*, May 24, 2012; K. Higgins, "Microsoft Offers $250,000 for Rustock Botnet Operator Identity," *InformationWeek*, July 19, 2011; "Microsoft Offers Reward for Information on Rustock," *The Official Microsoft Blog*, July 18, 2011; C. Stewart, "Botnet Busters," *Bloomberg BusinessWeek*, June 20–26, 2011; C. Stewart, "FireEye: Botnet Busters," *Bloomberg BusinessWeek*, June 16, 2011; "Spammers Sought After Botnet Takedown," *BBC News*, March 25, 2011; M. Schwartz, "Microsoft, Feds Knock Rustock Botnet Offline," *InformationWeek*, March 18, 2011; N. Wingfield, "Spam Network Shut Down," *The Wall Street Journal*, March 18, 2011; M. Hickens, "Prolific Spam Network Is Unplugged," *The Wall Street Journal*, March 17, 2011; "Operation b107—Rustock Botnet Takedown," *Microsoft Malware Protection Center*, March 17, 2011; www.fireeye.com, accessed March 5, 2013.

Questions

1. Describe why it was so important for law enforcement officials to capture all 96 Rustock command servers at one time.
2. If the perpetrators of Rustock are ever caught, will it be possible to prove that the perpetrators were responsible for the malware? Why or why not? Support your answer.

Anti-malware systems are generally reactive. Whereas firewalls filter network traffic according to categories of activities likely to cause problems, anti-malware systems filter traffic according to a database of specific problems. These systems create definitions, or signatures, of various types of malware and then update these signatures in their products. The anti-malware software then examines suspicious computer code to determine whether it matches a known signature. If the software identifies a match, it removes the code. For this reason organizations regularly update their malware definitions.

Because malware is such a serious problem, the leading vendors are rapidly developing anti-malware systems that function proactively as well as reactively. These systems evaluate behavior rather than relying entirely on signature matching. In theory, therefore, it is possible to catch malware before it can infect systems.

Whitelisting and Blacklisting.   A report by the Yankee Group (*www.yankeegroup.com*), a technology research and consulting firm, stated that 99 percent of organizations had installed anti-malware systems, but 62 percent still suffered malware attacks. As we have seen, anti-malware systems are usually reactive, and malware continues to infect companies.

One solution to this problem is **whitelisting**. Whitelisting is a process in which a company identifies the software that it will allow to run on its computers. Whitelisting permits acceptable software to run, and it either prevents any other software from running or it lets new software run in a quarantined environment until the company can verify its validity.

Whereas whitelisting allows nothing to run unless it is on the whitelist, **blacklisting** allows everything to run unless it is on the blacklist. A blacklist, then, includes certain types of software that are not allowed to run in the company environment. For example, a company might blacklist peer-to-peer file sharing on its systems. In addition to software, people, devices, and Web sites can also be whitelisted and blacklisted.

Encryption.   Organizations that do not have a secure channel for sending information use encryption to stop unauthorized eavesdroppers. **Encryption** is the process of converting an original message into a form that cannot be read by anyone except the intended receiver.

All encryption systems use a key, which is the code that scrambles and then decodes the messages. The majority of encryption systems use public-key encryption. **Public-key encryption**—also known as *asymmetric encryption*—uses two different keys: a public key and a private key (see Figure 4.4). The public key (locking key) and the private key (the unlocking key) are created simultaneously using the same mathematical formula or algorithm. Because the two keys are mathematically related, the data encrypted with one key can be decrypted by using the other key. The public key is publicly available in a directory that all parties can access. The private key is kept secret, never shared with anyone, and never sent across the Internet. In this system, if Hannah wants to send a message to Harrison, she first obtains Harrison's public key (locking key), which she uses to encrypt her message (put the message in the "two lock box"). When Harrison receives Hannah's message, he uses his private key to decrypt it (open the box).

Although this arrangement is adequate for personal information, organizations that conduct business over the Internet require a more complex system. In these cases, a third party, called a **certificate authority**, acts as a trusted intermediary between the companies. The certificate authority issues digital certificates and verifies the integrity of the certificates. A **digital certificate** is an electronic document attached to a file that certifies that the file is from the organization it claims to be from and has not been modified from its original format. As you can see in Figure 4.5, Sony requests a digital certificate from VeriSign, a certificate authority, and uses this certificate when it conducts business with Dell. Note that the digital certificate contains an identification number, the issuer, validity dates, and the requester's public key. For examples of certificate authorities, see *www.entrust.com*, *www.verisign.com*, *www.cybertrust .com*, *www.secude.com*, and *www.thawte.com*.

Virtual Private Networking.   A **virtual private network** is a private network that uses a public network (usually the Internet) to connect users. VPNs essentially integrate the global connectivity of the Internet with the security of a private network and thereby extend the reach of the organization's networks. VPNs are called *virtual* because they have no separate

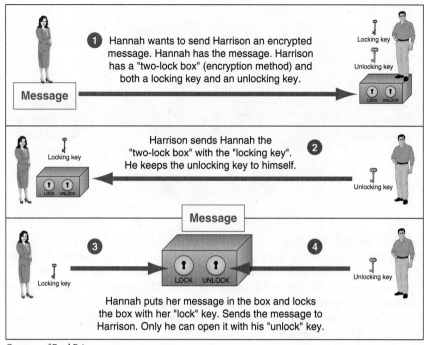

FIGURE 4.4 How public key encryption works. (Omnisec AG.)

1 Hannah wants to send Harrison an encrypted message. Hannah has the message. Harrison has a "two-lock box" (encryption method) and both a locking key and an unlocking key.

Message

Locking key

Unlocking key

LOCK UNLOCK

2 Harrison sends Hannah the "two-lock box" with the "locking key". He keeps the unlocking key to himself.

Locking key

LOCK UNLOCK

Unlocking key

Message

3 Locking key

LOCK UNLOCK

4 Unlocking key

Hannah puts her message in the box and locks the box with her "lock" key. Sends the message to Harrison. Only he can open it with his "unlock" key.

Courtesy of Brad Prince.

physical existence. They use the public Internet as their infrastructure. They are created by using log-ins, encryption, and other techniques to enhance the user's **privacy**, the right to be left alone and to be free of unreasonable personal intrusion.

VPNs have several advantages. First, they allow remote users to access the company network. Second, they provide flexibility. That is, mobile users can access the organization's

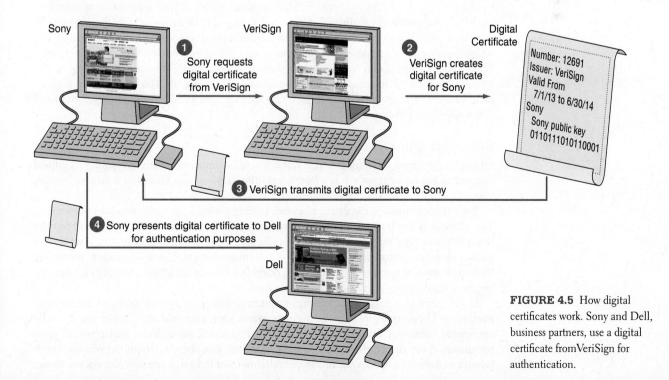

Sony

VeriSign

Digital Certificate

1 Sony requests digital certificate from VeriSign

2 VeriSign creates digital certificate for Sony

Number: 12691
Issuer: VeriSign
Valid From
7/1/13 to 6/30/14
Sony
Sony public key
0110111010110001

3 VeriSign transmits digital certificate to Sony

4 Sony presents digital certificate to Dell for authentication purposes

Dell

FIGURE 4.5 How digital certificates work. Sony and Dell, business partners, use a digital certificate from VeriSign for authentication.

FIGURE 4.6 Virtual private
network and tunneling.

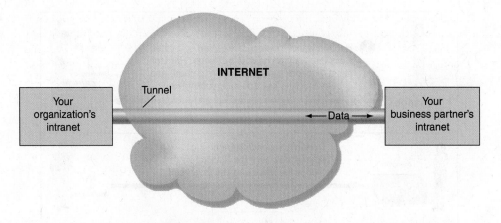

network from properly configured remote devices. Third, organizations can impose their
security policies through VPNs. For example, an organization may dictate that only corporate
e-mail applications are available to users when they connect from unmanaged devices.

To provide secure transmissions, VPNs use a process called tunneling. **Tunneling** encrypts
each data packet to be sent and places each encrypted packet inside another packet. In this
manner, the packet can travel across the Internet with confidentiality, authentication, and
integrity. Figure 4.6 illustrates a VPN and tunneling.

Secure Socket Layer.   **Secure socket layer**, now called **transport layer security (TLS)**, is
an encryption standard used for secure transactions such as credit card purchases and online
banking. TLS encrypts and decrypts data between a Web server and a browser end to end.

TLS is indicated by a URL that begins with "https" rather than "http," and it often displays
a small padlock icon in the browser's status bar. Using a padlock icon to indicate a secure connection and placing this icon in a browser's status bar are artifacts of specific browsers. Other
browsers use different icons (e.g., a key that is either broken or whole). The important thing to
remember is that browsers usually provide visual confirmation of a secure connection.

Employee Monitoring Systems.   Many companies are taking a proactive approach to
protecting their networks against what they view as one of their major security threats, namely,
employee mistakes. These companies are implementing **employee monitoring systems**,
which monitor their employees' computers, e-mail activities, and Internet surfing activities.
These products are useful to identify employees who spend too much time surfing on the
Internet for personal reasons, who visit questionable Web sites, or who download music illegally. Vendors that provide monitoring software include SpectorSoft (*www.spectorsoft.com*) and
Websense (*www.websense.com*).

Business Continuity Planning

An important security strategy for organizations is to be prepared for any eventuality. A critical
element in any security system is a *business continuity plan*, also known as a *disaster recovery
plan*.

Business continuity is the chain of events linking planning to protection and to recovery.
The purpose of the business continuity plan is to provide guidance to people who keep the
business operating after a disaster occurs. Employees use this plan to prepare for, react to, and
recover from events that affect the security of information assets. The objective is to restore the
business to normal operations as quickly as possible following an attack. The plan is intended
to ensure that critical business functions continue.

In the event of a major disaster, organizations can employ several strategies for business
continuity. These strategies include hot sites, warm sites, and cold sites. A **hot site** is a fully
configured computer facility, with all services, communications links, and physical plant
operations. A hot site duplicates computing resources, peripherals, telephone systems, applications, and workstations. A **warm site** provides many of the same services and options as the

hot site. However, it typically does not include the actual applications the company needs. A warm site includes computing equipment such as servers, but it often does not include user workstations. A **cold site** provides only rudimentary services and facilities, such as a building or a room with heating, air conditioning, and humidity control. This type of site provides no computer hardware or user workstations. The point of a cold site is that it takes care of long lead-time issues. Building, or even renting, space takes a long time. Installing high-speed communication lines, often from two or more carriers, takes a long time. Installing high-capacity power lines takes a long time. By comparison, buying and installing servers should not take a particularly long time.

Hot sites reduce risk to the greatest extent, but they are the most expensive option. Conversely, cold sites reduce risk the least, but they are the least expensive option.

Information Systems Auditing

Companies implement security controls to ensure that information systems work properly. These controls can be installed in the original system, or they can be added after a system is in operation. Installing controls is necessary but not sufficient to provide adequate security. In addition, people responsible for security need to answer questions such as: Are all controls installed as intended? Are they effective? Has any breach of security occurred? If so, what actions are required to prevent future breaches?

These questions must be answered by independent and unbiased observers. Such observers perform the task of *information systems auditing*. In an IS environment, an **audit** is an examination of information systems, their inputs, outputs, and processing.

Types of Auditors and Audits.   There are two types of auditors and audits: internal and external. IS auditing is usually a part of accounting *internal auditing*, and it is frequently performed by corporate internal auditors. An *external auditor* reviews the findings of the internal audit as well as the inputs, processing, and outputs of information systems. The external audit of information systems is frequently a part of the overall external auditing performed by a certified public accounting (CPA) firm.

IS auditing considers all of the potential hazards and controls in information systems. It focuses on issues such as operations, data integrity, software applications, security and privacy, budgets and expenditures, cost control, and productivity. Guidelines are available to assist auditors in their jobs, such as those from the Information Systems Audit and Control Association (*www.isaca.org*).

How is Auditing Executed?   IS auditing procedures fall into three categories: (1) auditing around the computer, (2) auditing through the computer, and (3) auditing with the computer.

Auditing around the computer means verifying processing by checking for known outputs using specific inputs. This approach is best used in systems with limited outputs. In *auditing through the computer*, auditors check inputs, outputs, and processing. They review program logic, and they test the data contained within the system. *Auditing with the computer* means using a combination of client data, auditor software, and client and auditor hardware. This approach enables the auditor to perform tasks such as simulating payroll program logic using live data.

before you go on...

1. What is the single most important information security control for organizations?

2. Differentiate between authentication and authorization. Which of these processes is always performed first?

3. Compare and contrast whitelisting and blacklisting.

4. What is the purpose of a disaster recovery plan?

5. What is information system auditing?

What's In IT For Me?

For the Accounting Major

Public companies, their accountants, and their auditors have significant information security responsibilities. Accountants are now being held professionally responsible for reducing risk, assuring compliance, eliminating fraud, and increasing the transparency of transactions according to Generally Accepted Accounting Principles (GAAP). The SEC and the Public Company Accounting Oversight Board (PCAOB), among other regulatory agencies, require information security, fraud prevention and detection, and internal controls over financial reporting. Forensic accounting, a combination of accounting and information security, is one of the most rapidly growing areas in accounting today.

For the Finance Major

Because information security is essential to the success of organizations today, it is no longer just the concern of the CIO. As a result of global regulatory requirements and the passage of Sarbanes-Oxley, responsibility for information security lies with the CEO and CFO. Consequently, all aspects of the security audit, including the security of information and information systems, are a key concern for financial managers.

In addition, CFOs and treasurers are increasingly involved with investments in information technology. They know that a security breach of any kind can have devastating financial effects on a company. Banking and financial institutions are prime targets for computer criminals. A related problem is fraud involving stocks and bonds that are sold over the Internet. Finance personnel must be aware of both the hazards and the available controls associated with these activities.

For the Marketing Major

Marketing professionals have new opportunities to collect data on their customers, for example, through business-to-consumer electronic commerce. Customers expect their data to be properly secured. However, profit-motivated criminals want those data. Therefore, marketing managers must analyze the risk of their operations. Failure to protect corporate and customer data will cause significant public relations problems, make customers very angry, may lead to lawsuits, and may result in losing customers to competitors. CRM operations and tracking customers' online buying habits can expose data to misuse (if they are not encrypted) or result in privacy violations.

For the Production/Operations Management Major

Every process in a company's operations—inventory purchasing, receiving, quality control, production, and shipping—can be disrupted by an information technology security breach or an IT security breach at a business partner. Any weak link in supply chain management or enterprise resource management systems puts the entire chain at risk. Companies may be held liable for IT security failures that impact other companies.

For the Human Resources Management Major

HR managers have responsibilities to secure confidential employee data. In addition, they must ensure that all employees explicitly verify that they understand the company's information security policies and procedures.

For the MIS Major

The MIS function provides the security infrastructure that protects the organization's information assets. This function is critical to the success of the organization, even though it is almost invisible until an attack succeeds. All application development, network deployment, and introduction of new information technologies have to be guided by IT security considerations. MIS personnel must customize the risk exposure security model to help the company identify security risks and prepare responses to security incidents and disasters.

Senior executives of publicly held companies look to the MIS function for help in meeting Sarbanes-Oxley requirements, particularly in detecting "significant deficiencies" or "material weaknesses" in internal controls and remediating them. Other functional areas also look to the MIS function to help them meet their security responsibilities.

[Summary]

1. Identify the five factors that contribute to the increasing vulnerability of information resources, and provide a specific example of each one.

The five factors are:

- Today's interconnected, interdependent, wirelessly networked business environment
  Example: The Internet
- Smaller, faster, cheaper computers and storage devices
  Examples: Netbooks, thumb drives, iPads
- Decreasing skills necessary to be a computer hacker
  Example: Information system hacking programs circulating on the Internet
- International organized crime taking over cybercrime
  Example: Organized crime has formed transnational cybercrime cartels. Because it is difficult to know exactly where cyber attacks originate, these cartels are extremely hard to bring to justice.
- Lack of management support
  Example: Suppose that your company spent $10 million on information security countermeasures last year, and they did not experience any successful attacks on their information resources. Short-sighted management might conclude that the company could spend less during the next year and obtain the same results. Bad idea.

2. Compare and contrast human mistakes and social engineering, and provide a specific example of each one.

Human mistakes are unintentional errors. However, employees can also make unintentional mistakes as a result of actions by an attacker, such as social engineering. *Social engineering* is an attack where the perpetrator uses social skills to trick or manipulate a legitimate employee into providing confidential company information.

An example of a human mistake is tailgating. An example of social engineering is when an attacker calls an employee on the phone and impersonates a superior in the company.

3. Discuss the ten types of deliberate attacks.

The ten types of deliberate attacks are:

Espionage or trespass occurs when an unauthorized individual attempts to gain illegal access to organizational information.

Information extortion occurs when an attacker either threatens to steal, or actually steals, information from a company. The perpetrator demands payment for not stealing the information, for returning stolen information, or for agreeing not to disclose the information.

Sabotage and vandalism are deliberate acts that involve defacing an organization's Web site, possibly causing the organization to lose its image and experience a loss of confidence by its customers.

Theft of equipment and information is becoming a larger problem because computing devices and storage devices are becoming smaller yet more powerful with vastly increased storage, making these devices easier and more valuable to steal.

Identity theft is the deliberate assumption of another person's identity, usually to gain access to his or her financial information or to frame him or her for a crime.

Preventing *compromises to intellectual property* is a vital issue for people who make their livelihood in knowledge fields. Protecting intellectual property is particularly difficult when that property is in digital form.

Software attacks occur when malicious software penetrates an organization's computer system. Today, these attacks are typically profit-driven and Web-based.

Alien software is clandestine software that is installed on your computer through duplicitous methods. It typically is not as malicious as viruses, worms, or Trojan horses, but it does use up valuable system resources.

Supervisory control and data acquisition refers to a large-scale, distributed measurement and control system. SCADA systems are used to monitor or control chemical, physical, and transport processes. A *SCADA attack* attempts to compromise such a system in order to cause damage to the real-world processes that the system controls.

With both *cyberterrorism* and *cyberwarfare*, attackers use a target's computer systems, particularly via the Internet, to cause physical, real-world harm or severe disruption, usually to carry out a political agenda.

4. **Define the three risk mitigation strategies, and provide an example of each one in the context of owning a home.**

The three risk mitigation strategies are:

Risk acceptance, where the organization accepts the potential risk, continues operating with no controls, and absorbs any damages that occur. If you own a home, you may decide not to insure it. Thus, you are practicing risk acceptance. Clearly, this is a bad idea.

Risk limitation, where the organization limits the risk by implementing controls that minimize the impact of threats. As a homeowner, you practice risk limitation by putting in an alarm system or cutting down weak trees near your house.

Risk transference, where the organization transfers the risk by using other means to compensate for the loss, such as by purchasing insurance. The vast majority of homeowners practice risk transference by purchasing insurance on their houses and other possessions.

5. **Identify the three major types of controls that organizations can use to protect their information resources, and provide an example of each one.**

Physical controls prevent unauthorized individuals from gaining access to a company's facilities. Common physical controls include walls, doors, fencing, gates, locks, badges, guards, and alarm systems. More sophisticated physical controls include pressure sensors, temperature sensors, and motion detectors.

Access controls restrict unauthorized individuals from using information resources. These controls involve two major functions: authentication and authorization. Authentication confirms the identity of the person requiring access. An example is biometrics. After the person is authenticated (identified), the next step is authorization. Authorization determines which actions, rights, or privileges the person has, based on his or her verified identity. Authorization is generally based on least privilege.

Communications (network) controls secure the movement of data across networks. Communications controls consist of firewalls, anti-malware systems, whitelisting and blacklisting, encryption, virtual private networking, secure socket layer, and vulnerability management systems.

[Chapter Glossary]

access controls Controls that restrict unauthorized individuals from using information resources and are concerned with user identification.

adware Alien software designed to help pop-up advertisements appear on your screen.

alien software Clandestine software that is installed on your computer through duplicitous methods.

anti-malware systems (antivirus software) Software packages that attempt to identify and eliminate viruses, worms, and other malicious software.

audit An examination of information systems, their inputs, outputs, and processing.

authentication A process that determines the identity of the person requiring access.

authorization A process that determines which actions, rights, or privileges the person has, based on verified identity.

back door Typically a password, known only to the attacker, that allows the attacker to access the system without having to go through any security procedures.

biometrics The science and technology of authentication (i.e., establishing the identity of an individual) by measuring the subject's physiologic or behavioral characteristics.

blacklisting A process in which a company identifies certain types of software that are not allowed to run in the company environment.

bot A computer that has been compromised by, and under the control of, a hacker.

botnet A network of computers that have been compromised by, and under control of a hacker, who is called the botmaster.

certificate authority A third party that acts as a trusted intermediary between computers (and companies) by issuing digital certificates and verifying the worth and integrity of the certificates.

cold site A backup location that provides only rudimentary services and facilities.

communications controls (also **network controls**) Controls that deal with the movement of data across networks.

controls Defense mechanisms (also called *countermeasures*).

cookie Small amounts of information that Web sites store on your computer, temporarily or more or less permanently.

copyright A grant that provides the creator of intellectual property with ownership of it for a specified period of time, currently the life of the creator plus 70 years.

cybercrime Illegal activities executed on the Internet.

cyberterrorism Can be defined as a premeditated, politically motivated attack against information, computer systems, computer programs, and data that results in violence against noncombatant targets by subnational groups or clandestine agents.

cyberwarfare War in which a country's information systems could be paralyzed from a massive attack by destructive software.

demilitarized zone (DMZ) A separate organizational local area network that is located between an organization's internal network and an external network, usually the Internet.

denial-of-service attack A cyber attack in which an attacker sends a flood of data packets to the target computer, with the aim of overloading its resources.

digital certificate An electronic document attached to a file certifying that this file is from the organization it claims to be from and has not been modified from its original format or content.

distributed denial-of-service (DDoS) attack A denial-of-service attack that sends a flood of data packets from many compromised computers simultaneously.

employee monitoring systems Systems that monitor employees' computers, e-mail activities, and Internet surfing activities.

encryption The process of converting an original message into a form that cannot be read by anyone except the intended receiver.

exposure The harm, loss, or damage that can result if a threat compromises an information resource.

firewall A system (either hardware, software, or a combination of both) that prevents a specific type of information from moving between untrusted networks, such as the Internet, and private networks, such as your company's network.

hot sites A fully configured computer facility, with all information resources and services, communications links, and physical plant operations, that duplicates your company's computing resources and provides near-real-time recovery of IT operations.

identity theft Crime in which someone uses the personal information of others to create a false identity and then uses it for some fraud.

information security Protecting an organization's information and information systems from unauthorized access, use, disclosure, disruption, modification, or destruction.

intellectual property The intangible property created by individuals or corporations, which is protected under trade secret, patent, and copyright laws.

least privilege A principle that users be granted the privilege for some activity only if there is a justifiable need to grant this authorization.

logic bombs Segments of computer code embedded within an organization's existing computer programs.

malware Malicious software such as viruses and worms.

network controls (see **communications controls**)

password A private combination of characters that only the user should know.

patent A document that grants the holder exclusive rights on an invention or process for a specified period of time, currently 20 years.

phishing attack An attack that uses deception to fraudulently acquire sensitive personal information by masquerading as an official-looking e-mail.

physical controls Controls that restrict unauthorized individuals from gaining access to a company's computer facilities.

piracy Copying a software program (other than freeware, demo software, etc.) without making payment to the owner.

privacy The right to be left alone and to be free of unreasonable personal intrusion.

privilege A collection of related computer system operations that can be performed by users of the system.

public-key encryption (also called *asymmetric encryption*) A type of encryption that uses two different keys, a public key and a private key.

risk The likelihood that a threat will occur.

risk acceptance A strategy in which the organization accepts the potential risk, continues to operate with no controls, and absorbs any damages that occur.

risk analysis The process by which an organization assesses the value of each asset being protected, estimates the probability that each asset might be compromised, and compares the probable costs of each being compromised with the costs of protecting it.

risk limitation A strategy in which the organization limits its risk by implementing controls that minimize the impact of a threat.

risk management A process that identifies, controls, and minimizes the impact of threats, in an effort to reduce risk to manageable levels.

risk mitigation A process whereby the organization takes concrete actions against risks, such as implementing controls and developing a disaster recovery plan.

risk transference A process in which the organization transfers the risk by using other means to compensate for a loss, such as by purchasing insurance.

secure socket layer (SSL) (also known as **transport layer security**) An encryption standard used for secure transactions such as credit card purchases and online banking.

security The degree of protection against criminal activity, danger, damage, and/or loss.

social engineering Getting around security systems by tricking computer users inside a company into revealing sensitive information or gaining unauthorized access privileges.

spam Unsolicited e-mail.

spamware Alien software that uses your computer as a launch platform for spammers.

spyware Alien software that can record your keystrokes and/or capture your passwords.

threat Any danger to which an information resource may be exposed.

trade secret Intellectual work, such as a business plan, that is a company secret and is not based on public information.

transport layer security (TLS) (see **secure socket layer**)

trap doors (see **back door**)

Trojan horse A software program containing a hidden function that presents a security risk.

tunneling A process that encrypts each data packet to be sent and places each encrypted packet inside another packet.

virtual private network (VPN) A private network that uses a public network (usually the Internet) to securely connect users by using encryption.

viruses Malicious software that can attach itself to (or "infect") other computer programs without the owner of the program being aware of the infection.

vulnerability The possibility that an information resource will be harmed by a threat.

warm site A site that provides many of the same services and options of the hot site, but does not include the company's applications.

whitelisting A process in which a company identifies acceptable software and permits it to run, and either prevents anything else from running or lets new software run in a quarantined environment until the company can verify its validity.

worms Destructive programs that replicate themselves without requiring another program to provide a safe environment for replication.

zombie computer (see **bot**)

[Discussion Questions]

1. Why are computer systems so vulnerable?

2. Why should information security be a prime concern to management?

3. Is security a technical issue? A business issue? Both? Support your answer. (Hint: Read Kim Nash, "Why Technology Isn't the Answer to Better Security," *CIO* (*www.cio.com*), October 15, 2008.)

4. Compare information security in an organization with insuring a house.

5. Why are authentication and authorization important to e-commerce?

6. Why is cross-border cybercrime expanding rapidly? Discuss possible solutions.

7. Discuss why the Sarbanes-Oxley Act is having an impact on information security.

8. What types of user authentication are used at your university and/or place of work? Do these measures seem to be effective? What if a higher level of authentication were implemented? Would it be worth it, or would it decrease productivity?

9. Why are federal authorities so worried about SCADA attacks?

[Problem-Solving Activities]

1. A critical problem is assessing how far a company is legally obligated to go in order to secure personal data. Because there is no such thing as perfect security (i.e., there is always more that you can do), resolving this question can significantly affect cost.

   a. When are security measures that a company implements sufficient to comply with its obligations?

   b. Is there any way for a company to know if its security measures are sufficient? Can you devise a method for any organization to determine if its security measures are sufficient?

2. Assume that the daily probability of a major earthquake in Los Angeles is 0.07 percent. The chance that your computer center will be damaged during such a quake is 5 percent. If the center is damaged, the estimated damage to the computer center will be $4.0 million.

   a. Calculate the expected loss in dollars.

   b. An insurance agent is willing to insure your facility for an annual fee of $25,000. Analyze the offer, and discuss whether to accept it.

3. Enter *www.scambusters.org*. Find out what the organization does. Learn about e-mail scams and Web site scams. Report your findings.

4. Visit *www.dhs.gov/dhspublic* (Department of Homeland Security). Search the site for "National Strategy to Secure Cyberspace" and write a report on their agenda and accomplishments to date.

5. Enter *www.alltrustnetworks.com* and other vendors of biometrics. Find the devices they make that can be used to control access into information systems. Prepare a list of products and major capabilities of each vendor.

6. Software piracy is a global problem. Access the following Web sites: *www.bsa.org* and *www.microsoft.com/piracy/*. What can organizations do to mitigate this problem?

   Are some organizations dealing with the problem better than others?

7. Investigate the Sony PlayStation Network hack that occurred in April 2011.

   • What type of attack was it?

   • Was the success of the attack due to technology problems at Sony, management problems at Sony, or a combination of both? Provide specific examples to support your answer.

   • Which Sony controls failed?

   • Could the hack have been prevented? If so, how?

   • Discuss Sony's response to the hack.

   • Describe the damages that Sony incurred from the hack.

[Team Assignments]

1. Access *www.ftc.gov/sentinel* to learn more about how law enforcement agencies around the world work together to fight consumer fraud. Each team should obtain current statistics on one of the top five consumer complaint categories and prepare a report. Are any categories growing faster than others? Are any categories more prevalent in certain parts of the world?

2. Read "In the Matter of BJ's Wholesale Club, Inc., FTC File No. 042 3160, June 16, 2005, Agreement Containing Consent Order" at *www.ftc.gov/opa/2005/06/bjswholesale.htm*. Describe the security breach at BJ's Wholesale Club. What was the reason for this agreement? Identify some of the causes of the security breach, and discuss how BJ's can better defend itself against hackers and legal liability.

3. Read the article: "The Security Tools You Need" at *www.pcworld.com/downloads/collection/collid,1525/files.html*. Each team should download a product and discuss its pros and cons for the class. Be sure to take a look at all the comments posted about this article.

[Closing Case **Passwords Are No Longer Enough**]

The Problem

We bank online, track our finances online, do our taxes online, and store our photos, our documents, and our data online. As a result, the amount of personal information being stored online has exploded. Further, we typically link our online accounts, with our e-mail addresses acting as universal usernames, a problem that becomes worse as the number of our online accounts increases. The combination of our e-mail address as username with a password creates a single point of failure that can be exploited with devastating results.

How did this problem start? Companies conducting business over the Internet had to figure out a way to make people feel secure about conducting online transactions and storing personal information on merchants' Web sites. To function in the real world, the security systems provided by online merchants must effectively manage the trade-off between convenience and security. The most secure system is useless if it is too difficult for users to access. For example, if the merchant requires customer passwords to be 50 characters long and include special symbols, these passwords might keep their customers' accounts safe, but they would be impossible to remember.

Companies want the act of signing up and using their service to appear both totally private and perfectly simple. The problem with this scenario is that it makes security impossible. Therefore, these companies decided to employ combinations of usernames (the customer's e-mail address) and passwords.

We have all bought into the idea that a password is sufficient to protect all of our data, as long as it is elaborate enough. In reality, however, passwords by themselves are not enough. No matter how unique or complex you make them, passwords can no longer protect you.

There are many ways in which attackers can obtain our passwords, no matter how strong they are. How are our passwords compromised? Hackers have numerous strategies to discover them: They can guess them, lift them from an online password dump, crack them by brute force, and steal them using malware and phishing and spear phishing techniques. In addition, they can con a company's customer support department into resetting them. Let's examine these methods more closely.

- User carelessness is the biggest security risk of all. Therefore, the most basic hacking method is simply to guess correctly. Despite years of being told not to, people still use weak, predictable passwords. One security consultant compiled a list of the 10,000 most common passwords based on easily available sources, such as passwords dumped online by hackers and simple Google searches. He discovered that the most frequently used password was (believe it or not) "password." The second most popular password was the number 123456. If you use a weak password, then accessing your accounts becomes incredibly easy. Free software tools such as John the Ripper automate password-cracking to such an extent that anyone with rudimentary computer skills can do it. All they need is an Internet connection and a list of common passwords, which are often available online.

- Today, our laptops have more processing power than a mainframe did 20 years ago. Therefore, cracking a strong password with brute force computation takes just a few milliseconds longer than cracking a weak password. These computations simply try every possible combination of letters, numbers, and special characters until they discover the password.

- Since 2011, hackers have dumped more than 280 million "hashes"—that is, encrypted but readily crackable passwords—online for everyone to see. LinkedIn, Yahoo, Gawker, and eHarmony all have experienced security

breaches in which the usernames and passwords of millions of people were stolen and then dumped on the Internet. A comparison of just two dumps revealed that 49 percent of people had reused usernames and passwords. The implication here is that users should create a unique combination for every site that requires log in procedures. Unfortunately, this is not particularly feasible.

- Hackers also obtain our passwords through phishing and spear phishing attacks.

- Another means of stealing passwords is to use hidden malware that secretly sends your data to other people. According to a Verizon report, malware attacks accounted for 69 percent of data breaches in 2011. Malware is epidemic on Windows and, increasingly, Android. Malware typically works by installing a keylogger or some other form of malware that captures whatever you type or see (i.e., a screen grab). It frequently targets large organizations, where the goal is to gain access to the entire system.

  One example of this type of malware is ZeuS. Clicking a link from a phishing e-mail installs ZeuS on your computer. Then, when you log in to your online banking account, ZeuS captures your password and sends it back to a server controlled by the hacker. In one case in 2010, the FBI helped apprehend five individuals in the Ukraine who had used ZeuS to steal $70 million from 390 victims, primarily small businesses in the United States.

- Unfortunately, we still have to contend with human memory. Passwords must be difficult, or they can be routinely cracked or guessed. As we discussed, however, strong passwords are also the most difficult to remember. So, if you use strong passwords, there is a very good chance that you will forget them. To address this problem, every password-based system needs a mechanism to reset your account. Going further, the process of recovering a forgotten password, or creating a new one, cannot be too difficult, or customers will simply stop doing business with the Web site. Unfortunately, that process makes your account vulnerable to hackers who employ social engineering techniques. Hackers frequently con customer service agents into resetting passwords by getting past the "private security questions" that you set up in order to reset your forgotten passwords in the first place.

  You know how these security questions work. To reset a forgotten password, you supply answers to questions that supposedly only you know. In reality, hackers can obtain, or guess, the answers to your questions by searching for information on you on Google, LinkedIn, and Facebook. They can search the Facebook pages of your children, your spouse, your extended family, and your friends. The bottom line: If you have a Web presence, your answers to standard security questions are fairly easy to find. Your mother's maiden name is on Ancestry.com, your high school mascot is on Classmates, and your birthday and your best friend's name are on Facebook.

A Variety of Attempted Solutions

What kinds of actions do people take to prevent hackers from discovering our passwords? One common strategy is to create strong passwords. We now "live online" while depending large on the idea of the strong password. Unfortunately, strong passwords are no longer the cure. No matter how strong your password is, it can be compromised with the techniques we just discussed.

Another common solution is multifactor authentication. An example is the use of a password combined with a token (two-factor authentication). Although this strategy might be more secure than simply using a password by itself, it still can be compromised. As an example, in spring 2011, hackers broke into the security company RSA and stole data relating to its SecurID tokens, supposedly hack-proof devices that provide secondary codes to accompany passwords. RSA never divulged what was stolen, but it is widely believed that the hackers took enough data to duplicate the numbers that the tokens generate. If the hackers also learned the tokens' device IDs, then they would be able to penetrate the most secure systems in corporate America.

As another example, consider Google's two-factor authentication system for Gmail. It works like this: First you confirm a mobile phone number with Google. After that, whenever you try to log in from an unfamiliar IP address, the company sends an additional code to your phone, which is the second factor. Although this system does make your account safer, it can be hacked.

For example, hackers wanted to access a corporate executive's Google Apps account, but it was protected by two-factor authentication. So, they attacked his AT&T cell phone account instead. AT&T essentially uses Social Security numbers as over-the-phone passwords. Give the carrier those nine digits—or even just the last four digits—along with the name, phone number, and billing address on the account, and it lets anyone add a forwarding number to any account in its system. (Obtaining a Social Security number is simple, because they are sold openly online on hacker Web sites.) The hackers used the executive's Social Security number to add a forwarding number to his AT&T service. They then sent a password-reset request to Google. When the automated call came in, it was forwarded to them...... and his Google Apps account was theirs.

Still another proposed solution involves biometrics. However, two of the most common biometric systems, fingerprint readers and iris scanners, have two problems. First, there is little, if any, infrastructure to support them. Such infrastructure consists of the equipment, for example. Second, a fingerprint or an iris scan is a single piece of data, and single pieces of data can be stolen.

In addition, the biometrics systems themselves can be compromised. For example, Kevin Mitnick, the social engineer who spent five years in prison for his hacking, now runs his own security company. He is paid to break into systems and then explain to the owners how he did it. In one recent attack, his client was using voice authentication. To access the system, the user had to recite a series of randomly generated numbers, and both the sequence and the speaker's voice had to match a previous recording. Mitnick called his client and recorded their conversation, tricking him into using the numbers zero through nine in the conversation. Mitnick then split up the audio, played the numbers back in the correct sequence, and was able to access the client's system.

The Result

The ultimate problem with passwords is that they are a single point of failure, open to many types of attack. It is impossible to have a password-based security system that is memorable enough to allow mobile logins, flexible enough to vary from Web site to Web site, convenient enough to be easily reset, and yet also secure against brute-force hacking. Nevertheless, we continue to rely on passwords.

In the future, online identity verification will no longer be a password-based system. Instead, the password will be only one part of a multifactor process. Each online account will have to integrate many pieces of information: who we are and what we do; where we go and when; what we have with us; and how we act when we are there—true multifactor authentication.

Biometrics will undoubtedly play an important role in future authentication systems. In fact, these devices might require a biometric confirmation just to use them. Your computer or a remote Web site you are trying to access will confirm a particular device. Already, then, you have verified something you are and something you have. If you are logging in to your bank account from an entirely unlikely place, however, then you will have to go through additional steps. Maybe you will have to speak a phrase into the microphone and match your voiceprint. Maybe your phone's camera will snap a picture of your face and your bank's facial recognition software will have to identify you.

In many ways, businesses that we transact with online will have to act like credit card companies do today. These companies monitor patterns to flag anomalies, and then shut down activity if it seems like fraud. Google is already heading in this direction by moving beyond two-factor authentication to examine each login and compare it to the previous one in terms of location, device, and other signals that the company will not disclose. If Google sees something unexpected, then it will force the user to answer questions about the account.

Of course, as measures like these are implemented, future security systems will require significant sacrifices to our privacy. The system will need to draw upon our location and habits, and perhaps even our patterns of speech or our DNA. The only path to improved security is to allow our movements to be tracked in all sorts of ways and to have those movements and metrics tied to our actual identity. This shift will involve significant investment and inconvenience. Also, it will likely worry privacy advocates.

Fortunately, we don't have to wait until the future to protect ourselves from the threats we have just discussed. (Also see Technology Guide 5.) There are actions that you can take now; for example:

- Enable two-factor authentication whenever it is offered. Even though it can be hacked, it is better than doing nothing.

- Provide totally bogus answers to your security questions. For example, Your first car? "Sportscar AU Tigers." Just make certain your answers are memorable.

- Clean up your online presence. For example, Web sites such as Spokeo (www.spokeo.com) and WhitePages.com (www.whitepages.com) offer opt-out mechanisms that allow you to remove your information from their databases. You should take this action for every instance of your online presence.

- Use a unique, secure e-mail address for password recoveries. Create a special e-mail account that you never use for communications. Your username on this account should not be linked to your real name in any way.

Sources: Compiled from K. Hill, "Google Ordered to Teach America How to Put Passwords on Wi-Fi Networks," *Forbes*, March 13, 2013; R. Metz, "A Password You Wear on Your Wrist," *MIT Technology Review*, February 27, 2013; T. Simonite, "PayPal, Lenovo Launch New Campaign to Kill the Password," *MIT Technology Review*, February 12, 2013; J. Daly, "Passwords, Security, and the Future of Authentication," *EdTech Magazine*, February 11, 2013; C. Albanesius, "Sony Fined 250,000 British Pounds Over Playstation Hack," *PC Magazine*, January 24, 2013; R. Greenfield, "What the Future Without Passwords Will Look Like," *Yahoo! News*, January 22, 2013; M. Honan, "Kill the Password," *Wired*, December, 2012; R. Metz, "Instead of a Password, Security Software Just Checks Your Eyes," *MIT Technology Review*, December 3, 2012; S. Greengard, "Phishing Techniques Steal Sensitive Data," *Baseline Magazine*, October 11, 2012; T. Simonite, "To Keep Passwords Safe from Hackers, Just Break Them into Bits," *MIT Technology Review*, October 9, 2012; T. Claburn, "Mozilla Persona Aspires to Kill Passwords," *InformationWeek*, September 28, 2012; R. Metz, "More Passwords, More Problems," *MIT Technology Review*, September 21, 2012; "FBI Launches Face Recognition Project," *KurzweilAI .net*, September 10, 2012; S. Fox, "Goodbye Gibberish: Making Passwords Easier to Remember," *NBC News*, February 21, 2012.

Questions

1. Examine the strength of the passwords that you use. How vulnerable are your passwords to guessing? To brute-force hacking?

2. Does the security burden fall primarily on the user? On the company that the user is doing business with? On both? Support your answer.

3. Is it possible to ever have complete security in your online transactions? Why or why not? Explain your answer.

[Internship Activity]

Industry: Retail

Customer Relationship Management tools are excellent tools for managing relationships. You will learn more about these in Chapter 11. For now, let it suffice to know that they maintain massive amounts of data on customers, purchases, preferences, individuals, and products. This amount of data has to be kept secure.

For this activity you will be working for Hannah Shaw, Marketing Director for Caesars Entertainment in Las Vegas. Having chosen Salesforce.com as their CRM tool, they have set out to create a very unique experience for customers. They are now able to maintain a complete customer profile that includes hotel reservations, event attendance, preferences, and more in a system that is accessible organization-wide. However, Hannah is concerned about their data on certain "high-profile" customers.

Please visit the Book Companion Site to receive the full set of instructions on how you will help Hannah develop security policies and training programs to help keep high-profile customer data safe.

Chapter 5

Data and Knowledge Management

[LEARNING OBJECTIVES]	[CHAPTER OUTLINE]	[WEB RESOURCES]

[LEARNING OBJECTIVES]

1. Discuss ways that common challenges in managing data can be addressed using data governance.

2. Define Big Data, and discuss its basic characteristics.

3. Explain how to interpret the relationships depicted in an entity-relationship diagram.

4. Discuss the advantages and disadvantages of relational databases.

5. Explain the elements necessary to successfully implement and maintain data warehouses.

6. Describe the benefits and challenges of implementing knowledge management systems in organizations.

[CHAPTER OUTLINE]

5.1 Managing Data

5.2 Big Data

5.3 The Database Approach

5.4 Database Management Systems

5.5 Data Warehouses and Data Marts

5.6 Knowledge Management

[WEB RESOURCES]

- Student PowerPoints for note taking

WileyPLUS

- E-book
- Author video lecture for each chapter section
- Practice quizzes
- Flash Cards for vocabulary review
- Additional "IT's About Business" cases
- Video interviews with managers
- Lab Manuals for Microsoft Office 2010 and 2013

What's In IT For Me?

This Chapter Will Help Prepare You To...

ACCT	FIN	MKT	POM	HRM	MIS
ACCOUNTING	FINANCE	MARKETING	PRODUCTION OPERATIONS MANAGEMENT	HUMAN RESOURCES MANAGEMENT	MIS
Cost justify firm's databases	Use data for internal investment decisions	Use customer data to plan marketing campaigns	Analyze data for quality control	Use employee data for performance evaluations	Provide infrastructure to store firm's data

[Tapping the Power of Big Data]

Analysts have coined the term *Big Data* to refer to the vast and constantly increasing amounts of data that modern organizations need to capture, store, process, and analyze. Managing Big Data represents a very real problem that every business faces. The following case provides a variety of examples of companies that are utilizing Big Data in creative and profitable ways. The fundamental concept that underlies all of these cases is that Big Data will continue to get "bigger," so organizations will have to devise ever-more innovative solutions to manage these data.

Human Resources. Employee benefits, particularly healthcare, represent a major business expense. Consequently, some companies have turned to Big Data to better manage these benefits. Caesars Entertainment (www.caesars.com), for example, analyzes health-insurance claim data for its 65,000 employees and their covered family members. Managers can track thousands of variables that indicate how employees use medical services, such as the number of emergency room visits and whether employees choose a generic or brand name drug.

For instance, data revealed that too many employees with medical emergencies were being treated at hospital emergency rooms rather than at less-expensive urgent-care facilities. The company launched a campaign to remind employees of the high cost of emergency room visits, and they provided a list of alternative facilities. Subsequently, 10,000 emergencies shifted to less-expensive alternatives, for a total savings of $4.5 million.

Big Data is also having an impact on *hiring*. An example is Catalyst IT Services (www.catalystitservices.com), a technology outsourcing company that hires teams for programming jobs. In 2013, the company planned to screen more than 10,000 candidates. Not only is traditional recruiting too slow, but too often the hiring managers subjectively choose candidates who are not the best fit for the job. Catalyst addresses this problem by requiring candidates fill out an online assessment. It then uses the assessment to collect thousands of data points about each candidate. In fact, the company collects more data based on *how* candidates answer than on *what* they answer.

For example, the assessment might give a problem requiring calculus to an applicant who is not expected to know the subject. How the candidate reacts—laboring over an answer, answering quickly and then returning later, or skipping the problem entirely—provides insight into how that candidate might deal with challenges that he or she will encounter on the job. That is, someone who labors over a difficult question might be effective in an assignment that requires a methodical approach to problem solving, while whereas an applicant who takes a more aggressive approach might perform better in a different job setting.

The benefit of this big-data approach is that it recognizes that people bring different skills to the table and that there is no one-size-fits-all person for a job. Analyzing millions of data points can reveal which attributes candidates bring to specific situations.

As one measure of success, employee turnover at Catalyst averages about 15 percent per year, compared with more than 30 percent for its U.S. competitors and more than 20 percent for similar companies overseas.

Product Development. Big Data can help capture customer preferences and put that information to work in designing new products. In this area, both online companies and traditional companies are using Big Data to achieve competitive advantage.

Physical manufacturers are using Big Data to measure customer interest. For example, as Ford Motor Company (www.ford.com) was designing the first subcompact model on its new global platform—a common set of components that Ford would incorporate into its cars and trucks around the world—the company had to decide which features that were common in one region should be made available in all regions. One feature the company considered was a "three blink" turn indicator that had been available on its European cars for years. Unlike the turn signals on its U.S. vehicles, this indicator flashes three times at the driver's touch and then automatically shuts off.

Ford decided that conducting a full-scale market research test on this blinker would be too costly and time consuming. Instead, it examined auto-enthusiast Web sites and owner forums to discover what drivers were saying about turn indicators. Using text-mining algorithms, researchers culled more than 10,000 mentions and then summarized the most relevant comments.

The results? Ford introduced the three-blink indicator on the new Ford Fiesta in 2010, and by 2013 it was available on most Ford products. Although some Ford owners complained online that they have had trouble getting used to the new turn indicator, many others defended it. Ford managers note that the use of text-mining algorithms was critical in this effort because they provided the company with a complete picture that would not have been available using traditional market research.

Operations. For years, companies have been using information technology to make their operations more efficient. They can now use Big Data to capture much more information from a wealth of new sources.

Consider United Parcel Service (UPS). The company has long relied on data to improve its operations. Specifically, it uses sensors in its delivery vehicles that can, among other things, capture the truck's speed and location, the number of times it is placed in reverse, and whether the driver's seat belt is buckled. These data are uploaded at the end of each day to a UPS data center, where they are analyzed overnight. By combining GPS information and data from sensors installed on more than 46,000 vehicles, UPS in 2012 reduced fuel consumption by 8.4 million gallons, and it cut 85 million miles off its routes.

Marketing. Marketing managers have long used data to better understand their customers and to target their marketing efforts more directly. Today, Big Data enables marketers to craft much more personalized messages.

Like many hoteliers, United Kingdom's InterContinental Hotels Group (IHG; www.ihg.com) has gathered details about the 71 million members of its Priority Club rewards program, such as income levels and whether members prefer family-style or business-traveler accommodations. The company then consolidated all of this information into a single data warehouse that extracts information from social media Web sites and processes queries very quickly. A *data warehouse* is a repository of historical data that are organized by subject to support decision makers in the organization. Using its data warehouse and analytics software, the hotelier launched a new marketing campaign in January 2013. Where previous marketing campaigns generated, on average, between 7 and 15 customized marketing messages, the new campaign generated more than 1,500. IHG rolled out these messages in stages to an initial core of 12 customer groups, each of which is defined by 4,000 attributes. One group, for instance, tends to stay on weekends, redeem reward points for gift cards, and register through IHG marketing partners. Utilizing this information, IHG sent these customers a marketing message that alerted them to local weekend events.

The campaign proved to be highly successful. It generated a 35 percent higher rate of customer conversions, or acceptances, than previous, similar campaigns.

Sources: Compiled from S. Sikular, "Gartner's Big Data Definition Consists of Three Parts, Not to Be Confused with Three 'V's," *Forbes*, March 27, 2013; G. Fowler, "Data, Data Everywhere," *The Wall Street Journal*, March 13, 2013; G. Press, "What's To Be Done About Big Data?" *Forbes*, March 11, 2013; S. Rosenbush and M. Totty, "How Big Data Is Changing the Whole Equation for Business," *The Wall Street Journal*, March 11, 2013; D. Clark, "How Big Data Is Transforming the Hunt for Talent," *Forbes*, March 8, 2013; G. Satell, "The Limits of Big Data Marketing," *Forbes*, March 6, 2013; V. Mayer-Schonberger and K. Cukier, "Big Data: A Revolution That Will Transform How We Live, Work, and Think," Eamon Dolan/Houghton Mifflin Harcourt, March 5, 2013; "Big Data: What's Your Plan?" *McKinsey & Company Insights*, March, 2013; D. Henschen, "Big Data Revolution Will Be Led by Revolutionaries," *InformationWeek*, December 12, 2012; "Integrate for Insight," *Oracle White Paper*, October 27, 2012; "Big Data Now," *O'Reilly Media*, October, 2012; S. Greengard, "Big Data Challenges Organizations," *Baseline Magazine*, June 13, 2012; S. Lohr, "The Age of Big Data," *The New York Times*, February 11, 2012; "Big Data: Lessons From the Leaders," *The Economist (Economist Intelligence Unit)*, 2012; www.the-bigdatainstitute.com, accessed April 17, 2013.

What We Learned from This Case

Information technologies and systems support organizations in managing—that is, acquiring, organizing, storing, accessing, analyzing, and interpreting—data. As you noted in Chapter 1, when these data are managed properly, they become *information* and then *knowledge*. Information and knowledge are invaluable organizational resources that can provide a competitive advantage.

So, just how important are data and data management to organizations? From confidential customer information, to intellectual property, to financial transactions, to social media posts, organizations possess massive amounts of data that are critical to organizational success and that they need to manage. Managing these data, however, comes at a huge cost. According to Symantec's (www.symantec.com) State of Information Survey, digital information annually costs organizations worldwide $1.1 trillion, and it also makes up roughly half of an organization's total value. Large organizations spend an average of $38 million annually to maintain and utilize data, and small-to-medium-sized businesses spend $332,000.

This chapter will examine the processes data first into information and then into knowledge. Managing data is critically important in large organizations. However, it is equally important to small organizations, as you see in IT's About Business 5.1.

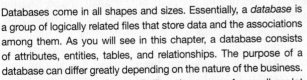

IT's about [small] business

5.1 Rollins Automotive POM

Databases come in all shapes and sizes. Essentially, a *database* is a group of logically related files that store data and the associations among them. As you will see in this chapter, a database consists of attributes, entities, tables, and relationships. The purpose of a database can differ greatly depending on the nature of the business.

Take, for example, Dennis Rollins, the owner of a small car lot in Bowdon, Georgia. Dennis needed an effective way to manage the data pertaining to his car lot. Achieving a solid online presence can be difficult for small used car dealers because there are so many makes and models of cars to sell and so many online outlets through which to advertise. Had Dennis opted to manage his data himself, he would have needed at least one database to manage

his inventory and at least one other database to allow his customers to view product information. He would also have to hire a full-time employee to oversee Internet sales. Adding two databases and a full-time employee was far beyond Dennis' capacity, so he sought an easier solution.

That solution came in the form of Dealer Car Search (http://dealercarsearch.com), a company that specializes in creating Web sites for car dealers. Dealer Car Search provides products for small businesses, dealers, and dealer chains. What ultimately makes the company so successful, however, is its database. This database provides the data-entry capabilities, analysis capabilities, reporting, and search features.

Now, when Dennis has a new vehicle to sell, he has to enter his data just once onto his customer page on Dealer Car Search. The data then automatically appear on his Web site (http://rollinsautomotive.com) as well as on other car sites (such as http://autotrader.com). Dealer Car Search also supplies Dennis with an inventory management system that provides a view of his inventory along with reports to help him determine his pricing. If Dennis changes a price or updates any other information, the change automatically appears on all of the other sites.

The result? The database turned out to be the one-stop solution that Dennis needed. It provides inventory management,

Internet advertising, mobile apps, performance reporting, lead management, and much more. Simply put, this database application provides a seamless experience that benefits Dealer Car Search, Rollins Automotive, and Rollins's customers.

Sources: Compiled from http://dealercarsearch.com, http://rollinsautomotive .com, accessed February 28, 2013.

Questions
1. Why is Dealer Car Search's database largely responsible for its success?
2. Why didn't Dennis Rollins simply build his own database using Access? Support your answer.

Few business professionals are comfortable making or justifying business decisions that are not based on solid information. This is especially true today, when modern information systems make access to that information quick and easy. For example, we have technology that formats data in a way that managers and analysts can easily understand. Consequently, these professionals can access these data themselves and analyze them according to their needs, using a variety of tools. The result is useful *information*. Executives can then apply their experience to use this information to address a business problem, thereby producing *knowledge*. Knowledge management, enabled by information technology, captures and stores knowledge in forms that all organizational employees can access and apply, thereby creating the flexible, powerful "learning organization."

Clearly, data and knowledge management are vital to modern organizations. But, why should *you* learn about them? The reason is that you will play an important role in the development of database applications. The structure and content of your organization's database depends on how users (you) define your business activities. For example, when database developers in the firm's MIS group build a database, they use a tool called entity-relationship (ER) modeling. This tool creates a model of how users view a business activity. When you understand how to create and interpret an ER model, then you can evaluate whether the developers have captured your business activity correctly.

Keep in mind that decisions about data last longer, and have a broader impact, than decisions about hardware or software. If decisions concerning hardware are wrong, then the equipment can be replaced relatively easily. If software decisions turn out to be incorrect, they can be modified, though not always painlessly or inexpensively. Database decisions, in contrast, are much harder to undo. Database design constrains what the organization can do with its data for a long time. Remember that business users will be stuck with a bad database design, while the programmers who created the database will quickly move on to their next projects. This is why it is so important to get database designs right the first time—and you will play a key role in these designs.

Relational databases (discussed in detail later in this chapter) store data in flat, two-dimensional tables, consisting of rows and columns. When you know how data are stored in these tables, then you know what types of data are available for analysis and decision making. Of course, your familiarity with data warehouses will serve the same purpose. Also, understanding relational databases will help you work with database developers in defining a new database or suggesting improvements to an existing one. It is one thing for you to say to a database developer, "I wish I could get this information from the database." It is quite another thing to say, "If you could add this column of data to Table A and this other column of data to Table B, then I could get this information from the database." An important note: Don't be concerned that database developers will be insulted if you provide such detailed instructions. They actually enjoy responding to specific, knowledgeable requests from users!

In addition, you might want to create a small, personal database using a software product such as Microsoft Access. In that case, you will need to be familiar with at least the basics of the product.

After the data are stored in your organization's databases, they must be accessible to users in a form that helps users make decisions. Organizations accomplish this objective by developing data warehouses. You should become familiar with data warehouses because they are invaluable decision-making tools.

You will also make extensive use of your organization's knowledge base to perform your job. For example, when you are assigned a new project, you will likely research your firm's knowledge base to identify factors that contributed to the success (or failure) of previous, similar projects.

You begin this chapter by taking a look at the Big Data phenomenon. You continue by examining the multiple problems involved in managing data and the database approach that organizations use to solve those problems. You will then see how database management systems enable organizations to access and use the data stored in the databases. Next, you study data warehouses and data marts and how to utilize them for decision making. You finish the chapter by examining knowledge management.

Managing Data

5.1

All IT applications require data. These data should be of high quality, meaning that they should be accurate, complete, timely, consistent, accessible, relevant, and concise. Unfortunately, the process of acquiring, keeping, and managing data is becoming increasingly difficult.

The Difficulties of Managing Data

Because data are processed in several stages and often in multiple locations, they are frequently subject to problems and difficulties. Managing data in organizations is difficult for many reasons.

First, the amount of data increases exponentially with time. Much historical data must be kept for a long time, and new data are added rapidly. For example, to support millions of customers, large retailers such as Walmart have to manage petabytes of data. (A petabyte is approximately 1,000 terabytes, or trillions of bytes; see Technology Guide 1.)

In addition, data are also scattered throughout organizations, and they are collected by many individuals using various methods and devices. These data are frequently stored in numerous servers and locations and in different computing systems, databases, formats, and human and computer languages. IT's About Business 5.2 demonstrates how New York City is benefiting from the system it utilizes to manage its data management problems.

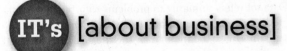

5.2 New York City Opens Its Data to All

Obtaining and using government data has never been easy. In most cases, these data are stored in proprietary formats. Historically it has been impossible to obtain these data and then to reconfigure them into accessible and open formats. To address this problem, New York City passed Local Law 11, which mandated that city agencies systematically categorize data and make them available to the public.

To accommodate this initiative, the city had to redefine its data practices. So, in September 2012, it created an "Open Data Policy and Technical Standards Manual," which outlines how city agencies can gather, structure, and automate data flows to meet the requirements of Local Law 11. To ensure that the process was collaborative and that it met the needs of city residents, the city's

Department of Information Technology and Telecommunications (DoITT) enlisted the help of the civic technology community and city agencies to create the document. The agency also launched a wiki (http://nycopendata.pediacities.com/wiki/index.php/NYC_Open_Data) that let citizens amend or comment on the document as it was being created.

This initiative has changed the way that the New York City government functions. As of mid-2013, the city had made approximately 1,750 unique representations of more than 1,000 raw data sets available at no charge via NYC OpenData. These data sets include more than 60 city agencies, commissions, and business improvement districts. They span the breadth of city operations, including cultural affairs, education, health, housing, property, public safety, social services, and transportation. Most of the data can be viewed through a standard Web browser and downloaded in multiple file formats. The data include:

- 10 years of city performance data; building information, including building complaints, permits, and building jobs;
- Emergency information encompassing evacuation zones and evacuation centers;
- Crime data spanning the previous 12 years;
- A list of licensed taxi drivers that is updated on a daily basis.

New York City is now using data and analysis in unprecedented ways to develop policies, drive operations, and improve services for its citizens. The goal is to enable developers, entrepreneurs, and academics to put data to work in new and innovative ways. Literally anyone can employ his or her skills and creativity to utilize these data to improve the city's quality of life.

One of the initiative's fundamental objectives is to encourage creative projects aimed at defining and illuminating public policy questions—for example, overlays of data pertaining to gang activity and the availability of youth programs, in-depth analysis of traffic crashes, school performance, noise problems, affordable housing, and homelessness. These are all age-old urban problems that can

be examined in new ways as the data become available online and people use them in innovative ways.

This effort is ongoing. In September 2013, the DoITT was scheduled to publish an open-data compliance plan that (1) categorizes all public data sets held by the city and (2) outlines plans to make these data sets available by the end of 2018. As New York City Council Member Gale Brewer noted, "We are putting an end to the days of city agencies posting information in confusing formats that cannot be searched or manipulated."

Sources: Compiled from J. Naidoo, "Open Data Platforms: A Tool to Revolutionise Governance," *The Guardian;* April 16, 2013; S. Greengard, "New York City Takes an Open Approach to Data," *Baseline Magazine,* March 20, 2013; S. Goodyear, "Why New York City's Open Data Law Is Worth Caring About," *The Atlantic Cities,* March 8, 2013; B. Morrissey, "New York's Data Deluge Begins," *The New York World,* March 7, 2013; J. Pollicino, "Bloomberg Signs NYC 'Open Data Policy' into Law, Plans Web Portal for 2018," *Engadget.com,* March 12, 2012; "New York City to Mandate Open Data," *Government Technology,* March 2, 2012; www.nyc.gov, accessed April 15, 2013.

Questions
1. What are some other creative applications addressing city problems that could be developed using NYC's open data policy?
2. List some disadvantages of providing all city data in an open, accessible format.

Another problem is that data are generated from multiple sources: internal sources (e.g., corporate databases and company documents), personal sources (e.g., personal thoughts, opinions, and experiences), and external sources (e.g., commercial databases, government reports, and corporate Web sites). Data also come from the Web, in the form of clickstream data. **Clickstream data** are those data that visitors and customers produce when they visit a Web site and click on hyperlinks (described in Chapter 4). Clickstream data provide a trail of the users' activities in the Web site, including user behavior and browsing patterns.

Adding to these problems is the fact that new sources of data, such as blogs, podcasts, videocasts, and radio frequency identification (RFID) tags and other wireless sensors, are constantly being developed. In addition, data degrade over time. For example, customers move to new addresses or change their names, companies go out of business or are bought, new products are developed, employees are hired or fired, and companies expand into new countries.

Data are also subject to *data rot*. Data rot refers primarily to problems with the media on which the data are stored. Over time, temperature, humidity, and exposure to light can cause physical problems with storage media and thus make it difficult to access the data. The second aspect of data rot is that finding the machines needed to access the data can be difficult. For example, it is almost impossible today to find 8-track players. Consequently, a library of 8-track tapes has become relatively worthless, unless you have a functioning 8-track player or you convert the tapes to a modern medium such as CDs.

Data security, quality, and integrity are critical, yet they are easily jeopardized. In addition, legal requirements relating to data differ among countries as well as among industries, and they change frequently.

Another problem arises from the fact that, over time, organizations have developed information systems for specific business processes, such as transaction processing, supply chain management, and customer relationship management. Information systems that specifically support these processes impose unique requirements on data, which results in repetition and conflicts across the organization. For example, the marketing function might maintain information on customers, sales territories, and markets. These data might be duplicated within the billing or customer service functions. This situation can produce inconsistent data within the enterprise. Inconsistent data prevent a company from developing a unified view of core business information—data concerning customers, products, finances, and so on—across the organization and its information systems.

Two other factors complicate data management. First, federal regulations (e.g., Sarbanes-Oxley) have made it a top priority for companies to better account for how they are managing information. Sarbanes-Oxley requires that (1) public companies evaluate and disclose the effectiveness of their internal financial controls and (2) independent auditors for these companies agree to this disclosure. The law also holds CEOs and CFOs personally responsible for such disclosures. If their companies lack satisfactory data management policies and fraud or a security breach occurs, the company officers could be held liable and face prosecution.

Second, companies are drowning in data, much of which is unstructured. As you have seen, the amount of data is increasing exponentially. To be profitable, companies must develop a strategy for managing these data effectively.

There are two additional problems with data management: Big Data and data hoarding. Big Data, which we discussed in the chapter-opening case, is so important that we devote Section 5.2 to this topic. We examine data hoarding in the chapter-closing case.

Data Governance

To address the numerous problems associated with managing data, organizations are turning to data governance. **Data governance** is an approach to managing information across an entire organization. It involves a formal set of business processes and policies that are designed to ensure that data are handled in a certain, well-defined fashion. That is, the organization follows unambiguous rules for creating, collecting, handling, and protecting its information. The objective is to make information available, transparent, and useful for the people who are authorized to access it, from the moment it enters an organization until it is outdated and deleted.

One strategy for implementing data governance is master data management. **Master data management** is a process that spans all organizational business processes and applications. It provides companies with the ability to store, maintain, exchange, and synchronize a consistent, accurate, and timely "single version of the truth" for the company's master data.

Master data are a set of core data, such as customer, product, employee, vendor, geographic location, and so on, that span the enterprise information systems. It is important to distinguish between master data and transaction data. *Transaction data*, which are generated and captured by operational systems, describe the business's activities, or transactions. In contrast, master data are applied to multiple transactions and are used to categorize, aggregate, and evaluate the transaction data.

Let's look at an example of a transaction: You (Mary Jones) purchase one Samsung 42-inch plasma television, part number 1234, from Bill Roberts at Best Buy, for $2,000, on April 20, 2013. In this example, the master data are "product sold," "vendor," "salesperson," "store," "part number," "purchase price," and "date." When specific values are applied to the master data, then a transaction is represented. Therefore, transaction data would be, respectively, "42-inch plasma television," "Samsung," "Best Buy," "Bill Roberts," "1234," "$2,000," and "April 20, 2013."

An example of master data management is Dallas, Texas, which implemented a plan for digitizing the city's public and private records, such as paper documents, images, drawings, and video and audio content. The master database can be utilized by any of the 38 government departments that have appropriate access. The city is also integrating its financial and billing processes with its customer relationship management program. (You will learn about customer relationship management in Chapter 11.)

How will Dallas utilize this system? Imagine that the city experiences a water-main break. Before it implemented the system, repair crews had to search City Hall for records that were filed haphazardly. Once the workers found the hard-copy blueprints, they would take them to the site and, after examining them manually, would decide on a plan of action. In contrast, the new system delivers the blueprints wirelessly to the laptops of crews in the field, who can magnify or highlight areas of concern to generate a rapid response. This process reduces the time it takes to respond to an emergency by several hours.

Along with data governance, organizations use the database approach to efficiently and effectively manage their data. We discuss the database approach in the Section 5.3.

before you go on...

1. What are some of the difficulties involved in managing data?

2. Define *data governance*, *master data*, and *transactional data*.

5.2 Big Data

We are accumulating data and information at an increasingly rapid pace from such diverse sources as company documents, e-mails, Web pages, credit card swipes, phone messages, stock trades, memos, address books, and radiology scans. New sources of data and information include blogs, podcasts, videocasts (think of YouTube), digital video surveillance, and RFID tags and other wireless sensors (discussed in Chapter 8). In fact, organizations are capturing data about almost all events—including events that, in the past, firms never used to think of as data at all, such as a person's location, the vibrations and temperature of an engine, or the stress at numerous points on a bridge—and then analyzing those data.

Organizations and individuals must process an unimaginably vast amount of data that is growing ever more rapidly. According to IDC (a technology research firm), the world generates exabytes of data each year (an exabyte is one trillion terabytes). Furthermore, the amount of data produced worldwide is increasing by 50 percent each year. As we discussed at the beginning of the chapter, we refer to the superabundance of data available today as Big Data. (We capitalize *Big Data* to distinguish the term from large amounts of traditional data.) We are awash in data that we have to make sense of and manage. To deal with the growth and the diverse nature of digital data, organizations must employ sophisticated techniques for data management.

At its core, Big Data is about predictions. Predictions do not come from "teaching" computers to "think" like humans. Instead, predictions come from applying mathematics to huge quantities of data to infer probabilities. Consider these examples:

- The likelihood that an e-mail message is spam;
- The likelihood that the typed letters "teh" are supposed to be "the";
- The likelihood that the trajectory and velocity of a person jaywalking indicates that he will make it across the street in time—meaning that a self-driving car need only slow down slightly.

Big Data systems perform well because they contain huge amounts of data on which to base their predictions. Moreover, they are configured to improve themselves over time by searching for the most valuable signals and patterns as more data are input.

Defining Big Data

It is difficult to define Big Data. Here we present two descriptions of the phenomenon. First, the technology research firm Gartner (www.gartner.com) defines **Big Data** as diverse, high-volume, high-velocity information assets that require new forms of processing to enable enhanced decision making, insight discovery, and process optimization. Second, the Big Data Institute (TBDI; www.the-bigdatainstitute.com) defines Big Data as vast data sets that:

- Exhibit variety;
- Include structured, unstructured, and semi-structured data;
- Are generated at high velocity with an uncertain pattern;
- Do not fit neatly into traditional, structured, relational databases (discussed later in this chapter); and

- Can be captured, processed, transformed, and analyzed in a reasonable amount of time only by sophisticated information systems.

Big Data generally consists of the following. Keep in mind that this list is not inclusive. It will expand as new sources of data emerge.

- Traditional enterprise data—examples are customer information from customer relationship management systems, transactional enterprise resource planning data, Web store transactions, operations data, and general ledger data.
- Machine-generated/sensor data—examples are smart meters; manufacturing sensors; sensors integrated into smartphones, automobiles, airplane engines, and industrial machines; equipment logs; and trading systems data.
- Social data—examples are customer feedback comments; microblogging sites such as Twitter; and social media sites such as Facebook, YouTube, and LinkedIn.
- Images captured by billions of devices located throughout the world, from digital cameras and camera phones to medical scanners and security cameras.

Let's take a look at a few specific examples of Big Data:

- When the Sloan Digital Sky Survey in New Mexico was launched in 2000, its telescope collected more data in its first few weeks than had been amassed in the entire history of astronomy. By 2013, the survey's archive contained hundreds of terabytes of data. However, the Large Synoptic Survey Telescope in Chile, due to come online in 2016, will collect that quantity of data every five days.
- In 2013 Google was processing more than 24 petabytes of data every day.
- Facebook members upload more than 10 million new photos every hour. In addition, they click a "like" button or leave a comment nearly 3 billion times every day.
- The 800 million monthly users of Google's YouTube service upload more than an hour of video every second.
- The number of messages on Twitter grows at 200 percent every year. By mid-2013 the volume exceeded 450 million tweets per day.
- As recently as the year 2000, only 25 percent of the stored information in the world was digital. The other 75 percent was analog; that is, it was stored on paper, film, vinyl records, and the like. By 2013, the amount of stored information in the world was estimated to be around 1,200 exabytes, of which less than 2 percent was non-digital.

Characteristics of Big Data

Big Data has three distinct characteristics: volume, velocity, and variety. These characteristics distinguish Big Data from traditional data.

- *Volume:* We have noted the incredible volume of Big Data in this chapter. Although the sheer volume of Big Data presents data management problems, this volume also makes Big Data incredibly valuable. Irrespective of their source, structure, format, and frequency, data are always valuable. If certain types of data appear to have no value today, it is because we have not yet been able to analyze them effectively. For example, several years ago when Google began harnessing satellite imagery, capturing street views, and then sharing these geographical data for free, few people understood its value. Today, we recognize that such data are incredibly useful (e.g., consider the myriad of uses for Google Maps).

   Consider machine-generated data, which are generated in much larger quantities than nontraditional data. For instance, sensors in a single jet engine can generate 10 terabytes of data in 30 minutes. With more than 25,000 airline flights per day, the daily volume of data from just this single source is incredible. Smart electrical meters, sensors in heavy industrial equipment, and telemetry from automobiles increase the volume of Big Data.

- *Velocity:* The rate at which data flow into an organization is rapidly increasing. Velocity is critical because it increases the speed of the feedback loop between a company and its customers. For example, the Internet and mobile technology enable online retailers to compile histories not only on final sales, but on their customers' every click and interaction. Companies that can quickly utilize that information—for example, by recommending additional purchases—gain competitive advantage.

- *Variety:* Traditional data formats tend to be structured, relatively well described, and they change slowly. Traditional data include financial market data, point-of-sale transactions, and much more. In contrast, Big Data formats change rapidly. They include satellite imagery, broadcast audio streams, digital music files, Web page content, scans of government documents, and comments posted on social networks.

Managing Big Data

Big Data makes it possible to do many things that were previously impossible; for example, spot business trends more rapidly and accurately, prevent disease, track crime, and so on. When properly analyzed, Big Data can reveal valuable patterns and information that were previously hidden because of the amount of work required to discover them. Leading corporations, such as Walmart and Google, have been able to process Big Data for years, but only at great expense. Today's hardware, cloud computing (see Technology Guide 3), and open- source software make processing Big Data affordable for most organizations.

The first step for many organizations toward managing Big Data was to integrate information silos into a database environment and then to develop data warehouses for decision making. After completing this step, many organizations turned their attention to the business of information management—making sense of their proliferating data. In recent years, Oracle, IBM, Microsoft, and SAP have spent billions of dollars purchasing software firms that specialize in data management and business intelligence. (You will learn about business intelligence in Chapter 12.)

In addition, many organizations are turning to NoSQL databases (think of them as "not only SQL" databases) to process Big Data. These databases provide an alternative for firms that have more and different kinds of data (Big Data) in addition to the traditional, structured data that fit neatly into the rows and columns of relational databases.

As you will see later in this chapter, traditional relational databases such as Oracle and MySQL store data in tables organized into rows and columns. Each row is associated with a unique record, for instance a customer account, and each column is associated with a field that defines an attribute of that account (e.g., customer name, customer identification number, customer address, etc.).

In contrast, **NoSQL databases** can manipulate structured as well as unstructured data and inconsistent or missing data. For this reason, NoSQL databases are particularly useful when working with Big Data. Many products utilize NoSQL databases, including Cassandra (http://cassandra.apache.org), CouchDB (http://couchdb.apache.org), MongoDB (www.mongodb.org), and Hadoop (http://hadoop.apache.org). The following example focuses on MongoDB, a leading NoSQL database vendor.

Example

Pay-Television Provider Uses MongoDB

As consumers watch increasing amounts of video online, pay-TV providers have had to adapt. Many providers have pursued "TV Everywhere" strategies that enable their customers to watch content on devices other than their televisions. A few providers have pursued standalone Internet-based video services to compete directly with Netflix and other streaming-video providers.

One major pay-TV provider launched an online video site that offers its users the option of subscribing on a monthly basis or ordering movies a la carte. Users can choose from a catalog containing more than 1,500 films and pause, rewind, or fast-forward programs easily. They can also mark films for future viewing and automatically receive recommendations for other films they might like.

This provider chose MongoDB for its database management system because of the system's flexibility and scalability. The company needed a system that could support 70,000 concurrent users during peak hours, many of whom constantly access the database to search for, browse, rewind, pause, and fast-forward films. The database also stores data indicating where viewers pause a film so they can return to the content later.

The ease of adding new fields to records in MongoDB permits developers to rapidly incorporate new metadata (discussed later in this chapter) to classify films in a variety of ways, in addition to traditional tags such as actor, director, and genre. Over time, the recommendation engine becomes smarter as it leverages a growing base of content, metadata, and information about user behavior.

Sources: Compiled from "Agility in the Age of Apps," *10gen White Paper*, February, 2013; S. Taparia, "5 Ways Big Data Will Change Lives in 2013," *Forbes*, January 9, 2013; D. Merriman, "Seven Best Practices for Revolutionizing Your Data," *Forbes*, June 6, 2012; www.mongodb.org, accessed April 16, 2013.

Leveraging Big Data

Organizations must do more than simply manage Big Data; they must also gain value from it. In general, there are six broadly applicable ways to leverage Big Data to gain value.

Creating Transparency. Simply making Big Data easier for relevant stakeholders to access in a timely manner can create tremendous business value. In the public sector, for example, making relevant data more readily accessible across otherwise separate departments can sharply reduce search and processing times. In manufacturing, integrating data from R&D, engineering, and manufacturing units to enable concurrent engineering can significantly reduce time to market and improve quality.

Enabling Experimentation. Experimentation allows organizations to discover needs and improve performance. As organizations create and store more data in digital form, they can collect more accurate and detailed performance data (in real or near-real time) on everything from product inventories to personnel sick days. IT enables organizations to set up controlled experiments.

For example, Amazon constantly experiments by offering slightly different "looks" on its Web site. These experiments are called A/B experiments, because each experiment has only two possible outcomes. Here is how the experiment works: Hundreds of thousands of people who click on Amazon.com will see one version of the Web site, and hundreds of thousands of others will see the other version. One experiment might change the location of the "Buy" button on the Web page. Another might change the size of a particular font on the Web page. (Amazon conducts literally hundreds of A/B experiments when evaluating its Web page.) Amazon captures data on an assortment of variables from all of the clicks, including which pages users visited, the time they spent on each page, and whether the click led to a purchase. It then analyzes all of these data to "tweak" its Web site to provide the optimal user experience.

Segmenting Population to Customize Actions. Big Data allows organizations to create narrowly defined customer segmentations and to tailor products and services to precisely meet customer needs. For example, companies are able to perform micro-segmentation of customers in real time to precisely target promotions and advertising. Suppose, for instance, that a company knows you are in one of its stores, considering a particular product. (They can obtain this information from your smartphone, from in-store cameras, and from facial recognition software.) They can send a coupon directly to your phone offering 10 percent off if you buy the product within the next five minutes.

Replacing/Supporting Human Decision Making with Automated Algorithms. Sophisticated analytics can substantially improve decision making, minimize risks, and unearth valuable insights. For example, tax agencies use automated risk-analysis software tools to identify tax returns that warrant for further examination, and retailers can use algorithms to fine-tune inventories and pricing in response to real-time in-store and online sales.

Innovating New Business Models, Products, and Services. Big Data enables companies to create new products and services, enhance existing ones, and invent entirely new business models. For example, manufacturers utilize data obtained from the use of actual products to improve the development of the next generation of products and to create innovative after-sales service offerings. The emergence of real-time location data has created an entirely new set of location-based services ranging from navigation to pricing property and casualty insurance based on where, and how, people drive their cars.

Organizations Can Analyze Far More Data. In some cases, organizations can even process all the data relating to a particular phenomenon, meaning that they do not have to rely as much on sampling. Random sampling works well, but it is not as effective as analyzing an entire dataset. In addition, random sampling has some basic weaknesses. To begin with, its accuracy depends on ensuring randomness when collecting the sample data. However, achieving such randomness is tricky. Systematic biases in the process of data collection can cause the results to be highly inaccurate. For example, consider political polling using landline phones. This sample tends to exclude people who use only cell phones. This bias can seriously skew the results, because cell phone users are typically younger and more liberal than people who rely primarily on landline phones.

before you go on...

1. Define Big Data.
2. Describe the characteristics of Big Data.
3. Describe how companies can use Big Data to gain competitive advantage.

5.3 The Database Approach

From the time that businesses first adopted computer applications (mid-1950s) until the early 1970s, organizations managed their data in a *file management environment*. This environment evolved because organizations typically automated their functions one application at a time. Therefore, the various automated systems developed independently from one another, without any overall planning. Each application required its own data, which were organized in a data file.

A **data file** is a collection of logically related records. In a file management environment, each application has a specific data file related to it. This file contains all of the data records the application requires. Over time, organizations developed numerous applications, each with an associated, application-specific data file.

For example, you can relate to a situation where most of your information is stored in your university's central database, but a club to which you belong has its own files, the athletics department has separate files for student athletes, and your instructors maintain grade data on their personal computers. It is easy for your name to be misspelled in one of these databases or files but not in others. Similarly, if you move, then your address might be updated correctly in one database or file but not in others.

Using databases eliminates many problems that arose from previous methods of storing and accessing data, such as file management systems. Databases are arranged so that one set of software programs—the database management system—provides all users with access to all of the data. (You will study database management systems later in this chapter.) This system minimizes the following problems:

- *Data redundancy*: The same data are stored in multiple locations.
- *Data isolation*: Applications cannot access data associated with other applications.
- *Data inconsistency*: Various copies of the data do not agree.

In addition, database systems maximize the following:

- *Data security*: Because data are "put in one place" in databases, there is a risk of losing a lot of data at once. Therefore, databases have extremely high security measures in place to minimize mistakes and deter attacks.

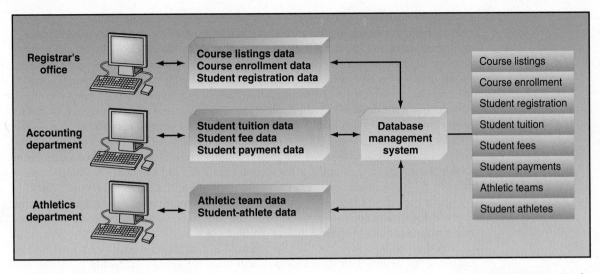

FIGURE 5.1 Database management system.

- *Data integrity*: Data meet certain constraints; for example, there are no alphabetic characters in a Social Security number field.
- *Data independence*: Applications and data are independent of one another; that is, applications and data are not linked to each other, so all applications are able to access the same data.

Figure 5.1 illustrates a university database. Note that university applications from the registrar's office, the accounting department, and the athletics department access data through the database management system.

A database can contain vast amounts of data. To make these data more understandable and useful, they are arranged in a hierarchy. In the next section, you will become familiar with the data hierarchy. You will then see how databases are designed.

The Data Hierarchy

Data are organized in a hierarchy that begins with bits and proceeds all the way to databases (see Figure 5.2). A **bit** (*bi*nary dig*it*) represents the smallest unit of data a computer can process. The term *binary* means that a bit can consist only of a 0 or a 1. A group of eight bits, called a **byte**, represents a single character. A byte can be a letter, a number, or a symbol. A logical

FIGURE 5.2 Hierarchy of data for a computer-based file.

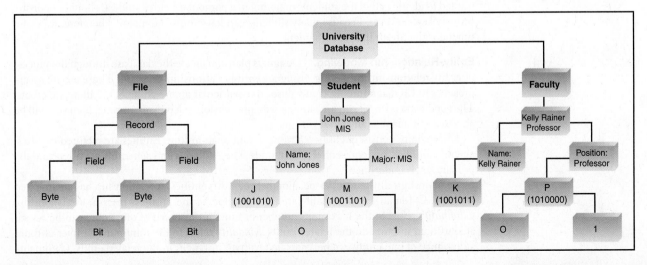

grouping of characters into a word, a small group of words, or an identification number is called a **field**. For example, a student's name in a university's computer files would appear in the "name" field, and her or his Social Security number would appear in the "Social Security number" field. Fields can also contain data other than text and numbers. They can contain an image, or any other type of multimedia. Examples are a motor vehicle department's licensing database that contains a driver's photograph and a field that contains a voice sample to authorize access to a secure facility. In the Apple iTunes Store, a song is a field in a record, with other fields containing the song's title, its price, and the album on which it appears.

A logical grouping of related fields, such as the student's name, the courses taken, the date, and the grade, comprises a **record**. A logical grouping of related records is called a **data file** or a **table**. For example, a grouping of the records from a particular course, consisting of course number, professor, and students' grades, would constitute a data file for that course. Continuing up the hierarchy, a logical grouping of related files constitutes a *database*. Using the same example, the student course file could be grouped with files on students' personal histories and financial backgrounds to create a student database.

Now that you have seen how data are arranged in a database, you will learn how modern organizations design their databases. You will focus on entity-relationship modeling and normalization procedures.

Designing the Database

To be valuable, a database must be organized so that users can retrieve, analyze, and understand the data they need. A key to designing an effective database is the data model. A **data model** is a diagram that represents entities in the database and their relationships. An **entity** is a person, place, thing, or event—such as a customer, an employee, or a product—about which information is maintained. Entities can typically be identified in the user's work environment. A record generally describes an entity. An **instance** of an entity is a specific, unique representation of the entity. For example, an instance of the entity STUDENT would be a particular student.

Each characteristic or quality of a particular entity is called an **attribute**. For example, if our entities were a customer, an employee, and a product, entity attributes would include customer name, employee number, and product color.

Every record in a file must contain at least one field that uniquely identifies that record so that it can be retrieved, updated, and sorted. This identifier field is called the **primary key**. For example, a student record in a U.S. university would use a unique student number as its primary key. (Note: In the past, your Social Security number served as the primary key for your student record. However, for security reasons, this practice has been discontinued.) In some cases, locating a particular record requires the use of **secondary keys**. A secondary key is another field that has some identifying information but typically does not identify the record with complete accuracy. For example, the student's major might be a secondary key if a user wanted to identify all of the students majoring in a particular field of study. It should not be the primary key, however, because many students can have the same major. Therefore, it cannot uniquely identify an individual student.

Entity-Relationship Modeling. Designers plan and create the database through the process of **entity-relationship modeling**, using an **entity-relationship diagram**. There are many approaches to ER diagramming. You will see one particular approach here, but there are others. The good news is that if you are familiar with one version of ER diagramming, then you will be able to easily adapt to any other version.

ER diagrams consist of entities, attributes, and relationships. Entities are pictured in boxes, and relationships are represented as diamonds. The attributes for each entity are listed, and the primary key is underlined.

Relationships illustrate an association between two entities. A relationship has a name that is a verb. Cardinality and modality are the indicators of the business rules in a relationship. *Cardinality* refers to the maximum number of times an instance of one entity can be associated with an instance in the related entity. *Modality* refers to the minimum number of times an instance of one entity can be associated with an instances in the related entity. Cardinality can be 1 or Many, and its symbol is placed on the outside of the relationship line, closest to the entity. Modality can be 1 or 0, and its symbol is placed on the inside of the relationship line, next to the cardinality symbol. Figure 5.3 displays the cardinality and modality symbols. Figure 5.4 depicts an ER diagram.

As defined earlier, an **entity** is a person, place, or thing that can be identified in the users' work environment. For example, consider student registration at a university. Students register for courses, and they also register their cars for parking permits. In this example, STUDENT, PARKING PERMIT, CLASS, and PROFESSOR are entities, as illustrated in Figure 5.4.

Entities of a given type are grouped in *entity classes*. In our example, STUDENT, PARKING PERMIT, CLASS, and PROFESSOR are entity classes. An instance of an entity class is the representation of a particular entity. Therefore, a particular STUDENT (James Smythe, 145-89-7123) is an instance of the STUDENT entity class; a particular parking permit (91778) is an instance of the PARKING PERMIT entity class; a particular class (76890) is an instance of the CLASS entity class; and a particular professor (Margaret Wilson, 115-65-7632) is an instance of the PROFESSOR entity class.

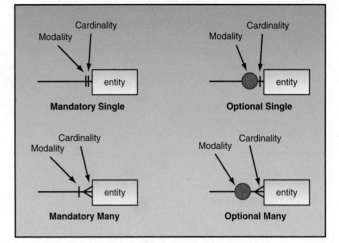

FIGURE 5.3 Cardinality and modality symbols.

Entity instances have **identifiers**, which are attributes (attributes and identifiers are synonymous) that are unique to that entity instance. For example, STUDENT instances can be identified with Student Identification Number; PARKING PERMIT instances can be identified with Permit Number; CLASS instances can be identified with Class Number; and PROFESSOR instances can be identified with Professor Identification Number. These identifiers (or primary keys) are underlined on ER diagrams, as in Part b of Figure 5.4.

Entities have **attributes**, or properties, that describe the entity's characteristics. In our example, examples of attributes for STUDENT are Student Name and Student Address. Examples of attributes for PARKING PERMIT are Student Identification Number and Car Type. Examples of attributes for CLASS are Class Name, Class Time, and Class Place. Examples of attributes for PROFESSOR are Professor Name and Professor Department. (Note that each course at this university has one professor—no team teaching.)

Why is Student Identification Number an attribute of both the STUDENT and PARKING PERMIT entity classes? That is, why do we need the PARKING PERMIT entity class? If you consider all of the interlinked university systems, the PARKING PERMIT entity class is needed for other applications, such as fee payments, parking tickets, and external links to the state Department of Motor Vehicles.

Entities are associated with one another in relationships, which can include many entities. (Remember that relationships are represented by diamonds on ER diagrams.) The number of entities in a relationship is the degree of the relationship. Relationships between two items are called *binary relationships*. There are three types of binary relationships: one-to-one, one-to-many, and many-to-many.

In a *one-to-one* (1:1) relationship, a single-entity instance of one type is related to a single-entity instance of another type. Figure 5.4a labels STUDENT–PARKING PERMIT as a 1:1 relationship. The relationship means that a student can have a parking permit but does not need to have one. (Clearly, if a student does not have a car, then he or she will not need a parking permit.) Note that the relationship line on the PARKING PERMIT side shows zero or one—that is, a cardinality of 1, and a modality of 0. On the STUDENT side of the relationship, only one parking permit can be assigned to one student. Note that the relationship line on the STUDENT side shows one and only one—that is, a cardinality of 1 and a modality of 1.

The second type of relationship, *one-to-many* (1:M), is represented by the CLASS–PROFESSOR relationship in Figure 5.4a. This relationship means that a professor can have

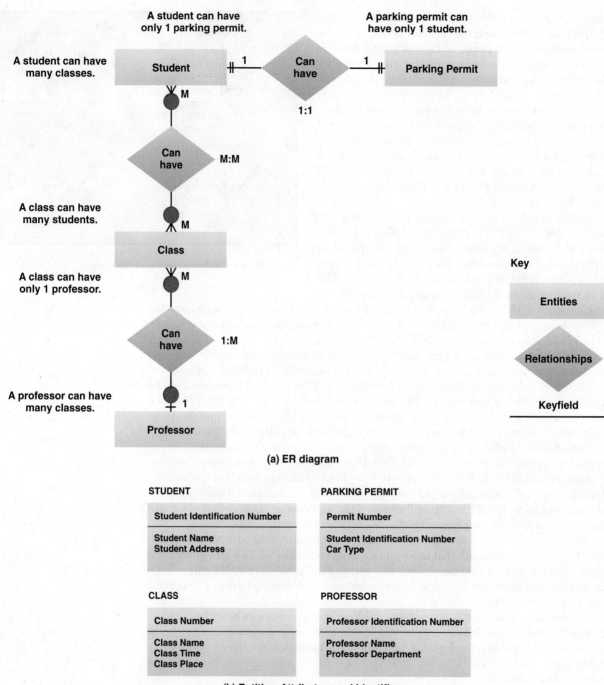

FIGURE 5.4 Entity-relationship diagram model.

one or more courses, but each course can have only one professor. Note that the relationship line on the PROFESSOR side shows one and only one—that is, a cardinality of 1 and a modality of 1. In contrast, the relationship line on the CLASS side shows one or many—that is, a cardinality of Many and a modality of 1.

The third type of relationship, *many-to-many* (M:M), is represented by the STUDENT–CLASS relationship in Figure 5.4a. This M:M relationship indicates that a student can have one or more courses, and a course can have one or more students. Note that the relationship line on the STUDENT side shows one or more—that is, a cardinality of Many and a modality of 1.

Further, the relationship line of the CLASS side also shows one or more—that is, a cardinality of Many and a modality of 1.

ER modeling is valuable because it allows database designers to communicate with users throughout the organization to ensure that all entities and the relationships among the entities are represented. This process underscores the importance of taking all users into account when designing organizational databases. Notice that all entities and relationships in our example are labeled in terms that users can understand. Now that you understand how a database is designed, you can turn your attention to database management systems.

before you go on...

1. What is a data model?

2. What is a primary key? A secondary key?

3. What is an entity? An attribute?

Database Management Systems

5.4

A **database management system (DBMS)** is a set of programs that provide users with tools to add, delete, access, modify, and analyze data stored in a single location. An organization can access the data by using query and reporting tools that are part of the DBMS or by using application programs specifically written to perform this function. DBMSs also provide the mechanisms for maintaining the integrity of stored data, managing security and user access, and recovering information if the system fails. Because databases and DBMSs are essential to all areas of business, they must be carefully managed.

There are a number of different database architectures, but we focus on the relational database model because it is popular and easy to use. Other database models (e.g., the hierarchical and network models) are the responsibility of the MIS function and are not used by organizational employees. Popular examples of relational databases are Microsoft Access and Oracle.

The Relational Database Model

Most business data—especially accounting and financial data—traditionally were organized into simple tables consisting of columns and rows. Tables allow people to compare information quickly by row or column. In addition, users can retrieve items rather easily by locating the point of intersection of a particular row and column.

The **relational database model** is based on the concept of two-dimensional tables. A relational database generally is not one big table—usually called a *flat file*—that contains all of the records and attributes. Such a design would entail far too much data redundancy. Instead, a relational database is usually designed with a number of related tables. Each of these tables contains records (listed in rows) and attributes (listed in columns).

These related tables can be joined when they contain common columns. The uniqueness of the primary key tells the DBMS which records are joined with others in related tables. This feature allows users great flexibility in the variety of queries they can make. Despite these features, however, the relational database model has some disadvantages. Because large-scale databases can be composed of many interrelated tables, the overall design can be complex, leading to slow search and access times.

Consider the relational database example about students diagrammed in Figure 5.5. The table contains data about the entity called students. Attributes of the entity are student name, undergraduate major, grade point average, and graduation date. The rows are the records on Sally Adams, John Jones, Jane Lee, Kevin Durham, Juan Rodriguez, Stella Zubnicki,

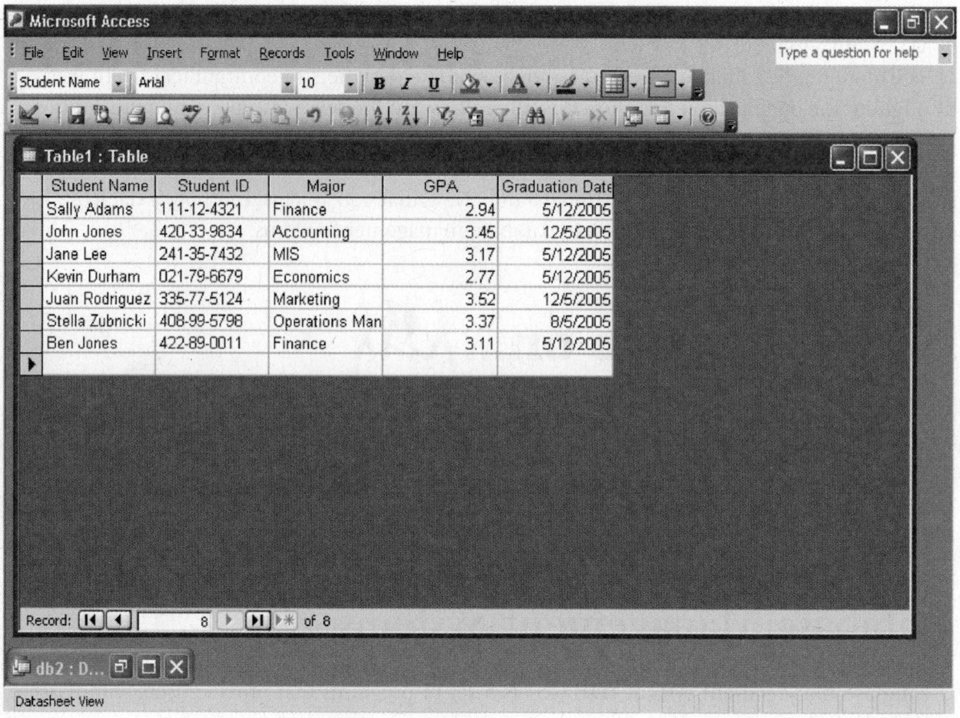

Student Name	Student ID	Major	GPA	Graduation Date
Sally Adams	111-12-4321	Finance	2.94	5/12/2005
John Jones	420-33-9834	Accounting	3.45	12/5/2005
Jane Lee	241-35-7432	MIS	3.17	5/12/2005
Kevin Durham	021-79-6679	Economics	2.77	5/12/2005
Juan Rodriguez	335-77-5124	Marketing	3.52	12/5/2005
Stella Zubnicki	408-99-5798	Operations Man	3.37	8/5/2005
Ben Jones	422-89-0011	Finance	3.11	5/12/2005

FIGURE 5.5 Student database example.

and Ben Jones. Of course, your university keeps much more data on you than our example shows. In fact, your university's student database probably keeps hundreds of attributes on each student.

Query Languages. The most commonly performed database operation is requesting information. **Structured query language (SQL)** is the most popular query language used for this operation. SQL allows people to perform complicated searches by using relatively simple statements or key words. Typical key words are SELECT (to specify a desired attribute), FROM (to specify the table to be used), and WHERE (to specify conditions to apply in the query).

To understand how SQL works, imagine that a university wants to know the names of students who will graduate cum laude (but not magna or summa cum laude) in May 2014. The university IS staff would query the student relational database with an SQL statement such as SELECT Student Name, FROM Student Database, WHERE Grade Point Average >= 3.40 and Grade Point Average <= 3.60. The SQL query would return John Jones and Juan Rodriguez.

Another way to find information in a database is to use *query by example* (*QBE*). In QBE, the user fills out a grid or template—also known as a *form*—to construct a sample or a description of the data desired. Users can construct a query quickly and easily by using drag-and-drop features in a DBMS such as Microsoft Access. Conducting queries in this manner is simpler than keying in SQL commands.

Data Dictionary. When a relational model is created, the **data dictionary** defines the required format for entering the data into the database. The data dictionary provides information on each attribute, such as its name, whether it is a key or part of a key, the type of data expected (alphanumeric, numeric, dates, and so on), and valid values. Data dictionaries can also provide information on why the attribute is needed in the database; which business functions, applications, forms, and reports use the attribute; and how often the attribute should be updated.

Data dictionaries benefit organizations in many ways. Because they provide names and standard definitions for all attributes, they reduce the chances that the same attribute will be used in different applications but with a different name. In addition, data dictionaries

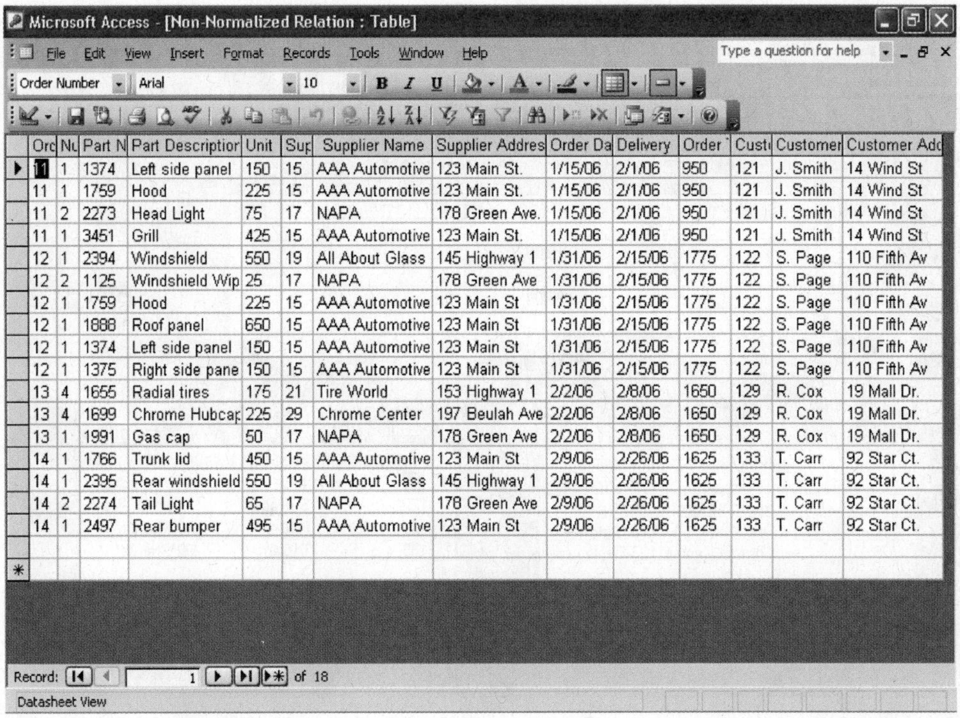

Orc	Nu	Part N	Part Descriptior	Unit	Sup	Supplier Name	Supplier Addres	Order Da	Delivery	Order	Custi	Customer	Customer Adc
11	1	1374	Left side panel	150	15	AAA Automotive	123 Main St.	1/15/06	2/1/06	950	121	J. Smith	14 Wind St
11	1	1759	Hood	225	15	AAA Automotive	123 Main St.	1/15/06	2/1/06	950	121	J. Smith	14 Wind St
11	2	2273	Head Light	75	17	NAPA	178 Green Ave.	1/15/06	2/1/06	950	121	J. Smith	14 Wind St
11	1	3451	Grill	425	15	AAA Automotive	123 Main St.	1/15/06	2/1/06	950	121	J. Smith	14 Wind St
12	1	2394	Windshield	550	19	All About Glass	145 Highway 1	1/31/06	2/15/06	1775	122	S. Page	110 Fifth Av
12	2	1125	Windshield Wip	25	17	NAPA	178 Green Ave	1/31/06	2/15/06	1775	122	S. Page	110 Fifth Av
12	1	1759	Hood	225	15	AAA Automotive	123 Main St	1/31/06	2/15/06	1775	122	S. Page	110 Fifth Av
12	1	1888	Roof panel	650	15	AAA Automotive	123 Main St	1/31/06	2/15/06	1775	122	S. Page	110 Fifth Av
12	1	1374	Left side panel	150	15	AAA Automotive	123 Main St	1/31/06	2/15/06	1775	122	S. Page	110 Fifth Av
12	1	1375	Right side pane	150	15	AAA Automotive	123 Main St	1/31/06	2/15/06	1775	122	S. Page	110 Fifth Av
13	4	1655	Radial tires	175	21	Tire World	153 Highway 1	2/2/06	2/8/06	1650	129	R. Cox	19 Mall Dr.
13	4	1699	Chrome Hubcap	225	29	Chrome Center	197 Beulah Ave	2/2/06	2/8/06	1650	129	R. Cox	19 Mall Dr.
13	1	1991	Gas cap	50	17	NAPA	178 Green Ave	2/2/06	2/8/06	1650	129	R. Cox	19 Mall Dr.
14	1	1766	Trunk lid	450	15	AAA Automotive	123 Main St	2/9/06	2/26/06	1625	133	T. Carr	92 Star Ct.
14	1	2395	Rear windshield	550	19	All About Glass	145 Highway 1	2/9/06	2/26/06	1625	133	T. Carr	92 Star Ct.
14	2	2274	Tail Light	65	17	NAPA	178 Green Ave	2/9/06	2/26/06	1625	133	T. Carr	92 Star Ct.
14	1	2497	Rear bumper	495	15	AAA Automotive	123 Main St	2/9/06	2/26/06	1625	133	T. Carr	92 Star Ct.

FIGURE 5.6 Nonnormalized relation.

supply organizations with an inventory of their data resources, enabling them to manage these resources more effectively.

Normalization. To use a relational database management system productively, the data must be analyzed to eliminate redundant data elements. **Normalization** is a method for analyzing and reducing a relational database to its most streamlined form to ensure minimum redundancy, maximum data integrity, and optimal processing performance. When data are *normalized*, attributes in the table depend only on the primary key.

As an example of normalization, consider an automotive repair garage. This business takes orders from customers whose cars need to be repaired. In this example, ORDER, PART, SUPPLIER, and CUSTOMER are entities. There can be many PARTS in an ORDER, but each PART can come from only one SUPPLIER. In a nonnormalized relation called ORDER (see Figure 5.6), each ORDER would have to repeat the name, description, and price of each PART needed to complete the ORDER, as well as the name and address of each SUPPLIER. This relation contains repeating groups and describes multiple entities.

For example, consider the table in Figure 5.6, and notice the very first column (labeled Order). This column contains multiple entries for each order—four rows for Order 11, six rows for Order 12, and so on. These multiple rows for an order are called *repeating groups*. The table in Figure 5.6 also contains multiple entities: ORDER, PART, SUPPLIER, and CUSTOMER. When you normalize the data, you want to eliminate repeating groups and have normalized tables, each containing only a single entity.

You might think that four entities would mean four normalized tables. (The ORDER, SUPPLIER, and CUSTOMER tables are shown in Figure 5.7a, and the PART table is shown in Figure 5.7b.) To fully normalize the data in this example, however, you must create an extra table, called ORDERED-PARTS. This table, presented in Figure 5.7b, contains the particular parts and how many of each part are included in a particular order.

The normalization process, illustrated in Figure 5.8, breaks down the relation, ORDER, into smaller relations: ORDER, SUPPLIER, and CUSTOMER (Figure 5.7a) and ORDERED PARTS and PART (Figure 5.7b). Each of these relations describes a single entity. This process is conceptually simpler, and it eliminates repeating groups. For example, consider an order at

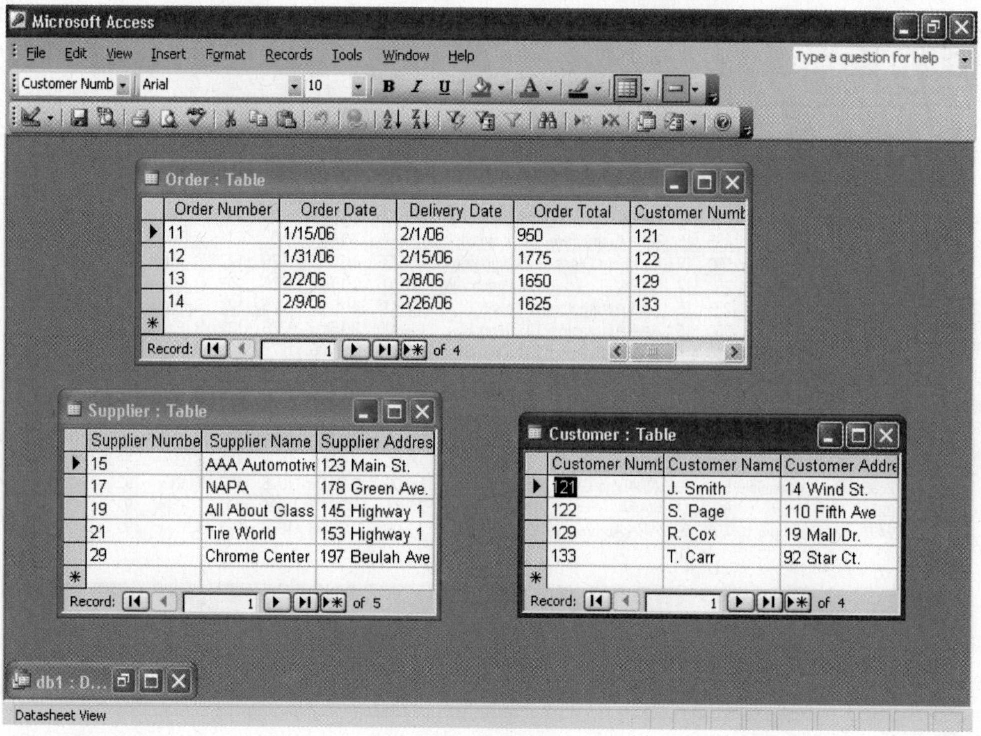

Order Number	Order Date	Delivery Date	Order Total	Customer Numb
11	1/15/06	2/1/06	950	121
12	1/31/06	2/15/06	1775	122
13	2/2/06	2/8/06	1650	129
14	2/9/06	2/26/06	1625	133

Supplier Numbe	Supplier Name	Supplier Addres
15	AAA Automotive	123 Main St.
17	NAPA	178 Green Ave.
19	All About Glass	145 Highway 1
21	Tire World	153 Highway 1
29	Chrome Center	197 Beulah Ave

Customer Numb	Customer Name	Customer Addre
121	J. Smith	14 Wind St.
122	S. Page	110 Fifth Ave
129	R. Cox	19 Mall Dr.
133	T. Carr	92 Star Ct.

(a)

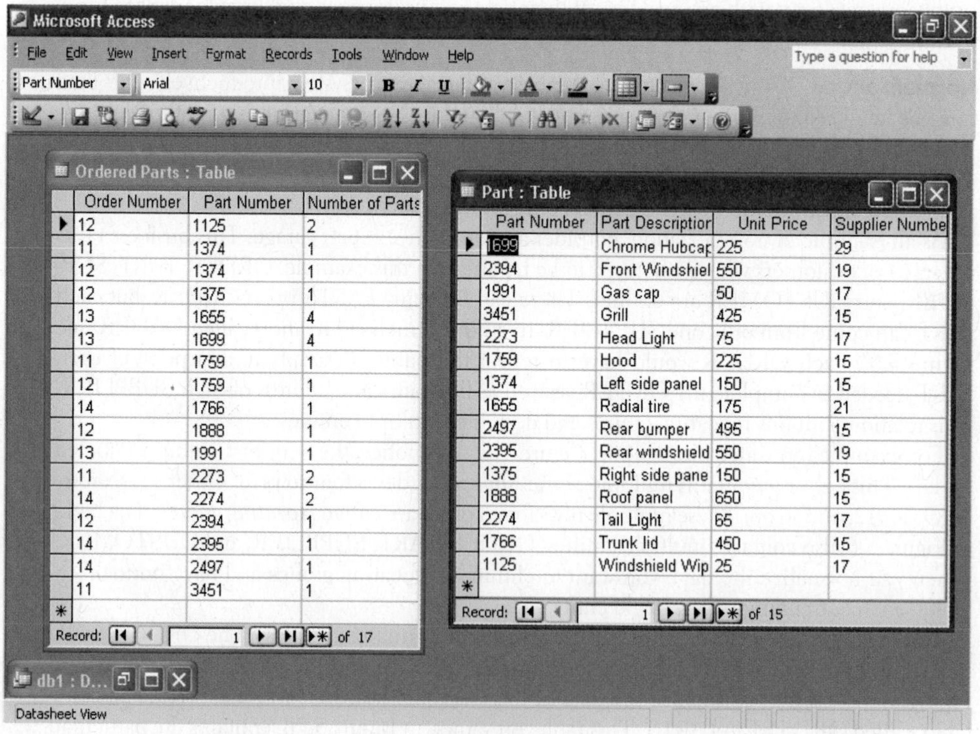

Order Number	Part Number	Number of Parts
12	1125	2
11	1374	1
12	1374	1
12	1375	1
13	1655	4
13	1699	4
11	1759	1
12	1759	1
14	1766	1
12	1888	1
13	1991	1
11	2273	2
14	2274	2
12	2394	1
14	2395	1
14	2497	1
11	3451	1

Part Number	Part Descriptior	Unit Price	Supplier Numbe
1699	Chrome Hubcap	225	29
2394	Front Windshiel	550	19
1991	Gas cap	50	17
3451	Grill	425	15
2273	Head Light	75	17
1759	Hood	225	15
1374	Left side panel	150	15
1655	Radial tire	175	21
2497	Rear bumper	495	15
2395	Rear windshield	550	19
1375	Right side pane	150	15
1888	Roof panel	650	15
2274	Tail Light	65	17
1766	Trunk lid	450	15
1125	Windshield Wip	25	17

(b)

FIGURE 5.7 Smaller relationships broken down from the nonnormal relations. (a) Order, Supplier, Customer. (b) Ordered Parts, Part.

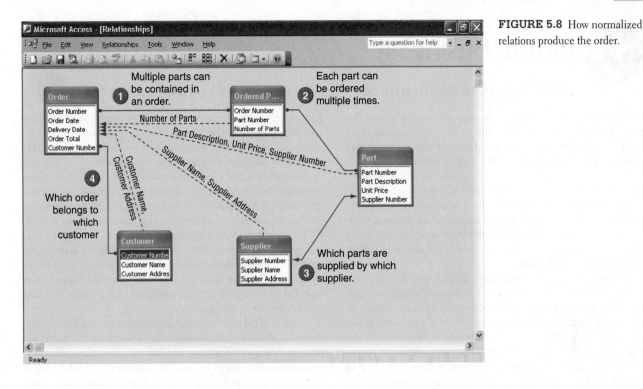

FIGURE 5.8 How normalized relations produce the order.

the automobile repair shop. The normalized relations can produce the order in the following manner (see Figure 5.8).

- The ORDER relation provides the Order Number (the primary key), Order Date, Delivery Date, Order Total, and Customer Number.
- The primary key of the ORDER relation (Order Number) provides a link to the ORDERED PARTS relation (the link numbered 1 in Figure 5.8).
- The ORDERED PARTS relation supplies the Number of Parts information to ORDER.
- The primary key of the ORDERED PARTS relation is a composite key that consists of Order Number and Part Number. Therefore, the Part Number component of the primary key provides a link to the PART relation (the link numbered 2 in Figure 5.8).
- The PART relation supplies the Part Description, Unit Price, and Supplier Number to ORDER.
- The Supplier Number in the PART relation provides a link to the SUPPLIER relation (the link numbered 3 in Figure 5.8).
- The SUPPLIER relation provides the Supplier Name and Supplier Address to ORDER.
- The Customer Number in ORDER provides a link to the CUSTOMER relation (the link numbered 4 in Figure 5.8).
- The CUSTOMER relation supplies the Customer Name and Customer Address to ORDER.

Databases in Action

It is safe to say that almost all organizations have one or more databases. Further, there are numerous interesting database applications. IT's About Business 5.3 illustrates how a database can provide the foundation for many functions within an organization.

Organizations implement databases to efficiently and effectively manage their data. However, because databases typically process data in real time (or near real time), it is not practical to allow users access to the databases. After all, the data will change while the user is looking at them! As a result, data warehouses have been developed to allow users to access data for decision making. You will learn about data warehouses in the next section.

IT's [about business]

5.3 Database Solution for the German Aerospace Center

There are hundreds of operational satellites in orbit around the earth. Each one completes an orbit of the Earth approximately every 100 minutes. The cameras and sensors that many of these satellites carry have made satellite imagery pervasive in today's society. As just one example, recreational Internet users can zoom in on houses and neighborhoods anywhere in the world.

Satellite imagery is more than simply entertainment, however. Population research, environmental studies, crisis response planning, inner-city traffic planning, military surveillance, and many other applications benefit from the "eyes in the sky" that remote sensing technology provides.

The explosive growth in the volume of photographic and digital images from satellites has become a challenge for data management and archiving. Consider the German Aerospace Center, or Deutsches Zentrum für Luft und Raumfahrt (DLR; www.dlr.de), with 7,000-plus employees at 16 locations in Germany. As the country's aerospace agency, the DLR maintains a research operation, known as the German Remote Sensing Data Center (DFD) that focuses on the Earth and on atmospheric observation for global monitoring, environmental studies, and security. In the past, the DFD attempted to manage the exponentially growing satellite data using multiple information management systems, with increasingly poor results.

The DLR was convinced that the DFD needed a single information management system designed to meet the DFD's various needs, the needs of its commercial clients, and the needs of the German nation. As a result, the DFD developed a Data and Information System (DIMS) to solve the challenge of data storage and archiving.

The system's primary goals were to store data and to manage all business workflows. Long-term preservation of satellite image data was particularly important, because the longer the data are stored, the more valuable they become. This observation is especially applicable in environmental studies, where scientists can identify changes in ice flows, coastlines, and other geological entities. In addition, the system had to address other pressing needs such as preparing and delivering orders and disseminating data to users.

The DFD team worked collaborated with a third-party software company to develop a reliable and highly scalable database that provided efficient access to multiple petabytes of archived satellite-image data. The database had to fulfill long-term preservation policies and offer a high level of availability and scalability to accommodate future exponential data growth.

In addition to the images themselves, the database contains metadata that describe the images—for example, acquisition time and location data. The metadata also include administrative information such as the internal location of the files in the archive.

The database system supports the business of the DFD, executing long-term preservation policies and retrieving and delivering Earth observation images to users of the system. When a user initiates a request for data, a digital library matches the metadata from the user request with the metadata of the image files and delivers the files to the user.

The size of the satellite image archive has grown to 2 petabytes. The value of these data is inestimable. For instance, by utilizing the pictures stored in the archive and the metadata managed by the database system, the DLR was able to respond to the March 2011 earthquake and tsunami in Japan with "before" pictures and "after" imagery taken on the morning of the earthquake. These side-by-side pictures helped local authorities to estimate the size of the disaster and to guide rescue teams on the ground.

When the DFD delivers data, it has to follow security regulations, some of which are defined by German law. For example, persons from certain geographic locations cannot receive images of certain other geographic locations, depending on the resolution of the data. DFD has to cancel delivery if the matchups are positive. The database system enables the DLR to monitor these matchups very efficiently.

The administrative requirements for the system are reasonable. The system requires less than one full-time employee's time to administer.

Sources: Compiled from E. Mittelbach, "Satellite Images for Emergencies," *DLR Magazine*, April, 2013; "The German Aerospace Center," *IBM Customer Case Study*, January 30, 2013; M. Fleischmann, "A Handful of Satellite," *DLR Magazine*, December, 2012; www.ibm.com, www.dlr.de, accessed April 15, 2013.

Questions
1. What are the main functions of the DLR database system?
2. What are the advantages of the DLR database system?

before you go on...

1. What are the advantages and disadvantages of relational databases?
2. What are the benefits of data dictionaries?
3. Describe how structured query language works.

Data Warehouses and Data Marts

Today, the most successful companies are those that can respond quickly and flexibly to market changes and opportunities. A key to this response is the effective and efficient use of data and information by analysts and managers. The problem is providing users with access to corporate data so that they can analyze the data to make better decisions. Let's look at an example. If the manager of a local bookstore wanted to know the profit margin on used books at her store, she could obtain that information from her database, using SQL or QBE. However, if she needed to know the trend in the profit margins on used books over the past 10 years, she would have to construct a very complicated SQL or QBE query.

This example illustrates several reasons why organizations are building data warehouses and/or data marts. First, the bookstore's databases contain the necessary information to answer the manager's query, but this information is not organized in a way that makes it easy for her to find what she needs. Second, the organization's databases are designed to process millions of transactions every day. Therefore, complicated queries might take a long time to answer, and they also might degrade the performance of the databases. Third, transactional databases are designed to be updated. This update process requires extra processing. Data warehouses and data marts are read-only, and the extra processing is eliminated because data already contained in the data warehouse are not updated. Fourth, transactional databases are designed to access a single record at a time. Data warehouses are designed to access large groups of related records.

As a result of these problems, companies are using a variety of tools with data warehouses and data marts to make it easier and faster for users to access, analyze, and query data. You will learn about these tools in Chapter 12 on Business Intelligence.

Describing Data Warehouses and Data Marts

In general, data warehouses and data marts support business intelligence (BI) applications. As you will see in Chapter 12, business intelligence is a broad category of applications, technologies, and processes for gathering, storing, accessing, and analyzing data to help business users make better decisions. A **data warehouse** is a repository of historical data that are organized by subject to support decision makers in the organization.

Because data warehouses are so expensive, they are used primarily by large companies. A **data mart** is a low-cost, scaled-down version of a data warehouse that is designed for the end-user needs in a strategic business unit (SBU) or an individual department. Data marts can be implemented more quickly than data warehouses, often in less than 90 days. Further, they support local rather than central control by conferring power on the user group. Typically, groups that need a single or a few BI applications require only a data mart, rather than a data warehouse.

The basic characteristics of data warehouses and data marts include the following:

- *Organized by business dimension or subject.* Data are organized by subject—for example, by customer, vendor, product, price level, and region. This arrangement differs from transactional systems, where data are organized by business process, such as order entry, inventory control, and accounts receivable.

- *Use online analytical processing.* Typically, organizational databases are oriented toward handling transactions. That is, databases use online transaction processing (OLTP), where business transactions are processed online as soon as they occur. The objectives are speed and efficiency, which are critical to a successful Internet-based business operation. Data warehouses and data marts, which are designed to support decision makers but not OLTP, use online analytical processing. *Online analytical processing (OLAP)* involves the analysis of accumulated data by end users. We consider OLAP in greater detail in Chapter 12.

- *Integrated.* Data are collected from multiple systems and then integrated around subjects. For example, customer data may be extracted from internal (and external) systems and then integrated around a customer identifier, thereby creating a comprehensive view of the customer.

- *Time variant.* Data warehouses and data marts maintain historical data (i.e., data that include time as a variable). Unlike transactional systems, which maintain only recent data (such as for the last day, week, or month), a warehouse or mart may store years of data. Organizations utilize historical data to detect deviations, trends, and long-term relationships.
- *Nonvolatile.* Data warehouses and data marts are nonvolatile—that is, users cannot change or update the data. Therefore the warehouse or mart reflects history, which, as we just saw, is critical for identifying and analyzing trends. Warehouses and marts are updated, but through IT-controlled load processes rather than by users.
- *Multidimensional.* Typically the data warehouse or mart uses a multidimensional data structure. Recall that relational databases store data in two-dimensional tables. In contrast, data warehouses and marts store data in more than two dimensions. For this reason, the data are said to be stored in a **multidimensional structure**. A common representation for this multidimensional structure is the *data cube*.

The data in data warehouses and marts are organized by *business dimensions*, which are subjects such as product, geographic area, and time period that represent the edges of the data cube. If you look ahead briefly to Figure 5.11 for an example of a data cube, you see that the product dimension is comprised of nuts, screws, bolts, and washers; the geographic area dimension is comprised of east, west, and central; and the time period dimension is comprised of 2011, 2012, and 2013. Users can view and analyze data from the perspective of these business dimensions. This analysis is intuitive because the dimensions are presented in business terms that users can easily understand.

A Generic Data Warehouse Environment

The environment for data warehouses and marts includes the following:

- Source systems that provide data to the warehouse or mart
- Data-integration technology and processes that prepare the data for use
- Different architectures for storing data in an organization's data warehouse or data marts
- Different tools and applications for the variety of users. (You will learn about these tools and applications in Chapter 5.)
- Metadata, data-quality, and governance processes that ensure that the warehouse or mart meets its purposes

Figure 5.9 a generic data warehouse/data mart environment. Let's drill-down into the component parts.

Source Systems. There is typically some "organizational pain" (i.e., business need) that motivates a firm to develop its BI capabilities. Working backward, this pain leads to information requirements, BI applications, and source system data requirements. The data requirements can range from a single source system, as in the case of a data mart, to hundreds of source systems, as in the case of an enterprisewide data warehouse.

Modern organizations can select from a variety of source systems: operational/transactional systems, enterprise resource planning (ERP) systems, Web site data, third-party data (e.g., customer demographic data), and more. The trend is to include more types of data (e.g., sensing data from RFID tags). These source systems often use different software packages (e.g., IBM, Oracle) and store data in different formats (e.g., relational, hierarchical).

A common source for the data in data warehouses is the company's operational databases. To differentiate between relational databases and multidimensional data warehouses and marts, imagine your company manufactures four products—nuts, screws, bolts, and washers—and has sold them in three territories—East, West, and Central—for the previous three years—2011, 2012, and 2013. In a relational database, these sales data would resemble Figures 5.10a, b, and c. In a multidimensional database, in contrast, these data would be represented by a three-dimensional matrix (or data cube), as depicted in Figure 5.11. This matrix represents sales *dimensioned by* products and regions and year. Notice that Figure 5.10a presents only sales for 2011. Sales for 2012 and 2013 are presented in Figures 5.10b and 5.10c, respectively.

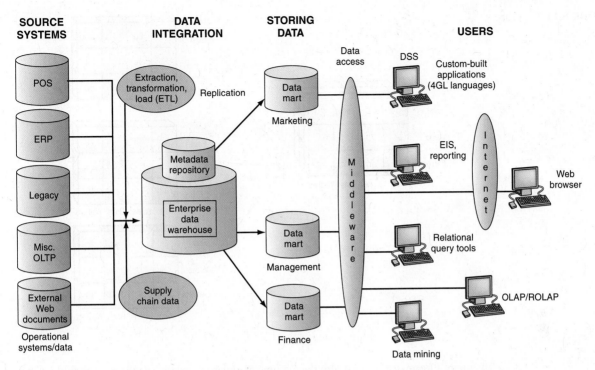

FIGURE 5.9 Data warehouse framework.

Figures 5.12a, b, and c illustrate the equivalence between these relational and multidimensional databases.

Unfortunately, many source systems that have been in use for years contain "bad data" (e.g., missing or incorrect data) and are poorly documented. As a result, data-profiling software should be used at the beginning of a warehousing project to better understand the data. For example, this software can provide statistics on missing data, identify possible primary and foreign keys, and reveal how derived values (e.g., column 3 = column 1 + column 2) are calculated. Subject area database specialists (e.g., marketing, human resources) can also assist in understanding and accessing the data in source systems.

Organizations need to address other source systems issues as well. Often there are multiple systems that contain some of the same data and the best system must be selected as the source

FIGURE 5.10 Relational databases.

(a) 2011

Product	Region	Sales
Nuts	East	50
Nuts	West	60
Nuts	Central	100
Screws	East	40
Screws	West	70
Screws	Central	80
Bolts	East	90
Bolts	West	120
Bolts	Central	140
Washers	East	20
Washers	West	10
Washers	Central	30

(b) 2012

Product	Region	Sales
Nuts	East	60
Nuts	West	70
Nuts	Central	110
Screws	East	50
Screws	West	80
Screws	Central	90
Bolts	East	100
Bolts	West	130
Bolts	Central	150
Washers	East	30
Washers	West	20
Washers	Central	40

(c) 2013

Product	Region	Sales
Nuts	East	70
Nuts	West	80
Nuts	Central	120
Screws	East	60
Screws	West	90
Screws	Central	100
Bolts	East	110
Bolts	West	140
Bolts	Central	160
Washers	East	40
Washers	West	30
Washers	Central	50

FIGURE 5.11 Data cube.

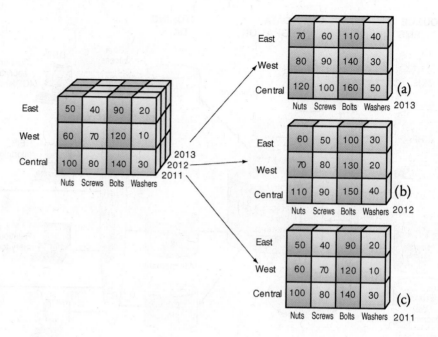

system. Organizations must also decide how granular (i.e., detailed) the data should be. For example, does the organization need daily sales figures or data at the individual transaction level? The conventional wisdom is that it is best to store data at a highly granular level because someone will likely request the data at some point.

Data Integration. In addition to storing data in their source systems, organizations need to extract the data, transform them, and then load them into a data mart or warehouse. This process is often called ETL, but the term *data integration* is increasingly being used to reflect the growing number of ways that source system data can be handled. For example, in some cases, data are extracted, loaded into a mart or warehouse, and then transformed (i.e., ELT rather than ETL).

Data extraction can be performed either by handwritten code (e.g., SQL queries) or by commercial data-integration software. Most companies employ commercial software. This software makes it relatively easy to specify the tables and attributes in the source systems that are to be used, map and schedule the movement of the data to the target (e.g., a data mart or warehouse), make the required transformations, and ultimately load the data.

After the data are extracted they are transformed to make them more useful. For example, data from different systems may be integrated around a common key, such as a customer identification number. Organizations adopt this approach to create a 360-degree view of all of their interactions with their customers. As an example of this process, consider a bank. Customers can engage in a variety of interactions: visiting a branch, banking online, using an ATM, obtaining a car loan, and more. The systems for these touchpoints—defined as the numerous ways that organizations interact with customers, such as e-mail, the Web, direct contact, and the telephone—are typically independent of one another. To obtain a holistic picture of how customers are using the bank, the bank must integrate the data from the various source systems in a data mart or warehouse.

Other kinds of transformations also take place. For example, format changes to the data may be required, such as using *male* and *female* to denote gender, as opposed to 0 and 1 or M and F. Aggregations (summaries) may be performed, say on sales figures, so that queries can use the summaries rather than recalculating them each time. Data-cleansing software may be used to "clean up" the data; for example, eliminating duplicate records for the same customer.

Finally, data are loaded into the warehouse or mart during a specific period known as the "load window." This window is becoming smaller as companies seek to store ever-fresher data

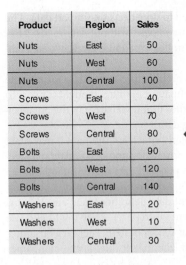

Product	Region	Sales
Nuts	East	50
Nuts	West	60
Nuts	Central	100
Screws	East	40
Screws	West	70
Screws	Central	80
Bolts	East	90
Bolts	West	120
Bolts	Central	140
Washers	East	20
Washers	West	10
Washers	Central	30

2011

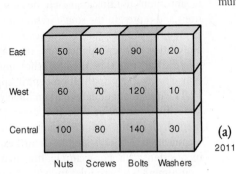

(a)
2011

Product	Region	Sales
Nuts	East	60
Nuts	West	70
Nuts	Central	110
Screws	East	50
Screws	West	80
Screws	Central	90
Bolts	East	100
Bolts	West	130
Bolts	Central	150
Washers	East	30
Washers	West	20
Washers	Central	40

2012

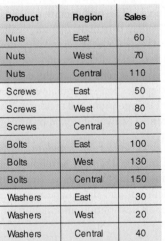

(b)
2012

Product	Region	Sales
Nuts	East	70
Nuts	West	80
Nuts	Central	120
Screws	East	60
Screws	West	90
Screws	Central	100
Bolts	East	110
Bolts	West	140
Bolts	Central	160
Washers	East	40
Washers	West	30
Washers	Central	50

2013

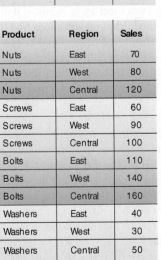

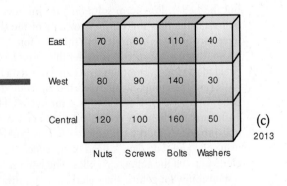

(c)
2013

in their warehouses. For this reason, many companies have moved to real-time data warehousing where data are moved (using data-integration processes) from source systems to the data warehouse or mart almost instantly. For example, within 15 minutes of a purchase at Walmart, the details of the sale have been loaded into a warehouse and are available for analysis.

Storing the Data.   A variety of architectures can be used to store decision-support data. The most common architecture is *one central enterprise data warehouse*, without data marts. Most organizations use this approach, because the data stored in the warehouse are accessed by all users and represent the *single version of the truth*.

Another architecture is *independent data marts*. This architecture stores data for a single application or a few applications, such as marketing and finance. Limited thought is given to how the data might be used for other applications or by other functional areas in the organization. This is a very application-centric approach to storing data.

The independent data mart architecture is not particularly effective. Although it may meet a specific organizational need, it does not reflect an enterprisewide approach to data management. Instead, the various organizational units create independent data marts throughout the organization. Not only are these marts expensive to build and maintain, but they often contain inconsistent data. For example, they may have inconsistent data definitions (such as, What is a customer? Is a particular individual a potential or current customer?). They might also use different source systems (which may have different data for the same item, such as a customer address). Although independent data marts are an organizational reality, larger companies have increasingly moved to data warehouses.

Still another data warehouse architecture is the *hub and spoke*. This architecture contains a central data warehouse that stores the data plus multiple dependent data marts that source their data from the central repository. Because the marts obtain their data from the central repository, the data in these marts still comprise the *single version of the truth* for decision-support purposes.

The dependent data marts store the data in a format that is appropriate for how the data will be used and for providing faster response times to queries and applications. As you have learned, users can view and analyze data from the perspective of business dimensions and measures. This analysis is intuitive because the dimensions are in business terms, easily understood by users.

Metadata.   It is important to maintain data about the data, known as *metadata*, in the data warehouse. Both the IT personnel who operate and manage the data warehouse and the users who access the data need metadata. IT personnel need information about data sources; database, table, and column names; refresh schedules; and data-usage measures. Users' needs include data definitions, report/query tools, report distribution information, and contact information for the help desk.

Data Quality.   The quality of the data in the warehouse must meet users' needs. If it does not, the data will not be trusted and ultimately will not be used. Most organizations find that the quality of the data in source systems is poor and must be improved before the data can be used in the data warehouse. Some of the data can be improved with data-cleansing software, but the better, long-term solution is to improve the quality at the source system level. This approach requires the business owners of the data to assume responsibility for making any necessary changes to implement this solution.

To illustrate this point, consider the case of a large hotel chain that wanted to conduct targeted marketing promotions using zip code data it collected from its guests when they checked in. When the company analyzed the zip code data, analysts discovered that many of the zip codes were 99999. How did this error occur? The answer is that the clerks were not asking customers for their zip codes, but they needed to enter something to complete the registration process. A short-term solution to this problem was to conduct the marketing campaign using city and state data instead of zip codes. The long-term solution was to make certain the clerks entered the actual zip codes. The latter solution required the hotel managers to take the responsibility for getting their clerks to enter the correct data.

Governance.   To ensure that BI is meeting their needs, organizations must implement governance to plan and control their BI activities. Governance requires that people, committees, and processes be in place. Companies that are effective in BI governance often create a senior-level committee comprised of vice-presidents and directors who (1) ensure that the business objectives and BI strategies are in alignment, (2) prioritize projects, and (3) allocate resources. These companies also establish a middle management–level committee that oversees the various projects in the BI portfolio to ensure that these projects are being completed in accordance with the company's objectives. Finally, lower-level operational committees perform tasks such as creating data definitions and identifying and solving data problems. All of these committees rely on the collaboration and contributions of business-unit personnel and IT personnel.

Users.   Once the data are loaded in a data mart or warehouse, they can be accessed. At this point the organization begins to obtain business value from BI; all of the prior stages constitute creating BI infrastructure.

There are many potential BI users, including IT developers; frontline workers; analysts; information workers; managers and executives; and suppliers, customers, and regulators. Some of these users are *information producers* whose primary role is to create information for other users. IT developers and analysts typically fall into this category. Other users—including managers and executives—are *information consumers*, because they utilize information created by others.

Companies have reported hundreds of successful data-warehousing applications. You can read client success stories and case studies at the Web sites of vendors such as NCR Corp. (www.ncr.com) and Oracle (www.oracle.com). For a more detailed discussion, visit the Data Warehouse Institute (http://tdwi.org). The benefits of data warehousing include the following:

- End users can access needed data quickly and easily via Web browsers because these data are located in one place.
- End users can conduct extensive analysis with data in ways that were not previously possible.
- End users can obtain a consolidated view of organizational data.

These benefits can improve business knowledge, provide competitive advantage, enhance customer service and satisfaction, facilitate decision making, and streamline business processes. IT's About Business 5.4 demonstrates the benefits of data warehousing to the Soon Chun Hyang University Hospital in South Korea.

Despite their many benefits, data warehouses have some limitations. First, they can be very expensive to build and to maintain. Second, incorporating data from obsolete mainframe systems can be difficult and expensive. Finally, people in one department might be reluctant to share data with other departments.

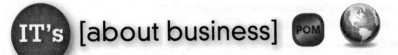

IT's [about business] POM

5.4 Hospital Improves Patient Care with Data Warehouse

Founded in 1972, Soon Chun Hyang University Hospital (SCHUH; http://www.schmc.ac.kr/seoul/eng/index.do) has evolved into one of the largest healthcare institutions in South Korea. The hospital operates 2,800 beds in four different cities across the country—Seoul, Gumi, Cheonan, and Bucheon.

As the number of patients and the amount of patient data dramatically increased, SCHUJ faced a growing challenge in continuing to offer an excellent care experience. To maintain its high standards, the hospital needed to reduce admission times, process patient test results more quickly, and transfer patients for diagnosis or treatment at different locations more efficiently.

In the past, each of SCHUH's four sites had utilized different information technology systems, including systems for electronic medical records (EMRs), electronic payment systems, and picture archiving and communications systems (PaCS), which manage imaging data from magnetic resource imaging (MRI) and computed tomography (CT) scanning systems. As a result, when patients were transferred from one hospital site to another, they had to bring all of their relevant medical records and data with them. This

information then had to be manually entered into that hospital's electronic systems. This process was incredibly time-consuming and expensive. Further, because different hospital sites could not easily share patient histories, they sometimes performed the same diagnostic tests twice, duplicating the effort and the costs.

Delivering test results from X-ray, MRI, or CT scans in a timely manner was also difficult using the hospital's four existing legacy systems. Preparing imaging data to send to a patient's physician for analysis could take up to three days, which significantly slowed down the diagnostic process.

To resolve these problems, SCHUH launched the Integrated Medical Information System (IMIS) project. The purpose of this project was to replace the information silos located at each of the hospital's four sites with a centralized source of patient information; namely, a data warehouse.

The first step was to submit a request for proposals (RFP) that outlined the requirements for the data warehouse. Security was a significant requirement, because the storage and transfer of patient data is strictly regulated by the South Korean Protection of Medical Information Act. Another requirement was scalability. That is, vendors had to demonstrate that their IT solutions would accommodate the rapidly expanding volumes of data from the hospital's growing number of patients.

After a number of demonstrations and meetings, SCHUH engaged IBM (www.ibm.com) to deliver the data warehouse. The hospital's IT team worked with IBM to implement the new patient data warehouse at an integrated datacenter in Bucheon. The warehouse includes storage systems for each hospital's medical records and PaCS data. Each storage system is backed up offsite to provide protection and resiliency for patient records. After historical patient data have been held for a predetermined period of time, they are archived as magnetic tape.

To ensure regulatory compliance, the system transmits data between the hospitals through a secure private network. Further, the system applies a database security solution to all four hospitals, which restricts access to patient data to authorized employees.

Each hospital can now access the data warehouse using a Web browser. Because patient data collected at each of SCHUH's four sites are now consolidated in the warehouse, the hospital has eliminated the inefficiencies associated with its legacy system silos.

The warehouse makes patient data available to all hospital sites the moment the data are entered. This process has reduced the unnecessary duplication of diagnostic tests and accelerated patient transfers and readmissions. By substantially improving its operational efficiency, the hospital aims to reduce its annual operating costs by 40 percent. Significantly, it plans to reinvest these savings to further improve patient care.

The warehouse has also driven improvements in the processing of imaging data. Specifically, it has reduced the time required to share imaging data with another hospital department from 3 days to just 30 minutes, an improvement of more than 95 percent. All imaging data are now digital, which significantly reduces the risks associated with losing physical copies of imaging results.

Having a single source of patient data will also help SCHUH make advances in medical research. In addition, the data warehouse contains all of the hospital's EMR and PaCS imaging data. It has thus become an invaluable resource for clinical trials, because it allows researchers to perform statistical analyses of the effectiveness of new drugs and treatment programs.

Sources: Compiled from "Soon Chun Hyang Hospital Augments Its Care Experience," *IBM Customer Case Study*, March 19, 2013; J. Taitsman, J. Grimm, and S. Agrawal, "Protecting Patient Privacy and Security," The New England Journal of Medicine," March 14, 2013; T. Samson, "Hospitals Far From Immune from Patient-Data Theft," *InfoWorld*, January 3, 2013; S. Yeo, "Electronic Medical Records Are Streamlining Healthcare," *Advantech Digital Healthcare*, December 27, 2012; J. Thompson, "Korean Hospital System Builds Country's First Integrated Hospital Infrastructure," *Healthcare IT News*, March 29, 2012; http://www.schmc.ac.kr/seoul/eng/index.do, accessed April 15, 2013.

Questions

1. Describe the benefits of the hospital's data warehouse.
2. Describe potential disadvantages of the hospital's data warehouse.

---

before you go on...

1. Differentiate between data warehouses and data marts.
2. Describe the characteristics of a data warehouse.
3. What are three possible architectures for data warehouses and data marts in an organization?

5.6 Knowledge Management

As we have noted throughout this text, data and information are critically important organizational assets. Knowledge is a vital asset as well. Successful managers have always valued and utilized intellectual assets. These efforts were not systematic, however, and they did not ensure that knowledge was shared and dispersed in a way that benefited the overall organization. Moreover, industry analysts estimate that most of a company's knowledge assets are not housed in relational databases. Instead, they are dispersed in e-mail, word processing documents, spreadsheets, presentations on individual computers, and in people's heads. This arrangement makes it extremely difficult for companies to access and integrate this knowledge. The result frequently is less-effective decision making.

Concepts and Definitions

Knowledge management (KM) is a process that helps organizations manipulate important knowledge that comprises part of the organization's memory, usually in an unstructured format. For an organization to be successful, knowledge, as a form of capital, must exist in a format that can be exchanged among persons. In addition, it must be able to grow.

Knowledge.   In the information technology context, knowledge is distinct from data and information. As you learned in Chapter 1, data are a collection of facts, measurements, and statistics; information is organized or processed data that are timely and accurate. Knowledge is information that is *contextual*, *relevant*, and *useful*. Simply put, knowledge is *information in action*. **Intellectual capital** (or **intellectual assets**) is another term for knowledge.

To illustrate with an example, a bulletin listing all of the courses offered by your university during one semester would be considered data. When you register, you process the data from the bulletin to create your schedule for the semester. Your schedule would be considered information. Awareness of your work schedule, your major, your desired social schedule, and characteristics of different faculty members could be construed as knowledge, because it can affect the way you build your schedule. You see that this awareness is contextual and relevant (to developing an optimal schedule of classes) as well as useful (it can lead to changes in your schedule). The implication is that knowledge has strong experiential and reflective elements that distinguish it from information in a given context. Unlike information, knowledge can be utilized to solve a problem.

Numerous theories and models classify different types of knowledge. Here you will focus on the distinction between explicit knowledge and tacit knowledge.

Explicit and Tacit Knowledge.   **Explicit knowledge** deals with more objective, rational, and technical knowledge. In an organization, explicit knowledge consists of the policies, procedural guides, reports, products, strategies, goals, core competencies, and IT infrastructure of the enterprise. In other words, explicit knowledge is the knowledge that has been codified (documented) in a form that can be distributed to others or transformed into a process or a strategy. A description of how to process a job application that is documented in a firm's human resources policy manual is an example of explicit knowledge.

In contrast, **tacit knowledge** is the cumulative store of subjective or experiential learning. In an organization, tacit knowledge consists of an organization's experiences, insights, expertise, know-how, trade secrets, skill sets, understanding, and learning. It also includes the organizational culture, which reflects the past and present experiences of the organization's people and processes, as well as the organization's prevailing values. Tacit knowledge is generally imprecise and costly to transfer. It is also highly personal. Finally, because it is unstructured, it is difficult to formalize or codify, in contrast to explicit knowledge. A salesperson who has worked with particular customers over time and has come to know their needs quite well would possess extensive tacit knowledge. This knowledge is typically not recorded. In fact, it might be difficult for the salesperson to put into writing, even if he or she were willing to share it.

Knowledge Management Systems

The goal of knowledge management is to help an organization make the most productive use of the knowledge it has accumulated. Historically, management information systems have focused on capturing, storing, managing, and reporting explicit knowledge. Organizations now realize they need to integrate explicit and tacit knowledge into formal information systems. **Knowledge management systems (KMSs)** refer to the use of modern information technologies—the Internet, intranets, extranets, databases—to systematize, enhance, and expedite intrafirm and interfirm knowledge management. KMSs are intended to help an organization cope with turnover, rapid change, and downsizing by making the expertise of the organization's human capital widely accessible.

Organizations can realize many benefits with KMSs. Most importantly, they make **best practices**, the most effective and efficient ways of doing things, readily available to a wide range of employees. Enhanced access to best-practice knowledge improves overall organizational performance. For example, account managers can now make available their tacit knowledge about how best to manage large accounts. The organization can then utilize this knowledge when it trains new account managers. Other benefits include improved customer service, more efficient product development, and improved employee morale and retention.

At the same time, however, implementing effective KMSs presents several challenges. First, employees must be willing to share their personal tacit knowledge. To encourage this behavior, organizations must create a knowledge management culture that rewards employees who add

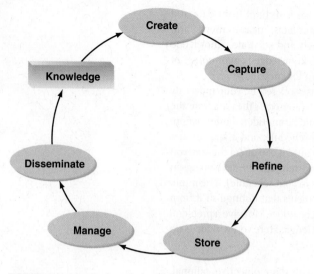

FIGURE 5.13 The knowledge management system cycle.

their expertise to the knowledge base. Second, the organization must continually maintain and upgrade its knowledge base. Specifically, it must incorporate new knowledge and delete old, outdated knowledge. Finally, companies must be willing to invest in the resources needed to carry out these operations.

The KMS Cycle

A functioning KMS follows a cycle that consists of six steps (see Figure 5.13). The reason the system is cyclical is that knowledge is dynamically refined over time. The knowledge in an effective KMS is never finalized because the environment changes over time and knowledge must be updated to reflect these changes. The cycle works as follows:

1. *Create knowledge.* Knowledge is created as people determine new ways of doing things or develop know-how. Sometimes external knowledge is brought in.
2. *Capture knowledge.* New knowledge must be identified as valuable and be represented in a reasonable way.
3. *Refine knowledge.* New knowledge must be placed in context so that it is actionable. This is where tacit qualities (human insights) must be captured along with explicit facts.
4. *Store knowledge.* Useful knowledge must then be stored in a reasonable format in a knowledge repository so that others in the organization can access it.
5. *Manage knowledge.* Like a library, the knowledge must be kept current. It must be reviewed regularly to verify that it is relevant and accurate.
6. *Disseminate knowledge.* Knowledge must be made available in a useful format to anyone in the organization who needs it, anywhere and anytime.

before you go on...

1. What is knowledge management?

2. What is the difference between tacit knowledge and explicit knowledge?

3. Describe the knowledge management system cycle.

What's In IT For Me?

For the **Accounting Major**

ACCT

The accounting function is intimately concerned with keeping track of the transactions and internal controls of an organization. Modern databases enable accountants to perform these functions more effectively. Databases help accountants manage the flood of data in today's organizations so that they can keep their firms in compliance with the standards imposed by Sarbanes-Oxley.

Accountants also play a role in cost justifying the creation of a knowledge base and then auditing its cost-effectiveness. In addition, if you work for a large CPA company that provides management services or sells knowledge, you will most likely use some of your company's best practices that are stored in a knowledge base.

For the **Finance Major**

FIN

Financial managers make extensive use of computerized databases that are external to the organization, such as CompuStat or Dow Jones, to obtain financial data on organizations in their industry. They can use these data to determine if their organization meets industry benchmarks in return on investment, cash management, and other financial ratios.

Financial managers, who produce the organization's financial status reports, are also closely involved with Sarbanes-Oxley. Databases help these managers comply with the law's standards.

For the Marketing Major

Databases help marketing managers access data from the organization's marketing transactions, such as customer purchases, to plan targeted marketing campaigns and to evaluate the success of previous campaigns. Knowledge about customers can make the difference between success and failure. In many databases and knowledge bases, the vast majority of information and knowledge concerns customers, products, sales, and marketing. Marketing managers regularly use an organization's knowledge base, and they often participate in its creation.

For the Production/Operations Management Major

Production/operations personnel access organizational data to determine optimum inventory levels for parts in a production process. Past production data enable production/operations management (POM) personnel to determine the optimum configuration for assembly lines. Firms also collect quality data that inform them not only about the quality of finished products but also about quality issues with incoming raw materials, production irregularities, shipping and logistics, and after-sale use and maintenance of the product.

Knowledge management is extremely important for running complex operations. The accumulated knowledge regarding scheduling, logistics, maintenance, and other functions is very valuable. Innovative ideas are necessary for improving operations and can be supported by knowledge management.

For the Human Resources Management Major

Organizations keep extensive data on employees, including gender, age, race, current and past job descriptions, and performance evaluations. HR personnel access these data to provide reports to government agencies regarding compliance with federal equal opportunity guidelines. HR managers also use these data to evaluate hiring practices, evaluate salary structures, and manage any discrimination grievances or lawsuits brought against the firm.

Databases help HR managers provide assistance to all employees as companies turn over more and more decisions about healthcare and retirement planning to the employees themselves. The employees can use the databases for help in selecting the optimal mix among these critical choices.

HR managers also need to use a knowledge base frequently to find out how past cases were handled. Consistency in how employees are treated not only is important, but it also protects the company against legal actions. In addition, training for building, maintaining, and using the knowledge system sometimes is the responsibility of the HR department. Finally, the HR department might be responsible for compensating employees who contribute their knowledge to the knowledge base.

For the MIS Major

The MIS function manages the organization's data as well as the databases. MIS database administrators standardize data names by using the data dictionary. This process ensures that all users understand which data are in the database. Database personnel also help users access needed data and generate reports with query tools.

[Summary]

1. **Discuss ways that common challenges in managing data can be addressed using data governance.**

   The following are three common challenges in managing data:

   - Data are scattered throughout organizations and are collected by many individuals using various methods and devices. These data are frequently stored in numerous servers and locations and in different computing systems, databases, formats, and human and computer languages.
   - Data come from multiple sources.
   - Information systems that support particular business processes impose unique requirements on data, which results in repetition and conflicts across an organization.

   One strategy for implementing data governance is master data management. Master data management provides companies with the ability to store, maintain, exchange, and synchronize a consistent, accurate, and timely "single version of the truth" for the company's core master data. Master data management consistently manages data gathered from across an organization, consistently manages data from multiple sources, and consistently manages data across business processes in an organization.

2. **Define Big Data, and discuss its basic characteristics.**

   Big Data is composed of high volume, high velocity, and high variety information assets that require new forms of processing to enable enhanced decision making, insight discovery, and process optimization. Big Data has three distinct characteristics, which are volume, velocity, and variety. These characteristics distinguish Big Data from traditional data.

   - *Volume*: Big Data consists of vast quantities of data.
   - *Velocity*: Big Data flows into an organization at incredible speeds.
   - Variety: Big Data includes a huge variety of different data in differing data formats.

3. **Explain how to interpret the relationships depicted in an entity-relationship diagram.**

   See Figure 5.4 and its accompanying explanation for a demonstration of interpreting relationships in an ER diagram.

4. **Discuss the advantages and disadvantages of relational databases.**

   Relational databases allow people to compare information quickly by row or column. In addition, items are easy to retrieve by finding the point of intersection of a particular row and column. On the other hand, large-scale relational databases can be composed of many interrelated tables, making the overall design complex with slow search and access times.

5. **Explain the elements necessary to successfully implement and maintain data warehouses.**

   To successfully implement and main a data warehouse, an organization must:

   - Link source systems that provide data to the warehouse or mart.
   - Prepare the necessary data for the data warehouse using data integration technology and processes.
   - Decide on an appropriate architecture for storing data in the data warehouse or data mart.
   - Select the tools and applications for the variety of organizational users.
   - Ensure that metadata, data quality, and governance processes are in place to ensure that the data warehouse or mart meets its purposes.

6. **Describe the benefits and challenges of implementing knowledge management systems in organizations.**

   Organizations can realize many benefits with KMSs.

   - Best practices are readily available to a wide range of employees;
   - Improved customer service;

- More efficient product development;
- Improved employee morale and retention.

Challenges to implementing KMSs include:

- Employees must be willing to share their personal tacit knowledge;
- Organizations must create a knowledge management culture that rewards employees who add their expertise to the knowledge base;
- The knowledge base must be continually maintained and updated;
- Companies must be willing to invest in the resources needed to carry out these operations.

Organizations can use knowledge management to develop best practices, to establish the most effective and efficient ways of doing things, and to make these practices readily available to a wide range of employees. Other benefits of knowledge management include improved customer service, more efficient product development, and improved employee morale and retention.

A functioning KMS follows a cycle that consists of six steps: create knowledge, capture knowledge, refine knowledge, store knowledge, manage knowledge, and disseminate knowledge.

[Chapter Glossary]

attribute Each characteristic or quality describing a particular entity.

best practices The most effective and efficient ways to do things.

Big Data Diverse, high-volume, high-velocity information assets that require new forms of processing to enable enhanced decision making, insight discovery, and process optimization.

bit A binary digit—that is, a 0 or a 1.

byte A group of eight bits that represents a single character.

clickstream data Data collected about user behavior and browsing patterns by monitoring users' activities when they visit a Web site.

data dictionary Collection of definitions of data elements; data characteristics that use the data elements; and the individuals, business functions, applications, and reports that use this data element.

data file A collection of logically related records (see **table**).

data governance An approach to managing information across an entire organization.

data mart A low-cost, scaled-down version of a data warehouse that is designed for the end-user needs in a strategic business unit (SBU) or a department.

data model Definition of the way data in a DBMS are conceptually structured.

data warehouse A repository of historical data that are organized by subject to support decision makers in the organization.

database A group of logically related files that stores data and the associations among them.

database management system (DBMS) The software program (or group of programs) that provides access to a database.

entity A person, place, thing, or event about which information is maintained in a record.

entity classes Groupings of entities of a given type.

entity-relationship (ER) diagram Document that shows data entities and attributes and relationships among them.

entity-relationship (ER) modeling The process of designing a database by organizing data entities to be used and identifying the relationships among them.

explicit knowledge The more objective, rational, and technical types of knowledge.

field A grouping of logically related characters into a word, a small group of words, or a complete number.

file A grouping of logically related records.

identifiers Attributes that are unique to an entity instance.

instance A particular entity within an entity class.

intellectual capital (or intellectual assets) Other terms for knowledge.

knowledge management (KM) A process that helps organizations identify, select, organize, disseminate, transfer, and apply information and expertise that are part of the organization's memory and that typically reside within the organization in an unstructured manner.

knowledge management systems (KMSs) Information technologies used to systematize, enhance, and expedite intra- and interfirm knowledge management.

master data A set of core data, such as customer, product, employee, vendor, geographic location, and so on, that spans an enterprise's information systems.

master data management A process that provides companies with the ability to store, maintain, exchange, and synchronize a consistent, accurate, and timely "single version of the truth" for the company's core master data.

multidimensional structure Storage of data in more than two dimensions; a common representation is the *data cube*.

normalization A method for analyzing and reducing a relational database to its most streamlined form for minimum redundancy, maximum data integrity, and best processing performance.

NoSQL databases Databases that can manipulate structured as well as unstructured data and inconsistent or missing data; are useful when working with Big Data.

online transaction processing (OLTP) Processing of business transactions online as soon as they occur.

primary key The identifier field or attribute that uniquely identifies a record.

query by example (QBE) Database language that enables the user to fill out a grid (form) to construct a sample or description of the data wanted.

record A grouping of logically related fields; describes an entity.

relational database model Data model based on the simple concept of tables in order to capitalize on characteristics of rows and columns of data.

secondary key An identifier field or attribute that has some identifying information but typically does not identify the file with complete accuracy.

structured query language (SQL) Popular relational database language that enables users to perform complicated searches with relatively simple instructions.

table A grouping of logically related records (see data file).

tacit knowledge The cumulative store of subjective or experiential learning, which is highly personal and hard to formalize.

[Discussion Questions]

1. Is Big Data really a problem on its own, or are the use, control, and security of the data the true problem? Provide specific examples to support your answer.

2. What are the implications of having incorrect data points in your Big Data? What are the implications of incorrect or duplicated customer data? How valuable are decisions that are made based on faulty information derived from incorrect data?

3. Explain the difficulties involved in managing data.

4. What are the problems associated with poor-quality data?

5. What is master data management? What does it have to do with high-quality data?

6. Explain why master data management is so important in companies that have multiple data sources.

7. Describe the advantages of relational databases.

8. Explain why it is important to capture and manage knowledge.

9. Compare and contrast tacit knowledge and explicit knowledge.

[Problem-Solving Activities]

1. Access various employment Web sites (e.g., www.monster.com and www.dice.com) and find several job descriptions for a database administrator. Are the job descriptions similar? What are the salaries offered in these positions?

2. Access the Web sites of several real estate companies. Find the sites that take you through a step-by-step process for buying a home, that provide virtual reality tours of homes in your price range and location, that provide mortgage and interest rate calculators, and that offer financing for your home. Do the sites require that you register to access their services? Can you request that an e-mail be sent to you when properties in which you might be interested become available?

3. It is possible to find many Web sites that provide demographic information. Access several of these sites and see what they offer. Do the sites differ in the types of demographic information they offer? If so, how? Do the sites require a fee for the information they offer? Would demographic information be useful to you if you wanted to start a new business? If so, how and why?

4. The Internet contains many Web sites that provide information on financial aid resources for students. Access several of these sites. Do you have to register to access the information? Can you apply for financial aid on the sites, or do you have to request paper applications that you must complete and return?

5. Draw an entity-relationship diagram for a small retail store. You wish to keep track of the product name, description, unit price, and number of items of that product sold to each customer. You also wish to record customer name, mailing address, and billing address. You must track each transaction (sale) as to date, product purchased, unit price, number of units, tax, and total amount of the sale.

6. Draw the entity-relationship diagram for the following patient appointment system. The business rules of this system are the following:

A doctor can be scheduled for many appointments but might not have any scheduled at all. Each appointment is scheduled with exactly one doctor. A patient can schedule one or more appointments. One appointment is scheduled with exactly one patient. An appointment must generate exactly one bill, and a bill is generated by only one appointment. One payment is applied to exactly one bill, and one bill can be paid off over time by several payments. A bill can be outstanding, having nothing yet paid on it at all. One patient can make many payments, but a single payment is made by only one patient. Some patients are insured by an insurance company. If they are insured, they can only carry insurance with one insurance company. An insurance company can have many patients carry their policies. For patients who carry insurance, the insurance company will make payments, with each single payment made by exactly one insurance company.

7. Access the Web sites of IBM (www.ibm.com), Sybase (www.sybase.com), and Oracle (www.oracle.com), and trace the capabilities of their latest data management products, including Web connections.

8. Enter the Web site of the Gartner Group (www.gartner .com). Examine the company's research studies pertaining to data management. Prepare a report on the state of the art.

9. Calculate your personal digital footprint at http://www.emc .com/digital_universe/downloads/web/personal-ticker.htm.

10. Diagram a knowledge management system cycle for a fictional company that sells customized T-shirts to students.

[Closing Case **Can Organizations Have Too Much Data?**] MIS

The Problem

Organizations are hoarding (over-retaining) data that they no longer need. This massive accumulation of unnecessary data results from several technological and organizational factors. From a technology standpoint, the growth of high-bandwidth Internet connections (discussed in Chapter 6) and the decrease in the price of hard drive storage (discussed in Technology Guide 1) have made it relatively easy and inexpensive to move and store vast amounts of documents and files.

From an organizational perspective, few managers are concerned about what is being stored when it seems on the surface to be so cheap to simply keep everything. In fact, in most organizations, no one is responsible for limiting the amount of data that is being stored. Business unit managers typically do not see a budget line item for all of the costs associated with unused or unneeded data, so they do not make it a management priority—at least, not until huge amounts of corporate data are involved in a legal matter or a government investigation.

Although storing vast amounts of hoarded data seems to be cheap, this is not really the case. Hoarding data actually involves significant costs. These costs fall into three broad categories: infrastructure costs; hidden costs; and legal, compliance, and regulatory costs.

Infrastructure Costs. When companies closely analyze their data, they typically find that 80 percent of their ostensibly "active" files and folders have not been accessed for three to five years. This situation results in unnecessary IT expenditures for electronic data storage, disaster recovery, and data migration as old servers and systems are retired. Some organizations also have tens of thousands of backup tapes in storage, many of which are essentially useless. Nevertheless, they are generating storage fees and excess costs if they are included in the discovery process for litigation (discussed below).

Hidden Costs. Other costs associated with unnecessary data hoarding are hidden—out of sight, and out of mind. One example of hidden costs is lost productivity when employees have to search through volumes of unused and unwanted materials to find the information they need.

Legal, Compliance, and Regulatory Costs. The largest costs of over-retained data frequently arise when a company becomes entangled in legal actions. When a legal matter arises, the court issues a legal hold for all data pertaining to the matter; that is, a company cannot dispose of *any* relevant data after the hold is issued. In essence, the legal hold supersedes the company's right to dispose of information that is not required for any specific operational or regulatory requirements. The process of examining a company's data to find if they are pertinent to the case is called discovery.

The discovery process can be extraordinarily expensive. In many cases, companies must hire attorneys to examine data files to determine whether they are pertinent to discovery requests or subpoenas. Even if companies use electronic discovery software, the costs are still substantial. For example, although an e-discovery company, Blackstone Discovery (www.blackstonediscovery.com), helped one company analyze 1.5 million documents for less than $100,000, that firm still incurred those costs. The key point here is that if the company had disposed of the data before the legal matter arose, these costs would have been substantially lower. As this example illustrates, companies should proactively and appropriately dispose of unnecessarily hoarded data.

In addition, companies increasingly must adhere to state privacy legislation that requires them to notify state officials and implicated state citizens if private information such as Social Security numbers or credit card numbers is breached or disclosed. For example, Belmont Bank in Massachusetts discovered that a backup tape had been left on a table and disposed of by the cleaning crew. It appeared that the tape had been incinerated and therefore was not actually disclosed to any third parties. Nevertheless, the bank had to pay a $7,500 civil penalty.

Companies also incur costs when legal problem arise from incidents involving the actual loss of credit card information. Security experts estimate the cost of the TJX breach to be $256 million or more. At the risk of stating the obvious, hackers and thieves cannot take what organizations no longer possess. One excellent protection against a breach is to dispose of data as soon as they are no longer needed for business purposes or legal matters.

The Solution

So, how can a company reduce the risks and costs associated with data hoarding? First, companies must understand that the key to avoiding legal difficulties is to make good-faith, reasonable efforts to meet record-keeping obligations and to document those efforts. Perfection is not required for legal purposes. Furthermore, companies normally are obligated to keep only "a" copy of relevant information, not "all" copies. That is, there is little or no need to keep all backups. Companies that recognize this simple fact can sometimes dispose of tens of thousands of unneeded backup files, thereby generating enormous savings.

Second, companies should hire a properly insured external consultant or expert who will go on record as authorizing the final disposition of data files. Organizational employees are not typically comfortable saying "throw out those data," and many employees are too busy to devote the time that an electronic data housecleaning (e-housecleaning) project requires. Going further, employees may not be familiar with the legal standards governing the disposition of information. As a result, organizations are more comfortable delegating the responsibility for directing data disposal to external experts. In fact, these experts are frequently the persons whose deposition is ultimately taken if anyone questions the disposition decision.

Third, companies should launch an e-housecleaning project. The first step is to review company policies regulating records retention and legal holds to confirm that the company is operating in a reasonable and defensible manner. The basic inquiry here is whether the company appears to be placing the proper documents and information on hold when litigation arises.

The next step is to inventory physical data containers, such as hard drives, servers, tapes, and other media, and make reasonable efforts to determine their source. If the data are required for business, regulatory or legal hold purposes, then they should be placed on retention schedules. If not, then companies should dispose them off.

Finally, for maximum protection, the external expert should draft an opinion letter explaining the process and directing the final disposition of unneeded data. This step ensures that if the data disposition is ever challenged, the company can point to this process and its associated documentation as evidence of their good-faith effort to comply with their record-keeping obligations.

The Results

Properly performed e-housecleaning efforts offer a large return on investment. Some companies have been able to remove thousands of backup files that have been determined to be irrelevant to legal hold, and others have freed up significant amounts of storage space—all of this in addition to avoiding discovery and data breach costs.

In some firms, an executive or business unit insists on holding onto unused data, claiming that they may someday need to access those data. The most effective strategy for dealing with "just-in-case hoarders" is to allow them keep their data, but with the understanding that they are now the "owner" of the data, meaning they must accept all of the responsibilities that ownership entails. Therefore, they will assume all ownership costs, including data storage, backup, and data breach responsibility, as well as all legal costs associated with reviewing and producing the data if the data are ever swept into litigation discovery or governmental investigations. Once these individuals understand the full costs associated with ownership, they usually opt to dispose of the data instead.

Sources: Compiled from S. Mathieson, "Civil Servants Are Not to Blame for Government Data Hoarding," *The Guardian*, April 10, 2013; J. Clark, "Big Data or Big Data Hoarding?" *The Datacenter Journal*, March 14, 2013; "Security Implications of Improper Data Disposal?" *InfoShield Security*, March 11, 2013; A. Kidman, "Data Disposal 101: Don't Use Rubbish Bins," *lifehacker.com.au*, February 21, 2013; J. Jaeger, "Changing Your Data-Hoarding Ways," *Compliance Week*, February 5, 2013; A. Samuel, "E-Discovery Trends for 2013," *CMS Wire*, January 17, 2013; J. Dvorak, "Stop Your Data Hoarding!" *PC Magazine*, December 11, 2012; L. Luellig, "A Modern Governance Strategy for Data Disposal," *CIO Insight*, December 5, 2012; A. Kershaw, "Hoarding Data Wastes Money," *Baseline Magazine*, April 16, 2012; T. Claburn, "Google Apps Vault Promises Easy E-Discovery," *Information-Week*, March 29, 2012; T. Harbert, "E-Discovery in the Cloud? Not So Easy," *Computerworld*, March 6, 2012; B. Kerschberg, "E-Discovery and the Rise of Predictive Coding," Forbes, March 23, 2011; M. Miller, "Data Theft: Top 5 Most Expensive Data Breaches," *The Christian Science Monitor*, May 4, 2011; E. Savitz, "The Problem with Packrats: The High Cost of Digital Hoarding," *Forbes*, March 25, 2011; J. Markoff, "Armies of Expensive Lawyers, Replaced by Cheaper Software," *The New York Times*, March 4, 2011.

Questions

1. Compare and contrast this case with the material in this chapter on Big Data. That is, given the disadvantages of over-retained data, how should an organization manage Big Data?

2. Are there any advantages to over-retaining data? Support your answer.

3. Storage media are becoming much cheaper, with increasing capacity. Would it be easier and cheaper to over-retain data than it would be to pay employees to dispose of data properly and to hire an outside expert to oversee this process?

[Internship Activity]

Industry: Banking

Data is "huge" when it comes to understanding customer patterns. The more data you have, and the more analysis you are able to do, the better you will understand what makes customers tick. In fact, data is such a "big" part of understanding customers we have a unique name for it...BIG DATA.

Noble Bank (as well as any bank) uses historical data to create profiles of applicants to determine who will get a loan and who will not. However, they also use data to determine how much they can change product offerings and not lose existing customers. Because there is a certain amount of effort involved with moving your entire checking account to a new bank (new checks, new debit cards, automatic deposits to be updated, and more) banks hold a certain amount of "staying power" in the inconvenience of "change" (no pun intended).

Please visit the Book Companion Site to receive the full set of instructions on how you will help Noble Bank analyze their latest customer survey data to determine how much staying power they have over their competitions incentives.

Chapter 6

Telecommunications and Networking

[LEARNING OBJECTIVES]	[CHAPTER OUTLINE]	[WEB RESOURCES]

[LEARNING OBJECTIVES]

1. Compare and contrast the two major types of networks.

2. Describe the wireline communications media and transmission technologies.

3. Describe the most common methods for accessing the Internet.

4. Explain the impact that networks have had on business and everyday life for each of the six major categories of network applications.

[CHAPTER OUTLINE]

6.1 What Is a Computer Network?

6.2 Network Fundamentals

6.3 The Internet and the World Wide Web

6.4 Network Applications

[WEB RESOURCES]

- Student PowerPoints for note taking

WileyPLUS

- E-book
- Author video lecture for each chapter section
- Practice quizzes
- Flash Cards for vocabulary review
- Additional "IT's About Business" cases
- Video interviews with managers
- Lab Manuals for Microsoft Office 2010 and 2013

What's In IT For Me?

This Chapter Will Help Prepare You To...

ACCT	FIN	MKT	POM	HRM	MIS
ACCOUNTING	FINANCE	MARKETING	PRODUCTION OPERATIONS MANAGEMENT	HUMAN RESOURCES MANAGEMENT	MIS
Collaborate with external auditors	Integrate internal and industry financial data	Coordinate activities of sales force	Collaborate project team	Deliver online training to employees	Implement and manage firm's networks

The Problem

Although the steady progress of communications technologies has generated bandwidth (the transmission capacity of a network) that is commensurate with user traffic on most Web sites, the explosion of streaming video and mobile technologies is beginning to create bandwidth problems. The Internet was designed to transmit content such as e-mails and Web pages. However, media items being transmitted through the Web today, such as high-definition movies, are several magnitudes greater in size than the types of information the Internet was originally designed to handle. To compound this problem, there are now more than 50 million smartphone users in the United States, many of whom use the Internet to stream video content to their phones. Put simply, the number of users uploading large content such as videos has skyrocketed within the past few years and will likely continue to increase.

In a widely cited estimate, Cisco Systems (www.cisco.com) predicted that Internet traffic will triple by 2014, increasing to 64 exabytes (1 exabyte is 1 million terabytes) per month. To provide a reference point, monthly traffic in 2006 was 5 exabytes, enough to store every word ever spoken. Moreover, by 2014, more than 90 percent of Internet traffic will consist of video uploads, downloads, and streaming. As startling as Cisco's statistics may sound, market researcher Infonetics (www.infonetics.com) contends that Cisco's numbers may be conservative. Infonetics proposed several possible scenarios of how Internet development could unfold. One frightening example is that large telecommunications companies might cease upgrading their technologies, leaving consumers with slow connections and hindering Internet innovation.

The Internet bandwidth issue is as much about economics as it is about technology. Currently, consumers can send 1-kilobyte e-mails or watch the latest 30-gigabyte movie on their large-screen televisions for the same monthly *broadband* (defined later in this chapter) fee. Unlike the system used for power and water bills where higher usage equals higher fees, monthly broadband fees are not tied to bandwidth usage.

A study from Juniper Networks (www.juniper.net) highlights this "revenue-per-bit" problem. The report predicts that Internet revenue for carriers such as AT&T (www.att.com) and Comcast (www.comcast.com) will grow by 5 percent per year through 2020. At the same time,

[Network Neutrality Wars]

MIS

Internet traffic will increase by 27 percent annually, meaning that carriers will have to increase their bandwidth investment by 20 percent per year just to keep up with demand. Under this model, the carriers' business models will break down by 2014, because their total necessary investment will come to exceed revenue growth.

Few industry analysts expect carriers to stop investing in new capacity, but analysts agree that a financial crunch is coming. As Internet traffic soars, analysts expect revenue per megabit to fall from 43 cents in 2010 to just 2 cents in 2014. These figures translate into a far lower return on investment (ROI). Although carriers can find ways to increase their capacity, it will be difficult for them to reap any revenue benefits from doing so.

The heart of the problem is that, even if the technology is equal to the task of transmitting huge amounts of data, no one is sure how to pay for these technologies. One proposed solution is to eliminate network neutrality.

A Possible Solution

Network neutrality is the current model under which Internet service providers (ISPs) operate. Under this model, ISPs must allow customers equal access to content and applications, regardless of the source or nature of the content. That is, *Internet backbone carriers* (discussed later in this chapter) must treat all Web traffic equally on a first-come, first-serve basis.

Telecommunications and cable companies want to replace network neutrality with an arrangement in which they can charge differentiated prices based on the amount of bandwidth consumed by the content that is being delivered over the Internet. These companies believe that differentiated pricing is the most equitable method by which they can finance the necessary investments in their network infrastructures.

To bolster their argument, ISPs point to the enormous amount of bandwidth required to transmit pirated versions of copyrighted materials over the Internet. In fact, Comcast (the second largest ISP in the United States) reported in 2010 that illegal file sharing of copyrighted material was consuming 50 percent of its network capacity. In 2008, the company slowed down the transmission of BitTorrent (www.bittorrent.com) files, a form of peer-to-peer transmissions that is frequently used for piracy and illegal sharing of copyrighted materials. (We discuss BitTorrent later in this chapter.) In response, the Federal Communications Commission (FCC) ordered Comcast to restore its previous service. Comcast then filed a lawsuit challenging the FCC's authority to enforce network neutrality. In April 2010, the Washington DC Circuit Court of Appeals ruled in favor of Comcast, declaring that the FCC did not have the authority to regulate how an ISP manages its network. By endorsing differentiated pricing, the court struck a major blow against network neutrality.

ISPs further contend that mandating net neutrality will hinder U.S. international competitiveness by decreasing innovation and discouraging capital investments in new network technologies. According to this scenario, ISPs will be unable to handle the exploding demand for Internet and wireless data transmission.

Meanwhile, proponents of network neutrality are petitioning Congress to regulate the industry to prevent network providers from adopting strategies similar to Comcast. They argue that the risk of censorship increases when network providers can selectively block or slow access to certain content, such as access to competing low-cost services such as Skype and Vonage. They also assert that a neutral network encourages everyone to innovate because they do not have to obtain permission from phone companies, cable companies, or other authorities. Finally, they contend that the neutral Internet has helped to create many new businesses.

Most analysts expect that those users who consume the most data eventually will have to pay more, most likely in the form of tiered pricing plans. Americans, however, have never had to contend with limits on the amount of data they upload and download, so there may be some pushback from users.

Despite the 2010 court ruling against network neutrality, on December 21, 2010, the FCC approved network neutrality rules that prohibited broadband providers from blocking customer access to legal Web content. The new rules bar wireline-based broadband providers—but not mobile broadband providers—from "unreasonable discrimination" against Web traffic.

In January 2011, Verizon filed a legal appeal challenging the FCC's authority to enforce these new rules.

The Results

U.S. wireless networks have already moved in the direction of tiered-pricing plans. In June 2010, for example, AT&T discontinued its all-you-can-use $30 per month data plan, replacing it tiered-pricing plans for its mobile consumers.

One iPhone user related the following story. For 4 years, he had been using his iPhone to perform the same basic functions: checking e-mail, listening to Pandora Internet radio, accessing Google Maps, browsing the Web, and shopping online. In 2011 he averaged about 1.76 gigabytes of data per month. In January 2012, however, he surpassed a limit established by AT&T (his wireless carrier). In response, AT&T sent him an e-mail, suggesting that he consider using Wi-Fi whenever possible for applications that use the greatest amounts of data, such as streaming video apps and remote Web camera apps. To state that he was unhappy would be an understatement. He promptly began searching wireless plans at competing companies. Further complicating this issue is the fact that there is little, if any, agreement on what constitutes excessive data usage.

On October 1, 2011, AT&T began to reduce speeds for the 5 percent of their unlimited-plan customers who used the most bandwidth. Significantly, AT&T subscribers who sign up for tiered plans do not have any bandwidth limitations. Instead, they have to pay a higher price if they exceed the data limits specified in their plans. In addition, new customers are no longer allowed to sign up for unlimited plans. The AT&T model may foreshadow the direction that many Internet and cable providers will need to take in the future to remain profitable in the face of skyrocketing bandwidth demands.

In 2012, Verizon initiated a legal challenge to the FCC's network neutrality rules, claiming that these rules violate the company's right to free speech. (Verizon characterizes the transmission of data across its networks as "speech.") Specifically, Verizon argued that the FCC overstepped its authority and that its network neutrality rules are unconstitutional. Significantly, the court that will hear this case is the same one that ruled in favor of Comcast.

Verizon may have a valid point. The FCC can regulate the physical infrastructure over which packets travel on the network. It is less clear, however, whether it can also regulate the actual service or content those packets deliver.

As of March 2013, the court was expected to wait until September before hearing arguments in the Verizon vs. the FCC case. This would delay a decision until the end of 2013 or early 2014. The battle over network neutrality continues.

Sources: S. Higginbotham, "Analyst: Verizon's Network Neutrality Challenge May Have to Wait Until Fall," *GigaOM*, March 25, 2013; J. Brodkin, "Time Warner, Net Neutrality Foes Cry Foul Over Netflix Super HD Demands," *Ars Technica*, January 17, 2013; M. Reardon, "Verizon to FCC: Free Speech Trumps Net Neutrality Rules," *CNET News*, July 3, 2012; J. Hamilton, "AT&T Must Give Shareholders Net Neutrality Vote," *Bloomberg*, February 14, 2012; W. Plank, "Confessions of an iPhone Data Hog," *The Wall Street Journal*, January 27, 2012; J. Engebretson, "Verizon Confirms It Will Appeal Newly Published Net Neutrality Rules Soon," *Connected Planet*, September 27, 2011; E. Wyatt, "House Votes Against 'Net Neutrality'," *The New York Times*, April 8, 2011; L. Segall, "Verizon Challenges FCC Net Neutrality Rules," *CNN Money*, January 21, 2011; K. Corbin, "Net Neutrality 2011: What Storms May Come," *Internet News*, December 30, 2010; C. Albanesius, "What Do the FCC's Net Neutrality Rules Mean for You?" *PC Magazine*, December 22, 2010; G. Gross, "FCC Approves Compromise Net Neutrality Rules," *Network World*, December 21, 2010; P. Burrows, "Will Video Kill the Internet, Too?" *Bloomberg BusinessWeek*, December 6–12, 2010; J. Nocera, "The Struggle for What We Already Have," *New York Times*, September 4, 2010; C. Miller, "Web Plan Is Dividing Companies," *New York Times*, August 11, 2010; A. Schatz and S. Ante, "FCC Web Rules Create Pushback," *Wall Street Journal*, May 6, 2010; www.comcast.com, www.att.com, accessed March 13, 2013.

What We Learned from This Case

You need to know three fundamental points about network computing. First, computers do not work in isolation in modern organizations. Rather, they constantly exchange data with one another. Second, this exchange of data—facilitated by telecommunications technologies—provides companies with a number of very significant advantages. Third, this exchange can take place over any distance and over networks of any size.

Without networks, the computer on your desk would be merely another productivity-enhancement tool, just as the typewriter once was. The power of networks, however, turns your computer into an amazingly effective tool for accessing information from thousands of sources, thereby making both you and your organization more productive. Regardless of the type of organization (profit/not-for-profit, large/small, global/local) or industry (manufacturing, financial services, healthcare), networks in general, and the Internet in particular, have transformed—and will continue to transform—the way we do business.

Networks support new ways of doing business, from marketing to supply chain management to customer service to human resources management. In particular, the Internet and private intranets—networks located within a single organization—have an enormous impact on our lives, both professionally and personally. In fact, for all organizations regardless of their size, having an Internet strategy is no longer just a source of competitive advantage. Rather, it is necessary for survival, as you see in IT's About Business 6.1.

Computer networks are essential to modern organizations, for many reasons. First, networked computer systems enable organizations to be more flexible so they can adapt to rapidly changing business conditions. Second, networks enable companies to share hardware, computer applications, and data across the organization and among different organizations. Third, networks make it possible for geographically dispersed employees and work groups to share documents, ideas, and creative insights. This sharing encourages teamwork, innovation, and more efficient and effective interactions. In addition, networks are a critical link between businesses, their business partners, and their customers.

Clearly, networks are essential tools for modern businesses. But, why do *you* need to be familiar with networks? The simple fact is that if you operate your own business or work in a business, you cannot function without networks. You will need to communicate rapidly with your customers, business partners, suppliers, employees, and colleagues. Until about 1990, you would have used the postal service or the telephone system with voice or fax capabilities for business communication. Today, however, the pace of business is much faster—almost real time. To keep up with this incredibly fast pace, you will need to use computers, e-mail, the Internet, cell phones, and mobile devices. Further, all of these technologies will be connected via networks to enable you to communicate, collaborate, and compete on a global scale.

Networking and the Internet are the foundations for commerce in the 21st century. Recall that one important objective of this book is to help you become an informed user of information systems. A knowledge of networking is an essential component of modern business literacy.

You begin this chapter by learning what a computer network is and identifying the various types of networks. You then study network fundamentals and follow by turning your attention to the basics of the Internet and the World Wide Web. You conclude the chapter by seeing the many network applications available to individuals and organizations—that is, what networks help you do.

IT's [about business]

6.1 Studio G   MIS

Sometimes, using the right network can make all the difference. What is the right network? The answer is, it depends. As an organization grows, its network needs to change and evolve to meet its ever-changing needs. This is exactly the case with Studio G Architects, Inc., an architecture firm based in San José, California. The firm began with only two employees, and they needed only two telephone lines to communicate with their customers. However, as the business grew, Studio G needed a better communication solution.

Solving the communication problem initially seemed simple. Just add more telephone lines, right? Not quite. Studio G did not want to

hire a receptionist, so they needed some type of networked phone system that could route calls and help customers reach the appropriate contact. The only type of system capable of routing calls in this way is a private branch exchange (PBX). A PBX is a telephone exchange that serves a particular business or office, as opposed to a telephone exchange operated by a telephone company that serves several businesses or the general public. A PBX makes connections among the internal telephones of a private organization and connects them to the public switched telephone network.

Studio G chose Cisco's Small Business Unified Communications Series as their PBX provider. Cisco's system provides excellent flexibility in routing calls and voice mails, transferring calls, and so on. Further, because PBX provides these functions, Studio G did not have to hire a receptionist.

What is the result? Studio G is now able to keep pace with their larger competitors because they can communicate with their customers at a fraction of the cost spent by other organizations. Kelly Simcox, the owner of Studio G, asserted: "We have grown substantially . . . [and] are competing for projects against firms that are substantially larger than ours."

In this situation the right telecommunication solution was a PBX. Many similar solutions are available today to help small businesses communicate with their customers more efficiently. As you

have seen in this case, networking solutions will continue to allow small businesses to compete on a more level playing field with their larger competitors.

Sources: Compiled from "Small Architecture Firm Keeps Pace with Large Competitors," *Cisco Customer Case Study*; "Small Business PBX: A 5 Minute Lesson," www.vocalocity.com, accessed March 5, 2013; "Small Business PBX: The Basics," *Cisco Resource Center*, accessed March 11, 2013; www.cisco.com, www.studio-g-architects.com, accessed March 11, 2013.

Questions

1. As a business grows, why does its communication network needs grow?
2. What advantages does the Cisco system provide for Studio G?

What Is a Computer Network?

6.1

A **computer network** is a system that connects computers and other devices (e.g., printers) via communications media so that data and information can be transmitted among them. Voice and data communication networks are continually becoming faster—that is, their bandwidth is increasing—and cheaper. **Bandwidth** refers to the transmission capacity of a network; it is stated in bits per second.

The broadband industry itself has difficulty defining the term, broadband. The Federal Communications Commission originally defined broadband as the transmission capacity of a communications medium (discussed later in this chapter) faster than 256,000 (256 Kbps) bits per second. The FCC then upgraded its definition to 768 Kbps downstream (e.g., downloading a syllabus from your university's network) and 256 Kbps upstream (e.g., uploading content to Facebook). In 2010, the FCC upgraded its definition of broadband to 4 Mbps (million bits per second) downstream and 1 Mbps upstream. In 2013, the FCC says that it is considering another definitional upgrade for broadband. Therefore, we define **broadband** as the transmission capacity of a communications medium faster than 4 Mbps downstream and 1 Mbps upstream. The definition of broadband is fluid, and will undoubtedly be changed to reflect larger transmission capacities in the future.

You are familiar with certain types of broadband connections, such as **digital subscriber line (DSL)** and cable to your homes and dorms. DSL and cable fall within the range of transmission capacity mentioned here and are thus defined as broadband connections.

The various types of computer networks range from small to worldwide. They include (from smallest to largest) personal area networks (PANs), local area networks (LANs), metropolitan area networks (MANs), wide area networks (WANs), and the Internet. PANs are short-range networks—typically a few meters—that are used for communication among devices close to one person. PANs can be wired or wireless. (You will learn about wireless PANs in Chapter 8.) MANs are relatively large computer networks that cover a metropolitan area. MANs fall between LANs and WANs in size. WANs typically cover large geographic areas; in some cases they can span the entire planet.

Local Area Networks

Regardless of their size, networks represent a compromise among three objectives: speed, distance, and cost. Organizations typically must select two of the three. To cover long distances, organizations can have fast communication if they are willing to pay for it, or cheap communication if they are willing to accept slower speeds. A third possible combination of the three trade-offs is fast, cheap communication with distance limitations. This is the idea behind local area networks.

A **local area network (LAN)** connects two or more devices in a limited geographical region, usually within the same building, so that every device on the network can communicate with

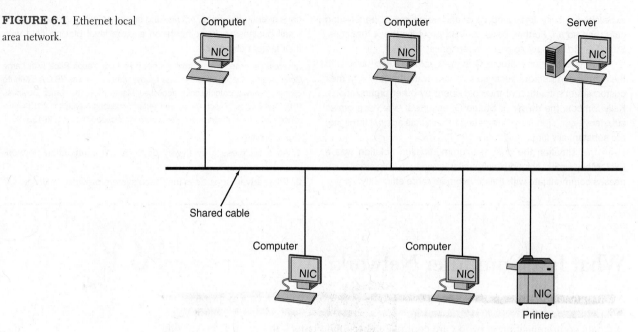

FIGURE 6.1 Ethernet local area network.

every other device. Most LANs today use Ethernet (discussed later in this chapter). Figure 6.1 illustrates an Ethernet LAN that consists of four computers, a server, and a printer, all of which connect via a shared cable. Every device in the LAN has a *network interface card* (NIC) that allows the device to physically connect to the LAN's communications medium. This medium is typically unshielded twisted-pair wire (UTP).

Although it is not required, many LANs have a **file server** or **network server**. The server typically contains various software and data for the network. It also houses the LAN's network operating system, which manages the server and routes and manages communications on the network.

Wide Area Networks

When businesses have to transmit and receive data beyond the confines of the LAN, they use wide area networks. Interestingly, the term *wide area network* did not even exist until local area networks appeared. Before that time, what we call a wide area network today was simply called a "network."

A **wide area network (WAN)** is a network that covers a large geographic area. WANs typically connect multiple LANs. They are generally provided by common carriers such as telephone companies and the international networks of global communications services providers. WANs have large capacity, and they typically combine multiple channels (e.g., fiber-optic cables, microwave, and satellite). The Internet is an example of a WAN.

WANs also contain routers. A **router** is a communications processor that routes messages from a LAN to the Internet, across several connected LANs, or across a wide area network such as the Internet.

Enterprise Networks

Organizations today have multiple LANs and may have multiple WANs. All of these networks are interconnected to form an **enterprise network**. Figure 6.2 displays a model of enterprise computing. Note that the enterprise network in the figure has a **backbone network**. Corporate backbone networks are high-speed central networks to which multiple smaller networks (such as LANs and

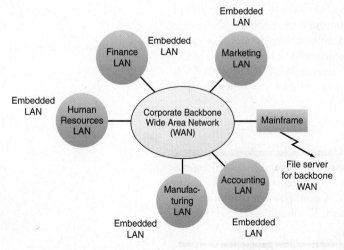

FIGURE 6.2 Enterprise network.

smaller WANs) connect. The LANs are called *embedded LANs* because they connect to the backbone WAN.

before you go on...

1. What are the primary business reasons for using networks?

2. What is the difference between LANs and WANs?

3. Describe an enterprise network.

Network Fundamentals

6.2

In this section, you will learn the basics of how networks actually operate. You will then distinguish between analog and digital signals and understand how modems enable computer networks to "translate" among them. You follow by studying wireline communications media, which enable computers in a network to transmit and receive data. You conclude this section by looking at network protocols and types of network processing.

Analog and Digital Signals

Networks transmit information with two basic types of signals, analog and digital. **Analog signals** are continuous waves that transmit information by altering the characteristics of the waves. Analog signals have two parameters, *amplitude* and *frequency*. For example, all sounds—including the human voice—are analog, traveling to human ears in the form of waves. The higher the waves (or amplitude), the louder the sound; the more closely packed the waves, the higher the frequency or pitch. In contrast, **digital signals** are discrete pulses that are either on or off, representing a series of *bits* (0s and 1s). This quality allows digital signals to convey information in a binary form that can be interpreted by computers. Figure 6.3 illustrates both analog and digital signals.

The function of a **modem** is to convert digital signals to analog signals—a process called *modulation*—and analog signals to digital signals—a process called *demodulation*. (The name

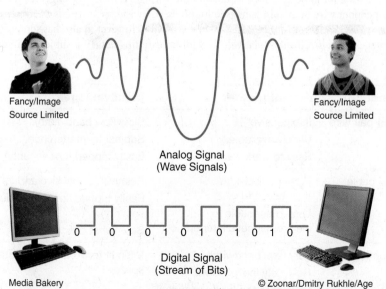

FIGURE 6.3 Analog and digital signals.

Fancy/Image
Source Limited

Fancy/Image
Source Limited

Analog Signal
(Wave Signals)

0 1 0 1 0 1 0 1 0 1 0 1 0 1 0 1

Digital Signal
(Stream of Bits)

Media Bakery

© Zoonar/Dmitry Rukhle/Age
Fotostock America, Inc.

modem is a contraction of *modulator-dem*odulator.) Modems are used in pairs. The modem at the sending end converts a computer's digital information into analog signals for transmission over analog lines, such as telephone lines. At the receiving end, another modem converts the analog signal back into digital signals for the receiving computer. There are three types of modems: dial-up modems, cable modems, and DSL modems.

The U.S. public telephone system was originally designed as an analog network to carry voice signals or sounds in an analog wave format. In order for this type of circuit to carry digital information, that information must be converted into an analog wave pattern by a *dial-up modem*. Dial-up modems have transmission speeds of up to 56 kilobytes per second (Kbps) and are almost extinct in most parts of the developed world.

Cable modems are modems that operate over coaxial cable—for example, cable TV. They offer broadband access to the Internet or corporate intranets. Cable modem speeds vary widely. Most providers offer bandwidth between 1 and 6 million bits per second (Mbps) for downloads (from the Internet to a computer) and between 128 and 768 thousand bits per second (Kbps) for uploads. Cable modem services share bandwidth among subscribers in a locality. That is, the same cable line connects to many households. Therefore, when large numbers of neighbors access the Internet at the same time, cable speeds can decrease significantly during those times.

DSL (discussed later in this chapter) *modems* operate on the same lines as voice telephones and dial-up modems. DSL modems always maintain a connection, so an Internet connection is immediately available.

Communications Media and Channels

Communicating data from one location to another requires some form of pathway or medium. A **communications channel** is such a pathway. It is comprised of two types of media: cable (twisted-pair wire, cable, or fiber-optic cable) and broadcast (microwave, satellite, radio, or infrared).

Cable media or wireline media use physical wires or cables to transmit data and information. Twisted-pair wire and coaxial cables are made of copper, and fiber-optic cable is made of glass. The alternative is communication over **broadcast media** or **wireless media**. The key to mobile communications in today's rapidly moving society is data transmissions over electromagnetic media—the "airwaves." In this section you will study the three wireline channels. Table 6.1 summarizes the advantages and disadvantages of each of these channels. You will become familiar with wireless media in Chapter 8.

Twisted-Pair Wire. **Twisted-pair wire** is the most prevalent form of communications wiring; it is used for almost all business telephone wiring. As the name suggests, it consists of strands of copper wire twisted in pairs (see Figure 6.4). Twisted-pair wire is relatively inexpensive to purchase, widely available, and easy to work with. However, it also has some significant disadvantages. Specifically, it is relatively slow for transmitting data, it is subject to interference

Table 6.1

Advantages and Disadvantages of Wireline Communications Channels

Channel	Advantages	Disadvantages
Twisted-pair wire	Inexpensive. Widely available. Easy to work with.	Slow (low bandwidth). Subject to interference. Easily tapped (low security).
Coaxial cable	Higher bandwidth than twisted-pair. Less susceptible to electromagnetic interference.	Relatively expensive and inflexible. Easily tapped (low-to-medium security). Somewhat difficult to work with.
Fiber-optic cable	Very high bandwidth. Relatively inexpensive. Difficult to tap (good security).	Difficult to work with (difficult to splice).

from other electrical sources, and it can be easily tapped by unintended receivers to gain unauthorized access to data.

Coaxial Cable.   **Coaxial cable** (Figure 6.5) consists of insulated copper wire. Compared to twisted-pair wire, it is much less susceptible to electrical interference, and it can carry much more data. For these reasons, it is commonly used to carry high-speed data traffic as well as television signals (thus the term *cable TV*). However, coaxial cable is more expensive and more difficult to work with than twisted-pair wire. It is also somewhat inflexible.

Fiber Optics.   **Fiber-optic cable** (Figure 6.6) consists of thousands of very thin filaments of glass fibers that transmit information via light pulses generated by lasers. The fiber-optic cable is surrounded by cladding, a coating that prevents the light from leaking out of the fiber.

Fiber-optic cables are significantly smaller and lighter than traditional cable media. They also can transmit far more data, and they provide greater security from interference and tapping. As of mid-2013, optical fiber had reached data transmission rates of more than 50 trillion bits (terabits) per second in laboratory experiments. Fiber-optic cable is typically used as the backbone for a network, whereas twisted-pair wire and coaxial cable connect the backbone to individual devices on the network.

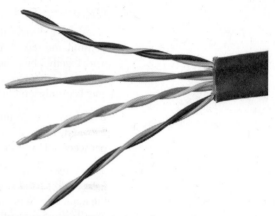

©David Schliepp/iStockphoto

FIGURE 6.4 Twisted-pair wire.

FIGURE 6.5 Two views of coaxial cable.

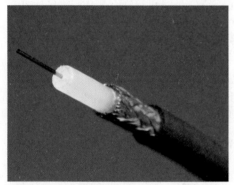

GIPhotoStock/Science Source

Cross-section view

©Piotr Malczyk/iStockphoto

How coaxial cable looks to us

FIGURE 6.6 Two views of fiber-optic cable.

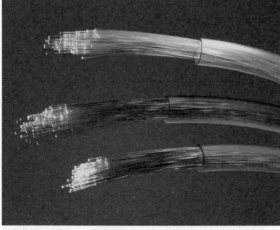

Philip Hatson/Science Source

Cross-section view

Chris Knapton/Science Source

How fiber-optic cable looks to us

Network Protocols

Computing devices that are connected to the network must access and share the network to transmit and receive data. These devices are often referred to as *nodes* of the network. They work together by adhering to a common set of rules and procedures—known as a **protocol**—that enable them to communicate with one another. The two major protocols are the Ethernet and Transmission Control Protocol/Internet Protocol.

Ethernet. A common LAN protocol is Ethernet. Most large corporations use 10-gigabit Ethernet, where the network provides data transmission speeds of 10 gigabits (10 billion bits) per second. However, 100-gigabit Ethernet is emerging.

Transmission Control Protocol/Internet Protocol. The **Transmission Control Protocol/Internet Protocol (TCP/IP)** is the protocol of the Internet. TCP/IP uses a suite of protocols, the main ones being the Transmission Control Protocol (TCP) and the Internet Protocol (IP). The TCP performs three basic functions: (1) It manages the movement of packets between computers by establishing a connection between the computers, (2) it sequences the transfer of packets, and (3) it acknowledges the packets that have been transmitted. The **Internet Protocol (IP)** is responsible for disassembling, delivering, and reassembling the data during transmission.

Before data are transmitted over the Internet, they are divided into small, fixed bundles called *packets*. The transmission technology that breaks up blocks of text into packets is called *packet switching*. Each packet carries the information that will help it reach its destination—the sender's IP address, the intended receiver's IP address, the number of packets in the message, and the number of the particular packet within the message. Each packet travels independently across the network and can be routed through different paths in the network. When the packets reach their destination, they are reassembled into the original message.

It is important to note that packet-switching networks are reliable and fault tolerant. For example, if a path in the network is very busy or is broken, packets can be dynamically ("on the fly") rerouted around that path. Also, if one or more packets does not get to the receiving computer, then only those packets need to be resent.

Why do organizations use packet switching? The main reason is to achieve reliable end-to-end message transmission over sometimes unreliable networks that may have transient (short-acting) or persistent (long-acting) faults.

The packets use the TCP/IP protocol to carry their data. TCP/IP functions in four layers (see Figure 6.7). The *application layer* enables client application programs to access the other layers, and it defines the protocols that applications use to exchange data. One of these application protocols is the **Hypertext Transfer Protocol (HTTP)**, which defines how messages are

FIGURE 6.7 The four layers of the TCP/IP reference model.

©CostinT / iStockphoto

©CostinT / iStockphoto

Email: Sending a Message via SMPT (Simple Mail Transfer Protocol)	Application	Email: Message received
Break Message into packets and determine order	Transport	Packets reordered and replaced (if lost)
Assign sending and receiving IP addresses and apply to each packet	Internet	Packets routed through internal network to desired IP address
Determine path across network/Internet to intended destination	Network Interface	Receipt of packets

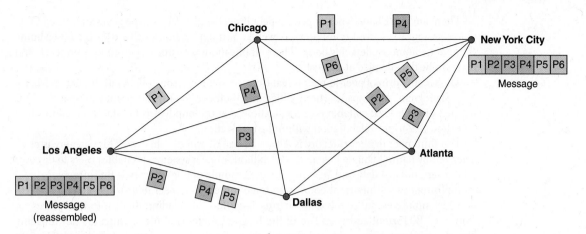

FIGURE 6.8 Packet switching.

formulated and how they are interpreted by their receivers. The *transport layer* provides the application layer with communication and packet services. This layer includes TCP and other protocols. The *Internet layer* is responsible for addressing, routing, and packaging data packets. The IP is one of the protocols in this layer. Finally, the *network interface layer* places packets on, and receives them from, the network medium, which can be any networking technology.

Two computers using TCP/IP can communicate even if they use different hardware and software. Data sent from one computer to another proceed downward through all four layers, beginning with the sending computer's application layer and going through its network interface layer. After the data reach the receiving computer, they travel up the layers.

TCP/IP enables users to send data across sometimes unreliable networks with the assurance that the data will arrive in uncorrupted form. TCP/IP is very popular with business organizations because of its reliability and the ease with which it can support intranets and related functions.

Let's look at an example of packet-switching across the Internet. Figure 6.8 illustrates a message being sent from New York City to Los Angeles over a packet-switching network. Note that the different colored packets travel by different routes to reach their destination in Los Angeles, where they are reassembled into the complete message.

Types of Network Processing

Organizations typically use multiple computer systems across the firm. **Distributed processing** divides processing work among two or more computers. This process enables computers in different locations to communicate with one another via telecommunications links. A common type of distributed processing is client/server processing. A special type of client/server processing is peer-to-peer processing.

Client/Server Computing. **Client/server computing** links two or more computers in an arrangement in which some machines, called *servers*, provide computing services for user PCs, called *clients*. Usually, an organization performs the bulk of its processing or application/data storage on suitably powerful servers that can be accessed by less powerful client machines. The client requests applications, data, or processing from the server, which acts on these requests by "serving" the desired commodity.

Client/server computing leads to the ideas of "fat" clients and "thin" clients. As discussed in Technology Guide 1, *fat clients* have large storage and processing power and therefore can run local programs (such as Microsoft Office) if the network goes down. In contrast, *thin clients* may have no local storage and only limited processing power. Thus, they must depend on the network to run applications. For this reason, they are of little value when the network is not functioning.

Peer-to-Peer Processing. **Peer-to-peer (P2P) processing** is a type of client/server distributed processing where each computer acts as *both* a client and a server. Each computer can access (as assigned for security or integrity purposes) all files on all other computers.

There are three basic types of peer-to-peer processing. The first type accesses unused CPU power among networked computers. A well-known application of this type is **SETI@home** (http://setiathome.ssl.berkeley.edu). These applications are from open-source projects, and they can be downloaded at no cost.

The second form of peer-to-peer is real-time, person-to-person collaboration, such as Microsoft SharePoint Workspace (http://office.microsoft.com/en-us/sharepoint-workspace). This product provides P2P collaborative applications that use buddy lists to establish a connection and allow real-time collaboration within the application.

The third peer-to-peer category is advanced search and file sharing. This category is characterized by natural-language searches of millions of peer systems. It enables users to discover other users, not just data and Web pages. One example of this category is BitTorrent.

BitTorrent (www.bittorrent.com) is an open-source, free, peer-to-peer file-sharing application that simplifies the problem of sharing large files by dividing them into tiny pieces, or "torrents." BitTorrent addresses two of the biggest problems of file sharing: (1) downloading bogs down when many people access a file at once, and (2) some people leech, meaning they download content but refuse to share it. BitTorrent eliminates the bottleneck by enabling all users to share little pieces of a file at the same time—a process called *swarming*. The program prevents leeching because users must upload a file while they download it. Thus, the more popular the content, the more efficiently it zips over a network.

before you go on...

1. Compare and contrast the three wireline communications channels.

2. Describe the various technologies that enable users to send high-volume data over any network.

3. Describe the Ethernet and TCP/IP protocols.

4. Differentiate between client/server computing and peer-to-peer processing.

6.3 The Internet and the World Wide Web

The **Internet ("the Net")** is a global WAN that connects approximately 1 million organizational computer networks in more than 200 countries on all continents, including Antarctica. It has become so widespread that it features in the daily routine of almost 2 billion people. Participating computer systems include smartphones, PCs, LANs, databases, and mainframes.

The computers and organizational nodes on the Internet can be of different types and makes. They are connected to one another by data communications lines of different speeds. The primary network connections and telecommunications lines that link the nodes are referred to as the **Internet backbone**. For the Internet, the backbone is a fiber-optic network that is operated primarily by large telecommunications companies.

As a network of networks, the Internet enables people to access data in other organizations and to communicate, collaborate, and exchange information seamlessly around the world, quickly and inexpensively. Thus, the Internet has become a necessity for modern businesses.

The Internet grew out of an experimental project of the Advanced Research Project Agency (ARPA) of the U.S. Department of Defense. The project began in 1969 as the *ARPAnet*. Its purpose was to test the feasibility of a WAN over which researchers, educators, military personnel, and government agencies could share data, exchange messages, and transfer files.

Today, Internet technologies are being used both within and among organizations. An **intranet** is a network that uses Internet protocols so that users can take advantage of familiar applications and work habits. Intranets support discovery (easy and inexpensive browsing and search), communication, and collaboration inside an organization. For the numerous uses of intranets, see www.intranetjournal.com.

In contrast, an **extranet** connects parts of the intranets of different organizations. In addition, it enables business partners to communicate securely over the Internet using virtual private networks (VPNs, explained in Chapter 4). Extranets offer limited accessibility to the intranets of participating companies, as well as necessary interorganizational communications. They are widely used in the areas of business-to-business (B2B) electronic commerce (see Chapter 7) and supply chain management (SCM; see Chapter 10).

No central agency manages the Internet. Instead, the costs of its operation are shared among hundreds of thousands of nodes. Thus, the cost for any one organization is small. Organizations must pay a small fee if they wish to register their names, and they need to have their own hardware and software to operate their internal networks. The organizations are obliged to move any data or information that enter their organizational network, regardless of the source, to their destination, at no charge to the senders. The senders, of course, pay the telephone bills for using either the backbone or regular telephone lines.

Accessing the Internet

The Internet may be accessed in several ways. From your place of work or your university, you can access the Internet via your organization's LAN. A campus or company backbone connects all of the various LANs and servers in the organization to the Internet. You can also log onto the Internet from your home or on the road, using either wireline or wireless connections.

Connecting via an Online Service. You can also access the Internet by opening an account with an Internet service provider. An **Internet service provider** is a company that provides Internet connections for a fee. Large ISPs include America Online (www.aol.com), Juno (www.juno.com), Earthlink (www.earthlink.com), and NetZero (www.netzero.net). In addition, many telephone providers and cable companies sell Internet access, as do computer companies such as Microsoft. To use this service you need a modem and standard communication software.

ISPs connect to one another through **network access points (NAPs)**. NAPs are exchange points for Internet traffic. They determine how traffic is routed. NAPs are key components of the Internet backbone. Figure 6.9 displays a schematic of the Internet. The white links at the top of the figure represent the Internet backbone; the brown dots where the white links meet are the NAPs.

Connecting via Other Means. There have been several attempts to make access to the Internet cheaper, faster, and easier. For example, terminals known as Internet kiosks have been

FIGURE 6.9 Internet (backbone in white). (*Source:* © Mark Stay/iStockphoto)

Table **6.2** **Internet Connection Methods**	Service	Description
	Dial-up	Still used in the United States where broadband is not available.
	DSL	Broadband access via telephone companies.
	Cable modem	Access over your cable TV coaxial cable. Can have degraded performance if many of your neighbors are accessing the Internet at once.
	Satellite	Access where cable and DSL are not available.
	Wireless	Very convenient, and WiMAX will increase the use of broadband wireless.
	Fiber-to-the-home (FTTH)	Expensive and usually only placed in new housing developments.

located in such public places as libraries and airports (and even in convenience stores in some countries) for use by people who do not have their own computers. Accessing the Internet from smartphones and iPads is common, and fiber-to-the-home (FTTH) is growing rapidly. FTTH involves connecting fiber-optic cable directly to individual homes. This system initially was restricted to new residential developments, but it is rapidly spreading. Table 6.2 summarizes the various means of connecting to the Internet.

Addresses on the Internet. Each computer on the Internet has an assigned address, called the **Internet Protocol (IP) address** that distinguishes it from all other computers. The IP address consists of sets of numbers, in four parts, separated by dots. For example, the IP address of one computer might be 135.62.128.91. You can access a Web site by typing this number in the address bar of your browser.

Currently, there are two IP addressing schemes. The first scheme, IPv4, is the most widely used. IP addresses using IPv4 consist of 32 bits, meaning that there are 2^{32} possibilities for IP addresses, or 4,294,967,295 distinct addresses. Note that the IP address in the preceding paragraph (135.62.128.91) is an IPv4 address. At the time that IPv4 was developed, there were not as many computers that need addresses as there are today. Therefore, a new IP addressing scheme has been developed, IPv6.

IP addresses using IPv6 consist of 128 bits, meaning that there are 2^{128} possibilities for distinct IP addresses, which is an unimaginably large number. IPv6, which is replacing IPv4, will accommodate the rapidly increasing number of devices that need IP addresses, such as smartphones.

IP addresses must be unique so that computers on the Internet know where to find one another. The Internet Corporation for Assigned Names (ICANN) (www.icann.org) coordinates these unique addresses throughout the world. Without that coordination, we would not have one global Internet.

Because the numeric IP addresses are difficult to remember, most computers have names as well. ICANN accredits certain companies called *registrars* to register these names, which are derived from a system called the domain name system (DNS). Domain names consist of multiple parts, separated by dots that are read from right to left. For example, consider the domain name *business.auburn.edu*. The rightmost part (or zone) of an Internet name is its top-level domain (TLD). The letters *edu* in business.auburn.edu indicate that this is an educational site. The following are popular U.S. TLDs:

com   commercial sites
edu   educational sites
mil   military government sites
gov   civilian government sites
org   organizations

To finish our domain name example, *auburn* is the name of the organization (Auburn University), and *business* is the name of the particular machine (server) within the organization to which the message is being sent.

A top-level domain is the domain at the highest level in the hierarchical Domain Name System of the Internet. The top-level domain names are located in the root zone (rightmost zone) of the name. Management of most TLDs is delegated to responsible organizations by ICANN. ICANN operates the Internet Assigned Numbers Authority (IANA), which is in charge of maintaining the DNS root zone. Today, IANA distinguishes the following groups of TLDs:

- Country-code top-level domains (ccTLD): Two letter domains established for countries or territories. For example, *de* stands for Germany, *it* for Italy, and *ru* for Russia.
- Internationalized country code top-level domains (IDN ccTLD): These are ccTLDs in non-Latin character sets (e.g., Arabic or Chinese).
- Generic top-level domains (gTLD): Top-level domains with three or more characters. gTLDs initially consisted of .gov, .edu, .com, .mil, .org, and .net. In late 2000, ICANN introduced .aero, .biz, .coop, .info, .museum, .name, and .pro. In June 2012, ICANN revealed nearly 2,000 applications for new top-level domains.

The Future of the Internet

Consumer demand for content delivered over the Internet is increasing rapidly. Recall that Cisco estimates that Internet traffic will total some 64 exabytes per month in 2014. Many experts are now concerned that Internet users will experience brownouts from three factors: (1) the increasing number of people who work online, (2) the soaring popularity of Web sites such as YouTube that require large amounts of bandwidth, and (3) the tremendous demand for high-definition television delivered over the Internet. These brownouts will cause computers to go offline for several minutes at a time. Researchers assert that if Internet bandwidth is not improved rapidly, then within a few years the Internet will be able to function only at a much reduced speed.

Even today, the Internet sometimes is too slow for data-intensive applications such as full-motion video files (movies) or large medical files (X-rays). In addition, the Internet is unreliable and is not secure. As a result, Internet2 has been developed by more than 200 U.S. universities collaborating with industry and government. **Internet2** develops and deploys advanced network applications such as remote medical diagnosis, digital libraries, distance education, online simulation, and virtual laboratories. It is designed to be fast, always on, everywhere, natural, intelligent, easy, and trusted. Note that Internet2 is not a separate physical network from the Internet. For more detail, see www.internet2.edu.

The World Wide Web

Many people equate the Internet with the World Wide Web. However, they are not the same thing. The Internet functions as a transport mechanism, whereas the World Wide Web is an application that uses those transport functions. Other applications, such as e-mail, also run on the Internet.

The **World Wide Web (The Web, WWW, or W3)** is a system of universally accepted standards for storing, retrieving, formatting, and displaying information via a client/server architecture. The Web handles all types of digital information, including text, hypermedia, graphics, and sound. It uses graphical user interfaces (GUIs; explained in Technology Guide 2), so it is very easy to navigate.

Organizations that wish to offer information through the Web must establish a *home page*, which is a text and graphical screen display that usually welcomes the user and provides basic information on the organization that has established the page. In most cases, the home page will lead users to other pages. All the pages of a particular company or individual are collectively known as a **Web site**. Most Web pages provide a way to contact the organization or the individual. The person in charge of an organization's Web site is its *Webmaster*. (Note: *Webmaster* is a gender-neutral title.)

To access a Web site, the user must specify a **uniform resource locator (URL)**, which points to the address of a specific resource on the Web. For instance, the URL for Microsoft is http://www.microsoft.com. Recall that HTTP stands for hypertext transport protocol. The remaining letters in this URL—www.microsoft.com—indicate the domain name that identifies the Web server that stores the Web site.

Users access the Web primarily through software applications called **browsers**. Browsers provide a graphical front end that enables users to point-and-click their way across the Web, a process called *surfing*. Web browsers became a means of universal access because they deliver the same interface on any operating system under which they run.

before you go on...

1. Describe the various ways that you can connect to the Internet.
2. Identify each part of an Internet address.
3. What are the functions of browsers?
4. Describe the difference between the Internet and the World Wide Web.

6.4 Network Applications

Now that you have a working knowledge of what networks are and how you can access them, the key question is, How do businesses use networks to improve their operations? This section addresses that question. Stated in general terms, networks support businesses and other organizations in all types of functions.

This section will explore numerous network applications, including discovery, communication, collaboration, e-learning and distance learning, virtual universities, and telecommuting. These applications, however, are merely a sampling of the many network applications currently available to users. Even if these applications formed an exhaustive list today, they would not do so tomorrow when something new will be developed. Further, placing network applications in categories is difficult because there will always be borderline cases. For example, the difference between chat rooms (in the communications category) and teleconference (in the collaboration category) is only one of degree.

Discovery

The Internet enables users to access or discover information located in databases all over the world. By browsing and searching data sources on the Web, users can apply the Internet's discovery capability to areas ranging from education to government services to entertainment to commerce. Although having access to all this information is a great benefit, it is critically important to realize that there is no quality assurance for information on the Web. The Web is truly democratic in that *anyone* can post information to it. Therefore, the fundamental rule about information on the Web is "User beware!"

In addition, the Web's major strength—the vast stores of information it contains—also presents a major challenge. The amount of information on the Web can be overwhelming, and it doubles approximately each year. As a result, navigating through the Web and gaining access to necessary information are becoming more and more difficult. To accomplish these tasks, people increasingly are using search engines, directories, and portals.

Search Engines and Metasearch Engines. A **search engine** is a computer program that searches for specific information by key words and then reports the results. A search engine maintains an index of billions of Web pages. It uses that index to find pages that match a set of user-specified keywords. Such indexes are created and updated by *webcrawlers*, which are

FIGURE 6.10 The KartOO home page (www.kartoo.com).

computer programs that browse the Web and create a copy of all visited pages. Search engines then index these pages to provide fast searches.

In mid-2013, four search engines accounted for almost all searches in the United States. They are, in order: Google (www.google.com), Bing (www.bing.com), Yahoo! (www.yahoo.com), and Ask (www.ask.com). In addition, there are an incredible number of other search engines that are quite useful, many of which perform very specific searches. (See an article on "The Top 100 Alternative Search Engines" that appeared on www.readwriteweb.com.) The leading search engine in China is Baidu, which claimed 78 percent of the Chinese market in April 2013.

For an even more thorough search, you can use a metasearch engine. Metasearch engines search several engines at once and then integrate the findings to answer users' queries. Examples are Surf-wax (www.surfwax.com), Metacrawler (www.metacrawler.com), Mamma (www.mamma.com), KartOO (www.kartoo.com), and Dogpile (www.dogpile.com). Figure 6.10 illustrates the KartOO home page.

One interesting search engine is known as Summly. IT's About Business 6.2 explains how Summly works.

IT's [about business]

6.2 A New Search Engine **MIS**

When Nick D'Aloisio was 12, he created an app called SongStumblr, which used Bluetooth to let users know what music people nearby were listening to. Next, he taught himself the basics of artificial intelligence (AI) software and built an app called Facemood, which updates you on the emotional state of your friends by monitoring their Facebook status. Over the next 3 years, Nick earned about $30,000 from profits from one-time sales of his apps, netting about $1.50 for each app download after deducting Apple's 30 percent share of the profits. By age 15, he had set up his own company. (His mother had to sign all of his legal documents because he was underage.)

In 2011, while studying for a history exam, Nick grew frustrated with the huge amount of text that showed up on Google search results. To save himself time, he wrote a program that summarized content in an easily digestible preview. He used his flair for languages—he was studying Latin, Mandarin Chinese, and French at the time—to create a program, which he named Summly, that would extract the most relevant sentences out of the long text that Google searches provide. Microsoft Word had already marketed a summarizing tool that searched for the most frequent keywords sequentially. However, Nick was convinced he could do better with a genetic algorithm that could choose important sentences as

a human does. Therefore, he created a program that detects the topic of a text and uses that information to determine what metrics to apply. Then, the program utilizes those metrics to determine, for example, if numbers are more important than descriptive words, and to extract critical sentences accordingly.

Nick realized that his program could be used as much more than just a personal study tool. It could be used as a service for media companies, financial institutions, law firms, or any organization that faces the challenge of extracting key points from huge amounts of data. For example, if you visit a Web site that contains excessive amounts of information, Summly will provide you with a more user-friendly version of the information condensed into three to five bullet points. Summly works especially well with news articles, because it bullet-points the main headlines. Summly also provides key words for the article.

D'Aloisio first honed his knowledge of AI and writing computer code. He then contacted a linguistics researcher at MIT's Semantics Lab and paid him $250 to analyze his algorithm. The researcher's conclusion: Summly constructed summaries in a way that was 40 percent more similar to the process humans use than its competitors. This finding was enough validation for D'Aloisio to release a free app (then called Trimit), which ran on an iPhone and received regular updates as he refined it. He set up a Web site and a demo video of the app on YouTube. A patent search revealed that, although similar apps existed in the market, none featured the trained AI component or the tie-in to the iPhone that Trimit could boast.

Shortly after the app's release, two investment funds contacted D'Aloisio via his Web site. One was Horizons Ventures, whose founder and manager had seen a story about Trimit on TechCrunch (a technology blog) and was interested in the technology behind the app. After thoroughly examining D'Aloisio's app, in September 2011 Horizons purchased a 25 percent stake in the product for $300,000.

Over the course of the next 3 months, Summly was downloaded 130,000 times. The downloads were made available free of charge to build name recognition for the product.

You might ask, if the downloads are free, how does D'Aloisio plan to make a profit? Rather than make money from users, he licensed Summly to media and financial companies, Web browsers, and search engines. He will charge these outlets either a regular subscription fee or a fee for every 1,000 summaries. He has yet to set the exact pricing for his product.

D'Aloisio then hired full-time programmers who trained his genetic algorithm to mimic choices made by humans. This process was tedious and time-consuming, and it involved reading thousands and thousands of Web articles (such as Wikipedia, movie reviews, and many other sources), choosing the three to five most important sentences, and feeding them into the algorithm.

D'Aloisio believes his product will be successful because search interfaces like Google have not changed in many years, despite a dramatic increase in the amount of content that is available on the Web. He maintains that he has developed an entirely new type of search engine that can revolutionize the search-engine field.

In March 2013, Yahoo! purchased Summly for $30 million, and it hired D'Aloisio and two other Summly employees. D'Aloisio pulled Summly's app off the market, but he claimed that the technology behind Summly would soon be incorporated into Yahoo! products.

Sources: Compiled from H. Tsukayama, "Summly and Its Teen Founder Snapped Up by Yahoo," *The Washington Post*, March 26, 2013; B. Stelter, "He Has Millions and a New Job at Yahoo. Soon He'll Be 18." *The New York Times*, March 25, 2013; P. Olson, "Search Engine Wunderkind," *Forbes*, March 12, 2012; J. Wakefield, "British Designer of Summly App Hits Jackpot," *BBC News*, December 28, 2011; M. Kirkpatrick, "Summly: New App Helps You Read All Your Bookmarked Links in Minutes," *ReadWrite-Web*, December 13, 2011; P. Olson, "Teenage Programmer Backed by Hong Kong Billionaire Li Ka Shing," *Forbes*, December 13, 2011; C. Bonnington, "Teen's IOS App Uses Complex Algorithms to Summarize the Web," *Wired*, December 13, 2011; www.summly.com, accessed March 2, 2013.

Questions

1. What are the advantages of the Summly app? Do you see any disadvantages in using the product?
2. Has D'Aloisio actually created a new kind of search engine? Support your answer.

Publication of Material in Foreign Languages. Not only is there a huge amount of information on the Internet, but it is written in many different languages. How, then, do you access this information? The answer is that you use an *automatic translation* of Web pages. Such translation is available to and from all major languages, and its quality is improving with time. Some major translation products are Microsoft's Bing translator (http://www.microsofttranslator .com) and Google (www.google.com/language_tools) (see Figure 6.11), as well as products and services available at Trados (www.trados.com).

Should companies invest their time and resources to make their Web sites accessible in multiple languages? The answer is, absolutely. In fact, multilingual Web sites are now a competitive necessity because of the global nature of the business environment. Companies increasingly are looking outside their home markets to grow revenues and attract new customers. When companies are disseminating information around the world, getting that information correct is

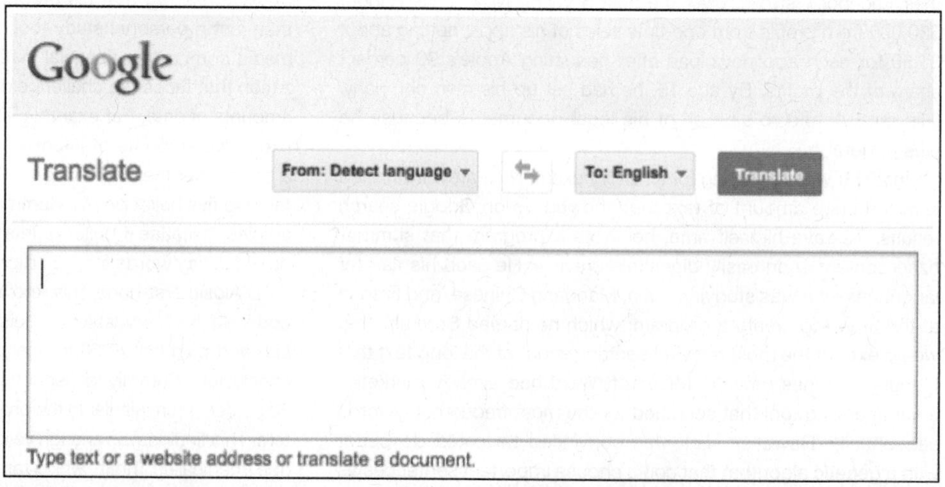

FIGURE 6.11 Google Translate.

essential. It is not enough for companies to translate Web content. They must also localize that content and be sensitive to the needs of the people in local markets.

To reach 80 percent of the world's Internet users, a Web site needs to support a minimum of ten languages: English, Chinese, Spanish, Japanese, German, Korean, French, Italian, Russian, and Portuguese. At 20 cents and more per word, translation services are expensive. Companies supporting ten languages can spend $200,000 annually to localize information and another $50,000 to maintain the Web sites. Translation budgets for major multinational companies can run in the millions of dollars. Many large companies use Systran S.A. (www .systransoft.com) for high-quality machine translation services.

Portals.   Most organizations and their managers encounter information overload. Information is scattered across numerous documents, e-mail messages, and databases at different locations and systems. Finding relevant and accurate information is often time-consuming and may require users to access multiple systems.

One solution to this problem is to use portals. A **portal** is a Web-based, personalized gateway to information and knowledge that provides relevant information from different IT systems and the Internet using advanced search and indexing techniques. After reading the next section, you will be able to distinguish among four types of portals: commercial, affinity, corporate, and industrywide. The four types of portals are distinguished by the audiences they serve.

A **commercial (public) portal** is the most popular type of portal on the Internet. It is intended for broad and diverse audiences, and it offers routine content, some of it in real time (e.g., a stock ticker). Examples are Lycos (www.lycos.com) and Microsoft Network (www.msn.com).

In contrast, an **affinity portal** offers a single point of entry to an entire community of affiliated interests, such as a hobby group or a political party. Your university most likely has an affinity portal for its alumni. Figure 6.12 displays the affinity portal for the University of West Georgia. Other examples of affinity portals are www.techweb.com and www.zdnet.com.

As the name suggests, a **corporate portal** offers a personalized, single point of access through a Web browser to critical business information located inside and outside an organization. These portals are also known as *enterprise portals*, *information portals*, and *enterprise information portals*. In addition to making it easier to find needed information, corporate portals offer customers and employees self-service opportunities. IT's About Business 6.3 provides an example of an effective corporate portal maintained by Marriott.

FIGURE 6.12 University of West Georgia affinity portal (Courtesy of the University of West Georgia).

Welcome to myUWG

Welcome to the University of West Georgia's myUWG website.
Please login to the right.

Pay Fees By Credit Card
Click here to pay fees by credit card.

What's Inside?
E-mail: Send and receive e-mail, and create your own personal address book.

Calendar: Access and manage your personal, course and school calendars.

Groups: Create, manage and join group homepages for clubs, affiliations and interests.

and much more...

Secure Access Login

User Name:

Password:

Login   Cancel

Having problems logging in?
Click here for new Password Change Rules and supported browsers.

Lost your password?

Lookup your Username

Top   **UNIVERSITY of West Georgia**

IT's [about business]

6.3 Marriott's Corporate Portal

Marriott International operates more than 3,500 hotel properties worldwide under its portfolio of brands, including Marriott Hotels & Resorts, JW Marriott, Renaissance, Edition, Autograph Collection, and Courtyard by Marriott. These properties fall into the following categories: luxury, collections, lifestyle and boutique, signature, select service, and extended stay.

Until 2011, Marriott used a "one size fits all" approach for its advertising, marketing, and branding efforts, despite the fact that independent franchisers own most of its properties. For years, regardless of location or brand, each property was offered the same (low) level of marketing support. One major limitation of this strategy was that different brands targeted different types of customers. For example, leisure travelers use very different criteria than business travelers when choosing a hotel.

As a result of this policy, each Marriott property was largely responsible for its own marketing efforts. Consequently, there was little consistency from location to location or from brand to brand. Furthermore, many properties did not have the funds to support their own marketing efforts. Finally, to compound the problem, Marriott had failed to create an easy method for sharing marketing materials between corporate headquarters and the various properties.

As customer attitudes and preferences changed, Marriott realized that its corporate marketing practices needed to evolve as well. Consequently, the company launched a rebranding effort to tailor its marketing and branding decisions to each unique brand and target market. To fully implement this shift in strategy, the company needed a better strategy to share and leverage its marketing assets. Therefore, it created a user-friendly online corporate portal to manage the creation, distribution, and review of marketing practices and material, as well as to support its new brand standards.

To address its marketing concerns, Marriott International created BrandWorks, an automated online marketing portal, in all of its locations. BrandWorks makes it quick, easy, and cost-effective for each of the company's properties to create their own customized marketing materials. Marriot hotels, advertising agencies, and marketing managers use the portal to share and/or download stock photography, view brand standards and guidelines, download marketing templates, and use document wizards to create customized marketing materials.

Going further, BrandWorks enables Marriott to offer different programs and strategies to each of its distinct brands that are designed specifically to appeal to their respective target audiences. Using BrandWorks, Marriott compiled a comprehensive catalog of updated brand guidelines, templates, strategies, and materials so that it could implement its promotions and marketing activities properly and cost-effectively across all of its markets, and in multiple languages.

Marriott also deployed a centralized offer-management system in BrandWorks. This system allows its properties worldwide to create Marriott Rewards offers and deals and then promote them on the Marriott Web site and via other marketing channels.

BrandWorks also has built-in tracking capabilities to report on promotional programs, as well as automated analyses to identify which offers, programs, and marketing campaigns are most successful. In 2012, Marriott integrated social media strategies for all of its brands and properties into the portal.

BrandWorks enabled Marriott to improve information sharing and collaboration among its global locations and corporate teams. Internal users can report on total log-ins, the number of documents currently in the system based on brand and category, and the number of offers created and disseminated through each marketing channel. These data enable the company to determine what marketing information to activate for each brand and for each audience. Consequently, Marriott can now deliver a better customer experience, ensure consistency across locations and languages, and help executives make better decisions.

In addition, the offer management system within BrandWorks enables Marriott marketing managers to deliver revenue-generating offers to customers more rapidly. Because BrandWorks has built-in capabilities to tailor its offers to distinct audiences, demographics, and marketing channels, marketing staffers have submitted more than 3 times as many offers through the portal than they did prior to implementing the system.

Other Marriott departments have started to use BrandWorks as well. For example, the HR department has begun posting its presentations on the portal. The food and beverage department also posts its menus to the portal, as well as information on group sales and event management.

From 2009 to 2011, user log-ins to Marriott's portal increased by 186 percent, and the amount of marketing material distributed through the portal increased by more than 100 percent. In 2011 alone, more than 6,000 users from Marriott properties, corporate headquarters, and regional departments logged in to Brand-Works. The users came from 70 countries and territories, and they represented 16 different brands. These individuals accessed BrandWorks remotely through any Internet browser using desktops, laptops, tablets, and smartphones.

Sources: Compiled from S. Brier, "How Marriott Got Marketing Right," *Baseline Magazine*, January 17, 2012; S. Brier, "Marriott Saves Estimated $9.2 Million in Marketing Costs with Online Portal," *Hospitality Technology*, December 19, 2011; T. McQuilken, "Marriott Brings Marketing to Next Level with BrandWorks," *Hotel Business*, September 21, 2011; "Case Study: Marriott International," *Excella Consulting*, accessed February 28, 2012; www.marriott.com, accessed March 27, 2013.

Questions

1. Provide examples of the advantages BrandWorks brought to Marriott's franchisees.
2. Provide examples of how BrandWorks could be used for functional areas of Marriott other than marketing.

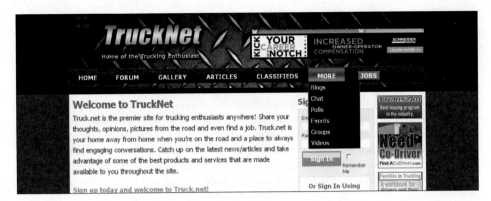

FIGURE 6.13 TruckNet portal.

Whereas corporate portals are associated with a single company, an **industrywide** portal serves entire industries. An example is TruckNet (www.truck.net), a portal for the trucking industry and the trucking community, including professional drivers, owner/operators, and trucking companies (see Figure 6.13). TruckNet provides drivers with personalized Web-based e-mail, access to applications to leading trucking companies in the United States and Canada, and access to the Drivers Round Table, a forum where drivers can discuss issues of interest. The portal also provides a large database of trucking jobs and general information related to the trucking industry.

Communication

The second major category of network applications is communication. There are many types of communication technologies, including e-mail, call centers, chat rooms, and voice. You learn about each one in this section. You will read about another type of communication, blogging, in Chapter 9.

Electronic Mail. Electronic mail (e-mail) is the largest-volume application running over the Internet. Studies have found that almost all companies conduct business transactions via e-mail, and the vast majority confirm that e-mail is tied to their means of generating revenue. In fact, for many users, e-mail has all but replaced the telephone.

Web-Based Call Centers. Effective personalized customer contact is becoming an important aspect of Web-based customer support. Such service is provided through *Web-based call centers*, also known as *customer care centers*. For example, if you need to contact a software vendor for technical support, you will usually be communicating with the vendor's Web-based call center, using e-mail, a telephone conversation, or a simultaneous voice/Web session. Web-based call centers are sometimes located in foreign countries such as India. Such *offshoring* is an important issue for U.S. companies. (We discuss offshoring in detail in Chapter 13.)

For several reasons, some U.S. companies are moving their call center operations back to the United States. First, they believe they have less control of their overseas call center operations. They must depend on the vendor company to uphold their standards, such as quality of service. A second difficulty is language differences, which can create serious communication problems. Third, companies that manage sensitive information risk breaching customer confidentiality and security. Finally, the call center representatives typically work with many companies. As a result, they may not deliver the same level of customer services that each company requires.

Electronic Chat Rooms. *Electronic chat* refers to an arrangement whereby participants exchange conversational messages in real time. A chat room is a virtual meeting place where many people (in fact, anyone) come to chat. Chat programs allow you to send messages to people who are connected to the same channel of communication at the same time. Anyone can join in the conversation. Messages are displayed on your screen as they arrive, even if you are in the middle of typing a message.

There are two major types of chat programs. The first type is Web based, which allows you to send messages to Internet users by using a Web browser and visiting a Web chat site (e.g., http://messenger.yahoo.com). The second type is e-mail based (text only); it is called *Internet Relay Chat (IRC)*. A business can use IRC to interact with customers, provide online experts for answers to questions, and so on.

Voice Communication.   When people need to communicate with one another from a distance, they use the telephone more frequently than any other communication device. With the plain old telephone service (POTS), every call opened up a dedicated circuit for the duration of the call. A dedicated circuit connects you to the person with whom you are talking and is devoted only to your call. In contrast, as you saw earlier in this chapter, the Internet divides data into packets, which traverse the Internet in random order and are reassembled at their destination.

With **Internet telephony**, also known as **voice-over Internet protocol** or **VoIP**, phone calls are treated as just another kind of data. That is, your analog voice signals are digitized, sectioned into packets, and then sent over the Internet. In the past, to utilize VoIP you needed a computer with a sound card and a microphone. Today, however, you do not need special phones or headsets for your computer.

VoIP can reduce your monthly phone bills. However, packet switching can cause garbled communications. For example, if the packets of a message arrive out of order, that is not a problem when you are sending an e-mail or transmitting a photo. Incorrect reassembly of the packets of a voice message, however, will garble the message. Fortunately, this is less of a problem than in the past, because VoIP software continues to improve, and typical communications links have become much faster. So, although VoIP is not perfect, it is ready for prime time.

Skype (www.skype.com) provides several VoIP services for free: voice and video calls to users who also have Skype, instant messaging, short message service, voice mail, one-to-one and group chats, and conference calls with up to nine people (see Figure 6.14). As of mid-2013, the most current version of Skype offered full-screen, high-definition video calling, Skype Access (to access WiFi hotspots), call transfer to a Skype contact on a mobile or landline, improved quality of calls, and ease of use. In addition, it offers other functions for which users pay. For example, SkypeOut allows you to make calls to landline phones and mobile

FIGURE 6.14 Skype 5.5 interface.

phones. SkypeIn provides a number that your friends can call from any phone and you pick up the call in Skype.

Vonage (www.vonage.com) also provides VoIP services, but for a fee (approximately $25 per month). With Vonage you make and receive calls with your existing home phone through your broadband Internet connection. Your phone actually connects to Vonage instead of an actual phone company. The person whom you are calling does not need to have Vonage or even an Internet connection.

Unified Communications. In the past, organizational networks for wired and wireless data, voice communications, and videoconferencing operated independently, and the IT department managed each network separately. This arrangement increased costs and reduced productivity.

Unified communications (UC) simplifies and integrates all forms of communications—voice, voice mail, fax, chat, e-mail, instant messaging, short message service, presence (location) services, and videoconferencing—on a common hardware and software platform. *Presence services* enable users to know where their intended recipients are and if they are available, in real time.

UC unifies all forms of human and computer communications into a common user experience. For example, UC allows an individual to receive a voice mail message and then read it in his or her e-mail inbox. In another example, UC enables users to seamlessly collaborate with another person on a project, regardless of where the users are located. One user could quickly locate the other user by accessing an interactive directory, determining whether that user is available, engaging in a text messaging session, and then escalating the session to a voice call or even a video call, all in real time.

Collaboration

The third major category of network applications is collaboration. An important feature of modern organizations is that people collaborate to perform work. **Collaboration** refers to efforts by two or more entities—that is, individuals, teams, groups, or organizations—who work together to accomplish certain tasks. The term **work group** refers specifically to two or more individuals who act together to perform some task.

Workflow is the movement of information as it progresses through the sequence of steps that make up an organization's work procedures. Workflow management makes it possible to pass documents, information, and tasks from one participant to another in a way that is governed by the organization's rules or procedures. Workflow systems are tools for automating business processes.

If group members are working in different locations, they constitute a **virtual group (team)**. Virtual groups conduct *virtual meetings*—that is, they "meet" electronically. **Virtual collaboration** (or *e-collaboration*) refers to the use of digital technologies that enable organizations or individuals who are geographically dispersed to collaboratively plan, design, develop, manage, and research products, services, and innovative applications. Organizational employees frequently collaborate virtually with one another. In addition, organizations collaborate virtually with customers, suppliers, and other business partners to become more productive and competitive.

One type of collaboration is **crowdsourcing**, in which an organization outsources a task to an undefined, generally large group of people in the form of an open call. Crowdsourcing provides many potential benefits to organizations. First, crowds can explore problems—and often resolve them—at relatively low cost, and often very quickly. Second, the organization can tap a wider range of talent than might be present among its employees. Third, by listening to the crowd, organizations gain firsthand insight into their customers' desires. Finally, crowdsourcing taps into the global world of ideas, helping companies work through a rapid design process. Let's look at some examples of crowdsourcing.

- *Crowdsourcing help desks:* IT help desks are a necessary service on college campuses because students depend on their computers and Internet access to complete their schoolwork and attend class online. At Indiana University at Bloomington, new IT help desks use crowdsourcing to alleviate the cost and pressure of having to answer so many calls.

Students and professors post their IT problems on an online forum, where other students and amateur IT experts answer them.

- *Recruitment:* Champlain College in Vermont developed a Champlain For Reel program, inviting students to share via YouTube videos recounting their experiences at the school and the ways they benefited from their time there. The YouTube channel serves to recruit prospective students and even updates alumni on campus and community events.

- *Scitable* (www.nature.com/scitable) combines social networking and academic collaboration. Through crowdsourcing, students, professors, and scientists discuss problems, find solutions, and swap resources and journals. Scitable is a free site that lets each individual user turn to crowdsourcing for answers even while helping others.

- *The Great Sunflower Project* (www.greatsunflower.org): Gretchen LeBuhn, an associate biology professor at San Francisco State University, needed help with her studies of honeybees, but she had limited grant money. So, she contacted gardening groups around the country. Through this crowdsourcing strategy, LeBuhn ultimately created a network of more than 25,000 gardeners and schools to assist with her research. She then sent these participants seeds for plants that attract bees. In return, the participants recorded honeybee visits and activity for her on her Web site.

- Procter & Gamble (P&G) uses InnoCentive (www.innocentive.com), where company researchers post their problems. P&G offers cash rewards to problem solvers.

- At defense contractor HCL Technologies (www.hcltech.com), crowdsourcing provides the foundation for strategic business planning. More than 8,000 employees review internal business plans to create transparency across business units and open up the strategic planning process across the company. The process has provided honest assessments and excellent overall business analysis. As a result of this process, HCL has changed its strategic focus from providing application support to providing strategic services to its clients.

Although crowdsourcing has numerous success stories, there are many questions and concerns about this system, including the following:

- How accurate is the content created by the nonexperts in the crowd? How is accuracy maintained?

- How is crowd-created content being updated? How can companies be certain that the content is relevant?

- Should the crowd be limited to experts? If so, then how would a company go about implementing this policy?

- The crowd may submit too many ideas, with most of them being worthless. In this scenario, evaluating all of these ideas can be prohibitively expensive. For example, during the BP oil spill in 2010, crowds submitted more than 20,000 suggestions on how to stem the flow of oil. The problem was very technical, so there were many poor suggestions. Nevertheless, despite the fact that BP was under severe time constraints, the company had to evaluate all of the ideas.

- Content contributors may violate copyrights, either intentionally or unintentionally.

- The quality of content (and therefore subsequent decisions) depends on the composition of the crowd. The best decisions may come if the crowd is made up of people with diverse opinions and ideas. In many cases, however, companies do not know the makeup of the crowd in advance.

Collaboration can be *synchronous*, meaning that all team members meet at the same time. Teams may also collaborate *asynchronously* when team members cannot meet at the same time. Virtual teams, whose members are located throughout the world, typically must collaborate asynchronously.

A variety of software products are available to support all types of collaboration. Among the most prominent are Microsoft SharePoint Workspace, Google Docs, IBM Lotus Quickr, and Jive. In general, these products provide online collaboration capabilities, workgroup e-mail, distributed databases, bulletin whiteboards, electronic text editing, document management, workflow capabilities, instant virtual meetings, application sharing, instant messaging, consensus building, voting, ranking, and various application development tools.

These products also provide varying degrees of content control. Wikis, Google Docs, Microsoft SharePoint Workspace, and Jive provide for shared content with *version management*, whereas Microsoft SharePoint Workspace and IBM Lotus Quickr offer *version control*. Products that provide version management track changes to documents and provide features to accommodate multiple people working on the same document at the same time. In contrast, version-control systems provide each team member with an account that includes a set of permissions. Shared documents are located in shared directories. Document directories are often set up so that users must check out documents before they can edit them. When one team member checks out a document, no other member can access it. Once the document has been checked in, it becomes available to other members.

In this section, we review the major collaboration software products. We then shift our attention to two tools that support collaboration—electronic teleconferencing and videoconferencing.

Microsoft SharePoint. Microsoft's SharePoint product (www.microsoft.com/Sharepoint/default.mspx) provides shared content with version control. SharePoint supports document directories and has features that enable users to create and manage surveys, discussion forums, wikis, member blogs, member Web sites, and workflow. It also has a rigorous permissions structure, which allows organizations to control users' access based on their organizational role, team membership, interest, security level, or other criteria.

One company that has used SharePoint effectively is Continental Airlines. When new federal regulations regarding long runway delays went into effect, Continental responded by implementing a SharePoint system that puts various aspects of flight operations—aircraft status, pilots, crews, and customer care—on the same page. Under this system, the 135 general managers at the airline's domestic airports fill out a 16-page form online. The form includes the names and numbers of airport workers, from the airport authority to the person who drives the stairs to planes waiting on the runway. The general managers have to specify how they would manage delays of an hour, two hours, and two-and-one-half hours. The Sharepoint system includes a dashboard for Continental's centralized system operations center. People in the center can use the dashboard to quickly find information about delays and to communicate with pilots, crews, and dispatchers to decide what to do to mitigate any delays.

Google Docs. Google Docs (http://docs.google.com) is a free Web-based word processor, spreadsheet, and presentation application. It enables users to create and edit documents online while collaborating with other users. In contrast to Microsoft SharePoint Workspace, Google Docs allows multiple users to open, share, and edit documents at the same time.

IBM Lotus Quickr. IBM's Lotus Quickr (www.ibm.com/lotus/quickr) product provides shared content with version control in the form of document directories with check-in and check-out features based on user privileges. Quickr provides online team spaces where members can share and collaborate by utilizing team calendars, discussion forums, blogs, wikis, and other collaboration tools for managing projects and other content.

Jive. Jive's (www.jivesoftware.com) newest product, Clearspace, uses Web collaboration and communication tools such as forums, wikis, and blogs to allow people to share content with version management, via discussion rooms, calendars, and commotion lists. For example, Nike originally used Clearspace Community to run a technical support forum on Nike Plus (http://nikerunning.nike.com), a Web site where runners track their miles and calories burned using a sensor in their shoes. The company soon noticed that runners were also using the forum to meet other athletes. In response, Nike expanded its forum to include a section where runners could meet and challenge one another to races. Since that time, 40 percent of visitors to the site who did not own the Nike Plus sensor ended up buying the product.

Electronic Teleconferencing. **Teleconferencing** is the use of electronic communication technology that enables two or more people at different locations to hold a conference. There are several types of teleconferencing. The oldest and simplest is a telephone conference call,

FIGURE 6.15 Telepresence System.

HO Marketwire Photos/NewsCom

where several people talk to one another from multiple locations. The biggest disadvantage of conference calls is that they do not allow the participants to communicate face to face. In addition, participants in one location cannot see graphs, charts, and pictures at other locations.

To overcome these shortcomings, organizations are increasingly turning to video tele-conferencing, or videoconferencing. In a **videoconference**, participants in one location can view participants, documents, and presentations at other locations. The latest version of videoconferencing, called *telepresence*, enables participants to seamlessly share data, voice, pictures, graphics, and animation by electronic means. Conferees can also transmit data along with voice and video, which allows them to work together on documents and to exchange computer files.

Several companies are offering high-end telepresence systems. For example, Hewlett-Packard's Halo system (www.hp.com), Cisco's TelePresence 3000 (www.cisco.com), and Polycom's HDX (www.polycom.com) use massive high-definition screens up to eight feet wide to show people sitting around conference tables (see Figure 6.15). Telepresence systems also have advanced audio capabilities that let everyone talk at once without canceling out any voices. Financial and consulting firms are quickly adopting telepresence systems, such as the Blackstone Group (www.blackstone.com), a private equity firm, and Deloitte & Touche (www.deloitte.com), a consulting firm.

Let's look at two examples of how organizations use these various collaboration technologies.

- Burr & Forman (www.burr.com), a full-service law firm based in Atlanta, Georgia, uses Microsoft SharePoint as a content and document repository. SharePoint allowed users to find and share the documents they need faster and with less effort. Further, Burr could quickly, easily, and securely provide its clients with access to whatever documents they need. The firm was also able to consolidate nine different document libraries into a single library that all of its employees can access.

  Burr also uses AdobeConnect (www.adobe.com) to provide online training. This feature enables the firm train multiple people in different offices at one time. Burr also uses the tool for continuing education training, which requires input to prove that the person watches the entire video session.

  In addition, Burr employs Cisco System's (www.cisco.com) Tandberg video conferencing system for internal meetings, depositions, interviews, and other events. The firm has realized decreased travel costs as a result of using video conferencing.

- Ellegro Learning Solutions (www.ellegrolearning.com), a provider of customized corporate training and development programs, uses collaboration tolls to increase efficiency,

streamline operations, and increase profitability. One tool from LiquidPlanner (www
.liquidplanner.com) helps project team members work more efficiently. LiquidPlanner
allows the company to consolidate project-related information in one place, so developers,
programmers, consultants, managers, executives, and customers can easily access information and collaborate on development during the course of a project. This capability was
extremely important for Ellegro, which lacked a consistent approach to project tracking.
The firm needed to view priorities, resources, and timelines across multiple projects and
clients. They also needed to dynamically adjust their plans and compare their progress to
forecasted results, such as timelines, resource constraints, and delivery dates. By having
access to real-time updates on project development, managers can quickly shift priorities
as necessary, ensuring that the most important projects receive the resources and attention
they need.

Ellegro is also using the WebEx online conferencing platform to implement real-time
collaboration and virtual meetings, as well as to demonstrate learning programs to customers. Online conferencing reduces the firm's need for travel. Ellegro estimates that WebEx
saves the company about $8,000 per project through reduced travel and other expenses.
Further, because employees travel less, they are more productive.

E-Learning and Distance Learning

E-learning and distance learning are not the same thing, but they do overlap. E-learning refers
to learning supported by the Web. It can take place inside classrooms as a support to conventional teaching, such as when students work on the Web during class. It also can take place in
virtual classrooms, in which all coursework is done online and classes do not meet face-to-face.
In these cases, e-learning is a part of distance learning. **Distance learning (DL)** refers to any
learning situation in which teachers and students do not meet face-to-face.

Today, the Web provides a multimedia interactive environment for self-study. Web-enabled
systems make knowledge accessible to those who need it, when they need it, anytime, anywhere. For this reason, e-learning and DL can be useful both for formal education and for
corporate training. IT's About Business 6.4 illustrates how university students can take online
classes from anywhere in the world via Massive Online Open Courses or MOOCs.

IT's [about business]

6.4 Massive Open Online Courses   MIS

Massive open online courses—known as MOOCs—are a tool for
democratizing higher education. Hundreds of thousands of students around the world who lack access to elite universities have
been embracing MOOCs as a way to acquire sophisticated skills
and high-paying jobs without having to pay tuition or secure a
college degree.

Consider Stanford University's experience. In fall 2011,
160,000 students in 190 countries enrolled in a single AI course
offered by Stanford. An additional 200 students registered for
the course on campus. A few weeks into the semester, attendance for the on-campus course decreased to about 30, as
students decided to watch online videos instead of physically
attending the class. The course gave rise to its own community,
including a Facebook group, online discussions among participants, and volunteer translators who made the course available
in 44 languages.

The 23,000 students who completed the course received
a PDF file (suitable for framing) by e-mail that indicated their

percentile score. However, the file did not contain the name
"Stanford University." A total of 248 students, none of them from
Stanford, earned grades of 100 percent.

Besides the AI course, Stanford offered two other MOOCs in fall
2011—Machine Learning (104,000 registered, 13,000 completed
the course), and Introduction to Databases (92,000 registered, 7,000
completed the course). In Spring 2012, Stanford offered 13 MOOCs,
including Anatomy, Cryptography, Game Theory, and Natural
Language Processing.

On February 13, 2012, the Massachusetts Institute of Technology (MIT), which had been posting course materials online for
10 years, opened registration for its first MOOC, a circuits and
electronics course. The course served as a prototype for the university's MITx (www.mitx.org) project, which will eventually offer a
wide range of courses and will provide some sort of credential for
students who complete them.

Several factors contributed to the dramatic growth of MOOCs,
including improved technology and the rapidly increasing costs of

traditional universities. MOOCs are highly automated, with computer-graded assignments and exams. Nonetheless, they provide many opportunities for social interaction. The Stanford MOOCs, for example, offered virtual office hours and online discussion forums where students could ask and answer questions—and vote on which questions were important enough to filter up to the professors.

One Stanford professor observed that in a classroom, when a professor asks a question to the class, one student answers, and the others do not get a chance to participate. In contrast, in an online environment with embedded quizzes, *everyone* has to try to answer the questions. Students who do not know the answer can go back and listen to the lecture over and over until they do. The professor also noted that MOOCs allow students to work at their own pace and keep practicing until they master the content.

A student in one of Stanford's Fall 2011 MOOCs had not been a technology major, nor did she follow a technological career path. She studied psychology at the University of Pittsburgh and was a physician's assistant in charge of the presurgical ward at New York Downtown Hospital. She took the Stanford MOOC on technology to better understand her husband's career (he was a developer at Foursquare). Despite the fact that she did not take the class to affect her own job, she has since used her new software skills to automate some of the routine tasks she performs at work, such as keeping track of which patients require follow-up before surgery. Her skills also help her communicate with the information technology specialists who are installing electronic medical records systems at the hospital.

In what some academicians see as a threat to higher education, some MOOCs now offer an informal credential, although in most cases it is not free. The provost at Stanford notes that there are many issues to consider with MOOCs, from questions of copyright of course materials to implications for Stanford's accreditation if the university provides an official credential for these courses.

One of the professors who taught Stanford's first MOOC cofounded Udacity (www.udacity.com), a for-profit startup that offers a variety of MOOCs. Udacity is not the only such startup. Udemy (www.udemy.com), founded in 2010, is a similar startup. Both sites plan to help their students find jobs and obtain their permission to sell leads to recruiters, thereby helping the students find jobs. Both companies will maintain detailed records on thousands of students who have learned new skills, and many of those students will want to make those skills known to potential employers. For example, if a recruiter was searching for the top 100 people in a certain geographic area who have knowledge about machine learning (artificial intelligence), Udacity and Udemy would be able to provide that information for a fee.

In early 2013, San José State University (www.sjsu.edu) announced a pilot project with Udacity to jointly create three introductory mathematics classes. The courses are offered free online, but students who want credit from San José State must pay a fee of $150 for each class. Significantly, this amount is substantially less than the $450 to $750 that students would typically pay for a credit-bearing course. The college is also working on another MOOC pilot with a nonprofit provider, edX (www.edx.org), which is led by MIT and Harvard University.

Sources: Compiled from J. Young, "California State U. Will Experiment With Offering Credit for MOOCs," *The Chronicle of Higher Education*, January 15, 2013; T. Lewin, "Instruction for Masses Knocks Down Campus Walls," *The New York Times*, March 4, 2012; B. Sheridan and B. Greeley, "Computer Coding: Not for Geeks Only," *Bloomberg BusinessWeek*, January 26, 2012; L. Chamberlin and T. Parish, "MOOCs: Massive Open Online Courses or Massive and Often Obtuse Courses?" *eLearn Magazine*, August 2011; I. de Waard, "Explore a New Learning Frontier: MOOCs," *Learning Solutions Magazine*, July 25, 2011; R. Kop, "The Challenges to Connectivist Learning on Open Online Networks: Learning Experiences During a Massive Open Online Course," *International Review of Research in Open and Distance Learning*, v. 12, no. 3, 2011; K. Masters, "A Brief Guide to Understanding MOOCs," *The Internet Journal of Medical Education*, v. 1, no. 2, 2011; E. Fuller, "Top 10 Benefits of a College Degree," *Christian Science Monitor*, October 2010; www.udacity.com, www.stanford.edu, www.mit.edu, accessed February 25, 2013.

Questions

1. Discuss possible quality control issues with MOOCs. For each issue that you list, describe how you would solve the problem.
2. What are some specific examples of the impact that MOOCs could have on traditional higher education? Explain your answer.
3. Would you be willing to enroll in a MOOC as a full-time student at your university? Would you be willing to enroll in a MOOC after you graduate? Why or why not?

There are many benefits to e-learning. For example, online materials can deliver very current content that is of high quality (created by content experts) and consistent (presented the same way every time). It also gives students the flexibility to learn at any place, at any time, and at their own pace. In corporate training centers that use e-learning, learning time generally is shorter, which means that more people can be trained within a given timeframe. This system reduces training costs and eliminates the expense of renting facility space.

Despite these benefits, e-learning has some drawbacks. For one, students must be computer literate. Also, they may miss the face-to-face interaction with instructors. In addition, accurately assessing students' work can be problematic because instructors really do not know who completed the assignments.

E-learning does not usually replace the classroom setting. Rather, it enhances it by taking advantage of new content and delivery technologies. Advanced e-learning support environments, such as Blackboard (www.blackboard.com), add value to traditional learning in higher education.

Virtual Universities

Virtual universities are online universities in which students take classes via the Internet at home or an off-site location. A large number of existing universities offer online education of some form. Some universities, such as the University of Phoenix (www.phoenix.edu), California Virtual Campus (www.cvc.edu), and the University of Maryland (www.umuc.edu), offer thousands of courses and dozens of degrees to students worldwide, all of them online. Other universities offer limited online courses and degrees, but they employ innovative teaching methods and multimedia support in the traditional classroom.

Telecommuting

Knowledge workers are being called the distributed workforce, or digital nomads. This group of highly prized workers is now able to work anywhere and anytime, a process called **telecommuting**. Distributed workers are those who have no permanent office at their companies, preferring to work at home offices, in airport lounges or client conference rooms, or on a high school stadium bleacher. The growth of the distributed workforce is driven by globalization, extremely long commutes to work, rising gasoline prices, ubiquitous broadband communications links (wireline and wireless), and powerful laptop computers and computing devices.

Telecommuting offers a number of potential advantages for employees, employers, and society. For employees, the benefits include reduced stress and improved family life. In addition, telecommuting offers employment opportunities for housebound people such as single parents and persons with disabilities. Employer benefits include increased productivity, the ability to retain skilled employees, and the ability to attract employees who do not live within commuting distance.

However, telecommuting also has some potential disadvantages. For employees, the major disadvantages are increased feelings of isolation, possible loss of fringe benefits, lower pay (in some cases), no workplace visibility, the potential for slower promotions, and lack of socialization. In a 2013 study, researchers at Stanford University found that telecommuting employees are 50 percent less likely to get a promotion than those workers who come into the office. The researchers concluded that a lack of "face time" with bosses caused careers to stall.

In addition, telecommuting employees often have difficulties "training" their families to understand that they are at work even though they are physically at home. Families have to understand that they should not disturb the telecommuter for anything that they would not have disturbed him or her about in a "real" office. The major disadvantages to employers are difficulties in supervising work and potential data security problems. IT's About Business 6.5 underscores the intense debate about telecommuting in today's workplace.

 IT's [about business]

6.5 Yahoo! CEO Marissa Mayer Bans Telecommuting

According to the U.S. Census Bureau, approximately 9 percent of American workers work from home at least one day per week, and that percentage is increasing rapidly. However, Yahoo! (www.yahoo.com) seems to be reversing this trend.

In February 2013, Yahoo! CEO Marissa Mayer controversially terminated the company's policy of allowing its employees to work offsite. According to an anonymous source, Mayer checked the logins on Yahoo's virtual private network and discovered that her remote employees did not log in to the company network often enough. In addition, Mayer was frustrated because the Yahoo! parking lot was slow to fill up in the morning and quick to empty by 5:00 PM, a situation not typical of the company's rivals in Silicon Valley.

In an internal memo republished in multiple media outlets, Mayer announced: "To become the absolute best place to work, communication and collaboration will be important, so we need to be working side-by-side. That is why it is critical that we are all present in our offices. Some of the best decisions and insights come from hallway and cafeteria discussions, meeting new people, and impromptu team meetings. Speed and quality are often sacrificed when we work from home." Some observers speculated that Mayer was trying to trim unproductive workers without incurring the costs associated with layoffs, and in the process may have received more negative publicity than she had anticipated. Hundreds of Yahoo employees—including those who work from home one or two days per week—will have to decide whether to come to the office every day or lose their jobs.

For her part, Mayer is a well-known workaholic. She created a controversy when she took the top job at Yahoo when she was five months pregnant and then took only two weeks of maternity leave. When she returned to work she built a nursery next to her office at Yahoo! at her own expense so she could be closer to her infant son and yet work even longer hours.

A backlash to Mayer's announcement threatened to overshadow any progress that she had made in reversing Yahoo!'s long decline. For example, working mothers are protesting because they believe that Mayer is setting them back by taking away their flexible working arrangements. Many people view telecommuting as the only way time-stressed women who do not enjoy the pay, privilege, and perks that come with being the chief executive of a Fortune 500 company can care for young children and advance their careers at the same time.

Mayer's decision to ban telecommuting intensifies the debate about the subject. In contrast to Mayer's claims that working in house makes employees more productive and creative, several studies have found that telecommuting brings positive outcomes to organizations. For example, one broad, inclusive study by the consulting firm Workshifting (www.workshifting.com) discovered, on average, a 27 percent increase in productivity among telecommuting employees. Overall, more than two-thirds of the employers surveyed, including British Telecom (www.bt.com), Dow Chemical (www.dow.com), and American Express (www.americanexpress.com), reported higher productivity among telecommuting employees than those working in-house. One of the most impressive examples of telecommuting advantages is at Cisco (www.cisco.com), which, in contrast to Mayer's assertion, found that its telecommuters communicated and collaborated effectively. Cisco has also benefitted from improved employee retention, and it saves $277 million annually by allowing its employees to telecommute. Similarly, a 2011 study by WorldatWork (www.worldatwork.org) concluded that

companies that embrace flexibility had lower turnover rates and greater employee satisfaction, motivation, and engagement.

Going further, a study by Global Workplace Analytics (www.teleworkresearchnetwork.com) revealed that telecommuting generates significant environmental savings. Specifically, allowing employees to telecommute half-time could reduce carbon emissions by more than 51 million metric tons per year—the equivalent of taking all of greater New York's commuters off the road.

Mayer's ban on telecommuting is widely viewed as a risky step that could further damage Yahoo! employee morale and performance and undermine recruiting efforts in a very competitive job market. As of March 2013, the impact of Yahoo's ban on telecommuting remained to be seen. That is, is Marissa Mayer right or wrong?

About a month after Mayer's announcement, electronics retailer Best Buy (www.bestbuy.com) followed suit by banning telecommuting for the roughly 4,000 employees at its headquarters. This move eliminated an innovative program called Results Only Work Environment, which had allowed workers to complete projects out of the office. Employees essentially had free rein as long as they met their superiors' expectations. As with Yahoo!, the impact of Best Buy's ban on telecommuting remains to be seen.

Sources: Compiled from J. Kotkin, "Marissa Mayer's Misstep and the Unstoppable Rise of Telecommuting," *Forbes*, March 26, 2013; M. Patrick, "Yahoo! Ban on Telecommuting Causes Debate," *U.S. News and World Report*, March 22, 2013; T. Hsu, "After Yahoo, Best Buy Also Rethinks Telecommuting," *Los Angeles Times*, March 6, 2013; B. Belton, "Best Buy Copies Yahoo, Reins in Telecommuting," *USA Today*, March 6, 2013; R. Silverman and Q. Fottrell, "The Home Office in the Spotlight," *The Wall Street Journal*, February 27, 2013; J. Guynn, "Yahoo CEO Marissa Mayer Causes Uproar with Telecommuting Ban," *Los Angeles Times*, February 26, 2013; www.yahoo.com, accessed March 27, 2013.

Questions

1. Do you feel that Yahoo! is making the correct decision in banning telecommuting?
   a. Debate the pro side of this issue (i.e., Mayer's side).
   b. Debate the con side of this issue.
2. This IT's About Business was written in March 2013. Take a look at www.yahoo.com to see how the company is doing. Also, check on news articles about the ongoing fallout from Mayer's decision.
3. Discuss Mayer's internal memo quoted above. Do you agree or disagree with it? Support your answer.

before you go on...

1. Discuss the network applications that you studied in this section and the tools and technologies that support each one.
2. Identify the business conditions that have made videoconferencing more important.
3. Differentiate between e-learning and distance learning.
4. Describe virtual universities.
5. What is telecommuting? Do you think you would like to telecommute? Why or why not?

What's In IT For Me?

For the Accounting Major

Accounting personnel use corporate intranets and portals to consolidate transaction data from legacy systems to provide an overall view of internal projects. This view contains the current costs charged to each project, the number of hours spent on each project by individual employees, and an analysis of how actual costs compare to projected costs. Finally, accounting personnel use Internet access to government and professional Web sites to stay informed on legal and other changes affecting their profession.

For the Finance Major

Corporate intranets and portals can provide a model to evaluate the risks of a project or an investment. Financial analysts use two types of data in the model: historical transaction data from corporate databases via the intranet and industry data obtained via the Internet. In addition, financial services firms can use the Web for marketing and to provide services.

For the Marketing Major

Marketing managers use corporate intranets and portals to coordinate the activities of the sales force. Sales personnel access corporate portals via the intranet to discover updates on pricing, promotion, rebates, customer information, and information about competitors. Sales staff can also download and customize presentations for their customers. The Internet, particularly the Web, opens a completely new marketing channel for many industries. Just how advertising, purchasing, and information dispensation should occur appears to vary from industry to industry, product to product, and service to service.

For the Production/Operations Management Major

Companies are using intranets and portals to speed product development by providing the development team with three-dimensional models and animation. All team members can access the models for faster exploration of ideas and enhanced feedback. Corporate portals, accessed via intranets, enable managers to carefully supervise their inventories as well as real-time production on assembly lines. Extranets are also proving valuable as communication formats for joint research and design efforts among companies. The Internet is also a great source of cutting-edge information for POM managers.

For the Human Resources Management Major

Human resources personnel use portals and intranets to publish corporate-policy manuals, job postings, company telephone directories, and training classes. Many companies deliver online training obtained from the Internet to employees through their intranets. Human resources departments use intranets to offer employees healthcare, savings, and benefit plans, as well as the opportunity to take competency tests online. The Internet supports worldwide recruiting efforts; it can also be the communications platform for supporting geographically dispersed work teams.

For the MIS Major

As important as the networking technology infrastructure is, it is invisible to users (unless something goes wrong). The MIS function is responsible for keeping all organizational networks up and running all the time. MIS personnel, therefore, provide all users with an "eye to the world" and the ability to compute, communicate, and collaborate anytime, anywhere. For example, organizations have access to experts at remote locations without having to duplicate that expertise in multiple areas of the firm. Virtual teaming allows experts physically located in different cities to work on projects as though they were in the same office.

[Summary]

1. Compare and contrast the two major types of networks.

The two major types of networks are local area networks (LANs) and wide area networks (WANs). LANs encompass a limited geographic area and are usually composed of one communications medium. In contrast, WANs encompass a broad geographical area and are usually composed of multiple communications media.

2. Describe the wireline communications media and channels.

Twisted-pair wire, the most prevalent form of communications wiring, consists of strands of copper wire twisted in pairs. It is relatively inexpensive to purchase, widely available, and easy to work with. However, it is relatively slow for transmitting data, it is subject to interference from other electrical sources, and it can be easily tapped by unintended receivers.

Coaxial cable consists of insulated copper wire. It is much less susceptible to electrical interference than is twisted-pair wire and it can carry much more data. However, coaxial cable is more expensive and more difficult to work with than twisted-pair wire. It is also somewhat inflexible.

Fiber-optic cables consist of thousands of very thin filaments of glass fibers that transmit information via light pulses generated by lasers. Fiber-optic cables are significantly smaller and lighter than traditional cable media. They also can transmit far more data, and they provide greater security from interference and tapping. Fiber-optic cable is often used as the backbone for a network, whereas twisted-pair wire and coaxial cable connect the backbone to individual devices on the network.

3. Describe the most common methods for accessing the Internet.

Common methods for connecting to the Internet include dial-up, DSL, cable modem, satellite, wireless, and fiber to the home.

4. Explain the impact that networks have had on business and everyday life for each of the six major categories of network applications.

- *Discovery* involves browsing and information retrieval, and provides users the ability to view information in databases, download it, and/or process it. Discovery tools include search engines, directories, and portals. Discovery tools enable business users to efficiently find needed information.

- Networks provide fast, inexpensive *communications*, via e-mail, call centers, chat rooms, voice communications, and blogs. Communications tools provide business users with a seamless interface among team members, colleagues, business partners, and customers.

- *Collaboration* refers to mutual efforts by two or more entities (individuals, groups, or companies) who work together to accomplish tasks. Collaboration is enabled by workflow systems. Collaboration tools enable business users to collaborate with colleagues, business partners, and customers.

- *E-learning* refers to learning supported by the Web. Distance learning refers to any learning situation in which teachers and students do not meet face-to-face. E-learning provides tools for business users to enable their lifelong learning.

- *Virtual universities* are online universities in which students take classes via the Internet at home or an off-site location. Virtual universities make it possible for students to obtain degrees while working full time, thus increasing their value to their firms.

- *Telecommuting* is the process whereby knowledge workers are able to work anywhere and anytime. Telecommuting provides flexibility for employees, with many benefits and some drawbacks.

[Chapter Glossary]

affinity portal A Web site that offers a single point of entry to an entire community of affiliated interests.

analog signals Continuous waves that transmit information by altering the amplitude and frequency of the waves.

backbone networks High-speed central networks to which multiple smaller networks (such as LANs and smaller WANs) connect.

bandwidth The transmission capacity of a network, stated in bits per second.

broadband The transmission capacity of a communications medium faster than 4 Mbps downstream and 1 Mbps upstream.

broadcast media (also called wireless media) Communications channels that use electromagnetic media (the "airwaves") to transmit data.

browsers Software applications through which users primarily access the Web.

cable media (also called wireline media) Communications channels that use physical wires or cables to transmit data and information.

chat room A virtual meeting place where groups of regulars come to "gab" electronically.

client/server computing Form of distributed processing in which some machines (servers) perform computing functions for end-user PCs (clients).

clients Computers, such as users' personal computers, that use any of the services provided by servers.

coaxial cable Insulated copper wire; used to carry high-speed data traffic and television signals.

collaboration Mutual efforts by two or more individuals who perform activities in order to accomplish certain tasks.

commercial (public) portal A Web site that offers fairly routine content for diverse audiences; offers customization only at the user interface.

communications channel Pathway for communicating data from one location to another.

computer network A system that connects computers and other devices via communications media so that data and information can be transmitted among them.

corporate portal A Web site that provides a single point of access to critical business information located inside and outside of an organization.

crowdsourcing A process in which an organization outsources a task to an undefined, generally large group of people in the form of an open call.

digital signals A discrete pulse, either on or off, that conveys information in a binary form.

digital subscriber line (DSL) A high-speed, digital data-transmission technology using existing analog telephone lines.

distance learning (DL) Learning situations in which teachers and students do not meet face-to-face.

distributed processing Network architecture that divides processing work between two or more computers, linked together in a network.

domain name system (DNS) The system administered by the Internet Corporation for Assigned Names (ICANN) that assigns names to each site on the Internet.

domain names The name assigned to an Internet site, consisting of multiple parts, separated by dots, which are translated from right to left.

e-learning Learning supported by the Web; can be done inside traditional classrooms or in virtual classrooms.

enterprise network An organization's network composed of interconnected multiple LANs and WANs.

Ethernet A common local area network protocol.

extranet A network that connects parts of the intranets of different organizations.

fiber-optic cable A communications medium consisting of thousands of very thin filaments of glass fibers, surrounded by cladding, that transmit information via light pulses generated by lasers.

file server (also called network server) A computer that contains various software and data files for a local area network and contains the network operating system.

Hypertext Transport Protocol (HTTP) The communications standard used to transfer pages across the WWW portion of the Internet; defines how messages are formulated and transmitted.

industrywide portal A Web-based gateway to information and knowledge for an entire industry.

Internet (The Net) A massive global WAN that connects approximately 1 million organizational computer networks in more than 200 countries on all continents, including Antarctica, and features in the daily routine of almost 2 billion people. Participating computer systems include smartphones, PCs, LANs, databases, and mainframes.

Internet backbone The primary network connections and telecommunications lines that link the computers and organizational nodes of the Internet.

Internet Protocol (IP) A set of rules responsible for disassembling, delivering, and reassembling packets over the Internet.

Internet Protocol (IP) address An assigned address that uniquely identifies a computer on the Internet.

Internet service provider (ISP) A company that provides Internet connections for a fee.

Internet telephony (Voice-over Internet Protocol or VoIP) The use of the Internet as the transmission medium for telephone calls.

Internet2 A new, faster telecommunications network that deploys advanced network applications such as remote medical diagnosis, digital libraries, distance education, online simulation, and virtual laboratories.

intranet A private network that uses Internet software and TCP/IP protocols.

local area network (LAN) A network that connects communications devices in a limited geographical region, such as a building, so that every user device on the network can communicate with every other device.

metasearch engine A computer program that searches several engines at once and integrates the findings of the various search engines to answer queries posted by users.

modem Device that converts signals from analog to digital and vice versa.

network access points (NAPs) Computers that act as exchange points for Internet traffic and determine how traffic is routed.

network server (see file server)

packet switching The transmission technology that divides blocks of text into packets.

peer-to-peer (P2P) processing A type of client/server distributed processing that allows two or more computers to pool their resources, making each computer both a client and a server.

portal A Web-based personalized gateway to information and knowledge that provides information from disparate information systems and the Internet, using advanced search and indexing techniques.

protocol The set of rules and procedures governing transmission across a network.

router A communications processor that routes messages from a LAN to the Internet, across several connected LANs, or across a wide area network such as the Internet.

search engine A computer program that searches for specific information by key words and reports the results.

servers Computers that provide access to various network services, such as printing, data, and communications.

synchronous optical network (SONET) An interface standard for transporting digital signals over fiber-optic lines; allows the integration of transmissions from multiple vendors.

telecommuting A work arrangement whereby employees work at home, at the customer's premises, in special workplaces, or while traveling, usually using a computer linked to their place of employment.

teleconferencing The use of electronic communication that allows two or more people at different locations to have a simultaneous conference.

Transmission Control Protocol/Internet Protocol (TCP/IP) A file transfer protocol that can send large files of information across sometimes unreliable networks with assurance that the data will arrive uncorrupted.

twisted-pair wire A communications medium consisting of strands of copper wire twisted together in pairs.

unified communications Common hardware and software platform that simplifies and integrates all forms of communications—voice, e-mail, instant messaging, location, and videoconferencing—across an organization.

uniform resource locator (URL) The set of letters that identifies the address of a specific resource on the Web.

videoconference A virtual meeting in which participants in one location can see and hear participants at other locations and can share data and graphics by electronic means.

virtual collaboration The use of digital technologies that enable organizations or individuals to collaboratively plan, design, develop, manage, and research products, services, and innovative information systems and electronic commerce applications.

virtual group (team) A work group whose members are in different locations and who meet electronically.

virtual universities Online universities in which students take classes via the Internet at home or an off-site location.

Voice-over Internet Protocol (VOIP; see Internet telephony)

Web site Collectively, all of the Web pages of a particular company or individual.

wide area network (WAN) A network, generally provided by common carriers, that covers a wide geographic area.

wireless media (see broadcast media)

wireline media (see cable media)

work group Two or more individuals who act together to perform some task, on either a permanent or temporary basis.

workflow The movement of information as it flows through the sequence of steps that make up an organization's work procedures.

World Wide Web (The Web, WWW, or W3) A system of universally accepted standards for storing, retrieving, formatting, and displaying information via a client/server architecture; it uses the transport functions of the Internet.

[Discussion Questions]

1. What are the implications of having fiber-optic cable to everyone's home?
2. What are the implications of BitTorrent for the music industry? For the motion picture industry?
3. Discuss the pros and cons of P2P networks.
4. Should the Internet be regulated? If so, by whom?
5. Discuss the pros and cons of delivering this book over the Internet.
6. Explain how the Internet works. Assume you are talking with someone who has no knowledge of information technology (in other words, keep it very simple).

7. How are the network applications of communication and collaboration related? Do communication tools also support collaboration? Give examples.

8. Search online for the article from *The Atlantic*: "Is Google Making Us Stupid?" *Is* Google making us stupid? Support your answer.

9. Refer to the chapter opening case:
   a. How do you feel about the net neutrality issue?
   b. Do you believe heavier bandwidth users should pay for more bandwidth?

   c. Do you believe wireless carriers should operate under different rules than wireline carriers?
   d. Evaluate your own bandwidth usage. (e.g., do you upload and download large files, such as movies?) If network neutrality were to be eliminated, what would the impact be for you?
   e. Should businesses monitor network usage? Do see a problem with employees using company-purchased bandwidth for personal use? Please explain your answer.

[Problem-Solving Activities]

1. Calculate how much bandwidth you consume when using the Internet every day. How many e-mails do you send daily and what is the size of each? (Your e-mail program may have e-mail file size information.) How many music and video clips do you download (or upload) daily and what is the size of each? If you view YouTube often, surf the Web to find out the size of a typical YouTube file. Add up the number of e-mail, audio, and video files you transmit or receive on a typical day. When you have calculated your daily Internet usage, determine if you are a "normal" Internet user or a "power" Internet user. What impact does network neutrality have on you as a "normal" user? As a "power" user?

2. Access several P2P applications, such as SETI@home. Describe the purpose of each application, and indicate which ones you would like to join.

3. Access http://ipv6.com and www.ipv6news.info and learn about more advantages of IPv6.

4. Access www.icann.org and learn more about this important organization.

5. Set up your own Web site using your name for the domain name (e.g., KellyRainer).
   • Explain the process for registering a domain.
   • Which top-level domain will you use and why?

6. Access www.icann.org and obtain the name of an agency or company that can register a domain for the TLD that you selected. What is the name of that agency or company?

7. Access the Web site for that agency or company (in question 6) to learn the process that you must use. How much will it initially cost to register your domain name? How much will it cost to maintain that name in the future?

8. You plan to take a two-week vacation in Australia this year. Using the Internet, find information that will help you plan the trip. Such information includes, *but is not limited to*, the following:
   a. Geographical location and weather conditions at the time of your trip
   b. Major tourist attractions and recreational facilities
   c. Travel arrangements (airlines, approximate fares)
   d. Car rental; local tours

   e. Alternatives for accommodation (within a moderate budget) and food
   f. Estimated cost of the vacation (travel, lodging, food, recreation, shopping, etc.)
   g. Country regulations regarding the entrance of your dog
   h. Shopping
   i. Passport information (either to obtain one or to renew one)
   j. Information on the country's language and culture
   k. What else do you think you should research before going to Australia?

9. From your own experience or from the vendor's information, list the major capabilities of Lotus Notes/Domino. Do the same for Microsoft Exchange. Compare and contrast the products. Explain how the products can be used to support knowledge workers and managers.

10. Visit Web sites of companies that manufacture telepresence products for the Internet. Prepare a report. Differentiate between telepresence products and videoconferencing products.

11. Access Google (or YouTube) videos and search for "Cisco Magic." This video shows Cisco's next-generation telepresence system. Compare and contrast it with current telepresence systems.

12. Access the Web site of your university. Does the Web site provide high-quality information (right amount, clear, accurate, etc.)? Do you think a high-school student who is thinking of attending your university would feel the same way?

13. Compare and contrast Google Sites (www.google.com/sites) and Microsoft Office Live (www.liveoffice.com). Which site would you use to create your own Web site? Explain your choice.

14. Access the Web site of the Recording Industry Association of America (www.riaa.com). Discuss what you find there regarding copyright infringement (i.e, downloading music files). How do you feel about the RIAA's efforts to stop music downloads? Debate this issue from your point of view and from the RIAA's point of view.

15. Research the companies involved in Internet telephony (Voice-over IP). Compare their offerings as to price, necessary technologies, ease of installation, and so on. Which company is the most attractive to you? Which company might be the most attractive for a large company?

16. Access various search engines other than Google. Search for the same terms on several of the alternative search engines and on Google. Compare the results on breadth (number of results found) and precision (results are what you were looking for).

17. Second Life (www.secondlife.com) is a three-dimensional, online world built and owned by its residents. Residents of Second Life are avatars who have been created by real people. Access Second Life, learn about it, and create your own avatar to explore this world. Learn about the thousands of people who are making "real-world" money from operations in Second Life.

18. Access Microsoft's Bing translator (http://www.microsoft-translator.com) or Google (www.google.com/language_tools) translation pages. Type in a paragraph in English and select, for example, English-to-French. When you see the translated paragraph in French, copy it into the text box, and select French-to-English. Is the paragraph that you first entered the same as the one you are looking at now? Why or why not? Support your answer.

[Closing Case **Fiber to All of Us?**]

The Problem

In 2013, the United States ranked a distant 24th among the world's developed nations in Internet access speeds, with average download speeds of only 11.6 megabits per second. In many Asian and European countries, customers can typically buy affordable service providing hundreds of megabits per second or more.

Cable distribution giants such as Verizon (www.verizon.com), Time Warner Cable (www.timewarnercable.com), and Comcast (www.comcast.com) are enjoying a healthy profit margin on their Internet services. Verizon's (www.verizon.com) fiber-optic network, called FiOS, serves the largest number of home subscribers in the United States. Verizon has made FiOS available to some 18 million U.S. households at a cost to Verizon of $23 billion. FiOS offers basic service starting at 15 megabits per second, which can be upgraded in some areas to as much as 300 megabits per second. Comcast's Xfinity Platinum service also offers 300 megabits per second download cable service in some locations for about $300 per month.

None of these companies, however, plans to extend these services to additional geographic areas. Rather, their business goal is to sign up more people in their existing service areas. Why have they adopted this strategy? The answer is that this approach adds the most revenue without increasing the companies' capital costs. Essentially, there are no compelling business incentives for the established cable companies to expand their service offerings. This policy is unfortunate because most Americans have no choice but to do business with their local cable company. To compound this problem, few companies have the money to compete with the existing, cash-heavy telecommunications companies who control existing cable networks. Given these realities, what would it take to implement ultrafast fiber service throughout the United States?

Possible Solutions

One possible solution involves Google (www.google.com), which is installing and operating ultrafast fiber-optic cable service, known as Google Fiber, to homes in Kansas City (Kansas and Missouri). Google secured guarantees from the Kansas City government that the company would receive rapid responses on matters such as city inspections, access to rights-of-way, and permission to place fiber in sewers.

Google's fiber and connections are off-the-shelf technology, and Google's fiber service is priced at just $70 per month, or $120 with bundled television. For the television service, Google made content deals that include some sports channels, although HBO is not yet part of Google's service content. Google's fiber service offerings come with two terabytes of DVR storage, one additional terabyte of cloud storage, plus a Nexus 7 Android tablet for use as a remote control.

How can Google offer this level of service for so low a price? The answer is that Google appears to be willing to accept lower operating margins and profits for compelling business reasons. The company's long-term corporate fortunes are closely linked to heavy Web usage. Therefore, more Web traffic, and more people watching that traffic, means more ad revenue for Google.

There are many cities where it may not be feasible to deploy fiber; for example, cities that have areas that are not densely populated or where construction costs are too high. Further, in California, the provisions for securing environmental permits make such a project cost-prohibitive.

Google is not the only organization that is bringing ultrafast fiber services to areas of the United States. Some cities are taking matters into their own hands as well. For example, in 2010 the local power utility in Chattanooga Tennessee, received $111 million in federal stimulus money to accelerate the build-out of a one-gigabit per second network for a smart electric grid. In 2013, the utility began offering one-gigabit Internet access for about $300 per month, depending on the television service the customer chooses.

The Results

Kansas City families are delighted with Google's fiber service. For instance, in late 2012, an installer wired one home with

Google Fiber, making the Internet access speed 50 times faster while substantially improving the television service. This entire package cost $125 per month, which was just a few dollars more than the family had been paying Time Warner Cable for their previous, slower service. The family was able to simultaneously stream four high-definition television shows, recording three of them on the included two-terabyte DVR. That was two more shows than they could previously watch at once, with plenty of capacity to spare.

At one level, this project reflects Google's desire to keep developing new businesses by providing customers with ultra-fast speeds and then offering them experimental services such as Google TV. However, if Google's business model for deploying fiber services works, then it may create a new era for privately built broadband.

On another level, ultrafast Internet access may help local entrepreneurship. For example, Kansas City wants to attract information technology startups. An effort called Homes for Hackers is trying to convince Kansas City homeowners with Google Fiber service to give free rooms to developers for three months in hopes that they will form startup companies. Consider RareWire (www.rarewire.com), a Kansas City startup that develops apps for mobile devices. Google Fiber gave RareWire a chance to compete on a much larger scale, and hopefully a better chance to be successful.

Despite these successes, however, there are problems associated with expanding ultrafast fiber in the United States. One of the major impediments is industry lobbying. For example, in 2011, after the city of Wilson, North Carolina, built its own fast network—which competed with the existing carriers—the North Carolina legislature, under pressure from industry lobbyists, passed a law that made it more difficult for local governments to build their own networks. In addition, the law prevented Wilson from expanding its network beyond the county line.

The FCC has called for broadband providers and state and city officials to build out at least one "gigabit community" in all 50 states by 2015. In fact, Google is expanding its Google Fiber service to Olathe, Kansas, Austin, Texas, and Provo, Utah. And the bottom line? Efforts such as Google's are an encouraging start. Nevertheless, the United States has a long way to go to achieve widespread one gigabit per second service.

And how will the existing cable companies respond to Google's "fiber challenge?" They can continue their lobbying efforts against Google fiber; they can lower their prices; they can increase their download and upload speeds; or some combination. Just one example: In Kansas City in January 2013, Time Warner Cable boosted speeds and lowered prices, likely in response to Google Fiber. In fact, data from Akamai, which delivers a hefty portion of all Web traffic, produced an interesting finding. In the fourth quarter of 2012, Kansas saw the largest increase in average Internet connection speeds of all the U.S. states.

Sources: Compiled from D. Talbot, "Google Fiber's Ripple Effect," *MIT Technology Review*, April 26, 2013; J. Calacanis, "Google's Fiber Takeover Plan Expands, Will Kill Cable and Carriers," *Pandodaily.com*, April 19, 2013; P. Olson, "Google Turns Up the Heat on Cable Companies, Expanding Fiber to Austin, Texas," *Forbes*, April 9, 2013; S. Gustin, "Google Fiber Expanding Superfast Internet Service to Olathe, Kansas," *Time*, March 20, 2013; D. Talbot, "When Will the Rest of Us Get Google Fiber?" *MIT Technology Review*, February 4, 2013; P. Kafka, "A Peak at TV's Future, Via Google Fiber," *All Things Digital*, November 21, 2012; D. Talbot, "Google's Internet Service Might Actually Bring the U.S. Up to Speed," *MIT Technology Review*, November 19, 2012; "Google Fiber Installations Kick Off Today," *Google Fiber Blog*, November 13, 2012; A. Knapp, "The Google Highway," *Forbes*, October 22, 2012; S. Gustin, "Google Fiber Issues Public Challenge: Get Up to Speed!" *Time*, September 14, 2012; "Super-Fast Google Fiber for Kansas City," *KurzweilAI.net*, July 27, 2012; R. Metz, "Google Launches a Superfast Internet and TV Business," *MIT Technology Review*, July 26, 2012; D. Talbot, "City with Superfast Internet Invites Innovators to Play," *MIT Technology Review*, February 28, 2012; R. Hof, "Searching for the Future of Television," *MIT Technology Review*, December 21, 2010; http://fiber.google.com/about/, accessed March 25, 2013.

Questions

1. Why would a "search company" such as Google decided to enter the fiber services business? Describe the benefits that Google expects to obtain from this new business venture.

2. Describe the various outcomes that might occur in an area that receives ultrafast fiber, regardless of the provider.

[Internship Activity]

Industry: Healthcare

Networks create the connections that allow data to be shared with the right people at the right time. User needs change (data, devices, access, etc.) and networks must also change to work fulfill those new requirements.

When Chad Prince took on the role of Practice Administrator at Anniston Orthopaedics, he was faced with the task of updating their entire network because they were implementing a new Practice Management/Electronic Health Records system and it required new hardware and network components. Less than 3 years later, the PM/HER software vendor is pushing their clients to move into the "cloud" rather than trying to constantly update their networks. Chad is concerned about the latency of receiving information when it is housed 50-600 miles away rather than on a server around the corner.

Please visit the Book Companion Site to receive the full set of instructions on how you will help Chad determine if the cloud can help meet their networking needs.

Chapter 7

E-Business and E-Commerce

[LEARNING OBJECTIVES]	[CHAPTER OUTLINE]	[WEB RESOURCES]
1. Describe the six common types of electronic commerce.	7.1 Overview of E-Business and E-Commerce	• Student PowerPoints for note taking
2. Describe the various online services of business-to-consumer (B2C) commerce, providing specific examples of each.	7.2 Business-to-Consumer (B2C) Electronic Commerce	**WileyPLUS** • E-book
3. Describe the three business models for business-to-business electronic commerce.	7.3 Business-to-Business (B2B) Electronic Commerce	• Author video lecture for each chapter section • Practice quizzes
4. Identify the ethical and legal issues related to electronic commerce, providing examples.	7.4 Ethical and Legal Issues in E-Business	• Flash Cards for vocabulary review • Additional "IT's About Business" cases • Video interviews with managers • Lab Manuals for Microsoft Office 2010 and 2013

What's In IT For Me?

This Chapter Will Help Prepare You To...

ACCT	FIN	MKT	POM	HRM	MIS
ACCOUNTING	FINANCE	MARKETING	PRODUCTION OPERATIONS MANAGEMENT	HUMAN RESOURCES MANAGEMENT	MIS
Audit e-commerce transactions	Trade securities online	Manage firm's virtual marketplace	Transition from push to pull model	Manage e-commerce legal issues	Provide IT infrastructure for e-commerce

The Problem

[The Flash Crash]

FIN

On May 6, 2010, the U.S. stock market experienced a crash in which the Dow Jones Industrial Average lost almost 9 percent of its total value, only to recover those losses within minutes. It was the second-largest point swing—1,010.14 points—and the biggest one-day point decline—998.5 points—on an intraday basis in the history of Dow Jones. This crash became known as the Flash Crash.

That day, the market was already under pressure as a result of a massive debt crisis in Greece. Then, an automated sale of a large block of futures touched off a chain reaction of events. A futures contract is an agreement, traded on an exchange, to buy or sell assets—particularly commodities or shares of stock—at a fixed price but to be delivered and paid for later. After the automated sale, a mutual fund's computer program began selling $4.1 billion of futures contracts.

Normally, a sale of this size would take place over as many as 5 hours. In this case, however, the sell algorithm installed on the mutual fund's computer placed 75,000 contracts on the market in 20 minutes. The algorithm was programmed to execute the trade "without regard to price or time," which meant that it continued to sell even as prices rapidly dropped.

Many of the contracts sold by the algorithm were purchased by high-frequency traders (HFTs). HFTs are computerized traders who buy and sell at high speed. They account for more than one-half of the overall trading in today's markets. The HFT programs detected that they had amassed excessive "long" positions, meaning that they had purchased a large amount of stock with the expectation that its price would rise. They immediately began to sell these stocks aggressively, which in turn caused the mutual fund's algorithm to accelerate its selling. As the HFT and mutual fund programs traded contracts back and forth, they created a "hot potato" effect, where contracts changed hands 27,000 times in 14 seconds. Despite this frenzied trading, however, only 200 contracts were actually bought or sold. In most cases, the same contracts moved back and forth between the mutual funds and the HFTs in microseconds.

The only buy orders originated from automated systems, which were submitting orders known as "stub quotes." Stub quotes are offers to buy stocks at prices so low that the purchasers are unlikely to ever be the only buyers of that stock. However, during the flash crash, the stub quotes were the only offers from buyers. When the only available offer to buy available is a penny-priced stub quote, then a market order, by definition, will buy the stock at that price. In this respect, automated trading systems will follow their algorithms regardless of the outcome. This process caused shares of some prominent companies, such as Procter & Gamble and Accenture, to trade down as low as a penny per share. Significantly, human involvement probably would have prevented these orders from executing at absurdly low prices.

Critics of high-frequency trading charge that firms that dominate the HFT market often stop trading during times of crisis, which is exactly when they are needed the most. The critics also contend that ordinary investors are paying more for their stocks, not less, because HFT traders pick up information about stock orders and push up prices before orders can be filled.

A Stopgap Solution

The U.S. Securities and Exchange Commission (SEC) responded to the crash by instituting circuit breakers on all stocks in the S&P 500 stock index. Circuit breakers halt trading in a stock for 5 minutes if the price moves by 10 percent or more within a 5-minute period. After a short time, the SEC expanded the circuit breakers to include a broader range of stocks. However, no one knows for certain if the circuit breakers can prevent future "flash crashes."

Lawmakers are also proposing another possible solution: enacting a small tax on each equity trade. Such a tax would likely discourage some high-frequency trading, slow the market's overall pace, and raise billions of dollars in revenue for the federal government. Some of the tax revenues could be used to enhance the SEC's monitoring efforts.

Some trading firms are proposing rules that require HFT firms to honor the prices they offer for a stock for at least 50 milliseconds. This time seems incredibly short, but it is a lifetime in high-frequency trading.

The Results

The circuit breakers are now in place as a hopeful, preventative measure for future market crashes. However, flash crashes continue to occur.

- In the spring of 2012, a computer problem scuttled the initial public offering (IPO) of one of the nation's largest electronic exchanges, BATS. Similarly, computer problems at the Nasdaq stock market troubled the IPO of Facebook.

- In August 2012, Knight Capital, a brokerage firm, nearly collapsed after it incurred more than $400 million in losses in minutes, because of errant technology.

- In October 2012, a single mysterious computer program that placed orders—and subsequently canceled them—made up 4 percent of all quote traffic for one day in the U.S. stock market. According to the market data firm Nanex (www.nanex.com), the program placed orders in 25-millisecond bursts that involved about 500 stocks. In reality, however, the algorithm never executed a single trade. The most problematic issue is that this single computer program accounted for 10 percent of the entire bandwidth that is allowed for trading on any given day.

Indeed, the Flash Crash raises a larger question about the stock market. In recent years, the market has grown exponentially faster and more diverse. The primary venue for stock trading is no longer the New York Stock Exchange, but rather computer servers run by companies around the world. This diversity has made stock trading more affordable, which benefits both institutional and individual investors. Unfortunately, it has also made ensuring an orderly market more difficult.

Significantly, one study claims that flash events actually happen routinely, at such rapid speeds that they do not register on regular market records. If this conclusion is accurate, then these events could have troubling consequences for market stability. The study analyzed stock market trades executed between 2006 and 2011 that occurred faster than 950 milliseconds, and it identified 18,520 crashes and spikes. These trades happened so quickly that human traders had no time to react. In addition, they fell into market patterns that did not fit the patterns observed at slower time scales. The study concluded that ultrahigh-frequency trading has created a new world, one where the usual rules do not apply and where the computer algorithms that run the trading are only dimly understood by humans—even those humans who created the algorithms.

Circuit breakers or not, traders are still searching for ways to trade even faster. For example, one company designed a new computer chip specifically for high-frequency trading that can execute trades in .000000074 seconds.

A major danger facing the financial industry is that regulators, politicians, and industry leaders—already distracted by the major challenge of reforming Wall Street in the wake of the broader credit crisis of 2008—will shrug off the Flash Crash as an aberration that does not indicate the need for any fundamental rethinking of how humans, machines, and markets interact. Left unchecked, Wall Street's computer models will remain susceptible to unpredictable disasters, making future flash crashes likely. The unfortunate bottom line is that many ordinary Americans have grown wary of the stock market, which they see as the playground of algorithms, powerful banks, and secretive, fast-money trading firms.

In fact, it does not look like HFT is going away. Hibernia Atlantic, a company that operates undersea telecommunications cables, placed a new $300 million transatlantic fiber optic cable line connecting the financial markets in London and New York. A small group of U.S. and European HFT firms will pay steep fees to use the cable. The new line is the fastest cable across the Atlantic, and it will likely encourage even more ultrahigh-frequency trading on an international scale.

Sources: Compiled from "Mysterious Algorithm Was 4% of Trading Activity Last Week," *KurzweilAI.net*, October 11, 2012; J. Adler, "Raging Bulls," *Wired*, September 2012; N. Popper, "In Search of a Market Speed Limit," *The New York Times*, September 9, 2012; M. Phillips, "Trading at the Speed of Light," *Bloomberg BusinessWeek*, April 2–8, 2012; B. Keim, "Nanosecond Trading Could Make Markets Go Haywire," *Wired*, February 16, 2012; M. Millar, "'Lightning Fast Future Traders Working in Nanoseconds," *BBC News*, November 17, 2011; L. Salamone, "On Wall Street, the Race to Zero Continues," *HPC Wire*, September 27, 2011; "New $300 Million Transatlantic Cable Makes Stock Trades 6 Milliseconds Faster," *Public Intelligence*, September 14, 2011; E. Macbride, "Flash Crash Update: Why the Multi-Asset Meltdown Is a Real Possibility," *Forbes*, March 2, 2011; T. McCabe, "When the Speed of Light Is Too Slow: Trading at the Edge," Kurzweilai.net, November 11, 2010; Spicer, J. "Special Report: Globally, the Flash Crash Is No Flash in the Pan," *Reuters*, October 15, 2010; E. Lambert, "The Truth About the Flash Crash," *Forbes*, October 1, 2010; S. Schaefer, "Dissecting the Flash Crash," *Forbes*, October 1, 2010; L. Mearian, "Regulators Blame Computer Algorithm for Stock Market 'Flash Crash'," *Computerworld*, October 1, 2010; G. Bowley, "Lone $4.1 Billion Sale Led to 'Flash Crash' in May," *New York Times*, October 1, 2010; S. Patterson, "Letting the Machines Decide," *Wall Street Journal*, July 13, 2010; N. Mehla, "The Machines That Ate the Market," *Bloomberg BusinessWeek*, May 20, 2010; S. Patterson, "How the 'Flash Crash' Echoed Black Monday," *Wall Street Journal*, May 17, 2010; L. Harris, "How to Prevent Another Trading Panic," *Wall Street Journal*, May 12, 2010; E. Wyatt, "Regulators Vow to Find Way to Stop Rapid Dives," *New York Times*, May 10, 2010; S. Patterson and T. Lauricella, "Did a Big Bet Help Trigger 'Black Swan' Stock Swoon?" *Wall Street Journal*, May 10, 2010; A. Lucchetti, "Exchanges Point Fingers Over Human Hands," *Wall Street Journal*, May 9, 2010.

What We Learned from This Case

One of the most profound changes in the modern world of business is the emergence of electronic commerce. **Electronic commerce** (**EC** or **e-commerce**) describes the process of buying, selling, transferring, or exchanging products, services, or information via computer networks, including the Internet. E-commerce is transforming all of the business functional areas we discussed in Chapter 1 as well as their fundamental tasks, from advertising to paying bills. Its impact is so widespread that it is affecting almost every modern organization. Regardless of where you land a job, your organization likely will be practicing electronic commerce.

Electronic commerce influences organizations in many significant ways. First, it increases an organization's *reach*, defined as the number of potential customers to whom the company can market its products. In fact, e-commerce provides unparalleled opportunities for companies to expand worldwide at a small cost, to increase market share, and to reduce costs. By utilizing electronic commerce, many small businesses can now operate and compete in market spaces that formerly were dominated by larger companies.

Another major impact of electronic commerce has been to remove many of the barriers that previously impeded entrepreneurs seeking to start their own businesses. E-commerce offers amazing opportunities for you to open your own business by developing an e-commerce Web site. IT's About Business 7.1 illustrates how one person used e-commerce to create an extremely successful business.

Electronic commerce is also drastically changing the nature of competition due to the development of new online companies, new business models, and the diversity of EC-related

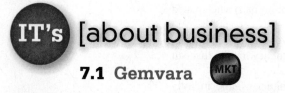

IT's [about business]

7.1 Gemvara [MKT]

When Matt Lauzon was a senior at Babson College in Wellesley, Massachusetts, he created an interesting business plan. He developed a Web site, Gemvara (www.gemvara.com), that enables consumers to design custom, high-end jewelry without ever having to visit a jewelry store.

To find varied opinions and advice about his business plan, Lauzon signed 50 brick-and-mortar jewelers (i.e., jewelers having physical stores) to a network that lets their clients customize items both in their stores and online. He discovered that customers were very excited about the experience of customizing from home, because they had more control over the design process. Lauzon's business plan concentrated on the concept of electronic commerce for what Lauzon calls "Generation Me."

Gemvara's Web site allows its customers to custom-design the piece of jewelry they want. Gemvara then sends the design specifications to one of its brick-and-mortar jewelry store partners. Each design is made to order by integrating the customer's vision with gemstones, precious metals, and processes.

Lauzon launched Gemvara in February 2011. Since that time, the Web site has experienced double-digit monthly revenue growth, received more than 1 million page views per month, and enjoyed an average order price of approximately $1,000.

Lauzon attributes much of his company's success to its superb customer service, which his company provides 24/7

via phone, e-mail, or live chat. He notes that establishing trust between his company and customers, especially for expensive purchases like fine jewelry, is essential. Nearly half of Gemvara's customers have never purchased a piece of jewelry online before, and 24/7 customer service goes a long way toward overcoming the trust barrier.

Sources: Compiled from "Gemvara Welcomes Summer with Launch of Black and White Collection," *12News.com*, June 19, 2013; J. Brooks, "Oprah names Gemvara Earrings to 'Favorite Things' List," *Boston Business Journal*, 2012; "America's Most Promising Companies: Gemvara," *Forbes*, November 30, 2011; L. Indvik, "How Gemvara Is Changing the Way Fine Jewelry Is Bought Online," *Mashable*, March 27, 2011; J. Holland, "The Bling King," *Entrepreneur*, March, 2011; www.gemvara.com, accessed March 2, 2013.

Questions

1. Access the Gemvara Web site. What are its strengths? Its weaknesses? Would you design and purchase jewelry on the site? Why or why not?
2. Search out Web sites for Gemvara competitors. Discuss each site's strengths and weaknesses. In light of your findings, do you think Gemvara will be successful in the long term? Why or why not?
3. How would a traditional brick-and-mortar jewelry store compete against Gemvara and other similar Web sites?

---

products and services. Recall your study of competitive strategies in Chapter 2, particularly the impact of the Internet on Porter's five forces. You learned that the Internet can both endanger and enhance a company's position in a given industry.

This chapter's opening case illustrates how e-commerce has fundamentally altered the nature of competition in the futures markets and stock markets. Despite all of the advantages that e-commerce offers, the Flash Crash demonstrates that the reliance on computers (and thus on e-commerce) can lead to disaster if humans fail to properly monitor the process.

It is important for you to have a working knowledge of electronic commerce because your organization almost certainly will be employing e-commerce applications that will affect its strategy and business model. This knowledge will make you more valuable to your organization, and it will enable you to quickly contribute to the e-commerce applications employed in your functional area. As you read What's In IT For Me? at the end of the chapter, envision yourself performing the activities discussed in your functional area.

Going further, you may decide to become an entrepreneur and start your own business, as illustrated in IT's About Business 9.1 and 9.2. In this case, it is even more essential for you to understand electronic commerce, because e-commerce, with its broad reach, will probably be critical for your business to survive and thrive.

In this chapter, you will discover the major applications of e-business, and you will be able to identify the services necessary for its support. You will then study the major types of electronic commerce: business-to-consumer (B2C), business-to-business (B2B), consumer-to-consumer (C2C), business-to-employee (B2E), and government-to-citizen (G2C). You conclude by examining several legal and ethical issues that have arisen as a result of the rapid growth of e-commerce.

IT's [about business]

7.2 Finding A Doctor Right Now

ZocDoc (www.zocdoc.com) is a Web site that allows patients to make doctors' appointments, in much the same way that Open Table (www.opentable.com) allows customers to make dinner reservations. More specifically, ZocDoc enables patients to read verified reviews written by real patients, find doctors in their vicinity who accept their insurance, and instantly book appointments with local medical professionals online or via a free iPhone or Android app that patients can download.

ZocDoc is free for patients, but it charges doctors a $250 monthly fee to be included in their database. ZocDoc's software catalogs each physician's insurance plans and appointment calendars. It also sends checkup reminders to patients. On their 50th birthdays, ZocDoc members receive an e-mail that reads: "There was recently a 13% drop in new cases [of colon cancer] . . . because more people are getting colonoscopies."

In addition to encouraging patients to visit the doctor more frequently, ZocDoc helps patients select the right doctor for them. After their visits, the software asks patients to rate their experience, and most do so via comments and one-to-five star ratings in three categories—overall recommendation, bedside manner, and wait time.

In the beginning, it was difficult to get ZocDoc off the ground. Days before debuting Zocdoc at a technology conference in San Francisco, the Web site's founder had gathered the names of only three doctors in his database. In desperation, he staked out the waiting room of a practice with five doctors.

The doctors finally agreed to join his list, giving him enough names to fill out a scroll-down menu. He also dug into his savings to hire salespeople to recruit doctors and computer programmers to write code to integrate ZocDoc software

Today, nearly 1 percent of the U.S. population uses ZocDoc each month. Further, the Web site now includes medical specialists located in 1,600 cities. In just one example, the New York Eye & Ear Infirmary estimates that the practice's 120 doctors who have signed up with ZocDoc have gained, among them, 9,000 new patients in just over 2 years.

In early 2013, ZocDoc released its first new product since it launched its Web site: ZocDoc CheckIn. This app lets patients fill out their medical paperwork online when they book an appointment. ZocDoc digitally transfers the information to doctors, so patients can get in and out more efficiently.

Sources: S. Snow, "Inside ZocDoc's Quest to Reinvent Health Care," *Mashable.com*, January 8, 2013; V. Barret, "What the Patient Ordered," *Forbes*, February 27, 2012; S. Lohr, "Lessons from ZocDoc, a Health Tech Start-up That Works," *New York Times*, January 30, 2012; Z. Moukheiber, "Is ZocDoc the Fastest Growing Health Information Technology Company?" *Forbes*, August 8, 2011; C. Meyers, "ZocDoc Sweeps the Nation, Revolutionizing Doctor-Patient Relationships," *TheNextWeb*, June 2, 2011; www.zocdoc.com, accessed February 11, 2013.

Questions

1. Describe ZocDoc's business model.
2. What are the disadvantages of ZocDoc's business model for the company? For the patients?

Overview of E-Business and E-Commerce 7.1

Any entrepreneur or company that decides to practice electronic commerce must develop a strategy to do so effectively. The first step is to determine exactly *why* you want to do business over the Internet using a Web site. There are several reasons for employing Web sites:

- To sell goods and services
- To induce people to visit a physical location
- To reduce operational and transaction costs
- To enhance your reputation

A Web site can accomplish any of these goals. Unless a company (or you) has substantial resources, however, it is difficult to accomplish all of them at the same time. The appropriate Web site for achieving each goal will be somewhat different. As you set up your Web site, you must consider how the site will generate and retain traffic, as well as a host of other issues. The point here is that, when you are studying the various aspects of electronic commerce, you should keep the strategy of the organization or entrepreneur in mind. This will help you determine the type of Web site to use.

This section examines the basics of e-business and e-commerce. First, we define these two concepts. You then become familiar with pure and partial electronic commerce. You then take a look at the various types of electronic commerce. Next, you focus on e-commerce mechanisms, which are the ways that businesses and people buy and sell over the Internet. You conclude this section by considering the benefits and limitations of e-commerce.

Definitions and Concepts

Recall that electronic commerce describes the process of buying, selling, transferring, or exchanging products, services, or information via computer networks, including the Internet. **Electronic business** (e-business) is a somewhat broader concept. In addition to the buying and selling of goods and services, **e-business** refers to servicing customers, collaborating with business partners, and performing electronic transactions within an organization.

Electronic commerce can take several forms depending on the degree of digitization involved. The *degree of digitization* is the extent to which the commerce has been transformed from physical to digital. This concept can relate to both the product or service being sold and the delivery agent or intermediary. In other words, the product can be either physical or digital, and the delivery agent can be either physical or digital.

In traditional commerce, both dimensions are physical. Purely physical organizations are referred to as **brick-and-mortar organizations.** (You may also see the term *bricks-and-mortar.*) In contrast, in *pure EC* all dimensions are digital. Companies engaged only in EC are considered **virtual** (or **pure-play**) **organizations.** All other combinations that include a mix of digital and physical dimensions are considered *partial* EC (but not pure EC). **Clicks-and-mortar organizations** conduct some e-commerce activities, yet their primary business is carried out in the physical world. A common alternative to the term *clicks-and-mortar* is *clicks-and-bricks.* You will encounter both terms. Therefore, clicks-and-mortar organizations are examples of partial EC. E-commerce is now so well established that people generally expect companies to offer this service in some form.

Purchasing a shirt at Walmart Online or a book from **Amazon.com** is an example of partial EC because the merchandise, although bought and paid for digitally, is physically delivered by FedEx or UPS. In contrast, buying an e-book from **Amazon.com** or a software product from **Buy.com** constitutes pure EC because the product itself as well as its delivery, payment, and transfer are digital. To avoid confusion, we use the term *electronic commerce* to denote both pure and partial EC.

Types of E-Commerce

E-commerce can be conducted between and among various parties. In this section, you will identify the six common types of e-commerce, and you will learn about three of them—C2C, B2E, and e-government—in detail. You then consider B2C and B2B in separate sections because they are very complex.

- **Business-to-consumer electronic commerce (B2C).** In B2C, the sellers are organizations, and the buyers are individuals. You learn about B2C electronic commerce in Section 7.2.

- **Business-to-business electronic commerce (B2B).** In B2B transactions, both the sellers and the buyers are business organizations. B2B comprises the vast majority of EC volume. You will learn more about B2B electronic commerce in Section 7.3. Figure 1.5 also illustrates B2B electronic commerce.

- **Consumer-to-consumer electronic commerce (C2C).** In C2C (also called customer-to-customer), an individual sells products or services to other individuals. The major strategies for conducting C2C on the Internet are auctions and classified ads.

In dozens of countries, the volume of C2C selling and buying on auction sites is exploding. Most auctions are conducted by intermediaries such as eBay (www.ebay.com). Consumers can also select general sites such as www.auctionanything.com, a company that sells software and services that help individuals and organizations conduct their own auctions. In addition, many individuals are conducting their own auctions.

The major categories of online classified ads are similar to those found in print ads: vehicles, real estate, employment, pets, tickets, and travel. Classified ads are available through most Internet service providers (AOL, MSN, etc.), at some portals (Yahoo!, etc.), and from Internet directories and online newspapers. Many of these sites contain search engines that help shoppers narrow their searches. Craigslist (www.craigslist.org) is the largest online classified ad provider.

Internet-based classified ads have one major advantage over traditional types of classified ads: They provide access to an international, rather than a local, audience. This wider audience greatly increases both the supply of goods and services and the number of potential buyers. It is important to note that the value of expanded geographic reach depends greatly on what is being bought or sold. For example, you might buy software from a company located 1,000 miles from you, but you would not buy firewood from someone at such a distance.

- **Business-to-employee (B2E).** In B2E, an organization uses EC internally to provide information and services to its employees. For example, companies allow employees to manage their benefits and to take training classes electronically. In addition, employees can buy discounted insurance, travel packages, and tickets to events on the corporate intranet. They also can order supplies and materials electronically. Finally, many companies have electronic corporate stores that sell the company's products to its employees, usually at a discount.

- **E-government.** E-government is the use of Internet technology in general and e-commerce in particular to deliver information and public services to citizens (called government-to-citizen or G2C EC) and to business partners and suppliers (called government-to-business or G2B EC). G2B EC is much like B2B EC, usually with an overlay of government procurement regulations. That is, G2B EC and B2B EC are similar conceptually. However, the functions of G2C EC are conceptually different from anything that exists in the private sector (e.g., B2C EC).

  E-government is also an efficient way of conducting business transactions with citizens and businesses and within the governments themselves. E-government makes government more efficient and effective, especially in the delivery of public services. An example of G2C electronic commerce is electronic benefits transfer, in which governments transfer benefits, such as Social Security and pension payments, directly to recipients' bank accounts.

- **Mobile commerce (m-commerce).** The term *m-commerce* refers to e-commerce that is conducted entirely in a wireless environment. An example is using cell phones to shop over the Internet. You will learn about m-commerce in Chapter 10.

Each type of EC is executed in one or more business models. A **business model** is the method by which a company generates revenue to sustain itself. Table 7.1 summarizes the major EC business models.

Major E-Commerce Mechanisms

Businesses and customers can buy and sell on the Internet through a number of mechanisms. The most widely used mechanisms are:

- Electronic catalogs,
- Electronic auctions,
- E-storefronts,
- E-malls, and
- E-marketplaces.

Let's look at each one more closely.

Catalogs have been printed on paper for generations. Today, however, they are available on CD-ROM and the Internet. Electronic catalogs consist of a product database, a directory and search capabilities, and a presentation function. They are the backbone of most e-commerce sites.

An **auction** is a competitive buying and selling process in which prices are determined dynamically by competitive bidding. Electronic auctions (e-auctions) generally increase revenues for sellers by broadening the customer base and shortening the cycle time of the auction. Buyers generally benefit from e-auctions because they can bargain for lower prices. In addition, they do not have to travel to an auction at a physical location.

The Internet provides an efficient infrastructure for conducting auctions at lower administrative costs and with many more involved sellers and buyers. Individual consumers and corporations alike can participate in auctions.

Table **7.1**

E-Commerce Business Models

Online direct marketing	Manufacturers or retailers sell directly to customers. Very efficient for digital products and services. Can allow for product or service customization. (www.dell.com)
Electronic tendering system	Businesses request quotes from suppliers. Uses B2B with a reverse auction mechanism.
Name-your-own-price	Customers decide how much they are willing to pay. An intermediary tries to match a provider. (www.priceline.com)
Find-the-best-price	Customers specify a need; an intermediary compares providers and shows the lowest price. Customers must accept the offer in a short time or may lose the deal. (www.hotwire.com)
Affiliate marketing	Vendors ask partners to place logos (or banners) on partner's site. If customers click on logo, go to vendor's site, and buy, then vendor pays commissions to partners.
Viral marketing	Receivers send information about your product to their friends.
Group purchasing (e-coops)	Small buyers aggregate demand to create a large volume; the group then conducts tendering or negotiates a low price.
Online auctions	Companies run auctions of various types on the Internet. Very popular in C2C, but gaining ground in other types of EC. (www.ebay.com)
Product customization	Customers use the Internet to self-configure products or services. Sellers then price them and fulfill them quickly (*build-to-order*). (www.jaguar.com)
Electronic marketplaces	Transactions are conducted efficiently (more information and exchanges to buyers and sellers, lower transaction costs) in electronic marketplaces (private or public).
Bartering online	Intermediary administers online exchange of surplus products and/or company receives "points" for its contribution, which it can use to purchase other needed items. (www.bbu.com)
Deep discounters	Company offers deep price discounts. Appeals to customers who consider only price in their purchasing decisions. (www.half.com)
Membership	Only members can use the services provided, including access to certain information, conducting trades, etc. (www.egreetings.com)

There are two major types of auctions: forward and reverse. In **forward auctions**, sellers solicit bids from many potential buyers. Usually, sellers place items at sites for auction, and buyers bid continuously for them. The highest bidder wins the items. Both sellers and buyers can be either individuals or businesses. The popular auction site **eBay.com** is a forward auction.

In **reverse auctions**, one buyer, usually an organization, wants to purchase a product or a service. The buyer posts a request for quotation (RFQ) on its Web site or on a third-party site. The RFQ provides detailed information on the desired purchase. Interested suppliers study the RFQ and then submit bids electronically. Everything else being equal, the lowest-price bidder wins the auction. The reverse auction is the most common auction model for large purchases (in terms of either quantities or price). Governments and large corporations frequently use this approach, which may provide considerable savings for the buyer.

Auctions can be conducted from the seller's site, the buyer's site, or a third party's site. For example, eBay, the best-known third-party site, offers hundreds of thousands of different items in several types of auctions. Overall, more than 300 major companies, including **Amazon.com** and **Dellauction.com**, sponsor online auctions.

An *electronic storefront* is a Web site that represents a single store. An *electronic mall*, also known as a *cybermall* or *e-mall*, is a collection of individual shops under one Internet address.

Electronic storefronts and electronic malls are closely associated with B2C electronic commerce. You study each one in more detail in Section 7.2.

An *electronic marketplace (e-marketplace)* is a central, virtual market space on the Web where many buyers and many sellers can conduct e-commerce and e-business activities. Electronic marketplaces are associated with B2B electronic commerce. You learn about electronic marketplaces in Section 7.3.

Electronic Payment Mechanisms

Implementing EC typically requires electronic payments. **Electronic payment mechanisms** enable buyers to pay for goods and services electronically, rather than writing a check or using cash. Payments are an integral part of doing business, whether in the traditional manner or online. Traditional payment systems have typically involved cash and/or checks. In most cases, traditional payment systems are not effective for EC, especially for B2B. Cash cannot be used because there is no face-to-face contact between buyer and seller. Not everyone accepts credit cards or checks, and some buyers do not have credit cards or checking accounts. Finally, contrary to what many people believe, it may be *less* secure for the buyer to use the telephone or mail to arrange or send payments, especially from another country, than to complete a secured transaction on a computer. For all of these reasons, a better method is needed to pay for goods and services in cyberspace. This method is electronic payment systems. Let's take a closer look at four types of electronic payment: electronic checks, electronic credit cards, purchasing cards, and electronic cash.

Electronic Checks.   *Electronic checks (e-checks)*, which are used primarily in B2B, are similar to regular paper checks. A customer who wishes to use e-checks must first establish a checking account with a bank. Then, when the customer buys a product or a service, he or she e-mails an encrypted electronic check to the seller. The seller deposits the check in a bank account, and the funds are transferred from the buyer's account into the seller's account.

Like regular checks, e-checks carry a signature (in digital form) that can be verified (see www.authorize.net). Properly signed and endorsed e-checks are exchanged between financial institutions through electronic clearinghouses. (See www.eccho.org and www.troygroup.com for details.)

Electronic Cards.   There are a variety of electronic cards, and they are used for different purposes. The most common types are electronic credit cards, virtual credit cards, purchasing cards, stored-value money cards, and smart cards.

Electronic credit cards allow customers to charge online payments to their credit card account. These cards are used primarily in B2C and in shopping by small-to-medium enterprises (SMEs). Here is how e-credit cards work (see Figure 7.1).

- Step 1: When you buy a book from Amazon, for example, your credit card information and purchase amount are encrypted in your browser. This way the information is safe while it is "traveling" on the Internet to Amazon.

- Step 2: When your information arrives at Amazon, it is not opened. Rather, it is transferred automatically (in encrypted form) to a *clearinghouse*, where it is decrypted for verification and authorization.

- Step 3: The clearinghouse asks the bank that issued you your credit card (the card issuer bank) to verify your credit card information.

- Step 4: Your card issuer bank verifies your credit card information and reports this to the clearinghouse.

- Step 5: The clearinghouse reports the result of the verification of your credit card to Amazon.

- Step 6: Amazon reports a successful purchase and amount to you.

- Step 7: Your card issuer bank sends funds in the amount of the purchase to Amazon's bank.

- Step 8: Your card issuer bank notifies you (either electronically or in your monthly statement) of the debit on your credit card.

- Step 9: Amazon's bank notifies Amazon of the funds credited to its account.

FIGURE 7.1 How e-credit cards work. (The numbers 1–9 indicate the sequence of activities.)

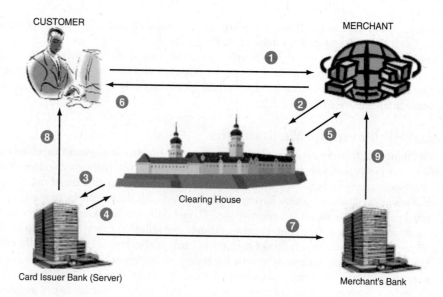

Virtual credit cards allow customers to shop online (see Figure 7.2). These cards can be used only once. The reason for this limitation is to thwart criminals by using a different, random card number every time you shop online. Going further, a virtual number is good only on the Web site where you make your purchase. An online purchase made with a virtual card number shows up on your bill just like any other purchase.

Purchasing cards are the B2B equivalent of electronic credit cards (see Figure 7.3). In some countries, purchasing cards are the primary form of payment between companies. Unlike credit cards, where credit is provided for 30 to 60 days (for free) before payment is made to the merchant, payments made with purchasing cards are settled within a week.

Stored-value money cards allow you to store a fixed amount of prepaid money and then spend it as necessary. These cards are used to pay for photocopies in your library, for transportation, and for telephone calls. Each time you use the card, the amount is reduced by the amount you spent. Figure 7.4 illustrates a New York City Metro (subway and bus) card.

FIGURE 7.2 Example of virtual credit card.

Finally, **smart cards** contain a chip that can store a considerable amount of information—more than 100 times the amount contained on a stored-value money card (see Figure 7.5). Smart cards are frequently multipurpose—that is, you can use them as a credit card, a debit card, a stored-value money card, or a loyalty card. Smart cards are ideal for *micropayments*, which are small payments of a few dollars or less.

Person-to-Person Payments. **Person-to-person payments** enable two individuals, or an individual and a business, to transfer funds without using a credit card. One of the first companies to offer this service was PayPal (an eBay company). An attractive security feature of PayPal is that you have to put only enough money in the account to cover any upcoming transactions. Therefore, if anyone should gain access to your account, that person will not have access to all of your money.

Person-to-person payment services work this way. First, you select a service and open up an account. Basically, this process entails creating a user name, selecting a password, and providing the service with a credit card or bank account number. Next, you transfer funds from your credit card or bank account to your

Mike Clarke/AFP/Getty Images/NewsCom

FIGURE 7.3 Example of purchasing card.

© Clarence Holmes Photography/Alamy Limited

FIGURE 7.4 The New York City Metro Card.

© MARKA/Alamy Limited

FIGURE 7.5 Smart cards are frequently multipurpose.

new account. Now you are ready to send money to someone over the Internet. You access the service—for example, PayPal—with your user name and password, and you specify the e-mail address of the person to receive the money, along with the dollar amount that you want to send. The service then sends an e-mail to the payee's e-mail address. The e-mail contains a link back to the service's Web site. When the recipient clicks on the link, he or she is taken to the service. There, the recipient is asked to set up an account to which the money that you sent will be credited. The recipient can then credit the money from this account to either a credit card or a bank account. The service charges the payer a small amount, roughly $1 per transaction.

Benefits and Limitations of E-Commerce

Few innovations in human history have provided as many benefits to organizations, individuals, and society as e-commerce has. E-commerce benefits organizations by making national and international markets more accessible and by lowering the costs of processing, distributing, and retrieving information. Customers benefit by being able to access a vast number of products and services, around the clock. The major benefit to society is the ability to easily and conveniently deliver information, services, and products to people in cities, rural areas, and developing countries.

Despite all these benefits, EC has some limitations, both technological and nontechnological, that have restricted its growth and acceptance. One major technological limitation is the lack of universally accepted security standards. Also, in less-developed countries, telecommunications bandwidth often is insufficient, and accessing the Web is expensive. Nontechnological limitations include the perceptions that EC is insecure, has unresolved legal issues, and lacks a critical mass of sellers and buyers. As time passes, these limitations, especially the technological ones, will diminish or be overcome.

before you go on...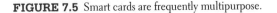

1. Define e-commerce and distinguish it from e-business.
2. Differentiate among B2C, B2B, C2C, and B2E electronic commerce.
3. Define e-government.
4. Discuss forward and reverse auctions.
5. Discuss the various online payment mechanisms.
6. Identify some benefits and limitations of e-commerce.

7.2 Business-to-Consumer (B2C) Electronic Commerce

B2B EC is much larger than B2C EC by volume, but B2C EC is more complex. The reason is that B2C involves a large number of buyers making millions of diverse transactions per day with a relatively small number of sellers. As an illustration, consider Amazon, an online retailer that offers thousands of products to its customers. Each customer purchase is relatively small, but Amazon must manage every transaction as if that customer were its most important one. The company needs to process each order quickly and efficiently, and ship the products to the customer in a timely manner. In addition, it has to manage returns. Multiply this simple example by millions, and you get an idea of how complex B2C EC can be. Overall, B2B complexities tend to be more business related, whereas B2C complexities tend to be more technical and volume related.

This section addresses the primary issues in B2C EC. We begin by studying the two basic mechanisms that customers utilize to access companies on the Web: electronic storefronts and electronic malls. In addition to purchasing products over the Web, customers also access online services. Therefore, the next section covers several online services, such as banking, securities trading, job searching, and travel. The complexity of B2C EC creates two major challenges for sellers: channel conflict and order fulfillment. We examine these two topics in detail. Finally, companies engaged in B2C EC must "get the word out" to prospective customers. Therefore, this section concludes with a look at online advertising.

Electronic Storefronts and Malls

For several generations, home shopping from catalogs, and later from television shopping channels, has attracted millions of customers. Today, shopping online offers an alternative to catalog and television shopping. **Electronic retailing (e-tailing)** is the direct sale of products and services through electronic storefronts or electronic malls, usually designed around an electronic catalog format and/or auctions.

Like any mail-order shopping experience, e-commerce enables you to buy from home and to do so 24 hours a day, 7 days a week. Compared to mail order, however, EC offers a wider variety of products and services, including the most unique items, often at lower prices. Furthermore, within seconds, shoppers can access very detailed supplementary product information. In addition, they can easily locate and compare competitors' products and prices. Finally, buyers can find hundreds of thousands of sellers. Two popular online shopping mechanisms are electronic storefronts and electronic malls.

Electronic Storefronts. As we saw earlier in the chapter, an **electronic storefront** is a Web site that represents a single store. Today, Internet shoppers can access hundreds of thousands of electronic storefronts. Each storefront has a unique uniform resource locator (URL), or Internet address, at which buyers can place orders. Some electronic storefronts are extensions of physical stores such as Hermes, The Sharper Image, and Walmart. Others are new businesses started by entrepreneurs who discovered a niche on the Web (e.g., **Restaurant.com** and **Alloy.com**). Manufacturers (e.g., www.dell.com) and retailers (e.g., www.officedepot.com) also use storefronts. IT's About Business 7.3 illustrates how Macy's is expanding its online presence.

Electronic Malls Whereas an electronic storefront represents a single store, an **electronic mall**, also known as a *cybermall* or an *e-mall*, is a collection of individual shops grouped under a single Internet address. The basic idea of an electronic mall is the same as that of a regular shopping mall: to provide a one-stop shopping place that offers a wide range of products and services. A cybermall may include thousands of vendors. For example, Microsoft Shopping (now Bing shopping, www.bing.com/shopping) includes tens of thousands of products from thousands of vendors.

There are two types of cybermalls. In the first type, known as *referral malls* (e.g., www.hawaii.com), you cannot buy anything. Instead, you are transferred from the mall to a participating

IT's [about business]

7.3 Macy's Increases Its Online Presence

For decades, Macy's was a prominent brick-and-mortar enterprise, with more than 800 store locations in 45 states. (Think of the backdrop for the Thanksgiving Day Parade.) Today, however, the store is adapting to the digital age by dramatically expanding its e-commerce business. In fiscal years 2008, 2009, and 2010, Macy's online sales increased by 30 percent, 20 percent, and 29 percent, respectively. Macy's e-commerce group oversees Web sites such as www.macys.com and www.bloomingdales.com. The group's overall goals are to make Macy's Web sites the primary contact interface for all of their Internet-using customers and to drive customer traffic into their physical stores.

In January 2011, Macy's announced that it was adding more than 700 new positions over the next two years to support the growth of its online business. The company's strategy for its online business is to provide a multichannel mechanism for its customers to shop seamlessly in stores, online, and via mobile devices. The company is also building an online fulfillment center in West Virginia while expanding its existing fulfillment center in Tennessee.

Macy's has implemented Splunk (www.splunk.com) software to support its e-commerce initiatives. Splunk is a software company whose products enable business users to access data directly without having to go through their IT department. Macy's utilizes Splunk software to monitor, report, and analyze both its historical data and its live clickstream data from the Web.

Macy's also uses Splunk software to proactively identify network and systems issues that could cause its Web site to crash, thereby preventing customers from researching products or making online purchases. For example, in late 2010, Splunk alerted Macy's technicians to a problem that would have been catastrophic to online operations if it had not been addressed quickly. The technicians solved the problem within 30 minutes without incurring any downtime for the company's Web site. This type of quick resolution would not have been possible before Macy's starting using Splunk. In those days its technicians used a manual process to respond to problems after they had occurred. With that system, Macy's technicians required 48 hours—compared with 30 minutes—to resolve a problem. These long delays in restoring Web site connectivity resulted in significant dollar losses and damaged the company's brand.

In addition to proactively preventing downtimes, another key benefit of the Splunk software is that it enables Macy's to gather a variety of data that executives and analysts can use to determine how customers are utilizing the company's Web sites. As you might expect, this feature is especially valuable during the Christmas shopping season.

In addition to Splunk, Macy's uses other tools to help keep its online operations operating smoothly. One tool, DynaTrace Software, enables the store to test the performance of new e-commerce applications that they deploy. Macy's integrates DynaTrace with an application from Coradiant called TruSight. These integrated applications allow company analysts to examine Web site performance from the perspective of users by providing real-time visibility into the performance and availability of Web applications. The applications provide this feature by capturing and measuring information on user transactions as they happen. Macy's integrated software has helped it identify user problems that were not being reported to the company's customer service department. For example, during the 2010 holiday shopping season, DynaTrace and TruSight enabled analysts to identify a sign-in issue during the online checkout process that could have damaged Macy's online operations and reduced customer satisfaction.

Sources: Compiled from K. Talley, "Macy's Strategy Paying Off," The Wall Street Journal, February 27, 2013; T. Henschen, "Splunk Answers Business Demand for Big Data Analysis," *InformationWeek*, January 12, 2012; T. Groenfeldt, "Security Data is Big Data and a Business Advantage," *Forbes*, December 14, 2011; T. Taulli, "Splunk: Patience Can Make Billions," *Forbes*, April 12, 2011; B. Violino, "Macy's Ramps Up Online Operations," *Baseline Magazine*, January 27, 2011; www.macys.com, www.splunk.com, www.dynatrace.com, accessed February 24, 2013.

Questions
1. Why is it so important that the Macy's Web sites function as optimally as possible?
2. What is the relationship between Macy's Web sites and increasing customer traffic in their physical stores?

---

storefront. In the second type of mall (e.g., http://shopping.google.com), you can actually make a purchase (see Figure 7.6). At this type of mall, you might shop from several stores, but you make only one purchase transaction at the end. You use an *electronic shopping cart* to gather items from various vendors and then pay for all of them in a single transaction. The mall organizer, such as Google, takes a commission from the sellers for this service.

Online Service Industries

In addition to purchasing products, customers can also access needed services via the Web. Selling books, toys, computers, and most other products on the Internet can reduce vendors' selling costs by 20 to 40 percent. Further reduction is difficult to achieve because the products

FIGURE 7.6 Electronic malls include products from many vendors.

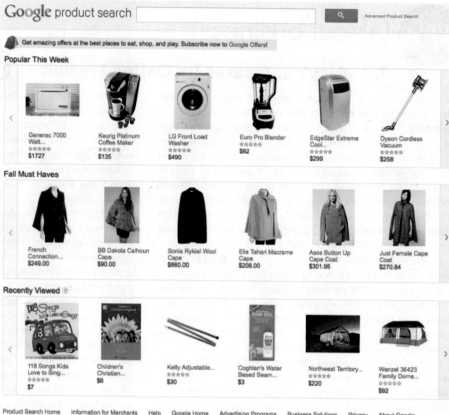

must be delivered physically. Only a few products, such as software and music, can be digitized and then delivered online for additional savings. In contrast, services, such as buying an airline ticket and purchasing stocks or insurance, can be delivered entirely through e-commerce, often with considerable cost reduction. Not surprisingly, then, online delivery of services is growing very rapidly, with millions of new customers being added each year.

One of the most pressing EC issues relating to online services (as well as in marketing tangible products) is **disintermediation**. Intermediaries, also known as middlemen, have two functions: (1) They provide information, and (2) they perform value-added services such as consulting. The first function can be fully automated and most likely will be assumed by e-marketplaces and portals that provide information for free. When this occurs, the intermediaries who perform only (or primarily) this function are likely to be eliminated. The process whereby intermediaries are eliminated is called disintermediation.

In contrast, performing value-added services requires expertise. Unlike the information function, then, this function can be only partially automated. Thus, intermediaries who provide value-added services not only are likely to survive, but they may actually prosper. The Web helps these employees in two situations: (1) when the number of participants is enormous, as with job searches, and (2) when the information that must be exchanged is complex.

In this section, you will examine some leading online service industries: banking, trading of securities (stocks, bonds), job matching, travel services, and advertising.

Cyberbanking.   *Electronic banking*, also known as **cyberbanking**, involves conducting various banking activities from home, at a place of business, or on the road instead of at a physical bank location. Electronic banking has capabilities ranging from paying bills to applying for a loan. For customers, it saves time and is convenient. For banks, it offers an inexpensive alternative to branch banking—for example, about 2 cents cost per transaction versus $1.07 at a

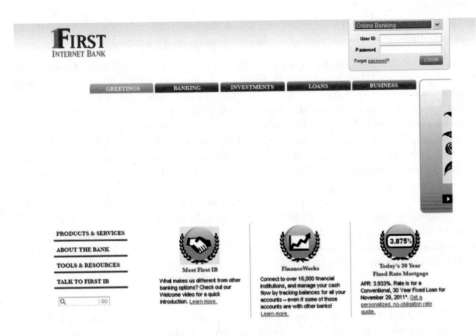

FIGURE 7.7 First Internet Bank of Indiana.

physical branch. It also enables banks to attract remote customers. In addition to regular banks with added online services, **virtual banks**, which are dedicated solely to Internet transactions, are emerging. An example of a virtual bank is First Internet Bank of Indiana (www.firstib.com) (see Figure 7.7).

International banking and the ability to handle trading in multiple currencies are critical for international trade. Transfers of electronic funds and electronic letters of credit are vital services in international banking. An example of support for EC global trade is provided by TradeCard, in conjunction with MasterCard. TradeCard is an international company that provides a secure method for buyers and sellers to make digital payments anywhere on the globe (see the demo at www.tradecard.com). In another example, banks and companies such as Oanda (www.oanda.com) provide conversions of more than 160 currencies.

Online Securities Trading. Millions of people in the United States use computers to trade stocks, bonds, and other financial instruments. In fact, several well-known securities companies, including E*Trade, Ameritrade, and Charles Schwab, offer only online trading. In Korea, more than half of stock traders are already using the Internet for that purpose. Why? Because it is cheaper than a full-service or discount broker. On the Web, investors can find a considerable amount of information regarding specific companies or mutual funds in which to invest (e.g., http://money.cnn.com and www.bloomberg.com).

For example, let's say you have an account with Scottrade. You access Scottrade's Web site (www.scottrade.com) from your personal computer or your Internet-enabled mobile device, enter your account number and password to access your personalized Web page, and then click on "stock trading." Using a menu, you enter the details of your order—buy or sell, margin or cash, price limit, market order, and so on. The computer informs you of the current "ask" and "bid" prices, much as a broker would do over the telephone. You can then approve or reject the transaction.

The Online Job Market. The Internet offers a promising new environment for job seekers and for companies searching for hard-to-find employees. Thousands of companies and government agencies advertise available positions, accept resumes, and take applications via the Internet.

Job seekers use the online job market to reply online to employment ads, to place resumes on various sites, and to use recruiting firms (e.g., www.monster.com, www.simplyhired.com, www.linkedin.com, and www.truecareers.com). Companies that have jobs to offer advertise these openings on their Web sites, and they search the bulletin boards of recruiting firms. In many countries, governments must advertise job openings on the Internet.

Travel Services.   The Internet is an ideal place to plan, explore, and arrange almost any trip economically. Online travel services allow you to purchase airline tickets, reserve hotel rooms, and rent cars. Most sites also offer a fare-tracker feature that sends you e-mail messages about low-cost flights. Examples of comprehensive online travel services are **Expedia.com, Travelocity.com,** and **Orbitz.com.** Online services are also provided by all major airline vacation services, large conventional travel agencies, car rental agencies, hotels (e.g., www.hotels.com), and tour companies. In a variation of this process, **Priceline.com** allows you to set a price you are willing to pay for an airline ticket or hotel accommodations. It then attempts to find a vendor that will match your price.

One costly problem that e-commerce can cause is "mistake fares" in the airline industry. For example, on August 6, 2012, El Al (www.elal.com), Israel's national airline, offered flights to Israel worth up to $1,600 for as little as some $300. This price was incorrect; the actual price was higher. By the time El Al noticed the mistake and pulled the fare, however, some tickets had been sold, thanks in part to online travel discussion groups.

Online Advertising.   *Advertising* is the practice of disseminating information in an attempt to influence a buyer–seller transaction. Traditional advertising on TV or in newspapers involves impersonal, one-way mass communication. In contrast, direct-response marketing, or telemarketing, contacts individuals by direct mail or telephone and requires them to respond in order to make a purchase. The direct-response approach personalizes advertising and marketing. At the same time, however, it can be expensive, slow, and ineffective. It can also be extremely annoying to the consumer.

Internet advertising redefines the advertising process, making it media rich, dynamic, and interactive. It improves on traditional forms of advertising in a number of ways. First, Internet ads can be updated any time at minimal cost and therefore can be kept current. In addition, these ads can reach very large numbers of potential buyers all over the world. Further, they are generally cheaper than radio, television, and print ads. Finally, Internet ads can be interactive and targeted to specific interest groups and/or individuals.

Advertising Methods.   The most common online advertising methods are banners, pop-ups, and e-mail. **Banners** are simply electronic billboards. Typically, a banner contains a short text or graphical message to promote a product or a vendor. It may even contain video clips and sound. When customers click on a banner, they are transferred to the advertiser's home page. Banner advertising is the most commonly used form of advertising on the Internet (see Figure 7.8).

A major advantage of banners is that they can be customized to the target audience. If the computer system knows who you are or what your profile is, it might send you a banner that is specifically intended to match your interests. A major disadvantage of banners is that they can convey only limited information because of their small size. Another drawback is that many viewers simply ignore them.

Pop-up and pop-under ads are contained in a new browser window that is automatically launched when you enter or exit a Web site. A **pop-up ad** appears in front of the current browser window. A **pop-under ad** appears underneath the active window; when users close the active window, they see the ad. Many users strongly object to these ads, which they consider intrusive. Modern browsers let users block pop-up ads, but this feature must be used with caution because some Web sites depend on pop-up capabilities to present content other than advertising. For example, when you log on to your Verizon e-mail page, you also see a brief

FIGURE 7.8 When customers click on a banner ad, they are transferred to the vendor's homepage.

Banner (468 x 60)

(one line each) summary of recent news stories. If you hover your mouse over one of them, you get a pop-up window with an extended summary (a few paragraphs) of that story. Another example is the WebCT Vista software for online instruction, where discussion group posts appear in pop-up windows. In the first example, blocking pop-ups would make the feature less useful. In the second example it would eliminate important functionality.

E-mail is emerging as an Internet advertising and marketing channel. It is generally cost-effective to implement, and it provides a better and quicker response rate than other advertising channels. Marketers develop or purchase a list of e-mail addresses, place them in a customer database, and then send advertisements via e-mail. A list of e-mail addresses can be a very powerful tool because the marketer can target a group of people or even individuals.

As you have probably concluded by now, there is a potential for misuse of e-mail advertising. In fact, some consumers receive a flood of unsolicited e-mail, or *spam*. **Spamming** is the indiscriminate distribution of electronic ads without the permission of the receiver. Unfortunately, spamming is becoming worse over time.

Two important responses to spamming are permission marketing and viral marketing. **Permission marketing** asks consumers to give their permission to voluntarily accept online advertising and e-mail. Typically, consumers are asked to complete an electronic form that asks what they are interested in and requests permission to send related marketing information. Sometimes, consumers are offered incentives to receive advertising.

Permission marketing is the basis of many Internet marketing strategies. For example, millions of users periodically receive e-mails from airlines such as American and Southwest. Users of this marketing service can ask to be notified of low fares from their hometown or to their favorite destinations. Significantly, they can easily unsubscribe at any time. Permission marketing is also extremely important for market research (e.g., search for "Media Metrix" at www.comscore.com).

In one particularly interesting form of permission marketing, companies such as Clickdough.com, ExpressPaidSurveys.com, and CashSurfers.com have built customer lists of millions of people who are happy to receive advertising messages whenever they are on the Web. These customers are paid $0.25 to $0.50 an hour to view messages while they do their normal surfing.

Viral marketing refers to online word-of-mouth marketing. The strategy behind viral marketing is to have people forward messages to friends, family members, and other acquaintances suggesting they "check this out." For example, a marketer can distribute a small game program embedded with a sponsor's e-mail that is easy to forward. The marketer releases only a few thousand copies, with the expectation that the recipients in turn will forward the program to many more thousands of potential customers. In this way, viral marketing enables companies to build brand awareness at a minimal cost without having to spam millions of uninterested users.

Issues in E-Tailing

Despite e-tailing's increasing popularity, many e-tailers continue to face serious issues that can restrict their growth. Perhaps the two most significant issues are channel conflict and order fulfillment.

Clicks-and-mortar companies may face a conflict with their regular distributors when they sell directly to customers online. This situation, known as **channel conflict**, can alienate the distributors. Channel conflict has forced some companies to avoid direct online sales. For example, Walmart, Lowe's, and Home Depot would rather have customers come to their stores. Therefore, although all three companies maintain e-commerce Web sites, their sites place more emphasis on providing information—products, prices, specials, and store locations—than on online sales.

Channel conflict can arise in areas such as pricing and resource allocation—for example, how much money to spend on advertising. Another potential source of conflict involves the logistics services provided by the offline activities to the online activities. For example, how should a company handle returns of items purchased online? Some companies have completely separated the "clicks" (the online portion of the organization) from the "mortar" or "bricks" (the traditional bricks-and-mortar part of the organization). However, this approach can increase expenses, reduce the synergy between the two organizational channels, and alienate customers. As a result, many companies are integrating their online and offline channels, a process known as **multichanneling**. IT's About Business 7.4 illustrates how the online channel is causing problems for brick-and-mortar retailers. From a more positive perspective, eBay sees great potential in the hybrid online/offline shopping experience. IT's About Business 7.5 describes how the company has developed or bought the necessary information technology for its e-commerce initiative.

IT's [about business]

7.4 Can Traditional Retailers Survive?

Many shoppers walk into brick-and-mortar retail stores, see products that interest them, and conduct research on their smartphones. Many of these shoppers ultimately make their purchases online and they may make their purchases from the Web site of the store they are in, or from another online vendor. This comparison process is called *showrooming*.

Showrooming occurs when shoppers visit a store to examine a product in person but then proceed to buy it from a rival online, frequently at a lower price. This process is presenting a worsening problem for brick-and-mortar retailers, including Target, Best Buy, Walmart, Barnes & Noble, and many others. At the same time, showrooming benefits Amazon, eBay, and other online retailers.

For example, Amazon's Price Check app has made showrooming even more widespread. Amazon awards customers with an additional 5 percent discount (up to $5) on up to three qualifying products if they use this app to check the price of those products while shopping in a physical retail store. Eligible categories of products include electronics, toys, music, sporting goods, and DVDs. Shoppers can utilize this app to price-check in four ways: by scanning a bar code, by snapping a photo of the product, by pronouncing the product's name, or by typing in a search query.

Online-only retailers have two significant advantages over traditional retailers. First, their labor costs are significantly lower. Second, at least for the time being, they do not collect sales tax in most states, which makes them very appealing to their customers. Going further, sites such as Amazon are based on an entirely different business model than are traditional retailers. That is, Amazon can sell products so cheaply because it uses its other profitable business units—such as cloud data storage and the fees it charges merchants to sell on its Web site—to subsidize the rest of its businesses. Traditional retailers that do not use this model are unable to match Amazon's low prices, which puts them at a fundamental disadvantage. In addition, consumer preferences in general are moving to online venues.

Traditional retailers like Target, Best Buy, and Walmart are playing catch-up in online retailing, which is becoming an increasingly important avenue for sales. It is critical for traditional retailers to become more attractive to their customers, so they are fighting back against the online retailing giants.

Target's Attempt. In fall 2011, Target (www.target.com) relaunched and upgraded its Web site, which had been operated by Amazon for the last decade. During that time, the site had crashed several times, most notably when shoppers rushed to buy a special line of items made by the Italian fashion house Missoni.

Target also asked its suppliers for help in limiting showrooming. In January 2012, Target sent a letter to its vendors, suggesting that they create special products for Target so that they could set themselves apart from their competitors and shield themselves from the price comparisons that have become so easy for shoppers to perform on their computers and smartphones. When this option is not possible, Target asked its suppliers to help it match their rivals' prices. Vendors are likely to try to meet Target's requests because Target is a very large and prominent retail chain.

Maurices's Attempt. Other traditional retailers are using geofencing. A *geofence* is a virtual perimeter for a real-world, physical geographic area. For example, Maurices (www.maurices.com), the women's clothing chain, sends promotions to the smartphones of people who come within a few hundred yards of its stores. Only consumers who opt in to the service are sent messages about in-store sales.

Meijer's Attempt. Meijer (www.meijer.com), a chain of supermarkets, is adopting a different approach. The chain is using sensors in its stores to offer customized information and virtual coupons via smartphone. In addition, it provides a special service for customers who prepare shopping lists online. These shoppers can open up the retailer's app inside the store, and the app will reorder their list based on their location in the store, thus speeding up the shopping process.

The approaches of Maurices and Meijer are of questionable value. After all, not everyone has a smartphone. Perhaps Best Buy (www.bestbuy.com) has a better plan to compete with online retailers.

Best Buy's Attempt. Just a few years ago, Best Buy was regarded as one of the finest retailers in the world. However, the firm's profits declined by 91 percent between 2011 and 2012, and its share price fell dramatically.

Despite these depressing financials, Best Buy is still the largest personal computer retailer, the largest independent phone retailer, and the largest camera dealer in the world. It also sells more tablets than any other retailer.

Best Buy decided to focus on the strengths of physical retail that online companies cannot match. For example, showrooming is a threat, but it also exposes a major limitation of online commerce: People want to try before they buy, and they cannot do that on a Web site.

Even more importantly, Best Buy has a vast logistics network that delivers products quickly and reliably to 1,400 stores across the country. Order a product online from Best Buy, and you can pick it up the same day from one of its physical stores.

In essence, Best Buy is combining its physical storefronts and digital infrastructure into a single, unified organic package. For instance, Best Buy is embracing the showrooming trend with a pilot project that it launched in 50 stores. When a customer comes in to test out, say, high-end cameras, a sales rep with a tablet meets him or her to compare specifications on the various models. Meanwhile, specially trained reps try to provide the kind of service that customers cannot easily find online. For example, if the customer finds a camera he or she likes, the rep can pull up a list of comparison sites to locate the lowest price. (Best Buy is trying to match competitors' prices whenever possible. This process could become easier as states try to require Amazon to charge sales tax on its transactions.)

Going further, if the customer wants a camera that is not in stock, the rep can help him or her place an order through BestBuy.com. The customer then has a choice of delivery methods—same-day in-store pickup or home delivery.

As Best Buy's CEO explained, "What beats Amazon Prime and free shipping? It's something that's in stock, near me, and right now. And if you can add a knowledgeable rep and a price match, you are golden."

It remains to be seen whether low price points at online retailers will spell ruin for their more traditional competitors. Traditional retailers will have to offer customers a truly exceptional shopping and buying experience to be able to compete in the marketplace.

It may be that Best Buy has the best idea: integrate its physical stores with the process of showrooming.

Sources: Compiled from M. Copeland, "Death by a Billion Clicks," *Wired*, December, 2012; B. Tuttle, "Put Down the Mouse," *Time*, November 26, 2012; M. Townsend, S. Maheshwari, and C. Timberlake, "The War Over Christmas," *Bloomberg BusinessWeek*, November 5–11, 2012; D. Mattoli and M. Bustillo, "Can Texting Save Stores?" *The Wall Street Journal*, May 9, 2012; N. Potter, "'Showrooming': People Shopping in Stores, Then Researching by Cell Phone, Says Pew Survey," *ABC News*, January 31, 2012; A. Zimmerman, "Showdown Over 'Showrooms'," *The Wall Street Journal*, January 23, 2012; J. Milliot, "The Amazon Price Check App and the Battle Over 'Showrooming'," *Publishers Weekly*, December 9, 2011; T. Novellino, "The Amazon App Attack," *Portfolio.com*, December 8, 2011; E. Straub, "Browse at a Bookstore, Buy at Amazon: The Evil of Showrooming," *Time*, December 8, 2011; A. Chang, "Retail Groups Lash Out After Amazon Announces Price Check App Promotion," *The Los Angeles Times*, December 7, 2011; A. Chang, "Amazon Giving Shoppers Up to $15 for Using Its Price Check App," *The Los Angeles Times*, December 6, 2011; www.target.com, www.pewresearch.org, www.bestbuy.com, www.amazon.com, accessed February 28, 2013.

Questions

1. What other strategies could Target and other brick-and-mortar retailers implement to combat showrooming? Provide examples of IT solutions and non-IT solutions that were not discussed in this case.
2. Do you practice showrooming? If not, why not? If so, why? Do you showroom only to compare prices? List other reasons why shoppers might practice showrooming.
3. Are there categories of goods other than the ones mentioned in this case that might lend themselves to showrooming? Provide specific examples to support your answer.

IT's [about business]

7.5 The Future of Shopping   MKT POM

Once a retail pioneer, by late 2011 eBay (www.ebay.com) had become an auction wasteland saddled with outdated technology. In order to save the company, John Donahoe, eBay's new CEO, completely remodeled the company's business practices. He removed layers of bureaucracy between management and engineers, opened up PayPal to outside developers, created a Web site that consumers could experiment with and comment on, and invested in new e-commerce technology. Donahoe also worked to reduce eBay's dependence on auctions as a source of revenue. By mid-2012, only 24 percent of eBay's revenue came from auctions, compared with 35 percent in previous years.

Donahoe also shifted eBay's focus as a Web site. He realized that the increased use of mobile devices was blurring the lines between online and offline shopping, and he wanted to locate eBay at the center of the hybrid online/offline shopping experience. According to Forrester Research, the financial opportunity of this hybrid experience dwarfs the space of simple e-commerce (i.e., browsing and buying online), which represents just 9 percent of all retail sales. Donahoe's vision for eBay's future is for the company to provide its customers with the ability to shop wherever they want, however they want, for the best price, and with the greatest convenience.

How did eBay go about accomplishing this goal and transitioning into a hybrid online/offline shopping experience? The retailer followed the progression outlined below:

- Step 1: eBay purchased RedLaser (www.redlaser.com). RedLaser is a company whose technology allows consumers to scan bar codes, vehicle identification numbers, gift cards, asset tags, and QR codes with their mobile devices.

- Step 2: eBay purchased Milo (www.milo.com), a company that enables shoppers to view the inventory of offline stores online 24/7. Although Milo had been able to land major retailers for its inventory network, the company was still a relatively small player. eBay, however, had the designers and developers who could help Milo overcome its technical challenges. In addition, eBay had more than 30 million sellers and merchants in its marketplace, many of whom had offline inventory that Milo could tap. As a result, Milo's technology could help eBay list far more products than was previously possible.

- Step 3: eBay purchased GSI Commerce (www.gsicommerce .com), a company that builds e-commerce platforms for several hundred offline retailers. GSI concentrates on customer care and on interactive marketing for its clients. This purchase, helped eBay was able to improve its online customer interactions, strengthen its customer relationships, and provide superior customer service.

- Step 4: eBay purchased Where (www.where.com). Where builds location-based mobile apps for every major mobile device platform, including Android, iPhone, and BlackBerry. The company boasts 4 million active users per month. Where provides local listings for restaurants, bars, merchants, and events, and it suggests places and deals for its users based on their location and past behavior. The absorption of Where into eBay allowed eBay customers to shop from any location. Further, Where enabled eBay to suggest additional products to customers based on their location.

- Step 5: eBay purchased Fig Card (http://figcard.com, bought by PayPal in 2011). Fig Card allows merchants to accept payments from mobile devices in stores by using a simple USB device that plugs into the cash register or point-of-sale terminal. To participate, customers simply need to download the Fig app onto their smartphone. Going further, once consumers set up their payment information and designate PayPal as a payment option, Fig Card is able to integrate with PayPal. This new functionality allowed eBay to expand the options that its customers could use to pay for purchases.

- Step 6: eBay already owns PayPal (www.paypal.com). eBay wants every transaction to end with PayPal.

Consider these scenarios:

- You have met your girlfriend for lunch, and you are admiring her new handbag. You take a picture of her purse with your smartphone. Your smartphone then uses an eBay app to reveal all of the boutiques within a 3-mile radius that have the same color and style bag in stock, along with the price that each store charges. You then decide which store has your ideal combination of price and location, and you order the bag via your phone. After lunch, you visit that store, and you bypass the checkout lines by showing the salesperson the digital receipt on your phone.

- The local Starbucks "sees" you (i.e., it senses your smartphone's location) when you are two blocks away, and it offers you a dollar toward your next Frappuccino purchase. Starbucks puts the dollar into your PayPal account, where it sits until it expires in one hour.

- What about that new Canon camera you are thinking about, but are not yet ready to purchase? Scan its bar code (or RFID tag or QR code) into your PayPal "wish list." Then, when you walk by a retailer who has the camera in stock, that store can make you a special pricing offer that is better than you have found anywhere else.

Here is the model: eBay + RedLaser + Milo + GSI + PayPal + Fig Card + Where = Success!

Recall that eBay's new CEO wants to establish a complete shopping experience for the company's customers. With each piece of the puzzle, eBay has made it easier, faster, and more convenient for its customers to shop. Furthermore, the company's customers have more choices than ever before, and many of those choices are relevant to the customer's location. eBay's new model appears to be working. The company claims that, although all the pieces are not yet integrated, the model still facilitated nearly $4 billion in mobile transactions in 2011.

Sources: Compiled from I. Steiner, "eBay's New X.Commerce Is Getting Some Legs," *eCommerce Bytes*, July 23, 2012; P. Demery, "eBay Turns to Technology," *Internet Retailer*, June 1, 2012; R. Kim, "With X.Commerce, eBay Eyes a Bigger Prize as Sales Enabler," *GigaOM*, October 12, 2011; D. Sacks, "How Jack Abraham Is Reinventing eBay," *Fast Company*, June 22, 2011; L. Rao, "eBay Closes $2.4 Billion Acquisition of GSI Commerce," *TechCrunch*, June 20, 2011; S. Kirsner, "eBay Buys Mobile Payments Startup Fig Card, Second Boston Acquisition in April," *Boston.com*, April 28, 2011; www.milo.com, www.ebay.com, accessed March 20, 2013.

Questions

1. What are the advantages of eBay's hybrid shopping experience vision for the customer?
2. What are potential disadvantages of eBay's hybrid shopping experience vision for the customer?

The second major issue confronting e-commerce is order fulfillment, which can create problems for e-tailers as well. Any time a company sells directly to customers, it is involved in various order-fulfillment activities. It must perform the following activities: quickly find the products to be shipped; pack them; arrange for the packages to be delivered speedily to the customer's door; collect the money from every customer, either in advance, by COD, or by individual bill; and handle the return of unwanted or defective products.

It is very difficult to accomplish these activities both effectively and efficiently in B2C, because a company has to ship small packages to many customers and do it quickly. For this reason, companies involved in B2C activities often experience difficulties in their supply chains.

In addition to providing customers with the products they ordered and doing it on time, order fulfillment provides all related customer services. For example, the customer must receive assembly and operation instructions for a new appliance. In addition, if the customer is unhappy with a product, the company must arrange an exchange or a return. (Visit www.fedex .com to learn how FedEx manages returns.)

In the late 1990s, e-tailers faced continuous problems in order fulfillment, especially during the holiday season. These problems included late deliveries, delivering wrong items, high delivery costs, and compensation to unsatisfied customers. For e-tailers, taking orders over the Internet is the easy part of B2C e-commerce. Delivering orders to customers' doors is the hard part. In contrast, order fulfillment is less complicated in B2B. These transactions are much larger, but they are fewer in number. In addition, these companies have had order fulfillment mechanisms in place for many years.

before you go on...

1. Describe electronic storefronts and malls.

2. Discuss various types of online services, such as cyberbanking, securities trading, job searches, travel services, and so on.

3. Discuss online advertising, its methods, and its benefits.

4. Identify the major issues related to e-tailing.

5. What are spamming, permission marketing, and viral marketing?

Business-to-Business (B2B) Electronic Commerce

7.3

In *business to business* (B2B) e-commerce, the buyers and sellers are business organizations. B2B comprises about 85 percent of EC volume. It covers a broad spectrum of applications that enable an enterprise to form electronic relationships with its distributors, resellers, suppliers, customers, and other partners. Organizations can use B2B to restructure their supply chains and their partner relationships.

B2B applications utilize any of several business models. The major models are sell-side marketplaces, buy-side marketplaces, and electronic exchanges.

Sell-Side Marketplaces

In the **sell-side marketplace** model, organizations attempt to sell their products or services to other organizations electronically from their own private e-marketplace Web site and/or from a third-party Web site. This model is similar to the B2C model in which the buyer is expected to come to the seller's site, view catalogs, and place an order. In the B2B sell-side marketplace, however, the buyer is an organization.

The key mechanisms in the sell-side model are forward auctions and electronic catalogs that can be customized for each large buyer. Sellers such as Dell Computer (www .dellauction.com) use auctions extensively. In addition to conducting auctions from their own Web sites, organizations can use third-party auction sites, such as eBay, to liquidate items. Companies such as Ariba (www.ariba.com) are helping organizations to auction old assets and inventories.

The sell-side model is used by hundreds of thousands of companies. It is especially powerful for companies with superb reputations. The seller can be either a manufacturer (e.g., Dell or IBM), a distributor (e.g., www.avnet.com), or a retailer (e.g., www.bigboxx.com). The seller uses EC to increase sales, reduce selling and advertising expenditures, increase delivery speed, and lower administrative costs. The sell-side model is especially suitable to customization. Many companies allow their customers to configure their orders online. For example, at Dell (www.dell.com), you can determine the exact type of computer that you want. You can choose the type of chip (e.g., Itanium 2), the size of the hard drive (e.g., 1 terabyte), the type of monitor (e.g., 22-inch flat screen), and so on. Similarly, the Jaguar Web site (www .jaguar.com) allows you to customize the Jaguar you want. Self-customization greatly reduces any misunderstandings concerning what customers want, and it encourages businesses to fill orders more quickly.

Buy-Side Marketplaces

Procurement is the overarching function that describes the activities and processes to acquire goods and services. Distinct from purchasing, procurement involves the activities necessary to establish requirements, sourcing activities such as market research and vendor evaluation, and negotiation of contracts. *Purchasing* refers to the process of ordering and receiving goods and services. It is a subset of the procurement process.

The **buy-side** marketplace is a model in which organizations attempt to procure needed products or services from other organizations electronically. A major method of procuring goods and services in the buy-side model is the reverse auction.

The buy-side model uses EC technology to streamline the procurement process. The goal is to reduce both the costs of items procured and the administrative expenses involved in procuring them. In addition, EC technology can shorten the procurement cycle time.

Procurement by using electronic support is referred to as e-procurement. **E-procurement** uses reverse auctions, particularly group purchasing. In **group purchasing**, multiple buyers combine their orders so that they constitute a large volume and therefore attract more seller attention. In addition, when buyers place their combined orders on a reverse auction, they can negotiate a volume discount. Typically, the orders of small buyers are aggregated by a third-party vendor, such as the United Sourcing Alliance (www.usa-llc.com).

Electronic Exchanges

Private exchanges have one buyer and many sellers. Electronic marketplaces (e-marketplaces), called **public exchanges** or just **exchanges**, are independently owned by a third party, and they connect many sellers and many buyers. Public exchanges are open to all business organizations. They frequently are owned and operated by a third party. Public exchange managers provide all of the necessary information systems to the participants. Thus, buyers and sellers merely have to "plug in" in order to trade. B2B public exchanges are often the initial point for contacts between business partners. Once the partners make contact, they may move to a private exchange or to private trading rooms provided by many public exchanges to conduct their subsequent trading activities.

Electronic exchanges deal in direct materials and indirect materials. *Direct materials* are inputs to the manufacturing process, such as safety glass used in automobile windshields and windows. *Indirect materials* are those items, such as office supplies, that are needed for maintenance, operations, and repairs (MRO).

There are three basic types of public exchanges: vertical, horizontal, and functional. All three types offer diversified support services, ranging from payments to logistics.

Vertical exchanges connect buyers and sellers in a given industry. Examples of vertical exchanges are www.plasticsnet.com in the plastics industry and www.papersite.com in the paper industry. The vertical e-marketplaces offer services that are particularly suited to the community they serve. Vertical exchanges are frequently owned and managed by a *consortium*, a term for a group of major players in an industry. For example, Marriott and Hyatt own a procurement consortium for the hotel industry, and Chevron owns an energy e-marketplace.

Horizontal exchanges connect buyers and sellers across many industries. They are used primarily for MRO materials. Examples of horizontal exchanges are TradersCity (www.traderscity .com), Globalsources (www.globalsources.com), and Alibaba (www.alibaba.com).

Finally, in *functional exchanges*, needed services such as temporary help or extra office space are traded on an "as-needed" basis. For example, Employease (www.employease.com) can find temporary labor by searching employers in its Employease Network.

before you go on...

1. Briefly differentiate between the sell-side marketplace and the buy-side marketplace.
2. Briefly differentiate among vertical exchanges, horizontal exchanges, and functional exchanges.

Ethical and Legal Issues in E-Business   7.4

Technological innovation often forces a society to reexamine and modify its ethical standards. In many cases, the new standards are incorporated into law. In this section, you will learn about two important ethical considerations—privacy and job loss—as well as various legal issues arising from the practice of e-business.

Ethical Issues

Many of the ethical and global issues related to IT also apply to e-business. Here you will learn about two basic issues: privacy and job loss.

By making it easier to store and transfer personal information, e-business presents some threats to privacy. To begin with, most electronic payment systems know who the buyers are. It may be necessary, then, to protect the buyers' identities. Businesses frequently use encryption to provide this protection.

Another major privacy issue is tracking. For example, individuals' activities on the Internet can be tracked by cookies (discussed in Chapter 7). Cookies store your tracking history on your personal computer's hard drive, and any time you revisit a certain Web site, the server recognizes the cookie. In response, antivirus software packages routinely search for potentially harmful cookies.

In addition to compromising individual privacy, the use of EC may eliminate the need for some of a company's employees, as well as brokers and agents. The manner in which these unneeded workers, especially employees, are treated can raise ethical issues: How should the company handle the layoffs? Should companies be required to retrain employees for new positions? If not, how should the company compensate or otherwise assist the displaced workers?

Legal and Ethical Issues Specific to E-Commerce

Many legal issues are related specifically to e-commerce. A business environment in which buyers and sellers do not know one another and cannot even see one another creates opportunities for dishonest people to commit fraud and other crimes. During the first few years of EC, the public witnessed many such crimes. These illegal actions ranged from creating a virtual bank that disappeared along with the investors' deposits to manipulating stock prices on the Internet. Unfortunately, fraudulent activities on the Internet are increasing. In the following section, you explore some of the major legal issues that are specific to e-commerce.

Fraud on the Internet.   Internet fraud has grown even faster than Internet use itself. In one case, stock promoters falsely spread positive rumors about the prospects of the companies they touted in order to boost the stock price. In other cases, the information provided might have been true, but the promoters did not disclose that they were paid to talk up the companies. Stock promoters specifically target small investors who are lured by the promise of fast profits.

Stocks are only one of many areas where swindlers are active. Auctions are especially conducive to fraud, by both sellers and buyers. Other types of fraud include selling bogus investments and setting up phantom business opportunities. Because of the growing use of e-mail, financial criminals now have access to many more people. The U.S. Federal Trade Commission (FTC, www.ftc.gov) regularly publishes examples of scams that are most likely to be spread via e-mail or to be found on the Web. Later in this section, you will see some ways in which consumers and sellers can protect themselves from online fraud.

Domain Names. Another legal issue is competition over domain names. Domain names are assigned by central nonprofit organizations that check for conflicts and possible infringement of trademarks. Obviously, companies that sell goods and services over the Internet want customers to be able to find them easily. In general, the closer the domain name matches the company's name, the easier the company is to locate.

A domain name is considered legal when the person or business who owns the name has operated a legitimate business under that name for some time. Companies such as Christian Dior, Nike, Deutsche Bank, and even Microsoft have had to fight or pay to get the domain name that corresponds to their company's name. Consider the case of Delta Air Lines. Delta originally could not obtain the Internet domain name delta.com because Delta Faucet had purchased it first. Delta Faucet had been in business under that name since 1954 and therefore had a legitimate business interest in the domain name. Delta Air Lines had to settle for delta-airlines.com until it bought the domain name from Delta Faucet. Delta Faucet is now at deltafaucet.com. Several cases of disputed domain names are currently in court.

Cybersquatting. **Cybersquatting** refers to the practice of registering or using domain names for the purpose of profiting from the goodwill or the trademark that belongs to someone else. The Anti-Cybersquatting Consumer Protection Act (1999) permits trademark owners in the United States to sue for damages in such cases.

However, some practices that could be considered cybersquatting are not illegal, although they may well be unethical. Perhaps the more common of these practices is "domain tasting." Domain tasting lets registrars profit from the complex money trail of pay-per-click advertising. The practice can be traced back to the policies of the organization responsible for regulating Web names, the Internet Corporation for Assigned Names and Numbers (ICANN) (www.icann.org) (see Figure 7.9). In 2000, ICANN established the "create grace period," a five-day period during which a company or person can claim a domain name and then return it for a full refund of the $6 registry fee. ICANN implemented this policy to allow someone who mistyped a domain to

FIGURE 7.9 Internet Corporation for Assigned Names and Numbers (ICANN) Web site (*Source:* www.icann.org).

return it without cost. In some cases, companies engage in cybersquatting by registering domain names that are very similar to their competitors' domain names in order to generate traffic from people who misspell Web addresses.

Domain tasters exploit this policy by claiming Internet domains for five days at no cost. These domain names frequently resemble those of prominent companies and organizations. The tasters then jam these domains full of advertisements that come from Yahoo! and Google. Because this process involves zero risk and 100 percent profit margins, domain tasters register millions of domain names every day—some of them over and over again. Experts estimate that registrants ultimately purchase less than 2 percent of the sites they sample. In the vast majority of cases, they use the domain names for only a few days to generate quick profits.

Taxes and Other Fees. In offline sales, most states and localities tax business transactions that are conducted within their jurisdiction. The most obvious example is sales taxes. Federal, state, and local authorities now are scrambling to create some type of taxation policy for e-business. This problem is particularly complex for interstate and international e-commerce. For example, some people claim that the state in which the *seller* is located deserves the entire sales tax (in some countries, it is a value-added tax, or VAT). Others contend that the state in which the *server* is located also should receive some of the tax revenues.

In addition to the sales tax, there is a question about where—and in some cases, whether—electronic sellers should pay business license taxes, franchise fees, gross-receipts taxes, excise taxes, privilege taxes, and utility taxes. Furthermore, how should tax collection be controlled? Legislative efforts to impose taxes on e-commerce are opposed by an organization named the Internet Freedom Fighters. So far, their efforts have been successful.

However, that situation may change. A bill that would give states the authority to collect sales taxes on all Internet purchases passed a major procedural hurdle in the U.S. Senate in late-April, 2013. If the bill becomes law, it would hand state and local governments as much as $11 billion per year in added revenue that they are legally owed.

Even before electronic commerce over the Internet emerged, the basic law was that as long as a retailer did not have a physical presence in the state where the consumer was shopping, that retailer did not have to collect a sales tax. Shoppers are supposed to track such purchases and then pay the taxes owed in their annual tax filings. Few people, however, do this or are even aware of it.

The result is that online retailers have been able to undercut the prices of their non-Internet (e.g., brick-and-mortar stores) competitors for years. As state and local governments have had increasingly large cash shortcomings since the U.S. recession, officials have fought back. In mid-2013, nine states require Amazon to collect sales taxes.

Copyright. Recall from Chapter 6 that intellectual property is protected by copyright laws and cannot be used freely. This point is significant because many people mistakenly believe that once they purchase a piece of software, they have the right to share it with others. In fact, what they have bought is the right to *use* the software, not the right to *distribute* it. That right remains with the copyright holder. Similarly, copying material from Web sites without permission is a violation of copyright laws. Protecting intellectual property rights in e-commerce is extremely difficult, however, because it involves hundreds of millions of people in some 200 countries with differing copyright laws who have access to billions of Web pages. (Recall the case of Kim Dotcom in the opening case of Chapter 4.)

before you go on...

1. List and explain some ethical issues in EC.
2. Discuss the major legal issues of EC.
3. Describe buyer protection and seller protection in EC.

What's In IT For Me?

For the Accounting Major

Accounting personnel are involved in several EC activities. Designing the ordering system and its relationship with inventory management requires accounting attention. Billing and payments are also accounting activities, as are determining cost and profit allocation. Replacing paper documents with electronic means will affect many of the accountant's tasks, especially the auditing of EC activities and systems. Finally, building a cost-benefit and cost-justification system to determine which products/services to take online and creating a chargeback system are critical to the success of EC.

For the Finance Major

The worlds of banking, securities and commodities markets, and other financial services are being reengineered because of EC. Online securities trading and its supporting infrastructure are growing more rapidly than any other EC activity. Many innovations already in place are changing the rules of economic and financial incentives for financial analysts and managers. Online banking, for example, does not recognize state boundaries, and it may create a new framework for financing global trades. Public financial information is now accessible in seconds. These innovations will dramatically change the manner in which finance personnel operate.

For the Marketing Major

A major revolution in marketing and sales is taking place because of EC. Perhaps its most obvious feature is the transition from a physical to a virtual marketplace. Equally important, however, is the radical transformation to one-on-one advertising and sales and to customized and interactive marketing. Marketing channels are being combined, eliminated, or recreated. The EC revolution is creating new products and markets and significantly altering existing ones. Digitization of products and services also has implications for marketing and sales. The direct producer-to-consumer channel is expanding rapidly and is fundamentally changing the nature of customer service. As the battle for customers intensifies, marketing and sales personnel are becoming the most critical success factor in many organizations. Online marketing can be a blessing to one company and a curse to another.

For the Production/Operations Management Major

EC is changing the manufacturing system from product-push mass production to order-pull mass customization. This change requires a robust supply chain, information support, and reengineering of processes that involve suppliers and other business partners. Suppliers can use extranets to monitor and replenish inventories without the need for constant reorders. In addition, the Internet and intranets help reduce cycle times. Many production/operations problems that have persisted for years, such as complex scheduling and excess inventories, are being solved rapidly with the use of Web technologies. Companies can now use external and internal networks to find and manage manufacturing operations in other countries much more easily. Also, the Web is reengineering procurement by helping companies conduct electronic bids for parts and subassemblies, thus reducing cost. All in all, the job of the progressive production/operations manager is closely tied in with e-commerce.

For the Human Resources Management Major

HR majors need to understand the new labor markets and the impacts of EC on old labor markets. Also, the HR department may use EC tools for such functions as procuring office supplies. Moreover, becoming knowledgeable about new government online initiatives and online training is critical. In addition, HR personnel must be familiar with the major legal issues related to EC and employment.

[Summary]

1. Describe the six common types of electronic commerce.

In *business-to-consumer* (B2C) electronic commerce, the sellers are organizations and the buyers are individuals. In *business-to-business* (B2B) electronic commerce, the sellers and the buyers are businesses. In *consumer-to-consumer* (C2C) electronic commerce, an individual sells products or services to other individuals. In *business-to-employee* (B2E) electronic commerce, an organization uses EC internally to provide information and services to its employees. *E-government* is the use of Internet technology in general and e-commerce in particular to deliver information and public services to citizens (called government-to-citizen or G2C EC) and business partners and suppliers (called government-to-business or G2B EC). *Mobile commerce* refers to e-commerce that is conducted entirely in a wireless environment. We leave the examples of each type to you.

2. Describe the various online services of business-to-consumer (B2C) commerce, providing specific examples of each.

Electronic *banking*, also known as cyberbanking, involves conducting various banking activities from home, at a place of business, or on the road instead of at a physical bank location.

Online securities trading involves buying and selling securities over the Web.

Online job matching over the Web offers a promising environment for job seekers and for companies searching for hard-to-find employees. Thousands of companies and government agencies advertise available positions, accept resumes, and take applications via the Internet.

Online travel services allow you to purchase airline tickets, reserve hotel rooms, and rent cars. Most sites also offer a fare-tracker feature that sends you e-mail messages about low-cost flights. The Internet is an ideal place to plan, explore, and arrange almost any trip economically.

Online advertising over the Web makes the advertising process media-rich, dynamic, and interactive.

We leave the examples to you.

3. Describe the three business models for business-to-business electronic commerce.

In the *sell-side marketplace* model, organizations attempt to sell their products or services to other organizations electronically from their own private e-marketplace Web site and/or from a third-party Web site. Sellers such as Dell Computer (**www.dellauction.com**) use sell-side auctions extensively. In addition to auctions from their own Web sites, organizations can use third-party auction sites, such as eBay, to liquidate items.

The *buy-side marketplace* is a model in which organizations attempt to buy needed products or services from other organizations electronically.

E-marketplaces, in which there are many sellers and many buyers, are called *public exchanges*, or just exchanges. Public exchanges are open to all business organizations. They frequently are owned and operated by a third party. There are three basic types of public exchanges: vertical, horizontal, and functional. *Vertical exchanges* connect buyers and sellers in a given industry. *Horizontal exchanges* connect buyers and sellers across many industries. In *functional exchanges*, needed services such as temporary help or extra office space are traded on an "as-needed" basis.

4. **Identify the ethical and legal issues related to electronic commerce, providing examples.**

E-business presents some threats to privacy. First, most electronic payment systems know who the buyers are. It may be necessary, then, to protect the buyers' identities with encryption. Another major privacy issue is tracking, where individuals' activities on the Internet can be tracked by cookies.

The use of EC may eliminate the need for some of a company's employees, as well as brokers and agents. The manner in which these unneeded workers, especially employees, are treated can raise ethical issues: How should the company handle the layoffs? Should companies be required to retrain employees for new positions? If not, how should the company compensate or otherwise assist the displaced workers?

We leave the examples to you.

[Chapter Glossary]

auction A competitive process in which either a seller solicits consecutive bids from buyers or a buyer solicits bids from sellers, and prices are determined dynamically by competitive bidding.

banner Electronic billboards, which typically contain a short text or graphical message to promote a product or a vendor.

brick-and-mortar organizations Organizations in which the product, the process, and the delivery agent are all physical.

business model The method by which a company generates revenue to sustain itself.

business-to-business electronic commerce (B2B) Electronic commerce in which both the sellers and the buyers are business organizations.

business-to-consumer electronic commerce (B2C) Electronic commerce in which the sellers are organizations and the buyers are individuals; also known as e-tailing.

business-to-employee electronic commerce (B2E) An organization using electronic commerce internally to provide information and services to its employees.

buy-side marketplace B2B model in which organizations buy needed products or services from other organizations electronically, often through a reverse auction.

channel conflict The alienation of existing distributors when a company decides to sell to customers directly online.

clicks-and-mortar organizations Organizations that do business in both the physical and digital dimensions.

consumer-to-consumer electronic commerce (C2C) Electronic commerce in which both the buyer and the seller are individuals (not businesses).

cyberbanking Various banking activities conducted electronically from home, a business, or on the road instead of at a physical bank location; also known as *electronic banking*.

cybersquatting Registering domain names in the hope of selling them later at a higher price.

disintermediation Elimination of intermediaries in electronic commerce.

e-government The use of electronic commerce to deliver information and public services to citizens, business partners,

and suppliers of government entities, and those working in the public sector.

electronic business (e-business) A broader definition of electronic commerce, including buying and selling of goods and services, and servicing customers, collaborating with business partners, conducting e-learning, and conducting electronic transactions within an organization.

electronic commerce (EC or e-commerce) The process of buying, selling, transferring, or exchanging products, services, or information via computer networks, including the Internet.

electronic mall A collection of individual shops under one Internet address; also known as a *cybermall* or an *e-mall*.

electronic marketplace A virtual market space on the Web where many buyers and many sellers conduct electronic business activities.

electronic payment mechanisms Computer-based systems that allow customers to pay for goods and services electronically, rather than writing a check or using cash.

electronic retailing (e-tailing) The direct sale of products and services through storefronts or electronic malls, usually designed around an electronic catalog format and/or auctions.

electronic storefront The Web site of a single company, with its own Internet address, at which orders can be placed.

e-procurement Purchasing by using electronic support.

e-wallets Software components in which a user stores secured personal and credit card information for one-click reuse.

exchanges (see **public exchanges**)

forward auctions Auctions that sellers use as a selling channel to many potential buyers; the highest bidder wins the items.

group purchasing The aggregation of purchasing orders from many buyers so that a volume discount can be obtained.

mobile commerce (m-commerce) Electronic commerce conducted in a wireless environment.

multichanneling A process in which a company integrates its online and offline channels.

permission marketing Method of marketing that asks consumers to give their permission to voluntarily accept online advertising and e-mail.

person-to-person payments A form of electronic cash that enables the transfer of funds between two individuals, or between an individual and a business, without the use of a credit card.

pop-under ad An advertisement that is automatically launched by some trigger and appears underneath the active window.

pop-up ad An advertisement that is automatically launched by some trigger and appears in front of the active window.

public exchanges (or **exchanges**) Electronic marketplaces in which there are many sellers and many buyers, and entry is open to all; frequently owned and operated by a third party.

reverse auctions Auctions in which one buyer, usually an organization, seeks to buy a product or a service, and suppliers submit bids; the lowest bidder wins.

sell-side marketplace B2B model in which organizations sell to other organizations from their own private e-marketplace and/or from a third-party site.

smart cards Cards that contains a microprocessor (chip) that enables the card to store a considerable amount of information (including stored funds) and to conduct processing.

spamming Indiscriminate distribution of e-mail without the receiver's permission.

stored-value money cards A form of electronic cash on which a fixed amount of prepaid money is stored; the amount is reduced each time the card is used.

viral marketing Online word-of-mouth marketing.

virtual banks Banking institutions dedicated solely to Internet transactions.

virtual (or pure play) organizations Organizations in which the product, the process, and the delivery agent are all digital.

[Discussion Questions]

1. Discuss the major limitations of e-commerce. Which of these limitations are likely to disappear? Why?

2. Discuss the reasons for having multiple EC business models.

3. Distinguish between business-to-business forward auctions and buyers' bids for RFQs.

4. Discuss the benefits to sellers and buyers of a B2B exchange.

5. What are the major benefits of G2C electronic commerce?

6. Discuss the various ways to pay online in B2C. Which method(s) would you prefer and why?

7. Why is order fulfillment in B2C considered difficult?

8. Discuss the reasons for EC failures.

9. Should Mr. Coffee sell coffeemakers online? (Hint: Take a look at the discussion of channel conflict in this chapter.)

10. In some cases, individuals engage in cybersquatting so that they can sell the domain names to companies expensively. In other cases, companies engage in cybersquatting by registering domain names that are very similar to their competitors' domain names in order to generate traffic from people who misspell Web addresses. Discuss each practice in terms of its ethical nature and legality. Is there a difference between the two practices? Support your answer.

11. Do you think information technology has made it easier to do business? Or has IT only raised the bar on what is required to be able to do business in the 21st century? Support your answer with specific examples.

12. With the rise of electronic commerce, what do you think will happen to those without computer skills, Internet access, computers, smart phones, and so on? Will they be able to survive and advance by hard work?

[Problem-Solving Activities]

1. Assume you are interested in buying a car. You can find information about cars at numerous Web sites. Access five Web sites for information about new and used cars, financing, and insurance. Decide which car you want to buy. Configure your car by going to the car manufacturer's Web site. Finally, try to find the car from www.autobytel.com. What information is most supportive of your decision-making process? Write a report about your experience.

2. Compare the various electronic payment methods. Specifically, collect information from the vendors cited in this chapter and find additional vendors using **Google .com**. Pay attention to security level, speed, cost, and convenience.

3. Conduct a study on selling diamonds and gems online. Access such sites as www.bluenile.com, www.diamond.com,

www.thaigem.com, www.tiffany.com, and www.jewelry-exchange.com.

   a. What features do these sites use to educate buyers about gemstones?

   b. How do these sites attract buyers?

   c. How do these sites increase customers' trust in online purchasing?

   d. What customer service features do these sites provide?

4. Access www.nacha.org. What is NACHA? What is its role? What is the ACH? Who are the key participants in an ACH e-payment? Describe the "pilot" projects currently underway at ACH.

5. Access www.espn.com. Identify at least five different ways the site generates revenue.

6. Access www.queendom.com. Examine its offerings and try some of them. What type of electronic commerce is this? How does this Web site generate revenue?

7. Access www.ediets.com. Prepare a list of all the services the company provides. Identify its revenue model.

8. Access www.theknot.com. Identify the site's revenue sources.

9. Access www.mint.com. Identify the site's revenue model. What are the risks of giving this Web site your credit and debit card numbers, as well as your bank account number?

10. Research the case of www.nissan.com. Is Uzi Nissan cybersquatting? Why or why not? Support your answer. How is Nissan (the car company) reacting to the www.nissan.com Web site?

11. Enter www.alibaba.com. Identify the site's capabilities. Look at the site's private trading room. Write a report. How can such a site help a person who is making a purchase?

12. Enter www.grubhub.com. Explore the site. Why is the site so successful? Could you start a competing site? Why or why not?

13. Enter www.dell.com, go to "Desktops," and configure a system. Register to "My Cart" (no obligation). What calculators are used there? What are the advantages of this process as compared with buying a computer in a physical store? What are the disadvantages?

14. Enter www.checkfree.com and www.lmlpayment.com to identify their services. Prepare a report.

15. Access various travel sites such as www.travelocity.com, www.orbitz.com, www.expedia.com, www.kayak.com, and www.pinpoint.com. Compare these Web sites for ease of use and usefulness. Note differences among the sites. If you ask each site for the itinerary, which one gives you the best information and the best deals?

16. Access www.outofservice.com, and answer the musical taste and personality survey. When you have finished, click on "Results" and see what your musical tastes say about your personality. How accurate are the findings about you?

Chapter Addendum: Tips for Safe Electronic Shopping

- Look for reliable brand names at sites such as Walmart Online, Disney Online, and Amazon. Before purchasing, make sure that the site is authentic by entering the site directly and not from an unverified link.

- Search any unfamiliar selling site for the company's address and phone and fax numbers. Call up and quiz the employees about the seller.

- Check out the vendor with the local Chamber of Commerce or Better Business Bureau (www.bbbonline.org). Look for seals of authenticity such as TRUSTe.

- Investigate how secure the seller's site is by examining the security procedures and by reading the posted privacy policy.

- Examine the money-back guarantees, warranties, and service agreements.

- Compare prices with those in regular stores. Too-low prices are too good to be true and some catch is probably involved.

- Ask friends what they know. Find testimonials and endorsements on community Web sites and well-known bulletin boards.

- Find out what your rights are in case of a dispute. Consult consumer protection agencies and the National Consumer League's Fraud Center (www.fraud.org).

- Check Consumerworld (www.consumerworld.org) for a collection of useful resources.

- For many types of products, www.resellerratings.com is a useful resource.

[Closing Case **What's Your eScore?**]

The Problem

Between your credit score, your grade point average, and your blood pressure and cholesterol levels, you have plenty of scores to worry about. But, what about your eScore? *eScores* are digital scores, also known as consumer valuation or buying-power scores, that measure your potential value as a customer. They are produced by a company known as eBureau.

Credit scores, based on personal credit reports, have been around for decades. Also, direct marketing companies have long ranked consumers based on their socioeconomic status. eScores, however, go further. They take into account factors ranging from occupation, salary, and home value to how much customers spend on luxury goods or pet food. They then analyze these data to predict how much a customer will spend. Businesses use eScores to locate potential customers and assess whether these customers will be profitable.

One Solution

An increasing number of companies, including banks, credit and debit card providers, insurers, and online educational institutions are using eScores to determine which potential customers they should solicit on the Web. eScores work this way:

A client submits a data set containing the names of tens of thousands of sales leads it has already purchased, along with the names of leads who became customers. eBureau then adds several thousand details—such as age, income, occupation, property value, length of residence, and retail history—from its databases to each customer profile. From those raw data points, the system extrapolates up to 50,000 additional variables per person. It then analyzes those data to identify the common factors among the existing customer base. The resulting algorithm then scores prospective customers based on their resemblance to these existing customers.

For example, eBureau ranked prospective customers for a national prepaid debit card issuer, assigning each prospect a score between 0 and 998. People who scored above 950 were considered likely to become highly profitable customers, who would generate an estimated $213 of revenue per card over a six-month period if they became customers. Those who scored less than 550 were predicted to be unprofitable clients, with an estimated revenue of $74 or less. Card issuers utilized this system to identify and solicit the high scorers while avoiding the low scorers.

Every month, eBureau scores roughly 20 million American adults on behalf of clients such as banks, payday lenders, and insurers, who are looking to acquire the names of prospective profitable customers. An eBureau spinoff, called TruSignal (www.tru-signal.com), scores about 110 million consumers monthly for advertisers seeking select audiences for online ads.

The Results

EScores increase the accuracy and speed with which companies can identify potential customers. However, public interest advocates assert that eScores raise serious questions concerning fairness because they create a two-tiered system that prioritizes online users without their knowledge. For example, consumers with high eScores might receive credit and insurance offers, while consumers with low eScores might be denied those same opportunities.

The Fair Credit Reporting Act, passed in 1970, requires consumer reporting agencies—that is, the companies that compile credit data—to show people their credit reports and allow them to correct errors. It also requires companies that use these reports to notify consumers if they take adverse action based on information contained in the reports. Companies such as eBureau, however, are able to circumvent the rules by using alternative financial data to calculate consumer eScores.

Federal regulators and consumer advocates worry that eScores could eventually put some consumers at a disadvantage, particularly consumers who are experiencing financial stress. eScores could create a new subprime class of consumers: people who are bypassed by companies online without even knowing it. Financial institutions, in particular, might avoid people with low eScores, thereby reducing those people's access to home loans, credit cards, and insurance.

As a result, federal regulators are investigating eBureau. They want to ensure that the company makes consumers aware of whether they have been secretly scored, particularly those consumers labeled less profitable or desirable.

For its part, eBureau claims that it maintains separate databases containing federally regulated data, such as credit or debt information used for purposes like risk management, from databases about consumers used to generate scores for marketing purposes. eBureau adds that its clients use the eScores only to narrow their field of prospective customers, not for the purposes of approving people for credit, loans, or insurance. Further, eBureau maintains that it does not sell consumer data to other companies, nor does it retain the eScores that it transmits to clients.

The bottom line for all of us? We do not know our eScores, which are secret, and we also do not know how our eScores are calculated.

Sources: Compiled from "Government Says It Is Investigating eBureau in St. Cloud," *Associated Press*, December 19, 2012; J. Guynn, "FTC Investigating Data Brokers That Mine Consumer Info," *The Los Angeles Times*, December 18, 2012; N. Singer, "F.T.C. Opens an Inquiry into Data Brokers," *The New York Times*, December 8, 2012; P. Koeppel, "E-Scores and the New Consumer Measurement," *Koeppeldirect.com*, December 7, 2012; K. Hill, "The Score That Companies Use to Decide Whether or Not They Want to Talk to You," *Forbes*, August 20, 2012; M. Reilly, "Are You a Good Customer? St. Cloud's eBureau Knows," *Minneapolis-St. Paul Business Journal*, August, 20, 2012; N. Singer, "Shoppers, Meet Your Scorekeeper," *The New York Times*, August 19, 2012; www.eburbureau.com, www.tru-signal.com, accessed March 29, 2013.

Questions

1. What are possible disadvantages to companies that use eBureau to rank potential customers?

2. Should consumers have access to their eScores? Why or why not? Support your answer.

[Internship Activity]

Industry: Retail

One difficulty of moving a small business from a traditional retail store to an online store is channel complications. In many cases, everything has to be reconsidered. For example, how will you communicate with your customers? How will they find product information? How will you accept orders? Manage payments? Shipping?

These questions and many more have kept Harrison Kirby from making the e-commerce plunge. Harrison runs a local golf course with a shop of around 150 products. He would love to have a website that would facilitate e-business for his golf course. He wants online scheduling of tee-times (including coordination of group play), online shopping, and social network integration.

Please visit the Book Companion Site to receive the full set of instructions on how you will help Harrison research ways other golf courses handle their e-business.

Chapter 8

Wireless, Mobile Computing, and Mobile Commerce

[LEARNING OBJECTIVES]	[CHAPTER OUTLINE]	[WEB RESOURCES]
1. Identify advantages and disadvantages of each of the four main types of wireless transmission media.	8.1 Wireless Technologies	• Student PowerPoints for note taking
2. Explain how businesses can use technology employed by short-range, medium-range, and long-range networks, respectively.	8.2 Wireless Computer Networks and Internet Access	**WileyPLUS**
3. Provide a specific example of how each of the five major m-commerce applications can benefit a business.	8.3 Mobile Computing and Mobile Commerce	• E-book • Author video lecture for each chapter section
4. Describe technologies that underlie pervasive computing, providing examples of how businesses can utilize each one.	8.4 Pervasive Computing	• Practice quizzes • Flash Cards for vocabulary review
5. Explain how the four major threats to wireless networks can damage a business.	8.5 Wireless Security	• Additional "IT's About Business" cases • Video interviews with managers • Lab Manuals for Microsoft Office 2010 and 2013

This Chapter Will Help Prepare You To...

ACCT	**FIN**	**MKT**	**POM**	**HRM**	**MIS**
ACCOUNTING	FINANCE	MARKETING	PRODUCTION OPERATIONS MANAGEMENT	HUMAN RESOURCES MANAGEMENT	MIS
Count and audit inventory	Manage wireless payment systems	Manage locationbased advertising	Increase productivity in warehouses	Improved employee communications	Provide firm's wireless infrastructure

The Problem

[**The Battle for the Mobile Wallet**]

Customers today are in more of a hurry than ever before. To satisfy them and keep their business, retailers are looking for strategies to speed up the checkout process and improve the overall customer experience. One strategy is to use customers' smartphones as a replacement for credit and debit cards. Instead of swiping a plastic card at the checkout counter, consumers merely wave their phones a few inches above a payment terminal. This process uses a contact-free technology called *near-field communications (NFC)*.

The technology described in the preceding paragraph, known as the *mobile wallet*, is already being installed on millions of phones in both the United States and overseas. However, wide adoption of this technology in the United States is being hindered by a major battle among large corporations that represent different components of the online commerce industry.

In one camp are the established credit card companies such as MasterCard, Visa, and American Express, in alliance with the banks that actually issue the cards to customers. The goal of these businesses is to maintain their traditional position at the center of any payment system and to continue to collect fees from merchants. However, they are facing intense competition from the other camp, which consists of technology companies such as Google and PayPal whose goal is to become major players in the new payment system. In addition, Apple and the mobile carriers such as Verizon, AT&T, and T-Mobile form a third camp that want to collect fees through their own control of the phones. Adding to the competitive mix are individual companies such as Starbucks that are developing proprietary mobile wallet technologies.

In the middle of this corporate battleground are the retailers, who may yet be the deciding factor in determining who wins the payment battle. To take advantage of mobile wallet technology, retailers have to install terminals that accept mobile payments. One final concerned party consists of consumer advocates, who are concerned that a mobile system would bring higher fees, which would ultimately be passed on to the customers.

The stakes in this competition are enormous because the small fees generated every time consumers swipe their cards add up to tens of billions of dollars of annual revenue in the United States alone. This revenue, of course, goes straight into the pocket of whoever controls the payment system. Before any individual company makes money, all of companies involved in electronic commerce need to sort out what role each one will play and who will collect the lucrative transaction fees from retailers.

A Variety of Solutions

Mobile Phone Carriers. In 2010, three of the four big mobile phone service providers—AT&T, T-Mobile, and Verizon, but not Sprint—along with Discover (www.discovercard.com) and Barclays Bank (www.barclays.co.uk) formed a joint venture named Isis. Their intention was to develop a new payment network that included both credit card companies and card-issuing banks. Isis creates a digital wallet into which customers of card-issuing banks can easily move their accounts. Consumers would interface with Isis through a mobile app, which would give them access to multiple credit and debit accounts. Retailers would participate by targeting offers to loyal members through Isis, while product companies and brands could also offer discounts to customers who opt in.

Credit Card Issuers. All three card issuers have mobile wallet applications: MasterCard has MasterCard PayPass (which is integrated into Google Wallet), Visa has the payWave mobile wallet, and American Express has American Express Serve (with Sprint).

The credit card companies claim that their mobile applications enable consumers to make online payments quickly, without having to enter card numbers and billing addresses over and over. For example, people who play smartphone games could buy add-ons, such as new weapons or extra ammunition, simply by clicking a Visa logo. Similarly, a caterer could e-mail a bill with a button that allows the client to pay with one click. Payers would authorize the transaction simply by entering a name and password.

Technology Companies. In May 2011, Google released a free Android app called the Google Wallet. The wallet securely stores multiple credit cards or a Google prepaid card linked to the customer's credit card. Google also introduced Google Offers, a location-based service that delivers daily, targeted, Groupon-like deals to the Google Wallet. The wallet also allows people to register their store loyalty cards and gift cards in the app.

Interestingly, if future models of the Apple iPhone incorporate NFC, the iPhone may route payments through Apple's iTunes store, which already has some 400 million accounts tied to credit cards. Apple iTunes could therefore be transformed into mobile wallets. Both Google Wallet and Apple iTunes, however, would need access to smartphone chips and to merchants' terminals. Apple could solve this problem by manufacturing its own smartphone chips, but Google could not because it makes only the software for Android smartphones, not the phones themselves.

In March 2012, eBay's PayPal unit released a card reader and a digital wallet that do not use NFC. Instead, to use the wallet customers simply need to enter a phone number and a PIN at the register. PayPal is also integrating check-in capabilities with its mobile application and location-based services so that smartphone users can identify nearby stores or restaurants.

One startup company, Square (www.squareup.com), has entered the field with several products. The Square Card Reader is a small plastic device attached to an iPod Touch, an iPhone, an Android phone, or an iPad. Merchants pay a 2.75 percent fee per transaction with no monthly charge, compared to a standard credit card rate of 3.5 percent with a 15 cent transaction fee.

Square's second product is an app called Pay With Square. Customers who install this app on their mobile devices can link to a credit or debit card and leave their wallets at home. At the checkout, the customer's name and photo appear on the merchant's point-of-sale system. The customer then digitally signs, and he or she receives a receipt via e-mail or text. This app also allows merchants to automatically identify Pay With Square users when they walk into a store or restaurant. Users can view all participating merchants via the app, and they can also receive coupons and incentives.

Square's third product is Square Register. Square developed this product to compete with the point-of-sale terminals used by retailers, a business now dominated by hardware makers such as VeriFone (www.verifone.com) and NCR (www.ncr.com). Register allows retailers to keep track of customers and inventory and to offer loyalty deals and discounts. In addition, it delivers analytics that inform merchants what their customers buy and when they buy it.

In August 2012 Starbucks invested $25 million in Square. The coffee giant plans to use Square to process all debit and credit transactions at its stores.

To compete directly with Square, in 2012 VeriFone introduced a card reader and a point-of-sale system that can work with products from other companies, such as digital wallets from Google and Isis. Both PayPal and VeriFone set their processing fees at 2.7 percent, undercutting Square by .05 of a percentage point. NCR launched its own card reader in July 2012.

Apple seems to be easing into the competition with its PassBook product. PassBook is an electronic wallet that customers can use to purchase boarding passes, movie tickets, and store cards. Keep in mind that Apple has some 400 million accounts with payment credentials in its iTunes store.

The Results

In December 2011, Verizon blocked its customers from installing Google Wallet on their smartphones. Verizon maintained that Google Wallet is not sufficiently secure to use on its phones because of technical issues The company further claimed that it is collaborating with Google to resolve those issues.

Despite this public statement, industry analysts charge that Verizon's move is likely related to its plan to team up with rival carriers AT&T and T-Mobile on the mobile payments venture, Isis. At the same time, Google is collaborating with MasterCard, Citigroup, and Sprint Nextel Corporation on its Google Wallet. Meanwhile, Visa is developing another digital wallet.

The battle for the transaction fees from mobile wallets is ongoing, and the results will not be evident for several years. However, the potential for large revenue streams is real, because mobile wallets have clear advantages. For example, which are you more likely to have with you at any given moment—your phone or your wallet? Also, keep in mind that if you lose your phone, it can be located on a map and remotely deactivated. Plus, your phone can be password protected. Your wallet cannot do these things.

When all of the digital wallet issues are sorted out, your smartphone or tablet may become your wallet, as well as a credit card reader and a register for merchants. You will use your mobile device as a coupon book, a comparison-shopping tool, and a repository for loyalty cards. In addition, when you walk into a store it will act as a beacon that can recommend products, provide reviews, and give directions to a product in a giant store.

Sources: Compiled from A. Johnson, "What's in Your Digital Wallet? Lucrative Data," *The Wall Street Journal*, March 22, 2013; S. Greengard, "Money Squared: The Digital Wallet," *Baseline Magazine*, October 1, 2012; "Bye-Bye Wallets," *Time*, August 27, 2012; L. Tucci, "What's a Wallet-Less Future Got to Do with Enterprise Computing?" *SearchCIO.com*, August 16, 2012; D. Goldman, "Mobile Pay War: Wal-Mart and Others Vs. Google," *CNN*, August 15, 2012; M. Helft, "The Death of Cash," *Fortune*, July 23, 2012; D. Zax, "Geode, the iPhone E-Wallet," *MIT Technology Review*, June 6, 2012; J. Leber, "A Banking Giant Makes a Mobile Payment Bet," *MIT Technology Review*, July 11, 2012; K. Kelleher, "PayPal's Bid for the Digital Wallet Looks Strong," *CNN*, March 21, 2012; A. Efrati and A. Troianovski, "War Over the Digital Wallet," *The Wall Street Journal*, December 7, 2011; B. Reed, "Verizon Cites Security Issue for Nixing Google Wallet," *Network World*, December 6, 2011; D. Goldman, "Verizon Blocks Google Wallet," *CNN Money*, December 6, 2011; C. Iozzio, "The Cash Killer," *Popular Science*, November, 2011; F. Graham, "Will NFC Make the Mobile Wallet Work?" *BBC News*, October 27, 2011; K. Boehret, "Google Mobile App Aims to Turn Phones Into Wallets," *The Wall Street Journal*, September 21, 2011; T. Duryee, "PayPal's Response to Google's Payment Plans," *AllThingsD.com*, September 15, 2011; M. Hachman, "Is Google Wallet What Mobile Payments Need to Succeed?" *PC Magazine*, May 27, 2011; B. Reed, "Google Wallet: Five Things You Need to Know," *Network World*, May 26, 2011; R. Kim, "Isis: Respect the Carriers; We'll Be Key to NFC Success," *GigaOM*, May 6, 2011; S. Marek, "AT&T, Verizon Wireless and T-Mobile Backpedal on Isis Joint Venture," *FierceWireless*, May 4, 2011; R. Sidel and S. Raice, "Pay By Phone Dialed Back," *Wall Street Journal*, May 4, 2011; T. Team, "American Express and Visa Squeeze PayPal's Crown Jewels," *Forbes*, April 4, 2011; A. Efrati and R. Sidel, "Google Sets Role in Mobile Payment," *Wall Street Journal*, March 28, 2011; T. Bernard and C. Miller, "Swiping Is the Easy Part," *New York Times*, March 23, 2011; D. Aamoth, "Pay Phone," *Time*, February 21, 2011; D. MacMillan, "Turning Smartphones into Cash Registers," *Bloomberg BusinessWeek*, February 14–20, 2011; K. Eaton, "The Race Is On to Make NFC Wireless Credit Card Dreams Come True (and Win Market Share)," *Fast Company*, February 2, 2011; M. Hamblen, "NFC: What You Need to Know," *Computerworld*, January 28, 2011; K. Heussner, "Is Your Next Credit Card Your Cell Phone?" *ABC News*, January 26, 2011; S. Greengard, "Mobile Payment, Please," *Baseline Magazine*, January 26, 2011; E. Zemen, "Will Apple, Google Lead Mobile Payment Revolution?" *InformationWeek*, January 25, 2011; B. Ellis, "The End of Credit Cards Is Coming," *CNNMoney*, January 24, 2011; C. Miller, "Now at Starbucks: Buy a Latte by Waving Your Phone," *New York Times*, January 18, 2011; O. Kharif, "In the Works: A Google Mobile Payment Service?" *Bloomberg BusinessWeek*, January 4, 2011; R. King, "Wells Fargo to Employees: Leave Wallets Home, Pay by Phone," *Bloomberg BusinessWeek*, January 4, 2011; www.iconcessionstand.com, www.paypal.com, accessed April 28, 2013.

What We Learned from This Case

The old, traditional working environment that required users to come to a wired computer was ineffective and inefficient. The solution was to build computers that are small enough to carry or wear and can communicate via wireless networks. The ability to communicate anytime and anywhere provides organizations with a strategic advantage by increasing productivity and speed and improving customer service. **Wireless** is a term that is used to describe telecommunications in which electromagnetic waves, rather than some form of wire or cable, carry the signal between communicating devices such as computers, smartphones, and iPads.

Before you continue, it is important to distinguish between the terms *wireless* and *mobile*, because they can mean different things. The term *wireless* means exactly what it says: without wires. In contrast, *mobile* refers to something that changes its location over time. Some wireless networks, such as MiFi (discussed later in this chapter), are also mobile. Others, however, are fixed. For example, microwave towers form fixed wireless networks.

Wireless technologies enable individuals and organizations to conduct mobile computing, mobile commerce, and pervasive computing. We define these terms here, and then we discuss each one in detail later in the chapter.

Mobile computing refers to a real-time, wireless connection between a mobile device and other computing environments, such as the Internet or an intranet. *Mobile commerce*—also known as *m-commerce*—refers to e-commerce (EC) transactions conducted with a mobile device. *Pervasive computing*, also called *ubiquitous computing*, means that virtually every object has processing power with either wireless or wired connections to a global network.

Wireless technologies and mobile commerce are spreading rapidly, replacing or supplementing wired computing. In fact, Cisco (www.cisco.com) predicts that the volume of mobile Web traffic will continue to rapidly increase over the next decade. As illustrated in this chapter's opening case, there is a huge battle underway to provide you with a mobile, digital wallet and to enable you to get rid of your physical wallet altogether, including all of the credit and debit cards you have in it. Billions of dollars are at stake, further highlighting the importance of wireless to you and your organization.

Almost all (if not all) organizations utilize wireless computing. Therefore, when you begin your career, you likely will be assigned a company smartphone and a wirelessly enabled computer. Clearly, then, it is important for you to learn about wireless computing not only because you will be using wireless applications but also because wireless computing will be so important to your organization. In your job, you will be involved with customers who conduct wireless transactions, with analyzing and developing mobile commerce applications, and with wireless security. And the list goes on.

Simply put, an understanding of wireless technology and mobile commerce applications will make you more valuable to your organization. When you look at "What's In IT For Me?" at the end of this chapter, envision yourself performing the activities discussed in your functional area. An understanding of wireless technology can also help you start and grow your own business, as illustrated in IT's About Business 8.1.

IT's [about business]

8.1 Big Wheel Mobile Truck & Square ⬤MKT ⬤POM

Have you ever gone into a restaurant, had a great time, and enjoyed a wonderful meal, only to find out that the restaurant does not accept credit cards? Naturally, you do not have enough cash on you, so you have to locate the nearest ATM that accepts your card. Why, you ask yourself, would a business not accept credit cards? The reason is that some businesses do not want to pay fees to the credit card companies. (These fees start from at least 2.75 percent of the transaction price.) Other businesses do not

accept credit cards for technological and logistical reasons. Such was the case for Tony Adams.

Chef and owner Tony Adams runs a mobile restaurant in Orlando, Florida (see http://bigwheeltruckmenu.com and http://bigwheelprovisions.com). Tony prides himself on his original recipes, which are made from fresh, locally sourced foods that Tony frequently purchases from the local farmers market. His Web site proudly advertises that "Local Is Lovely."

Tony sells his food from a food truck, and his location changes daily. He needed a mobile connection to accept credit card payments. Tony first tried a mobile app that allowed him to type in credit card numbers, but the app was cumbersome, and it did not allow him to customize his menus every day in the way that he needed to. In addition, he still had to total each order either on paper or with a calculator and then use the app only for accepting a credit card. Tony needed a much quicker method to calculate total amounts and accept credit card payments.

Then he heard about Square (http://squareup.com). Square offers an iPad point-of-sale (POS) system that allows Tony to customize his menus daily. As he logs in his menu items, Tony creates his POS for the day. Each item gets its own button, so he has to tap the menu items only to total each order. Square also offers a small device (it looks like a square) that plugs into the headphone jack of the iPad (and will also work on an iPhone). About the size of a postage stamp, this little gadget allows users to swipe the magnetic stripe of a credit card to enter the numbers into the POS. In sum, Square has provided a POS system that speeds up transactions for both Tony and his customers.

Do not confuse what Tony is doing with mobile payments. Tony is using technology to accept credit cards in a mobile environment. In fact, he is not alone in this endeavor. Mobile payment technologies have made it possible for many mobile vendors to accept credit cards with their iPads and iPhones. Mobile payments—that is, payments made with a mobile phone rather than with a debit/credit card—are an option for Tony's consumers who use Square's app called "Square Card Case." This app allows two Square users to connect app-to-app and complete a transaction without having to swipe a credit card.

Sources: Compiled from T. Bajarin, "Bringing the Checkout Counter to You," *PC Magazine*, June 24, 2013; D. Kucera, "Square Unveils All-in-One Point-of-Sale System for Stores," *Bloomberg.com*, February 20, 2013; http://squareup.com, http://squareup.com/register, http://bigwheelprovisions.com, http://bigwheeltruckmenu.com, accessed June 30, 2013.

Questions
1. Other than efficiency, what are additional benefits that Square provides for Tony?
2. Describe possible disadvantages of the Square app for Tony.

The wireless infrastructure upon which mobile computing is built may reshape the entire IT field. The technologies, applications, and limitations of mobile computing and mobile commerce are the focus of this chapter. You begin the chapter by learning about wireless devices and wireless transmission media. You continue by examining wireless computer networks and wireless Internet access. You then look at mobile computing and mobile commerce, which are made possible by wireless technologies. Next, you turn your attention to pervasive computing. You conclude by familiarizing yourself with a critical component of the wireless environment—namely, wireless security.

Wireless Technologies

8.1

Wireless technologies include both wireless devices, such as smartphones, and wireless transmission media, such as microwave, satellite, and radio. These technologies are fundamentally changing the ways organizations operate.

Individuals are finding wireless devices convenient and productive to use, for several reasons. First, people can make productive use of time that was formerly wasted—for example, while commuting to work on public transportation. Second, because people can take these devices with them, their work locations are becoming much more flexible. Third, wireless technology enables them to schedule their working time around personal and professional obligations.

Wireless Devices

Wireless devices provide three major advantages to users:

- They are small enough to easily carry or wear.
- They have sufficient computing power to perform productive tasks.
- They can communicate wirelessly with the Internet and other devices.

Modern smartphones provide capabilities that include cellular telephony, Bluetooth, Wi-Fi, a digital camera for images and video, global positioning system (GPS), an organizer, a scheduler, an address book, a calculator, access to e-mail and Short Message Service (SMS, sending and receiving short text messages up to 160 characters in length), instant messaging, text messaging, an MP3 music player, a video player, Internet access with a full-function browser, and a QWERTY keyboard.

One downside of smartphones is that people can use them to copy and pass on confidential information. For example, if you were an executive at Intel, would you want workers snapping pictures of their colleagues with your secret new technology in the background? Unfortunately, managers think of these devices as phones, not as digital cameras that can transmit wirelessly. New jamming devices are being developed to counter the threat. Some companies, such as Samsung (*www.samsung.com*), have recognized the danger and have banned these devices from their premises altogether. Regardless of any disadvantages, however, cell phones, and particularly smartphones, have had a far greater impact on human society than most of us realize, as you see in IT's About Business 8.2.

IT's [about business]

8.2 Cell Phones Revolutionize Healthcare in Uganda

Uganda's healthcare system needed an overhaul. The country has only 131 hospitals, and they need to serve 136 million people. This is a major reason why Ugandan children are dying of treatable diseases, particularly malaria, which accounts for up to 40 percent of medical visits and almost 25 percent of deaths among children under the age of 5. The Ugandan Ministry of Health and various other international organizations have tried to address the healthcare issue by building smaller clinics and utilizing volunteer village health team workers, some of whom dispense drugs. However, the results of these efforts have not been encouraging.

On the positive side, Uganda is well served by cellular carriers. One-third of Ugandans have mobile phones, which they share widely. These phones are not smartphones. The only app most of these $7 handsets offer is a flashlight. However, they can send text messages.

In an initiative called mTrac, principally sponsored by UNICEF, health workers are using these phones to text details of drug supplies and disease outbreaks that they had previously put on paper. This information is collected and entered into an online dashboard so that public-health officials can observe in real time what is happening. These officials can track which clinics have medicine and which ones do not. They then use this information to move medical supplies to locations where they are critically needed.

Local health clinics are not eager to report that they have extra medical supplies to avoid having these supplies sent to other clinics. Therefore, mTrac has developed an alternate data source: crowdsourcing. Specifically, mTrac has instituted a toll-free hotline where people can text complaints. Anyone who wants to report a problem about healthcare delivery can anonymously send information to a call center. At the center these complaints are gathered, checked out, and added to the online dashboard.

To support these activities, UNICEF has recruited about 140,000 members to a type of short-message-service social-networking group called U-report. Communicating entirely by text, U-reporters, who join the group much as people join Facebook, send and receive information about health issues. These texts can be targeted; for example, mothers can be alerted to free vaccinations in their area.

The ongoing cost of mTrac to the Ugandan Ministry of Health is negligible. Experts estimate that the ministry's outlay for mTrac is about $14 per district per month. UNICEF, the World Health Organization (WHO), and the United Kingdom's Department for International Development provided the initial capital, including money for developing the software and training workers, but the workers use their own phones.

The value of mTrac is incalculable. In January 2012, the health team in the Kotido district noticed an increase in reported cases of pneumonia. Upon investigation, it found that a village health team worker was misdiagnosing the disease and that patients were being treated with unnecessary and expensive antibiotics. The mistake was noted and fixed within weeks, and the worker was given additional training.

The mTrac program is now operating in all of Uganda's 113 districts. However, the system is not a cure-all. Being aware of the details of a health problem is not the same as developing a solution for that problem. The Ministry of Health receives 1,000 reports every week, and it sometimes struggles to respond. Despite these limitations, however, mTrac has changed expectations among people who formerly felt they had no voice. The Ugandan government contends that mTrac is helping to remake the social contract between the government and its citizens, no small matter indeed.

Sources: Compiled from J. de Vroeg, "Using Mobile Technology in TB Control in Uganda," *Text to Change*, January 8, 2013; B. Luscombe, "Disease Can't Hide," *Time*, August 27, 2012; C. Schultz, "Mobile Phones Helping to Control AIDS in Uganda," *iMedicalApps*, August 10, 2012; "mTrac Is Changing the Face of Health Operations in Uganda," *News Vision*, July 26, 2012; "Uganda's Free Health Care Systems 'in Crisis,' Daily Monitor Reports," *The Guardian*, October 4, 2011; B. Among, "Who Will Heal Uganda's Sick Health Sector," *The Daily Monitor*, October 1, 2011; www.mtrac.ug, accessed March 23, 2013.

Questions
1. Describe the problems with implementing mTrac in Uganda.
2. Describe how the use of smartphones (rather than simple cell phones) could change healthcare in Uganda. (Hint: Take a look at the thousands of healthcare apps available on smartphones today.)

Despite all of their advantages, however, the latest version of cell phones—smartphones—can cause problems as well. The following example demonstrates how smartphones can disrupt the court system.

Example

Smartphones in Court

Smartphones are now present in U.S. jury boxes, raising serious questions about juror impartiality and the ability of judges to control courtrooms. A Reuter's legal analysis revealed that jurors' forays onto the Internet via smartphones have resulted in dozens of mistrials, appeals, and overturned verdicts.

For decades, courts have instructed jurors not to seek information about cases outside the evidence introduced at trial. They also routinely warn jurors not to communicate about a case with anyone before they reach a verdict. Today, however, jurors can, with a few clicks on their smartphones, look up definitions of legal terms on Wikipedia, view crime scenes via Google Earth, and communicate with other people via their Facebook pages.

The consequences of these behaviors can be significant. In September 2010, for example, a Florida court overturned the manslaughter conviction of a man charged with killing his neighbor, citing the jury foreman's use of an iPhone to look up the definition of *prudent* in an online dictionary. That same month, the Nevada Supreme Court granted a new trial to a defendant convicted of sexually assaulting a minor, because the foreman had used his smartphone to search online for information about the types of physical injuries suffered by young victims of sexual assaults.

Courts are exploring ways to keep jurors "unplugged." Some judges now confiscate all smartphones from jurors when they enter a courtroom. In 2009, California updated its civil jury instructions to bar jurors from "all forms of electronic communication." From a different perspective, some legal experts argue that rather than try to stifle jurors from pursuing information on the Internet, courts need to figure out how to help them do so in a responsible way.

Sources: Compiled from H. Patel, "The Internet and Juries: The Role of the Factfinder?" *Rutgers Computer and Technology Law Journal*, March 3, 2013; D. Hefley, "New Jury Video Tackles Smartphones," *Herald Net*, December 18, 2012; "Juror Social Media Misconduct Can Lead to Mistrials," *Slater & Zurz LLP Law Firm Blog*, September 20, 2012; S. Eder, "Jury Files: The Temptation of Twitter," *The Wall Street Journal*, March 12, 2012; "Juries and the Internet: Justice Online," *The Guardian*, January 3, 2011; "As Jurors Go Online, U.S. Trials Go Off Track," *Reuters*, December 8, 2010.

Wireless Transmission Media

Wireless media, or broadcast media, transmit signals without wires. The major types of wireless media are microwave, satellite, radio, and infrared. Table 8.1 lists the advantages and disadvantages of each type.

Channel	Advantages	Disadvantages
Microwave	High bandwidth. Relatively inexpensive.	Must have unobstructed line of sight. Susceptible to environmental interference.
Satellite	High bandwidth. Large coverage area.	Expensive. Must have unobstructed line of sight. Signals experience propagation delay. Must use encryption for security.
Radio	High bandwidth. Signals pass through walls. Inexpensive and easy to install.	Creates electrical interference problems. Susceptible to snooping unless encrypted.
Infrared	Low to medium bandwidth. Used only for short distances.	Must have unobstructed line of sight.

Table

8.1

Advantages and Disadvantages of Wireless Media

Microwave. Microwave transmission systems transmit data via electromagnetic waves. These systems are used for high-volume, long-distance, line-of-sight communication. *Line-of-sight* means that the transmitter and receiver are in view of each other. This requirement creates problems because the Earth's surface is curved rather than flat. For this reason, microwave towers usually cannot be spaced more than 30 miles apart.

Clearly, then, microwave transmissions offer only a limited solution to data communications needs, especially over very long distances. In addition, microwave transmissions are susceptible to environmental interference during severe weather such as heavy rain and snowstorms. Although long-distance microwave data communications systems are still widely used, they are being replaced by satellite communications systems.

Satellite. **Satellite transmission** systems make use of communication satellites. Currently, there are three types of satellites circling Earth: geostationary (GEO), medium-earth-orbit (MEO), and low-earth-orbit (LEO). Each type has a different orbit, with the GEO being farthest from Earth and the LEO the closest. In this section, you examine the three types of satellites and then discuss two major satellite applications: Global positioning systems and Internet transmission via satellites. Table 8.2 compares and contrasts the three types of satellites.

As with microwave transmission, satellites must receive and transmit data via line-of-sight. However, the enormous *footprint*—the area of Earth's surface reached by a satellite's transmission—overcomes the limitations of microwave data relay stations. The most basic rule governing footprint size is simple: The higher a satellite orbits, the larger its footprint. Thus, medium-earth-orbit satellites have a smaller footprint than geostationary satellites, and low-earth-orbit satellites have the smallest footprint of all. Figure 8.1 compares the footprints of the three types of satellites.

In contrast to line-of-sight transmission with microwave, satellites use *broadcast* transmission, which sends signals to many receivers at one time. So, even though satellites are line-of-sight like microwave, they are high enough for broadcast transmission, thus overcoming the limitations of microwave.

TABLE 8.2

Three Basic Types of Telecommunications Satellites

Type	Characteristics	Orbit	Number	Use
GEO	• Satellites stationary relative to point on Earth • Few satellites needed for global coverage • Transmission delay (approximately .25 second) • Most expensive to build and launch • Longest orbital life (many years)	22,300 miles	8	TV signal
MEO	• Satellites move relative to point on Earth • Moderate number needed for global coverage • Requires medium-powered transmitters • Negligible transmission delay • Less expensive to build and launch • Moderate orbital life (6–12 years)	6,434 miles	10–12	GPS
LEO	• Satellites move rapidly relative to point on Earth • Large number needed for global coverage • Requires only low-power transmitters • Negligible transmission delay • Least expensive to build and launch • Shortest orbital life (as low as 5 years)	400–700 miles	Many	Telephone

Types of Orbits. *Geostationary earth orbit (GEO) satellites* orbit 22,300 miles directly above the equator. These satellites maintain a fixed position above Earth's surface because, at their altitude, their orbital period matches the 24-hour rotational period of Earth. For this reason, receivers on Earth do not have to track GEO satellites. GEO satellites are excellent for sending television programs to cable operators and for broadcasting directly to homes.

One major limitation of GEO satellites is that their transmissions take a quarter of a second to send and return. This brief pause, one kind of **propagation delay**, makes two-way telephone conversations difficult. Also, GEO satellites are large and expensive, and they require substantial amounts of power to launch.

Medium-earth-orbit (MEO) satellites are located about 6,000 miles above Earth's surface. MEO orbits require more satellites to cover Earth than GEO orbits because MEO footprints are smaller. MEO satellites have two advantages over GEO satellites: They are less expensive, and they do not have an appreciable propagation delay. However, because MEO satellites move with respect to a point on Earth's surface, receivers must track these satellites. (Think of a satellite dish slowly turning to remain oriented to a MEO satellite).

Low-earth-orbit (LEO) satellites are located 400 to 700 miles above Earth's surface. Because LEO satellites are much closer to Earth, they have little, if any, propagation delay. Like MEO satellites, however, LEO satellites move with respect to a point on Earth's surface and therefore must be tracked by receivers. Tracking LEO satellites is more difficult than tracking MEO satellites because LEO satellites move much more quickly relative to a point on Earth.

Unlike GEO and MEO satellites, LEO satellites can pick up signals from weak transmitters. This feature makes it possible for satellite telephones to operate via LEO satellites, because they can operate with less power using smaller batteries. Another advantage of LEO satellites is that they consume less power and cost less to launch.

At the same time, however, the footprints of LEO satellites are small, which means that many satellites are needed to cover the planet. For this reason, a single organization often produces multiple LEO satellites, known as *LEO constellations*. Two examples are Iridium and Globalstar.

Iridium (www.iridium.com) has placed a LEO constellation in orbit that consists of 66 satellites and 12 in-orbit spare satellites. The company maintains that it provides complete satellite communications coverage of Earth's surface, including the polar regions. Globalstar (www.globalstar.com) also has a LEO constellation in orbit.

Global Positioning Systems. The **global positioning system (GPS)** is a wireless system that utilizes satellites to enable users to determine their position anywhere on Earth. GPS is supported by 24 MEO satellites that are shared worldwide. The exact position of each satellite is always known because the satellite continuously broadcasts its position along with a time signal. By using the known speed of the signals and the distance from three satellites (for two-dimensional location) or four satellites (for three-dimensional location), it is possible to find the location of any receiving station or user within a range of 10 feet. GPS software can also convert the user's latitude and longitude to an electronic map.

Most of you are probably familiar with GPS in automobiles, which "talks" to drivers when giving directions. Figure 8.2 illustrates two ways for drivers to obtain GPS information in a car: a dashboard navigation system and a GPS app (in this case, TomTom; www.tomtom.com) on an iPhone.

Commercial use of GPS for activities such as navigating, mapping, and surveying has become widespread, particularly in remote areas. Cell phones in the United States now must have a GPS embedded in them so that the location of a person making an emergency call—for example, 911, known as **wireless 911**—can be detected immediately.

Three other global positioning systems are either planned or operational. The Russian GPS, *GLONASS*, was completed in 1995. However, the system fell into disrepair with the collapse of the Russian economy. In 2010, however, GLONASS achieved 100 percent coverage of

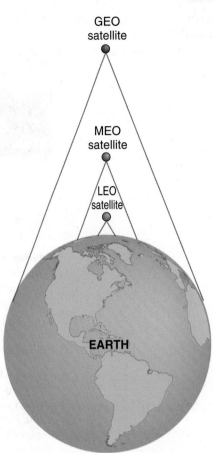

FIGURE 8.1 Comparison of satellite footprints. (*Source:* Drawn by Kelly Rainer.)

FIGURE 8.2 Obtaining GPS information in an automobile. (left: *Source:* Image Source.)

Dashboard GPS　　　　　　　　　TomTom app on iPhone

Russian territory. The European Union GPS, *Galileo*, has an anticipated completion date of 2015. China expects to complete its GPS, *Beidou*, by 2020.

Internet over Satellite (IoS).　In many regions of the world, Internet over Satellite (IoS) is the only option available for Internet connections because installing cables is either too expensive or physically impossible. IoS enables users to access the Internet via GEO satellites from a dish mounted on the side of their homes. Although IoS makes the Internet available to many people who otherwise could not access it, it has its drawbacks. Not only do GEO satellite transmissions involve a propagation delay, but they also can be disrupted by environmental influences such as thunderstorms.

Radio.　**Radio transmission** uses radio-wave frequencies to send data directly between transmitters and receivers. Radio transmission has several advantages. First, radio waves travel easily through normal office walls. Second, radio devices are fairly inexpensive and easy to install. Third, radio waves can transmit data at high speeds. For these reasons, radio increasingly is being used to connect computers to both peripheral equipment and local area networks (LANs; discussed in Chapter 6).

As with other technologies, however, radio transmission has its drawbacks. First, radio media can create electrical interference problems. Also, radio transmissions are susceptible to snooping by anyone who has similar equipment that operates on the same frequency.

Another problem with radio transmission is that when you travel too far away from the source station, the signal breaks up and fades into static. Most radio signals can travel only 30 to 40 miles from their source. However, satellite radio overcomes this problem. **Satellite radio** (or *digital radio*) offers uninterrupted, near CD-quality transmission that is beamed to your radio, either at home or in your car, from space. In addition, satellite radio offers a broad spectrum of stations, including many types of music, news, and talk.

XM Satellite Radio and Sirius Satellite Radio were competitors that launched satellite radio services. XM broadcast its signals from GEO satellites, while Sirius used MEO satellites. In July 2008, the two companies merged to form Sirius XM (www.siriusxm.com). Listeners subscribe to the service for a monthly fee.

Infrared.　The final type of wireless transmission is infrared transmission. **Infrared** light is red light that is not commonly visible to human eyes. Common applications of infrared light are found in remote control units for televisions, VCRs, and DVD and CD players. In addition, like radio transmission, infrared transceivers are used for short-distance connections between computers and peripheral equipment and local area networks. A *transceiver* is a device that can both transmit and receive signals.

before you go on...

1. Describe the most common types of wireless devices.

2. Describe the various types of transmission media.

Wireless Computer Networks and Internet Access

8.2

You have learned about various wireless devices and how these devices transmit wireless signals. These devices typically form wireless computer networks, and they provide wireless Internet access. In this section you will study wireless networks, which we organize by their effective distance: short range, medium range, and wide area.

Short-Range Wireless Networks

Short-range wireless networks simplify the task of connecting one device to another. In addition, they eliminate wires and enable users to move around while they use the devices. In general, short-range wireless networks have a range of 100 feet or less. In this section, you consider three basic short-range networks: Bluetooth, ultra-wideband (UWB), and near-field communications (NFC).

Bluetooth. **Bluetooth** (*www.bluetooth.com*) is an industry specification used to create small personal area networks. A **personal area network** is a computer network used for communication among computer devices—for example, telephones, personal digital assistants, and smartphones—located close to one person. Bluetooth 1.0 can link up to eight devices within a 10-meter area (about 30 feet) with a bandwidth of 700 kilobits per second (Kbps) using low-power, radio-based communication. Bluetooth 2.0 can transmit up to 2.1 megabits per second (Mbps) and, at greater power, up to 100 meters (roughly 300 feet). Ericsson, the Scandinavian mobile handset company that developed this standard, called it Bluetooth after the tenth-century Danish King Harald Blatan (*Blatan* means "Bluetooth"). Ericsson selected this named because Blatan unified previously separate islands into the nation of Denmark.

Common applications for Bluetooth are wireless handsets for cell phones and portable music players. Advantages of Bluetooth include low power consumption and the fact that it uses omnidirectional radio waves—that is, waves that are emitted in all directions from a transmitter. For this reason, you do not have to point one Bluetooth device at another to create a connection.

Ultra-Wideband. **Ultra-wideband (UWB)** is a high-bandwidth wireless technology with transmission speeds in excess of 100 Mbps. This very high speed makes UWB a good choice for applications such as streaming multimedia from, say, a personal computer to a television.

Time Domain (www.timedomain.com), a pioneer in UWB technology, has developed many UWB applications. One interesting application is the PLUS Real-Time Location System (RTLS). An organization can utilize PLUS to locate multiple people and assets simultaneously. Employees, customers, and/or visitors wear the PLUS Badge Tag. PLUS Asset Tags are placed on equipment and products. PLUS is extremely valuable for healthcare environments, where knowing the real-time location of caregivers (e.g., doctors, nurses, technicians) and mobile equipment (e.g., laptops, monitors) is critical.

Near-Field Communications. **Near-field communications (NFC)** has the smallest range of any short-range wireless networks. It is designed to be embedded in mobile devices such as cell phones and credit cards. For example, using NFC, you can swipe your device or card within a few centimeters of POS terminals to pay for items (see this chapter's opening case). NFC also has many other interesting uses. For example, IT's About Business 8.3 illustrates how NFC technology helps travelers in Japan.

Medium-Range Wireless Networks

Medium-range wireless networks are the familiar wireless local area networks (WLANs). The most common type of medium-range wireless network is Wireless Fidelity, or Wi-Fi. WLANs are useful in a variety of settings, some of which may be challenging.

IT's [about business]

8.3 Near-Field Communications Helps Travelers in Japan

Japan's smartphones are called *keitai*. These phones contain a high-resolution camera, a projector, and near-field communication capability. Consider the case of a Japanese woman who uses her keitai to scan a QR code (discussed later in this chapter) at a Tokyo bus stop. A timetable appears instantly on her screen, along with the estimated arrival time of the next bus. When her bus arrives, she uses her keitai to pay by simply waving it close to the payment terminal in the front of the bus.

Because the keitai are NFC equipped, they can function as boarding passes and tickets for trains, airplanes, and events. They also allow users to check into hotels, and they even serve as electronic room keys. Keitai also act as electronic wallets (e-wallets). Customers can input a credit of up to 50,000 yen over the Internet and then use their keitai to buy groceries at convenience stores, pay taxi drivers, and purchase goods from Japan's ubiquitous vending machines.

Japan's leading airline, All Nippon Airways (ANA), has been using e-wallets to compete with the country's fast trains for several years. As one ANA spokesperson explained, "The major drawback of flying compared to train travel is, of course, the time spent at the airport."

With ANA's all-in-one keitai ticket and boarding pass, passengers can arrive and board their planes in 15 minutes or less, even going through security checkpoints. This service, called SKiP, uses an e-wallet technology developed by communications company NTT.

Keitai are also equipped with GPS technology, which makes them very useful navigation tools. The Total Navigation site on a keitai displays three-dimensional maps and directions on the screen. If a user is holding the phone while navigating, it will vibrate to alert the driver to upcoming turns.

Keitai also help visitors cope with the Japanese language. For example, menus in Japanese restaurants are invariably written only in Japanese. Using a keitai, a visitor can take a picture of a meal, and the phone describes in English what the meal actually is. This is a valuable tool for many restaurants, because Japan relies on tourists for needed revenue. Other applications allow users to bring up menus, reviews, and translations by other users simply by focusing the phone's mobile camera at the restaurant itself.

In Kyoto, the Hyatt Regency offers an iPhone rental service that pinpoints guests' locations and beams target text, video, and graphics to inform, help, and guide them around the area. The hotel augments this service with advice and suggestions from the concierge.

The keitai are also equipped with *augmented reality (AR)*. AR apps know where users are, and they beam location-relevant information to their phones. This information is superimposed on the camera viewfinder on the phone's screen. AR apps in Japan also add tagging and social networking. Like other AR apps, the keitai calculates the user's position and then, using the camera, displays location-specific information graphically on top of the user's real-world view.

Interestingly, individuals and businesses can add their own information to these AR apps. They point the phone's camera at the landscape, adding "tags" that can include text, images, and sound that can be picked up later by other users in the area. Tags can translate into coupons from businesses or travel trips from friends and colleagues.

Sources: Compiled from D. Balaban, "Japan Airlines Set to Launch First NFC Boarding Passes," *NFC Times*, September 27, 2012; "NFC in the USA: Learning From Japan," *Travers Collins*, July 2, 2012; M. Keferl, "Near-Field Communication Is Shifting Marketing in Japan," *Advertising Age*, June 12, 2012; M. Fitzpatrick, "Near Field Communication Transforms Travel in Japan," *BBC News*, April 28, 2011; S. Clark, "NTT Adds New Mobile Marketing Capabilities to Japan's Osaifu-Keitai Mobile Wallet Service," *Near Field Communications World*, June 16, 2010; S. Toto, "Separate Keitai: Meet Japan's Sexiest New Handset," *TechCrunch*, February 5, 2010; "Japanese Cell Phone Culture," www.japaneselifestyle.com.au, accessed February 13, 2013.

Questions

1. As the Japanese travel industry creates more applications of technology for travel, what assumptions is it making about tourists?
2. Which of the keitai apps would you find most useful? Provide specific examples of the app(s) and the way(s) in which you would use them.
3. Do you see any problem with the social networking aspect of AR apps? Support your answer.

Wireless Fidelity (Wi-Fi). **Wireless fidelity (Wi-Fi)** is a medium-range WLAN, which is a wired LAN but without the cables. In a typical configuration, a transmitter with an antenna, called a **wireless access point** (see Figure 8.3), connects to a wired LAN or to satellite dishes that provide an Internet connection. A wireless access point provides service to a number of users within a small geographical perimeter (up to a couple of hundred feet), known as a hotspot. Multiple wireless access points are needed to support a larger number of users across a larger geographical area. To communicate wirelessly, mobile devices, such as laptop PCs, typically have a built-in wireless network interface capability.

Wi-Fi provides fast and easy Internet or intranet broadband access from public hotspots located at airports, hotels, Internet cafés, universities, conference centers, offices, and homes

Courtesy of Brad Prince

FIGURE 8.3 Wireless access point.

@ Marianna Day Massey/Zuma Press

FIGURE 8.4 Starbucks' patrons using Wi-Fi.

(see Figure 8.4). Users can access the Internet while walking across a campus, to their office, or through their homes. In addition, users can access Wi-Fi with their laptops, desktops, or PDAs by adding a wireless network card. Most PC and laptop manufacturers incorporate these cards in their PCs.

The Institute of Electrical and Electronics Engineers (IEEE) has established a set of standards for wireless computer networks. The IEEE standard for Wi-Fi is the 802.11 family. As of mid-2013, there were five standards in this family:

802.11a: supports wireless bandwidth up to 54 Mbps; high cost; short range; difficulty penetrating walls.

802.11b: supports wireless bandwidth up to 11 Mbps; low cost; longer range.

802.11g: supports wireless bandwidth up to 54 Mbps; high cost; longer range.

802.11n: supports wireless bandwidth exceeding 600 Mbps; higher cost than 802.11g; longer range than 802.11g.

802.11ac: a standard finalized in late 2012 that will support wireless bandwidth of 1 Gbps (1 billion bits per second); expected to reach the general market by early 2014.

The major benefits of Wi-Fi are its low cost and its ability to provide simple Internet access. It is the greatest facilitator of the wireless Internet—that is, the ability to connect to the Internet wirelessly.

Corporations are integrating Wi-Fi into their strategies. For example, Starbucks, McDonald's, Panera, and Barnes & Noble offer customers Wi-Fi in many of their stores, primarily for Internet access. The airlines are also getting in on the Wi-Fi act, as you see in IT's About Business 8.4.

Although Wi-Fi has become extremely popular, it is not without problems. Three factors are preventing the commercial Wi-Fi market from expanding even further: roaming, security, and cost.

- At this time, users cannot roam from hotspot to hotspot if the hotspots use different Wi-Fi network services. Unless the service is free, users have to log on to separate accounts and, where required, pay a separate fee for each service. (Some Wi-Fi hotspots offer free service, while others charge a fee.)

- Security is the second barrier to greater acceptance of Wi-Fi. Because Wi-Fi uses radio waves, it is difficult to shield from intruders.

- The final limitation to greater Wi-Fi expansion is cost. Even though Wi-Fi services are relatively inexpensive, many experts question whether commercial Wi-Fi services can survive when so many free hotspots are available to users.

IT's [about business]

8.4 Airlines Provide Wi-Fi to Passengers

After years of using drop-down televisions and expensive seat-back monitors, airlines now hope to entertain passengers on the screens that the travelers bring with them. The airlines are providing Wi-Fi, movies, and TV shows that travelers can view on their smartphones, tablets, and laptops. Although the airlines are experiencing economic difficulties, they are investing heavily in Wi-Fi capabilities. The airlines hope that this upfront investment will help them tap into a new source of revenue as they attract customers who need to be online while they are traveling.

By the time of this writing in mid-2013, some 2,000 commercial aircraft offer Internet access to passengers. Travelers can access their Internet connection at any point above 10,000 feet, the federal minimum altitude for using portable electronics. At least four companies are competing to provide Wi-Fi service to aircraft.

Five major U.S. carriers—Delta, American, AirTran, Alaska Airlines, and Virgin America—got into the wireless-providing business early. They signed contracts with Gogo (www.gogoair.com), the early option for in-flight Wi-Fi, and are now locked into contracts for a service that is quickly being bested by a number of rivals. Gogo beams its connection from cellular towers on the ground to antennas on the plane. This service has two major limitations. First, it is limited to the continental United States and Alaska. Second, it does not include live television.

Gogo's competitors offer expanded services and more features, but they have not yet proved themselves. Their promised services rely on satellites, which require heavier receivers that take longer to install than Gogo's receivers. Row 44 (http://row44.com), the Wi-Fi provider to Southwest Airlines, and Panasonic Avionics (www.mascorp.com), another in-flight Wi-Fi provider, offer global Wi-Fi via satellite. They stream live news and sports channels to flyers' devices.

ViaSat (www.viasat.com) provides more powerful in-flight Wi-Fi with the newest satellite technology, called Ka band. Ka band's competitive advantage is its higher bandwidth, which can service at least 10 times as many users as other in-flight Wi-Fi providers without affecting download speed. Gogo has announced plans to switch to Ka band by 2014 in the United States and to become a global Wi-Fi provider by 2015.

In the fall of 2012, Delta launched its on-demand service on 16 aircraft, offering $4 movies and $1 TV shows for flyers' laptops. American offers the same functions on 15 aircraft. Both airlines are running national ad campaigns that focus on their in-flight connectivity. Southwest charges $5 a flight for Row 44 Wi-Fi. Gogo charges $5 to $13 for Wi-Fi based on flight time, and it offers 15 minutes of Wi-Fi for $2. Virgin Atlantic plans to replace its seat-back touch screens with high-definition screens and to offer an enhanced Gogo Wi-Fi service that is four times as fast as its existing service.

Not surprisingly, passengers are unhappy with the cost of in-flight Wi-Fi access. Only about 7 percent of passengers currently avail themselves of the service. Although competition among in-flight Wi-Fi providers will drive down prices over time, in-flight Wi-Fi will not be an effective revenue-producing technology for airlines until this occurs.

Sources: Compiled from E. Perkins, "Perkins on Travel Wi-Fi Update, Airline by Airline," *Tribune Media Services*, March 13, 2013; H. Martin, "United Airlines Adds Wi-Fi for Overseas Flights," *Los Angeles Times*, February 10, 2013; R. Tomkins, "Airlines Cash In As In-Flight Wi-Fi Takes Off," *CNN*, November 22, 2012; N. Trajos, "More Airlines Add Wi-Fi, But Travelers Balk at Paying," *USA Today*, January 16, 2012; J. Nicas, "Playing the Wireless Card: Airlines Rush to Add Wi-Fi," *The Wall Street Journal*, October 11, 2011; www.gogoair.com, http://row44.com, www.mascorp.com, www.viasat.com, accessed March 20, 2013.

Questions

1. Would you use in-flight Wi-Fi if you had to pay the prices listed in this case? Why or why not?
2. How much would you pay to use in-flight Wi-Fi? (Your answer can be $0.)
3. What are the potential dangers of using in-flight Wi-Fi services?

Wi-Fi Direct. Until late 2010, Wi-Fi could operate only if the hotspot contained a wireless antenna. Because of this limitation, organizations have typically used Wi-Fi for communications of up to about 800 feet. For shorter, peer-to-peer connections they have used Bluetooth.

This situation changed following the introduction of a new iteration of Wi-Fi known as Wi-Fi Direct. Wi-Fi Direct enables peer-to-peer communications, so devices can connect directly. It allows users to transfer content among devices without having to rely on a wireless antenna. It can connect pairs or groups of devices at Wi-Fi speeds of up to 250 Mbps and at distances of up to 800 feet. Further, devices with Wi-Fi Direct can broadcast their availability to other devices just as Bluetooth devices can. Finally, Wi-Fi Direct is compatible with the more than 1 billion Wi-Fi devices currently in use.

Wi-Fi Direct will probably challenge the dominance of Bluetooth in the area of device-to-device networking. It offers a similar type of connectivity but with greater range and much faster data transfer.

MiFi. MiFi is a small, portable wireless device that provides users with a permanent Wi-Fi hotspot wherever they go. Thus, users are always connected to the Internet. The range of the MiFi device is about 10 meters (roughly 30 feet). Developed by Novatel, the MiFi device is also called an intelligent mobile hotspot. Accessing Wi-Fi through the MiFi device allows up to five persons to be connected at the same time, sharing the same connection. MiFi also allows users to use voice-over-IP technology to make free (or cheap) calls, both locally and internationally.

MiFi provides broadband Internet connectivity at any location that offers 3G cellular network coverage. One drawback with MiFi is that it is expensive both to acquire and to use.

Super Wi-Fi. Super Wi-Fi is a term coined by the U.S. Federal Communications Commission (FCC) to describe a wireless network proposal that creates long-distance wireless Internet connections. (The use of the trademark "Wi-Fi" in the name has been criticized because Super Wi-Fi is not based on Wi-Fi technology.) Super Wi-Fi uses the lower-frequency white spaces between television channel frequencies. These lower frequencies enable the signal to travel further and penetrate walls better than normal Wi-Fi frequencies.

Super Wi-Fi is already in use in Houston, Texas, and Wilmington, North Carolina. The technology threatens cell phone carriers' 3G technology, and it could eventually bring broadband wireless Internet access to rural areas.

Wireless Mesh Networks. **Mesh networks** use multiple Wi-Fi access points to create a wide area network that can be quite large. Mesh networks could have been included in the long-range wireless section, but you see them here because they are essentially a series of interconnected local area networks.

Around the United States, public wireless mesh programs have stalled and failed (e.g., in Philadelphia, in Boston, and on Long Island, New York). Service providers that partnered with cities to maintain the systems are dropping out, largely because the projects' costs are escalating and the revenue models are unclear. However, San José, California, is building a new "municipal Wi-Fi" network that shows promise, as the following example illustrates.

Example

Municipal Wi-Fi in San Jose, California

Municipal wireless networks (also called municipal Wi-Fi) are designed to turn an entire city into a wireless access zone in order to provide universal wireless access to the Internet. Cities provide municipal Wi-Fi via wireless mesh networks, using hundreds of wireless access points that are often located on utility poles. Unfortunately, some municipal wireless networks did not work as planned. They proved to be expensive to install and maintain. Further, they often did not provide adequate bandwidth for users to access the Internet.

A new downtown Wi-Fi network in San Jose, California, indicates a new beginning for the ill-fated and brief "muni Wi-Fi" attempts over the last decade. San Jose's municipal Wi-Fi network is now operating in the city's downtown area.

The city's goal is not to provide wireless Internet for all residents throughout the city. Rather, the city wants to make Wi-Fi available to all residents within the context of certain key municipal infrastructure applications. For instance, the new Wi-Fi network supports mobile Wi-Fi users in the city's parking guidance system, which can feed near real-time information about the location of empty spaces in the network of city-owned parking garages. The system also supports an expanding population of wireless parking meters. Both processes will generate city revenues, creating a sustainable foundation for the network's operations. This revenue generation is the basis for offering free, pervasive, high-bandwidth Wi-Fi connectivity as an end-user amenity in the 1.5-square-mile downtown area.

Sources: Compiled from E. Voss, "San Jose Free WiFi Network Launches in Downtown," *MuniWireless*, March 15, 2013; P. Shuler, "San Jose Launches 'Wickedly Fast' WiFi," *KQED News*, March 13, 2013; B. Reed, "South Carolina Clamps Down," *BGR.com*, June 29, 2012; M. Silbey, "Seattle Ends Free Wi-Fi," *Smart Planet*, May 8, 2012; J. Cox, "San Jose Wi-Fi Net Could Mark Rethinking of 'Muni Wi-Fi'," *Network World*, March 13, 2012; "Let Them Browse While They Eat Cake," *The Economist*, January 5, 2012; http://www.sanjoseca.gov/, accessed March 21, 2013.

Despite these problems, there are many examples of successful mesh-network applications. Consider the following:

- U.S. military forces are using wireless mesh networks to connect their laptops in field operations.
- Electric meters are now being placed on residences to transfer their readings to the central office for billing, without the need to employ human readers or to connect the meters with cables.
- The LEO Iridium constellation operates as a mesh network, with wireless links among adjacent satellites. Calls between two satellite phones are routed through the mesh, from one satellite to another across the constellation, without having to pass through an Earth-based station. As a result, the signal travels a shorter distance, reducing any transmission lag. In addition, the constellation can operate with fewer Earth stations.

Wide-Area Wireless Networks

Wide-area wireless networks connect users to the Internet over a geographically dispersed territory. These networks typically operate over the licensed spectrum—that is, they use portions of the wireless spectrum that are regulated by the government. In contrast, Bluetooth and Wi-Fi operate over the unlicensed spectrum and are therefore more prone to interference and security problems. In general, wide-area wireless network technologies fall into two categories: cellular radio and wireless broadband.

Cellular Radio.   **Cellular telephones** (**cell phones**) provide two-way radio communications over a cellular network of base stations with seamless handoffs. Cellular telephones differ from cordless telephones, which offer telephone service only within a limited range through a single base station attached to a fixed landline—for example, within a home or an office.

The cell phone communicates with radio antennas, or towers, placed within adjacent geographic areas called *cells* (see Figure 8.5). A telephone message is transmitted to the local cell—that is, the antenna—by the cell phone and then is passed from cell to cell until it

FIGURE 8.5 Cellular Radio Network. (*Sources*: Anthony Lee/OJO Images/Getty Images and Image Source Limited)

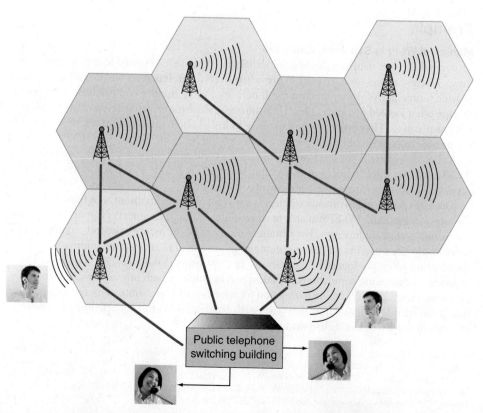

reaches the cell of its destination. At this final cell, the message either is transmitted to the receiving cell phone or it is transferred to the public switched telephone system to be transmitted to a wireline telephone. This is why you can use a cell phone to call other cell phones as well as standard wireline phones.

Until early 2011, large cell towers have been a "given" for cellular technology. The following example introduces an exciting new technology from Alcatel-Lucent (www.alcatel-lucent.com) that aims to replace these towers.

Cellular technology is quickly evolving, moving toward higher transmission speeds and richer features. The technology has progressed through several stages:

- *First generation* (1G) cellular used analog signals and had low bandwidth (capacity).
- *Second generation* (2G) uses digital signals primarily for voice communication; it provides data communication up to 10 Kbps.
- 2.5G uses digital signals and provides voice and data communication up to 144 Kbps.
- *Third generation* (3G) uses digital signals and can transmit voice and data up to 384 Kbps when the device is moving at a walking pace, 128 Kbps when it is moving in a car, and up to 2 Mbps when it is in a fixed location. 3G supports video, Web browsing, and instant messaging.

  3G does have disadvantages. Perhaps the most fundamental problem is that cellular companies in North America use two separate technologies: Verizon and Sprint use Code Division Multiple Access (CDMA), while Cingular and others use Global System for Mobile Communications (GSM). CDMA companies are currently using *Evolution-Data Optimized* (EV-DO) technology, which is a wireless broadband cellular radio standard.

  In addition, 3G is relatively expensive. In fact, most carriers limit how much information you can download and what you can use the service for. For instance, some carriers prohibit downloading or streaming audio or video. If you exceed the carriers' limits, they reserve the right to cut off your service.

- *Fourth generation* (4G) is still under development, and it is not one defined technology or standard. The International Telecommunications Union has specified speed requirements for 4G: 100 Mbps (million bits per second) for high-mobility communications such as cars and trains, and 1 Gbps (billion bits per second) for low-mobility communications such as pedestrians. A 4G system is expected to provide a secure all-IP (Internet Protocol)-based mobile broadband system to all types of mobile devices. Many of the current "4G" offerings do not meet the ITU specified speeds, but they call their service 4G nonetheless. See "IT's Personal" for more information.

Wireless Broadband or WiMAX. Worldwide Interoperability for Microwave Access, popularly known as WiMAX, is the name for IEEE Standard 802.16. WiMAX has a wireless access range of up to 31 miles, compared to 300 feet for Wi-Fi. WiMAX also has a data-transfer rate of up to 75 Mbps. It is a secure system, and it offers features such as voice and video. WiMAX antennas can transmit broadband Internet connections to antennas on homes and businesses located miles away. For this reason WiMAX can provide long-distance broadband wireless access to rural areas and other locations that are not currently being served.

IT's Personal: Wireless and Mobile

What the GSM3GHSDPA+4GLTE???

This chapter explains the many mobile platforms that are available to you as a consumer. Specifically, it discusses cellular, Bluetooth, Wi-Fi, satellite, and other wireless options. Within the cellular area, however, things get confusing because the telecommunications companies use so many acronyms these days. Have you ever wondered if Verizon 3G was equivalent to AT&T 3G? What about

4G and 4G LTE? Of course, most people assume that 4G is faster than 3G, but by how much?

For instance, when Apple released an update to its mobile operating system (iOS), AT&T suddenly began to display 4G on the iPhone rather than 3G! That was with no phone upgrade! Pretty nice, right? Wrong. In this instance, the "upgrade" was simply a change in terminology rather than a change in technology. The speed of the 3G/4G network had not changed. (Note: AT&T "4G LTE" is a different technology that does offer significantly higher speeds than AT&T 3G or 4G.)

Actual connection speeds are described in bit rates, meaning how many bits (1s or 0s) can be transmitted in one second. For example, a speed listed as 1.5 Mbps translates to 1.5 million bits per second. That sounds like a tremendous rate. Knowing the bits per second, however, is only part of understanding the actual speed. In reality, connection speed is not the same as throughput. Actual throughput will always be less than the connection speed.

To understand this point, consider how your car operates. Your car is probably capable of driving more than 100 mph. However, you are "throttled down" by various speed limits, so you never reach your potential speed. Your actual speed varies depending on the route you take, the speed limits imposed along that route, the weather, and many other factors. In the same way, even though AT&T, Verizon, Sprint, and other companies boast incredible wireless speeds ("Up to 20 Mbps!"), they will always say "up

to" because they know that you will never actually download a file at that rate.

The best method for determining the actual speeds of the various networks is to go to your local wireless store and run a speed test using the demo model they have on display. This will give you first-hand experience of the actual throughput speed you can expect from their network. This number is much more realistic than understanding terms such as 3G, 4G, and 4G LTE.

Here is how to perform the test: First, make sure the unit is connected only to a cellular network (not Wi-Fi). Then go to http://speedtest.net, and click "Begin Test." I just ran this test from my iPhone 4S on AT&T's 4G (not 4G LTE) network. My download speed was 3.80 Mbps, and my upload speed was 1.71 Mbps. These numbers are more informative than any name they are given (3G, 4G, etc.) because they indicate exactly what you can expect from your wireless connection. Run this test at competing stores (AT&T, Verizon, Sprint, T-Mobile, etc.), and you will have real data to compare. As names change, you can always run a test to find the facts.

---

before you go on...

1. What is Bluetooth? What is a WLAN?
2. Describe Wi-Fi, cellular service, and WiMAX.

8.3 Mobile Computing and Mobile Commerce

In the traditional computing environment, users come to a computer, which is connected with wires to other computers and to networks. Because these networks need to be linked by wires, it is difficult or even impossible for people on the move to use them. In particular, salespeople, repair people, service employees, law enforcement agents, and utility workers can be more effective if they can use IT while in the field or in transit. Mobile computing was designed for workers who travel outside the boundaries of their organizations as well as for anyone traveling outside his or her home.

Mobile computing refers to a real-time connection between a mobile device and other computing environments, such as the Internet or an intranet. This innovation is revolutionizing how people use computers. It is spreading at work and at home; in education, healthcare, and entertainment; and in many other areas.

Mobile computing has two major characteristics that differentiate it from other forms of computing: mobility and broad reach. *Mobility* means that users carry a device with them and can initiate a real-time contact with other systems from wherever they happen to be. *Broad reach* refers to the fact that when users carry an open mobile device, they can be reached instantly, even across great distances.

These two characteristics, mobility and broad reach, create five value-added attributes that break the barriers of geography and time: ubiquity, convenience, instant connectivity, personalization, and localization of products and services. A mobile device can provide information and communication regardless of the user's location (*ubiquity*). With an Internet-enabled mobile device, users can access the Web, intranets, and other mobile devices quickly and easily, without booting up a PC or placing a call via a modem (*convenience* and *instant connectivity*). A company can customize information and send it to individual consumers as a short message service (SMS) (*customization*). And, knowing a user's physical location helps a company advertise its products and services (*localization*). Mobile computing provides the foundation for mobile commerce (m-commerce).

Mobile Commerce

In addition to affecting our everyday lives, mobile computing is also transforming the way organizations conduct business by allowing businesses and individuals to engage in mobile commerce. As you saw at the beginning of this chapter, **mobile commerce** (or *m-commerce*) refers to electronic commerce (EC) transactions that are conducted in a wireless environment, especially via the Internet. Like regular EC applications, m-commerce can be transacted via the Internet, private communication lines, smart cards, and other infrastructures. M-commerce creates opportunities for businesses to deliver new services to existing customers and to attract new customers. To see how m-commerce applications are classified by industry, see www.wirelessresearch.eu.

The development of m-commerce is driven by the following factors:

- *Widespread availability of mobile devices.* By mid-2013, some 6 billion cell phones were in use throughout the world. Cell phones are spreading more quickly in the developing world than the developed world. Experts estimate that within a few years about 70 percent of cell phones in developed countries will have Internet access. Mobile Internet access in developing countries will increase rapidly as well. Thus, a mass market has developed for mobile computing and m-commerce.
- *Declining prices.* The price of wireless devices is declining and will continue to decline.
- *Bandwidth improvement.* To properly conduct m-commerce, you need sufficient bandwidth for transmitting text, voice, video, and multimedia. Wi-Fi, 4G cellular technology, and WiMAX all provide the necessary bandwidth.

Mobile computing and m-commerce include many applications, which result from the capabilities of various technologies. You will examine these applications and their impact on business activities in the next section.

Mobile Commerce Applications

Mobile commerce applications are many and varied. The most popular applications include location-based applications, financial services, intrabusiness applications, accessing information, and telemetry. The rest of this section examines these various applications and their effects on the ways people live and do business.

Location-Based Applications and Services. M-commerce B2C applications include location-based services and location-based applications. Location-based mobile commerce is called **location-based commerce (or L-commerce).**

Location-based services provide information that is specific to a given location. For example, a mobile user can (1) request the nearest business or service, such as an ATM or a restaurant; (2) receive alerts, such as a warning of a traffic jam or an accident; and (3) find a friend. Wireless carriers can provide location-based services such as locating taxis, service personnel, doctors, and rental equipment; scheduling fleets; tracking objects such as packages and train boxcars; finding information such as navigation, weather, traffic, and room schedules; targeting advertising; and automating airport check-ins.

Consider, for example, how location-based advertising can make the marketing process more productive. Marketers can use this technology to integrate the current locations and preferences of mobile users. They can then send user-specific advertising messages concerning nearby shops, malls, and restaurants to consumers' wireless devices. Despite these developments, however, mobile advertising is still in its early stages, as you see in IT's About Business 8.5.

Financial Services. Mobile financial applications include banking, wireless payments and micropayments, money transfers, wireless wallets, and bill-payment services. The bottom line for mobile financial applications is to make it more convenient for customers to transact business regardless of where they are or what time it is. Harried customers are demanding such convenience.

IT's [about business]

8.5 Mobile Ads Still Aren't Very Good

Experts classify mobile ads as the holy grail for companies that conduct business online. In fact, Pandora Media, Twitter, and many other companies often derive the majority of their revenue from mobile advertising. For example, in October 2012, Facebook's stock increased in value by more than 10 percent following news that the social network had earned 14 percent of its 2012 third-quarter revenue from mobile ads, up from almost nothing in the first quarter of that year.

Our smartphones are always with us, know where we are, and collect far more data about us than a desktop or laptop computer. So, if mobile computing has so much potential, why are mobile ads so mediocre?

Working with a tiny smartphone display, most mobile ads take one of two forms, each of which has serious limitations. The first form is the banner ad, which has little room to say anything other than "Click here for something!" The second form is the interstitial, which is the screen that pops up and interrupts you while you are trying to read something else. These two simple forms were borrowed from other media where they make more sense. For example, a print advertisement or a Web ad on a computer's large display is based on the concept of *adjacency*. We tolerate it because it is next to content that we want. Television ads function this way, but with the added dimension of time. Your TV show will be interrupted of course, but the show's story structure is designed with these interruptions in mind, and you will sit through commercials because you want to see what is going to happen next. Regardless of which of the two forms a mobile ad takes, it is disruptive to the viewer, and viewers simply do not like that.

According to research firm EMarketer (www.emarketer.com), worldwide mobile-ad spending will exceed $23 billion by 2016. Google is the largest beneficiary of that growth. Google realizes, however, that banner ads and interstitials do not work well on smartphones. Therefore, the company has been developing enhanced ad services like click-to-call buttons, which allow people to contact an advertiser directly about an offer using the phone in their hand. Another possible source of advertising is Google Now, a virtual personal assistant incorporated into Google's Android devices that keeps track of your frequently visited locations and repeating calendar entries and then tries to provide relevant information, such as a traffic report minutes before you head to work. As of mid-2013, Google had not sent any advertising through Google Now. However, industry analysts expect that it will at some point.

Google's mobile-payment system, Google Wallet (see the chapter-opening case), is another strategy the company is utilizing

to move beyond the existing mobile-advertising model. Storing a user's credit-card information does two things: It makes mobile purchases easier, and it provides a mechanism to track expenditures. Without a payment platform, Google and other companies have no way to determine whether an ad persuades a user to make an offline purchase. However, if you use Google Wallet to pay a florist after Google sent you an ad from that florist, Google can draw some conclusions about that ad's effectiveness, and it can then adjust prices accordingly.

Like Google, Facebook has expanded its mobile advertising. This expansion has been possible because more than 60 percent of Facebook users access the site via a mobile device. Facebook attributes its growth in mobile ads to the fact that its ads appear in the user's news feed, which the company calls a "sponsored story." (See the opening case in Chapter 9.) On Facebook, sponsored stories are first distributed to users who have chosen to be fans of an advertiser's Facebook page. If a fan likes the ad—which often consists of a coupon or another discount—in a sponsored story, then the ad is distributed to that fan's network of friends, regardless of whether they liked the advertiser's page. Facebook research has found that people recall an ad referred by a friend 10 times more often than they do a typical display ad.

The bottom line? Traditional advertising does not translate well to mobile devices, and companies are still having difficulty coming up with effective strategies for mobile advertising.

Sources: Compiled from T. Foran, "Native Advertising Strategies for Mobile Devices," *Forbes*, March 14, 2013; R. Hof, "Has Facebook Finally Mastered Mobile Marketing?" *Forbes*, March 6, 2013; A. Lashinsky, "Meet the Man Behind Facebook's Ad Revenue," *Fortune*, February 22, 2013; E. Spence, "Mobile Advertising in a Nutshell, Android for Show, Apple for Dough," *Forbes*, February 7, 2013; V. Kopytoff, "Cracking the Mobile Ad Market," *Fortune*, January 24, 2013; S. Olenski, "Is Location Based Advertising the Future of Mobile Marketing and Mobile Advertising?" *Forbes*, January 17, 2013; T. Worstall, "eBay Drops Mobile Advertising: Does This Hurt Facebook?" *Forbes*, December 20, 2012; S. Grobart, "Mobile Ads Are the Future. They're Also Lousy," *Bloomberg BusinessWeek*, November 5–11, 2012; J. Perez, "Zuckerberg Dazzles Wall Street with Q3 Mobile Progress," *CIO*, October 24, 2012.

Questions

1. Describe the advantages of mobile advertising to the advertiser. To the consumer.
2. Describe the disadvantages of mobile advertising to the advertiser. To the consumer.

In many countries, banks increasingly offer mobile access to financial and account information. For example, Citibank (www.citibank.com) alerts customers on their digital cell phones about changes to their account information.

If you took a taxi ride in Frankfurt, Germany, you could use your cell phone to pay the taxi driver. Such very small purchase amounts (generally less than $10) are called *micropayments*.

Web shoppers historically have preferred to pay with credit cards. Because credit card companies sometimes charge fees on transactions, however, credit cards are an inefficient way to make very small purchases. The growth of relatively inexpensive digital content, such as music (e.g., iTunes), ring tones, and downloadable games, is driving the growth of micropayments, as merchants seek to avoid paying credit card fees on small transactions.

Ultimately, however, the success of micropayment applications will depend on the costs of the transactions. Transaction costs will be small only when the volume of transactions is large. One technology that can increase the volume of transactions is wireless mobile wallets. Various companies offer mobile wallet (m-wallet) technologies that enable cardholders to make purchases with a single click from their mobile devices. This chapter's opening case discusses mobile wallets in detail.

In China, SmartPay allows people to use their mobile phones to pay their phone bills and utility bills, buy lottery tickets and airline tickets, and make other purchases. SmartPay launched 172.com (see www.172.com), a portal that centralizes the company's mobile, telephone, and Internet-based payment services for consumers. It designed the portal to provide a convenient, centralized source of information for all of these transactions.

Intrabusiness Applications. Although business-to-consumer (B2C) m-commerce gets considerable publicity, most of today's m-commerce applications actually are used *within* organizations. In this section, you will see how companies use mobile computing to support their employees.

Mobile devices increasingly are becoming an integral part of workflow applications. For example, companies can use nonvoice mobile services to assist in dispatch functions—that is, to assign jobs to mobile employees, along with detailed information about the job. Target areas for mobile delivery and dispatch services include transportation (delivery of food, oil, newspapers, cargo; courier services; tow trucks; taxis), utilities (gas, electricity, phone, water); field service (computers, office equipment, home repair); healthcare (visiting nurses, doctors, social services); and security (patrols, alarm installation).

Accessing Information. Another vital function of mobile technology is to help users obtain and utilize information. Two types of technologies—mobile portals and voice portals—are designed to aggregate and deliver content in a form that will work within the limited space available on mobile devices. These portals provide information to users anywhere and at any time.

A **mobile portal** aggregates and provides content and services for mobile users. These services include news, sports, and e-mail; entertainment, travel, and restaurant information; community services; and stock trading. The world's best-known mobile portal—i-mode from NTT DoCoMo (www.nttdocomo.com)—has more than 40 million subscribers, primarily in Japan. Major players in Europe are Vodafone, O2, and T-Mobile. Some traditional portals—for example, Yahoo!, AOL, and MSN—have mobile portals as well.

A **voice portal** is a Web site with an audio interface. Voice portals are not Web sites in the normal sense because they can also be accessed through a standard phone or a cell phone. A certain phone number connects you to a Web site, where you can request information verbally. The system finds the information, translates it into a computer-generated voice reply, and tells you what you want to know. Most airlines utilize voice portals to provide real-time information on flight status.

Another example of a voice portal is the voice-activated 511 travel-information line developed by Tellme.com. This technology enables callers to inquire about weather, local restaurants, current traffic, and other valuable information. In addition to retrieving information, some sites provide true interaction. For example, iPing (www.iping.com) is a reminder and notification service that allows users to enter information via the Web and receive reminder calls. This service can even call a group of people to notify them of a meeting or conference call.

Telemetry Applications. **Telemetry** is the wireless transmission and receipt of data gathered from remote sensors. Telemetry has numerous mobile computing applications. For example, technicians can use telemetry to identify maintenance problems in equipment. As another example, doctors can monitor patients and control medical equipment from a distance.

Car manufacturers use telemetry applications for remote vehicle diagnosis and preventive maintenance. For instance, drivers of many General Motors cars use its OnStar system (www .onstar.com) in numerous ways.

An interesting telemetry application for individuals is an iPhone app called Find My iPhone. Find My iPhone is a part of the Apple iCloud (www.apple.com/icloud). This app provides several very helpful telemetry functions. If you lose your iPhone, for example, it offers two ways to see its approximate location on a map. First, you can sign into the Apple iCloud from any computer. Second, you can use the Find My iPhone app on another iPhone, iPad, or iPod touch.

If you remember where you left your iPhone, you can write a message and display it on your iPhone's screen. The message might say, "Left my iPhone. Please call me at 301-555-1211." Your message appears on your iPhone, even if the screen is locked. And, if the map indicates that your iPhone is nearby—perhaps in your office under a pile of papers—you can tell Find My iPhone to play a sound that overrides the volume or silent setting.

If you left your iPhone in a public place, you may want to protect its contents. You can remotely set a four-digit passcode lock to prevent people from using your iPhone, accessing your personal information, or tampering with your settings. Going further, you can initiate a remote wipe (erase all contents) to restore your iPhone to its factory settings. If you eventually find your phone, then you can connect it to your computer and use iTunes to restore the data from your most recent backup.

If you have lost your iPhone and you do not have access to a computer, you can download the Find My iPhone app to a friend's iPhone, iPad, or iPod touch and then sign in to access all the Find My iPhone features.

before you go on...

1. What are the major drivers of mobile computing?

2. Describe mobile portals and voice portals.

3. Describe wireless financial services.

4. Discuss some of the major intrabusiness wireless applications.

8.4 Pervasive Computing

A world in which virtually every object has processing power and is connected to a global network either via a wireline or wirelessly is the world of **pervasive computing** (or **ubiquitous computing**). Pervasive computing is invisible "everywhere computing" that is embedded in the objects around us—the floor, the lights, our cars, the washing machine, our cell phones, our clothes, and so on.

For example, in a *smart home*, your home computer, television, lighting and heating controls, home security system, and many appliances can communicate with one another via a home network. You can control these linked systems through various devices, including your pager, cell phone, television, home computer, and even your automobile. One of the key elements of a smart home is the *smart appliance*, an Internet-ready appliance that can be controlled by a small handheld device or a desktop computer via a home network, either wireline or wireless. Two technologies provide the infrastructure for pervasive computing: radio-frequency identification and wireless sensor networks.

Radio-Frequency Identification

Radio-frequency identification (**RFID**) technology allows manufacturers to attach tags with antennas and computer chips on goods and then track their movement through radio signals. There are many uses for RFID tags, as you see in IT's About Business 8.6.

IT's [about business]

8.6 BP Uses Wireless Technologies

In 2009 the giant oil company BP (www.bp.com) launched a wide-ranging information technology initiative. The initiative, which BP calls "Track and Trace," involves deploying a web of networked RFID tags, cellular phones, and GPS devices to monitor key assets around the world. Its goals were to improve safety and compliance. Another goal was to save money by reducing BP's asset loss and theft, employee downtime, and material waste.

Track and Trace relies on a wide range of sensing technologies that had to be customized for the project. The technologies had to be safe enough to use around oil and gas and yet resilient enough to survive harsh conditions—from Arctic cold to desert heat to Gulf of Mexico humidity. For example, BP collaborated with a vendor to develop a GPS tracking device for pipeline inspectors, who often work alone in hazardous, remote conditions. To develop this technology, the vendor had to shrink its standard device and ensure that it would not emit sparks, so that it would be safe to use around combustible materials. Track and Trace technologies also had to be practical on a massive scale to influence the operations of a company with roughly 80,000 employees, thousands of facilities spread throughout the world, and millions of pieces of field equipment.

When the Deepwater Horizon oil rig exploded in 2010, killing 11 people and spewing oil into the Gulf of Mexico for 87 days, BP faced one of the industry's biggest and costliest oil cleanups. Track and Trace enabled BP to respond quickly in managing the cleanup, primarily through alerting spill responders about what equipment they had to work with and what condition the rig was in. BP deployed RFID-tagged Wave Gliders (self-powered robots that float around collecting data on air and water quality) in the Gulf of Mexico, and it tagged skimmers and other key assets across four U.S. Gulf states.

Another example of Track and Trace's usefulness is the role it played when BP had to perform routine refinery maintenance at the firm's Gelsenkirchen (GSK) refinery in Germany. To accomplish this process, GSK technicians worked section by section, sealing off one area before proceeding to the next. To do that, they used what is called a *blind* to close off pipe ends at the flange. Blinds were inserted and removed in a precise sequence. Engineers had to place RFID tags on 100,000 blinds at the refinery. They used Track and Trace to track the blinds with handheld readers. SAP software analyzed the data from Track and Trace to automatically determine which flanges should be blinded, and when.

In another Track and Trace project, BP outfitted oil trucks in Alaska with cellular equipment that transmits data to BP through the AT&T cellular network or, as a backup, through Iridium's satellites. The system monitors driver activity and sends alerts through e-mail and text about a suspected accident or unsafe activity by their truck drivers such as speeding and hard braking. The system monitors about 900 trucks, and it generates roughly 500,000 messages per week.

Sources: Compiled from T. Team, "BP Goes for Public Relations Makeover to Get Beyond Gulf Spill," *Forbes*, February 7, 2012; P. McDougall, "Asset Tracking Aids Huge BP Cleanup," *InformationWeek*, September 19, 2011; C. Swedberg, "BP Uses RFID Sensors to Track Pipe Corrosion," *RFID Journal*, January 31, 2011; www.bp.com, accessed March 11, 2013.

Questions

1. How did Track and Trace technologies help BP at least try to manage its catastrophic oil spill in the Gulf of Mexico?
2. What other uses might BP have for wireless sensor technologies?

RFID was developed to replace bar codes. A typical bar code, known as the *Universal Product Code* (*UPC*), is made up of 12 digits that are batched in various groups. The first digit identifies the item type, the next 5 digits identify the manufacturer, and the next 5 identify the product. The last digit is a check digit for error detection. Bar codes have worked well, but they have limitations. First, they require a line of sight to the scanning device. This system works well in a store, but it can pose substantial problems in a manufacturing plant or a warehouse or on a shipping/receiving dock. Second, because bar codes are printed on paper, they can be ripped, soiled, or lost. Third, the bar code identifies the manufacturer and product but not the actual item. Two systems are being developed to replace bar codes: *QR* (for quick response) *codes* and RFID systems. Figure 8.6 shows bar codes, QR codes, and an RFID tag.

A QR code is a two-dimensional code, readable by dedicated QR readers and camera phones. QR codes have several advantages over bar codes:

- QR codes can store much more information than bar codes.
- Data types stored in QR codes include numbers, text, URLs, and even Japanese characters.
- The size of QR codes is small because these codes store information horizontally and vertically.

QR code

RFID tag

Barcode

© Patrick Duinkerke/iStockphoto;
© raphotography/iStockphoto;
Media Bakery)

FIGURE 8.6 Barcodes, RFID tags, and QR codes.

- QR codes are more resistant to damage than bar codes.
- QR codes can be read from any direction or angle, so they are less likely to be misread.

RFID systems use tags with embedded microchips, which contain data, and antennas to transmit radio signals over a short distance to RFID readers. The readers pass the data over a network to a computer for processing. The chip in the RFID tag is programmed with information that uniquely identifies an item. It also contains information about the item such as its location and where and when it was made. Figure 8.7 shows an RFID reader and an RFID tag on a pallet.

There are two basic types of RFID tags: active and passive. *Active RFID tags* use internal batteries for power, and they broadcast radio waves to a reader. Because active tags contain batteries, they are more expensive than passive RFID tags, and they can be read over greater distances. Therefore, they are used primarily for more expensive items. In contrast, *passive RFID tags* rely entirely on readers for their power. They are less expensive than active tags, but they can be read only up to 20 feet. For these reasons they are generally applied to less-expensive merchandise. Problems with RFID include expense and the comparatively large size of the tags.

Wireless Sensor Networks

Wireless sensor networks (**WSNs**) are networks of interconnected, battery-powered, wireless sensors called *motes* that are placed into the physical environment. The motes collect data from many points over an extended space. Each mote contains processing, storage, and radio-frequency sensors and antennas. Each mote "wakes up" or activates for a fraction of a second when it has data to transmit. It then relays those data to its nearest neighbor. So, instead of every mote transmitting its data to a remote computer at a base station, the data are moved mote by mote until they reach a central computer where they can be stored and analyzed. An advantage of a wireless sensor network is that if one mote fails, then another one can pick up the data. This process makes WSNs very efficient and reliable. Also, if the network requires more bandwidth, it is easy to boost performance by placing new motes when and where they are required.

The motes provide information that enables a central computer to integrate reports of the same activity from different angles within the network. Therefore, the network can determine with much greater accuracy information such as the direction in which a person is moving, the weight of a vehicle, and the amount of rainfall over a field of crops.

There are many applications of wireless sensors. Nest Labs (*www.nest.com*) produces a "digital thermostat" that combines sensors and Web technology. The thermostat senses not only air temperature, but also the movements of people in a house. It then adjusts room temperatures accordingly to save energy.

Placing sensors in all kind of products makes the products "smart." Smart equipment includes sensors in bridges and oil rigs that alert their human minders when they need repairs, before equipment failure occurs. Sensors in jet engines produce data in real time on the operating performance of the engines. Sensors in fruit and vegetable cartons can track location and "sniff" the produce, warning in advance of spoilage, so shipments can be rerouted or rescheduled.

In Dubuque, Iowa, IBM has initiated a long-term project with the local government to use sensors, software, and the Internet to improve the city's use of water, electricity, and transportation. In a pilot project introduced in 2011, digital water meters were installed in 151 homes. These meters contain software that monitors water use and patterns. It then informs residents about ways to consume less, and it alerts them to likely leaks. The pilot program decreased water use by 65 million gallons per year in the city.

© Ecken, Dominique/
KeystonePressendienst/
Zuma Press

FIGURE 8.7 Small RFID reader and RFID tag.

A valuable application of sensors is to use them in smart electrical meters, thereby forming a smart grid. Smart meters monitor the usage of electricity, and they transmit that data to the utility company. IT's About Business 8.7 illustrates the advantages of utilizing smart meters in Brazil.

IT's [about business]

8.7 Brazil Uses Smart Meters

Reading electricity meters can be a dangerous job in Brazil, as AES Electropaulo (www.aeselectropaulo.com.br) meter readers well know. Robson Dourado, a São Paulo meter reader, claims that residents of São Paulo's Morro do Indio slum watch him carefully as he makes his rounds, worried that he will detect rogue wires that residents use to siphon away power illegally.

Electricity theft is rampant across much of Latin America, so much so that statisticians have devised a formula that uses the stolen wattage to measure the size of a country's informal economy. (The informal economy is that part of an economy that is not taxed or monitored by any form of government; for example bartering.) In some parts of Brazil, as much as 20 percent of electricity is stolen. To combat this problem and to avoid violent encounters with street gangs, utilities are using smart meters. These devices, which cost $150 to $400 each, allow power companies to monitor power usage remotely and in real time. The meters can detect unusually heavy demand, which may signal an illegal hookup. They can also shut off service to households and businesses that do not pay their bills.

The devices remove the human factor from meter reading, so customers can no longer collude with dishonest meter readers to cheat the power company. Smart meters are the perfect solution, says the chief technology officer of a Rio de Janeiro-based utility that has installed more than 150,000 of the devices. In his words, "They save us money, they are easy to install, and they require little maintenance." One Brazilian government official contends that the meters may save utility companies as much as $4.7 billion per year.

Sales of smart meters in Latin America are expected to generate $24 billion in revenue through 2020, with Brazil accounting for two-thirds of that total. Experts estimate that Brazilian utility companies may install as many as 63 million smart meters by 2020, while Mexico may install 22.4 million, Argentina 5 million, and Chile 3 million during the same time period.

In Rio de Janeiro, utility companies are taking advantage of preparations for the 2014 World Cup soccer championship and the 2016 Olympic Games to deploy the meters. Before August 2011, about 80 percent of the electricity in Tabajara and Morro dos Cabritos, two particularly violent slums, was stolen through illegal connections. After police established a constant presence in the slums, a utility company installed 50,000 smart meters. Electricity theft has dropped to zero since that time, proving the efficacy of the new technology.

Sources: Compiled from T. Woody, "How Europe Is Cashing in on Smart Meters as the U.S. Lags," *Forbes,* November 6, 2012; S. Nielsen, "Smart Meters Help Brazil Zap Electricity Theft," *Bloomberg BusinessWeek,* March 8, 2012; "Latin America's First Smart Grid Project Now Complete," *SmartGridNews,* December 22, 2011; "Brazil Will Adopt Smart Meters," *Gulfnews.com,* October 30, 2011; J. St. John, "Echelon Partners Up to Break into Brazil's Smart Meter Market," *Greentechmedia,* October 13, 2011; J. St. John, "Brazil: The Next Hot Smart Meter Market," *GigaOM.com,* November 24, 2010; www.aeselectropaulo.com.br, accessed March 20, 2013.

Questions

1. If smart meters are installed in large numbers, then what happens to the workers who are employed as meter readers? Do you see problems with this scenario?
2. Besides deterring theft, what other advantages might a smart meter provide to a utility company? To a homeowner? To a business?

before you go on...

1. Define pervasive computing, RFID, and wireless sensor networks.
2. Provide two specific business uses of RFID technology.

Wireless Security

8.5

Clearly, wireless networks provide numerous benefits for businesses. However, they also present a huge challenge to management—namely, their inherent lack of security. Wireless is a broadcast medium, and transmissions can be intercepted by anyone who is close enough and has access to the appropriate equipment. There are four major threats to wireless networks: rogue access points, war driving, eavesdropping, and radio-frequency jamming.

A *rogue access point* is an unauthorized access point to a wireless network. The rogue could be someone in your organization who sets up an access point meaning no harm but fails to inform the IT department. In more serious cases, the rogue is an "evil twin"—someone who wishes to access a wireless network for malicious purposes.

In an evil twin attack, the attacker is in the vicinity with a Wi-Fi-enabled computer and a separate connection to the Internet. Using a *hotspotter*—a device that detects wireless networks and provides information on them (see *www.canarywireless.com*)—the attacker simulates a wireless access point with the same wireless network name, or SSID, as the one that authorized users expect. If the signal is strong enough, users will connect to the attacker's system instead of the real access point. The attacker can then serve them a Web page asking for them to provide confidential information such as user names, passwords, and account numbers. In other cases, the attacker simply captures wireless transmissions. These attacks are more effective with public hotspots (e.g., McDonald's and Starbucks) than with corporate networks.

War driving is the act of locating WLANs while driving (or walking) around a city or elsewhere. To war drive or walk, you simply need a Wi-Fi detector and a wirelessly enabled computer. If a WLAN has a range that extends beyond the building in which it is located, then an unauthorized user might be able to intrude into the network. The intruder can then obtain a free Internet connection and possibly gain access to important data and other resources.

Eavesdropping refers to efforts by unauthorized users to access data that are traveling over wireless networks.

In *radio-frequency (RF) jamming*, a person or a device intentionally or unintentionally interferes with your wireless network transmissions.

As you see, wireless systems can be difficult to secure. Technology Guide 5 discusses a variety of techniques and technologies that you should implement to help you avoid these threats.

before you go on...

1. Describe the four major threats to the security of wireless networks.

2. Which of these threats is the most dangerous for a business? Which is the most dangerous for an individual? Support your answers.

What's In IT For Me?

For the Accounting Major

ACCT Wireless applications help accountants to count and audit inventory. They also expedite the flow of information for cost control. Price management, inventory control, and other accounting-related activities can be improved with the use of wireless technologies.

For the Finance Major

FIN Wireless services can provide banks and other financial institutions with a competitive advantage. For example, wireless electronic payments, including micropayments, are more convenient (anywhere, anytime) than traditional means of payment, and they are less expensive. Electronic bill payment from mobile devices is becoming more popular, increasing security and accuracy, expediting cycle time, and reducing processing costs.

For the Marketing Major

MKT Imagine a whole new world of marketing, advertising, and selling, with the potential to increase sales dramatically. Such is the promise of mobile computing. Of special interest for marketing are location-based advertising as well as the new opportunities resulting from pervasive computing and RFIDs. Finally, wireless technology also provides new opportunities in sales force automation (SFA), enabling faster and better communications with both customers (CRM) and corporate services.

POM For the Production/Operations Management Major

Wireless technologies offer many opportunities to support mobile employees of all kinds. Wearable computers enable off-site employees and repair personnel working in the field to service customers faster, better, and less expensively. Wireless devices can also increase productivity within factories by enhancing communication and collaboration as well as managerial planning and control. In addition, mobile computing technologies can improve safety by providing quicker warning signs and instant messaging to isolated employees.

HRM For the Human Resources Management Major

Mobile computing can improve HR training and extend it to any place at anytime. Payroll notices can be delivered as SMSs. In addition, wireless devices can make it even more convenient for employees to select their own benefits and update their personal data.

MIS For the MIS Major

MIS personnel provide the wireless infrastructure that enables all organizational employees to compute and communicate anytime, anywhere. This convenience provides exciting, creative, new applications for organizations to cut costs and improve the efficiency and effectiveness of operations (e.g., to achieve transparency in supply chains). Unfortunately, as you saw earlier, wireless applications are inherently insecure. This lack of security is a serious problem with which MIS personnel must contend.

[Summary]

1. **Identify advantages and disadvantages of each of the four main types of wireless transmission media.**

   Microwave transmission systems are used for high-volume, long-distance, line-of-sight communication. One advantage is the high volume. A disadvantage is that microwave transmissions are susceptible to environmental interference during severe weather such as heavy rain and snowstorms.

   Satellite transmission systems make use of communication satellites, and they receive and transmit data via line-of-sight. One advantage is that the enormous footprint—the area of Earth's surface reached by a satellite's transmission—overcomes the limitations of microwave data-relay stations. Like microwaves, satellite transmissions are susceptible to environmental interference during severe weather.

   Radio transmission systems use radio-wave frequencies to send data directly between transmitters and receivers. An advantage is that radio waves travel easily through normal office walls. A disadvantage is that radio transmissions are susceptible to snooping by anyone who has similar equipment that operates on the same frequency.

   Infrared light is red light that is not commonly visible to human eyes. Common applications of infrared light are in remote-control units for televisions, VCRs, and DVD and CD players. An advantage of infrared is that it does not penetrate walls and so does not interfere with other devices in adjoining rooms. A disadvantage is that infrared signals can be easily blocked by furniture.

2. **Explain how businesses can use technology employed by short-range, medium-range, and long-range networks, respectively.**

   Short-range wireless networks simplify the task of connecting one device to another, eliminating wires and enabling users to move around while they use the devices. In general, short-range wireless networks have a range of 100 feet or less. Short-range wireless networks include Bluetooth, ultra-wideband, and near-field communications. A business application of ultra-wideband is the PLUS Real-Time Location System from Time Domain. Using PLUS, an organization can locate multiple people and assets simultaneously.

Medium-range wireless networks include Wireless Fidelity (Wi-Fi) and mesh networks. *Wi-Fi* provides fast and easy Internet or intranet broadband access from public hotspots located at airports, hotels, Internet cafés, universities, conference centers, offices, and homes. *Mesh networks* use multiple Wi-Fi access points to create a wide area network that can be quite large.

Wide-area wireless networks connect users to the Internet over geographically dispersed territory. They include cellular telephones and wireless broadband. *Cellular telephones* provide two-way radio communications over a cellular network of base stations with seamless handoffs. *Wireless broadband* (WiMAX) has a wireless access range of up to 31 miles and a data-transfer rate of up to 75 Mbps. WiMAX can provide long-distance broadband wireless access to rural areas and remote business locations.

3. **Provide a specific example of how each of the five major m-commerce applications can benefit a business.**

Location-based services provide information specific to a location. For example, a mobile user can (1) request the nearest business or service, such as an ATM or restaurant; (2) receive alerts, such as a warning of a traffic jam or an accident; and (3) find a friend. With *location-based advertising*, marketers can integrate the current locations and preferences of mobile users. They can then send user-specific advertising messages about nearby shops, malls, and restaurants to wireless devices.

Mobile financial applications include banking, wireless payments and micropayments, money transfers, wireless wallets, and bill-payment services. The bottom line for mobile financial applications is to make it more convenient for customers to transact business regardless of where they are or what time it is.

Intrabusiness applications consist of m-commerce applications that are used *within* organizations. Companies can use nonvoice mobile services to assist in dispatch functions—that is, to assign jobs to mobile employees, along with detailed information about the job.

When it comes to *accessing information*, mobile portals and voice portals are designed to aggregate and deliver content in a form that will work within the limited space available on mobile devices. These portals provide information anywhere and anytime to users.

Telemetry is the wireless transmission and receipt of data gathered from remote sensors. Company technicians can use telemetry to identify maintenance problems in equipment. Car manufacturers use telemetry applications for remote vehicle diagnosis and preventive maintenance.

4. **Describe technologies that underlie pervasive computing, providing examples of how businesses can utilize each one.**

Pervasive computing is invisible and everywhere computing that is embedded in the objects around us. Two technologies provide the infrastructure for pervasive computing: *radio-frequency identification* (RFID) and *wireless sensor networks* (WSNs).

RFID is the term for technologies that use radio waves to automatically identify the location of individual items equipped with tags that contain embedded microchips. WSNs are networks of interconnected, battery-powered, wireless devices placed in the physical environment to collect data from many points over an extended space.

5. **Explain how the four major threats to wireless networks can damage a business.**

The four major threats to wireless networks are rogue access points, war driving, eavesdropping, and radio-frequency jamming. A *rogue access point* is an unauthorized access point to a wireless network. *War driving* is the act of locating WLANs while driving around a city or elsewhere. *Eavesdropping* refers to efforts by unauthorized users to access data that are traveling over wireless networks. *Radio-frequency jamming* occurs when a person or a device intentionally or unintentionally interferes with wireless network transmissions.

[Chapter Glossary]

Bluetooth Chip technology that enables short-range connection (data and voice) between wireless devices.

cellular telephones (cell phones) Phones that provide two-way radio communications over a cellular network of base stations with seamless handoffs.

Global Positioning System (GPS) A wireless system that uses satellites to enable users to determine their position anywhere on earth.

hotspot A small geographical perimeter within which a wireless access point provides service to a number of users.

infrared A type of wireless transmission that uses red light not commonly visible to human eyes.

location-based commerce (l-commerce) Mobile commerce transactions targeted to individuals in specific locations, at specific times.

mesh networks Networks composed of multiple Wi-Fi access points that create a wide area network that can be quite large.

microwave transmission A wireless system that uses microwaves for high-volume, long-distance, point-to-point communication.

mobile commerce (or m-commerce) Electronic commerce transactions that are conducted with a mobile device.

mobile computing A real-time connection between a mobile device and other computing environments, such as the Internet or an intranet.

mobile portal A portal that aggregates and provides content and services for mobile users.

mobile wallet (m-wallet) A technology that allows users to make purchases with a single click from their mobile devices.

near-field communications (NFC) The smallest of the short-range wireless networks that is designed to be embedded in mobile devices such as cell phones and credit cards.

personal area network A computer network used for communication among computer devices close to one person.

pervasive computing (or ubiquitous computing) A computer environment where virtually every object has processing power with wireless or wired connections to a global network.

propagation delay Any delay in communications from signal transmission time through a physical medium.

radio-frequency identification (RFID) technology A wireless technology that allows manufacturers to attach tags with antennas and computer chips on goods and then track their movement through radio signals.

radio transmission Uses radio-wave frequencies to send data directly between transmitters and receivers.

satellite radio (or digital radio) A wireless system that offers uninterrupted, near CD-quality music that is beamed to your radio from satellites.

satellite transmission A wireless transmission system that uses satellites for broadcast communications.

telemetry The wireless transmission and receipt of data gathered from remote sensors.

ubiquitous computing (see **pervasive computing**)

ultra-wideband (UWB) A high-bandwidth wireless technology with transmission speeds in excess of 100 Mbps that can be used for applications such as streaming multimedia from, say, a personal computer to a television.

voice portal A Web site with an audio interface.

wireless Telecommunications in which electromagnetic waves carry the signal between communicating devices.

wireless 911 911 emergency calls made with wireless devices.

wireless access point An antenna connecting a mobile device to a wired local area network.

Wireless Fidelity (Wi-Fi) A set of standards for wireless local area networks based on the IEEE 802.11 standard.

wireless local area network (WLAN) A computer network in a limited geographical area that uses wireless transmission for communication.

wireless sensor networks (WSNs) Networks of inter-connected, battery-powered, wireless sensors placed in the physical environment.

[Discussion Questions]

1. Given that you can lose a cell phone as easily as a wallet, which do you feel is a more secure way of carrying your personal data? Support your answer.

2. If mobile computing is the next wave of technology, would you ever feel comfortable with handing a waiter or waitress your cell phone to make a payment at a restaurant the way you currently hand over your credit or debit card? Why or why not?

3. What happens if you lose your NFC-enabled smartphone or it is stolen? How do you protect your personal information?

4. In your opinion, is the mobile (or digital) wallet a good idea? Why or why not?

5. Discuss how m-commerce can expand the reach of e-business.

6. Discuss how mobile computing can solve some of the problems of the digital divide.

7. List three to four major advantages of wireless commerce to consumers and explain what benefits they provide to consumers.

8. Discuss the ways in which Wi-Fi is being used to support mobile computing and m-commerce. Describe the ways in which Wi-Fi is affecting the use of cellular phones for m-commerce.

9. You can use location-based tools to help you find your car or the closest gas station. However, some people see location-based tools as an invasion of privacy. Discuss the pros and cons of location-based tools.

10. Discuss the benefits of telemetry in healthcare for the elderly.

11. Discuss how wireless devices can help people with disabilities.

12. Some experts say that Wi-Fi is winning the battle with 3G cellular service. Others disagree. Discuss both sides of the argument and support each one.

13. Which of the applications of pervasive computing do you think are likely to gain the greatest market acceptance over the next few years? Why?

[Problem-Solving Activities]

1. Investigate commercial applications of voice portals. Visit several vendors, e.g., Microsoft and Nuance (links to both websites are available via http://www.wiley.com/go/rainer/problemsolving). What capabilities and applications do these vendors offer?

2. Using a search engine, try to determine whether there are any commercial Wi-Fi hotspots in your area. (Hint: Access http://www.wiley.com/rainer/go/problemsolving.)

3. Examine how new data-capture devices such as RFID tags help organizations accurately identify and segment their customers for activities such as targeted marketing. Browse the Web, and develop five potential new applications not listed in this chapter for RFID technology. What issues would arise if a country's laws mandated that such devices be embedded in everyone's body as a national identification system?

4. Investigate commercial uses of GPS. Start with www.neigps.com. Can some of the consumer-oriented products be used in industry? Prepare a report on your findings.

5. Access www.bluetooth.com. Examine the types of products being enhanced with Bluetooth technology. Present two of these products to the class and explain how they are enhanced by Bluetooth technology.

6. Explore www.nokia.com. Prepare a summary of the types of mobile services and applications Nokia currently supports and plans to support in the future.

7. Enter www.ibm.com. Search for "wireless e-business." Research the resulting stories to determine the types of wireless capabilities and applications IBM's software and hardware support. Describe some of the ways these applications have helped specific businesses and industries.

8. Research the status of 3G and 4G cellular service by visiting the links available via http://www.wiley.com/go/rainer/problemsolving. Prepare a report on the status of 3G and 4G based on your findings.

9. Enter Pitney-Bowes Business Insight (www.pbinsight.com). Click on "MapInfo Professional," then click on the "Resources" tab, then on the "Demos" tab. Look for the location-based services demos. Try all the demos. Summarize your findings.

10. Enter www.packetvideo.com. Examine the demos and products and list their capabilities.

11. Enter www.onstar.com. What types of *fleet* services does OnStar provide? Are these any different from the services OnStar provides to individual car owners? (Play the movie.)

12. Access various search engines to find articles about "The Internet of Things." What is "the Internet of Things"? What types of technologies are necessary to support it? Why is it important?

[Closing Case Retailer Gains Many Benefits with RFID Item-Level Tagging]

The Problem

American Apparel (AA; www.americanapparel.net) is a vertically integrated clothing manufacturer, wholesaler, and retailer that also conducts its own design advertising, and marketing. The firm is best known for making basic, solid-color cotton knitwear such as T-shirts and underwear. However, in recent years it has expanded to include leggings, leotards, tank tops, vintage clothing, dresses, pants, denim, nail polish, and other products. In mid-2013, the company operated over 285 retail stores in 20 countries.

American Apparel retail stores operate boutique-style, stocking only one item of each style, color, and size on the floor at any time. Inventory turns over quickly in the apparel business, and with more than 26,000 stock-keeping units (SKUs) to manage, store staff constantly battled to keep inventory counts 100 percent accurate and the sales floor 100 percent stocked.

These efforts were time- and labor-intensive and expensive. However, the cost of inventory errors and stocking delays were even higher—lost sales and disappointed customers.

The IT Solution

AA searched for a more efficient and effective means to meet their goals and item-level radio frequency identification (RFID) that fit the company's needs. Before implementing RFID across the entire company, AA tested the system in one store.

The company gave careful consideration to its choice of store for the pilot test. They looked for a store that had average sales and a dedicated staff that would embrace the technology as well as a new process for inventory management. In addition, AA wanted a location with good traffic flow that was centrally located to other area AA stores, in order to facilitate a regional roll-out if the single store pilot test proved successful. The company chose the Columbia University area store in New York City.

AA partnered with Motorola (www.motorola.com) and used that company's handheld readers for the sales floor and the shipping dock. The store placed RFID tags on each item of clothing and merchandise. As the tags were affixed to each product, they were associated with the particular SKU in the system's software. From that point on, store associates used mobile (handheld) and fixed RFID readers to stock, inventory, and replenish the store's 40,000-piece store inventory.

The Results

American Apparel noted that its pilot RFID system contributed to a well-stocked store, increased sales, and allowed immediate and accurate responses to customers' requested design, size, and color of in-store merchandise. The RFID technology also allowed the retailer to better determine real-time buying behaviors of its customers and adjust inventory accordingly. This process made items easier for customers to find and for employees to replenish. In fact, the new system reduced the number of "missing" items (i.e, an item color or size that is not on the floor) from an average of 80 missing items on the floor

at any one time to fewer than 8, and these 8 were subsequently found misplaced on the floor.

Item-level RFID tagging also allowed inventory to be taken more accurately, in less time, enabling staff to spend more time on the sales floor assisting customers and making sales rather than restocking merchandise. Specifically, prior to implementing the RFID system, inventory took 6–8 people 6–8 hours. After the implementation, inventory takes two people 2.5 hours, and with improved accuracy.

The retailer is now able to fulfill its vision of consistently offering merchandise in every size and color on store floors at all times, creating a more rewarding customer experience and simplifying the inventory process. AA has also seen unexpected benefits from the RFID pilot test, namely a significant decline in employee theft.

American Apparel is now rolling out its RFID system across its stores around the world. By deploying the technology in all of its stores, the retailer expects to increase sales and improve customer service by having real-time visibility into product at nearby stores, enhancing the inter-store transfer process to balance stock. That is, if a store is out of a particular product, then the system will alert the staff to the nearest store with that product and how long it will take to transfer it where it is needed.

Sources: Compiled from "RFID News: JC Penney CEO Says Retailer Going All in on RFID, Perhaps With Significant Impact on Industry," *Supply Chain Digest*, August 15, 2012; M. Roberti, "Word Is Getting Out About RFID in Retail," *RFID Journal*, July 23, 2012; W. Loeb, "Macy's Wins With Technology," *Forbes*, July 10, 2012; "American Apparel Finds the Right Fit with Motorola RFID," *American Apparel Case Study*, 2012; www.americanapparel.net, www.motorola.com, accessed April 25, 2013.

Questions

1. What are the possible disadvantages of American Apparel's RFID system?

2. How could American Apparel measure the value of the RFID system? Provide specific examples of metrics that the retailer could use to justify the cost of the system. Also, provide non-quantifiable measures that the retailer could use to justify its system.

[Internship Activity]

Banking Industry

Mobile Communications have changed our lives dramatically in the past 15 years. We have progressed from a being connected to households by landline telephones to being connected to individuals by wireless devices. It is much more than just a phone… often referred to as a "smart" phone, these wireless devices allow us to stay connected via social media, text messages, video calls, photo sharing, email, and yes, even phone calls. It is no surprise, then, that businesses have used these powerful devices for their benefit in reaching out to customers.

For this Internship Activity, you will work for Jeremy Farr, Associate Vice President and IT Officer of Noble Bank & Trust in Anniston, AL. In particular, Jeremy is interested in learning about some of the new mobile developments his bank could use to allow their customers to access account information on the mobile web or through mobile apps. Your job will be to research potential providers and give feedback on the good and bad of different partners.

Please visit the Book Companion Site to receive the full set of instructions.

Chapter 9

Social Computing

[LEARNING OBJECTIVES]	[CHAPTER OUTLINE]	[WEB RESOURCES]
1. Describe six Web 2.0 tools and two major types of Web 2.0 sites.	9.1 Web 2.0	• Student PowerPoints for note taking
2. Describe the benefits and risks of social commerce to companies.	9.2 Fundamentals of Social Computing in Business	**WileyPLUS**
3. Identify the methods used for shopping socially.	9.3 Social Computing in Business: Shopping	• E-book
4. Discuss innovative ways to use social networking sites for advertising and market research.	9.4 Social Computing in Business: Marketing	• Author video lecture for each chapter section
5. Describe how social computing improves customer service.	9.5 Social Computing in Business: Customer Relationship Management	• Practice quizzes
6. Discuss different ways in which human resource managers make use of social computing.	9.6 Social Computing in Business: Human Resource Management	• Flash Cards for vocabulary review
		• Additional "IT's About Business" cases
		• Video interviews with managers
		• Lab Manuals for Microsoft Office 2010 and 2013

This Chapter Will Help Prepare You To...

ACCT	FIN	MKT	POM	HRM	MIS
ACCOUNTING	**FINANCE**	**MARKETING**	**PRODUCTION OPERATIONS MANAGEMENT**	**HUMAN RESOURCES MANAGEMENT**	**MIS**
Monitor social media for compliance	Collaborate with external financial experts	Receive real-time feedback from customers	Partners/ customers collaborate on product development	Enhance recruiting efforts	Develop internal company social networks

[Facebook Commerce]

The Problem

With some 1 billion members, Facebook is a very desirable Web site on which to advertise, sell, and conduct other social commerce activities. (**Social commerce** is the delivery of electronic commerce activities and transactions through social computing.) With its size, Facebook offers opportunities for companies to reach out to customers and conduct business transactions. What is the best way to take advantage of Facebook's size—as well as its existing customer base—to do business?

The Solutions

Facebook commerce (or *f-commerce*) refers to commerce executed on, or influenced by, the Facebook platform. Two major types of f-commerce are emerging: commerce-on Facebook and commerce-off Facebook.

Commerce-on Facebook. Commerce-on Facebook is a type of electronic commerce in which the transaction occurs completely inside Facebook. Vendors create Facebook stores for their customers, who conduct transactions without leaving Facebook.

There are many examples of Facebook stores:

- The P&G Pampers F-Store, powered by Amazon WebStore, sold 1,000 diaper packs directly to consumers in less than one hour after the store "went live" on Facebook.
- ASOS, Europe's first fully integrated F-store, makes it possible for consumers to complete purchases without ever leaving Facebook.
- Delta Airlines has built a complete ticketing system into its Facebook page. Although the airline allows the user to promote Delta by posting a general message on his or her Wall, it does not do much to help the user share details with friends involved in the trip, something that a Send Button could do nicely.

Facebook credits are just like tokens at an arcade or amusement park. Credits are a secure way to play games and purchase virtual and digital goods on Facebook. You can buy credits using your credit card, PayPal, mobile phone, or other payment methods. For instance, Warner Brothers allows consumers to use Facebook credits to stream movies in Facebook for 30 Facebook credits ($3) per movie.

Commerce-off Facebook. Commerce-off Facebook takes advantage of Facebook's Open Graph, which allows shoppers to sign in to Facebook from any Web site with any computing device (e.g., laptop, netbook, phone). Merchant integration with Facebook works in five ways: Facebook-enabled Web sites, Facebook in-store retail, Facebook-initiated selling, Facebook check-in deals, and Facebook mobile ads.

Facebook-enabled Web sites are traditional Web sites and e-commerce sites that integrate with Facebook to offer customers a Facebook experience while shopping or researching purchases. Brands can bring the Facebook experience to their Web sites, tapping users' connections and interests to support the purchasing process. The simplest examples involve using social plugins, which include the Like Button, Send Button, Subscribe Button, Recommendations, Login Button, and many others.

The Like Button is the most common plugin, and it is usually regarded as a content-sharing device. However, when it is used in conjunction with a product page, it can provide peer support by displaying the names and profile images of people who have Liked the product. For marketers and producers, the most appealing feature of the Like Button is the fact that it also highlights any of the user's Facebook friends who have Liked the product.

In *Facebook in-store retail*, brick-and-mortar retailers integrate with Facebook to offer customers a Facebook experience while shopping in their stores. For instance, Macy's Magic Fitting Room is a Facebook-connected fitting room equipped with a camera-enhanced 72-inch mirror and an iPad that allows customers to try on clothes and then share the experience with their Facebook friends.

With *Facebook-initiated selling*, businesses can set up a storefront for free on their Facebook pages. Customers begin the shopping process on Facebook and are then directed to the business's e-commerce pages at some point to complete the purchase process.

For example, Best Buy keeps shoppers in the Facebook environment and takes advantage of its social features while they are there. Best Buy's store app is labeled "Shop 1 Share." Users can search or browse for products. When they find something that interests them, they have two options: Ask Friends or Shop Now. Ask Friends leads to a Wall post asking about the product. Interestingly, Best Buy makes Ask Friends much more noticeable than Shop Now, which takes the user to the product page at *www.bestbuy.com* for the shopping cart and checkout process.

The *Facebook check-in deals* program allows local retailers to drive traffic to their stores by offering special discounts to consumers who check in to their location with Facebook Places on their mobile phones. For example, The Gap ran a promotion in which it leveraged check-in deals by offering a free pair of blue jeans to the first 10,000 consumers who checked in at Gap stores. Similarly, Mazda UK offered a 20 percent discount for the Mazda X5 for check-in deals when Facebook Places launched in the United Kingdom.

In October 2012, Facebook launched *mobile ads*. Several of Facebook's large advertising clients who used the mobile ads indicated that these ads can be used to develop e-commerce on Facebook, turning the social network into a mobile shopping and sales service. For example, Fab.com tested the service with Fab's shopping app (over Facebook) and noted that the app was 5 times more effective than any other mobile download channel that the company had ever used.

The Results

F-commerce is still in its infancy. In 2007, Facebook initiated Project Beacon, which collected e-commerce activity on third-party sites and announced a user's purchases on his or her friends' news feeds. Facebook quickly withdrew from that privacy nightmare. However, the damage done to its reputation for freely dispersing user data still deters f-commerce. Many Facebook users have become so accustomed to Facebook's aggressive data-sharing policies that they automatically assume the worst. In fact, studies have shown that a majority of Facebook users have concerns about Facebook's privacy and security.

Experienced e-commerce managers also perceive problems with Facebook itself. Facebook has relatively slow page loads and a smaller page size due to its advertising and navigation.

Analysts wonder why customers would bother shopping through Facebook when a faster and better experience is only a browser tab away, at the vendor's e-commerce site. Facebook advertising is also an issue. No matter how you structure your f-commerce store, the user will still be subjected to targeted Facebook ads during the buying process.

Going further, many Web marketers question the social nature of shopping itself. There is a widespread belief that people visit Facebook to catch up with their friends, not to be sold products. However, a J. Walter Thompson study reported that 48 percent of millennials (aged 20 to 33) would like the places where they shop to give them the ability to buy directly on Facebook.

In January 2012, P&G announced that the company was scaling back its $10 billion annual ad budget (primarily in traditional media) to take advantage of free impressions offered by Facebook in the form of Likes and status updates. Several months later, General Motors canceled its entire $10 million Facebook ad budget. The companies made these decisions for different reasons: GM was not convinced that Facebook ads are effective, and P&G was looking for free media advertising efficiencies.

Some industry analysts contend that advertising on Facebook is not as effective for some advertisers as advertising on search engine Web sites. Their reasoning is that people searching for information on purchase decisions are better targets for ads than are people checking out messages from friends. They also argue that advertising on Facebook is problematic because it interrupts personal conversations with impersonal branding.

WordStream (www.wordstream.com), a search marketing management company, compared advertising on Google with advertising on Facebook. WordStream's findings suggest that Facebook is a much less effective ad medium than Google. Let's take a look at the findings.

Total Reach
Facebook: 51 percent of all Internet users
Google: 90 percent of all Internet users

Fourth Quarter Revenues, 2012
Facebook: $5 billion
Google: $14 billion

Click-Through Rates
Facebook: 0.051 percent
Google: 0.4 percent
Average: 0.1 percent

The click-through rate of an advertisement is the number of clicks on an ad divided by the number of times the ad is shown, expressed as a percentage. The average click-through rate for an ad on the Internet is 0.1 percent. That is, an ad that appears 10,000 times on the Internet would be clicked on 10 times. An ad that is shown 10,000 times on Facebook would be clicked on 5 times. In contrast, if the same ad were displayed 10,000 times on Google, it would be clicked on 40 times. Thus, Google ads receive 8 times as many clicks as ads on Facebook, which represents a significant competitive advantage.

Regardless of the pros and cons of f-commerce, however, modern businesses must acknowledge one overwhelming fact: Facebook is where the customers are, and they should be able to buy wherever and whenever they like. Today, almost 70 percent of companies conduct transactions on or through Facebook.

Sources: Compiled from P. Rooke, "Why Is Facebook's E-Commerce Offering So Disappointing?" *GigaOM.com*, February 17, 2013; J. Edwards, "Facebook Is Building a Mobile E-Commerce Platform—And Advertisers Who've Seen It Love It," *Business Insider*, January 30, 2013; O. St. John, "Facebook Commerce a Hit with Small Retailers," *USA Today*, September 24, 2012; H. Elliott, "GM Retools: Goodbye Facebook, Hello Manchester United," *Forbes*, May 31, 2012; J. Edwards, "Here's the Real Reason GM Pulled $10 Million in Ads from Facebook," *Business Insider*, May 29, 2012; J. Edwards, "Facebook's Worst Nightmare: After GM, Here's How the Other Dominoes Could Fall," *Business Insider*, May 15, 2012; J. Edwards, "Data: Google Totally Blows Away Facebook on Ad Performance," *Business Insider*, May 15, 2012; J. Corpus, "F-Commerce for Hollywood: Turning Fans into Customers," *Forbes*, September 19, 2011; J. Ente, "The Beginner's Guide to Facebook Commerce,"

Mashable, July 14, 2011; E. Savitz, "Attention Facebook Shoppers: Get Ready for F-Commerce," *Forbes*, June 27, 2011; J. Hird, "101 Examples of F-Commerce," *EConsultancy*, May 19, 2011; J. Diner, "F-Commerce, the Arrival of the Facebook Consumer," *ClickZ.com*, May 10, 2011; www.facebook.com, accessed February 9, 2013.

Questions

1. What are the advantages for a business of conducting commerce on Facebook? The disadvantages?
2. What are the advantages for customers of conducting commerce on Facebook? The disadvantages?

What We Learned from This Case

Humans are social individuals; therefore, human behavior is innately social. Humans typically orient their behavior around other members of their community. As a result, people are sensitive to the behavior of people around them, and many of their decisions are influenced by their social context.

Traditional information systems support organizational activities and business processes and concentrate on cost reductions and productivity increases. A variation of this traditional model, **social computing**, is a type of IT that combines social behavior and information systems to create value. Social computing is focused on improving collaboration and interaction among people and on encouraging user-generated content. Significantly, in social computing, social information is not anonymous. Rather, it is important precisely because it is linked to particular individuals, who in turn are linked to their own networks of individuals.

Social computing makes socially produced information available to everyone. This information may be provided directly, as when users rate a movie (e.g., at Rotten Tomatoes), or indirectly, as with Google's PageRank algorithm, which sequences search results.

In social computing, users, rather than organizations, produce, control, use, and manage content via interactive communications and collaboration. As a result, social computing is transforming power relationships in organizations. Employees and customers are empowered by their ability to use social computing to organize themselves. Thus, social computing can influence people in power to listen to the concerns and issues of ordinary people. Organizational customers and employees are joining this social computing phenomenon, with serious consequences for most organizations.

Significantly, most governments and companies in modern developed societies are not prepared for the new social power of "ordinary people." Today, managers, executives, and government officials can no longer control the conversation around policies, products, and other issues.

In the new world of business and government, organizational leaders will have to demonstrate authenticity, even-handedness, transparency, good faith, and humility. If they do not, customers and employees may distrust them, to potentially disastrous effects. For example, customers who do not like a product or service can quickly broadcast their disapproval. Another example is that prospective employees do not have to take their employers at their word for what life is like at their companies—they can find out from people who already work there. A final example is that employees now have many more options to start their own companies, which could compete with their former companies.

As you see from these examples, the world is becoming more democratic and reflective of the will of ordinary people, enabled by the power of social computing. On the one hand, social power can help keep a company vital and can enable customers and employee activists to become a source of creativity, innovation, and new ideas that will move a company forward. On the other hand, companies that show insensitivity toward customers or employees quickly find themselves on a downward slide. Consider the following examples:

- Hershey faced public relations problems in August 2011 when 400 college students revolted, walking off their jobs. These students were hired through a foreign-exchange program sponsored by the U.S. State Department, and they did not like the stress of working in a candy-packing factory, sometimes on all-night shifts. The students, who came from

China, Nigeria, Turkey, and Ukraine, were excellent communicators, so they used You-Tube, Facebook, and other tools to bring attention to their plight.

- In 2011, Adidas came under attack in New Zealand when fans of the country's hugely popular national rugby team were outraged to learn that Adidas team jerseys were being sold for significantly higher prices in their country than in other countries. Fans discovered this information by researching product prices in New Zealand and the United States online. Armed with this information, they organized protests. Soon, national news programs picked up coverage of the protest and of Adidas's slow response to the consumer outrage. Customers started returning Adidas clothing to stores in disgust, and employees felt so threatened by the populace that they removed Adidas's logos from their company vehicles.

- In the Netherlands in 2011, a social media campaign against bankers' bonuses focused on the Amsterdam-based company ING. Bank customers began threatening en masse to withdraw deposits. In response, CEO Jan Hommen voluntarily waived his own upcoming $1.8 million bonus and then ordered all company directors to do the same.

Social computing is exploding worldwide, with China having the world's most active social media population. A McKinsey survey found that 91 percent of Chinese respondents reported that they had visited a social media site in the previous six months, compared with 70 percent in South Korea, 67 percent in the United States, and 30 percent in Japan. Interestingly, the McKinsey survey found that social media has a greater influence on purchasing decisions for Chinese consumers than for consumers anywhere else in the world.

Social computing is also increasing dramatically in Africa. Facebook in particular is growing rapidly in African countries, and it is the dominant social network in most of them. However, Facebook does have rivals in Africa, including the following:

- In South Africa, Mxit (www.mxit.com) has 10 million active users, more than double Facebook's number.
- In Ghana, a mobile social network called Saya.im (www.saya.im) gained more than 50,000 members in six weeks after the site launched.
- In Kenya, a mobile social network called iCow (www.icow.co.ke) provides farmers and other members with livestock management and other agricultural information.

Businesses today are using social computing in a variety of innovative ways, including marketing, customer relationship management, and human resource management. In fact, so many organizations are competing to use social computing in as many new ways as possible that an inclusive term for the use of social computing in business has emerged: *social commerce*. Because social computing is facilitated by Web 2.0 tools and sites, you begin this chapter by examining these technologies. You then turn your attention to a diverse number of social commerce activities, including shopping, advertising, market research, customer relationship management, and human resource management. You conclude by studying the risks and concerns associated with social computing.

When you complete this chapter, you will have a thorough understanding of social computing and the ways in which modern organizations use this technology. You will be familiar with the advantages and disadvantages of social computing as well as the risks and rewards it can bring to your organization. For example, most of you already have pages on social networking sites, so you are familiar with the positive and negative features of these sites. This chapter will enable you to apply this knowledge to your organization's efforts in the social computing arena. You will be in a position to contribute to your organization's policies on social computing. You will also be able to help your organization design its strategy to utilize social computing.

Significantly, social computing can help you start your own business. For example, many entrepreneurs have developed successful businesses on Facebook, as you see in IT's About Business 9.1.

As we noted earlier, social computing is facilitated by Web 2.0 tools and sites. In the next section, you will learn about Web 2.0 tools such as AJAX, tagging, Really Simple Syndication, blogs, microblogs, and wikis. You will also learn about two major types of Web 2.0 sites, social networking sites and mashups.

IT's [about business]

9.1 Tiger Tans and Gifts

Lisa Keiling owns a tanning salon in Wedowee, Alabama, that does very well from January through May. Unfortunately, during the rest of the year the demand for tanning beds is extremely low. In fact, the demand is so low that Lisa had to try some new strategies to bring in some income. First, she opened a small hunting/fishing shop in a room where she formerly kept a tanning bed. Even though hunting and fishing are very popular in Wedowee, that idea did not work well. Her next strategy was to sublease part of her space to a hairdresser. This idea generated a lot of extra revenue, and it became a very important part of her business. In fact, during the months when tanning was minimal, the hairdressing business became Lisa's primary source of income.

Despite the success of the hairdressing venture, however, Lisa still needed another source of revenue to make it through the slow times. After searching around for ideas for a small business, she found a machine that cut out vinyl designs that could be placed on cups, purses, bowls, plates, frames, and any other hard surface. With this machine, she could customize just about anything that she could imagine! Lisa purchased the machine and taught herself how to use it.

Once Lisa became proficient at producing vinyl designs, she needed a strategy to promote her new enterprise. She realized she needed to use the Internet, but she did not feel comfortable creating a Web site herself. However, Lisa was very familiar with Facebook. Because she had lived in the area for a long time and already had many "friends" on Facebook, the site was a natural

fit to advertise her new business. Lisa first created an account for her company. As she designed each new product, she posted a picture of it on Facebook and "liked" it herself from her personal page. Other people did the same because they liked the product. Her new creations were going viral in small-town Wedowee, and she was attracting new business!

For Lisa, the vinyl designs venture and Facebook combined to save her business during the winter months. If you visit her Facebook page, you will see that she is very active online every day. Her page made it possible for her customers to contact her and to purchase her products without having to come to her store.

Today, Lisa is exploring the option of adding a Web site to streamline the ordering process. This site would be synced with her Facebook page, and it would provide customers with a single location to place their orders. Lisa hopes that all of her efforts will continue to make her business a success. Her long-term goal is for the custom gift shop to function as her main source of income, with the tanning salon providing only supplemental income.

Sources: Compiled from authors' personal interviews with Lisa Keiling.

Questions

1. What other actions could Lisa take on Facebook to "get the word out" about her custom gifts?
2. Does Lisa really need a Web site for her business, or is her Facebook page sufficient? (Hint: Can she take orders via her Facebook page?)

9.1 Web 2.0

The World Wide Web, which you learned about in Chapter 6, first appeared in 1990. Web 1.0 was the first generation of the Web. We did not use this term in Chapter 4 because there was no need to say "Web 1.0" until Web 2.0 emerged.

The key developments of Web 1.0 were the creation of Web sites and the commercialization of the Web. Users typically had minimal interaction with Web 1.0 sites. Rather, they passively receive information from those sites.

Web 2.0 is a popular term that has proved difficult to define. According to Tim O'Reilly, a noted blogger, **Web 2.0** is a loose collection of information technologies and applications, plus the Web sites that use them. These Web sites enrich the user experience by encouraging user participation, social interaction, and collaboration. Unlike Web 1.0 sites, Web 2.0 sites are not so much online places to visit as Web locations that facilitate information sharing, user-centered design, and collaboration. Web 2.0 sites often harness collective intelligence (e.g., wikis); deliver functionality as services, rather than packaged software (e.g., Web services); and feature remixable applications and data (e.g., mashups).

In the following sections, we discuss six Web 2.0 information technology tools, which include AJAX, tagging, Really Simple Syndication, blogs, microblogs, and wikis. We then turn our attention to the two major types of Web 2.0 sites, social networking sites and mashups.

Ajax

Most Web 2.0 applications have rich, user-friendly interfaces based on AJAX. **AJAX** is a Web development technique that enables users to reload portions of Web pages with fresh data instead of having to reload the entire Web page. This process speeds up response time and increases user satisfaction.

Tagging

A **tag** is a keyword or term that describes a piece of information—for example, a blog, a picture, an article, or a video clip. Users typically choose tags that are meaningful to them. Tagging allows users to place information in multiple, overlapping associations rather than in rigid categories. For example, a photo of a car might be tagged with "Corvette," "sports car," and "Chevrolet." Tagging is the basis of *folksonomies*, which are user-generated classifications that use tags to categorize and retrieve Web pages, photos, videos, and other Web content.

One specific form of tagging, known as *geotagging*, refers to tagging information on maps. For example, Google Maps allows users to add pictures and information, such as restaurant or hotel ratings, to maps. Therefore, when users access Google Maps, their experience is enriched because they can see pictures of attractions, reviews, and things to do, posted by everyone and all related to the map location they are viewing.

Really Simple Syndication

Really Simple Syndication (RSS) is a Web 2.0 feature that allows you to receive the information you want (customized information), when you want it, without having to surf thousands of Web sites. RSS allows anyone to syndicate (publish) his or her blog, or any other content, to anyone who has an interest in subscribing to it. When changes to the content are made, subscribers receive a notification of the changes and an idea of what the new content contains. Subscribers can then click on a link that will take them to the full text of the new content.

For example, CNN.com provides RSS feeds for each of its main topic areas, such as world news, sports news, technology news, and entertainment news. NBC uses RSS feeds to allow viewers to download the most current version of shows such as *Meet the Press* and *NBC Nightly News*.

You can find thousands of Web sites that offer RSS feeds at Syndic8 (*www.syndic8.com*) and NewsIsFree (*www.newsisfree.com*). Figure 9.1 illustrates how to search an RSS and locate RSS feeds.

To use RSS, you can utilize a special newsreader that displays RSS content feeds from the Web sites you select. Many such readers are available, several of them for free. Examples are AmphetaDesk (*www.disobey.com/amphetadesk*) and Pluck (*www.pluck.com*). In addition, most browsers have built-in RSS readers. For an excellent RSS tutorial, visit *www.mnot.net/rss/tutorial*.

Blogs

A **weblog** (**blog** for short) is a personal Web site, open to the public, in which the site creator expresses his or her feelings or opinions via a series of chronological entries. *Bloggers*—people who create and maintain blogs—write stories, convey news, and provide links to other articles and Web sites that are of interest to them. The simplest method of creating a blog is to sign up with a blogging service provider, such as *www.blogger.com* (now owned by Google), *www.xanga.com* (see Figure 9.2), and *www.sixapart.com*. The **blogosphere** is the term for the millions of blogs on the Web.

Many companies listen to consumers in the blogosphere who express their views on the companies' products. Marketers refer to these views as *consumer-generated media*. For example, Nielsen (*www.nielsen-online.com*) "mines" the blogosphere to provide information for its clients in several areas. Nielsen helps clients find ways to serve potential markets, ranging from broad-based to niche markets. The company also helps clients detect false rumors before these rumors appear in the mainstream media, and it gauges the potency of a marketing push or the popularity of a new product.

Although blogs can be very useful, they also have shortcomings. Perhaps the primary value of blogs is their ability to bring current, breaking news to the public in the fastest time possible. Unfortunately, in doing so, bloggers sometimes cut corners, and their blogs can be inaccurate.

FIGURE 9.1 The Web site of National Public Radio (NPR) with RSS toolbar aggregator and search function. (Courtesy of NPR. Used with permission.)

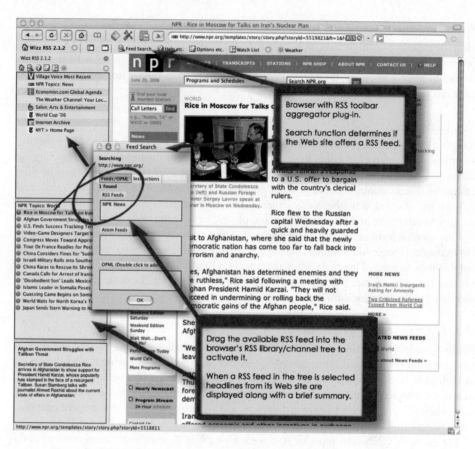

Regardless of their various problems, however, blogs have transformed the ways in which people gather and consume information.

Microblogging

Microblogging is a form of blogging that allows users to write short messages (or capture an image or embedded video) and publish them. These messages can be submitted via text messaging from mobile phones, instant messaging, e-mail, or simply over the Web. The content of a microblog differs from that of a blog because of the limited space per message (usually up to 140 characters). The most popular microblogging service is Twitter.

FIGURE 9.2 Xanga organizes blogs by common content (dating, beauty, food, and more) to help readers find multiple blogs on one Web site.

Twitter is a free microblogging service that allows its users to send messages and read other users' messages and updates, known as **tweets**. Tweets are displayed on the user's profile page and delivered to other users who have signed up to receive them.

Twitter is becoming a very useful business tool. It allows companies to quickly share information with people interested in their products, thereby creating deeper relationships with their customers. Businesses also use Twitter to gather real-time market intelligence and customer feedback. As an individual user, you can use Twitter to inform companies about your experiences with their business, offer product ideas, and learn about great offers.

It is possible to use Twitter for the wrong reasons, however. IT's About Business 9.2 illustrates how Twitter was used in the 2012 Mexican general elections.

IT's [about business]

9.2 Twitter Misuse in the Mexican Presidential Election

In Mexico's 2012 presidential campaign, the two top contenders engaged in a Twitter spam war, employing software robots (automated programs) that were designed to deliver negative tweets about opposing candidates and disrupt their social media efforts. This large-scale political spamming could foreshadow online efforts that campaigners in other countries will increasingly resort to.

One reason why Twitter was particularly prominent during this election is that Mexicans were already using Twitter as a source of information about events in northern areas of the country, where fear of violent retribution prevents news outlets from reporting about drug cartels.

In the presidential campaign, one political party in particular—the Institutional Revolutionary Party, or PRI—came under fire for unleashing tens of thousands of bots, or user accounts programmed to automatically tweet specific words and phrases. At the same time, they organized large groups of human Twitter users to simultaneously publish the same message. Their objective was to increase the likelihood that the message would land on Twitter's list of "trending" topics.

Spamming often makes use of *hashtags*—words and run-on phrases preceded by a hash sign (like #thishashtagexample). Twitter users can apply hashtags to their tweets to make them easily searchable, a strategy that has proved useful for groups like Occupy Wall Street.

The PRI's candidate, Pena Nieto, was both the target of hashtag organization and a possible beneficiary of hashtag mischief. During the spring of 2012, an anti-Pena Nieto hashtag emerged, #YoSoy132 (I am 132), after his campaign and several news outlets claimed that protesters at a campaign event at a university in Mexico City were not really students and had been planted by opposing parties. In response, 131 students who claimed to have attended the event posted a video on YouTube in which they displayed their student IDs and lashed out at the media coverage. The video launched a movement centered on the hashtag and variations of it, all of which implied that its user was the figurative 132nd protester. Before long, however, Pena Nieto supporters adopted that hashtag, and they added it to messages that praised him.

All three dominant political parties have used bots in various elections at the national and state levels in Mexico. Regardless of whether they employed bots, however, all three parties have deployed their young supporters to social networks. It is often difficult to determine whether their actions constitute honest political activism or spam.

Reports of similar politically motivated spamming have appeared in other countries, including Russia, Syria, and the United States. For example, in February 2013, U.S. Congressman Steve Stockman accused supporters of the anti-gun violence campaign of creating fake people on Twitter to post spam messages in support of stricter gun-control regulations. For its part, Twitter states clearly that spam is against its rules, citing 20 separate examples of behaviors it considers to be spamming.

In fact, Twitter engineers are trying to proactively reduce spam. For instance, Twitter collects data that could reveal malicious or abusive activity. It filed a lawsuit in the United States against five of the most aggressive spammers and providers of spamming tools. But Twitter also admits in its terms of service that ideas concerning what constitutes spamming will evolve as Twitter responds to new tricks and tactics employed by spammers.

And the results of the election? Pena Nieto won the election and became the President of Mexico.

Sources: Compiled from M. Weisbrot, "Irregularities Reveal Mexico's Election Far From Fair," *Common Dreams* (commondreams.org), March 19, 2013; R. Griffith, "The Dark Side of Twitter," *The Potomac Institute Cyber Center*, July 11, 2012; B. Gottlieb, "Mexico Elections: Reactions to Pena Nieto's Victory," *The Washington Post*, July 2, 2012; N. Flannery, "Mexico Journal: Twitter, Televisa, and the 2012 Election," *Forbes*, June 30, 2012; M. Orcutt, "Twitter Mischief Plagues Mexico's Election," *MIT Technology Review*, June 21, 2012; "#YoSoy132: Mexican Elections, Media, and Immigration," *The Huffington Post*, June 7, 2012; N. Flannery, "Twittocracy: Will Twitter and Social Media Change the Outcome of Mexico's Election?" *Forbes*, May 3, 2012;

Questions

1. Was Twitter really misused in the Mexican general election? Or, was the use of Twitter a legitimate campaign tactic? Support your answer.
2. Describe how any political campaigns could use Twitter to monitor the progress of the campaign. (Hint: Consider polling.)

Wikis

A **wiki** is a Web site made up entirely of content posted by users. Wikis have an "edit" link on each page that allows any user to add, change, or delete material, thus fostering easy collaboration.

Wikis take advantage of the combined input of many individuals. Consider Wikipedia (*www .wikipedia.org*), an online encyclopedia that is the largest existing wiki. Wikipedia contains more than 3.4 million articles in English, which get a combined total of nearly 500 million views every day. Wikipedia relies on volunteer administrators who enforce a neutral point of view, and it encourages users to delete copy that displays a clear bias. Nevertheless, there are still major debates over the reliability and accuracy of Wikipedia articles. Many educators will not allow students to cite references from Wikipedia because Wikipedia content is of uncertain origin. Moreover, Wikipedia does not provide any quality assessment or fact checking by experts. Therefore, academics and others still have major concerns about the accuracy of user-provided content.

Organizations use wikis in several ways. In project management, for example, wikis provide a central repository for capturing constantly updated product features and specifications, tracking issues, resolving problems, and maintaining project histories. In addition, wikis enable companies to collaborate with customers, suppliers, and other business partners on projects. Wikis are also valuable in knowledge management. For example, companies use wikis to keep enterprisewide documents, such as guidelines and frequently asked questions, accurate and current.

Social Networking Web Sites

A **social network** is a social structure composed of individuals, groups, or organizations linked by values, visions, ideas, financial exchange, friendship, kinship, conflict, or trade. **Social networking** refers to activities performed using social software tools (e.g., blogging) or social networking features (e.g., media sharing).

A social network can be described as a map of all relevant links or connections among the network's members. For each individual member that map is his or her **social graph**. Mark Zuckerberg of Facebook originally coined this term to refer to the social network of relationships among users of Facebook. The idea was that Facebook would take advantage of relationships among individuals to offer a richer online experience.

Social networks can also be used to determine the social capital of individual participants. **Social capital** refers to the number of connections a person has within and between social networks.

Participants congregate on *social networking Web sites* where they can create their own profile page for free and on which they can write blogs and wikis; post pictures, videos, or music; share ideas; and link to other Web locations they find interesting. Social networkers chat using instant messaging and Twitter, and they tag posted content with their own keywords, making content searchable and facilitating interactions and transactions. Social networkers converse, collaborate, and share opinions, experiences, knowledge, insights, and perceptions with one another. They also use these Web sites to find like-minded people online, either to pursue an interest or a goal or just to establish a sense of community among people who may never meet in the real world.

Table 9.1 shows the variety of online social networking platforms. Social networking Web sites allow users to upload their content to the Web in the form of text, voice, images, and videos.

Table 9.1
Categories of Social Networking Web Sites

Socially oriented: Socially focused public sites, open to anyone
- Facebook (*www.facebook.com*)
- Google Orkut (*www.orkut.com*)
- Google1 (*https://plus.google.com*)
- Hi5 (*www.hi5.com*)

Professional networking: Focused on networking for business professionals
- LinkedIn (*www.linkedin.com*)

Table
9.1 (continued)

Media sharing

- *Netcasting* includes podcasting (audio) and videocasting (audio and video). For example, educational institutions use netcasts to provide students with access to lectures, lab demonstrations, and sports events. In 2007, Apple launched iTunes U, which offers free content provided by major U.S. universities such as Stanford and MIT.
- *Web 2.0 media* sites allow people to come together and share user-generated digital media, such as pictures, audio, and video.
  - Video (Amazon Video on Demand, YouTube, Hulu, Facebook)
  - Music (Amazon MP3, Last.fm, Rhapsody, Pandora, Facebook, iTunes)
  - Photographs (Photobucket, Flickr, Shutterfly, Picasa, Facebook)

Communication

- *Blogs*: Blogger, LiveJournal, Open Diary, TypePad, WordPress, Vox, Expression Engine, Xanga
- *Microblogging/Presence applications*: Twitter, Plurk, Tumblr, Yammer, Qaiku

Collaboration: Wikis (Wikimedia, PBworks, Wetpaint)

Social bookmarking (or *social tagging*): Focused on helping users store, organize, search, and manage bookmarks of Web pages on the Internet

- Delicious (*www.delicious.com*)
- StumbleUpon (*www.stumbleupon.com*)
- Google Reader (*http://reader.google.com*)
- CiteULike (*www.citeulike.com*)

Social news: Focused on user-posted news stories that are ranked by popularity based on user voting

- Digg (*www.digg.com*)
- Chime.in (*http://chime.in*)
- Reddit (*www.reddit.com*)

Events: Focused on alerts for relevant events, people you know nearby, etc.

- Eventful (*www.eventful.com*)
- Meetup (*www.meetup.com*)
- Foursquare (*www.foursquare.com*)

Virtual meeting place: Sites that are essentially three-dimensional worlds, built and owned by the residents (the users)

- Second Life (*www.secondlife.com*)

Interesting New Social Networks

- Empire Avenue (*www.empireavenue.com*) is a social exchange network where members invest virtual currency in people and brands that interest them.
- Color (*www.color.com*) is a free mobile app that creates an instant social network based on users' locations and proximity to others. Users can instantly share images, videos, and text conversations with others nearby.
- Foursquare (*http://foursquare.com*) is a location-based mobile service that enables participants to share their location with friends by checking in via a smartphone app.
- Hunch (*www.hunch.com*) maps people's interests by asking them a series of questions. The site creates a "taste graph," which tracks everything that a user likes and dislikes.

Online Marketplaces for Microjobs

- For example, TaskRabbit (*www.taskrabbit.com*) and Zaarly (*www.zaarly.com*) enable people to farm out chores to a growing number of temporary personal assistants. Thousands of unemployed or underemployed workers use these sites. The part-time or full-time tasks are especially popular with stay-at-home moms, retirees, and students. Workers choose their jobs and negotiate their own rates.

Enterprise Social Networks

Business-oriented social networks can be public, such as LinkedIn.com. As such, they are owned and managed by an independent company.

However, an increasing number of companies have created in-house, private social networks for their employees, former employees, business partners, and/or customers. Such networks are "behind the firewall" and are often referred to as *corporate social networks*. Employees utilize these networks to create connections that allow them to establish virtual teams, bring new employees up to speed, improve collaboration, and increase employee retention by creating a sense of community. Employees are able to interact with their coworkers on a level that is typically absent in large organizations or in situations where people work remotely.

Corporate social networks are used for many processes, including

- Networking and community building, both inside and outside an organization
- *Social collaboration*: collaborative work and problem solving using wikis, blogs, instant messaging, collaborative office, and other special-purpose Web-based collaboration platforms; for example, see Laboranova (*www.laboranova.com*)
- *Social publishing*: employees and others creating either individually or collaboratively, and posting contents—photos, videos, presentation slides, and documents—into a member's or a community's accessible-content repository such as YouTube, Flickr, SlideShare, and DocStoc
- Social views and feedback
- *Social intelligence and social analytics*: monitoring, analyzing, and interpreting conversations, interactions, and associations among people, topics, and ideas to gain insights. Social intelligence is useful for examining relationships and work patterns of individuals and groups and for discovering people and expertise

Take IBM as an example. With more than 426,000 employees dispersed across 170 countries, more than 100,000 contractors, and a broad range of business partners and customers, IBM has no choice but to be a social business. In fact, IBM has become the largest corporate consumer of social technologies. On any given day, 50 percent of IBMers regularly work away from traditional IBM offices. Some of them work at home, while others are mobile workers.

To enable its social networking, IBM has deployed Social Blue (formerly Beehive), an internal social networking site that provides IBM employees with a rich connection to the people they work with on both a personal and a professional level. Social Blue helps employees make new connections, track current friends and coworkers, and renew contacts with people they have worked with in the past. When employees join Social Blue, they are assigned a profile page. They can then use the status message field and the free-form "About Me" section of this page to let other people at IBM know where they are and what they are doing.

Employees can also use Social Blue to post photos, create lists, and organize events. If users are hosting an event, they can create an event page in Social Blue and invite people to attend.

Another benefit of Social Blue is that employees can use it to create top-five lists, called "hive fives," to share their thoughts on any business-related topic they are passionate about. Social Blue also helps employees prepare for conference calls. If users do not know the other participants, they can check out their Social Blue profiles before the call and find out if they have common interests, either work related or recreational, or colleagues.

In addition to social goals, the Social Blue team created the site to help IBM employees meet the challenge of building relationships that are vital to working in large, distributed enterprises. Social Blue helps project leaders find people with the necessary skills for their projects.

Mashups

A **mashup** is a Web site that takes different content from a number of other Web sites and mixes them together to create a new kind of content. The launch of Google Maps is credited with providing the start for mashups. A user can take a map from Google, add his or her data, and then display a map mashup on his or her Web site that plots crime scenes, cars for sale, or anything else (see Figure 9.3).

FIGURE 9.3 Google Maps (*www.googlemaps.com*) is a classic example of a mashup. In this case, Google Maps is pulling in information from public transportation Web sites to provide the customer with transit directions.

There are many examples of mashups (for a complete list of mashups, see *www.program-mableweb.com*):

- Craigslist developed a dynamic map of all available apartments in the United States that are listed on their Web site (*www.housingmaps.com*).
- Everyblock.com is a mashup of Web services that integrates content from newspapers, blogs, and government databases to inform citizens of cities such as Chicago, New York, and Seattle about what is happening in their neighborhoods. This information includes criminal activities, restaurant inspections, and local photos posted on Flickr.

before you go on...

1. Differentiate between blogs and wikis.
2. Differentiate between social networking Web sites and corporate social networks.

Fundamentals of Social Computing in Business

9.2

Social computing in business, or social commerce, refers to the delivery of electronic commerce activities and transactions through social computing. Social commerce also supports social interactions and user contributions, allowing customers to participate actively in the marketing and selling of products and services in online marketplaces and communities. With social commerce, individuals can collaborate online, obtain advice from trusted individuals, and find and purchase goods and services. Below we list a few examples of social commerce:

- Disney allows people to book tickets on Facebook without leaving the social network.
- PepsiCo gives a live notification when its customers are close to physical stores (grocery, restaurants, gas stations) that sell Pepsi products. The company then uses Foursquare to send them coupons and discount information.

Table

9.2

Potential Benefits of Social Commerce

Benefits to Customers

- Better and faster vendor responses to complaints, because customers can air their complaints in public (on Twitter, Facebook, and YouTube)
- Customers can assist other customers (e.g., in online forums)
- Customers' expectations can be met more fully and quickly
- Customers can easily search, link, chat, and buy while staying on a social network's page

Benefits to Businesses

- Can test new products and ideas quickly and inexpensively
- Learn a lot about their customers
- Identify problems quickly and alleviate customer anger
- Learn about customers' experiences via rapid feedback
- Increase sales when customers discuss products positively on social networking site
- Create better marketing campaigns and brand awareness
- Use low-cost user-generated content, for example, in marketing campaigns
- Get free advertising through viral marketing
- Identify influential brand advocates and reward them

- Mountain Dew attracts video game lovers and sports enthusiasts via Dewmocracy contests (discussed later in the chapter). The company also encourages the most dedicated community members to contribute ideas on company products.
- Levi's advertises on Facebook by enabling consumers to populate a "shopping cart" based on what their friends think they would like.
- Wendy's uses Facebook and Twitter to award $50 gift cards to people who submit the funniest and quirkiest responses to various challenges.

Social commerce offers numerous benefits to both customers and vendors, as described in Table 9.2.

Despite all of its benefits, social computing does involve risks. It is problematic, for example, to advertise a product, brand, or company on social computing Web sites where content is user generated and is not edited or filtered. Companies that employ this strategy must be willing to accept negative reviews and feedback. Of course, negative feedback can be some of the most valuable information that a company receives, if it utilizes this information properly.

Companies that engage in social computing are always concerned with negative posts. For example, when a company creates a Facebook business page, by default the site allows other members of the Web site—potentially including disgruntled customers or unethical competitors—to post notes on the firm's Facebook Wall and to comment on what the firm has posted.

Going further, if the company turns off the feature that lets other users write on its Wall, people may wonder what the company is afraid of. The company will also be eliminating its opportunity to engage in great customer conversations, particularly conversations that could market the firm's products and services better than the company could do itself. Similarly, the company could delete posts. However, that policy only encourages the post author to scream even louder about being censored.

Another risk is the 20–80 rule of thumb, which posits that a minority of individuals (20 percent) contribute most of the content (80 percent) to blogs, wikis, social computing Web sites, etc. For example, in an analysis of thousands of submissions to the news voting site Digg over a three-week time frame, the *Wall Street Journal* reported that roughly 33 percent of the stories that made it to Digg's homepage were submitted by 30 contributors (out of 900,000 registered members).

Other risks of social computing include the following:

- Information security concerns
- Invasion of privacy

- Violation of intellectual property and copyright
- Employees' reluctance to participate
- Data leakage of personal information or corporate strategic information
- Poor or biased quality of users' generated content
- Cyberbullying/cyberstalking and employee harassment

Consider Rosetta Stone (*www.rosettastone.com*), which produces software for language translation. To obtain the maximum possible mileage out of social computing, Rosetta Stone implemented a strategy to control its customer interaction on Facebook. The strategy involves both human intervention and software to help monitor the firm's Facebook presence. Specifically, the software helps to monitor Wall posts and respond to them constructively.

Fans of facebook.com/Rosetta Stone who post questions on its Wall are likely to receive a prompt answer because the Facebook page is integrated with customer service software from Parature (*www.parature.com*). The software scans Wall posts and flags those posts that require a company response, as opposed to those in which fans of the company are talking among themselves. Rosetta Stone customer service representatives are also able to post responses to the Wall that are logged in the Parature issue tracking database.

Companies are engaged in many types of social commerce activities, including shopping, advertising, market research, customer relationship management, and human resource management. In the next sections of this chapter, you will learn about each social commerce activity.

before you go on...

1. Briefly describe the benefits of social commerce to customers.
2. Briefly describe the risks of social commerce to businesses.

Social Computing in Business: Shopping

9.3

Social shopping is a method of electronic commerce that takes all of the key aspects of social networks—friends, groups, voting, comments, discussions, reviews, etc.—and focuses them on shopping. Social shopping helps shoppers connect with one another based on tastes, location, age, gender, and other selected attributes.

The nature of shopping is changing, especially shopping for brand-name clothes and related items. For example, popular brands such as Gap, Shopbop, InStyle, and Lisa Klein are joining communities on Stylehive (*www.stylehive.com*) to help promote the season's latest fashion collections. Shoppers are using sites like ThisNext (*www.thisnext.com*) to create profiles and blogs about their favorite products in social communities. Shoppers can tag each item, so that all items become searchable. Moreover, searching within these Web sites can yield results targeted specifically to individual customers.

There are several methods to shop socially. You will learn about each of them in the next section.

Ratings, Reviews, and Recommendations

Prior to making a purchase, customers typically collect information such as what brand to buy, from which vendor, and at what price. Online customers do this by using shopping aids such as comparison agents and by visiting Web sites such as Epinions (*www.epinions.com*). Today, customers also use social networking to guide their purchase decisions. They are increasingly utilizing ratings, reviews, and recommendations from friends, fans, followers, and experienced customers.

Ratings, reviews, and recommendations are usually available in social shopping. In addition to seeing what is already posted, shoppers have an opportunity to contribute their own ratings

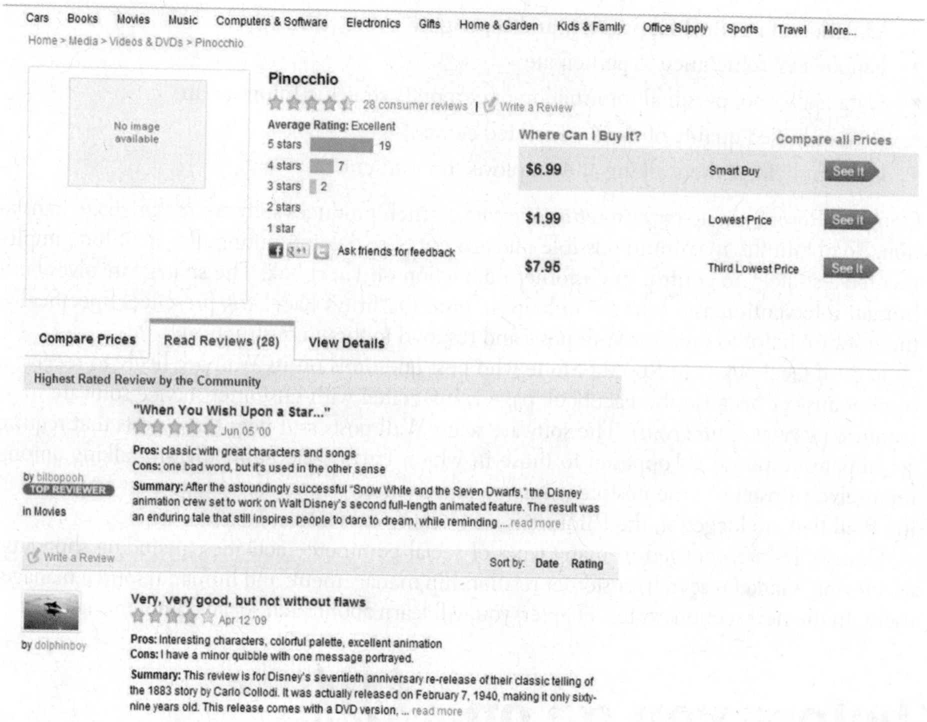

FIGURE 9.4 Epinions (*www
.epinions.com*) is a Web site that
allows customers to rate anything
from cars to music. In this
screenshot, customers review a
popular children's film.

FIGURE 9.4 Epinions (*www .epinions.com*) is a Web site that allows customers to rate anything from cars to music. In this screenshot, customers review a popular children's film.

and reviews and to discuss rating and reviews posted by other shoppers (see Figure 9.4). The ratings and reviews come from the following sources:

- *Customer ratings and reviews*: integrated into the vendor's Web page, a social network page, a customer review site, or in customer feeds (e.g., Amazon, iTunes, Buzzillions, Epinions).
- *Expert ratings and reviews*: views from an independent authority (e.g., see Metacritic).
- *Sponsored reviews*: paid-for reviews (e.g., SponsoredReviews, PayPerPost).
- *Conversational marketing*: individuals converse via e-mail, blog, live chat, discussion groups, and tweets. Monitoring these conversations yields rich data for market research and customer service.

For example, Maui Jim (*www.mauijim.com*), the sunglass company, used favorable word-of-mouth marketing as a key sales driver. The company uses Bazaarvoice's Ratings & Reviews to allow customers to contribute 5-point ratings and authentic product reviews on the company's entire line of sunglasses and accessories. In effect, Maui Jim extended customers' word-of-mouth reviews across the Web.

Maui Jim encourages its customers to share their candid opinions on the style, fit, and performance of all of its sunglass models. To accomplish this goal, the company integrates customer reviews into its Web site search function to ensure that shoppers who are interested in a particular product will see that product's rating in the search results. Customer response to this rating system has been overwhelmingly positive.

Social recommendation Web sites such as ShopSocially (*www.shopsocially.com*), Blippy (*www.blippy.com*), and Swipely (*www.swipely.com*) encourage conversations about purchases. The product recommendations are submitted by users' friends and acquaintances and arguably are more trustworthy than reviews posted by strangers.

ThisNext (*www.thisnext.com*) is a Web site where people recommend their favorite products to others. The site blends two powerful elements of real-world shopping: word-of-mouth recommendations from trusted sources and the ability to browse products in a way that naturally leads to discovery. IT's About Business 9.3 discusses a similar Web site, Pinterest (*www.pinterest.com*), in detail.

IT's [about business]

9.3 Pinterest

Social networks originated with blogging tools such as Blogger and WordPress, where users had to write an entire blog post to express themselves. Then Twitter and Facebook emerged, and a simple status update was all that was required to share a thought on the Web. These Web sites subsequently discovered even simpler ways to share opinions—for example, retweeting the updates of other users and "liking" Web pages on Facebook. Tumblr, now one of the largest blogging platforms, also fits this trend. Tumblr allows users to share images and to realign other people's posts.

Today, social sharing involves less effort, and it is more visual: "People-centric" recommendations are being augmented by "topic-centric" networks. Whereas Facebook lets users explore the Web through information shared by friends, newer social networks organize content by topics of interest.

Flipboard (*http://flipboard.com*) is an example of these trends. This network organizes content both by topics and by the "stuff" your friends enjoy. Flipboard turns the news into a more visual experience on your iPad, personalizing your experience by highlighting links shared by your online connections as well as topics that you find interesting.

Pinterest (*www.pinterest.com*) is a visual social network that organizes images by topic and allows users to reshare images with just one click. It also enables users to create online scrapbooks to share images of projects or products. The site is a kind of visual bulletin—or inspiration—board. Users, who currently must request an invitation to join Pinterest, create pinboards with categories like "Books I Love" or "Beautiful Places" or "Products That Save Me Time." Users can then link images from Web sites (using a Pinterest browser bookmark) or upload images from their computers and "pin" the images to the boards. As with Twitter, users can follow other users, and Pinterest images can be repinned and shared.

Pinterest has a devoted base of users—most of them female—who enjoy "pinning" items they find around the Web. Although clothing, home decor, and recipes dominate the site, inspirational quotes and humor are also popular topics.

According to comScore, unique visitors to Pinterest increased 400 percent from September 2011 to December 2011. In January 2013, Pinterest attracted more than 12 million visitors. Further, the following month Pinterest drove more visitors to third-party Web sites than Google, YouTube, and LinkedIn combined.

Despite its popularity, however, Pinterest is experiencing one major problem; namely, the site has no clearly defined strategy to make money. This situation is not unusual for an Internet startup.

After watching the growth of Facebook and Twitter—both of which grew quickly at first without employing a traditional business model—Pinterest cofounder Ben Silbermann is following the same path, and he plans to worry about money-making details later.

Historically, generating revenue from social networking sites, which are usually free to users, has been a challenge. Two options for Pinterest to consider are selling targeted advertising and selling data on users' interests. Neither option is original, and both run the risk of alienating Pinterest users.

Meanwhile, retailers are looking to piggyback off the popularity of Pinterest. For example, Bergdorf Goodman, a unit of the Neiman Marcus Group, is striving to develop a following for its high-end clothing and accessories on Pinterest. Similarly, Lands' End Canvas added a widget to its product pages, making it easier for users to immediately pin or repost images to their Pinterest profiles.

Etsy.com, an online crafts marketplace with more than 50,000 Pinterest followers, is using Pinterest's price display feature. When Pinterest users pin, for example, an Etsy chair on a board for their followers to see, the image of the chair will automatically include the chair's title and a banner displaying the price.

Pinterest has also been helpful to small businesses. Consider The Wedding Chicks (*www.weddingchicks.com*), a relatively new online retailer of wedding-party gifts. The company claims that Pinterest brings more than double the traffic to its Web site than Facebook and Twitter do, combined.

Sources: Compiled from T. Conneally, "Monetizing Pinterest? Pinbooster Has It Covered," *Forbes*, February 2013; T. Wilms, "The Interest in Pinterest: The Ten Things We Love (and Hate)," *Forbes*, August 13, 2012; A. Pragnell, "Why Pinterest Could Be the Next Social Media Giant," *Forbes*, July 2, 2012; K. Bischoff, "Winning the Mommy Market—Our StumbleUpon vs. Pinterest vs. Facebook Experiment," *Forbes*, March 8, 2012; D. Donston-Miller, "Pinterest: Why Your Company Should Take an Interest," *InformationWeek*, March 6, 2012; T. Watson, "Pinterest and the Hype Factor," *Forbes*, February 24, 2012; S. Needleman, "Start-Ups Follow Pinterest's Lead," *The Wall Street Journal*, February 23, 2012; S. Needleman and P. Tam, "The Rite of Web Passage—Huge Traffic, No Revenue," *The Wall Street Journal*, February 16, 2012; P. Cashmore, "Why Pinterest Is 2012's Hottest Website," *CNN Tech*, February 6, 2012; *www.pinterest.com*, accessed March 7, 2012.

Questions

1. Describe two other ways in which Pinterest could generate revenue without alienating its users.
2. Are Facebook and Pinterest competitors? Why or why not? Support your answer.

Group Shopping

Group shopping Web sites such as Groupon (*www.groupon.com*) and LivingSocial (*www.livingsocial.com*, see Figure 9.5) offer major discounts or special deals during a short time frame. Group buying is closely associated with special deals (flash sales).

FIGURE 9.5 LivingSocial (www.livingsocial.com) is a popular example of a group shopping Web site.

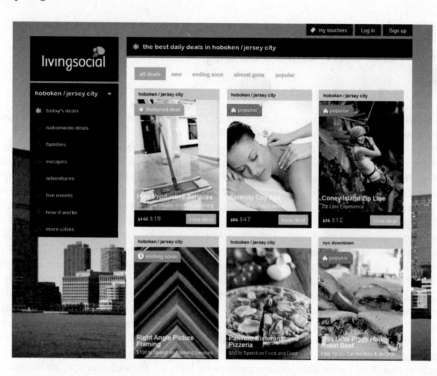

People who sign up with LivingSocial receive e-mails that offer deals at, for example, a restaurant, a spa, or an event in a given city. They can click on either "today's deal" or "past deal" (some past deals can still be active). They can also click on an icon and receive the deal the next day. Customers who purchase a deal receive a unique link to share with their friends. If a customer convinces three or more people to buy that specific deal using his or her link, then the customer's deal is free.

Vinobest is a French wine merchant that uses Facebook for group-buying and flash deals. The company offers opinions by oenologists (wine experts) and selections by sommeliers (wine stewards) for group-buying deals. Vinobest offers active pricing—the more people who buy, the cheaper the wine.

Individuals can also shop together virtually in real time. In this process, shoppers log on to a Web site and then contact their friends and family. Everyone then shops online at the same time. Some real-time shopping providers, such as DoTogether (*www.dotogether.com*) and Wet Seal (*www.wetseal.com*), have integrated their shopping service directly into Facebook. Customers log in to Facebook, install the firm's app, and invite their friends to join them on a virtual retail shopping experience.

Shopping Communities and Clubs

Shopping clubs host sales for their members that last just a few days and usually feature luxury brands at heavily discounted prices. Club organizers host three to seven sales per day, usually via e-mail messages that entice club members to shop at more than 70 percent off retail—but quickly, before supplies run out.

Luxury brands effectively partner with online shopping clubs to dispose of special-run, sample, overstock, or liquidation goods. These clubs are rather exclusive, which prevents the brands' images from being diminished. Examples are Beyond the Rack (*www.beyondtherack. com*), Gilt Groupe (*www.gilt.com*), Rue La La (*www.ruelala.com*), and One King's Lane (*www.onekingslane.com*).

Kaboodle (*www.kaboodle.com*) is another example of a shopping community. Kaboodle is a free service that lets users collect information from the Web and store it on a Kaboodle list that they can share with other shoppers. Kaboodle simplifies shopping by making it easier for people to find items they want in a catalog and by allowing users to share recommendations

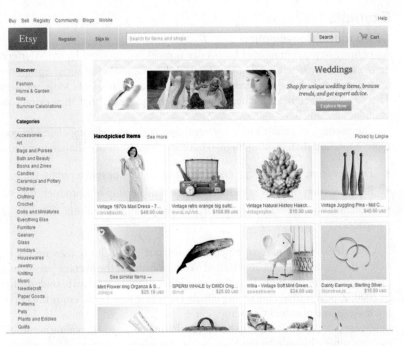

FIGURE 9.6 Etsy (*www.etsy .com*) is a social marketplace for all handmade or vintage items.

with one another using Kaboodle lists and groups. People can also use Kaboodle lists for planning vacations, sharing research for work and school, sharing favorite bands with friends, and basically everything else they might want to collect and share information about.

Social Marketplaces and Direct Sales

Social marketplaces act as online intermediaries that harness the power of social networks for introducing, buying, and selling products and services. A social marketplace helps members market their own creations (see Etsy in Figure 9.6). Other examples include the following:

- Craigslist (*www.craigslist.com*) provides online classifieds in addition to supporting social activities such as meetings and events.
- Fotolia (*www.fotolia.com*) is a social marketplace for the community of creative people who enjoy sharing, learning, and expressing themselves through images, forums, and blogs; members provide royalty-free stock images that other individuals and professionals can legally buy and share.
- Flipsy (*www.flipsy.com*) can be used by anyone to list, buy, and sell books, music, movies, and games.

Peer-to-Peer Shopping Models

Peer-to-peer shopping models are the high-tech version of old-fashioned bazaars and bartering systems. Individuals use these models to sell, buy, rent, or barter online with other individuals. For example, many Web sites have emerged to facilitate online sharing. SnapGoods created a community of people who rent goods to people in need, usually for the short term. SnapGoods helps these people connect over the Internet.

All of these peer-to-peer sites encourage **collaborative consumption**—that is, peer-to-peer sharing or renting. This trend is the result of the recession, because people had less money to spend and turned to sharing and renting. However, it has an environmentally "green" aspect as well. One of the most surprising benefits of collaborative consumption, however, turns out to be social. In an era when we may not know our neighbors that well, sharing things—even with strangers we have just met online—allows us to make meaningful connections. Some people share cars, and others invite travelers to stay in their homes for free. The following example illustrates the benefits of collaborative consumption.

Example
Collaborative Consumption

An entirely new generation of businesses is emerging, created by the intersection of the economic crisis, environmental concerns, and the maturation of social computing. These firms help interested parties share cars, clothing, couches, apartments, tools, meals, and even skills. The basic characteristic of these sharing marketplaces is that they extract value out of the "stuff" we already have.

The premise of collaborative consumption is simple: Having access to goods and skills is more important than owning them. There are three types of collaborative consumption:

- Product-service systems that enable people to share or rent a product (e.g., car sharing)
- Redistribution markets, which enable the reownership of a product (e.g., Craigslist)
- Collaborative lifestyles in which participants can share assets and skills (e.g., coworking spaces)

Consider our second-most expensive asset, our cars. (Our homes are the most expensive.) Across the United States, Canada, and Western Europe, the average person uses his or her car only 8 percent of the time. In fact, cars are the ultimate expensive, underutilized commodity. In 2000, Zipcar started convincing city dwellers that they could enjoy the perks of access without the expense of actually owning a car.

Zipcar is a U.S. membership-based car-sharing company providing automobile reservations to its members, billable by the hour or day. Members can reserve Zipcars online or by phone at any time. To access a car, members use an access card that works with the car's technology to unlock the door, where the keys are already located inside. Zipcar also offers an iPhone and Android application that allows members to honk the horn to locate a Zipcar, and unlock the doors. Zipcar charges a one-time application fee, an annual fee, and a reservation charge. Gas, parking, insurance, and maintenance are included in the price.

Competitors are emerging for Zipcar. Companies like RelayRides (*http://relayrides.com*), Zimride (*www.zimride.com*), Spride (*www.spride.com*), and Getaround (*www.getaround.com*) do not own any cars—they simply enable individuals to share them. For example, the average person who allows his or her car to be rented at RelayRides makes $250 per month. In fact, some users are making enough money on RelayRides to cover their entire car payment. Moreover, because RelayRides includes a $1 million insurance policy that covers both owners and renters during each reservation, renting from RelayRides is a low-risk arrangement.

In addition to its financial benefits, car sharing offers environmental benefits as well. When people's mobility costs shift from being fixed (ownership) to variable (renting), they make more efficient decisions about when and how frequently they actually need to drive. Research has demonstrated that the average car sharer drives 40 percent less than the average owner.

German car manufacturer Daimler is taking car sharing seriously. Its Car2Go (*www.car2go.com*) service is similar to Zipcar's, except that it does not require a reservation or a two-way trip. Car2Go's mobile app allows a person walking down a city street to locate a car on that block, access it immediately via a windshield card reader and PIN number, drive it anywhere locally, and leave it there for someone else to use. The fuel-efficient Smart car has a 100-watt solar roof, which powers the car's telematics (discussed in Chapter 8) and its battery.

Daimler is also developing an app called Car2Gether (*www.car2gether.com*), which matches local drivers with people who are looking for a ride. Riders submit a request to a driver of any type of car, and both profiles are linked to their Facebook pages and Twitter feeds. After the ride, both the driver and the rider rate each other.

Perhaps the greatest concern associated with car sharing is trust. Sharing works well only when the participants' reputations are involved. Most sharing platforms try to address this issue by creating a self-policing community. Almost all platforms require profiles of both parties, and they feature community rating systems.

Startups like TrustCloud (*http://trustcloud.com*) are endeavoring to become the portable reputation system for the Web. The company has built an algorithm that collects (if you choose to opt in) your online "data exhaust"—the trail you leave as you engage with others on Facebook,

LinkedIn, Twitter, commentary-filled sites like TripAdvisor, and others. It then calculates your reliability, consistency, and responsiveness. The result is a contextual badge that you carry to any Web site, a trust rating similar to the credit rating you have in the "offline" world.

Of course, Facebook is already collecting a huge amount of your data exhaust on its own site. Thus, Facebook could become the arbiter of online trust.

Collaborative consumption has the potential to become extremely disruptive to existing organizations. For example, if the people formerly known as "consumers" began consuming 10 percent less and sharing 10 percent more, traditional corporations would certainly see their profits decline.

Sources: Compiled from D. Brodwin, "The Rise of the Collaborative Consumption Economy," *U.S. News and World Report*, August 9, 2012; D. Sacks, "The Sharing Economy," *Fast Company*, May, 2011; www.collaborativeconsumption.com, www .car2go.com, http://trustcloud.com, accessed March 30, 2013.

Questions

1. What are some potential disadvantages of car sharing?
2. Describe how collaborative consumption can be disruptive to traditional organizations. How might the organizations respond to this challenge?

before you go on...

1. Why are ratings, reviews, and recommendations so important to potential customers?
2. Define collaborative consumption and describe how collaborative consumption is a "green" phenomenon.

Social Computing in Business: Marketing

9.4

Marketing can be defined as the process of building profitable customer relationships by creating value for customers and capturing value in return. There are many components to a marketing campaign, including (1) define your target audience; (2) develop your message (i.e., how you will solve their problem); (3) decide on how you will deliver your message (e.g., e-mail, snail mail, Web advertising, and/or social networks); and (4) follow up. Social computing is particularly useful for two marketing processes: advertising and market research.

Advertising

Social advertising refers to advertising formats that make use of the social context of the user viewing the ad. Social advertising is the first form of advertising to leverage user dynamics such as peer pressure, friend recommendations and likes, and other forms of social influence.

Many experts consider advertising to be the solution to the challenge of making money from social networking sites and social commerce sites. Advertisers have long noted the large number of visitors on social networks and the amount of time they spend there. As a result, they are willing to pay to place ads and run promotions on social networks. Advertisers now post ads on all major social networking Web sites.

Most ads in social commerce consist of branded content paid by advertisers. These ads belong to two major categories: *social advertisements* (or *social ads*) and *social apps*. Social advertisements are ads placed in paid-for media space on social media networks. Social apps are branded online applications that support social interactions and user contributions (e.g., Nike+).

Viral marketing—that is, word-of-mouth advertising—lends itself especially well to social networking. For example, Stormhoek Vineyards (*www.stormhoek.com*) initiated a marketing campaign by offering bloggers a free bottle of wine. Within six months, about 100 of these bloggers subsequently had posted voluntary comments—the majority of them positive—about the winery on their blogs. In turn, these comments were read by other bloggers.

There are other innovative ways to advertise in social media. Consider the following:

- Use a company Facebook page, including a store that attracts fans and lets them "meet" other customers. Then, advertise in your Facebook store.
- Tweet business success stories to your customers.
- Integrate ads into YouTube videos.
- Add a Facebook "Like" button with its sponsored story (advertisement) to your product. For example, Gatorade scored 1.2 million conversations in six months using their "Mission Control" campaign.
- Mercedes-Benz launched a "Tweet Race," which challenged four teams to drive across the country in Mercedes automobiles to Dallas, Texas, where the 2011 Super Bowl was being played. Each team collected Twitter followers with the help of a celebrity coach. Each tweet or retweet earned the team points, as did other activities, such as photographing other Mercedes cars during the road trip. The team that accumulated the most points by the end of the trip was declared the winner.
- Facebook has introduced a feature called the "sponsored story." When a member chats with friends and one of them indicates that he or she "checked into" a place or "liked it," say at Starbucks, a boxed "sponsored story" (an advertisement) will appear with the Starbucks logo (fee paid to Facebook). Furthermore, the name "Starbucks" will also appear in the user's news feed (another fee paid to Facebook). The users have the option to delete the boxed advertisement.

For an interesting example of aggressive social advertising, you need look no further than YouTube. IT's About Business 9.4 illustrates how YouTube is increasing its ad revenue in an incredible number of areas.

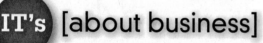

9.4 YouTube Is Redefining the Entertainment Business

When new cable channels such as CNN and ESPN emerged, they were underestimated by the traditional television networks. The question is: Can YouTube be as successful as CNN and ESPN?

YouTube (*www.youtube.com*) is utilizing its vast customer base (some 500 million viewers per month) to help define a new avenue for content creators to reach an audience. The concept is intriguing, but actually implementing the idea proved to be challenging for YouTube.

When YouTube was first created, it suffered from a reputation problem. Advertisers worried that their brands might end up next to a low-quality home video. Therefore, YouTube needed to create a business model that was unique to video. The site built a multitude of ad products that were crafted around the way people actually used the company's Web site. With the help of these new ad products, many of the activities regularly performed by YouTube users—specifically, starting their experience at the home page, searching for a video, visiting a channel, watching a movie trailer, or watching a music video—were translated into appropriate advertising opportunities. Google has predicted that by 2015 roughly 50 percent of display ads on YouTube will include video and 75 percent will have a social component.

The new ad products have begun to attract major brand advertisers to the Web site. Consider Philadelphia Cream Cheese, produced by Kraft Foods. The brand manager learned that YouTube is a haven for how-to videos about cooking. So, he came up with the "Real Women of Philadelphia" competition. On the launch day of the eight-month campaign, Kraft bought all of the advertising space on YouTube's home page, which cost more than $375,000. The ad invited women to invent Philly cream cheese recipes and cast themselves in their own videos as TV professionals. The goal was to drive viewers to Philly's Real Women community, which included Kraft's YouTube channel. More than 50 million people viewed the launch video. Ten million of them watched the entire video, and almost 100,000 clicked through to the Philly cream cheese Web site (an impressive number). In addition to the recipe views, Real Women helped boost Philly's revenue by 5 percent, the first increase in five years.

Promoted videos, which are video ads featured prominently on YouTube's search-results page, share prime space with the types of content that a particular user has searched for in the past. Research studies have indicated that these ads triple brand awareness, even without further action or follow-up on the part of the viewer.

YouTube has also devised a method to overhaul the way ads are consumed and sold on its site. This process, called TrueView, offers viewers the option to skip an ad entirely, but it charges advertisers a premium if viewers choose their content and watch it the entire way through.

In 2007, YouTube launched another marketing effort, known as the Partner program, to encourage audience-attracting producers to create more and better content. Under this program, YouTube sells ads next to its videos and gives audience-attracting producers more than half the revenue. By mid-2013, YouTube had recruited more than 10,000 partners to the program. Analysts estimate that the top 300 to 400 partners earned their living from content they produced for YouTube.

In December 2011, YouTube released Personalized Channels, which tries to replicate for video the predictive experience that Pandora creates for music.

YouTube has also enjoyed great success with globally broadcast live concerts that sites such as Hulu and Netflix, which are restricted to North America, cannot match. In November 2010, just before the release of Bon Jovi's greatest-hits album and international tour, the band gave an intimate concert in a 2,100-person venue in New York's Times Square, and they streamed it live via YouTube around the world. The YouTube team globally marketed the show, and they allowed Bon Jovi to use YouTube's new moderator tool to give fans an opportunity to interact by helping to pick the concert's song list. Following this campaign, Bon Jovi's greatest-hits album debuted in the top five in more than 20 markets around the world.

In 2006, less than 20 months after YouTube was founded, Google acquired the site for $1.65 billion. Since that time, YouTube has often been referred to as "Google's folly." Despite this moniker, by mid-2012 Google had evolved into the world's largest video platform. YouTube's success is largely a product of its strategy of cultivating its vibrant community.

Google believes that YouTube is emerging as the first global TV station. Video delivered via the Internet is creating a world with hundreds of thousands of "TV channels," and YouTube is helping people build these next-generation networks. Not only has YouTube created the largest online video community in the world, it is shaping the way video is produced, distributed, and monetized.

Not surprisingly, YouTube is also realizing increasing amounts of revenue. Google does not break out specific numbers for YouTube, but financial analysts who cover the company estimate that YouTube's revenue increased from somewhere between $100 million and $250 million in 2008 to approximately $4 billion in 2013.

Despite YouTube's phenomenal growth, many critics remain skeptical of the site's business model. They contend that YouTube still needs Hollywood content if it is to compete with Hulu and Netflix. Hollywood producers, however, still view YouTube primarily as a great promotion platform rather than a home for their content.

Take a look at YouTube's initiatives to expand programming and ad formats.

YouTube Content

Original Content: YouTube shares ad revenue with top content creators.

Examples: *The Annoying Orange*, Next New Networks, Machinma, Nigahiga, *The Young Turks*

Concerts: Live streaming concerts have drawn between 5 and 10 million live views. YouTube teamed up with Vevo and American Express in 2010 for its Unstaged series.

Examples: Bon Jovi, U2, The National, Alicia Keys, Arcade Fire, John Legend & The Roots

Sports: IPL, a cricket league in India, pulled in 55 million views during its first season on YouTube.

Examples: IPL and Major League Baseball

How To: YouTube has given rise to a generation of teaching stars. Michelle Phan's tutorial on Lady Gaga's "Poker Face" look has received 24 million views and paved the way for Phan's deals with Colgate, Lancome, and others.

Examples: Michelle Phan (makeup), Sal Khan (Khan Academy), ViewDo (guitar)

Movies/TV: YouTube tries to offer longer-form content not available elsewhere.

Examples: *Striker*, World Wrestling Entertainment, Sundance Film Festival, BBC Channels 4 and 5

Advertising as Content: To promote its Trivial Pursuit: Bet You Know It edition, Hasbro ads pit users against YouTube stars, generating more than 250 million views.

Examples: Kraft, Hasbro, *The Last Exorcism*

YouTube's Sources of Revenue

Home Page: The YouTube Homepage Roadblock allows brands to own the homepage for 24 hours with a 100 percent share. The homepage averages 50 million impressions and over 18 million unique daily visitors. Therefore, the home page enables brands to have a big impact on a concentrated audience.

Examples: Verizon, Hasbro, Kraft, Dreamworks, Fox

Promoted Videos: Like sponsored ads on Google, promoted videos pop up around search results. Advertisers pay only when users click "Play."

Examples: Evian, Panasonic, Stouffer's, Wrigley, Maybelline

Content ID: To avoid hosting illegally posted videos, YouTube learned how to identify them, a process called Content ID. YouTube then alerts copyright owners—including early adopter CBS—who decide whether to take down the video or sell ads against it.

Examples: CBS, Lionsgate (*Mad Men*), Sony

Click-to-Buy: Call-to-action spots with videos can transform viewers into consumers. For example, Monty Python videos directed viewers to the troupe's DVDs on Amazon, increasing sales by 23,000 percent.

Examples: Cee Lo Green (iTunes), Monty Python (Amazon)

Branded Channels: YouTube gives brands a great deal of latitude. For example, the CEO of the Visionaire Group claims that YouTube provides his company with the flexibility to engage users in a way that no other outlet does.

Examples: Lionsgate (*The Expendables*), Samsung, Tipp-Ex

Display: Google predicts that digital billboards will add more video and become more social in the next few years, eventually expanding into a $50 billion industry.

Examples: Blizzard Entertainment, HTC, Absolut, Volvo

Sources: Compiled from A. Knapp, "Indie Hip-Hop Star Destorm Power on YouTube and the Future of Music," *Forbes*, March 1, 2012; H. Shaughnessy, "YouTube Creators and the Rise of Social Entertainment," *Forbes*, February 21, 2012; A. Knapp, "Meredith Valiando Is Bringing YouTube to Concert Halls," *Forbes*, February 18, 2012; H. Shaughnessy, "Where Is the Big Time Headed? RockStar, Comic, Actor, and the Story of the Social Brand," *Forbes*, February 1, 2012; J. Perez, "YouTube to Boost Original,

Professional Programming," *CIO*, October 29, 2011; D. Jeffrey, "Viacom Tells Court YouTube Deliberately Violated Copyrights," *Bloomberg BusinessWeek*, October 18, 2011; A. Efrati, "YouTube Goes Professional," *The Wall Street Journal*, October 4, 2011; D. Sacks, "Blown Away," *Fast Company*, February 2011; F. Gillette, "On YouTube, Seven-Figure Views, Six-Figure Paychecks," *Bloomberg BusinessWeek*, September 23, 2010; T. Claburn, "YouTube Promises 15 Minutes of Fame," *InformationWeek*, July 29, 2010; E. Williams, "The YouTube Dilemma," *Bloomberg BusinessWeek*, March 18, 2009; *www.youtube.com*, accessed March 8, 2013.

Questions
1. Describe YouTube's basic model for revenue generation.
2. If you were the CEO of a television network, how would you combat YouTube?

Market Research

Traditionally, marketing professionals used demographics compiled by market research firms as one of their primary tools to identify and target potential customers. Obtaining this information was time-consuming and costly, because marketing professionals had to ask potential customers to provide it. Today, however, members of social networks provide this information voluntarily on their pages! (Think about all the information that you provide on your favorite social networking Web sites.) Because of the open nature of social networking, merchants can easily find their customers, see what they do online, and see who their friends are.

This information provides a new opportunity to assess markets in near real time. Word of mouth has always been one of the most powerful marketing methods—more often than not, people use products that their friends like and recommend. Social media sites can provide this type of data for numerous products and services.

Companies are utilizing social computing tools to obtain feedback from customers. This trend is referred to as *conversational marketing*. These tools enable customers to supply feedback via blogs, wikis, online forums, and social networking sites. Again, customers are providing much of this feedback to companies voluntarily and for free.

Social computing not only generates faster and cheaper results than traditional focus groups, but also fosters closer customer relationships. For example, Dell Computer operates a feedback Web site called IdeaStorm that allows customers to suggest and vote on improvements in its offerings (see Figure 9.7).

Retailers are aware that customers, especially younger ones, not only want to be heard, but also want to know whether other customers agree with them. Consequently, retailers increasingly are opening up their Web sites to customers, allowing them to post product reviews, ratings, and, in some cases, photos and videos.

As a result of this strategy, customer reviews are emerging as prime locations for online shoppers to visit. Approximately one-half of consumers consult reviews before making an online purchase, and almost two-thirds are more likely to purchase from a site that offers ratings and reviews.

For example, Del Monte (*www.delmonte.com*), through its "I Love My Dog" program, gathers data from pet owners that can help shape its marketing decisions. Del Monte's private social network helps the company to make decisions about products, test-market campaigns, understand buying preferences, and generate discussions about new items and product changes.

Using social computing for market research is not restricted to businesses. Customers also enjoy the capabilities that social computing offers when they are shopping. IT's About Business 9.5 illustrates how social computing helps shoppers perform market research utilizing Cars.com to find the car they want.

Conducting Market Research Using Social Networks

Customer sentiment expressed on Twitter, Facebook, and similar sites represents an incredibly valuable source of information for companies. Customer activities on social networking sites

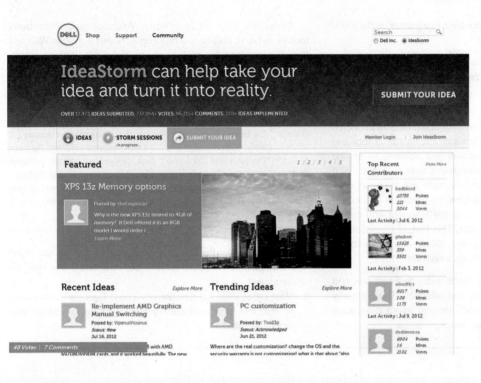

FIGURE 9.7 Customers share their ideas and feedback with Dell via IdeaStorm (*www.ideastorm.com*).

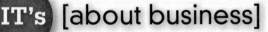

IT's [about business]

9.5 Buying a Vehicle Takes Work! MKT

With access to seemingly limitless amounts of information, American consumers can research nearly everything about automobiles, from car ratings and reviews to safety features and financing options. As a result, when they arrive at a dealership, they are better equipped to negotiate a sale than ever before.

Social media apps are helping to drive this customer empowerment, providing the most current vehicle and dealership information. Social media sites have become an integral part of the purchase process. A survey conducted by Capgemini (an international information technology consulting firm) found that the majority of respondents would be more likely to purchase a vehicle from a dealer if they found positive comments on social media sites.

Today's car dealers leverage social media (e.g., Facebook, Twitter, Tumblr, and many other sites) to build and engage communities through special promotions, coupons, and sales events. Dealers book showroom and service appointments over the Web, and they use apps like ClearMechanic, which lets dealer service operations explain repairs with photos and illustrations.

Cars.com is one of the Web sites that prospective car buyers turn to in their quest for information. Let's examine how the site uses social media to help its visitors.

Cars.com, a business unit of Classified Ventures (*www.classifiedventures.com*), serves approximately 10 million car shoppers per month. The company realizes that comparing features on different automobile models can be confusing to buyers. To make a wise buying decision, customers must compare many different types of information, including performance specifications, a variety of high-tech systems, and numerous safety features. To assist these customers, the Cars.com Web site (*www.cars.com*) integrates different types of data from different sources and presents them in a way that customers can use to shop for vehicles, compare features, read reviews, and obtain price quotes directly from dealerships.

To help customers understand and use all of the information contained on its Web site, the company is integrating Web 2.0 technology wherever it adds value and streamlines customer interactions. Cars.com is turning Web 2.0 into a competitive advantage. The company provides sophisticated Web capabilities and mobile tools that make it easier for customers to find, view, and extract the information they need to make a buying decision. Cars.com recognizes that a seamless experience on its Web site equals clicks, which in turn equals revenue. The company earns revenue from online classified ads placed by automakers, dealers, and private-party sellers. It also sells banner advertisements and provides lead-generation services.

Cars.com offers comprehensive pricing information, photo galleries, buying guides, side-by-side comparison tools, original editorial content, expert car reviews, and other relevant content from auto manufacturers. In addition, it provides user-generated content from customers themselves such as ratings of different makes and models. The company's Web site contains online portals for dealers and customers.

The company's Web site also contains many other useful tools. The following are a few examples:

- A tool focused on helping dealers list used vehicles at an optimal price when they place a classified ad.

- A tool that provides information about inventory levels, buying trends, and other factors.

- A tool that offers customers live data about incentives. When a potential buyer visits the Cars.com configuration tool and clicks through various automobiles and options, he or she sees any specific manufacturer and dealer incentives and rebates—matched to the specific vehicle and the exact configuration. This capability eliminates the problems associated with clicking to a different part of the Web site and manually searching for this information. This feature increases the "stickiness" factor of the Web site. (Stickiness refers to the amount of time a visitor spends on a Web site.)

Cars.com is also using social media such as Facebook and Twitter to further integrate content and offerings. The company wants to increase its visibility, while making information more accessible and useful to a larger audience.

Cars.com also offers iPhone, Android, and BlackBerry mobile apps. In addition, it has implemented a mobile Web site that is optimized for mobile phone browsers. Approximately 25 percent of the firm's total online traffic arrives through mobile devices.

Sources: Compiled from D. Vasquez, "How Social Media Has Changed Car Buying," *MediaLife Magazine*, February 28, 2013; "Is Social Media Changing Car Buying Decisions?" *Bloomberg BusinessWeek*, February 22, 2013; K. Casey, "Can Social Media Sell Cars?" *InformationWeek*, February 5, 2013; "The New Age Consumer," *Time*, November 5, 2012; B. Upbin, "Forbes Panel Tracks Footprints of the Elusive Customer," *Forbes*, February 7, 2012; S. Greengard, "Cars.com Drives Performance," *Baseline Magazine*, June 14, 2011; H. Elliot, "Common Car-Buying Mistakes," *Forbes*, May 9, 2011; *www.cars.com*, accessed February 22, 2013.

Questions

1. Is it possible for the Cars.com Web site to provide too much information to its customers? If so, how could this hurt the company?

2. What other Web 2.0 functionality could Cars.com include on its Web site to provide additional information for visitors who access the site?

---

generate huge amounts of data that must be analyzed, so that management can conduct better marketing campaigns and improve their product design and their service offerings. The monitoring, collection, and analysis of socially generated data and the resultant strategic decisions are combined in a process known as **social intelligence**.

An example of social intelligence is Wendy's International (www.wendys.com), which uses software to sift through the more than 500,000 customer messages the fast-food chain collects each year. Using Clarabridge (www.clarabridge.com) text analytics software, Wendy's analyzes comments from its online notes, e-mails, receipt-based surveys, and social media. Prior to adopting this software, the company used a combination of spreadsheets and keyword searches to review comments in what it describes as a slow and expensive manual approach. In contrast, the new software enables Wendy's to track customer experiences at the store level within minutes.

Social networks provide excellent sources of valuable information for market research. Here you see illustrative examples of how to use Facebook, Twitter, and LinkedIn for market research.

Using Facebook for Market Research. There are several ways to use Facebook for market research. Consider the following examples:

- Obtain feedback from your Facebook fans (and their friends if possible) on advertising campaigns, market research, etc. It is like having a free focus group.

- Test-market your messages. Provide two or three options, and ask fans which one they prefer and why.

- Use Facebook for survey invitations (i.e., to recruit participants). Essentially, turn Facebook into a giant panel, and ask users to participate in a survey. Facebook offers a self-service model for displaying ads, and these ads can be invitations to take a survey. Facebook also allows you to target your audience very specifically based on traditional demographic criteria (age, gender, etc.).

Using Twitter for Market Research. Your customers, your prospects, and industry thought leaders all use Twitter, making it a rich source of instantly updated information. Consider the following examples:

- Visit Twitter Search (*www.twitter.com/search*). Enter a company's Twitter name. Not only can you follow what companies are saying, you can also follow what everyone is saying to them. Monitoring replies to your competitors and their employees will help you develop your own Twitter strategy by enabling you to observe (a) what your competitors are doing and, more importantly, (b) what people think about it. You can also follow the company's response to this feedback.

- Take advantage of the tools that enable you to find people in the industries they operate in. Use *search.twitter.com* to monitor industry-specific keywords. Check out Twellow (*www.twellow.com*). This site automatically categorizes a Twitter user into one to three industries based on that person's bio and tweets.

- Do you want to know what topic is on most people's minds today? If so, then review the chart on TweetStats (*www.tweetstats.com*). It will show you the most frequently used words in all of Tweetdom, so you can be a part of those conversations.

- An increasing number of companies are utilizing Twitter to solicit information from customers and to interact with them. Examples are Dell (connecting with customers), JetBlue (learning about customers), Teusner Wines (gathering feedback, sharing information), and Pepsi (fast response time in dealing with complaints).

Using LinkedIn for Market Research. Post a question (e.g., solicit advice) regarding the topic or issue you are interested in. You may get a better result if you go to a specific LinkedIn group.

For example, let's take a look at how Mountain Dew uses social computing to conduct market research. The company has always appealed to consumers who were looking for high-caffeine beverages. However, the brand wanted to unite all of its customers into one community with its Dewmocracy contests, which let consumers pick the newest flavor.

Several brands have used social networks to help them choose new flavors, but Mountain Dew is expanding its scale from the most dedicated fans to the public at large. The first step of its market research involved sending seven flavors of soda to 50 Dew fanatics, who were also given cameras and told to debate and show their like or dislike for the brand on a video. The cameras were a great idea because it made the social media effort more personable. Rather than just looking at static images or tweets, Dew fans could see like-minded Dew fanatics in action. After narrowing the seven flavors to three, based in part on the videos, Mountain Dew turned to its Dew Labs Community, a 4,000-person group comprised of passionate soda fans. Those fans then created nearly every element of the three sodas, including color, name, packaging, and marketing campaigns. After that process was complete, Mountain Dew made the three flavors available in stores for a limited time, with the general public electing a winner (a drink named Voltage) via online voting. The Dewmocracy campaign utilized Facebook, Twitter, and YouTube to unite consumers through a common interest.

before you go on...

1. Is social advertising more effective than advertising without a social component? Why or why not?

2. Describe how marketing professionals use social networks to perform marketing research.

Social Computing in Business: Customer Relationship Management

9.5

The customer service profession has undergone a significant transformation, both in the ways that customer service professionals do business and in the ways that customers adapt to interacting with companies in a newly connected environment. Social computing has vastly altered both the expectations of customers and the capabilities of corporations in the area of customer relationship management.

How Social Computing Improves Customer Service

Customers are now incredibly empowered. Companies are closely monitoring social computing not only because they are mindful of the negative comments posted by social network members, but also because they perceive an opportunity to involve customers proactively to reduce problems by improved customer service.

Empowered customers know how to use the wisdom and power of crowds and communities to their benefit. These customers choose how they interact with companies and brands, and they have elevated expectations concerning their experiences with a company. They are actively involved with businesses, not just as purchasers, but also as advocates and influencers. As a result, businesses must respond to customers quickly and appropriately. Fortunately, social computing provides many opportunities for businesses to do just that, thereby giving businesses the opportunity to turn disgruntled customers into champions for the firm.

Consider the following examples:

- Qantas airlines (*www.qantas.com.au*) had a policy that required flyers to store large musical instruments in the cargo hold. Unfortunately, policy sometimes caused damage to the instruments. After suffering $1,200 in damage to his saxophone, one customer, Jamie Oehlers of Australia, organized a Facebook campaign to persuade the airline to eliminate this policy. When one person complains, he or she typically receives a nice letter, but company policy most likely will not change. When more than 8,700 people joined forces on Facebook (including members of national symphony orchestras), however, posting stories and pictures of instruments that had been damaged in the cargo hold and threatening to boycott the airline, Qantas had to listen carefully. The airline announced that they had listened to their customers and changed the policy. The new policy allows small musical instruments as carry-on baggage.

- Safeway, a large grocery chain, operates a customer club that provides members with in-store discounts. The company also sends e-mails to customers that contain coupons and a description of what is on sale as well as an online newsletter with health news and recipes, shopping tips, etc.

  To extend this service, Safeway invites you to become a Facebook fan and follow the company on Twitter. This way you will be the first to know about exclusive promotions and savings. Plus, you are able to connect and share information with other Safeway shoppers.

  You can also visit the company's blog, "Today at Safeway!" Team members post items from the floral department, the bakery department, and other departments throughout the stores. You can hear from Safeway's experts on nutrition, environmental sustainability, and more. The blog is a free vehicle that promotes active discussion among the Safeway community. Safeway moderates all communications, and it will not post any comments that contain offensive language, private or personal information, hateful or violent content, personal attacks, and self-serving promotion of goods, Web sites, or services. Also, the company asks members to post only original content.

- Best Buy is a large appliances retailer that sought to augment its in-store business by attracting online customers. The company developed a unique strategy to provide real-time customer service by utilizing its Twitter's @twelpforce account.

  Best Buy permitted the "blue shirt" members of its Geek Squad tech support service and corporate employees to staff its @twelpforce. In addition, any Best Buy employee working on company time can provide answers by using an @ reply to the customer. About 4,000 employees signed up to answer questions. By tagging their tweets with Twelpforce, these employees send their answers through the @twelpforce account. Anyone can then search the feed for topics they are researching.

- In December 2010, Groupon featured a discount to a restaurant delivery service in Tokyo for the New Year. The promotion was wildly successful, selling more than 500 "Groupons."

Unfortunately, the restaurant was not prepared for this level of success, so it was unable to accommodate all of the orders. Deliveries were late, and many of them were in terrible condition.

Andrew Mason, the CEO of Groupon, assumed responsibility for the failure. He acknowledged that he contracted to an organization that was not prepared to deal with the volume generated by the Groupon promotion. His company then refunded money to the customers who bought the coupons, and it gave away vouchers for future business. Groupon also created a video that featured a public apology about the incident. The apology was sincere and informative, explaining exactly what had happened and holding nothing back.

before you go on...

1. Discuss why social computing is so important in customer relationship management.
2. Describe how social computing improves customer service.

Social Computing in Business: Human Resource Management

9.6

Human resource (HR) departments in many organizations use social computing applications primarily in the areas of recruiting and training. For example, Deloite Touche Tohmatsu created a social network to assist its HR managers in downsizing and regrouping teams.

Recruiting

Both recruiters and job seekers are moving to online social networks as recruiting platforms. Enterprise recruiters are scanning online social networks, blogs, and other social resources to identify and find information about potential employees. If job seekers are online and active, there is a good chance that they will be seen by recruiters. In addition, on social networks there are many passive job seekers—people who are employed but would take a better job if one appeared. So, it is important that both active and passive job seekers maintain online profiles that truly reflect their background and skills. IT's About Business 9.6 takes a look at the difficulties inherent in the online recruiting process. It also provides some tips to assist you in a job search.

Training

Several companies use virtual worlds for training purposes. For example, Cisco uses its virtual campus in Second Life for product training and executive briefings. IBM runs management and customer interaction training sessions in Second Life as well.

before you go on...

1. Describe why LinkedIn has become so important in the recruiting process.
2. If you are looking for a job, what is major problem in restricting your search to social networks?

IT's [about business]

9.6 So You Want to Find a Job

The workplace you are about to enter has changed. In the past, the conventional wisdom was that companies provided a career for life. Going online to create a public profile that could win recruiters' attention would have seemed rude and risky.

Then came layoffs, mergers, and financial downturns. The average baby boomer was likely to hold 11 jobs over the course of his or her career. As a result of these developments, employees stopped feeling much loyalty to their employer of the moment. Suddenly, placing your public profile online became the smart thing to do.

Let's say you want to find a job. Like the majority of job hunters, you will probably conduct at least part of your search online, typically on job sites such as www.monster.com, www.careerbuilder.com, and www.simplyhired.com. After all, the vast majority of entry-level positions in the United States are now listed only online.

Using job sites has clear advantages for you: They are the cheapest, fastest, and most efficient way to connect employers with potential employees. Unfortunately, these sites can be overwhelmed with resumes, making it impossible for them to process these resumes efficiently and effectively. In the worst-case scenario, your resume will end up in a "black hole." For example, Starbucks attracted 7.6 million job applicants for 65,000 corporate and retail job openings, and Procter & Gamble received nearly 1 million applications for 2,000 available positions.

Luckily for you, job sites now have access to vast amounts of computing power (see cloud computing in Technology Guide 3), and they use new, more efficient search algorithms to help manage millions of resumes. In addition, you have access to many companies whose job is to assist you in your search.

On the other side of the job-search equation, employers have downsized their recruiting staffs in recent years, so they cannot keep up with the flood of applications produced by the various job sites. Some companies have attempted to replace human recruiters with software designed to sift applications; however, this process has serious downsides as well. If the company's sorting algorithm is too lax, it can yield numerous irrelevant results that waste time and money. If it is too rigid, the company can miss qualified applicants. Going further, less-qualified candidates can game the system by loading their resumes with the correct keywords that sorting programs typically search for. Finally, relying on software programs to sort applications removes any human interaction (e.g., actual human job interviews), which frequently signals a good fit between candidate and position.

In perhaps the most dramatic shift in the online employment business, job searchers are turning away from traditional job sites and toward social networks such as LinkedIn and Facebook, where many of them feel more comfortable and in control. Applicants like you have helped LinkedIn raise its market share in job search from 4.7 percent in 2010 to a projected 12.2 percent by the end of 2013. This shift explains why Simply Hired incorporated social networking into its search process, a move that enabled job seekers to integrate their networks with Simply Hired's job listings, making contacts and referrals to target companies easier.

To find a job, your best bet is to begin with LinkedIn (www.linkedin.com), which has roughly 165 million members. You should definitely have a profile on LinkedIn, which, by the way, is free. (See the end of this case for mistakes to avoid on your LinkedIn profile.)

Rather than try to obtain a few dollars here and there from individual users, LinkedIn has focused on selling a more powerful service to corporate talent scouts, namely, the company's flagship Recruiter product. Thousands of companies use the tool. In human resource departments, having your own Recruiter account is like being a bond trader with a Bloomberg terminal—it is a must-have tool.

LinkedIn's success comes from a dedication to selling services to recruiters who buy talent for a living. LinkedIn doubled its sales employees in 2012, and the company now spends 33 percent of its revenue on sales and marketing, a higher percentage than Oracle, Microsoft, Facebook, and Google. Each time LinkedIn has expanded its sales team for Recruiter and other hiring-solution products, the payoff has been rewarding.

Perhaps the fundamental reason for LinkedIn's success has been its ability to accurately identify its market segment. The company realizes that its automated approach does not lend itself well to the upper tier of the job market—for example, CEO searches—where traditional face-to-face searches continue to be the preferred strategy. At the other end of the spectrum—that is, low-paying, low-skill jobs such as cashiers and truck drivers—job boards provide faster results. LinkedIn targets the vast sweet spot between these two extremes, helping to fill high-skill jobs that pay anywhere from $50,000 to $250,000 or more per year. This is the spot you will likely be in when you graduate.

Let's take a look at a company that uses the LinkedIn Recruiter product. Adobe Systems (www.adobe.com) employs 10,000 people, and, at any time, the company will likely need to fill at least 750 openings worldwide. Traditionally, staffing agencies handled about 20 percent of Adobe's hunts for highly specialized engineers and digital experts. These search agencies were expensive, however, charging as much as $20,000 for each job they filled. Further, retention rates on their placements could be disappointing. In the past, there was no obvious alternative for Adobe to consider. Good people at other tech companies did not answer job ads. Such candidates would not switch employers unless another company found them and made them an excellent offer.

Then, a few years ago, Adobe recruiters staged a talent-scouting race. One pair of recruiters used the traditional method to locate 50 solid candidates for a technical job. Another pair used LinkedIn. The pair using LinkedIn completed the task in only hours. Weeks later, the other pair was still searching. Today, Adobe relies on search agencies for less than 2 percent of its job placements in the Americas.

LinkedIn is also invaluable in finding hidden candidates who would be overlooked in traditional searches. Consider the hiring manager for Wireless Vision, a mobile phone retailer. She was asked to find an accounting manager with entrepreneurial spirit. Regular job ads produced only 100 candidates, all of them unsuitable. So, the manager crafted a search on LinkedIn. Her target:

accountants who had worked in similar retail companies and whose profiles included keywords such as "launched," "created," and "built." Within days she had found an Avis veteran who had developed billing systems on his own. The two individuals talked, and Wireless Vision had its new accounting manager.

A number of job-search companies are competing with LinkedIn. These companies are trying to create better-targeted matching systems that leverage social networking functionality. Here are two examples:

- Beyond Credentials (www.beyondcredentials.com) uses specialized algorithms to shrink the applicant pool to a more manageable, higher-quality list by targeting young professionals with good grades from good schools. The firm also works only with employers who offer a minimum starting salary of $30,000 as well as room for advancement and working environments that Beyond Credentials staffers would want for themselves. The firm provides applicants with a personal pitch page that can even include video. Beyond Credentials charges $5,000 annually for one recruiter to use the site and $1,000 more per additional recruiter.

- Jobvite (www.jobvite.com) helps client companies by integrating social networking with the personal referrals that employers prefer. Clients' employees are allowed to send their online "friends" a "jobvite" to apply for an opening.

So, how are traditional search firms like Monster and Career-Builder responding? These two companies claim that they are no longer simply job sites. Instead, they offer an array of products, some of which include social networking features. Both companies have moved quickly to transfer their apps to mobile, which is particularly important in Asia, where job hunting is conducted on mobile phones rather than on desktop computers.

Despite these efforts, however, LinkedIn's disruptive impact on the $27 billion recruiting industry is evidenced in the declining stock prices of the recruiting sector's traditional companies. For example, the stock for Heidrick & Struggles (www.heidrick.com), a search firm that courts candidates the old-fashioned way, has lost 67 percent of its value since 2008. Monster Worldwide, which operates online job boards, has seen its stock price decline by more than 80 percent.

The bottom line for all job sites is that they do not want to produce 2,000 satisfactory candidates, but rather 20 great candidates. However, there is enormous overlap in what different sites offer, with each site borrowing from the others. By mid-2013, innovative technologies had increased job sites' revenues. Questions remain as to whether the job sites are making the process more effective for job seekers. However, career coaches offer valuable tips to help you find a job.

The most important secret to making online job-search sites work for you is to use them sparingly. When you are looking for a job, it is too easy to spend all day on your keyboard, combing through listings, trying endless search filters, and sending your resume into black holes. Job coaches advise you to spend 80 percent of your day networking and directly contacting the people in charge of jobs you want. Devote another 10 percent to head-hunters. Spend only the remaining 10 percent of your time online.

Here is how to make your time online count. To start with, as you saw above, you should have a profile on LinkedIn.

Next, access the Google-like job aggregators, such as Indeed (www.indeed.com) and Simply Hired. Both of them list millions of jobs, and they make it easy to narrow your search using filters. These filters include title, company name, location, and many others. Indeed allows you to search within a specific salary range. Simply Hired lets you sort for friendly, socially responsible, and even dog-friendly workplaces.

Both sites have advanced search options. Try plugging in the name of a company you might want to work for or an advanced degree that qualifies you for specialized work. For example, you could enter "CFA" if you are a certified financial analyst or "LEED" if you are a building engineer with expertise in environmental efficiency.

Simply Hired has a useful tool called "Who do I know." If you are on LinkedIn, this tool will instantly display your LinkedIn contacts with connections to various job listings. "Who do I know" also syncs with Facebook.

One more trick to using the aggregators: Configure them to deliver listings to your inbox. Set up an e-mail alert that delivers new job postings to you every day.

Also look for niche sites that are specific to your field. For technology-related jobs, for instance, Dice (www.dice.com) has a strong reputation. For nonprofit jobs, try Idealist (www.idealist.org). For government jobs, the U.S. government's site is an excellent resource: www.usajobs.gov.

One more great online resource is Craigslist (www.craigslist.com). It is one site the aggregators do not tap. Craigslist focuses on local listings, and it is especially useful for entry-level jobs and internships.

Beyond locating listings for specific jobs, career coaches contend that job sites can be a resource for keywords and phrases that you can pull from job descriptions and include in your resume, letters, and e-mails. Use the language from a job description in your cover letter.

Web sites like Vault (www.vault.com), Monster, and Career-Builder provide some helpful career tips. Vault, in particular, offers very useful career guides.

The bottom line: It is critical to extend most of your efforts *beyond* an online search. There is just too much competition online.

Mistakes Not To Make on Your LinkedIn Profile

- Do have a current, professional picture. (No dogs, no spouses, no babies, etc.)
- Do make sure that your LinkedIn Status is correct and current.
- Do join groups related to your field of study or even your personal interests.
- Do list an accurate skill set. Do not embellish.
- Do not use the standard connection request. Do some research on that person, and tailor your connection request to that person.
- Do not neglect LinkedIn's privacy settings. When you have a job and are looking for another one, you will want to be discreet. You can set your privacy settings so that your boss does not see that you are looking for opportunities.
- Do not skip the Summary. The Summary is a concise way of selling yourself. Write it in the first person.
- Do not eliminate past jobs or volunteer work.
- Do not say you have worked with someone when you have not.

Sources: Compiled from LearnVest, "8 Mistakes You Should Never Make on LinkedIn," *Forbes*, March 4, 2013; G. Anders, "LinkedIn's Fast-Lane Ambition: Watch These 5 Moves in 2013," *Forbes*, February 7, 2013; C. Ceniza-Levine, "What Recruiters Want from Job Seekers Today," *Forbes*, February 1, 2013; G. Anders, "The Other Social Network," *Forbes*, July 16, 2012; R. Sylvestre-Williams, "How Recruiters Use LinkedIn," *Forbes*, May 31, 2012; T. Team, "LinkedIn Looks to Hitch Ride from Mobile Ads," *Forbes*, February 14, 2012; R. Silverman, "No More Resumes, Say Some Firms," *The Wall Street Journal*, January 24, 2012; L. Weber, "Your Resume vs. Oblivion," *The Wall Street Journal*, January 24, 2012; S. Adams, "Secrets of Making the Most of Job Search Websites," *Forbes*, January 18, 2012; G. Anders, "The Rare Find," *Bloomberg BusinessWeek*, October 17–23, 2011; J. Francis, "Facebook Joins Labor Department in Online Job-Search Project," *Bloomberg BusinessWeek*, October 20, 2011; F. Russo, "The New Online Job Hunt," *Time*, October 3, 2011; S. Adams, "Unemployment: The Good News, the Bad News, and What to Do About It," *Forbes*, April 1, 2011; K. Jones, "Online Job Searches Rise as Economy Slides," *InformationWeek*, January 26, 2009; www.monster.com, www.linkedin.com, www.careerbuilder.com, www.jobvite.com, www.simplyhired.com, www.beyondcredentials.com, www.indeed.com, www.dice.com, www.idealist.org, www.usajobs.gov, www.craigslist.com, www.vault.com, accessed March 5, 2013.

Questions

1. What are the advantages of using online job sites when you look for your first job?
2. What are the disadvantages of using online job sites when you look for your first job?

What's In IT For Me?

For the Accounting Major

Audit teams use social networking technologies internally to stay in touch with team members who are working on multiple projects. These technologies serve as a common channel of communications. For example, an audit team manager can create a group, include his or her team members as subscribers, and then push information regarding projects to all members at once. Externally, these technologies are useful in interfacing with clients and other third parties for whom the firm and its staff provide services.

For the Finance Major

Many of the popular social networking sites have users who subscribe to finance-oriented subgroups. Among these groups are finance professionals who collaborate and share knowledge as well as nonfinancial professionals who are potential clients.

For the Marketing Major

Social computing tools and applications enable marketing professionals to become closer to their customers in a variety of ways, including blogs, wikis, ratings, and recommendations. Marketing professionals now receive almost real-time feedback on products.

For the Production/Operations Management Major

Social computing tools and applications allow production personnel to "enlist" business partners and customers in product development activities.

For the Human Resource Management Major

Social networks offer tremendous benefits to human resource professionals. HR personnel can perform a great deal of their recruiting activities by accessing such sites as LinkedIn. They can also check out potential new hires by accessing a large number of social networking sites. Internally, HR personnel can utilize private, internal social networks for employee expertise and experience in order to find the best person for a position or project team.

For the MIS Major

The MIS department is responsible for two aspects of social computing usage: (1) monitoring employee usage of social computing applications while at work, both time and content, and (2) developing private, internal social networks for company employees and then monitoring the content of these networks.

[Summary]

1. Describe six Web 2.0 tools and two major types of Web 2.0 sites.

AJAX is a Web development technique that enables portions of Web pages to reload with fresh data instead of requiring the entire Web page to reload.

A *tag* is a keyword or term that describes a piece of information (e.g., a blog, a picture, an article, or a video clip).

Really Simple Syndication allows you to receive the information you want (customized information), when you want it, without having to surf thousands of Web sites.

A *weblog* (*blog* for short) is a personal Web site, open to the public, in which the site creator expresses his or her feelings or opinions with a series of chronological entries.

Microblogging is a form of blogging that allows users to write short messages (or capture an image or embedded video) and publish them.

A *wiki* is a Web site on which anyone can post material and make changes to already posted material. Wikis foster easy collaboration and they harness the collective intelligence of Internet users.

Social networking Web sites allow users to upload their content to the Web in the form of text (e.g., blogs), voice (e.g., podcasts), images, and videos (e.g., videocasts).

A *mashup* is a Web site that takes different content from a number of other Web sites and mixes them together to create a new kind of content.

2. Describe the benefits and risks of social commerce to companies.

Social commerce refers to the delivery of electronic commerce activities and transactions through social computing.

Benefits of social commerce to customers include the following: better and faster vendors' response to complaints; customers can assist other customers; customers' expectations can be met more fully and quickly; customers can easily search, link, chat, and buy while staying in the social network's page.

Benefits of social commerce to vendors include the following: can test new products and ideas quickly and inexpensively; learn much about their customers; identify problems quickly and alleviate anger; learn from customers' experiences with rapid feedback; increase sales when customers discuss products positively on social networking site; create better marketing campaigns and brand awareness; use low-cost user-generated content, for example, in marketing campaigns; get free advertising through viral marketing; identify influential brand advocates and reward them.

Risks of social computing include information security concerns; invasion of privacy; violation of intellectual property and copyright; employees' reluctance to participate; data leakage of personal information or corporate strategic information; poor or biased quality of users' generated content; cyberbullying/cyberstalking and employee harassment.

3. Identify the methods used for shopping socially.

Social shopping is a method of electronic commerce that takes all of the key aspects of social networks—friends, groups, voting, comments, discussions, reviews, etc.—and focuses them on shopping.

Methods for shopping socially include what other shoppers say; group shopping; shopping communities and clubs; social marketplaces and direct sales; and peer-to-peer shopping.

4. Discuss innovative ways to use social networking sites for advertising and market research.

Social advertising represents advertising formats that employ the social context of the user viewing the ad.

Innovative ways to advertise in social media include the following: create a company Facebook page; tweet business success stories to your customers; integrate ads into You-Tube videos; add a Facebook "Like" button with its sponsored story to your product; use sponsored stories.

Using Facebook for market research: get feedback from your Facebook fans (and their friends if possible) on advertising campaigns, market research, etc.; test-market your messages; use Facebook for survey invitations.

Using Twitter for market research: use Twitter Search; use Twellow; look at the chart on TweetStats.

Using LinkedIn for market research: post a question (e.g., solicit advice) regarding the topic or issue you are interested in.

5. **Describe how social computing improves customer service.**

Customers are now incredibly empowered. Companies are closely monitoring social computing not only because they are mindful of the negative comments posted by social network members, but also because they see an opportunity to involve customers proactively to reduce problems by improved customer service.

Empowered customers know how to use the wisdom and power of crowds and communities to their benefit. These customers choose how they interact with companies and brands, and they have elevated expectations. These customers are participatory and have active involvement with businesses, not just as purchasers, but also as advocates and influencers. As a result, businesses must respond to customers quickly and accurately. Fortunately, social computing provides many opportunities for businesses to do just that, thereby giving businesses the opportunity to turn disgruntled customers into champions for the firm.

6. **Discuss different ways in which human resource managers make use of social computing.**

Recruiting: Both recruiters and job seekers are moving to online social networks as new recruiting platforms. Enterprise recruiters are scanning online social networks, blogs, and other social resources to identify and find information about potential employees. If job seekers are online and active, there is a good chance that they will be seen by recruiters. In addition, on social networks there are many passive job seekers—people who are employed but would take a better job if it appeared. So, it is important that both active and passive job seekers maintain profiles online that truly reflect them.

Training: Several companies use virtual worlds for training purposes. For example, Cisco uses its virtual campus in Second Life for product training and executive briefings. IBM runs management and customer interaction training sessions in Second Life as well.

[Chapter Glossary]

AJAX A Web development technique that allows portions of Web pages to reload with fresh data rather than requiring the entire Web page to reload.

blog (weblog) A personal Web site, open to the public, in which the site creator expresses his or her feelings or opinions with a series of chronological entries.

blogosphere The term for the millions of blogs on the Web.

collaborative consumption Peer-to-peer sharing or renting.

mashup Web site that takes different content from a number of other Web sites and mixes them together to create a new kind of content.

microblogging A form of blogging that allows users to write short messages (or capture an image or embedded video) and publish them.

Really Simple Syndication A technology that allows users to receive the information they want, when they want it, without having to surf thousands of Web sites.

social advertising Advertising formats that make use of the social context of the user viewing the ad.

social capital The number of connections a person has within and between social networks.

social commerce The delivery of electronic commerce activities and transactions through social computing.

social computing A type of information technology that combines social behavior and information systems to create value.

social graph A map of all relevant links or connections for one member of a social network.

social intelligence The monitoring, collection, and analysis of socially generated data and the resultant strategic decisions.

social marketplaces These act as online intermediaries that harness the power of social networks for introducing, buying, and selling products and services.

social network A social structure composed of individuals, groups, or organizations linked by values, visions, ideas, financial exchange, friendship, kinship, conflict, or trade.

social networking Activities performed using social software tools (e.g., blogging) or social networking features (e.g., media sharing).

social shopping A method of electronic commerce that takes all of the key aspects of social networks—friends, groups, voting, comments, discussions, reviews, etc.—and focuses them on shopping.

tag A keyword or term that describes a piece of information.

tweet Messages and updates posted by users on Twitter.

Twitter A free microblogging service that allows its users to send messages and read other users' messages and updates.

Web 2.0 A loose collection of information technologies and applications, plus the Web sites that use them.

Web 2.0 media Any Web site that provides user-generated media content and promotes tagging, rating, commenting, and other interactions among users and their media contributions.

weblog (see blog)

wiki A Web site on which anyone can post material and make changes to other material.

[Discussion Questions]

1. How would you describe Web 2.0 to someone who has not taken a course in information systems?

2. If you were the CEO of a company, would you pay attention to blogs about your company? Why or why not? If yes, would you consider some blogs to be more important or more reliable than are others? If so, which ones? How would you find blogs relating to your company?

3. Do you have a page on a social networking Web site? If yes, why? If no, what is keeping you from creating one? Is there any content that you definitely would *not* post on such a page?

4. How can an organization best employ social computing technologies and applications to benefit its business processes?

5. What factors might cause an individual, an employee, or a company to be cautious in the use of social networks?

6. Why are advertisers so interested in social networks?

7. What sorts of restrictions or guidelines should firms place on the use of social networks by employees? Are social computing sites a threat to security? Can they tarnish a firm's reputation? If so, how? Can they enhance a firm's reputation? If so, how?

8. Why are marketers so interested in social networks?

9. Why are human resource managers so interested in social networks?

[Problem-Solving Activities]

1. Enter *www.programmableweb.com* and study the various services that the Web site offers. Learn how to create mashups and then propose a mashup of your own. Present your mashup to the class.

2. Go to Amazon's Mechanical Turk Web site (*www.mturk.com*). View the available Human Intelligence Tasks (HITs). Are there any HITs that you would be interested in to make some extra money? Why or why not?

3. Access Pandora (*www.pandora.com*). Why is Pandora a social networking site?

4. Access ChatRoulette (*www.chatroulette.com*). What is interesting about this social networking site?

5. Using a search engine, look up the following:
   - *Most popular or most visited blogs*. Pick two and follow some of the posts. Why do you think these blogs are popular?
   - *Best blogs* (try *www.bloggerschoiceawards.com*). Pick two and consider why they might be the "best blogs."

6. Research how to be a successful blogger. What does it take to be a successful blogger? What time commitment might be needed? How frequently do successful bloggers post?

7. Design a mashup for your university. Include the purpose of the mashup, sources of data, and intended audience.

[Closing Case **Can Anyone Succeed with Local, Online Advertising?**]

The Problem

Local businesses buy online ads. In fact, in 2012 local businesses spent $19 billion on local advertising. Experts maintain that the local advertising business is potentially much larger, with estimates ranging from $90 billion to $130 billion. So, there is room for a great deal of growth in this area. Online businesses (e.g., Facebook, Google, Groupon, and LivingSocial), however, have traditionally not been profitable in local advertising. In addition, users of these Web sites typically access them via mobile devices, which are not "friendly" to ads. That is where Yelp (www.yelp.com) comes in.

A Potential Solution

Yelp was founded in 2004 primarily to help people connect with great local businesses. The Web site is like a large online bulletin board featuring user-generated content. The content consists of personal reviews based on experiences at local businesses. Yelp members are "in charge" as far as sharing, reviewing, and communicating is concerned. The main benefit of Yelp is the ease of communication that Yelpers experience. The site is like word-of-mouth for the digital world.

To write reviews or follow Yelp users, you must first sign up by creating a profile.

Yelp's service is free for consumers, but local businesses pay to advertise on the site and to add premium features to their Yelp pages. The founders initially focused on establishing the service in a single city, namely, San Francisco. They then replicated their success in other cities including Chicago, Boston, and New York.

Yelp differentiated itself from other social networking companies by hiring a sales force, which eventually grew to 500 people. The company adopted this strategy because they learned that small businesses depended on salespeople with whom they had developed a relationship.

Yelp established a loyal consumer following, due in large part to the fact that the company is vigilant in protecting consumers from suspect content. The company developed an automated review filter to identify suspicious content and minimize exposure to the consumers. Yelp's review algorithm assigns each establishment an average star ranking, and it filters out less-experienced contributors. The site also features a wide range of other features (lists, special offers, and events) that help people discover new businesses and communicate with one another.

Yelp then incorporated its reviews into Apple's Maps app (the one that replaced Google Maps). Consequently, the hundreds of millions of iPhone and iPad owners who use Maps are now Yelp users. Yelp's stand-alone apps, which attract 7 million users a month and are among the most popular free downloads in the Apple and Android stores, are now responsible for 40 percent of Yelp's searches.

The Results

The Yelp community has become known for sharing in-depth reviews and insights on all types of local businesses. From its modest beginnings in San Francisco, the company has mushroomed into an international phenomenon that spans 96 markets located in multiple countries. In August 2012, Yelp reported that it had 32,000 paying clients, more than double the total from the previous year. An additional 791,000 businesses had free accounts where they can post pictures and respond to users' reviews. As of March 2013, Yelp had some 84 million unique visitors to its site, and it received reviews from markets throughout the world. In total, "yelpers" have posted tens of millions of reviews.

Yelp's review algorithm has proved to be effective. In a recent study, an economist at the Harvard Business School compared Yelp ratings of restaurants in Washington State with actual sales figures reported to that state's Department of Revenue. He discovered that a one-star improvement in a business's Yelp rating was associated with, on average, a revenue increase of between 5 and 9 percent.

Perhaps surprisingly given its popularity, as of mid-2013 Yelp was not yet profitable. The company's biggest challenge is to convert more businesses into paying customers. In addition, the local advertising field is becoming competitive. Google has launched Google+ Local, a Yelp knockoff that includes links to almost every online review site except Yelp. Google also acquired Zagat, a site that has been publishing user-generated reviews in book form since the late 1970s. Not to be outdone, Facebook has launched Promoted Posts, a new advertising program that targets local businesses. In addition, it is testing a Yelp-like star-rating system.

Sources: Compiled from T. Hixon, "The Re, Reinvention of Search," *Forbes*, February 7, 2013; K. Eaton, "Yelp's Monthly Visitors Top 100 Million, But Profits Dip," *Fast Company*, February 7, 2013; A. Kanenetz, "Yelp Grades Cause New York City to Review Restaurant Health Ratings," *Fast Company*, January 25, 2013; "Yelp to Add Restaurants' Health Inspection Grades," *Associated Press*, January 27, 2013; M. Chafkin, "Not Just Another Web 2.0 Company, Yelp Basks in Its Star Power," *Fast Company*, December 2012/January 2013; Z. Gordon, "The Future of Local Online Is Commerce," *Forbes*, December 11, 2012; P. Gobry, "Now Amazon Can Easily Win the $100 Billion Local Commerce Market and the $150 Billion Smartphone Market," *Forbes*, October 27, 2012; J. Mangalindan, "How 'Local' Can Tech Get?" *Fortune*, July 27, 2011; www.yelp.com, accessed March 17, 2013.

Questions

1. What are the advantages of Yelp for local businesses? The disadvantages?
2. What are the advantages of Yelp for consumers? The disadvantages?
3. Can Yelp survive against similar offerings by Google and Facebook? Why or why not? Support your answer.

[Internship Activity]

Retail/Entertainment Industry

Social Computing has become a powerful tool used by retailers around the world. Group shopping; such as Groupon and LivingSocial offer discounts when a certain number of people purchase a given deal. This creates a bit of peer pressure when friends tell friends about a great deal that they really want and will only get if enough people will purchase it. This peer pressure can be very powerful in helping give customers incentive to open their wallets when they really did not have that particular purchase in mind.

For this Internship Activity, you will be working for Cinema 8, a local movie theatre that has recently lost ticket and concessions sales because a newer, bigger, nicer theatre has opened not far away. Hayden Blue is the Owner/Manager and your Internship Supervisor. He has a set of specific instructions for you to complete this project for him.

Please visit the Book Companion Site to receive the full set of instructions.

Chapter 10

Information Systems Within the Organization

[LEARNING OBJECTIVES]	[CHAPTER OUTLINE]	[WEB RESOURCES]
1. Explain the purpose of transaction processing systems.	10.1 Transaction Processing Systems	• Student PowerPoints for note taking
2. Explain the types of support information systems can provide for each functional area of the organization.	10.2 Functional Area Information Systems	**WileyPLUS** • E-book
3. Identify advantages and drawbacks to businesses implementing an enterprise resource planning system.	10.3 Enterprise Resource Planning (ERP) Systems	• Author video lecture for each chapter section
4. Describe the three main business processes supported by ERP systems.	10.4 ERP Support for Business Processes	• Practice quizzes • Flash Cards for vocabulary review
5. Discuss the three major types of reports generated by the functional area information systems and enterprise resource planning systems, providing examples of each type.	10.5 Reports	• Additional "IT's About Business" cases • Video interviews with managers • Lab Manuals for Microsoft Office 2010 and 2013

What's In IT For Me?

This Chapter Will Help Prepare You To...

ACCT	FIN	MKT	POM	HRM	MIS
ACCOUNTING	FINANCE	MARKETING	PRODUCTION OPERATIONS MANAGEMENT	HUMAN RESOURCES MANAGEMENT	MIS
Annual budget	Analyze cash flows	Understand customers' needs, wants	Manage materials handling	Manage recruiting	Responsible for firm's information systems

[IT Transformation at Ford Motor Company]

MIS

The Problem

Ford Motor Company underwent a "near-death" experience in the mid-2000s when it nearly declared bankruptcy. The old business model at Ford allocated a great deal of autonomy to each geographic region. One consequence of this arrangement was that the company's IT environment had become excessively complex and fragmented. The IT department had introduced initiatives that primarily addressed Ford's IT infrastructure. However, it had not proposed any initiatives to deal with the giant company's application portfolio. (An *application portfolio* is the term used for the entire group of applications used and maintained by an organization.) In fact, Ford often had at least three applications among its North American, South American, European, and Asia Pacific locations that fundamentally performed the same functions. Even worse, the IT department was not providing adequate support for the company's business initiatives.

The Solution

When Alan Mulally became Ford's CEO in 2006, he put several strategies in motion:

- Simplify the company's product line, focusing primarily on the Ford brand itself;
- Build vehicles people actually want to buy; create the best vehicle in every class in which Ford competes;
- Focus rigorously on data and facts in a weekly "Business Plan Review" that would involve all department heads;
- Integrate the company into one global enterprise, stop the infighting among divisions, and harness the power and scale of Ford's global resources.

Mulally called the last item the "One Ford" initiative. In parallel with One Ford, the IT group developed its "One IT" initiative. Consequently, Ford's entire IT group refocused on an initiative called One IT, which supported One Ford. The One IT initiative called for Ford to reorganize its IT group around four priorities:

- Integrate and standardize the applications in Ford's application portfolio;
- Support company growth;

- Encourage collaboration among business units and among all users;
- Drive internal efficiencies across the entire company.

To accomplish these priorities, the IT department first redirected funds from maintaining existing applications to investing in innovative new projects. Because those resources totaled 30 percent of IT's total budget, the department was able to devote hundreds of millions of dollars to new IT projects and applications. The IT department then realized savings from reducing staff and consolidating its six enterprise data centers into two. IT also retired numerous legacy applications and standardized business processes and applications across the company.

Another IT initiative involved transforming the company's historical, decentralized model into a centralized federated model. The *federated model* combines the essential features of centralization and decentralization. The underlying philosophy is to obtain the best of both worlds by creating shared best-of-breed services (e.g., corporate databases) that standardize Ford's IT architecture, while placing IT professionals in each of the business units (e.g., in research and development, product engineering, or manufacturing in any geographical region) so that they understand both the business details and the customers.

Essentially, Ford simplified its IT environment. The company now has a single shared service for IT infrastructure and operations and one for application development. The company is leveraging the scale of its IT department globally while supporting the unique requirements of its consumers and its product development and manufacturing facilities.

The federated model mirrors One Ford. One Ford provides "shared skill" teams for product engineering and manufacturing so that the company maintains consistent business processes around the world. In addition, One Ford has business units that support North America, South America, Europe, and Asia Pacific that ensure that the company tailors its product offerings to satisfy the unique requirements of each market.

Ford is currently building eight manufacturing plants around the world. The IT teams are delivering the automation that each plant requires. At the same time, they are integrating the new plants with Ford's global supply chain systems.

Ford also realized that to implement a successful IT transformation the company had to empower its employees. To accomplish this task, the automaker introduced a program called "Digital Worker" that examines all of the collaboration tools it needs to enable increased global capabilities. This initiative is partitioned into four areas, which are integrated to help teams situated throughout the world to collaborate:

- Traditional office productivity tools such as instant messaging, e-mail, and Microsoft Office;
- Data, audio, and video collaboration tools;
- Mobility solutions that enable remote access, employee bring-your-own-devices, tablet computing, etc.
- Microsoft SharePoint as a structured data repository and Yammer for social media.

The first phase of Digital Worker involved bringing these tools together. Next, Ford explored strategies to maximize business capability by considering not just the tools but the actual process of collaboration and how collaborative tools enable workers to be more productive.

Finally, the IT department is creating a tool called "How I Work," which employs a scenario-based approach that helps employees to identify the most effective and efficient collaborative tools to use within each context. For example, one scenario considers how to run an effective meeting.

The Results

Since the mid-2000s, Ford has experienced a remarkable turnaround. Significantly, the automaker's IT transformation played a key role in its comeback. The purpose of the IT transformation is to make Ford a faster, more agile, more innovative company. For example, IT support of Ford's new capabilities manifested itself when IT assisted in developing and deploying the Ford SYNC and in helping the company automate its new manufacturing plants.

Ford SYNC is a factory-installed, integrated in-vehicle communications and entertainment system that allows users to make hands-free telephone calls, control music, and perform other functions through voice commands. As of 2012, Ford offered SYNC in North America as a feature in fourteen Ford models and five Lincoln models.

Ford can now install all SYNC software in real time in the plant. Basically, as the vehicle progresses down the assembly line, the SYNC software is loaded wirelessly via Wi-Fi. Significantly, the SYNC functions are customized to meet the specifications of each vehicle. The SYNC language pack is based on whatever language needs to be configured for each vehicle. This wireless software installation process is now being used with other software modules on each vehicle (e.g., antilock braking system, power steering system, navigation system, etc.). Increasingly, IT applications in manufacturing plants are enabling Ford to provide more product functions than the company could provide historically when it had to physically load the software early on in the manufacturing process.

IT applications are also increasing the flexibility of Ford manufacturing plants. Because the tooling is more flexible, Ford can adjust its manufacturing capacity in real time to meet customer demand. (*Tooling* is the process of converting raw materials, such as steel and aluminum, into finished products, such as car bodies, doors, etc.) Historically, plants were configured to produce a certain number of one type of vehicle. Using IT and robots, Ford manufacturing plants are now able to adjust the mix of vehicles that are scheduled to be manufactured on a week-to-week basis.

Ford badly needs this amount of flexibility, particularly in light of the automaker's problems in the spring of 2012, when it could not manufacture enough vehicles to meet the increase in customer demand in North America. During this same period, Ford's rivals Chrysler and General Motors did not experience similar problems in increasing their capacity.

In sum, then, the IT function at Ford has evolved from being perceived internally as simply a tool provider to a true collaborator and innovator that actually helps the company solve its business problems.

Sources: Compiled from "SYNC Comes Different Ways," *Ford Motor Company*, 2013; J. Hiner, "How Ford Reimagined IT from the Inside-Out to Power Its Turnaround," *CNET News*, July 9, 2012; www.ford.com, accessed May 5, 2013.

What We Learned from This Case

The chapter-opening case illustrates the variety of information systems (IS) in organizations, as well as the integral part that IS play in an organization's success. IS are everywhere, and they affect organizations in countless ways. Although IS are frequently discussed within the context of large organizational settings, they also play a critical role in small organizations, as illustrated in IT's About Business 10.1.

Henthorn Mower & Engine Serviced needed a payroll solution, and ADP matched the company's requirements. As Henthorn Mower demonstrates, "systems within organizations" do not have to be owned by the organization itself. Instead, organizations can deploy very productive IS that are owned by an external vendor. The important point here is that "systems within an organization" are intended to support internal processes, regardless of who actually owns the systems.

It is important for you to have a working knowledge of IS within your organization, for a variety of reasons. First, your job will require you to access corporate data that are supplied primarily by your firm's transaction processing systems and enterprise resource planning systems. Second, you will have a great deal of input into the format and content of the reports that you receive from these systems. Third, you will utilize the information contained in these reports to perform your job more productively.

This chapter will teach you about the various information systems that modern organizations utilize. You begin by considering transaction processing systems, the most fundamental organizational information systems. You continue with the functional area management information systems, proceed to enterprise resource planning systems, and conclude with the reports that these information systems produce.

IT's about [small] business

10.1 Henthorn Mower & Engine Service and ADP

Information systems within an organization are not always computer based. Many small businesses still rely on systems where collection, storage, analysis, and distribution of information are all executed on paper. For example, paper payrolls include a time card that each employee "punches" every day when arriving at and leaving work (data collection). These "punches" are manually totaled at the end of each week (analysis) and then entered into a ledger for future reference (storage). At the appropriate time, this information will be sent to the accountant (distribution) to determine the amount of pay due to each employee (information).

In most cases, this process works. However, there are many ways this information could be more useful, if it were stored in a computer system that would help manage the entire process. Paper systems require significant manual effort, and they are especially subject to human error. Computerized information systems are much more reliable, and they provide many other benefits as well.

Consider the case of Rickie Star, who purchased his in-laws' mower business in 1978. The business—Henthorn Mower & Engine Service—remains a small, family-run business with about 12 employees. As is frequently true of family-owned businesses, many of the current information systems are paper based. Within Henthorn, the division of responsibilities was initially determined by history, preference, and the "way it has always been." In particular, the responsibility of managing time cards and payroll fell to Rickie's mother-in-law. She spent every Thursday morning going through the manual process outlined above. This process worked fine—that is, until she passed away, and the responsibility fell on Rickie's shoulders.

It did not take long for Rickie to realize that he needed a better solution to the payroll process. Even for his small business, he needed a quicker and more reliable system that would free him to spend his time performing other duties. After researching the possible solutions, he decided that the EasyPayNet (*https://easynet.adp.com*) and ezLaborManager (*https://ezlm.adp.com/*) solutions from ADP (*www.adp.com*) best suited his needs.

Rickie's time system moved from paper to the computer in a seamless fashion. Employees now use an electronic clock that scans a time card rather than the old manual clock that "punched" the card. This information is available in real time (no waiting until Thursday), so Rickie can see who is on time, who is late, and how many hours each employee has worked for each pay period. The system also calculates sick days, vacation days, taxes . . . and even cuts the employees' paychecks!

For Henthorn Mower & Engine Service, moving its paper-based system to the ADP solutions provided benefits beyond simply the time saved by not having to manually calculate payroll. Rather, the new IS added a level of reliability and quick access to information that employees had not even realized they were missing.

Sources: Compiled from "Henthorn Mower & Engine Service," *ADP Small Business Services Case Study*, 2011; *www.adp.com*, *https://easynet.adp.com*, *https://ezlm.adp.com*, accessed March 21, 2013.

Questions

1. Identify additional advantages (other than the ones described in this case) of computerizing Henthorn's payroll process.
2. What are some potential disadvantages of computerizing Henthorn's payroll process?

10.1 Transaction Processing Systems

Millions (sometimes billions) of transactions occur in large organizations every day. A **transaction** is any business event that generates data worthy of being captured and stored in a database. Examples of transactions are a product manufactured, a service sold, a person hired, and a payroll check generated. In another example, when you are checking out of Walmart, each time the cashier swipes an item across the bar code reader is one transaction.

A **transaction processing system (TPS)** supports the monitoring, collection, storage, and processing of data from the organization's basic business transactions, each of which generates data. The TPS collects data continuously, typically in *real time*—that is, as soon as the data are generated—and it provides the input data for the corporate databases. The TPSs are critical to the success of any enterprise because they support core operations.

In the modern business world, TPSs are inputs for the functional area information systems and business intelligence systems, as well as business operations such as customer relationship management, knowledge management, and e-commerce. TPSs have to efficiently handle both high volumes of data and large variations in those volumes (e.g., during

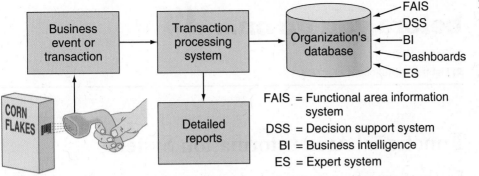

FIGURE 10.1 How transaction processing systems manage data.

FAIS = Functional area information system
DSS = Decision support system
BI = Business intelligence
ES = Expert system

periods of peak processing). In addition, they must avoid errors and downtime, record results accurately and securely, and maintain privacy and security. Figure 10.1 illustrates how TPSs manage data. Consider these examples of how TPSs manage the complexities of transactional data:

- When more than one person or application program can access the database at the same time, the database has to be protected from errors resulting from overlapping updates. The most common error is losing the results of one of the updates.

- When processing a transaction involves more than one computer, the database and all users must be protected against inconsistencies arising from a failure of any component at any time. For example, an error that occurs at some point in an ATM withdrawal can enable a customer to receive cash, although the bank's computer indicates that he or she did not. (Conversely, a customer might not receive cash although the bank's computer indicates that he or she did.)

- It must be possible to reverse a transaction in its entirety if it turns out to have been entered in error. It is also necessary to reverse a transaction when a purchased item is returned. For example, if you return a sweater that you have purchased, the store must credit your credit card for the amount of the purchase, refund your cash, or offer you an in-store credit to purchase another item. In addition, the store must update its inventory.

- It is frequently important to preserve an audit trail. In fact, for certain transactions an audit trail may be legally required.

These and similar issues explain why organizations spend millions of dollars on expensive mainframe computers. In today's business environment, firms must have the dependability, reliability, and processing capacity of these computers to handle their transaction processing loads.

Regardless of the specific data processed by a TPS, the actual process tends to be standard, whether it occurs in a manufacturing firm, a service firm, or a government organization. As the first step in this procedure, people or sensors collect data, which are entered into the computer via any input device. Generally speaking, organizations try to automate the TPS data entry as much as possible because of the large volume involved, a process called *source data automation* (discussed in Technology Guide 1).

Next, the system processes data in one of two basic ways: batch processing and online processing. In **batch processing**, the firm collects data from transactions as they occur, placing them in groups or *batches*. The system then prepares and processes the batches periodically (say, every night).

In **online transaction processing (OLTP)**, business transactions are processed online as soon as they occur. For example, when you pay for an item at a store, the system records the sale by reducing the inventory on hand by one unit, increasing sales figures for the item by one unit, and increasing the store's cash position by the amount you paid. The system performs these tasks in real time by means of online technologies.

before you go on...

1. Define TPS.

2. List the key functions of a TPS.

10.2 Functional Area Information Systems

Each department or functional area within an organization has its own collection of application programs, or information systems. Each of these **functional area information systems** (FAISs) supports a particular functional area in the organization by increasing each area's internal efficiency and effectiveness. FAISs often convey information in a variety of reports, which you will see in Section 10.5. Examples of FAISs include accounting IS, finance IS, production/operations management (POM) IS, marketing IS, and human resources IS.

As illustrated in Figure 10.1, the FAIS access data from the corporate databases. The following sections discuss the support that FAISs provide for these functional areas.

Information Systems for Accounting and Finance

A primary mission of the accounting and finance functional areas is to manage money flows into, within, and out of organizations. This mission is very broad because money is involved in all organizational functions. Therefore, accounting and finance information systems are very diverse and comprehensive. In this section, you focus on certain selected activities of the accounting/finance functional area.

Financial Planning and Budgeting. Appropriate management of financial assets is a major task in financial planning and budgeting. Managers must plan for both acquiring and utilizing resources.

- *Financial and economic forecasting.* Knowledge about the availability and cost of money is a key ingredient for successful financial planning. Cash flow projections are particularly important because they inform organizations what funds they need, when they need them, and how they will acquire them.

  Funds for operating organizations come from multiple sources, including stockholders' investments, bond sales, bank loans, sales of products and services, and income from investments. Decisions concerning funding for ongoing operations and for capital investment can be supported by decision support systems and business intelligence applications (discussed in Chapter 12), as well as expert systems (discussed in Technology Guide 4). In addition, numerous software packages for conducting economic and financial forecasting are available. Many of these packages can be downloaded from the Internet, some of them for free.

- *Budgeting.* An essential component of the accounting/finance function is the annual budget, which allocates the organization's financial resources among participants and activities. The budget allows management to distribute resources in the way that best supports the organization's mission and goals.

  Several software packages are available to support budget preparation and control and to facilitate communication among participants in the budget process. These packages can reduce the time involved in the budget process. Further, they can automatically monitor exceptions for patterns and trends.

Managing Financial Transactions. Many accounting/finance software packages are integrated with other functional areas. For example, Peachtree by Sage (*www.peachtree.com*) offers a sales ledger, a purchase ledger, a cash book, sales order processing, invoicing, stock control, a fixed assets register, and more.

Companies involved in electronic commerce need to access customers' financial data (e.g., credit line), inventory levels, and manufacturing databases (to determine available capacity and place orders). For example, Microsoft Dynamics GP (formerly Great Plains Software) offers 50 modules that meet the most common financial, project, distribution, manufacturing, and e-business needs.

Organizations, business processes, and business activities operate with, and manage, financial transactions. Consider these examples:

- *Global stock exchanges.* Financial markets operate in global, 24/7/365, distributed electronic stock exchanges that use the Internet both to buy and sell stocks and to broadcast real-time stock prices.

- *Managing multiple currencies.* Global trade involves financial transactions that are carried out in different currencies. The conversion ratios of these currencies are constantly in flux. Financial and accounting systems utilize financial data from different countries and convert the currencies from and to any other currency in seconds. Reports based on these data, which formerly required several days to generate, can now be produced in only seconds. In addition to currency conversions, these systems manage multiple languages as well.

- *Virtual close.* Companies traditionally closed their books (accounting records) quarterly, usually to meet regulatory requirements. Today, many companies want to be able to close their books at any time, on very short notice. Information systems make it possible to close the books quickly in what is called a *virtual close.* This process provides almost real-time information on the organization's financial health.

- *Expense management automation. Expense management automation* (EMA) refers to systems that automate the data entry and processing of travel and entertainment expenses. EMA systems are Web-based applications that enable companies to quickly and consistently collect expense information, enforce company policies and contracts, and reduce unplanned purchases as well as airline and hotel expenses. They also allow companies to reimburse their employees more quickly because expense approvals are not delayed by poor documentation.

Investment Management.   Organizations invest large amounts of money in stocks, bonds, real estate, and other assets. Managing these investments is a complex task, for several reasons. First, organizations have literally thousands of investment alternatives dispersed throughout the world to choose from. In addition, these investments are subject to complex regulations and tax laws, which vary from one location to another.

Investment decisions require managers to evaluate financial and economic reports provided by diverse institutions, including federal and state agencies, universities, research institutions, and financial services firms. In addition, thousands of Web sites provide financial data, many of them for free.

To monitor, interpret, and analyze the huge amounts of online financial data, financial analysts employ two major types of IT tools: (1) Internet search engines and (2) business intelligence and decision support software.

Control and Auditing.   One major reason why organizations go out of business is their inability to forecast and/or secure a sufficient cash flow. Underestimating expenses, overspending, engaging in fraud, and mismanaging financial statements can lead to disaster. Consequently, it is essential that organizations effectively control their finances and financial statements. Let us examine some of the most common forms of financial control.

- *Budgetary control.* After an organization has finalized its annual budget, it divides those monies into monthly allocations. Managers at various levels monitor departmental expenditures and compare them against the budget and the operational progress of corporate plans.

- *Auditing.* Auditing has two basic purposes: (1) to monitor how the organization's monies are being spent and (2) to assess the organization's financial health. Internal auditing is performed by the organization's accounting/finance personnel. These employees also prepare for periodic external audits by outside CPA firms.

- *Financial ratio analysis.* Another major accounting/finance function is to monitor the company's financial health by assessing a set of financial ratios. Included here are liquidity ratios (the availability of cash to pay debt), activity ratios (how quickly a firm converts noncash assets to cash assets), debt ratios (measure the firm's ability to repay long-term debt), and profitability ratios (measure the firm's use of its assets and control of its expenses to generate an acceptable rate of return).

Information Systems for Marketing

It is impossible to overestimate the importance of customers to any organization. Therefore, any successful organization must understand its customers' needs and wants and then develop its marketing and advertising strategies around them. Information systems provide numerous types of support to the marketing function. In fact, customer-centric organizations are so important that we devote one half of Chapter 11 to this topic.

Information Systems for Production/Operations Management

The POM function in an organization is responsible for the processes that transform inputs into useful outputs as well as for the overall operation of the business. Because of the breadth and variety of POM functions, you see only four here: in-house logistics and materials management, planning production and operation, computer-integrated manufacturing (CIM), and product life cycle management (PLM).

The POM function is also responsible for managing the organization's supply chain. Because supply chain management is vital to the success of modern organizations, the second half of Chapter 11 addresses this topic in detail.

In-House Logistics and Materials Management. Logistics management deals with ordering, purchasing, inbound logistics (receiving), and outbound logistics (shipping) activities. Related activities include inventory management and quality control.

Inventory Management. As the name suggests, inventory management determines how much inventory an organization should maintain. Both excessive inventory and insufficient inventory create problems. Overstocking can be expensive, because of storage costs and the costs of spoilage and obsolescence. However, keeping insufficient inventory is also expensive, because of last-minute orders and lost sales.

Operations personnel make two basic decisions: when to order and how much to order. Inventory models, such as the economic order quantity (EOQ) model, support these decisions. A large number of commercial inventory software packages that automate the application of these models are available.

Many large companies allow their suppliers to monitor their inventory levels and ship products as they are needed. This strategy, called *vendor-managed inventory* (VMI), eliminates the need for the company to submit purchasing orders. We discuss VMI in Chapter 11.

Quality Control. Quality-control systems used by manufacturing units provide information about the quality of incoming material and parts, as well as the quality of in-process semifinished and finished products. These systems record the results of all inspections and compare the actual results to established metrics. They also generate periodic reports containing information about quality—for example, the percentage of products that contain defects or that need to be reworked. Quality control data, collected by Web-based sensors, can be interpreted in real time. Alternatively, they can be stored in a database for future analysis.

Planning Production and Operations. In many firms, POM planning is supported by IT. POM planning has evolved from material requirements planning (MRP), to manufacturing resource planning (MRP II), to enterprise resource planning (ERP). We briefly discuss MRP and MRP II here, and we examine ERP in detail later in this chapter.

Inventory systems that use an EOQ approach are designed for items for which demand is completely independent—for example, the number of identical personal computers a computer manufacturer will sell. In manufacturing operations, however, the demand for some items is interdependent. Consider, for example, a company that makes three types of chairs, all of which use the same screws and bolts. In this case, the demand for screws and bolts depends on the total demand for all three types of chairs and their shipment schedules. The planning process that integrates production, purchasing, and inventory management of interdependent items is called *material requirements planning* (MRP).

MRP deals only with production scheduling and inventories. More complex planning also involves allocating related resources, such as money and labor. For these cases, more complex, integrated software, called *manufacturing resource planning* (MRP II), is available. MRP II integrates a firm's production, inventory management, purchasing, financing, and labor activities. Thus, MRP II adds functions to a regular MRP system. In fact, MRP II has evolved into enterprise resource planning.

Computer-Integrated Manufacturing. **Computer-integrated manufacturing (CIM;** also called *digital manufacturing*) is an approach that integrates various automated factory systems. CIM has three basic goals: (1) to simplify all manufacturing technologies and techniques, (2) to automate as many of the manufacturing processes as possible, and (3) to integrate and coordinate all aspects of design, manufacturing, and related functions via computer systems.

Product Life Cycle Management. Even within a single organization, designing and developing new products can be expensive and time consuming. When multiple organizations are involved, the process can become very complex. *Product life cycle management* is a business strategy that enables manufacturers to share product-related data that support product design and development and supply chain operations. PLM applies Web-based collaborative technologies to product development. By integrating formerly disparate functions, such as a manufacturing process and the logistics that support it, PLM enables these functions to collaborate, essentially forming a single team that manages the product from its inception through its completion.

Information Systems for Human Resource Management

Initial human resource information system (HRIS) applications dealt primarily with transaction processing systems, such as managing benefits and keeping records of vacation days. As organizational systems have moved to intranets and the Web, however, so have HRIS applications.

Many HRIS applications are delivered via an HR portal. For example, numerous organizations use their Web portals to advertise job openings and to conduct online hiring and training. In this section, you consider how organizations are using IT to perform some key HR functions: recruitment, HR maintenance and development, and HR planning and management.

Recruitment. Recruitment involves finding potential employees, evaluating them, and deciding which ones to hire. Some companies are flooded with viable applicants; others have difficulty finding the right people. IT can be helpful in both cases. In addition, IT can assist in related activities such as testing and screening job applicants.

With millions of resumes available online (in particular, LinkedIn), it is not surprising that companies are trying to find appropriate candidates on the Web, usually with the help of specialized search engines. Companies also advertise hundreds of thousands of jobs on the Web. Online recruiting can reach more candidates, which may bring in better applicants. In addition, the costs of online recruitment are usually lower than traditional recruiting methods such as advertising in newspapers or in trade journals.

Human Resources Development. After employees are recruited, they become part of the corporate human resources pool, which means they must be evaluated and developed. IT provides support for these activities.

Most employees are periodically evaluated by their immediate supervisors. In addition, in some organizations, peers or subordinates also evaluate other employees. Evaluations are typically digitized, and they are used to support many decisions, ranging from rewards to transfers to layoffs.

IT also plays an important role in training and retraining. Some of the most innovative developments are taking place in the areas of intelligent computer-aided instruction and the application of multimedia support for instructional activities. For example, companies conduct much of their corporate training over their intranet or via the Web.

Human Resources Planning and Management.

Managing human resources in large organizations requires extensive planning and detailed strategy. The following three areas are where IT can provide support:

- *Payroll and employees' records.* The HR department is responsible for payroll preparation. This process is typically automated with paychecks being printed or money being transferred electronically into employees' bank accounts.

- *Benefits administration.* Employees' work contributions to their organizations are rewarded by wages, bonuses, and other benefits. Benefits include health and dental care, pension contributions, wellness centers, and child care centers.

  Managing benefits is a complex task because of the multiple options offered and the tendency of organizations to allow employees to choose and trade off their benefits. In many organizations, employees can access the company portal to self-register for specific benefits.

- *Employee relationship management.* In their efforts to better manage employees, companies are developing *employee relationship management* (ERM) applications. A typical ERM application is a call center for employees' problems.

Table 10.1 provides an overview of the activities that the FAIS support. Figure 10.2 diagrams many of the information systems that support these five functional areas.

Table **10.1** Activities Supported by Functional Area Information Systems	
Accounting and Finance	
Financial planning—and cost of money	
Budgeting—allocates financial resources among participants and activities	
Capital budgeting—financing of asset acquisitions	
Managing financial transactions	
Handling multiple currencies	
Virtual close—the ability to close the books at any time on short notice	
Investment management—managing organizational investments in stocks, bonds, real estate, and other investment vehicles	
Budgetary control—monitoring expenditures and comparing them against the budget	
Auditing—ensuring the accuracy of the organization's financial transactions and assessing the condition of the organization's financial health	
Payroll	
Marketing and Sales	
Customer relations—know who customers are and treat them like royalty	
Customer profiles and preferences	
Sales force automation—using software to automate the business tasks of sales, thereby improving the productivity of salespeople	
Production/Operations and Logistics	
Inventory management—when to order new inventory, how much inventory to order, and how much inventory to keep in stock	

Table 10.1 (continued)

Quality control—controlling for defects in incoming material and defects in goods produced

Materials requirements planning—planning process that integrates production, purchasing, and inventory management of interdependent items (MRP)

Manufacturing resource planning—planning process that integrates an enterprise's production, inventory management, purchasing, financing, and labor activities (MRP II)

Just-in-time systems—a principle of production and inventory control in which materials and parts arrive precisely when and where needed for production (JIT)

Computer-integrated manufacturing—a manufacturing approach that integrates several computerized systems, such as computer-assisted design (CAD), computer-assisted manufacturing (CAM), MRP, and JIT

Product life cycle management—business strategy that enables manufacturers to collaborate on product design and development efforts, using the Web

Human Resource Management

Recruitment—finding employees, testing them, and deciding which ones to hire

Performance evaluation—periodic evaluation by superiors

Training

Employee records

Benefits administration—retirement, disability, unemployment, etc.

ACCOUNTING	FINANCE	HUMAN RESOURCES	PRODUCTION/OPERATIONS	MARKETING	
Profitability Planning	Financial Planning	Employment Planning, Outsourcing	Product Life Cycle Management	Sales Forecasting, Advertising Planning	STRATEGIC
Auditing, Budgeting	Investment Management	Benefits Administration, Performance Evaluation	Quality Control, Inventory Management	Customer Relations, Sales Force Automation	TACTICAL
Payroll, Accounts Payable, Accounts Receivable	Manage Cash, Manage Financial Transactions	Maintain Employee Records	Order Fulfillment, Order Processing	Set Pricing, Profile Customers	OPERATIONAL

FIGURE 10.2 Examples of information systems supporting the functional areas.

before you go on... 𝄃𝄃𝄃𝄃

1. Define a functional area information system and list its major characteristics.

2. How do information systems benefit the finance and accounting functional area?

3. Explain how POM personnel use information systems to perform their jobs more effectively and efficiently.

4. What are the most important HRIS applications?

10.3 Enterprise Resource Planning Systems

Historically, the functional area information systems were developed independently of one another, resulting in *information silos*. These silos did not communicate well with one another, and this lack of communication and integration made organizations less efficient. This inefficiency was particularly evident in business processes that involve more than one functional area, such as procurement and fulfillment.

Enterprise resource planning systems are designed to correct a lack of communication among the functional area IS. ERP systems resolve this problem by tightly integrating the functional area IS via a common database. For this reason, experts credit ERP systems with greatly increasing organizational productivity. **ERP systems** adopt a business process view of the overall organization to integrate the planning, management, and use of all of an organization's resources, employing a common software platform and database.

The major objectives of ERP systems are to tightly integrate the functional areas of the organization and to enable information to flow seamlessly across them. Tight integration means that changes in one functional area are immediately reflected in all other pertinent functional areas. In essence, ERP systems provide the information necessary to control the business processes of the organization.

It is important to understand here that ERP systems are an evolution of FAIS. That is, ERP systems have much the same functionality as FAIS, and they produce the same reports. ERP systems simply integrate the functions of the various FAIS.

Although some companies have developed their own ERP systems, most organizations use commercially available ERP software. The leading ERP software vendor is SAP (*www.sap.com*), which features its SAP R/3 package. Other major vendors include Oracle (*www.oracle.com*) and PeopleSoft (*www.peoplesoft.com*), now an Oracle company. (With more than 700 customers, PeopleSoft is the market leader in higher education). For up-to-date information on ERP software, visit *http://erp.ittoolbox.com*.

Although implementing ERP systems can be difficult because they are large and complicated, many companies have done so successfully. IT'S About Business 10.2 recounts a successful ERP deployment at a large European railway company.

ERP II Systems

ERP systems were originally deployed to facilitate business processes associated with manufacturing, such as raw materials management, inventory control, order entry, and distribution. However, these early ERP systems did not extend to other functional areas, such as sales and marketing. They also did not include any customer relationship management (CRM) capabilities that enable organizations to capture customer-specific information. Finally, they did not provide Web-enabled customer service or order fulfillment.

Over time, ERP systems evolved to include administrative, sales, marketing, and human resources processes. Companies now employ an enterprisewide approach to ERP that utilizes the Web and connects all facets of the value chain. (You might want to review our discussion of value chains in Chapter 2.)These systems are called ERP II.

IT's [about business]

10.2 European Railway Successfully Converts to SAP

A large European railway company transports millions of passengers and thousands of tons of cargo every year. The company has ambitious plans for growth, particularly in its freight-transport operations. As a result, it has invested heavily in expanding its information technology infrastructure. At the same time, the company faces rising operational expenses and increasing competition from other transport operators due to decreasing regulation of the transportation sector in its European markets. To successfully expand its operations as well as its market share, the railway must maximize savings and efficiencies, without sacrificing the exceptional service levels its customers have come to expect.

As the firm pursued its strategy of expansion, obtaining a unified view of its operations became increasingly difficult. The company's application portfolio was highly customized and fragmented, comprising more than 1,000 different information systems. This lack of IS integration and transparency across the company made it challenging for the business to obtain an accurate view of enterprise-wide cost structures and difficult to streamline operations across all of its divisions. The company needed to standardize its applications on a common platform.

The railway decided to replace its application portfolio with software solutions from SAP (www.sap.com). The company implemented SAP core modules, including financials, controlling, sales and delivery, materials management, plant maintenance, production planning and control, and project management. The firm also implemented the SAP real estate management module to support its complex property-management business. In addition, the railway relies on the SAP human capital management module for its staff and pension administration and billing. The SAP human resource solution is another critical application for the firm, which has thousands of current staff on its payroll and many former staff members who are receiving company pensions.

The entire corporate planning process and the consolidation of the company's divisions are based on SAP NetWeaver Business Warehouse. For analysis and business intelligence applications, the company implemented SAP BusinessObjects software. Approximately 25,000 users have access to the employee self-service portal, while a total of 2,500 users have access to the company's main SAP systems. To ensure that all users across all different systems comply with the company's access rights, the railway implemented SAP solutions for data governance, risk, and compliance.

Following the initial implementation of the core SAP modules, the railway leveraged its investment by replacing approximately 250 legacy applications without having to invest additional monies in SAP software licenses. Consolidating company data in the integrated SAP modules also substantially reduced the complexity of the overall information technology architecture, thereby reducing licensing, operational, and maintenance costs.

Overall, the SAP implementation lowered the total cost of ownership for corporate data management by 25 percent, and it reduced data backup times by 70 percent. Both enhancements enabled the company to reduce its operational costs. In addition, the new system reduced both application response times and batch processing times by 30 percent. Finally, the system reduced the time required to switch to backup systems in the event of a system failure by 97 percent, which dramatically improved both data security and business continuity.

Sources: Compiled from S. Kramer, "Belgian Railways Gets on Track for the Future with SAP and OpenText," *SAP Business Trends*, March 14, 2013; "A Large Railway Company Lays the Track for New Business Opportunities," *IBM Case Study*, April 12, 2013; "Belarusian Railways Transforms Operations and Reporting with SAP and IBM, *IBM Case Study*, October 1, 2012; www.ibm.com, www.sap.com, www.rw.by/en, accessed May 5, 2013.

Questions

1. Discuss why the railway decided to implement an ERP system.
2. Describe the benefits that the company realized after deploying its ERP system.

ERP II systems are interorganizational ERP systems that provide Web-enabled links among a company's key business systems—such as inventory and production—and its customers, suppliers, distributors, and other relevant parties. These links integrate internal-facing ERP applications with the external-focused applications of supply chain management and customer relationship management. Figure 10.3 illustrates the organization and functions of an ERP II system.

The various functions of ERP II systems are now delivered as e-business suites. The major ERP vendors have developed modular, Web-enabled software suites that integrate ERP, customer relationship management, supply chain management, procurement, decision support, enterprise portals, and other business applications and functions. Examples are Oracle's e-Business Suite and SAP's mySAP. The goal of these systems is to enable companies to execute most of their business processes using a single Web-enabled system of integrated software rather than a variety of separate e-business applications.

FIGURE 10.3 ERP II system.

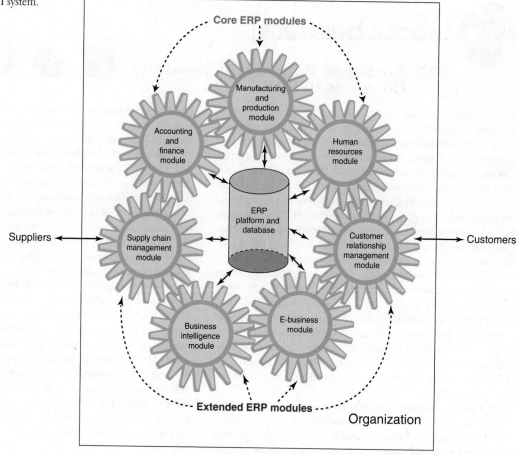

ERP II systems include a variety of modules that are divided into core ERP modules—financial management, operations management, and human resource management—and extended ERP modules—customer relationship management, supply chain management, business intelligence, and e-business. If a system does not have the core ERP modules, then it is not a legitimate ERP system. The extended ERP modules, in contrast, are optional. Table 10.2 describes each of these modules.

Benefits and Limitation of ERP Systems

ERP systems can generate significant business benefits for an organization. The major benefits fall into the following categories:

- *Organizational flexibility and agility.* As you have seen, ERP systems break down many former departmental and functional silos of business processes, information systems, and information resources. In this way, they make organizations more flexible, agile, and adaptive. The organizations can therefore respond quickly to changing business conditions and capitalize on new business opportunities.

- *Decision support.* ERP systems provide essential information on business performance across functional areas. This information significantly improves managers' ability to make better, more timely decisions.

- *Quality and efficiency.* ERP systems integrate and improve an organization's business processes, generating significant improvements in the quality of production, distribution, and customer service.

Table
10.2
ERP Modules

Core ERP Modules

Financial Management. These modules support accounting, financial reporting, performance management, and corporate governance. They manage accounting data and financial processes such as general ledger, accounts payable, accounts receivable, fixed assets, cash management and forecasting, product-cost accounting, cost-center accounting, asset accounting, tax accounting, credit management, budgeting, and asset management.

Operations Management. These modules manage the various aspects of production planning and execution such as demand forecasting, procurement, inventory management, materials purchasing, shipping, production planning, production scheduling, materials requirements planning, quality control, distribution, transportation, and plant and equipment maintenance.

Human Resource Management. These modules support personnel administration (including workforce planning, employee recruitment, assignment tracking, personnel planning and development, and performance management and reviews), time accounting, payroll, compensation, benefits accounting, and regulatory requirements.

Extended ERP Modules

Customer Relationship Management. (Discussed in detail in Chapter 11.) These modules support all aspects of a customer's relationship with the organization. They help the organization to increase customer loyalty and retention, and thus improve its profitability. They also provide an integrated view of customer data and interactions, helping organizations to be more responsive to customer needs.

Supply Chain Management. (Discussed in detail in Chapter 11.) These modules manage the information flows between and among stages in a supply chain to maximize supply chain efficiency and effectiveness. They help organizations plan, schedule, control, and optimize the supply chain from the acquisition of raw materials to the receipt of finished goods by customers.

Business Intelligence. (Discussed in detail in Chapter 12.) These modules collect information used throughout the organization, organize it, and apply analytical tools to assist managers with decision making.

E-Business. (Discussed in detail in Chapter 7.) Customers and suppliers demand access to ERP information including order status, inventory levels, and invoice reconciliation. Further, they want this information in a simplified format that can be accessed via the Web. As a result, these modules provide two channels of access into ERP system information—one channel for customers (B2C) and one for suppliers and partners (B2B).

Despite all of their benefits, however, ERP systems do have drawbacks. The major limitations of ERP implementations include:

- The business processes in ERP software are often predefined by the best practices that the ERP vendor has developed. *Best practices* are the most successful solutions or problem-solving methods for achieving a business objective. As a result, companies may need to change their existing business processes to fit the predefined business processes incorporated into the ERP software. For companies with well-established procedures, this requirement can create serious problems, especially if employees do not want to abandon their old ways of working and therefore resist the changes.

At the same time, however, an ERP implementation can provide an opportunity to improve and in some cases completely redesign inefficient, ineffective, or outdated procedures. In fact, many companies benefit from implementing best practices for their accounting, finance, and human resource processes, as well as other support activities that companies do not consider a source of competitive advantage.

Recall from Chapter 2, however, that different companies organize their value chains in different configurations to transform inputs into valuable outputs and achieve competitive advantage. Therefore, although the vendor's best practices, by definition, are appropriate for *most* organizations, they might not be the "best" one for your company if they change those processes that give you competitive advantage.

- ERP systems can be extremely complex, expensive, and time-consuming to implement. (We discuss the implementation of ERP systems in detail in the next section.) In fact, the costs and risks of failure in implementing a new ERP system are substantial. Quite a few companies have experienced costly ERP implementation failures. Large losses in revenue, profits, and market share have resulted when core business processes and information systems failed or did not work properly. In many cases, orders and shipments were lost, inventory changes were not recorded correctly, and unreliable inventory levels caused major-stock outs to occur. Companies such as Hershey Foods, Nike, A-DEC, and Connecticut General sustained losses in amounts up to hundreds of millions of dollars. In the case of FoxMeyer Drugs, a $5 billion pharmaceutical wholesaler, a failed ERP implementation caused the company to file for bankruptcy protection.

In almost every ERP implementation failure, the company's business managers and IT professionals underestimated the complexity of the planning, development, and training that were required to prepare for a new ERP system that would fundamentally change their business processes and information systems. The major causes of ERP implementation failure include:

- Failure to involve affected employees in the planning and development phases and in change management processes;
- Trying to do too much too fast in the conversion process;
- Insufficient training in the new work tasks required by the ERP system;
- The failure to perform proper data conversion and testing for the new system.

Implementing ERP Systems

Companies can implement ERP systems in two ways, using on-premise software or using software-as-a-service (SaaS). We differentiate between these two methods in detail in Technology Guide 3.

On-Premise ERP Implementation.   Depending on the types of value chain processes managed by the ERP system and a company's specific value chain, there are three strategic approaches to implementing an on-premise ERP system. These approaches are:

The *vanilla approach*: In this approach, a company implements a standard ERP package, using the package's built-in configuration options. When the system is implemented in this way, it will deviate only minimally from the package's standardized settings. The vanilla approach can make the implementation quicker, but the extent to which the software is adapted to the organization's specific processes is limited. Fortunately, a vanilla implementation provides general functions that can support the firm's common business processes with relative ease, even if they are not a perfect fit for those processes.

The *custom approach*: In this approach, a company implements a more customized ERP system by developing new ERP functions designed specifically for that firm. Decisions concerning the ERP's degree of customization are specific to each organization. To utilize the custom approach, the organization must carefully analyze its existing business processes to develop a system that conforms to the organizations particular characteristics and processes. In addition, customization is expensive and risky because computer code must be written and updated every time a new version of the ERP software is released. Going further, if the customization does not perfectly match the organization's needs, then the system can be very difficult to use.

The *best of breed approach*: This approach combines the benefits of the vanilla and customized systems while avoiding the extensive costs and risks associated with complete customization.

Companies that adopt this approach mix and match core ERP modules as well as other extended ERP modules from different software providers to best fit their unique internal processes and value chains. Thus, a company may choose several core ERP modules from an established vendor to take advantage of industry best practices—for example, for financial management and human resource management. At the same time, it may also choose specialized software to support its unique business processes—for example, for manufacturing, warehousing and distribution. Sometimes companies arrive at the best of breed approach the hard way. For example, Dell wasted millions of dollars trying to customize an integrated ERP system from a major vendor to match its unique processes before it realized that a smaller, more flexible system that integrated well with other corporate applications was the answer.

Software-as-a-Service ERP Implementation. Companies can acquire ERP systems without having to buy a complete software solution (i.e., on-premise ERP implementation). Many organizations are utilizing software-as-a-service (SaaS; discussed in Chapter 13 and Technology Guide 3) to acquire cloud-based ERP systems. (We discuss cloud computing in Technology Guide 3.)

In this business model, the company rents the software from an ERP vendor who offers its products over the Internet using the SaaS model. The ERP cloud vendor manages software updates and is responsible for the system's security and availability.

Cloud-based ERP systems can be a perfect fit for some companies. For instance, companies that cannot afford to make large investments in IT, yet which already have relatively structured business processes that need to be tightly integrated, might benefit from cloud computing.

The relationship between the company and the cloud vendor is regulated by contracts and by service level agreements (SLAs). The SLAs define the characteristics and quality of service; for instance, a guaranteed uptime, or the percentage of time that the system is available. Cloud vendors that fail to meet these conditions can face penalties.

The decision about whether to use on-premise ERP or SaaS ERP is specific to each organization, and it depends on how the organization evaluates a series of advantages and disadvantages. Three major advantages of using a cloud-based ERP system are:

- The system can be used from any location that provides Internet access. Consequently, users can work from any location using online shared and centralized resources (data and databases). Users access the ERP system via a secure virtual private network (VPN) connection (discussed in Chapter 4) with the provider.
- Companies using cloud-based ERP avoid the initial hardware and software expenses that are typical of on-premise implementations. For instance, to run SAP/R3 on-premise, a company must purchase SAP software as well as a license to use SAP. The magnitude of this investment can hinder small- to medium-size enterprises (SMEs) from adopting ERP.
- Cloud-based ERP solutions are scalable, meaning it is possible to extend ERP support to new business processes and new business partners (e.g., suppliers) by purchasing new ERP modules.

There are also disadvantages to adopting cloud-based ERP systems that a company must carefully evaluate. Three main disadvantages of using a cloud-based ERP system are:

- It is not clear whether cloud-based ERP systems are more secure than on-premise systems. In fact, a 2012 survey conducted by North Bridge Venture Partners indicated that security was the primary reason why organizations did not adopt cloud-based ERP.
- Companies that adopt cloud-based ERP systems sacrifice their control over a strategic IT resource. For this reason, some companies prefer to implement an on-premise ERP system, utilizing a strong in-house IT department that can directly manage the system.
- A third disadvantage is a direct consequence of the lack of control over IT resources. This disadvantage occurs when the ERP system experiences problems; for example, some ERP functions are temporarily slow or are not available. In such cases, having an internal IT

department that can solve problems immediately rather than dealing with the cloud vendor's system support can speed up the system recovery process.

This situation is particularly important for technology-intensive companies. In such companies, IT is crucial to conduct any kind of business with customers. Examples are e-commerce companies, banks, and government organizations that manage emergencies or situations that might involve individual and national security (e.g., healthcare organizations, police, secret services, homeland security department, anti-terrorism units, and others).

Finally, slow or unavailable software from a cloud-based ERP vendor creates business continuity problems for the client. (We discuss business continuity in Chapter 4.) That is, a sudden system problem or failure makes it impossible for the firm to operate. Companies lose money when they lose business continuity because customers cannot be serviced and employees cannot do their jobs. A loss of business continuity also damages the company's reputation because customers lose trust in the firm.

Enterprise Application Integration

For some organizations, integrated ERP systems are not appropriate. This situation is particularly true for companies that find the process of converting from their existing system too difficult or time-consuming.

Such companies, however, may still have isolated information systems that need to be connected with one another. To accomplish this task, these companies can use enterprise application integration. An **enterprise application integration (EAI) system** integrates existing systems by providing software, called *middleware*, that connects multiple applications. In essence, the EAI system allows existing applications to communicate and share data, thereby enabling organizations to utilize existing applications while eliminating many of the problems caused by isolated information systems. EAI systems also support implementation of "best of breed" ERP solutions by connecting software modules from different vendors.

before you go on...

1. Define ERP and describe its functions.
2. What are ERP II systems?
3. Differentiate between core ERP modules and extended ERP modules.
4. List some drawbacks of ERP software.
5. Highlight the differences between ERP configuration, customization, and best of breed implementation strategies.

10.4 ERP Support for Business Processes

ERP systems effectively support a number of standard business processes. In particular, ERP systems manage end-to-end, cross-departmental processes. A **cross-departmental process** is one that (1) originates in one department and ends in a different department or (2) originates and ends in the same department but involves other departments. Three prominent examples of cross-departmental processes are:

- The *procurement process*, which originates in the warehouse department (need to buy) and ends in the accounting department (send payment).
- The *fulfillment process*, which originates in the sales department (customer request to buy) and ends in the accounting department (receive payment).
- The *production process*, which originates and ends in the warehouse department (need to produce and reception of finished goods) but involves the production department as well.

Below, we examine these three processes in more detail, focusing on the steps that are specific to each one.

The Procurement, Fulfillment, and Production Processes

Three common cross-functional business processes are procurement, fulfillment, and production. In this section, we examine these processes in more detail, focusing on the steps that are specific to each one.

The Procurement Process. The **procurement process** originates when a company needs to acquire goods or services from external sources, and it concludes when the company receives and pays for them. Let's consider a procurement process where the company needs to acquire physical goods. This process involves three main departments—Warehouse, Purchasing, and Accounting—and consists of the following steps:

- The process originates in the Warehouse department, which generates a purchase requisition to buy the needed products.
- The Warehouse forwards the purchase requisition to the Purchasing department, which creates a purchase order (PO) and forwards it to a vendor. Generally, companies can choose from a number of vendors, and they select the one that best meets their requirements in terms of convenience, speed, reliability, and/or other characteristics.
- After the company places the order, it receives the goods in its Warehouse department, where someone physically checks the delivery to make certain that it corresponds to what the company ordered. He or she performs this task by comparing a packing list attached to the shipment against the PO.
- If the shipment matches the order, then the Warehouse issues a goods receipt document.
- At the same time or shortly thereafter, the Accounting department receives an invoice from the vendor. Accounting then checks that the PO, the goods receipt document, and the invoice match. This process is called the *three-way-match*.
- After Accounting verifies the match, it processes the payment and sends it to the vendor.

Figure 10.4 illustrates the procurement process.

The Order Fulfillment Process. In contrast to procurement, in which the company purchases goods from a vendor, in the **order fulfillment process**, also known as the order-to-cash process, the company sells goods to a customer. Fulfillment originates when the company receives a customer order, and it concludes when it receives a payment from the customer.

The fulfillment process can follow two basic strategies: sell-from-stock and configure-to-order. *Sell-from-stock* involves fulfilling customers directly using goods that are in the warehouse (stock). These goods are standard, meaning that the company does not customize them for buyers. In contrast, in *configure-to-order*, the company customizes the product in response to a customer request.

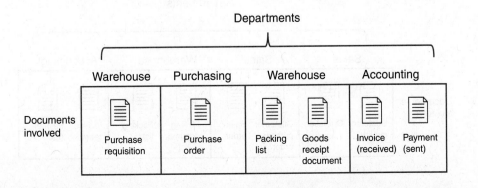

FIGURE 10.4 Departments and documents flow in the procurement process.

A fulfillment process involves three main departments: Sales, Warehouse, and Accounting. The steps in a fulfillment process include the following:

- The Sales department receives a customer inquiry, which essentially is a request for information concerning the availability and price of a specific good. (We restrict our discussion here to fulfilling a customer order for physical goods rather than services.)
- After Sales receives the inquiry, it issues a quotation that indicates availability and price.
- If the customer agrees to the price and terms, then Sales creates a customer purchase order and a sales order.
- Sales forwards the sales order to the Warehouse. The sales order is an inter-departmental document that helps the company keep track of the internal processes that are involved in fulfilling a specific customer order. In addition, it provides details of the quantity, price, and other characteristics of the product.
- The Warehouse prepares the shipment and produces two other internal documents: the picking document, which it uses to remove goods from the Warehouse, and the packing list, which accompanies the shipment and provides details about the delivery.
- At the same time, Accounting issues an invoice for the customer.
- The process concludes when Accounting receives a payment that is consistent with the invoice.

Figure 10.5 diagrams the fulfillment process. Note that it applies to both sell-from-stock and configure-to-order, because the basic steps are the same for both strategies.

The Production Process.   The **production process** does not occur in all companies because not all companies produce physical goods. In fact, many businesses limit their activities to buying (procurement) and selling products (e.g., retailers).

The production process can follow two different strategies: make-to-stock and make-to-order (see the discussion of the pull model and the push model in Chapter 11). *Make-to-stock* occurs when the company produces goods to create or increase an *inventory*; that is, finished products that are stored in the warehouse and are available for sales. In contrast, *make-to-order* occurs when the production is generated by a specific customer order.

Manufacturing companies that produce their own goods manage their inter-departmental production process across the Production and Warehouse departments. The steps in the production process are as follows:

- The Warehouse department issues a planned order when the company needs to produce a finished product, either because the Warehouse has insufficient inventory or because the customer placed a specific order for goods that are not currently in stock.
- Once the planned order reaches Production, the production controller authorizes the order and issues a production order, which is a written authorization to start the production of a certain amount of a specific product.

FIGURE 10.5 Departments and documents flow in the fulfillment process.

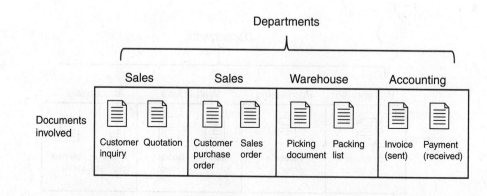

Departments

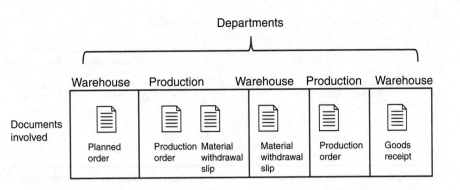

FIGURE 10.6 Departments and documents flow in the production process.

- To assemble a finished product, Production requires a number of materials (or parts). To acquire these materials, Production generates a material withdrawal slip, which lists all of the needed parts, and forwards it to the Warehouse.
- If the parts are available in the Warehouse, then the Warehouse delivers them to Production. If the parts are not available, then the company must purchase them via the procurement process.
- After Production has created the products, it updates the production order specifying that, as planned, a specific number of units of product can now be shipped to the Warehouse.
- As soon as the Warehouse receives the finished goods, it issues a goods receipt document that certifies how many units of a product it received that are available for sales.

This overview of the Production process is a highly simplified one. In reality, the process is very complex, and it frequently involves additional steps. In addition, ERP systems collect a number of other documents and pieces of information such as the bill of materials (a list of all materials needed to assemble a finished product), the list of work centers (locations where the production takes place), and the product routing (production steps). All of these topics require an in-depth analysis of the production process and are therefore beyond the scope of our discussion here. Figure 10.6 illustrates the production process.

A number of events can occur that create exceptions or deviations in the procurement, fulfillment, and production processes. Deviations can include:

- A delay in the receipt of products;
- Issues related to an unsuccessful three-way-match regarding a shipment and its associated invoice (procurement);
- Rejection of a quotation;
- A delay in a shipment;
- A mistake in preparing the shipment or in invoicing the customer (fulfillment);
- Overproduction of a product;
- Reception of parts that cannot be used in the production process;
- Non-availability of certain parts from a supplier.

Companies use ERP systems to manage procurement, fulfillment, and production because these systems track all of the events that occur within each process. Further, the system stores all of the documents created in each step of each process in a centralized database, where they are available as needed in real time. Therefore, any exceptions or mistakes made during one or more inter-departmental processes are handled right away by simply querying the ERP system and retrieving a specific document or piece of information that needs to be revised or examined more carefully. Therefore, it is important to follow each step in each process and to register the corresponding document into the ERP system.

Figure 10.7 portrays the three cross-functional business processes we just discussed. It specifically highlights the integration of the three processes, which is made possible by ERP systems.

FIGURE 10.7 Integrated
processes with ERP systems.

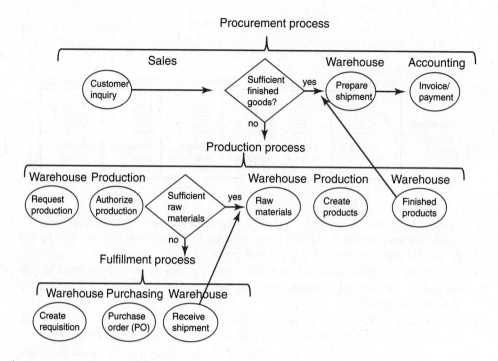

Interorganizational Processes: ERP with SCM and CRM

Although the procurement and the fulfillment processes involve suppliers and customers, they are considered (together with the production process) intraorganizational processes because they originate and conclude within the company. However, ERP systems can also manage processes that originate in one company and conclude in another company. These processes are called *interorganizational processes*, and they typically involve supply chain management (SCM) and customer relationship management (CRM) systems. You can find a more detailed description of CRM and SCM in Chapter 11. Here, we focus on the integration of these processes within a firm's industry value chain.

SCM and CRM processes help multiple firms in an industry coordinate activities such as the production-to-sale of goods and services. Let's consider a chain of grocery stores whose supply chain must properly manage perishable goods. On the one hand, store managers need to stock only the amount of perishable products that they are reasonably sure to sell before the products' expiration dates. On the other hand, they do not want to run out of stock of any products that customers need.

ERP SCM systems have the capability to place automatic requests to buy fresh perishable products from suppliers in real time. That is, as each perishable product is purchased, the system captures data on that purchase, adjusts store inventory levels, and transmits these data to the grocery chain's Warehouse as well as the products' vendors. The system executes this process by connecting the point-of-sale barcode-scanning system with the Warehouse and Accounting departments, as well as with the vendors' systems. In addition, SCM systems utilize historical data to predict when fresh products need to be ordered before the store's supply becomes too low.

ERP CRM systems also benefit businesses by generating forecasting analyses of product consumption based on critical variables such as geographical area, season, day of the week, and type of customer. These analyses help grocery stores coordinate their supply chains to meet customer needs for perishable products. Going further, CRM systems identify particular customer needs and then utilize this information to suggest specific product campaigns. These campaigns can transform a potential demand into sales opportunities, and convert sales opportunities into sales quotations and sales orders. This process is called the *demand-to-order* process.

before you go on...

1. What are the three main intraorganizational processes that are typically supported by ERP systems?
2. Why is it important that all steps in each process generate a document that is stored in the ERP system?
3. What is the difference between inter- and intra-company processes?
4. What are the two main ES systems that support interorganizational processes?

Reports

10.5

All information systems produce reports: transaction processing systems, functional area information systems, ERP systems, customer relationship management systems, business intelligence systems, and so on. We discuss reports here because they are so closely associated with FAIS and ERP systems. However, the important point is that *all* information systems produce reports. These reports generally fall into three categories: routine, ad-hoc (on-demand), and exception.

Routine reports are produced at scheduled intervals. They range from hourly quality control reports to daily reports on absenteeism rates. Although routine reports are extremely valuable to an organization, managers frequently need special information that is not included in these reports. At other times, they need the information that is normally included in routine reports, but at different times ("I need the report today, for the last three days, not for one week").

Such out-of-the routine reports are called **ad-hoc (on-demand) reports**. Ad-hoc reports also can include requests for the following types of information:

- **Drill-down reports** display a greater level of detail. For example, a manager might examine sales by region and decide to "drill down" to more detail by focusing specifically on sales by store and then by salesperson.
- **Key-indicator reports** summarize the performance of critical activities. For example, a chief financial officer might want to monitor cash flow and cash on hand.
- **Comparative reports** compare, for example, the performances of different business units or of a single unit during different times.

Some managers prefer exception reports. **Exception reports** include only information that falls outside certain threshold standards. To implement *management by exception*, management first creates performance standards. The company then creates systems to monitor performance (via the incoming data about business transactions such as expenditures), compare actual performance to the standards, and identify exceptions to the standards. The system alerts managers to the exceptions via exception reports.

Let us use sales as an example. First, management establishes sales quotas. The company then implements an FAIS that collects and analyzes all of the sales data. An exception report would identify only those cases where sales fell outside an established threshold—for example, more than 20 percent short of the quota. It would *not* report expenditures that fell *within* the accepted range of standards. By leaving out all "acceptable" performances, exception reports save managers time, thus helping them focus on problem areas.

before you go on...

1. Compare and contrast the three major types of reports.
2. Compare and contrast the three types of on-demand reports.

What's In IT For Me?

For the Accounting Major

Understanding the functions and outputs of TPSs effectively is a major concern of any accountant. It is also necessary to understand the various activities of all functional areas and how they are interconnected. Accounting information systems are a central component in any ERP package. In fact, all large CPA firms actively consult with clients on ERP implementations, using thousands of specially trained accounting majors.

For the Finance Major

IT helps financial analysts and managers perform their tasks better. Of particular importance is analyzing cash flows and securing the financing required for smooth operations. In addition, financial applications can support such activities as risk analysis, investment management, and global transactions involving different currencies and fiscal regulations.

Finance activities and modeling are key components of ERP systems. Flows of funds (payments), at the core of most supply chains, must be executed efficiently and effectively. Financial arrangements are especially important along global supply chains, where currency conventions and financial regulations must be considered.

For the Marketing Major

Marketing and sales expenses are usually targets in a cost-reduction program. Also, sales force automation not only improves salespeoples' productivity (and thus reduces costs), but it also improves customer service.

For the Production/Operations Management Major

Managing production tasks, materials handling, and inventories in short time intervals, at a low cost, and with high quality is critical for competitiveness. These activities can be achieved only if they are properly supported by IT. In addition, IT can greatly enhance interaction with other functional areas, especially sales. Collaboration in design, manufacturing, and logistics requires knowledge of how modern information systems can be connected.

For the Human Resources Management Major

Human resources managers can increase their efficiency and effectiveness by using IT for some of their routine functions. Human resources personnel need to understand how information flows between the HR department and the other functional areas. Finally, the integration of functional areas via ERP systems has a major impact on skill requirements and scarcity of employees, which are related to the tasks performed by the HRM department.

For the MIS Major

The MIS function is responsible for the most fundamental information systems in organizations: the transaction processing systems. The TPSs provide the data for the databases. In turn, all other information systems use these data. MIS personnel develop applications that support all levels of the organization (from clerical to executive) and all functional areas. The applications also enable the firm to do business with its partners.

[Summary]

1. **Explain the purpose of transaction processing systems.**

   TPSs monitor, store, collect, and process data generated from all business transactions. These data provide the inputs into the organization's database.

2. **Explain the types of support information systems can provide for each functional area of the organization.**

   The major business functional areas are production/operations management, marketing, accounting/finance, and human resources management. Table 10.1 provides an overview of the many activities in each functional area supported by FAIS.

3. **Identify advantages and drawbacks to businesses of implementing an ERP system.**

   Enterprise resource planning systems integrate the planning, management, and use of all of the organization's resources. The major objective of ERP systems is to tightly integrate the functional areas of the organization. This integration enables information to flow seamlessly across the various functional areas.

   The major benefits of ERP systems include the following:

   - Because ERP systems integrate organizational resources, they make organizations more flexible, agile, and adaptive. The organizations can therefore react quickly to changing business conditions and capitalize on new business opportunities.
   - ERP systems provide essential information on business performance across functional areas. This information significantly improves managers' ability to make better, more timely decisions.
   - ERP systems integrate organizational resources, resulting in significant improvements in the quality of customer service, production, and distribution.

   The major drawbacks of ERP systems include the following:

   - The business processes in ERP software are often predefined by the best practices that the ERP vendor has developed. As a result, companies may need to change existing business processes to fit the predefined business processes of the software. For companies with well-established procedures, this requirement can be a huge problem.
   - ERP systems can be extremely complex, expensive, and time-consuming to implement. In fact, the costs and risks of failure in implementing a new ERP system are substantial.

4. **Describe the three main business processes supported by ERP systems.**

   The *procurement process*, which originates in the warehouse department (need to buy) and ends in the accounting department (send payment).

   The *fulfillment process* that originates in the sales department (customer request to buy) and ends in the accounting department (receive payment).

   The *production process* that originates and ends in the warehouse department (need to produce and reception of finished goods), but involves the production department as well.

   We leave the details of the steps in each of these processes to you.

5. **Discuss the three major types of reports generated by the functional area information systems and enterprise resource planning systems, providing examples of each type.**

   Routine reports are produced at scheduled intervals. They range from hourly quality control reports to daily reports on absenteeism rates.

   Out-of-the routine reports are called *ad-hoc (on-demand) reports*. For example, a chief financial officer might want to monitor cash flow and cash on hand.

   Exception reports include only information that falls outside certain threshold standards. An exception report might identify only those cases where sales fell outside an established threshold—for example, more than 20 percent short of the quota.

[Chapter Glossary]

ad-hoc (on-demand) reports Nonroutine reports that often contain special information that is not included in routine reports.

batch processing Transaction processing system (TPS) that processes data in batches at fixed periodic intervals.

comparative reports Reports that compare performances of different business units or times.

computer-integrated manufacturing (CIM) An information system that integrates various automated factory systems; also called *digital manufacturing*.

cross-departmental process A business process that originates in one department and ends in another department, and/or originates and ends in the same department while involving other departments.

drill-down reports Reports that show a greater level of detail than is included in routine reports.

enterprise application integration (EAI) system A system that integrates existing systems by providing layers of software that connect applications together.

enterprise resource planning (ERP) systems Information systems that take a business process view of the overall organization to integrate the planning, management, and use of all of an organization's resources, employing a common software platform and database.

ERP II systems Interorganizational ERP systems that provide Web-enabled links among key business systems (such as inventory and production) of a company and its customers, suppliers, distributors, and others.

exception reports Reports that include only information that exceeds certain threshold standards.

functional area information systems (FAISs) Systems that provide information to managers (usually midlevel) in the functional areas, in order to support managerial tasks of planning, organizing, and controlling operations.

key-indicator reports Reports that summarize the performance of critical activities.

online transaction processing (OLTP) Transaction processing system (TPS) that processes data after transactions occur, frequently in real time.

order fulfillment process A cross-functional business process that originates when the company receives a customer order, and it concludes when it receives a payment from the customer.

procurement process A cross-functional business process that originates when a company needs to acquire goods or services from external sources, and it concludes when the company receives and pays for them.

production process A cross-functional business process in which a company produces physical goods.

routine reports Reports produced at scheduled intervals.

transaction Any business event that generates data worth capturing and storing in a database.

transaction processing system (TPS) Information system that supports the monitoring, collection, storage, and processing of data from the organization's basic business transactions, each of which generates data.

[Discussion Questions]

1. Why is it logical to organize IT applications by functional areas?
2. Describe the role of a TPS in a service organization.
3. Describe the relationship between TPS and FAIS.
4. Discuss how IT facilitates the budgeting process.
5. How can the Internet support investment decisions?
6. Describe the benefits of integrated accounting software packages.
7. Discuss the role that IT plays in support of auditing.
8. Investigate the role of the Web in human resources management.
9. What is the relationship between information silos and enterprise resource planning?

[Problem-Solving Activities]

1. Finding a job on the Internet is challenging as there are almost too many places to look. Visit the following sites: *www.careerbuilder.com*, *www.craigslist.org*, *www.linkedin.com*, *www.jobcentral.com*, and *www.monster.com*. What does each of these sites provide you as a job seeker?

2. Enter *www.sas.com* and access *revenue optimization* there. Explain how the software helps in optimizing prices.

3. Enter *www.eleapsoftware.com* and review the product that helps with online training (training systems). What are the most attractive features of this product?

4. Check out Microsoft Dynamics demos at *http://www.wiley.com/go/rainer/problemsolving*. View three of the demos in different functional areas of your choice. Prepare a report on each product's capabilities.

5. Examine the capabilities of the following (and similar) financial software packages: Financial Analyzer (from Oracle) and CFO Vision (from SAS Institute). Prepare a report comparing the capabilities of the software packages.

6. Surf the Net and find free accounting software. (Try CNet's software at *http://www.wiley.com/go/rainer/problemsolving*,

www.rkom.com, www.tucows.com, www.passtheshareware .com, and *www.freeware-guide.com.*) Download the software and try it. Compare the ease of use and usefulness of each software package.

7. Examine the capabilities of the following financial software packages: TekPortal (from *www.tekknowledge.com*), Financial Analyzer (from *www.oracle.com*), and Financial Management (from *www.sas.com*). Prepare a report comparing the capabilities of the software packages.

8. Find Simply Accounting Basic from Sage Software (*http://us.simplyaccounting.com*). Why is this product recommended for small businesses?

9. Enter *www.halogensoftware.com* and *www.successfactors .com.* Examine their software products and compare them.

10. Enter *www.iemployee.com* and find the support it provides to human resources management activities. View the demos and prepare a report on the capabilities of the products.

COLLABORATION EXERCISE

Background

Transaction processing systems, functional area systems, and enterprise resource planning systems provide much of the basis for decision support within an organization. All of the data often resides in a few databases or data warehouses and is then accessed by the various systems that provide support for making decisions.

Activity

Divide your team into the following positions based on major as much as possible (if you do not have enough majors to divide, then choose by preference): inventory, sales, production, labor, and accounting. Imagine that you are a manufacturing company that sells widgets and that your top salesperson just closed a deal for 10,000 units.

For each of the systems mentioned above (transaction, function, and enterprise), describe the information you think your area would need to capture, store, analyze, and distribute for this transaction.

Once everyone has completed their list of data needs, meet as a team and have a conversation about how similar or different your needs are. Is there any overlap? How would you use the information to make decisions?

Deliverable

Write up a description of the data that is needed by different areas and how important data capture is for providing the correct data points to the enterprise system. Submit your description to your professor.

[Closing Case Truck Manufacturer Incorporates Information Systems in Trucks]

The Problem

For more than a century, PACCAR (www.paccar.com) has been a manufacturer of Peterbilt, Kenworth, and DAF (in Europe) heavy trucks. For much of this period the company turned a handsome profit. During the U.S. recession of 2008, however, PACCAR's sales declined by 50 percent (but the company did report a profit that year). This problem convinced the company to take a risk by initiating a major information technology project.

IT leaders at PACCAR crafted a strategic vision for how electronic systems could change their trucking and freight-hauling business. This vision included identifying new features their trucks would need for PACCAR to remain competitive and profitable. IT envisioned two innovative systems: (1) a navigation system tailored to truckers' needs and (2) an onboard diagnostic system comprised of a network of data-collecting sensors that would warn of performance problems. Both systems would use pervasive wireless links to send data back to dispatchers. This system would allow PACCAR's customer companies to continuously monitor their trucks' location and performance.

The IT Solution

As a first step to implementing this vision, IT staffers communicated directly with employees from all of the firm's functional areas to emphasize the growing importance of in-vehicle electronic systems. Based on these talks, the company's business and IT leaders achieved a consensus that PACCAR should develop its electronic systems in house, even though the firm had no expertise in building either wireless consumer electronics or consumer-friendly computer interfaces.

To kick off the project, PACCAR convened a workshop for company design engineers, IT systems developers, and truck parts specialists. The workshop attendees decided their highest priority was to build a smart navigation system.

Then, financial problems hit the company. PACCAR reported revenue of $15 billion in 2008, but that revenue decreased by almost half to $8 billion in 2009. PACCAR eventually had to lay off roughly one-third of its workforce to keep its costs in line. The IT department had to reduce its staff as well, and it was prohibited from hiring new talent in wireless and mobile systems. Furthermore, because of the tough financial climate, the IT department had neither the research nor the development budget to create an innovative new system. Adding to these problems, PACCAR realized that in-vehicle electronic systems, a new territory for them, would evolve at a much faster pace than areas in which they possessed extensive expertise, such as engine technology.

To overcome these barriers, PACCAR decided to partner with outside organizations. For instance, the company utilized an automotive system that Microsoft had developed to build an in-cab electronics system. The PACCAR system contained a software development application that third parties could use to develop additional applications for PACCAR. In addition, PACCAR's system enabled high-resolution graphics on a touch screen in the cab of its trucks.

PACCAR's navigation system used Garmin geo-positioning integrated with the driver's user interface and related routing and mapping applications. Truck navigation systems are different from car systems in that they need to track details such as heights of bridges and weight restrictions along a route.

In addition to navigation, the touch screen presents the driver with six "virtual gauges" that display various metrics regarding engine performance. PACCAR plans to incorporate more than 20 additional gauges into the next generation of the system. Significantly, this change will require nothing more than a simple software update.

After developing its navigation system, PACCAR shifted its attention to its diagnostic system. PACCAR's system uses a modem from SignalSet (*www.signalset.com*) that automatically links to the strongest wireless signal that the truck can access. In August 2011, PACCAR announced that its diagnostic system was available as an add-on to its trucks. Less than a year later the system was available as a built-in option. To demonstrate the navigation and diagnostic systems for potential customers, PACCAR has built kiosks in 1,900 of its dealer showrooms.

The Results

PACCAR's electronic systems projects did more than place vital, customer-facing new systems into its products in the middle of a terrible economy. The projects also allowed the 275 PACCAR employees working on the projects to gain valuable experience collaborating with external talent.

Having made the leap into customer-facing systems and having made IT a critical part of its products, PACCAR understands that the pressure to continually update its IT systems to keep up with drivers' demands and rival products will be unrelenting. Therefore, the company now maintains a skilled IT staff dedicated to developing products and, when necessary, to collaborating with outside companies.

And the bottom line? PACCAR reported revenues of $17 billion in 2012, an increase of $700 million from 2011. Further, the company reported net income of $1.1 billion in 2012, an increase of $70 million over 2011. Interestingly, 2012 is the 73rd consecutive year that PACCAR has reported a profit.

Sources: Compiled from S. Kilcarr, "I'll Take Telematics With That Truck," *Fleet-Owner*, May 15, 2012; G. Conti, "Telematics: The Next Frontier," *Truckinginfo.com*, May 2012; P. Menig, "Top 12 Truck Electronics Issues - A Year's Worth of Subjects," *tech-i-m.com*, January 11, 2012; C. Babcock, "Heavy Truck Maker Revs Up IT Innovation Amid a Brutal Recession," *InformationWeek*, September 19, 2011; "PACCAR Truckerlink Uses Proprietary Cellular Network Technology," *Truckinginfo*, September 16, 2011; "PACCAR Parts Touts Cellular-Based Telematics Fleet Management Service," *Truck Parts and Service*, September 15, 2011; "Kenworth Truck Company Has Introduced the Revolutionary Kenworth NavPlus™, A PACCAR Proprietary Navigation and Infotainment Technology System for Class 5–8 Trucks," *The Street*, March 24, 2010; www.paccar.com, www.kenworth.com, www.peterbilt.com, www.truckerlink.com, www.signalset.com, accessed March 10, 2013.

Questions

1. Why did PACCAR turn to collaboration and commit resources to develop electronic systems during the recession?

2. What are the benefits of PACCAR's new navigation system and diagnostic system to truck drivers?

3. What are the benefits to PACCAR of collaborating with outside companies in building new systems?

[Internship Activity]

Manufacturing Industry

Implementation of an Enterprise Resource Planning system (ERP) is a very lofty goal for any organization. Especially if there are existing systems in place. Migrating to a new system takes more than just updating software. Sometimes it requires modifying processes, changing habits, providing training, and getting management and user buy-in.

For this activity, you will work for Halle Smith CIO of a wire manufacturing company. Halle has been charged with finding and implementing an ERP to help clean up the flow of data and operations within the organization. However, she knows it will be an uphill battle. Your task will be to research unsuccessful ERP implementations to help Halle understand the reasons why ERP implementations often fail.

Please visit the Book Companion Site to receive the full set of instructions.

Chapter 11

Customer Relationship Management and Supply Chain Management

[LEARNING OBJECTIVES]	[CHAPTER OUTLINE]	[WEB RESOURCES]

[LEARNING OBJECTIVES]

1. Identify the primary functions of both customer relationship management (CRM) and collaborative CRM.

2. Describe how businesses might utilize applications of each of the two major components of operational CRM systems.

3. Discuss the benefits of analytical CRM systems to businesses.

4. Explain the advantages and disadvantages of mobile CRM systems, on-demand CRM systems, and open-source CRM systems.

5. Describe the three components and the three flows of a supply chain.

6. Identify popular strategies to solving different challenges of supply chains.

7. Explain the utility of each of the three major technologies that supports supply chain management.

[CHAPTER OUTLINE]

11.1 Defining Customer Relationship Management

11.2 Operational Customer Relationship Management Systems

11.3 Analytical Customer Relationship Management Systems

11.4 Other Types of Customer Relationship Management Systems

11.5 Supply Chains

11.6 Supply Chain Management

11.7 Information Technology Support for Supply Chain Management

[WEB RESOURCES]

- Student PowerPoints for note taking

WileyPLUS

- E-book

- Author video lecture for each chapter section

- Practice quizzes

- Flash Cards for vocabulary review

- Additional "IT's About Business" cases

- Video interviews with managers

- Lab Manuals for Microsoft Office 2010 and 2013

ACCT	FIN	MKT	POM	HRM	MIS
ACCOUNTING	FINANCE	MARKETING	PRODUCTION OPERATIONS MANAGEMENT	HUMAN RESOURCES MANAGEMENT	MIS
Comply with cross-border data transfer laws	Analyze financial data from business partners	Manage consolidated customer data	Apply sales forecasts to demand	Train employees in CRM	Collect and store customer data

[Customer Relationship Management in the Internet Age]

Customer relationship management has become almost real time with the advent of social media. In this chapter-opening case, you will first read about two problems, which are examples of bad things that can happen very quickly to companies that treat customers poorly. You will then read about two solutions that exemplify the good things that can happen very quickly to companies that treat customers well.

A Problem (First Example)

A company called N-Control (www.avengercontroller.com) invented the Avenger video game console controller that was originally designed to help gamers with physical disabilities play video games. The Avenger was also marketed to enhance the performance of "hardcore gamers." On November 3, 2011, a customer—we'll call him Dave—ordered two Avenger controllers. N-Control's Web site advertised a shipping date of "early December." By December 16, however, Dave had not received any news regarding an official release date. He emailed Tom, the president of N-Control's marketing firm, Ocean Marketing. Tom promptly responded that the controllers would be shipped the following day.

Despite Tom's assurances, however, the controllers did not ship on December 17th, or on the 18th, or at any time in December. Making matters worse, N-Control awarded rebates to customers who ordered their Avengers after December 26th, but not to customers who had placed their orders prior to that date. The company did not explain this policy.

When Dave became aware of this policy, he contacted the marketing firm again to find out whether he could become eligible for the rebate by cancelling his initial order and reordering the Avenger. Tom responded with this statement: "Feel free to cancel we need the units we're back ordered 11,000 units so your 2 will be gone fast. Maybe I'll put them on eBay for 150.00 myself. Have a good day."

Understandably irritated by this response, Dave sent Tom a second e-mail in which he copied Mike Krahulik, co-creator of Penny Arcade (www.pennyarcade.com) and the founder of PAX East, one of the largest gaming conventions in the United States, along with various other gaming news Web sites. For some reason, instead of trying to defuse the situation by apologizing to Dave, Tom responded by calling Dave a child, and he laughed at Dave's complaints.

Krahulik was so offended by Tom's response that he guaranteed that Tom would not have a booth at PAX. Tom did not worry about being left out of PAX, claiming that he would be present at "bigger and better shows." In response, Krahulik informed Tom that he would be posting the entire e-mail conversation online. Tom responded, "Great! Love PR."

Krahulik posted the e-mail conversation on Penny Arcade. The story went viral in a matter of hours with the help of Reddit, Twitter, and Facebook. Tom's Twitter account was quickly bombarded with hostile messages. He changed his Twitter handle twice, to no avail.

Tom was not the only one to feel the "anger of the Internet." Amazon was flooded with negative reviews of the Avenger controller that characterized the company's customer service as abysmal.

A Problem (Second Example)

Musician Dave Carroll booked a flight with United Airlines. He checked his $3,500 Taylor guitar because it was difficult to bring guitars onto flights as carry-on luggage. When Carroll arrived at his destination, he discovered that his guitar had been severely damaged. In addition, he alleged that he heard a fellow passenger claim that baggage handlers on the tarmac at Chicago's O'Hare International Airport were throwing guitars during a layover on his flight. Carroll stated that he alerted three United Airlines employees, who showed complete indifference to his problem. Frustrated by this lack of response, Carroll filed a claim with United. In response, the airline informed him that he was ineligible for compensation because he had failed to make the claim within the company's stipulated "standard 24-hour timeframe."

Carroll maintained that he continued to negotiate for compensation with the airline for nine months, to no avail. At that point he wrote a song and created videos about his experience with United. The videos were released on YouTube, and they quickly collected more than 10 million hits.

A Solution (First Example)

While having lunch in a P.F. Chang's China Bistro restaurant (*www.pfchangs.com*), a woman in Florida sent out a Tweet about her delicious lettuce-wrap appetizer. An employee at P.F. Chang's headquarters in Scottsdale, Arizona, spotted the tweet. He alerted a manager, who immediately called the Florida restaurant. Using the customer's profile picture, the restaurant manager identified the woman, and he instructed a server to present her with lettuce wraps and a dessert for being an enthusiastic supporter of their company.

By having its finger on the pulse of its social media branding, P.F. Chang's executed a social media coup. Not only did the restaurant earn a fan for life—and one who has an active Twitter account—but the customer undoubtedly told her friends and coworkers about her lunchtime surprise, praising P.F. Chang's for caring about its customers. Further, in a short time, marketing executives in many organizations were presenting P.F. Chang's and its lettuce wraps in conferences and meetings as an example of intuitive branding.

A Solution (Second Example)

According to J.D. Power & Associates almost 20 percent of big bank customers have a problem with their bank. This problem is prevalent on the Web, where mishandled complaints can go viral and wreak havoc with a bank's reputation in minutes.

In 2010, Citibank issued a directive that required its social-media agents to obtain approval from managers at the bank before answering even the most mundane questions. This process extended the average response time to more than 24 hours—far too long for Web users. Consider Jane, who became so frustrated after spending 40 minutes on hold with Citibank customer service that she tweeted her displeasure. To her surprise, a Citibank agent tweeted right back saying, "Send us your phone number and we'll call you right now." In a few minutes, Jane was talking with a Citibank agent who had received special training in social media. The agent took such good care of Jane that now, whenever she has a problem, she bypasses the call center and instead tweets her concerns to the Twitter address @askCiti.

The Results

In the vignette of N-Control, Ocean Marketing fired Tom, and N-Control severed its relations with Ocean Marketing. N-Control then donated $10,000 to the Child's Play charity in an attempt to restore the brand's image.

In the vignette of United Airlines, Dave Carroll's videos created a public relations humiliation for United Airlines. Rob Bradford, the airline's managing director of customer solutions, telephoned Carroll personally to apologize for the mistake and to request permission to use the video internally for training. The belated compensation offer of $3,000, United donated to the Thelonious Monk Institute of Jazz as a "gesture of goodwill," failed to undo the damage done to its image.

Since the incident, Carroll has been in demand as a speaker on customer service. Ironically, on one of his trips, United lost his luggage. In January 2013, the German television and news service Tagesschau used the success of Carroll's online protest to exemplify a new kind of threat facing corporations in the Internet age.

In the vignette of P.F. Chang's, the restaurant used social media as an easy opportunity to make the most of the customer experience and to demonstrate to the organization that there is "gold" in Tweets.

In the vignette of Citibank, Jane was the beneficiary of a multiyear effort by Citibank to overhaul the way it interacts with customers via social networking sites. The bank persuaded its lawyers to give social media agents the latitude to respond to questions about customer accounts, products, and services without obtaining the approval of bank managers.

Banks now appreciate the value of courting customers via social media. These customers tend to be affluent and they are quick to adopt new technologies such as online and mobile banking. Further, winning these customers over pays quick dividends, because they are just as likely to comment about good experiences—such as the customer who recently thanked Citibank on Twitter for helping him with his mother's retirement account—as they are to complain about bad ones.

And the bottom line for Citibank? A 2012 study revealed that the organization performed markedly better than peer banks in responding to customer queries on Twitter.

Regardless of whether organizations have implemented a social media strategy, customers are increasingly using social media such as Twitter and Facebook. Significantly, these customers routinely inform the world how they feel about companies, their products, and their services. Their activities range from a Facebook group begging Trader Joe's (*www.traderjoes.com*) to open a store in a certain geographic location to a blogger complaining about a washing machine to a million followers. In today's highly technical and competitive environment, companies ignore social media at their peril.

Sources: Compiled from S. Kapner, "Citi Won't Sleep on Customer Tweets," *The Wall Street Journal*, October 5, 2012; S. Bennett, "Twitter Mobile Ads Give 'Staggering' Results, Says Advertiser," *MediaBistro.com*, June 29, 2012; S. Ovide, "Twitter's Mobile Ads Begin to Click," *The Wall Street Journal*, June 28, 2012; L. Brousell, "How Citibank Uses Twitter to Improve Customer Service," *The Wall Street Journal*, June 19, 2012; S. Haley, "Is a $10,000 Donation Enough To Make the World Forget about Ocean Marketing," *VentureBeat.com*, January 8, 2012; D. Smith, "Avenger Controller Fires Ocean Marketing After PR Fiasco," *International Business Times*, December 28, 2011; S. Haley, "Ocean Marketing: How to Self-Destruct Your Company With a Few Measly E-mails," *VentureBeat.com*, December 27, 2011; "City Integrates Customer Support on Twitter into Its First iPad App for the Mass Market," Visible Banking, August 2, 2011; W. Schuchart, "How P.F. Chang's Turned a Plate of Lettuce Wraps into a Twitter Win," *IT Knowledge Exchange*, March 16, 2011; J. McLean, "United Loses Luggage of 'United Breaks Guitars' guy," *Toronto Star*, October 29, 2009; "Singer Gets His Revenge on United Airlines and Soars to Fame," *The Guardian*, July 23, 2009; C. Ayers, "Revenge Is Best Served Cold—on YouTube," *The Times* (London), July 22, 2009; www.citibank.com, www.pfchangs.com, www.avengercontroller.com, www.davecarrollmusic.com, accessed March 16, 2013.

What We Learned from This Case

The chapter-opening case provides examples of the evolving nature of the business–customer relationship, particularly in today's social media arena. As personal technology usage changes, so too must the methods that businesses use to interface with their customers. Organizations increasingly are emphasizing a customer-centric approach to their business practices because they know that sustainable value is found in long-term customer relationships that extend beyond any given day's business transaction. The chapter-closing case addresses the critical importance of effectively managing complex warehouse operations.

Customer relationship management is not just for large organizations. CRM is essential for small organizations as well. IT's About Business 11.1 explains how induPlast uses information systems to improve their customer relationships.

IT's [about business]

11.1 induPlast   MKT

Have you ever paid attention to the hundreds of little plastic containers located in the cosmetics aisle of your grocery store? Or in the pharmaceutical aisle? Or, indeed, in every aisle in most stores? When you consider the plastic containers of all shapes, sizes, and colors that populate our world, it is really amazing! For some reason, every company feels the need to have a custom-designed container for each of its brands and for each product within that brand. Now, have you ever wondered whose job it is to make all of these different containers? In fact, the manufacturer of all of the containers you see likely comes from a very small pool of vendors.

One of these vendors is induPlast (www.induplast.it), based in Italy. With around 70 employees, induPlast manufactures injection-molded plastic containers, which can be customized for patrons. Unfortunately, induPlast began to experience problems providing adequate support to their customers. Specifically, information for a single customer ended up in different silos of information (i.e., different departments contained customer information, such as marketing, accounting, etc.). This setup made it very difficult for induPlast to track all of the various business dealings it conducted with a single customer. Not surprisingly, this problem created deficits in customer relationship management (CRM). Compounding this problem was the fact that each customer had multiple customized products.

Let's take a hypothetical example. (This situation is entirely fictional—the authors of this text are not familiar with specifics regarding induPlast clients.) Imagine that Johnson & Johnson (J&J) is a customer of induPlast. J&J has multiple divisions including skin and hair care, wound care and topicals, oral healthcare, women's health, and over-the-counter medicines. induPlast also has multiple divisions that focus on different product categories such as cosmetics and healthcare. Without a CRM tool, relationships between J&J and induPlast are developed at the division level rather than the corporate level. Therefore, each division of induPlast relates to each division of the customer company as a separate provider or customer, rather than as a department of a company with which induPlast has a unified customer relationship.

As you can see, without a CRM system, induPlast collects a great deal of customer data on J&J, but those data are confined to the individual division that gathered them, and they not available to other divisions. So, if induPlast finds it necessary to deal with J&J as a whole (not by division), it would experience major difficulties in assimilating all of the different data points to obtain a unified picture of its customer.

To solve problems similar to this fictional (though possible) example, induPlast needed a CRM system that would provide a 360-degree view of each customer. induPlast chose Sugar CRM, an open-source tool that enables the company to streamline its customer information and communication. The company was able to integrate Sugar with its existing systems to provide management with greater insight into the manufacturing process. Real-time tracking allowed induPlast to make decisions based on complete and current information rather than on stale or incomplete data gathered piecemeal across the company.

The result is that induPlast is now able to monitor trends in both the market and customer accounts in real time. As intended, the company now has a 360-degree view of customers across all divisions.

CRM tools serve many purposes. In some cases (this case included), they virtually consolidate data. This means that data are still housed in the existing systems where they were gathered, but the CRM connects those systems so that everyone in the company can access the data they need, regardless of which division they work in. In other cases, the CRM completely replaces existing systems and imports the existing data into the new system. Regardless of the method, the goal of CRM is to provide clean, current information on customers to help management make better decisions.

Sources: Compiled from www.induplast.it, www.sugarcrm.com, www.jnj.com/connect/healthcare-products/consumer, accessed March 23, 2012.

Questions

1. Why was information stored in "information silos" at induPlast in the first place?
2. Why is a 360-degree view of each customer so important to induPlast?

At this point, however, you may be asking yourself: Why should I learn about CRM and SCM? As you will see in this chapter, customers and suppliers are supremely important to *all* organizations. Regardless of the job you perform, you will have an impact, whether direct or indirect, on managing your firm's customers and suppliers. When you read the What's in IT For Me? section at the end of the chapter, you will learn about opportunities to make immediate contributions on your first job. Therefore, it is important that you gain a working knowledge of CRM, CRM systems, SCM, and SCM systems.

In Chapter 10, you learned about information systems that supported organizational activities within the organization. In this chapter, you study information systems that support organizational activities that extend outside the organization to customers (customer relationship management systems; CRM) and suppliers (supply chain management systems; SCM). Both of these systems are critical to the success of modern businesses. Accordingly, the first half of this chapter is devoted to CRM and CRM systems, and the second half to SCM and SCM systems.

Defining Customer Relationship Management 11.1

Before the supermarket, the mall, and the automobile, people purchased goods at their neighborhood store. The owners and employees recognized customers by name and knew their preferences and wants. For their part, customers remained loyal to the store and made repeated purchases. Over time, however, this personal customer relationship became impersonal as people moved from farms to cities, consumers became mobile, and supermarkets and department stores achieved economies of scale through mass marketing. Although prices were lower and products were more uniform in quality, the relationship with customers became nameless and impersonal.

The customer relationship has become even more impersonal with the rapid growth of the Internet and the World Wide Web. In today's hypercompetitive marketplace, customers are increasingly powerful; if they are dissatisfied with a product and/or a service from one organization, a competitor is often just one mouse click away. Further, as more and more customers shop on the Web, an enterprise does not even have the opportunity to make a good first impression *in person*.

Customer relationship management returns to personal marketing. That is, rather than market to a mass of people or companies, businesses market to each customer individually. By employing this approach, businesses can use information about each customer—for example, previous purchases, needs, and wants—to create offers that customers are more likely to accept. That is, the CRM approach is designed to achieve *customer intimacy*. This CRM approach is enabled by information technology in the form of various CRM systems and applications.

Customer relationship management is not only about the software. Sometimes the problem with managing relationships is simply time and information. Old systems may contain needed information, but this information may take too long to access and may not be usable across a variety of applications. The result is that companies have less time to spend with customers.

Customer relationship management (CRM) is a customer-focused and customer-driven organizational strategy. That is, organizations concentrate on assessing customers' requirements for products and services and then providing high-quality, responsive service. CRM is not a process or a technology per se; rather, it is a customer-centric way of thinking and acting. The focus of modern organizations has shifted from conducting business transactions to managing customer relationships. In general, organizations recognize that customers are the core of a successful enterprise, and the success of the enterprise depends on effectively managing relationships with them.

CRM builds sustainable long-term customer relationships that create value for the company as well as for the customer. That is, CRM helps companies acquire new customers and retain existing and expand their relationships with profitable existing customers. Retaining customers is particularly important because repeat customers are the largest generator of revenue for an enterprise. Also, organizations have long understood that winning back a customer who has switched to a competitor is vastly more expensive than keeping that customer satisfied in the first place.

Figure 11.1 depicts the CRM process. The process begins with marketing efforts, where the organization solicits prospects from a target population of potential customers. A certain number of these prospects will make a purchase and thus become customers. A certain number of these will become repeat customers. The organization then segments its repeat customers into low-value and high-value repeat customers. An organization's overall goal is to maximize the *lifetime value* of a customer, which is that customer's potential revenue stream over a number of years.

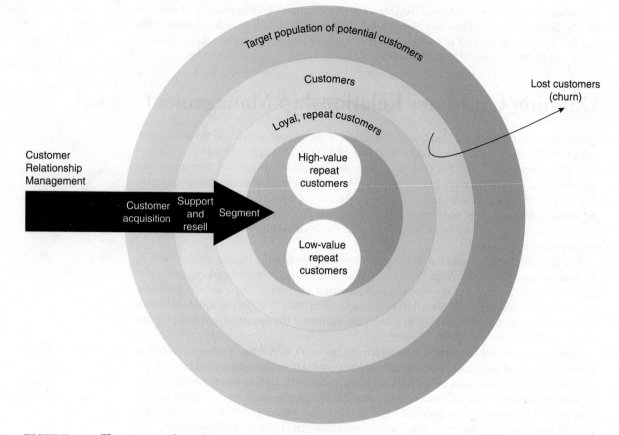

FIGURE 11.1 The customer relationship management process.

Over time all organizations inevitably lose a certain percentage of customers, a process called *customer churn*. The optimal result of the organization's CRM efforts is to maximize the number of high-value repeat customers while minimizing customer churn.

CRM is basically a simple idea: Treat different customers differently, because their needs differ, and their value to the company also may differ. A successful CRM strategy not only improves customer satisfaction, but it makes the company's sales and service employees more productive, which in turn generates increased profits. In fact, researchers at the National Quality Research Center at the University of Michigan discovered that a 1 percent increase in customer satisfaction can lead to as much as a 300 percent increase in a company's market capitalization, defined as the number of shares of the company's stock outstanding multiplied by the price per share of the stock. Put simply, a minor increase in customer satisfaction can lead to a major increase in a company's overall value.

Up to this point, you have been looking at an organization's CRM strategy. It is important to distinguish between a CRM *strategy* and CRM *systems*. Basically, CRM systems are information systems designed to support an organization's CRM strategy. For organizations to pursue excellent relationships with their customers, they need to employ CRM systems that provide the infrastructure needed to support those relationships. Because customer service and support are essential to a successful business, organizations must place a great deal of emphasis on both their CRM strategy and their CRM systems. IT's About Business 11.2 addresses CRM strategy and CRM systems at the SLS Hotel in Beverly Hills, California.

Broadly speaking, CRM systems lie along a continuum, from *low-end CRM systems* — designed for enterprises with many small customers — to *high-end CRM systems* — for enterprises

IT's [about business]

11.2 A Hotel Concierge in Your Pocket

Luxury hotels are renowned for their concierge services that cater discreetly to every guest. One such hotel, the SLS Hotel in Beverly Hills, California, is part of the Luxury Collection Hotel brand owned by SBE Entertainment Group LLC. Debuting in 2008 following a $230 million renovation of the former Le Meridien Beverly Hills, the 297-room SLS Hotel is all about delighting the senses. French modern designer Philippe Starck oversaw the $100 million décor. The food is the work of chef Jose Andres, 2011 recipient of the James Beard Foundation's award for most outstanding chef in North America.

Customer service, then, is a hallmark for the SLS Hotel. The hotel's IT manager, Eric Chao, notes that service is all about efficiency, gratification, and, most importantly, convenience. The last thing a luxury hotel wants is for its guests to feel that they have to work to get service during their stay. In fact, Chao maintains that many guests do not even want to speak directly with any of the hotel's employees. To satisfy these high customer expectations, SLS Hotel had to devise a strategy to discreetly improve the hotel's already sky-high-level service.

To achieve this objective, the hotel launched a mobile hotel app called GoSLSHotel (www.goslshotel.com) that offers convenient, around-the-clock service at the touch of an icon. Guests who want a late-night snack, an extra bottle of shampoo, or valet service no longer need to pick up their room phone, search for the correct button, and then interact with a hotel employee. Instead, they can request any service they need within seconds or minutes simply by clicking an icon on their smartphones or computers. GoSLSHotel even has a built-in timer. When a guest presses the "Send" button for an in-room dining order, the order immediately shows up on the kitchen's computer, where the time that the order was placed is shown by different-colored flags. The hotel claims that GoSLSHotel has generated "overwhelmingly positive comments."

GoSLSHotel not only drives better customer service. It also serves to drive business and to generate more revenue for the hotel. The first week after the app launched in 2010, it generated 30 service requests (spa, dining reservations, and housekeeping, among others), 15 room-service orders, and 2,500 guest "touches." Two years and many enhancements later, the hotel considers GoSLSHotel to be such a competitive advantage that it refused to allow Chao to discuss specific revenue numbers. Despite this secrecy that is imposed on the staff, the hotel closely monitors the app's numbers. Initially designed as a front-end (customer-touching; discussed in Section 11.2) guest service tool, GoSLSHotel now performs many back-end functions that track all guest touches, purchases, and requests and then use these data to generate reports that inform the hotel about guest preferences and trends. The app also has a feedback icon that allows guests to register complaints in real time to ensure they are addressed during their stay.

Consider the case of Linda, a fictional guest at SLS Hotel. Linda always uses GoSLSHotel to order Dom Perignon champagne upon arrival. Because the app records this information, after five stays the hotel might send a bottle of Dom to the room before Linda even arrives. Similarly, customers who frequent the hotel's 5,000-square-foot Ciel Spa might receive a discount on their next relaxation massage. The hotel recently offered gifts from the spa to guests who were willing to "like" SLS Hotel on its Facebook page.

Although GoSLSHotel provides a significant competitive advantage, customers are very concerned about the app's security. To alleviate these concerns, SLS Hotel takes great pains to communicate GoSLSHotel's security features so guests will feel comfortable using the app. GoSLSHotel users sign in with their room number and name, and they are not required to swipe their credit card for any purchase, thus easing the security fear factor.

As mentioned above, GoSLSHotel has driven new business, generated additional revenue, and provided SLS Hotel with a crucial competitive advantage over its competitors. However, the app's return on investment is just as much about the "intangibles" as it is about generating revenue. The level of convenience added by the app generates positive customer feelings, which in turn boost the hotel's reputation and ensure future business growth and stability.

Sources: Compiled from E. Savitz, "Rushing Mobile Apps Out Means Ushering Hackers In," *Forbes*, February 26, 2012; E. Savitz, "The Growing Problem of Privacy-Invading Mobile Apps," *Forbes*, February 23, 2012; L. Tucci, "Hotel App Pockets Revenue by Putting Concierge Service in Your Pocket," *SearchCIO.com*, February 23, 2012; P. Dailey, "SLS Hotel Adds Personal Touch to Guest Visits with Custom Mobile App," *Hospitality Technology*, May 13, 2010; "Runtriz Delivering Mobile Guest Facing App for SLS Hotel at Beverly Hills," *Hospitalitynet.com*, February 3, 2010; www.goslshotel.com, accessed March 5, 2013.

Questions

1. What is the SLS Hotel's CRM strategy?
2. What is the SLS Hotel's CRM system (used in the case)?
3. Why does GoSLSHotel give the hotel such a competitive advantage? Is this competitive advantage likely to be long-lived? Why or why not?
4. What are the privacy implications of the GoSLSHotel app?

---

with a few large customers. An example of a low-end system is Amazon, which uses its CRM system to recommend books to returning customers. An example of a high-end system is Boeing, which uses its CRM system to coordinate staff activities in a campaign to sell its new 787 aircraft to Delta Airlines. As you study the cases and examples in this chapter, consider where on the continuum a particular CRM system would fall.

Although CRM varies according to circumstances, all successful CRM policies share two basic elements. First, the company must identify the many types of customer touch points. Second, it needs to consolidate data about each customer. Let's examine these two elements in more detail.

Customer Touch Points

Organizations must recognize the numerous and diverse interactions that they have with their customers. These various types of interactions are referred to as **customer touch points**. Traditional customer touch points include telephone contact, direct mailings, and actual physical interactions with customers during their visits to a store. Organizational CRM systems, however, must manage many additional customer touch points that occur through the use of popular personal technologies. These touch points include e-mail, Web sites, and communications via smartphones (see Figure 11.2).

Data Consolidation

Data consolidation also is critical to an organization's CRM efforts. The organization's CRM systems must manage customer data effectively. In the past, customer data were stored in isolated systems (or silos) located in different functional areas across the business (e.g., in separate databases in the finance, sales, logistics, and marketing departments). Consequently, data for individual customers were difficult to share across the various functional areas. (Recall IT's About Business 11.1.)

FIGURE 11.2 Customer touch points.

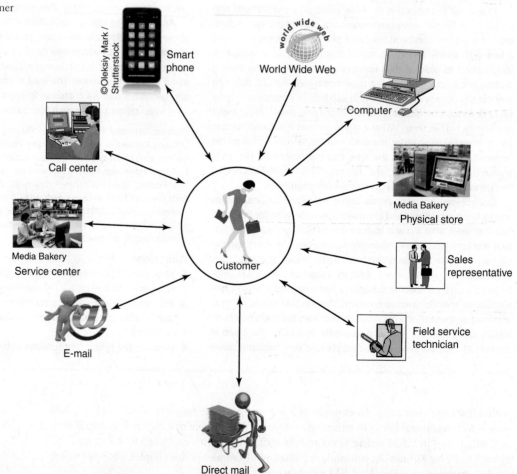

As you saw in Chapter 5, modern, interconnected systems built around a data warehouse now make all customer-related data available to every unit of the business. This complete data set on each customer is called a *360-degree view* of that customer. By accessing this view, a company can enhance its relationship with its customers and ultimately make more productive and profitable decisions.

Data consolidation and the 360-degree view of the customer enable the organization's functional areas to readily share information about customers. This information sharing leads to collaborative CRM. **Collaborative CRM systems** provide effective and efficient interactive communication with the customer throughout the entire organization. That is, collaborative CRM systems integrate communications between the organization and its customers in all aspects of marketing, sales, and customer support. Collaborative CRM systems also enable customers to provide direct feedback to the organization. As you read in Chapter 9, Web 2.0 applications such as blogs and Wikis are very important to companies that value customer input into their product and service offerings, as well as into new product development.

An organization's CRM system contains two major components: operational CRM systems and analytical CRM systems. You will learn about these components in the next two sections.

before you go on...

1. What is the definition of customer relationship management?
2. Why is CRM so important to any organization?
3. Define and provide examples of customer touch points.

Operational Customer Relationship Management Systems

11.2

Operational CRM systems support front-office business processes. **Front-office processes** are those that directly interact with customers; that is, sales, marketing, and service. The two major components of operational CRM systems are customer-facing applications and customer-touching applications (discussed below).

Operational CRM systems provide the following benefits:

- Efficient, personalized marketing, sales, and service;
- A 360-degree view of each customer;
- The ability of sales and service employees to access a complete history of customer interaction with the organization, regardless of the touch point.

An example of an operational CRM system involves Caterpillar, Inc. (*www.cat.com*), an international manufacturer of industrial equipment. Caterpillar uses its CRM tools to accomplish the following objectives:

- Improve sales and account management by optimizing the information shared by multiple employees and by streamlining existing processes (e.g., taking orders using mobile devices).
- Form individualized relationships with customers, with the aim of improving customer satisfaction and maximizing profits.
- Identify the most profitable customers, and provide them the highest level of service.
- Provide employees with the information and processes necessary to know their customers.
- Understand and identify customer needs, and effectively build relationships among the company, its customer base, and its distribution partners.

Customer-Facing Applications

In **customer-facing CRM applications,** an organization's sales, field service, and customer interaction center representatives interact directly with customers. These applications include customer service and support, sales force automation, marketing, and campaign management.

Customer Service and Support. Customer service and support refers to systems that automate service requests, complaints, product returns, and requests for information. Today, organizations have implemented **customer interaction centers (CIC),** where organizational representatives use multiple channels such as the Web, telephone, fax, and face-to-face interactions to communicate with customers. The CIC manages several different types of customer interaction.

One of the most well-known customer interaction centers is the *call center,* a centralized office set up to receive and transmit a large volume of requests by telephone. Call centers enable companies to respond to a large variety of questions, including product support and complaints.

Organizations also use the CIC to create a call list for the sales team, whose members contact sales prospects. This type of interaction is called *outbound telesales.* In these interactions, the customer and the sales team collaborate in discussing products and services that can satisfy customers' needs and generate sales.

Customers can communicate directly with the CIC to initiate a sales order, inquire about products and services before placing an order, and obtain information about a transaction that they have already made. These interactions are referred to as *inbound teleservice.* Teleservice representatives respond to requests either by utilizing service instructions found in an organizational knowledge base or by noting incidents that can be addressed only by field service technicians.

The CIC also provides the Information Help Desk. The Help Desk assists customers with their questions concerning products or services, and it also processes customer complaints. Complaints generate follow-up activities such as quality-control checks, delivery of replacement parts or products, service calls, generation of credit memos, and product returns.

New technologies are extending the traditional CIC's functionality to include e-mail and Web interaction. For example, Epicor (*www.epicor.com*) provides software solutions that combine Web channels, such as automated e-mail reply, and Web knowledge bases. The information the software provides is available to CIC representatives and field service personnel. Another new technology, live chat, allows customers to connect to a company representative and conduct an instant messaging session. The advantage of live chat over a telephone conversation is that live chat enables the participants to share documents and photos (see *www.livechatinc.com* and *www.websitealive.com*). Some companies conduct the chat with a computer using natural language processing rather than with a real person.

Sales Force Automation. **Sales force automation (SFA)** is the component of an operational CRM system that automatically records all of the components in a sales transaction process. SFA systems include a *contact management system,* which tracks all contacts that have been made with a customer, the purpose of each contact, and any follow-up that might be necessary. This system eliminates duplicated contacts and redundancy, which in turn reduces the risk of irritating customers. SFA also includes a *sales lead tracking system,* which lists potential customers or customers who have purchased related products.

Other elements of an SFA system can include a *sales forecasting system,* which is a mathematical technique for estimating future sales, and a *product knowledge system,* which is a comprehensive source of information regarding products and services. More-developed SFA systems also have online product-building features, called *configurators,* that enable customers to model the product to meet their specific needs. For example, you can customize your own running shoe at NikeID (*http://nikeid.nike.com*). Finally, many of the current SFA systems enable the salesperson in the field to connect remotely via Web-based interfaces that can be displayed on smartphones.

Marketing. Thus far, you have focused primarily on how sales and customer service personnel can benefit from CRM systems. However, CRM systems have many important applications for an organization's marketing department as well. For example, they enable marketers to identify and target their best customers, to manage marketing campaigns, and to generate quality leads for the sales teams. Additionally, CRM marketing applications can sift through volumes of customer data—a process known as data mining (discussed in Chapter 12)—to develop a *purchasing profile*; that is, a snapshot of a consumer's buying habits that may lead to additional sales through cross selling, up selling, and bundling.

Cross selling is the marketing of additional related products to customers based on a previous purchase. This sales approach has been used very successfully by banks. For example, if you have a checking and savings account at your bank, then a bank officer will recommend other products for you, such as certificates of deposit or other types of investments.

Up selling is a sales strategy in which the business person provides to customers the opportunity to purchase related products or services of greater value in place of, or along with, the consumer's initial product or service selection. For example, if a customer goes into an electronics store to buy a new television, a salesperson may show him a pricey 1080i HD LCD television placed next to a non-HD television in the hope of selling the more expensive set (assuming that the customer is willing to pay more for a sharper picture). Other common examples of up selling are warranties on electronics merchandise and the purchase of a car-wash after buying gas at the gas station.

Finally, **bundling** is a form of cross selling in which a business sells a group of products or services together at a lower price than their combined individual prices. For example, your cable company might bundle basic cable TV, broadband Internet access, and telephone service at a lower price than you would paid for each service separately.

Campaign Management. **Campaign management applications** help organizations plan campaigns that send the right messages to the right people through the right channels. Organizations manage their customers very carefully to avoid targeting people who have opted out of receiving marketing communications. Further, companies use these applications to personalize individual messages for each particular customer.

Customer-Touching Applications

Corporations have used manual CRM systems for many years. In the mid-1990s, organizations began using the Internet, the Web, and other electronic touch points (e.g., e-mail, point-of-sale terminals) to manage customer relationships. In contrast with customer-facing applications, where customers deal directly with a company representative, customers interact directly with these technologies and applications. Such applications are called **customer-touching CRM applications** or **electronic CRM (e-CRM) applications**. Customers typically can use these applications to help themselves. There are many types of e-CRM applications. Let's examine some of the major ones.

Search and Comparison Capabilities. It is often difficult for customers to find what they want from the vast array of products and services available on the Web. To assist customers, many online stores and malls offer search and comparison capabilities, as do independent comparison Web sites (see *www.mysimon.com*).

Technical and Other Information and Services. Many organizations offer personalized experiences to induce customers to make purchases or to remain loyal. For example, Web sites often allow customers to download product manuals. One example is General Electric's Web site (*www.ge.com*), which provides detailed technical and maintenance information and sells replacement parts to customers who need to repair outdated home appliances. Another example is Goodyear's Web site (*www.goodyear.com*), which provides information about tires and their use.

Customized Products and Services. Another customer-touching service that many online vendors use is mass customization, a process in which customers can configure their own products. For example, Dell Computer (*www.dell.com*) allows customers to configure their own computer systems. The Gap (*www.gap.com*) allows customers to "mix and match" an entire wardrobe. Web sites such as Hitsquad (*www.hitsquad.com*), MusicalGreeting (*www.musicalgreeting.com*), and Surprise (*www.surprise.com*) allow customers to pick individual music titles from a library and customize a CD, a feature that traditional music stores do not offer.

In addition, customers now can view account balances or check the shipping status of orders at any time from their computers or smartphones. If you order books from Amazon, for example, you can look up the anticipated arrival date. Many other companies, including FedEx and UPS, provide similar services (see *www.fedex.com* and *www.ups.com*).

Personalized Web Pages. Many organizations permit their customers to create personalized Web pages. Customers use these pages to record purchases and preferences, as well as problems and requests. For example, American Airlines generates personalized Web pages for each of its approximately 800,000 registered travel-planning customers.

FAQs. Frequently asked questions (FAQs) are a simple tool for answering repetitive customer queries. Customers may find the information they need by using this tool, thereby eliminating the need to communicate with an actual person.

E-mail and Automated Response. The most popular tool for customer service is e-mail. Inexpensive and fast, e-mail is used not only to answer inquiries from customers but also to disseminate information, send alerts and product information, and conduct correspondence on any topic.

Loyalty Programs. **Loyalty programs** recognize customers who repeatedly use a vendor's products or services. Loyalty programs are appropriate when two conditions are met: a high frequency of repeat purchases, and limited product customization for each customer. IT's About Business 11.3 illustrates how Starbucks has extended its loyalty program to mobile devices.

IT's [about business]

11.3 Starbucks' Loyalty Program Goes Mobile

Starbucks is leveraging mobile phones to drive sales and improve its much-vaunted loyalty program. In December 2011, the company disclosed that it had successfully handled 26 million transactions via its new mobile payment system, which allows smartphone users to pay for Starbucks' products using their phones. By the end of 2012, Starbucks was processing more than 2 million mobile payments per week, representing between 1 and 2 percent of the company's total sales.

The app is also tied directly to Starbucks' loyalty program. About 3.6 million customers belong to the My Starbucks Rewards program, and 2 million of them have achieved gold status. When My Starbucks customers pay for purchases electronically, their accounts are automatically credited, and any qualifying discounts are applied. Starbucks' loyalty members earn one star for each purchase they make using the company's loyalty card. When they earn 30 stars, they attain gold status.

Starbucks believes the success of its mobile loyalty system is due to the convenience it offers its customers. It is simply a faster and easier way for customers to pay.

Sources: C. Tode, "Starbucks Caffeinates Mobile Payments With Over 2M Mobile Transactions Per Week," *Mobile Commerce Daily*, November 5, 2012; E. Morphy, "The Rise of Self-Service Mobile CRM," *CRM Buyer*, September 4, 2012; C. Tode, "Starbucks Is Worldwide Leader in Mobile Payment Transactions," *Mobile Commerce Daily*, January 31, 2012; S. Greengard, "Mobile Loyalty Program Scores at Starbucks," *Baseline Magazine*, December 20, 2011; T. Wasserman, "One in Four Starbucks Transactions Now Done Via Card, Including Mobile," *CNN*, December 6, 2011; www .starbucks.com, accessed March 19, 2013.

Questions

1. Do you see any disadvantages to Starbucks' mobile loyalty program? Provide specific examples to support your answer.

2. Refer to the case regarding the digital wallet in Chapter 8. How does Starbucks' mobile loyalty program fit in with the concept of the digital wallet?

The purpose of loyalty programs is not to reward past behavior, but to influence future behavior. Note that the most profitable customers are not necessarily those whose behavior can be most easily influenced. As one example, most major U.S. airlines provide some "elite" benefits to anyone who flies 25,000 miles with them and their partners over the course of a year. Customers who fly first class pay much more for a given flight than those who fly in discount economy. Nevertheless, they reach elite status only 1.5 to 2 times faster than economy-class passengers. Why is this true? The reason is that, although first-class passengers are far more profitable than discount seekers, they also are less influenced by loyalty programs. Discount flyers respond much more enthusiastically to the benefits of frequent flyer programs. Therefore, airlines award more benefits to discount flyers than to first-class flyers (relative to their spending).

The airlines' frequent flyer programs are probably the best-known loyalty programs. Other popular loyalty programs are casino players' clubs, which reward frequent players, and supermarkets, which reward frequent shoppers. Loyalty programs use a database or data warehouse to keep a record of the points (or miles) a customer has accrued and the rewards to which he or she is entitled. The programs then use analytical tools to mine the data and learn about customer behavior.

before you go on...

1. Differentiate between customer-facing applications and customer-touching applications.

2. Provide examples of cross selling, up selling, and bundling (other than the examples presented in the text).

Analytical Customer Relationship Management Systems

11.3

Whereas operational CRM systems support front-office business processes, **analytical CRM systems** provide business intelligence by analyzing customer behavior and perceptions. For example, analytical CRM systems typically provide information concerning customer requests and transactions, as well as customer responses to the organization's marketing, sales, and service initiatives. These systems also create statistical models of customer behavior and the value of customer relationships over time, as well as forecasts about acquiring, retaining, and losing customers. Figure 11.3 illustrates the relationship between operational CRM systems and analytical CRM systems.

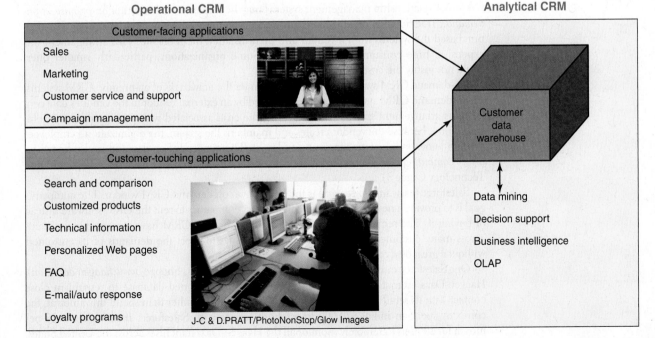

J-C & D.PRATT/PhotoNonStop/Glow Images

FIGURE 11.3 The relationship between operational CRM and analytical CRM.

Important technologies in analytical CRM systems include data warehouses, data mining, decision support, and other business intelligence technologies (discussed in Chapter 12). After these systems have completed their various analyses, they supply information to the organization in the form of reports and digital dashboards (discussed in Chapter 12).

Analytical CRM systems analyze customer data for a variety of purposes, including:

- Designing and executing targeted marketing campaigns;
- Increasing customer acquisition, cross selling, and up selling;
- Providing input into decisions relating to products and services (e.g., pricing and product development);
- Providing financial forecasting and customer profitability analysis.

before you go on...

1. What is the relationship between operational CRM systems and analytical CRM systems?

2. What are some of the functions of analytical CRM systems?

11.4 Other Types of Customer Relationship Management Systems

Now that you have examined operational and analytical CRM systems, let's shift our focus to other types of CRM systems. Three exciting developments in this area are on-demand CRM systems, mobile CRM systems, and open-source CRM systems.

On-Demand CRM Systems

Customer relationship management systems may be implemented as either *on-premise* or *on-demand*. Traditionally, organizations utilized on-premise CRM systems, meaning that they purchased the systems from a vendor and then installed them on site. This arrangement was expensive, time consuming, and inflexible. Some organizations, particularly smaller ones, could not justify the cost of these systems.

On-demand CRM systems became a solution for the drawbacks of on-premise CRM systems. An **on-demand CRM system** is one that is hosted by an external vendor in the vendor's data center. This arrangement spares the organization the costs associated with purchasing the system. In addition, because the vendor creates and maintains the system, the organization's employees need to know only how to access and utilize it. The concept of on-demand is also known as *utility computing* (see Technology Guide 3) or *software-as-a-service* (SaaS; see Chapter 13 and Technology Guide 3).

Salesforce (*www.salesforce.com*) is the best-known on-demand CRM vendor. The company's goal is to provide a new business model that allows companies to rent the CRM software instead of buying it. The secret to their success appears to be that CRM has common requirements across many customers, allowing Salesforce's product to meet the demands of its customers without a great deal of customization.

One Salesforce customer is Minneapolis-based Haagen-Dazs Shoppe (*www.haagen-dazs.com*). Haagen-Dazs estimated that designing its own custom-designed database to remain in close contact with its retail franchises would have cost $65,000. Rather than spend this amount, the company spent an initial $20,000 to establish service with Salesforce. It now pays $125 per month for 20 users to remotely monitor all the Haagen-Dazs franchises across the United States, via the Web or a smartphone.

Despite their benefits, on-demand CRM systems have potential problems. First, the vendor could prove to be unreliable, in which case the company would have no CRM functionality at all. Second, hosted software is difficult or impossible to modify, and only the vendor can upgrade it. Third, vendor-hosted CRM software may be difficult to integrate with the organization's existing software. Finally, giving strategic customer data to vendors always carries risks.

Mobile CRM Systems

A **mobile CRM** system is an interactive system that enables an organization to conduct communications related to sales, marketing, and customer service activities through a mobile medium for the purpose of building and maintaining relationships with its customers. Simply put, mobile CRM systems involve interacting directly with consumers through portable devices such as smartphones. Many forward-thinking companies believe that mobile CRM systems have tremendous potential to create personalized customer relationships that may be accessed anywhere and at any time. In fact, the potential opportunities provided through mobile marketing appear so rich that many companies already have identified mobile CRM systems as a cornerstone of their future marketing activities. IT's About Business 11.4 discusses a mobile CRM application at the Nutricia.

 IT's **[about business]**

11.4 Mobile CRM at Nutricia

A unit of the international food company Danone (www.danone.com), Nutricia (www.nutricia.com) develops, markets, and sells medical nutrition for people who are sick or who need extra energy. The company records most of its sales in Europe, but it is expanding its services throughout the world. Nutricia interacts with many stakeholders, including government organizations, nursing homes, hospitals, doctors, pharmacies, and patients.

One of Nutricia's greatest challenges is government regulation. The company must obtain government approval for its products so that users can be eligible for government reimbursement. The company must also manage its wide geographic reach. Its sales and customer service representatives must cover a great deal of territory, and they need tools to help them work efficiently. Nutricia had an existing CRM system that was unable to keep up with the rapid changes in the company's regulatory environment. The old system was not user friendly and did not supply a 360-degree view of its customers. Consequently, only 20 percent of the firm's agents utilized it. Compounding this problem was the fact that most of Nutricia's field staff are former nurses who are unaccustomed to working with computers.

Nutricia decided to implement CWR Mobile CRM (www.cwrmobility.com) because the software matched the company's demanding requirements. Nutricia found that using mobile devices instead of notebook computers improved the quality of the conversation between the field agent and the doctor by removing the physical barrier of the computer screen. Some agents also used their smartphones to record parts of their conversations with physicians (with permission). By adding the audio file directly from the smartphone to the contact record, the information is instantly available to anyone working on that particular account.

The percentage of field representatives who utilize the new mobile CRM system has risen to 85 percent, and it is growing. The new system has increased Nutricia's productivity to an unprecedented level. Prior to implementing the system, Nutricia had eight representatives who visited 9,000 customers per year. The company now has six agents who make 20,000 customer visits per year.

Sources: R. Grainger, "The Future of Mobile CRM," *CRM Magazine,* February 22, 2013; P. Hernandez, "CRM Is Most Wanted Mobile Enterprise App: Survey," *Enterprise Apps Today,* February 8, 2013; D. Henschen, "Microsoft CRM Embraces iPhone, iPad, Android," *InformationWeek,* February 6, 2012; "Nutricia Boosts Its Productivity and Sales Health with Mobile CRM Solution," *CWR Mobility Customer Case Study,* 2012; www.danone.com, www.nutricia.com, www.cwrmobility.com, accessed March 16, 2013.

Questions

1. What are disadvantages of mobile CRM for Nutricia? (Hint: Nutricia is a healthcare company.)
2. Identify two additional advantages of Nutricia's mobile CRM application.

Open-Source CRM Systems

As explained in Technology Guide 2, the source code for open-source software is available at no cost. **Open-source CRM systems**, therefore, are CRM systems whose source code is available to developers and users.

Open-source CRM systems provide the same features or functions as other CRM software, and they may be implemented either on-premise or on-demand. Leading open-source CRM vendors include SugarCRM (*www.sugarcrm.com*), Concursive (*www.concursive.com*), and vtiger (*www.vtiger.com*).

The benefits of open-source CRM systems include favorable pricing and a wide variety of applications. In addition, these systems are easy to customize. This is an attractive feature for organizations that need CRM software designed for their specific needs. Finally, updates and bug (software error) fixes for open-source CRM systems are rapidly distributed, and extensive support information is available free of charge.

Like all software, however, open-source CRM systems have certain risks. The most serious risk involves quality control. Because open-source CRM systems are created by a large community of unpaid developers, there sometimes is no central authority responsible for overseeing the quality of the product. Further, for best results, companies must have the same information technology platform in place as the one on which the open-source CRM system was developed.

before you go on...

1. Define on-demand CRM.
2. Define mobile CRM.
3. Define open-source CRM.

11.5 Supply Chains

Modern organizations are increasingly concentrating on their core competencies and on becoming more flexible and agile. To accomplish these objectives, they rely on other companies, rather than on companies they themselves own, to supply the necessary goods and services they need. Organizations recognize that these suppliers can perform these activities more efficiently and effectively than they can. This trend toward relying on an increasing number of suppliers has led to the concept of supply chains. A **supply chain** is the flow of materials, information, money, and services from raw material suppliers, through factories and warehouses, to the end customers. A supply chain also includes the *organizations* and *processes* that create and deliver products, information, and services to end customers.

Supply chains improve trust and collaboration among supply chain partners, thus improving supply chain visibility and inventory velocity. **Supply chain visibility** is the ability for all organizations in a supply chain to access or view relevant data on purchased materials

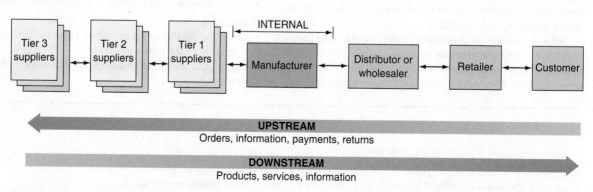

FIGURE 11.4 Generic supply chain.

as these materials move through their suppliers' production processes and transportation networks to their receiving docks. In addition, organizations can access or view relevant data on outbound goods as they are manufactured, assembled, or stored in inventory and then shipped through their transportation networks to their customers' receiving docks. The sooner a company can deliver products and services after receiving the materials required to make them—that is, the higher the **inventory velocity**—the more satisfied the company's customers will be.

Supply chains are a vital component of the overall strategies of many modern organizations. To utilize supply chains efficiently, a business must be tightly integrated with its suppliers, business partners, distributors, and customers. A critical component of this integration is the use of information systems to facilitate the exchange of information among the participants in the supply chain.

You might ask, "Why do I need to study supply chain management?" The answer is that supply chains are critical to modern organizations. Therefore, regardless of your position within an organization, you will be involved with some aspect of your company's supply chain. You might think that supply chain management is only for large organizations. However, as you see in IT's About Business 11.5, small organizations must carefully manage their supply chains as well.

IT's [about business]

11.5 Campus Quilts Partners with UPS to Manage Its Supply Chain

What do you plan to do with all of the T-shirts you collect in your college years? Store them in a box somewhere? Wear them for the next 30 years? Give them away? Leigh Lowe of Louisville, Kentucky, has a different alternative for you—make a quilt out of them. Leigh is the owner of a small business that takes T-shirts, ties, baby clothes, sweatshirts, hats, and other memorable clothing items and sews them into pillowcases or quilts. Making this unique product offering is very time intensive—a single quilt can take up to 3 weeks—but the end product is highly personalized and valuable to the customer.

The supply chain management and logistics for this type of business are different from your typical commercial retailer. In this situation, the supplier of the raw materials and the customer who receives the final product are the same. Additionally, both the raw materials and the final product are unique and irreplaceable items. Therefore, it is imperative that Campus Quilts take the utmost care with the product throughout the product life cycle, from acquiring the raw materials to delivering the final product. Although Leigh is an incredibly talented quilt maker, she had no experience with protecting the security of irreplaceable items. Therefore, Leigh realized she would need a reliable third-party logistics/supply chain partner to manage this part of the job.

Leigh turned to UPS to handle all of her logistical needs. She opened an account with UPS that allows her to initiate and track three separate shipments for each custom product via the Web. The process works like this: The customer initiates the process by placing an order either online or by phone. After the customer makes a deposit, Campus Quilts sends a package to the customer that includes information on the product he or she has chosen, design instructions, a prepaid shipping label, and instructions for sending the raw materials (T-shirts or other memorable clothing) to Campus Quilts. The customer then follows the instructions and ships the materials using the prepaid label. Leigh creates the finished product from the raw materials. She then ships the finished quilt back to the address specified in the order.

Relying on UPS to handle the logistics allows Leigh to focus on producing a quality product while expanding her potential customer base. Campus Quilts is able to reach customers worldwide via the Web and UPS. Without a shipping solution, Leigh's business would be confined to the local area. With a reliable shipping partner, she can expand far beyond her local area. Together, Campus Quilts and UPS provide a seamless customer experience. Customers feel "touched" all the way through the process because they always know where their personal items are—even during shipping. This sense of involvement helps customers trust Campus Quilts, brings Leigh closer to her customers, and is leading to a steadily increasing business.

Sources: Compiled from www.campusquilt.com, www.ups.com, accessed March 22, 2013.

Questions
1. Describe why the supply chain for Campus Quilts differs from a "normal" supply chain. Discuss the implications of these differences for Leigh's supply chain management.
2. Why would Leigh's business be confined to her local area without a shipping solution?

The Structure and Components of Supply Chains

The term *supply chain* comes from a picture of how the partnering organizations are linked together. Figure 11.4 illustrates a typical supply chain. (Recall that Figure 1.5 also illustrated a supply chain, in a slightly different way.) Note that the supply chain involves three segments:

1. *Upstream*, where sourcing or procurement from external suppliers occurs.

   In this segment, supply chain (SC) managers select suppliers to deliver the goods and services the company needs to produce its product or service. Further, SC managers develop the pricing, delivery, and payment processes between a company and its suppliers. Included here are processes for managing inventory, receiving and verifying shipments, transferring goods to manufacturing facilities, and authorizing payments to suppliers.

2. *Internal*, where packaging, assembly, or manufacturing takes place.

   SC managers schedule the activities necessary for production, testing, packaging, and preparing goods for delivery. SC managers also monitor quality levels, production output, and worker productivity.

3. *Downstream*, where distribution takes place, frequently by external distributors.

   In this segment, SC managers coordinate the receipt of orders from customers, develop a network of warehouses, select carriers to deliver products to customers, and develop invoicing systems to receive payments from customers.

   The flow of information and goods can be bidirectional. For example, damaged or unwanted products can be returned, a process known as *reverse flows* or *reverse logistics*. In the retail clothing industry, for example, reverse logistics involves clothing that customers return, either because the item had defects or because the customer did not like the item.

Tiers of Suppliers.   Figure 11.4 shows several tiers of suppliers. As the diagram indicates, a supplier may have one or more subsuppliers, a subsupplier may have its own subsupplier(s), and so on. For an automobile manufacturer, for example, Tier 3 suppliers produce basic products such as glass, plastic, and rubber; Tier 2 suppliers use these inputs to make windshields, tires, and plastic moldings; and Tier 1 suppliers produce integrated components such as dashboards and seat assemblies.

The Flows in the Supply Chain.   There are typically three flows in the supply chain: material, information, and financial. *Material flows* are the physical products, raw materials, supplies, and so forth that flow along the chain. Material flows also include the reverse flows discussed above. A supply chain thus involves a *product life cycle* approach, from "dirt to dust."

Information flows consist of data related to demand, shipments, orders, returns, and schedules, as well as changes in any of these data. Finally, *financial flows* involve money transfers, payments, credit card information and authorization, payment schedules, e-payments, and credit-related data.

Significantly, different supply chains have different numbers and types of flows. For instance, in service industries there may be no physical flow of materials, but frequently there is a flow of information, often in the form of documents (physical or electronic copies). For example, the digitization of software, music, and other content can create a supply chain without any physical flow. Notice, however, that in such a case, there are two types of information flows: one that replaces materials flow (digitized software), and another that provides the supporting information (orders, billing, and so on). To manage the supply chain, an organization must coordinate all of the above flows among all of the parties involved in the chain, a topic we turn to next.

before you go on... ⋀⋀⋀⋀

1. What is a supply chain?
2. Describe the three segments of a supply chain.
3. Describe the flows in a supply chain.

Supply Chain Management

11.6

The function of **supply chain management (SCM)** is to improve the way a company finds the raw materials it needs to produce a product or service and deliver it to its customers. That is, supply chain management is the process of planning, organizing, and optimizing the various activities performed along the supply chain. There are five basic components of SCM:

1. *Plan*: Planning is the strategic component of SCM. Organizations must have a strategy for managing all the resources that go toward meeting customer demand for their product or service. Planning involves the development of a set of metrics (measurable deliverables) to monitor the organization's supply chain to ensure that it is efficient and it delivers high quality and value to customers for the lowest cost.

2. *Source*: In the sourcing component, organizations choose suppliers to deliver the goods and services they need to create their product or service. Supply chain managers develop pricing, delivery, and payment processes with suppliers, and they create metrics to monitor and improve their relationships with their suppliers. They also develop processes for managing their goods and services inventory, including receiving and verifying shipments, transferring them to manufacturing facilities, and authorizing supplier payments.

3. *Make*: This is the manufacturing component. Supply chain managers schedule the activities necessary for production, testing, packaging, and preparation for delivery. This component is the most metric-intensive part of the supply chain, where organizations measure quality levels, production output, and worker productivity.

4. *Deliver*: This component, often referred to as *logistics*, is where organizations coordinate the receipt of customer orders, develop a network of warehouses, select carriers to transport their products to their customers, and set up an invoicing system to receive payments.

5. *Return*: Supply chain managers must create a responsive and flexible network for receiving defective, returned, or excess products back from their customers, as well as supporting customers who have problems with delivered products.

Like other functional areas, SCM utilizes information systems. The goal of SCM systems is to reduce the problems, or friction, along the supply chain. Friction can lead to increased time, costs, and inventories as well as decreased customer satisfaction. SCM systems, therefore, reduce uncertainty and risks by decreasing inventory levels and cycle time while improving business processes and customer service. All of these benefits make the organization more profitable and competitive.

Significantly, SCM systems are a type of interorganizational information system. In an **interorganizational information system (IOS)**, information flows among two or more organizations. By connecting the information systems of business partners, IOSs enable the partners to perform a number of tasks:

- Reduce the costs of routine business transactions;
- Improve the quality of the information flow by reducing or eliminating errors;
- Compress the cycle time involved in fulfilling business transactions;
- Eliminate paper processing and its associated inefficiencies and costs;
- Make the transfer and processing of information easier for users.

The Push Model versus the Pull Model

Many SCM systems use the **push model**. In this model, also known as *make-to-stock*, the production process begins with a forecast, which is simply an educated guess as to customer demand. The forecast must predict which products customers will want as well as the desired quantity of each product. The company then produces the amount of products in the forecast, typically by using mass production, and sells, or "pushes," those products to consumers.

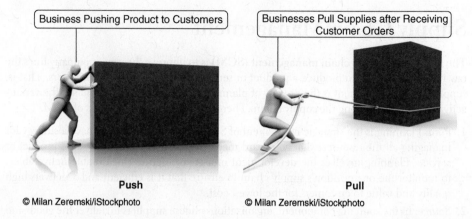

Push

© Milan Zeremski/iStockphoto

Pull

© Milan Zeremski/iStockphoto

Unfortunately, these forecasts are often incorrect. Consider, for example, an automobile manufacturer that wants to produce a new car. Marketing managers conduct extensive research, including customer surveys and analyses of competitors' cars, and then provide the results to forecasters. If the forecasters' predictions are too high—that is, if they predict that customers will purchase a certain number of these new cars but actual demand falls below this amount—then the automaker has excess cars in inventory and will incur large carrying costs. Further, the company will probably have to sell the excess cars at a discount.

From the opposite perspective, if the forecasters' predictions are too low—that is, actual customer demand exceeds expectations—then the automaker probably will have to run extra shifts to meet the demand, thereby incurring substantial overtime costs. Further, the company risks losing business to its competitors if the car that customers want is not available. Using the push model in supply chain management can cause problems, as you will see in the next section.

To avoid the uncertainties associated with the push model, many companies now employ the pull model of supply chain management, using Web-enabled information flows. In the **pull model**, also known as *make-to-order*, the production process begins with a customer order. Therefore, companies make only what customers want, a process closely aligned with mass customization.

A prominent example of a company that uses the pull model is Dell Computer. Dell's production process begins with a customer order. This order not only specifies the type of computer the customer wants, but it also alerts each Dell supplier as to the parts of the order for which that supplier is responsible. That way, Dell's suppliers ship only the parts that Dell needs to produce the computer.

Not all companies can use the pull model. Automobiles, for example, are far more complicated and more expensive to manufacture than computers, so automobile companies require longer lead times to produce new models. Automobile companies do use the pull model, but only for specific automobiles that some customers order (e.g., Rolls-Royce, Bentley, and other extremely expensive cars).

Problems along the Supply Chain

As you saw earlier, friction can develop within a supply chain. One major consequence of ineffective supply chains is poor customer service. In some cases, supply chains do not deliver products or services when and where customers—either individuals or businesses—need them. In other cases, the supply chain provides poor-quality products. Other problems associated with supply chain friction are high inventory costs and revenue loss.

The problems along the supply chain arise primarily from two sources: (1) uncertainties, and (2) the need to coordinate multiple activities, internal units, and business partners. A major source of supply chain uncertainties is the *demand forecast*. Demand for a product can be influenced by numerous factors such as competition, prices, weather conditions, technological developments, overall economic conditions, and customers' general confidence.

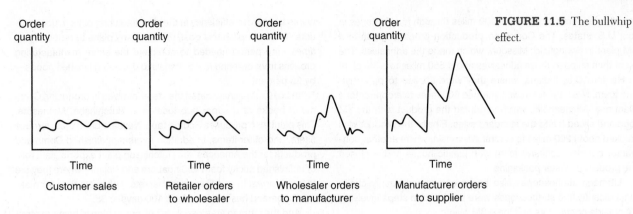

| Order quantity | Order quantity | Order quantity | Order quantity |

Time | Time | Time | Time

Customer sales | Retailer orders to wholesaler | Wholesaler orders to manufacturer | Manufacturer orders to supplier

FIGURE 11.5 The bullwhip effect.

Another uncertainty is delivery times, which can be affected by numerous factors ranging from production machine failures to road construction and traffic jams. In addition, quality problems in materials and parts can create production delays, which also generate supply chain problems.

One major challenge that managers face in setting accurate inventory levels throughout the supply chain is known as the bullwhip effect. The **bullwhip effect** refers to erratic shifts in orders up and down the supply chain (see Figure 11.5). Basically, the variables that affect customer demand can become magnified when they are viewed through the eyes of managers at each link in the supply chain. If each distinct entity that makes ordering and inventory decisions places its interests above those of the chain, then stockpiling can occur at as many as seven or eight locations along the chain. Research has shown that in some cases such hoarding has led to as much as a 100-day supply of inventory that is waiting "just in case," versus the 10- to 20-day supply manufacturers normally keep at hand. IT's About Business 11.6 illustrates how 3M is solving its supply chain problems.

IT's [about business]

11.6 3M Deals with Supply Chain Problems POM

3M (www.3m.com) manufactures 65,000 products, ranging from Scotch tape to film for solar-energy panels to dental braces. It makes these products in 214 plants located in 41 countries. Over the years, 3M had developed long, complicated supply chains for many of its products.

One reason why the supply chains became so complicated was the company's risk-averse culture. Specifically, the culture at 3M is "make a little, sell a little." That is, do not buy new machinery and construct plants until a product has proved itself in the market. Instead, 3M product developers would utilize existing

machines and expertise even if they were located hundreds of miles away. This strategy enabled 3M to keep its machinery running around the clock, thereby achieving efficiency. It also resulted in higher shipping costs and longer production cycles.

Let's take a look at two 3M products with convoluted supply chains: Command picture-hanging hooks and Littmann stethoscopes.

3M's Command picture-hanging hooks are made of plastic and strips of sticky foam, and they do not look complicated. However, as recently as 2010, the Command production process literally wandered more than 1,300 miles through four factories in four U.S. states. The Command production process began at a 3M plant in Springfield, Missouri, which made the adhesives. The plant then shipped those adhesives about 550 miles to a 3M plant in Hartford City, Indiana, where they were applied to polyethylene foam. Next, the foam was shipped 600 miles to a contractor's plant near Minneapolis, which imprinted the product with the 3M logo and sliced it into the standard sizes. Finally, the product was trucked about 200 miles to central Wisconsin, where another contractor bundled adhesive foam with plastic hooks and enclosed the product in blister packaging.

Littmann stethoscopes also had a convoluted supply chain. Until recently, the stethoscopes were produced in steps involving 14 outside contractors and three 3M plants.

When 3M became aware of these problems, it developed a strategic plan to simplify its supply chains, in order to reduce costs and increase flexibility in the company's manufacturing processes and along its supply chains. Long, convoluted supply chains increase inventory costs because each separate production stage maintains a buffer stock of unfinished items to cope with any disruptions in the flow from another plant or from suppliers. Holding that inventory is expensive in terms of space and cash spent for materials waiting to become merchandise. 3M set out to speed up production when it has a hit product and to avoid convoluted supply chains.

3M has also developed 10 larger, more efficient plants, called *super hubs*, that are capable of making multiple products for a particular region of the world. Six of these hubs are located in the United States, and the remaining four are situated in Singapore, Japan, Germany, and Poland. By moving production closer to its customers, 3M can reduce shipping costs and currency risks while customizing its products to match regional tastes. Essentially, 3M wants to improve efficiency in the manufacturing of its major products. To accomplish this goal, the company plans to reduce *cycle times*—the period needed to complete the entire manufacturing process from ordering raw materials to delivering finished goods—by 25 percent.

In 2010, 3M consolidated the steps involved in producing Command hooks at a super hub located in Hutchinson, Minnesota. This plant also produces Scotch tape, Nexcare bandages, furnace filters, and other items. In addition to creating finished Command products for the Americas, the Hutchinson plant exports giant rolls of unfinished sticky foam to Singapore and Poland, where they are tailored for Asian and European markets. The cycle time for making Command has dropped from 100 days to 35.

And the Littman stethoscopes? All production is being centralized in a plant in Columbia, Missouri. The cycle time has fallen from 165 days to 50.

Sources: Compiled from S. Culp, "Supply Chain Disruption a Major Threat to Business," *Forbes*, February 15, 2013; "3M to Establish Super Hub in Turkey," *Hurriyet Daily News*, October 10, 2012; "Industrial Giant 3M on Mission to Remove Its Supply Chain 'Hairballs'," *Supply Chain Digest*, June 6, 2012; J. Hagerty, "3M Begins Untangling Its 'Hairballs'," *The Wall Street Journal*, May 17, 2012; M. Mangelsdorf, "Understanding the 'Bullwhip' Effect in Supply Chains," *MIT Technology Review*, January 27, 2010; www.3m.com, accessed March 15, 2013.

Questions

1. Describe how large, complex organizations such as 3M can develop large, complex supply chains. Can this situation occur by accident? By design? Support your answer.
2. Describe the advantages of 3M using "super hubs."
3. Describe disadvantages of 3M using "super hubs."
4. Is 3M experiencing the bullwhip effect in this case? Why or why not? Support your answer.

Solutions to Supply Chain Problems

Supply chain problems can be very costly. Therefore, organizations are motivated to find innovative solutions. During the oil crises of the 1970s, for example, Ryder Systems, a large trucking company, purchased a refinery to control the upstream part of the supply chain and to ensure it had sufficient gasoline for its trucks. Ryder's decision to purchase a refinery is an example of vertical integration. **Vertical integration** is a business strategy in which a company purchases its upstream suppliers to ensure that its essential supplies are available as soon as they are needed. Ryder later sold the refinery because it could not manage a business it did not understand and because oil became more plentiful.

Ryder's decision to vertically integrate was not the best method for managing its supply chain. In the remainder of this section, you will look at some other possible solutions to supply chain problems, many of which are supported by IT.

Using Inventories to Solve Supply Chain Problems. Undoubtedly, the most common solution to supply chain problems is *building inventories* as insurance against supply chain uncertainties. As you have learned, holding too much inventory can be very costly. Thus, companies make major attempts to optimize and control inventories. IT's About Business 11.7 illustrates how Airbus is using a "smart" supply chain to manage its parts inventory.

One widely utilized strategy to minimize inventories is the **just-in-time (JIT) inventory system**. Essentially, JIT systems deliver the precise number of parts, called *work-in-process* inventory, to be assembled into a finished product at precisely the right time.

IT's [about business]

11.7 Airbus Moves to a "Smart Supply Chain"

Supply chain information that was previously generated manually is increasingly being generated by sensors, RFID tags, meters, GPS, and other devices and systems. How does this reality affect supply chain managers? For one thing, it means they will have real-time information on all products moving through their supply chains. Supply chains will therefore rely less on labor-based tracking and monitoring, because the new technology will allow shipping containers, trucks, products, and parts to report on their own status.

Airbus is one of the world's largest commercial aircraft manufacturers, producing more than of the world's new aircraft with more than 100 seats per plane. As its suppliers became more geographically dispersed, Airbus was finding it increasingly difficult to track parts, components, and other assets as they moved from the warehouses of various suppliers to the company's 18 manufacturing sites.

To make its supply chain more visible, Airbus created a smart sensing solution that can detect any deviations of inbound shipments from their intended path. Here is how the sensing solution works: As parts move from suppliers' warehouses to the Airbus assembly line, they travel in smart containers fitted with RFID tags that hold important information. (We discuss RFID in detail in Chapter 8.) At each stop along the supply chain, RFID readers communicate with each tag. If shipments end up at the wrong location or they do not contain the correct parts, the RFID readers alert employees so they can fix the problem before it disrupts production.

Airbus's supply chain solution, the largest of its kind in manufacturing, has significantly reduced the number and severity of incorrect shipments and deliveries as well as the costs associated with correcting these problems. In turn, alleviating these problems has allowed Airbus to reduce the number of overall travel containers by 8 percent, to avoid significant inventory carrying costs, and to increase the overall efficiency of its parts flow.

Sources: Compiled from D. Pearson and D. Michaels, "Airbus Wants Suppliers to Consolidate," *The Wall Street Journal*, November 8, 2012; "At Airbus, It's Clear Skies and High Visibility," *The Smarter Supply Chain of the Future* (IBM Corporation), 2012; "Examining Airbus and Boeing Supply Chain Issues," *Manufacturing Business Technology*, September 22, 2011; "The Smarter Supply Chain of the Future," *IBM Corporation*, 2009; www .airbus.com, accessed March 22, 2013.

Questions

1. Discuss the value to Airbus of supply chain transparency (i.e., knowing where every part is in real time).
2. What are potential problems with using RFID tags throughout Airbus's parts supply chain?

Although JIT offers many benefits, it has certain drawbacks as well. To begin with, suppliers are expected to respond instantaneously to requests. As a result, they have to carry more inventory than they otherwise would. In this sense, JIT does not *eliminate* excess inventory; rather, it simply *shifts* it from the customer to the supplier. This process can still reduce the overall inventory size if the supplier can spread the increased inventory over several customers. However, that is not always possible.

In addition, JIT replaces a few large supply shipments with a large number of smaller ones. In terms of transportation, then, the process is less efficient.

Information Sharing.   Another common approach to solving supply chain problems, and especially to improving demand forecasts, is *sharing information* along the supply chain. Information sharing can be facilitated by electronic data interchange and extranets, topics you will learn about in the next section.

One notable example of information sharing occurs between large manufacturers and retailers. For example, Walmart provides Procter & Gamble with access to daily sales information from every store for every item that P&G makes for Walmart. This access enables P&G to manage the *inventory replenishment* for Walmart's stores. By monitoring inventory levels, P&G knows when inventories fall below the threshold for each product at any Walmart store. These data trigger an immediate shipment.

Information sharing between Walmart and P&G is executed automatically. It is part of a vendor-managed inventory strategy. **Vendor-managed inventory** (VMI) occurs when the supplier, rather than the retailer, manages the entire inventory process for a particular product or group of products. Significantly, P&G has similar agreements with other major retailers. The benefit for P&G is accurate and timely information on consumer demand for its products. Thus, P&G can plan production more accurately, minimizing the bullwhip effect.

before you go on...

1. Differentiate between the push model and the pull model.

2. Describe various problems that can occur along the supply chain.

3. Discuss possible solutions to problems along the supply chain.

11.7 Information Technology Support for Supply Chain Management

Clearly, SCM systems are essential to the successful operation of many businesses. As you have seen, these systems—and IOSs in general—rely on various forms of IT to resolve problems. Three technologies, in particular, provide support for IOSs and SCM systems: electronic data interchange, extranets, and Web services. You will learn about Web services in Technology Guide 3. In this section you examine the other two technologies.

Electronic Data Interchange (EDI)

Electronic data interchange (EDI) is a communication standard that enables business partners to exchange routine documents, such as purchasing orders, electronically. EDI formats these documents according to agreed-upon standards (e.g., data formats). It then transmits messages over the Internet using a converter, called a *translator*.

EDI provides many benefits that are not available with a manual delivery system. To begin with, it minimizes data entry errors, because each entry is checked by the computer. In addition, the length of the message can be shorter, and the messages are secured. EDI also reduces cycle time, increases productivity, enhances customer service, and minimizes paper usage and storage. Figure 11.6 contrasts the process of fulfilling a purchase order with and without EDI.

EDI does have some disadvantages. Business processes sometimes must be restructured to fit EDI requirements. Also, there are many EDI standards in use today, so one company might have to use several standards in order to communicate with multiple business partners.

In today's world, where every business has a broadband connection to the Internet and where multi-megabyte design files, product photographs, and PDF sales brochures are routinely e-mailed, the value of reducing a structured e-commerce message from a few thousand XML bytes to a few hundred EDI bytes is negligible. As a result, EDI is being replaced by XML-based Web services. (You will learn about XML in Technology Guide 3.)

Extranets

To implement IOSs and SCM systems, a company must connect the intranets of its various business partners to create extranets. **Extranets** link business partners over the Internet by providing them access to certain areas of each other's corporate intranets (see Figure 11.7).

The primary goal of extranets is to foster collaboration between and among business partners. A business provides extranet access to selected B2B suppliers, customers, and other partners. These individuals access the extranet through the Internet. Extranets enable people located outside a company to collaborate with the company's internal employees. They also allow external business partners to enter the corporate intranet, via the Internet, to access data, place orders, check the status of those orders, communicate, and collaborate. Finally, they make it possible for partners to perform self-service activities such as checking inventory levels.

Extranets use virtual private network (VPN) technology to make communication over the Internet more secure. The major benefits of extranets are faster processes and information flow, improved order entry and customer service, lower costs (e.g., for communications, travel, and administrative overhead), and overall improved business effectiveness.

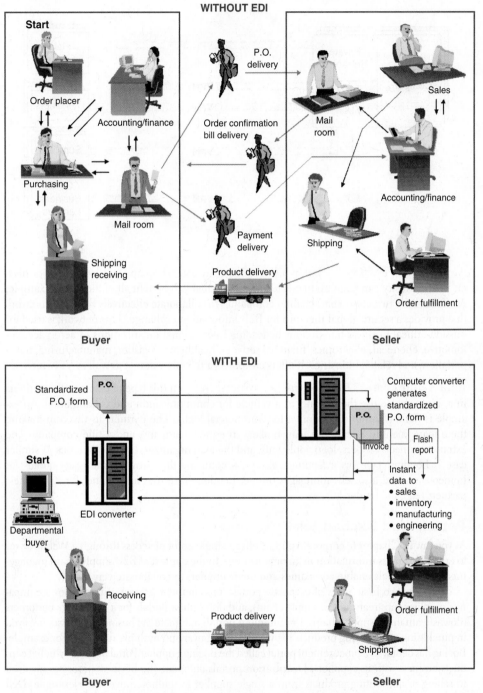

FIGURE 11.6 Comparing purchase order (PO) fulfillment with and without EDI. (*Source:* Drawn by E. Turban.)

There are three major types of extranets. The type that a company chooses depends on the business partners involved and the purpose of the supply chain. We present each type below, along with its major business applications.

A Company and Its Dealers, Customers, or Suppliers.   This type of extranet centers on a single company. An example is the FedEx extranet, which allows customers to track the status of a delivery. Customers use the Internet to access a database on the FedEx intranet. Enabling customers to monitor deliveries saves FedEx the cost of hiring human operators to perform that task over the phone.

FIGURE 11.7 The structure
of an extranet.

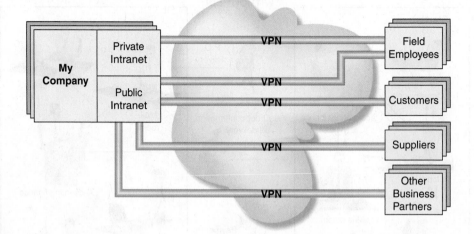

FIGURE 11.7 The structure of an extranet.

An Industry's Extranet. Just as a single company can set up an extranet, the major players in an industry can team up to create an extranet that will benefit all of them. For example, ANXeBusiness (*www.anx.com*) enables companies to collaborate effectively through a network that provides a secure global medium for B2B information exchange. This network is used for mission-critical business transactions by leading international organizations in aerospace, automotive, chemical, electronics, financial services, healthcare, logistics, manufacturing, transportation, and related industries. It offers customers a reliable extranet as well as VPN services.

Joint Ventures and Other Business Partnerships. In this type of extranet, the partners in a joint venture use the extranet as a vehicle for communication and collaboration. An example is Bank of America's extranet for commercial loans. The partners involved in making these loans include a lender, a loan broker, an escrow company, and a title company. The extranet connects lenders, loan applicants, and the loan organizer, Bank of America. A similar case is Lending Tree (*www.lendingtree.com*), a company that provides mortgage quotes for homeowners and also sells mortgages online. Lending Tree uses an extranet for its business partners (e.g., the lenders).

Portals and Exchanges

As you saw in Chapter 6, corporate portals offer a single point of access through a Web browser to critical business information in an organization. In the context of B2B supply chain management, these portals enable companies and their suppliers to collaborate very closely.

There are two basic types of corporate portals: procurement (sourcing) portals for a company's suppliers (upstream in the supply chain), and distribution portals for a company's customers (downstream in the supply chain). **Procurement portals** automate the business processes involved in purchasing or procuring products between a single buyer and multiple suppliers. For example, Boeing has deployed a procurement portal called the Boeing Supplier Portal through which it conducts business with its suppliers. **Distribution portals** automate the business processes involved in selling or distributing products from a single supplier to multiple buyers. For example, Dell services its business customers through its distribution portal at *http://premier.dell.com*.

before you go on...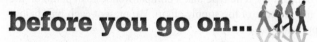

1. Define EDI, and list its major benefits and limitations.

2. Define an extranet, and explain its infrastructure.

3. List and briefly define the major types of extranets.

4. Differentiate between procurement portals and distribution portals.

What's In **IT** For **Me?**

For Accounting Majors

Customer Relationship Management. CRM systems can help companies establish controls for financial reporting related to interactions with customers in order to support compliance with legislation. For example, Sarbanes-Oxley requires companies to establish and maintain an adequate set of controls for accurate financial reporting that can be audited by a third party. Other sections [302 and 401(b)] have implications for customer activities, including the requirements that sales figures reported for the prior year be correct. Section 409 requires companies to report material changes to financial conditions, such as the loss of a strategic customer or significant customer claims about product quality.

CRM systems can track document flow from a sales opportunity, to a sales order, to an invoice, to an accounting document, thus enabling finance and accounting managers to monitor the entire flow. CRM systems that track sales quotes and orders can be used to incorporate process controls that identify questionable sales transactions. CRM systems can provide exception-alert capabilities to identify instances outside defined parameters that put companies at risk.

Supply Chain Management. The cost accountant will play an important role in developing and monitoring the financial accounting information associated with inventory and cost of goods sold. In a supply chain, much of the data for these accounting requirements will flow into the organization from various partners within the chain. It is up to the chief accountant, the comptroller or CFO, to prepare and review this data.

Going further, accounting rules and regulations and the cross-border transfer of data are critical for global trade. IOSs can facilitate such trade. Other issues that are important for accountants are taxation and government reports. In addition, creating information systems that rely on EDI requires the attention of accountants. Finally, fraud detection in global settings (e.g., transfers of funds) can be facilitated by appropriate controls and auditing.

For the Finance Major

Customer Relationship Management. CRM systems allow companies to track marketing expenses, collecting appropriate costs for each individual marketing campaign. These costs then can be matched to corporate initiatives and financial objectives, demonstrating the financial impact of the marketing campaign.

Pricing is another key area that impacts financial reporting. For example, what discounts are available? When can a price be overridden? Who approves discounts? CRM systems can put controls into place for these issues.

Supply Chain Management. In a supply chain, the finance major will be responsible for analyzing the data created and shared among supply chain partners. In many instances, the financial analyst will recommend actions to improve supply chain efficiencies and cash flow. This may benefit all the partners in the chain. These recommendations will be based on financial models that incorporate key assumptions such as supply chain partner agreements for pricing. Through the use of extensive financial modeling, the financial analyst helps to manage liquidity in the supply chain.

Many finance-related issues exist in implementing IOSs. For one thing, establishing EDI and extranet relationships involves structuring payment agreements. Global supply chains may involve complex financial arrangements, which may have legal implications.

For the Marketing Major

Customer Relationship Management. CRM systems are an integral part of every marketing professional's work activities. CRM systems contain the consolidated customer data that provides the foundation for making informed marketing decisions. Using this data, marketers develop well-timed and targeted sales campaigns with customized product mixes and established price points that enhance potential sales opportunities and therefore increase revenue. CRM systems also support the development of forecasting models for future sales to existing clients through the use of historical data captured from previous transactions.

Supply Chain Management. A tremendous amount of useful sales information can be derived from supply chain partners through the supporting information systems. For example, many of the customer support activities take place in the downstream portion of the supply chain. For the marketing manager, an understanding of how the downstream activities of the supply chain relate to prior chain operations is critical.

Further, a tremendous amount of data is fed from the supply chain supporting information systems into the CRM systems that are used by marketers. The information and a complete understanding of its genesis are vital for mixed-model marketing programs.

For the Production/Operations Management Major

Customer Relationship Management. Production is heavily involved in the acquisition of raw materials, conversion, and distribution of finished goods. However, all of these activities are driven by sales. Increases or decreases in the demand for goods result in a corresponding increase or decrease in a company's need for raw materials. Integral to a company's demand is forecasting future sales, an important part of CRM systems. Sales forecasts are created from the historical data stored in CRM systems.

This information is critically important to a production manager who is placing orders for manufacturing processes. Without an accurate future sales forecast, production managers may face inventory problems (discussed in detail in this chapter). The use of CRM systems for production and operational support is critical to efficiently managing the resources of the company.

Supply Chain Management. The production/operations management major plays a major role in the supply chain development process. In many organizations, the production/operations management staff may even lead the supply chain integration process because of their extensive knowledge of the manufacturing components of the organization. Because they are in charge of procurement, production, materials control, and logistical handling, a comprehensive understanding of the techniques of SCM is vital for the production/operations staff.

The downstream segment of supply chains is where marketing, distribution channels, and customer service are conducted. An understanding of how downstream activities are related to the other segments is critical. Supply chain problems can reduce customer satisfaction and negate marketing efforts. It is essential, then, that marketing professionals understand the nature of such problems and their solutions. Also, learning about CRM, its options, and its implementation is important for designing effective customer services and advertising.

As competition intensifies globally, finding new global markets becomes critical. Use of IOSs provides an opportunity to improve marketing and sales. Understanding the capabilities of these technologies as well as their implementation issues will enable the marketing department to excel.

For the Human Resources Major

Customer Relationship Management. Companies trying to enhance their customer relationships must recognize that employees who interact with customers are critical to the success of CRM strategies. Essentially, the success of CRM is based on the employees' desire and ability to promote the company and its CRM initiatives. In fact, research analysts have found that customer loyalty is based largely on employees' capabilities and their commitment to the company.

As a result, human resource managers know that a company that desires valued customer relationships needs valued relationships with its employees. Therefore, HR managers are implementing programs to increase employee satisfaction and are training employees to execute CRM strategies

Supply Chain Management. Supply chains require interactions among the employees of partners in the chain. These interactions are the responsibility of the Human Resources Manager. The HR Manager must be able to address supply chain issues that relate to staffing, job descriptions, job rotations, and accountability. All of these areas are complex within a supply chain and require the HR function to understand the relationship among partners as well as the movement of resources.

Preparing and training employees to work with business partners (frequently in foreign countries) requires knowledge about how IOSs operate. Sensitivity to cultural differences and extensive communication and collaboration can be facilitated with IT.

For the MIS Major

MIS

Customer Relationship Management. The IT function in the enterprise is responsible for the corporate databases and data warehouse, as well as the correctness and completeness of the data in them. That is, the IT department provides the data used in a 360-degree-view of the customer. Further, IT personnel provide the technologies underlying the customer interaction center.

Supply Chain Management. The MIS staff will be instrumental in the design and support of information systems—both internal organizational and interorganizational—that will underpin the business processes that are part of the supply chain. In this capacity, the MIS staff must have a concise knowledge of the business, the systems, and the points of intersection between the two.

[Summary]

1. **Identify the primary functions of both customer relationship management (CRM) and collaborative CRM.**

   Customer relationship management (CRM) is an organizational strategy that is customer focused and customer driven. That is, organizations concentrate on assessing customers' requirements for products and services and then providing high-quality, responsive service. CRM functions include acquiring new customers, retaining existing customers, and growing relationships with existing customers.

   Collaborative CRM is an organizational CRM strategy where data consolidation and the 360-degree view of the customer enable the organization's functional areas to readily share information about customers. The functions of collaborative CRM include integrating communications between the organization and its customers in all aspects of marketing, sales, and customer support processes, and enabling customers to provide direct feedback to the organization.

2. **Describe how businesses might use applications of each of the two major components of operational CRM systems.**

   Operational CRM systems support the front-office business processes that interact directly with customers (i.e., sales, marketing, and service). The two major components of operational CRM systems are customer-facing applications and customer-touching applications.

   Customer-facing CRM applications include customer service and support, sales force automation, marketing, and campaign management. *Customer-touching applications* include search and comparison capabilities, technical and other information and services, customized products and services, personalized Web pages, FAQs, e-mail and automated response, and loyalty programs.

3. Discuss the benefits of analytical CRM systems to businesses.

Analytical CRM systems analyze customer behavior and perceptions in order to provide business intelligence. Organizations use analytical systems for many purposes, including designing and executing targeted marketing campaigns; increasing customer acquisition, cross selling, and up selling; providing input into decisions relating to products and services (e.g., pricing, and product development); and providing financial forecasting and customer profitability analysis.

4. Explain the advantages and disadvantages of mobile CRM systems, on-demand CRM systems, and open-source CRM systems.

On-demand CRM systems are those hosted by an external vendor in the vendor's data center. Advantages of on-demand CRM systems include lower costs and a need for employees to know only how to access and utilize the software. Drawbacks include possibly unreliable vendors, difficulty in modifying the software, and difficulty in integrating vendor-hosted CRM software with the organization's existing software.

Mobile CRM systems are interactive systems where communications related to sales, marketing, and customer service activities are conducted through a mobile medium for the purpose of building and maintaining customer relationships between an organization and its customers. Advantages of mobile CRM systems include convenience for customers and the chance to build a truly personal relationship with customers. A drawback could be difficulty in maintaining customer expectations; that is, the company must be extremely responsive to customer needs in a mobile, near-real-time environment.

Open-source CRM systems are those whose source code is available to developers and users. The benefits of open-source CRM systems include favorable pricing, a wide variety of applications, easy customization, rapid updates and bug (software error) fixes, and extensive free support information. The major drawback of open-source CRM systems is quality control.

5. Describe the three components and the three flows of a supply chain.

A *supply chain* is the flow of materials, information, money, and services from raw material suppliers, through factories and warehouses, to the end customers. A supply chain involves three segments: upstream, where sourcing or procurement from external suppliers occurs; internal, where packaging, assembly, or manufacturing takes place; and downstream, where distribution takes place, frequently by external distributors.

There are three flows in the supply chain: *material flows*, which are the physical products, raw materials, supplies, and so forth; *information flows*, which consist of data related to demand, shipments, orders, returns, and schedules, as well as changes in any of these data; and *financial flows*, which involve money transfers, payments, credit card information and authorization, payment schedules, e-payments, and credit-related data.

6. Identify popular strategies to solving different challenges of supply chains.

Two major challenges in setting accurate inventory levels throughout a supply chain are the *demand forecast* and the bullwhip effect. Demand for a product can be influenced by numerous factors such as competition, prices, weather conditions, technological developments, economic conditions, and customers' general confidence. The *bullwhip effect* refers to erratic shifts in orders up and down the supply chain.

The most common solution to supply chain problems is *building inventories* as insurance against SC uncertainties. Another solution is the *just-in-time* (JIT) inventory system, which delivers the precise number of parts, called *work-in-process inventory*, to be assembled into a finished product at precisely the right time. The third possible solution is *vendor-managed inventory* (VMI), which occurs when the vendor, rather than the retailer, manages the entire inventory process for a particular product or group of products.

7. **Explain the utility of each of the three major technologies that supports supply chain management.**

Electronic data interchange (EDI) is a communication standard that enables the electronic transfer of routine documents, such as purchasing orders, between business partners.

Extranets are networks that link business partners over the Internet by providing them access to certain areas of each other's corporate intranets. The main goal of extranets is to foster collaboration among business partners.

Corporate portals offer a single point of access through a Web browser to critical business information in an organization. In the context of business-to-business supply chain management, these portals enable companies and their suppliers to collaborate very closely.

[Chapter Glossary]

analytical CRM system CRM system that analyzes customer behavior and perceptions in order to provide actionable business intelligence.

bullwhip effect Erratic shifts in orders up and down the supply chain.

bundling A form of cross selling where an enterprise sells a group of products or services together at a lower price than the combined individual price of the products.

campaign management applications CRM applications that help organizations plan marketing campaigns that send the right messages to the right people through the right channels.

collaborative CRM system A CRM system where communications between the organization and its customers are integrated across all aspects of marketing, sales, and customer support processes.

cross selling The practice of marketing additional related products to customers based on a previous purchase.

customer-facing CRM applications Areas where customers directly interact with the organization, including customer service and support, sales force automation, marketing, and campaign management.

customer interaction center (CIC) A CRM operation where organizational representatives use multiple communication channels to interact with customers in functions such as inbound teleservice and outbound telesales.

customer relationship management (CRM) A customer-focused and customer-driven organizational strategy that concentrates on addressing customers' requirements for products and services, and then providing high-quality, responsive service.

customer-touching CRM applications (also called **electronic CRM** or **e-CRM**) Applications and technologies with which customers interact and typically help themselves.

customer touch point Any interaction between a customer and an organization.

distribution portals Corporate portals that automate the business processes involved in selling or distributing products from a single supplier to multiple buyers.

electronic CRM (e-CRM) (see **customer-touching CRM applications**)

electronic data interchange (EDI) A communication standard that enables the electronic transfer of routine documents between business partners.

extranets Networks that link business partners over the Internet by providing them access to certain areas of each other's corporate intranets.

front-office processes Those processes that directly interact with customers; that is, sales, marketing, and service.

interorganizational information system (IOS) An information system that supports information flow among two or more organizations.

inventory velocity The speed at which a company can deliver products and services after receiving the materials required to make them.

just-in-time (JIT) inventory system A system in which a supplier delivers the precise number of parts to be assembled into a finished product at precisely the right time.

loyalty program Programs that offer rewards to customers to influence future behavior.

mobile CRM system An interactive CRM system where communications related to sales, marketing, and customer service activities are conducted through a mobile medium for the purpose of building and maintaining customer relationships between an organization and its customers.

on-demand CRM system A CRM system that is hosted by an external vendor in the vendor's data center.

open-source CRM system CRM software whose source code is available to developers and users.

operational CRM system The component of CRM that supports the front-office business processes that directly interact with customers (i.e., sales, marketing, and service).

procurement portals Corporate portals that automate the business processes involved in purchasing or procuring products between a single buyer and multiple suppliers.

pull model A business model in which the production process begins with a customer order and companies make only what customers want, a process closely aligned with mass customization.

push model A business model in which the production process begins with a forecast, which predicts the products that customers will want as well as the quantity of each product. The company then produces the amount of products in the forecast, typically by using mass production, and sells, or "pushes," those products to consumers.

sales force automation (SFA) The component of an operational CRM system that automatically records all the aspects in a sales transaction process.

supply chain The coordinated movement of *resources* from organizations through *conversion* to the end consumer.

supply chain management (SCM) An activity in which the leadership of an organization provides extensive oversight for the partnerships and processes that compose the supply chain and leverages these relationships to provide an operational advantage.

supply chain visibility The ability of all organizations in a supply chain to access or view relevant data on purchased materials as these materials move through their suppliers' production processes.

up selling A sales strategy where the organizational representative provides to customers the opportunity to purchase higher-value related products or services in place of, or along with the consumer's initial product or service selection.

vendor-managed inventory (VMI) An inventory strategy where the supplier monitors a vendor's inventory for a product or group of products and replenishes products when needed.

vertical integration Strategy of integrating the upstream part of the supply chain with the internal part, typically by purchasing upstream suppliers, in order to ensure timely availability of supplies.

[Discussion Questions]

1. How do customer relationship management systems help organizations achieve customer intimacy?
2. What is the relationship between data consolidation and CRM systems?
3. Discuss the relationship between CRM and customer privacy.
4. Distinguish between operational CRM systems and analytical CRM systems.
5. Differentiate between customer-facing CRM applications and customer-touching CRM applications.
6. Explain why Web-based customer interaction centers are critical for successful CRM systems.
7. Why are companies so interested in e-CRM applications?
8. Discuss why it is difficult to justify CRM applications.
9. You are the CIO of a small company with a rapidly growing customer base. Which CRM system would you use: an on-premise CRM system, an on-demand CRM system, or an open-source CRM system? Remember that open-source CRM systems may be implemented either on-premise or on-demand. Discuss the pros and cons of each type of CRM system for your business.
10. Refer to the example concerning the CRM efforts of Caterpillar. Where on the CRM continuum (low-end to high-end) does the company's CRM strategy fit? Explain your answer.
11. List and explain the important components of a supply chain.
12. Explain how a supply chain approach may be part of a company's overall strategy.
13. Explain the important role that information systems play in supporting a supply chain strategy.
14. Would Rolls-Royce Motorcars (*www.rolls-roycemotorcars.com*) use a push model or a pull model in its supply chain? Support your answer.
15. Why is planning so important in supply chain management?

[Problem-Solving Activities]

1. Access *www.ups.com* and *www.fedex.com*. Examine some of the IT-supported customer services and tools provided by the two companies. Compare and contrast the customer support provided on the two companies' Web sites.
2. Enter *www.anntaylor.com*, *www.hermes.com*, and *www.tiffany.com*. Compare and contrast the customer service activities offered by these companies on their Web sites. Do you see marked similarities? Differences?
3. Access your university's Web site. Investigate how your university provides for customer relationship management. (Hint: First decide who your university's customers are.)
4. Access *www.sugarcrm.com*, and take the interactive tour. Prepare a report on SugarCRM's functionality to the class.
5. Access *www.ups.com* and *www.fedex.com*. Examine some of the IT-supported customer services and tools provided by the two companies. Write a report on how the two companies contribute to supply chain improvements.
6. Enter *www.supply-chain.org*, *www.cio.com*, *www.findarticles.com*, and *www.google.com*, and search for recent information on supply chain management.
7. Surf the Web to find a procurement (sourcing) portal, a distribution portal, and an exchange (other than the examples presented in this chapter). List the features they have in common and those features that are unique.

[Team Assignments]

1. Assign each group to an open-source CRM vendor. Each group should examine the vendor, its products, and the capabilities of those products and make a presentation to the class detailing how its vendor's product is superior to the other open-source CRM products. See Sugar-CRM (*www.sugarcrm.com*), Concursive (*www.concursive.com*), vtiger (*www.vtiger.com*), SplendidCRM Software (*www.splendidcrm.com*), Compiere (*www.compiere.com*), Hipergate (*http://sourceforge.net/projects/hipergate/*), and openCRX (*www.opencrx.com*).

2. Assign each group to an on-demand CRM vendor. Each group should examine each vendor, its products, and the capabilities of those products and make a presentation to the class detailing how its vendor's product is superior to the other on-demand CRM products. See Salesforce (*www.salesforce.com*), Oracle (*http://crmondemand.oracle.com*), Aplicor (*www.aplicor.com*), NetSuite (*www.netsuite.com*), SalesNexus (*www.salesnexus.com*), SageCRM (*www.sagecrm.com*), Commence (*www.commence.com*), and eSalesTrack (*www.esalestrack.com*).

3. Create groups to investigate the major CRM applications and their vendors.

   - Sales force automation (Microsoft Dynamics, Oracle, FrontRange Solutions, RightNow Technologies, Maximizer Software)

   - Call centers (LivePerson, Cisco, Oracle)
   - Marketing automation (SalesNexus, Marketo, Chordiant, Infor, Consona, Pivotal, Oracle)
   - Customer service (Oracle, Amazon, Dell, Sage)

   Start with *www.searchcrm.com* and *www.customerthink.com* (to ask questions about CRM solutions). Have each group present arguments to convince the class members to use the product(s) the group investigated.

4. Assign each group in the class to a major supply chain management vendor, such as SAP, Oracle, i2, IBM, and so on. Each group will investigate topics such as (a) the products, (b) major capabilities, (c) relationship to customer relationship management, and (d) customer success stories. Each group will prepare a presentation for the class, trying to convince the class why that group's software product is best.

5. Have each team locate several organizations that use IOSs, including one with a global reach. Students should contact the companies to find out what IOS technology support they use (e.g., an EDI, an extranet, etc.) and what issues they faced in implementation. Prepare a report.

[Closing Case Cengage Uses Information Technology to Improve Warehouse Operations] POM

The Problem

Cengage Learning (www.cengage.com) is the second-largest higher-education textbook company in the United States. It has 5,500 employees, generates revenues of approximately $2 billion, and operates in more than 20 countries. The company provides teaching, learning, and research solutions for academic, professional, and library markets globally. Cengage Learning purchases educational materials from suppliers all over the world. Many of these materials arrive in print form at the Cengage Learning Distribution Center (CLCD), where they are stored until they are shipped out to Cengage customers. The CLDC stores 81 million textbooks. To manage this vast inventory, Cengage needs to optimize the CLDC's performance.

The IT Solutions

To operate the CLDC at peak efficiency and effectiveness, Cengage utilizes a warehouse management system called Logistics PRO, produced by Manhattan Associates (www.manh.com). Logistics PRO continuously tracks the location and status of every textbook in the warehouse. In addition,

the system calculates the lowest shipping cost for each parcel. Finally, it calculates the amount of labor required to ship each day's orders on time.

As books enter the CLDC, Logistics PRO records their dimensions and then assigns them to their proper storage location in the building. When customers place orders for books, the system calculates the most efficient way to pack the books in shipping boxes and then to pack the boxes on the trucks that take the parcels from the facility. It then feeds those calculations into a voice-directed picking system called Jennifer Voice Plus, designed by Lucas Systems (www.lucasware.com). The Jennifer system translates the information into spoken directions—for example, how many books to pick, how to pack the box, where to ship them—and then conveys that information to warehouse workers wearing headsets.

Because the new system performs all of the essential calculations, the warehouse workers no longer need to carry a bar-code scanner. Therefore, they can use both hands to select and pack books for shipment. As a result, they have become more productive, and the overall process has become more efficient. Jennifer guides the workers, very precisely, through their workday.

The CLDC also utilizes a high-speed package-conveying system from Automotion Conveyors (www.automotionconveyors.com). This system enables employees to move boxes of books—many of them quite heavy—from different parts of the warehouse without injuring themselves. Eight miles of conveyer track connect to a 600-foot-long, high-speed sorter that funnels 130 units per minute into one of 36 diversion lanes. Workers on those lanes—all listening to instructions from Jennifer—sort, pick, pack, and ship 100,000 custom orders each day. These learning materials often go from a storage shelf in the CLDC to a customer's mailbox in just 24 hours.

The Results

The implementation of the warehouse management, voice direction, and conveyer systems has enormously improved productivity at the CLDC. Ten years ago, 300 employees working at full capacity could ship only 50 million units annually. Today, 250 employees ship 63 million parcels, an increase of roughly 50 percent per employee.

In addition to increased productivity, the three systems have produced many benefits for the CLDC. Per-unit shipping costs have decreased, while the quality of outbound shipments (e.g., accuracy of the order, timeliness, and other metrics) has increased. Workers make fewer mistakes. Training times for new and temporary workers have decreased from an average of four days to just four hours. Interestingly, since the installation of the conveyer system, the CLDC has enjoyed a near-perfect OSHA record.

In sum, then, the new systems have dramatically transformed the way the CLDC operates and the way that Cengage customers view their interactions with the company. In addition to these immediate benefits, these systems support the company's long-term growth strategy.

Sources: Compiled from M. Hendricks, "How Voice Technology Could Revolutionize Supply Chain Management, *AllBusiness.com*, March 15, 2013; P. Barlas, "Manhattan Associates Carve Niche in Retail," *Investors.com*, November 1, 2012; J. Steffney and R. Eby, "Textbook Technology," *Baseline Magazine*, May 8, 2012; L. Rogers, "Voice Technology Speaks to Workers," *Supply Chain Management Review*, February 1, 2012; "Jennifer Voice Has Extraordinary Client Roster," *SB Wire*, June 9, 2011; "Voice Picking Productivity as Part of Jennifer VoicePlus Enhanced with Speedometer," *SB Wire*, June 1, 2011; "Lucas Systems Enhances Jennifer VoicePlus System With Serenade Speech Recognition Platform," *Speech Technology Magazine*, October 15, 2010; www.manh.com, www.automotionconveyors.com, www.lucasware.com, www.cengage.com, accessed March 15, 2013.

Questions

1. Describe the advantages that the LucasPRO system provides for the operation of the CLDC.

2. Describe the advantages that the Jennifer system provides for the operation of the CLDC.

3. Discuss possible positive and negative reactions that CLDC workers might have to automating the operations of the CLDC.

[Internship Activity]

Manufacturing Industry

Customer Relationship Management and Supply Chain Management tools are useful because they help the organization manage external relationships. In fact, CRM tools provide information that will be very useful to the SCM systems even though the external entities they interact with are on opposite sides of the supply chain model.

Mileah Jones is a Quality Control Manager and her primary responsibility is to investigate product issues reported by her customers and to communicate with the supply chain to resolve issues. For this activity, your task is to help Mileah understand how the information generated by a CRM can be helpful to her and the her business partners that are connected across the SCM system.

Please visit the Book Companion Site to receive the full set of instructions.

Chapter 12

Business Analytics

[LEARNING OBJECTIVES]	[CHAPTER OUTLINE]	[WEB RESOURCES]
1. Explain different ways in which IT supports decision making.	12.1 Managers and Decision Making	• Student PowerPoints for note taking
2. Provide examples of different ways that organizations make use of business intelligence (BI).	12.2 What Is Business Intelligence?	**WileyPLUS** • E-book
3. Explain the value that different BI applications provide to large and small businesses.	12.3 Business Intelligence Applications for Data Analysis	• Author video lecture for each chapter section
4. Offer examples of how businesses and government agencies can use different BI applications to analyze data.	12.4 Business Intelligence Applications for Presenting Results	• Practice quizzes • Flash Cards for vocabulary review
5. Explain how your university could use CPM to effect solution to two campus problems.	12.5 Business Intelligence in Action: Corporate Performance Management	• Additional "IT's About Business" cases • Video interviews with managers • Lab Manuals for Microsoft Office 2010 and 2013

What's In IT For Me?

This Chapter Will Help Prepare You To...

ACCT	FIN	MKT	POM	HRM	MIS
ACCOUNTING	FINANCE	MARKETING	PRODUCTION OPERATIONS MANAGEMENT	HUMAN RESOURCES MANAGEMENT	MIS
Uncover fraudulent transactions	Make stock market investment decisions	Allocate advertising budgets	Schedule production activities	Control job applicant process	Provide information in dashboards

The Problem

The aging physical infrastructure of the city of South Bend, Indiana, was causing significant problems for civic leaders. For instance, the city's 1950s-era combination water delivery and sewer system was experiencing as many as 30 overflow incidents every year. During these overflows, dislodged debris would collect at the feeder ramps to the main sewer arteries. Further, sewage would overflow dams, back up into homes, and cause other damage, resulting in frequent threats of multimillion dollar fines from state and federal regulators. The only way for the city to minimize those incidents was to have field workers physically observe each of the system's 36 major feeder ramp junctions, and, if possible, remove the debris. This approach was inefficient, and it failed to provide adequate public health and environmental safeguards.

The IT Solution

To alleviate South Bend's water and sewer problems, city information technology personnel implemented two technologies. The first was a real-time sewer-monitoring system, and the second was an analytics software tool designed to help cities monitor and manage services. The city installed credit-card-sized sensors at 116 locations in its sewer system. These sensors fed data via wireless Internet connections into a database for use by the analytics software.

The Results

Managers, sewer technicians, and operators at South Bend's Board of Public Works now had Web-based access to the software. The analytics tool works like a GPS traffic report, using color codes on a map of the sewer system to indicate where potential problems are starting, and allocating sewer technicians to prevent backups and overflows before they happen. In addition, the mayor has a Web-based dashboard (discussed later in this chapter) that lets him keep tabs on the state of the water and sewer systems.

The data provided by the analytics tools revealed that some sewer pipes have extra capacity, whereas others over flow during heavy rainstorms. With the system of real-time sensors in place, technicians and operators can now ensure that when rainfall is heavier in a certain part of town, the resulting sewer flows can be routed to areas where the pipes have greater capacity.

Since South Bend implemented this new system, the city has reduced the number of overflows by 95 percent. Even better, the entire system cost the city $6 million, which is significantly less than the $120 million in sewer improvements it faced if it had opted to make traditional repairs.

[Developing Smarter Cities through Analytics]

In fact, the system is delivering far more additional value than originally anticipated. Water distribution system operators are using the system to monitor instances when they flush out iron and manganese buildup, a process that can cause overflows if it is not carefully controlled. In addition, the city uses system data regarding water service shutoffs to inform the police about the locations of abandoned and foreclosed homes. This information alerts the police to provide additional patrols in those areas, thereby avoiding unnecessary urban blight.

South Bend has identified an additional $23 million in potential operational savings they will achieve from adding the sensors and using the system's data to deliver a variety of services more efficiently. One such service involves closely monitoring sidewalk temperatures to more accurately plan for purchases of de-icing materials.

Sources: Compiled from K. Makovsky, "Smart-City; Smart PR Pros," *Forbes*, March 14, 2013; S. Lohr, "SimCity for Real: Measuring an Untidy Metropolis," *The New York Times*, February 23, 2013; T. Kontzer, "Business Analytics Turns Data into Intelligence," *Baseline Magazine*, September 10, 2012; "IBM, Notre Dame, Emnet Help South Bend, Indiana Protect Public Health, Reduce Pollution with Smarter Cities Cloud Analytics," *IBM Press Release*, June 27, 2012; "The CEO Guide to Smart Cities," *Bloomberg BusinessWeek*, December 21, 2011; www.ibm.com/smartercities, accessed April 20, 2013.

Questions

1. Describe the benefits South Bend realized by implementing the sensors and analytics software. Can any city do what South Bend has done? Why or why not? Support your answer.
2. Describe additional applications for sensors tied to analytics software within an urban setting.

What We Learned from This Case

The "smart cities" case illustrates the importance and far-reaching nature of business intelligence applications. **Business intelligence (BI)** is a broad category of applications, technologies, and processes for gathering, storing, accessing, and analyzing data to help business users make better decisions. BI applications enable decision makers to quickly ascertain the status of a business enterprise by examining key information. South Bend civic leaders needed current, timely, and accurate information that their old system could not provide. Implementing the BI applications generated significant benefits throughout the city, supporting important decisions about South Bend's overall goal: providing the highest levels of benefits to citizens while staying within the budget.

This chapter describes information systems that support *decision making*. It begins by reviewing the manager's job and the nature of modern managerial decisions. This discussion will help you to understand why managers need computerized support. It then considers how business intelligence can support individuals, groups, and entire organizations.

It is impossible to overstate the importance of business intelligence within modern organizations. Recall from Chapter 1 that the essential goal of information systems is to provide the right information to the right person, in the right amount, at the right time, in the right format. In essence, BI achieves this goal. BI systems provide business intelligence that you can act on in a timely fashion.

It is also impossible to overstate the importance of your input into the BI process within an organization, for several reasons. First, you (the user community) will decide what data should be stored in your organization's data warehouse. You will then work closely with the MIS department to obtain these data.

Further, you will use your organization's BI applications, probably from your first day on the job. With some BI applications such as data mining and decision support systems, you will decide how you want to analyze the data (user-driven analysis). With other BI applications such as dashboards, you will decide which data you need and in which format. Again, you will work closely with your MIS department to ensure that these applications meet your needs.

Much of this chapter is concerned with large-scale BI applications. You should keep in mind, however, that smaller organizations, and even individual users, can implement small-scale BI applications as well. For example, Excel spreadsheets provide some BI functions, as do SQL queries of a database. IT's About [Small] Business 12.1 illustrates how a startup uses analytics to help beef and dairy farmers.

IT's about [small] business

12.1 Analytics Helps Farmers

Farmers have always had plenty of data but few tools to help them analyze the data. For example, they receive data from their feeding machines as well as reports on health status, reproductive status, and milk production from their veterinarians. Historically they had to sit down, collate the printed reports, and try to make sense of them.

Today, farmers have another option: They can use Fameron (https://www.farmeron.com). Founded by Matija Kopic, a Croatian, Fameron (launched in November 2011) is a Web-based service that farmers use to analyze the various types of information they receive concerning their animals: diet, health, reproduction, milk production, and medicine or drug dosages. Farmeron connects the data generated by the farm machinery directly to the Web. Farmeron provides analysis and dashboards (discussed later in this chapter) to its clients to help them achieve insights into how well their farms are performing. The company's services are extremely fast and appealing to use. Where it once took days for a dairy farmer to input and analyze months of diet and medical data, Farmeron's service makes the conclusions available instantly.

One Croatian dairy farmer with 400 cows claimed that Farmeron helped him to meet laws for animal tracking and sales and also to report animal deaths to the insurance companies. The farmer also uses Farmeron to manage daily feed rations and feed purchases, which is critical because feed can represent up to 70 percent of his farm's expenses.

As of mid-2013, Farmeron focused largely on dairy and beef cows. It charged farmers who own up to 75 cows about 25 cents per head monthly; those with up to 600 cows pay about 45 cents per month. Larger farms pay on a custom plan. Kopic is considering expanding his operation to include chickens and pigs. In one instance a frog farmer requested his service. Because Farmeron collects data across many farms, the company can make broad conclusions about what works concerning best practices. A *best practice* is a method or technique that has consistently shown superior results to those achieved with other means; for this reason it is used as a benchmark. Fameron can also provide recommendations for improving production. Kopic believes that Farmeron can be particularly useful in emerging markets where knowledge concerning best practices.

Farmeron runs on the Web, so farmers can access its services on their tablet computers. Although some tablets are dropped in the "wrong" places on farms and get filthy, farmers appreciate having all of the relevant data with them. That way, they do not have to go inside to search through a pile of hard-copy spreadsheets on their desk.

More than 600 corporate farms use Farmeron services. Forty-five percent of these farms are located in North America, with the largest having 4,000 animals. In May 2012, Farmeron signed a partnership with Neelsen Agrar, a large German equipment company with operations in more than 30 countries. Agrar is selling Farmeron to its clients.

Farmeron does have competitors, including Farmlogs (http://farmlogs.com), Farm Works (www.farmworks.com), and equipment manufacturer John Deere, which provides software and Web support for managing agricultural operations.

Sources: Compiled from A. Chowdhry, "FarmLogs Is Going to Change the Way Farmers Manage Their Business," *Forbes*, February 14, 2013; "7 Craziest Things Connected to the Internet: Cows and Crops," *CNN Money*, September 2012; T. Geron, "Cows in the Cloud," *Forbes*, August 20, 2012; M. Butcher, "SaaS for Cows!," *TechCrunch*, May 10, 2012; https://www.farmeron.com, http://farmlogs.com, www.farmworks.com, accessed April 19, 2013.

Questions

1. Why is having instantaneous data availability so important for farmers? Provide examples to support your answer.
2. What other agricultural applications might Kopic develop that would be useful to farmers? Provide examples to support your answer.

The most popular BI tool by far is Excel. For years, BI vendors "fought" against the use of Excel. Eventually, however, they decided to "join it" by designing their software so that it interfaces with Excel. How does this process work? Essentially, users download plug-ins that add functionality (e.g., the ability to list the top 10 percent of customers, based on sales) to Excel. This process can be thought of as creating "Excel on steroids." Excel then connects to the vendor's application server—which provides additional data-analysis capabilities—which in turn connects to a backend database, such as a data mart or warehouse. This arrangement gives Excel users the functionality and access to data typical of sophisticated BI products, while allowing them to work with a familiar client—Excel.

Microsoft has made similar changes to its product line. Specifically, Excel now can be used with MS SQL Server (a database product), and it can be utilized in advanced BI applications, such as dashboards and data mining/predictive analysis.

After you finish this chapter, you will have a basic understanding of decision making, the business intelligence process, and BI applications employed in modern organizations. This knowledge will enable you to immediately and confidently provide input into your organization's BI processes and applications. Further, the hands-on exercises in this chapter will familiarize you with the actual use of BI software. These exercises will enable you to use your organization's BI applications to effectively analyze data and thus make better decisions. Enjoy!

12.1   Managers and Decision Making

Management is a process by which an organization achieves its goals through the use of resources (people, money, materials, and information). These resources are considered to be *inputs*. Achieving the organization's goals is the *output* of the process. Managers oversee this process in an attempt to optimize it. A manager's success often is measured by the ratio between the inputs and outputs for which he or she is responsible. This ratio is an indication of the organization's **productivity**.

The Manager's Job and Decision Making

To appreciate how information systems support managers, you first must understand the manager's job. Managers do many things, depending on their position in the organization, the type and size of the organization, the organization's policies and culture, and the personalities of the managers themselves. Despite these variations, however, all managers perform three basic roles (Mintzberg, 1973):

1. *Interpersonal roles:* figurehead, leader, liaison
2. *Informational roles:* monitor, disseminator, spokesperson, analyzer
3. *Decisional roles:* entrepreneur, disturbance handler, resource allocator, negotiator

Early information systems primarily supported the informational roles. In recent years, information systems have been developed that support all three roles. In this chapter, you will focus on the support that IT can provide for decisional roles.

A **decision** refers to a choice among two or more alternatives that individuals and groups make. Decisions are diverse and are made continuously. Decision making is a systematic process. Economist Herbert Simon (1977) described decision making as composed of three major phases: intelligence, design, and choice. Once the choice is made, the decision is implemented. Figure 12.1 illustrates this process, indicating which tasks are included in each phase. Note that there is a continuous flow of information from intelligence, to design, to choice (bold lines), but at any phase there may be a return to a previous phase (broken lines).

This model of decision making is quite general. Undoubtedly, you have made decisions where you did not construct a model of the situation, validate your model with test data, or conduct a sensitivity analysis. The model we present here is intended to encompass all of the conditions that might occur when making a decision. For some decisions, some steps or phrases may be minimal, implicit (understood), or absent.

The decision-making process starts with the *intelligence phase*, in which managers examine a situation and identify and define the problem or opportunity. In the *design phase*, decision makers construct a model for the situation. They do this by making assumptions that simplify reality and by expressing the relationships among all the relevant variables. Managers then validate the model by using test data. Finally, decision makers set criteria for evaluating all of the potential solutions that are proposed. The *choice phase* involves selecting a solution or course of action that seems best suited to resolve the problem. This solution (the decision) is then implemented. Implementation is successful if the proposed solution solves the problem or seizes the opportunity. If the solution fails, then the process returns to the previous phases. Computer-based decision support assists managers in the decision-making process.

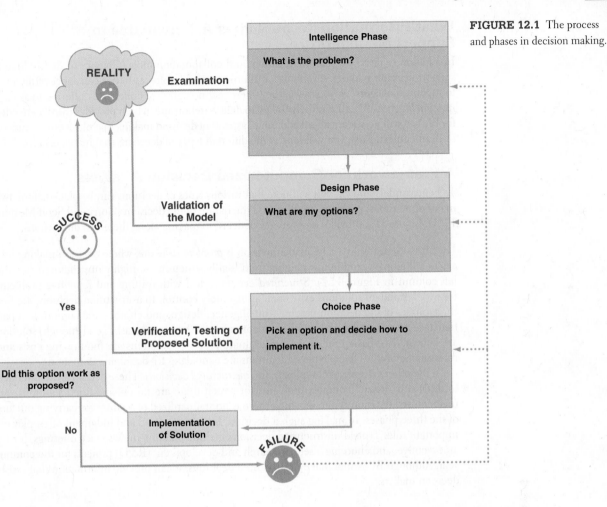

FIGURE 12.1 The process and phases in decision making.

Why Managers Need IT Support

Making good decisions is very difficult without solid information. Information is vital for each phase and activity in the decision-making process. Even when information is available, however, decision making is difficult due to the following trends:

- The *number of alternatives* is constantly *increasing,* due to innovations in technology, improved communications, the development of global markets, and the use of the Internet and e-business. A key to good decision making is to explore and compare many relevant alternatives. The greater the number of alternatives, the more a decision maker needs computer-assisted searches and comparisons.

- Most decisions must be made *under time pressure.* It often is not possible to manually process information fast enough to be effective.

- Due to increased uncertainty in the decision environment, decisions are becoming more complex. It is usually necessary to *conduct a sophisticated analysis* in order to make a good decision.

- It often is necessary to rapidly access remote information, consult with experts, or conduct a group decision-making session, all without incurring large expenses. Decision makers, as well as the information, can be situated in different locations. Bringing everything together quickly and inexpensively can be a major challenge.

These trends create major difficulties for decision makers. Fortunately, as you will see throughout this chapter, a computerized analysis can be of enormous help.

What Information Technologies Are Available to Support Managers?

In addition to discovery, communication, and collaboration tools (Chapter 6) that indirectly support decision making, several other information technologies have been successfully used to support managers. As you saw earlier, these technologies are collectively referred to as *business intelligence* (BI). BI is closely linked to data warehousing, which provides the data needed for BI. You will now learn about additional aspects of decision making that place our discussion of BI in context. First, you will look at the different types of decisions that managers face.

A Framework for Computerized Decision Analysis

To better understand BI, you will note that various types of decisions can be placed along two major dimensions: problem structure and the nature of the decision (Gorry and Scott Morton, 1971). Figure 12.2 provides an overview of decision making along these two dimensions.

Problem Structure.   The first dimension is *problem structure*, where decision-making processes fall along a continuum ranging from highly structured to highly unstructured (see the left column in Figure 12.2). *Structured decisions* deal with routine and repetitive problems for which standard solutions exist, such as inventory control. In a structured decision, the first three phases of the decision process—intelligence, design, and choice—are laid out in a particular sequence, and the procedures for obtaining the best (or at least a good enough) solution are known. Two basic criteria used to evaluate proposed solutions are minimizing costs and maximizing profits. These types of decisions are candidates for decision automation.

At the other extreme of complexity are *unstructured decisions*. These decisions are intended to deal with "fuzzy," complex problems for which there are no cut-and-dried solutions. An unstructured decision is one in which there is no standardized procedure for carrying out any of the three phases. In making such a decision, human intuition and judgment often play an important role. Typical unstructured decisions include planning new service offerings, hiring an executive, and choosing a set of research and development (R&D) projects for the coming year. Although BI cannot make unstructured decisions, it can provide information that assists decision makers.

	Operational Control	Management Control	Strategic Planning	IS Support
Structured	Accounts receivable, order entry 1	Budget analysis, short-term forecasting, personnel reports, make-or-buy analysis 2	 3	MIS, statistical models (management science, financial, etc.)
Semistructured	Production scheduling, inventory control 4	Credit evaluation, budget preparation, plant layout, project scheduling, reward systems design 5	Building a new plant, mergers and acquisitions, planning (product, quality assurance, compensation, etc.) 6	Decision support systems, business intelligence
Unstructured	 7	Negotiating, recruiting an executive, buying hardware, lobbying 8	New technology development, product R&D, social responsibility planning 9	Decision support systems, expert systems, enterprise resource planning, neural networks, business intelligence, big data

FIGURE 12.2 Decision support framework. Technology is used to support the decisions shown in the column at the far right and in the bottom row.

Located between structured and unstructured decisions are *semistructured* decisions, in which only some of the decision process phases are structured. Semistructured decisions require a combination of standard solution procedures and individual judgment. Examples of semistructured decisions are evaluating employees, setting marketing budgets for consumer products, performing capital acquisition analysis, and trading bonds.

The Nature of Decisions.   The second dimension of decision support deals with the *nature of decisions*. All managerial decisions fall into one of three broad categories:

1. *Operational control*—executing specific tasks efficiently and effectively.
2. *Management control*—acquiring and using resources efficiently in accomplishing organizational goals.
3. *Strategic planning*—the long-range goals and policies for growth and resource allocation.

These categories are displayed along the top row of Figure 12.2.

Note that strategic decisions define the context in which management control decisions are made. In turn, management control decisions define the context in which operational control decisions are made.

The Decision Matrix.   The three primary classes of problem structure and the three broad categories of the nature of decisions can be combined in a decision-support matrix that consists of nine cells, as diagrammed in Figure 12.2. Lower-level managers usually perform tasks in cells 1, 2, and 4. The tasks in cells 3, 5, and 7 are usually the responsibility of middle managers and professional staff. Finally, tasks in cells 6, 8, and 9 are generally carried out by senior executives.

Computer Support for Structured Decisions.   Examples of computer support that might be used for the nine cells in the matrix are displayed in the right-hand column and the bottom row of Figure 12.2. Structured and some semistructured decisions, especially of the operational and management control type, have been supported by computers since the 1950s. Decisions of this type are made in all functional areas, but particularly in finance and operations management.

Problems that lower-level managers encounter on a regular basis typically have a high level of structure. Examples are capital budgeting (e.g., replacement of equipment), allocating resources, distributing merchandise, and controlling inventory. For each type of structured decision, prescribed solutions have been developed, which often include mathematical formulas. This approach is called *management science* or *operations research*, and it also is executed with the aid of computers.

before you go on...

1. Describe the decision-making process proposed by Simon.
2. You are registering for classes next semester. Apply the decision-making process to your decision about how many and which courses to take. Is your decision structured, semistructured, or unstructured?
3. Consider your decision-making process when registering for classes next semester. Explain how information technology supports (or does not support) each phase of this process.

What Is Business Intelligence?

12.2

To provide users with access to corporate data, many organizations are implementing data warehouses and data marts, which you learned about in Chapter 5. Users analyze the data in warehouses and marts using a wide variety of BI tools. Many vendors offer integrated packages of these tools under the overall label of *business intelligence (BI) software*. Major

BI software vendors include SAS (*www.sas.com*), Hyperion (*www.hyperion.com*, now owned by Oracle), Business Objects (*www.businessobjects.com*, now owned by SAP), Information Builders (*www.informationbuilders.com*), SPSS (*www.spss.com*, now owned by IBM), and Cognos (*www.ibm.com/cognos*).

As you have seen, BI is vital to modern decision making and organizational performance. Let's consider in greater detail the technical foundation for BI and the variety of ways that BI can be used.

The phrase *business intelligence* is relatively new. Business and IT analyst Howard Dresner coined the term in 1989 while he was an analyst at Gartner, a market research firm. The expression is especially popular in industry, where it is used as an umbrella term that encompasses all decision-support applications.

BI encompasses not only applications, but also technologies and processes. It includes both "getting data in" (to a data mart or warehouse) and "getting data out" (through BI applications).

In addition, a significant change is taking place within the BI environment. In the past, organizations used BI only to support management. Today, however, BI applications are increasingly available to front-line personnel (e.g., call center operators), suppliers, customers, and even regulators. These groups rely on BI to provide them with the most current information.

The Scope of Business Intelligence

The use of BI in organizations varies considerably. In smaller organizations, BI may be limited to Excel spreadsheets. In larger ones, BI often is enterprisewide, and it includes applications such as data mining/predictive analytics, dashboards, and data visualization. It is important to recognize that the importance of BI to organizations continues to grow. It is not an exaggeration to say that for many firms, BI is now a requirement for competing in the marketplace, as illustrated in IT's About Business 12.2.

IT's [about business]

12.2 Can We Predict the Weather? POM

If you were in the business of supplying heating oil in the northeastern United States, would it be useful to know if a big winter snowstorm with subzero temperatures was likely to hit Massachusetts the following month? If you were a firefighter in the backcountry of California and you knew that the odds of intense Santa Anna winds would increase dramatically in three weeks, how would you react? If you were a Home Depot manager, wouldn't you want to have snow shovels in stock if a large snowstorm was approaching? If you worked in the Federal Emergency Management Agency (FEMA), would you want to receive a 30-day advance warning of the next hurricane?

Although meteorologists currently make widespread use of satellite imaging and computer modeling, the founders of EarthRisk Technologies (www.earthrisktech.com) maintain it is nearly impossible to use current weather forecasting models to make anything more than the most general predictions about weather more than two weeks into the future. To address this limitation, EarthRisk has implemented weather forecasting software to estimate the likelihood of extreme weather events 30 to 40 days in advance, which is twice as long as conventional forecasts.

EarthRisk draws on 60 years of weather data to identify conditions that could lead to major temperature swings several weeks later. The weather events that precede a hot or cold stretch are like dominoes toppling in sequence. The company's software predicts

the probability of each domino falling over, and it sells that information to energy companies that want to lock in fuel prices before demand peaks.

For instance, the U.S. division of Iberdrola Renewables (www.iberdrolausa.com), the Spanish energy company, uses EarthRisk's service to plan its natural gas purchases. In the fall of 2011, the experts' consensus was that the winter of 2012 would be cold, and natural gas prices rose accordingly. But as EarthRisk analyzed the historical data, its projections showed a warming trend in the Midwest and the East. Further, that trend would accelerate as the winter wore on. As EarthRisk predicted, the winter of 2012 had the second-highest number of extreme heat events and the lowest number of extreme cold events since 1948. Natural gas prices dropped, and Iberdrola profited by buying less natural gas, at a lower price.

EarthRisk's next project is to detect Atlantic hurricanes days in advance by analyzing conditions such as ocean temperatures, sea level pressures, and vertical wind shear. The company also wants to make its software intuitive enough to be used by nonmeteorologists at insurance companies and other businesses.

Climate Corporation (www.climate.com) also analyzes weather patterns, but it applies the results of their analyses in a different way than EarthRisk. Climate provides crop insurance to help farmers manage their risk. The company uses analytics to price their insurance products. It analyzes decades of data from the National Weather Service and other sources to derive knowledge of rainfall, temperature, and soil conditions in farmlands across America. The data sets are so fine-tuned that Climate can determine how the average weather at one spot differs from another spot just 2.5 miles away. The firm uses this information, along with historic crop yields, to predict how next year's crop is going to look.

For each location, Climate simulates the weather for the next two years, performing this operation10,000 times. This analysis enables the company to customize insurance prices according to each farm's risk factors and to offer protection that supplements federal assistance. Historically, farmers have relied on crop insurance sold by the federal government. Unfortunately, this program suffers from bureaucratic red tape. Farmers must plant their fields on a schedule determined by the government and then consent to inspections. To estimate crop value, farmers have to record and turn over years' worth of data pertaining to yields. When disasters strike, claims take months to process, and the payout often covers only costs, not lost profits.

Today, farmers can log on to Climate's Web site and input details about their planting plans. An algorithm then produces multiple policy options. Farmers choose the option that best fits their needs.

Because Climate's servers are always recording weather data, the company knows when a policy is triggered by, for instance, a drought, and it automatically issues payments to the affected farmers. Climate also makes its data available to its customers, showing them the range of yields and profits they can expect based on likely weather conditions.

Consider John Stevens, a farmer who owns 5,300 acres of farmland. Stevens spends much of the winter trying to find the perfect "prescriptions," as he calls them, for his fields. Stevens analyzes weather data, takes soil moisture readings, and studies the latest news on seed hybrids, all to maximize his crop yields. During the last few years, however, his meticulous planning has been undermined by severe weather. Heavy rains fell during his brief five-day planting windows. Then, unusually high temperatures suffocated his crops.

To protect his operation, Stevens now purchases crop insurance from Climate. He appreciates the additional peace of mind that Climate provides. Each year he spends hundreds of thousands of dollars during the planting season. If a weather event damages his crops in May, Climate will pay him quickly enough to buy more seed and replant. In contrast, the federal insurance program does not pay out until after the planting season.

Sources: "The Climate Corporation Launches Climate Corporation Press Release, October 9, 2012; T. Woody, "Weather Men," *Forbes*, April 9, 2012; A. Vance, "Algorithms on the Prairie," *Bloomberg BusinessWeek*, March 26–April 1, 2012; B. Bigelow, "EarthRisk Figures Odds in Long-Range Forecasts of 'Extreme Weather'," *Xconomy*, January 25, 2012; D. Rice, "Team Seeks to Provide More Advance Warning on Hurricanes," *USA Today*, October 11, 2011; Q. Hardy, "Big Data in the Dirt (and the Cloud)," *The New York Times*, October 11, 2011; J. Tozzi, "Weather Seer," *Bloomberg BusinessWeek*, September 26–October 2, 2011; G. Robbins, "EarthRisk Seeks Business Niche Spotting Severe Weather," *San Diego Union Tribune*, August 2011; www.earthrisktech.com, accessed February 27, 2013.

Questions

1. What impact will EarthRisk and/or Climate Corporation have on the business model of The Weather Channel? If you were a Weather Channel executive, what would you do to counter the threat from these two companies?
2. Provide examples of other organizations to whom long-range weather forecasts would be valuable.

Not all organizations use BI in the same way. For example, some organizations employ only one or a few applications, whereas others utilize enterprisewide BI. In this section you will examine three specific BI targets that represent different levels of change:

- The development of one or a few related BI applications
- The development of infrastructure to support enterprisewide BI
- Support for organizational transformation

These targets differ in terms of their focus; scope; level of sponsorship, commitment, and required resources; technical architecture; impact on personnel and business processes; and benefits.

The Development of One or a Few Related BI Applications.   This BI target often is a point solution for a departmental need, such as campaign management in marketing. Sponsorship, approval, funding, impacts, and benefits typically occur at the departmental level. For this target, organizations usually create a data mart to store the necessary data. Organizations must be careful that the data mart—an "independent" application—does not become a "data silo" that stores data that are inconsistent with, and cannot be integrated with, data used elsewhere in the organization.

The Development of Infrastructure to Support Enterprisewide BI.   This BI target supports both current and future BI needs. A crucial component of BI at this level is an enterprise data warehouse. Because it is an enterprisewide initiative, senior management often provides sponsorship, approval, and funding. In addition, the impacts and benefits are felt throughout the organization.

An example of this target is the 3M corporation. Traditionally, 3M's various divisions had operated independently, using separate decision-support platforms. Not only was this arrangement costly, but it prevented 3M from integrating the data and presenting a "single face" to its customers. For example, sales representatives did not know whether or how business customers were interacting with other 3M divisions. The solution was to develop an enterprise data warehouse that enabled 3M to operate as an integrated company. As an added benefit, the costs of implementing this system were offset by savings resulting from the consolidation of the various platforms.

Support for Organizational Transformation.   With this target, BI is used to fundamentally transform the ways in which a company competes in the marketplace. BI supports a new business model, and it enables the business strategy. Because of the scope and importance of these changes, critical elements such as sponsorship, approval, and funding originate at the highest organizational levels. The impact on personnel and processes can be significant, and the benefits are organizationwide.

Harrah's Entertainment (a brand of Caesars Entertainment; *www.caesars.com*) provides a good example of this BI target. Harrah's developed a customer loyalty program, known as *Total Rewards*. To implement the program, Harrah's created a BI infrastructure (a data warehouse) that collected data from casino, hotel, and special event systems (e.g., wine tasting weekends) across all the various customer touchpoints (e.g., slot machines, table games, and Internet). Harrah's used this data to reward loyal customers and reach out to them in personal and appealing ways, such as through promotional offers. As a result, the company became a leader in the gaming industry.

Interestingly, Seminole Gaming has taken Harrah's original analytics model and extended it to transform how it does business. IT's About Business 12.3 illustrates how Seminole uses analytics to predict customer behavior.

In Chapter 5, you studied the basics of data warehouses and data marts. In this section, you have seen how important data warehouses and marts are to the different ways that organizations use BI. In the next section, you will learn how the user community can analyze the data in warehouses and marts, how the results of these analyses are presented to users, and how organizations can use the results of these analyses.

IT's [about business]

12.3 Predicting Customer Behavior

Seminole Gaming (www.theseminolecasinos.com) operates seven casinos in Florida on behalf of the Seminole Tribe. Two of the facilities are Hard Rock-branded hotel casinos. The company has more than 11,000 slot machines, 300 table games, dozens of restaurants, and nearly 10,000 employees.

Despite the breadth of its operations, however, Seminole Gaming considered its customer analysis to be inadequate. The company's customer segmentation strategy relied entirely on prior customer behavior, which it analyzed using traditional RFS (recency, frequency, spend) metrics. This system did not enable the company to predict customer behavior, or as they put it, "to be able to see into the future." To achieve this objective, the company decided to implement SAS (www.sas.com) Enterprise Miner, a business intelligence package.

Seminole generates a large volume of direct mail. Whereas many other industries employ newer electronic channels such as e-mail and social media as marketing tools, Seminole maintains that in the casino business, direct mail is a much more effective channel. To make this strategy more efficient, Seminole needed to eliminate the cost of sending mail to prospective customers who are unlikely to respond.

Consequently, Seminole utilized Enterprise Miner to build an analytic model for a direct mail campaign for concerts at Hard Rock Live, located on the grounds of the Seminole Hard Rock Hotel & Casino in Hollywood, Florida. The model helped the company identify the 35 percent of its customers who were most likely to respond to one of their direct-mail offers. Seminole sent each of these customers a specific mailing for each concert. For the remaining 65 percent, the company consolidated mailers—that is, it advertised multiple concerts, instead of a single concert, in each mailer. While the single-mailer-per-concert approach proved most effective for those customers who were likely to respond, advertising multiple concerts in a single mailer to the other customers not only reduced the company's mail costs, but it increased the customer response rate. Overall this new response model generated more than $1 million in profit annually.

After the casino identified people to whom they should not be mailing, its next strategy was to identify prospective customers to whom they should be mailing, but were not. This strategy is important for companies that rely heavily on direct mail.

Seminole also utilizes Enterprise Miner to gather a wealth of data about its customers' purchases. A significant portion of its player base uses its casino rewards card. For each of these players, the casino knows their play choices as well as the outcomes for every machine or table on every day.

Traditional casino direct-mail programs rely heavily on metrics such as average daily actual (a measure of how much money a player loses on a given day), average daily theoretical (a measure of how much a player would have lost if he or she had been either more or less lucky than expected, per day), average daily worth (a calculation that combines the previous two metrics), and points earned (a measure of how much total play a player has given the casino). It is unprofitable to mail every customer for every marketing campaign, so casinos use these metrics to decide to whom they will mail , and how often.

Let's look at an example. Suppose Seminole launches a campaign that offers $5 in free play to any customer whose average daily worth is greater than $50. In effect, the casino has determined that offering $5 to such customers generates enough additional casino visits to cover the expense of the offer to customers who were going to visit anyway.

The question now becomes: How can the casino find the "hidden gems" among the customers whose average daily worth is less than $50? The answer is to go back in time and look at all customers whose value prior to time period X was less than $50 but who came back after that time period and increased their daily worth to more than $50. This is a basic change-of-behavior model that Enterprise Miner handles easily. In fact, models such as these are driving strong, profitable results at Seminole.

Seminole Gaming also engages in projects that might not generate an immediate direct return. One such project is to perform market basket analyses of the slot machines that their customers play. *Market basket analysis* is a technique that identifies co-occurrence relationships among activities performed by specific individuals.

As a simple example, suppose a casino had only three slot machine games—A, B, and C—and two customers—Bob and Rita. Bob and Rita each spend $100 per visit, but while Rita plays only game C, Bob splits his money between games A and B. In this example, the casino would say that games A and B are associated with each other, whereas game C is not associated with any other games. If you add millions of customers and thousands of slot machines to the analysis, the model becomes extremely complex. Fortunately, Enterprise Miner is able to process these huge models.

When Seminole initiated this project, they did not know what they would find. The analytics ultimately revealed surprising relationships among games on the slot floor. The company would not publicize those relationships, but it conceded that it revised its entire slot-machine decision-making process as a result of these analyses.

In its next project, Seminole is analyzing slot-machine data to uncover unknown groupings of customers and slot machines. For example, where should slot machines be physically located in the casino to attract the most customers. As of mid-2013, the results were not definitive. Nevertheless, Seminole is confident that it has established an entirely new way to segment customers, as well as an entirely new model for locating its slot machines inside its casinos, as a result of the hidden groupings.

And the bottom line? In terms of benefits, the models that Seminole has utilized for direct-mail marketing campaigns are providing an annual benefit of more than $5 million.

Source: Compiled from R. Thomas, "Analytics Tool Predicts Customer Behavior," *Baseline Magazine*, August 3, 2012.

Questions
1. What other analyses should Seminole perform? Provide examples to support your answer.
2. Are there disadvantages to Seminole's use of analytics to predict customer behavior? (Hint: Is it possible to know too much about customers from the casino's viewpoint? What about from the customer's viewpoint?)

---

before you go on...

1. Define BI.
2. Discuss the breadth of support provided by BI applications to organizational employees.
3. Identify and discuss the three basic targets of BI.

Business Intelligence Applications for Data Analysis

12.3

A good strategy to study the ways in which organizations use business intelligence applications is to consider how the users analyze data, how they present the results of their analyses, and how managers and executives (who can also be users) implement these results. Recall from Chapter 5 that the data are stored in a data warehouse or data mart. The user community analyzes these data employing a variety of BI applications. The results of these analyses can be presented to users via other BI applications. Finally, managers and executives put the overall results to good use. You will become familiar with data analysis, data presentation, and data use in the next three sections.

A variety of BI applications for analyzing data are available. They include multidimensional analysis (also called *online analytical processing*, or *OLAP*), data mining, and decision support systems.

Multidimensional Analysis or Online Analytical Processing (OLAP)

Some BI applications include **online analytical processing (OLAP)**, also referred to as **multidimensional analysis** capabilities. OLAP involves "slicing and dicing" data stored in a dimensional format, drilling down in the data to greater detail, and aggregating the data.

Consider our example from Chapter 5. Recall Figure 5.11 showing the data cube. The product is on the x-axis, geography is on the y-axis, and time is on the z-axis. Now, suppose you want to know how many nuts the company sold in the West region in 2009. You would slice and dice the cube, using *nuts* as the specific measure for product, *West* as the measure for geography, and *2009* as the measure for time. The value or values that remain in the cell(s) after our slicing and dicing is (are) the answer to our question. As an example of drilling down, you also might want to know how many nuts were sold in January 2009. Alternatively, you might want to know how many nuts were sold during 2008–2010, which is an example of aggregation, also called "rollup."

Data Mining

Data mining refers to the process of searching for valuable business information in a large database, data warehouse, or data mart. Data mining can perform two basic operations: (1) predicting trends and behaviors, and (2) identifying previously unknown patterns. BI applications typically provide users with a view of what has happened; data mining helps to explain *why* it is happening, and it predicts what will happen in the future.

Regarding the first operation, data mining automates the process of finding predictive information in large databases. Questions that traditionally required extensive hands-on analysis now can be answered directly and quickly from the data. For example, *targeted marketing* relies on predictive information. Data mining can use data from past promotional mailings to identify those prospects who are most likely to respond favorably to future mailings. Another business problem that uses predictive information is the forecasting of bankruptcy and other forms of default.

Data mining can also identify previously hidden patterns in a single step. For example, it can analyze retail sales data to discover seemingly unrelated products that people often purchase together. The classic example is beer and diapers. Data mining found that young men tend to buy beer and diapers at the same time when shopping at convenience stores.

One significant pattern-discovery operation is detecting fraudulent credit card transactions. As you use your credit card, a pattern emerges over time of the typical ways you use your card and your typical shopping behaviors—the places in which you use your card, the amounts you spend, and so on. If your card is stolen and used fraudulently, the usage often varies noticeably from your established pattern. Data mining tools can discern this difference and bring the issue to your attention.

Numerous data mining applications are used in business and in other fields. According to a Gartner report (*www.gartner.com*), most Fortune 1000 companies worldwide currently use data mining, as the following representative examples illustrate. Note that in most cases the purpose of data mining is to identify a business opportunity to create a sustainable competitive advantage.

- *Retailing and sales.* Predicting sales, preventing theft and fraud, and determining correct inventory levels and distribution schedules among outlets. For example, retailers such as AAFES (stores on military bases) use Fraud Watch from SAP (*www.sap.com*) to combat fraud by employees in their 1,400 stores.

- **Banking.** Forecasting levels of bad loans and fraudulent credit card use, predicting credit card spending by new customers, and determining which kinds of customers will best respond to (and qualify for) new loan offers.

- **Manufacturing and production.** Predicting machinery failures, and finding key factors that help optimize manufacturing capacity.

- **Insurance.** Forecasting claim amounts and medical coverage costs, classifying the most important elements that affect medical coverage, and predicting which customers will buy new insurance policies.

- **Policework.** Tracking crime patterns, locations, and criminal behavior; identifying attributes to assist in solving criminal cases (e.g., see the chapter-closing case).

- **Healthcare.** Correlating demographics of patients with critical illnesses, and developing better insights on how to identify and treat symptoms and their causes. IT's About Business 12.4 illustrates how a professional rugby team in Great Britain uses analytics to help prevent injuries to its players.

- **Marketing.** Classifying customer demographics that can be used to predict which customers will respond to a mailing or buy a particular product.

IT's [about business]

12.4 Analytics Helps to Reduce Injuries to Rugby Players

Professional sports are much more than just a game. Instead, they are increasingly becoming a scientific undertaking that is driven by data and numbers. Gone are the days of relying on raw talent and gut instinct to succeed. Although sports organizations have used analytics for years—the book and film *Moneyball* highlights the use of analytics to make player decisions in major league baseball in the 1990s—analytics software is becoming ever-more sophisticated. The use of analytics is now spreading to professional rugby, a popular sport in Great Britain that bears some resemblance to U.S. football.

Rugby historically has been a brutal contact sport in which players use minimal protective equipment. In fact, about 25 percent of all players are injured during a typical season, and some suffer season-ending injuries. For the players, the injuries are frustrating and can cause them to sit out games, sometimes even an entire season. For the teams, the absence of key players on the field frequently results in lost games, as well as diminished ticket sales and attendance.

Teams such as the Leicester Tigers in the United Kingdom are now embracing analytics to conduct deep analyses of raw injury data. The Tigers worked with IBM to develop more efficient methods to understand why injuries occur and how the organization can reduce their frequency. Analysts studied a variety of factors, including fatigue and game intensity levels, to detect hidden patterns and anomalies that provide insights into which players were likely to get injured and what types of injuries they would suffer.

For example, if a player displays a statistically significant change in one or more of his fatigue parameters (e.g., the level of lactic acid in his blood is statistically too high) and the current intensity level of training is high, these data might indicate that his chances of being injured are 80 percent greater than normal. One of his teammates might register a 60 percent greater risk. This level of real-time information makes it possible for the team to adjust each player's training regimen as well as the team's substitution patterns in games to reduce the risk of injury.

Going further, analytics allows the Tigers to analyze psychological data to reveal other key factors that could affect their players' performance. These factors include the additional stress of playing on the road, as well as social or environmental elements (e.g., family problems) that could impact the way players perform during a match. The goal is to tailor the team's training programs to each player's physical and psychological state.

Sources: Compiled from A. Smith, "Sports Analytics: How 'Moneyball' Meets Big Data," *ZDNet*, March 14, 2013; R. Bluey, "From 'Moneyball' to Money Bombs: What Sports Analytics Can Teach Political Nerds," *The Atlantic*, March 8, 2013; P. Dizikes, "Sports Analytics: A Real Game-Changer," *MIT News*, March 4, 2013; S. Greengard, "Putting Predictive Analytics Into Play," *Baseline Magazine*, May 2, 2012; B. Alamar and V. Mehrotra, "Beyond Moneyball: The Future of Sports Analytics," *Analytics Magazine*, February 24, 2012; www.leicestertigers.com, accessed April 3, 2013.

Questions

1. If you were a player for the Leicester Tigers, would you want to have that much personal data analyzed? Is there a "creepiness" factor here? Support your answer.

2. What are some potential disadvantages of Leicester's analytics system? Provide specific examples.

3. Would you encourage your favorite U.S. sports teams to adopt a similar analytics system? Why or why not?

Decision Support Systems

Decision support systems (DSSs) combine models and data in an attempt to analyze semi-structured problems and some unstructured problems that involve extensive user involvement. **Models** are simplified representations, or abstractions, of reality. DSSs enable business managers and analysts to access data interactively, to manipulate these data, and to conduct appropriate analyses.

Decision support systems can enhance learning and contribute to all levels of decision making. DSSs also employ mathematical models. Finally, they have the related capabilities of sensitivity analysis, what-if analysis, and goal-seeking analysis, which you will learn about next. You should keep in mind that these three types of analysis are useful for any type of decision-support application. Excel, for example, supports all three.

Sensitivity Analysis. *Sensitivity analysis* is the study of the impact that changes in one or more parts of a decision-making model have on other parts. Most sensitivity analyses examine the impact that changes in input variables have on output variables.

Most models include two types of input variables: decision variables and environmental variables. "What is our reorder point for these raw materials?" is a decision variable (internal to the organization). "What will the rate of inflation be?" is an environmental variable (external to the organization). The output in this example is the total cost of raw materials. Companies generally perform a sensitivity analysis to determine the impact of environmental variables on the result of the analysis.

Sensitivity analysis is extremely valuable because it enables the system to adapt to changing conditions and to the varying requirements of different decision-making situations. It provides a better understanding of the model as well as of the problem that the model purports to describe.

What-if Analysis. A model builder must make predictions and assumptions regarding the input data, many of which are based on the assessment of uncertain futures. The results depend on the accuracy of these assumptions, which can be highly subjective. *What-if analysis* attempts to predict the impact of a change in the assumptions (input data) on the proposed solution. For example, what will happen to the total inventory cost *if* the originally assumed cost of carrying inventories is 12 percent rather than 10 percent? In a well-designed BI system, managers themselves can interactively ask the computer these types of questions as often as they need to.

Goal-Seeking Analysis. *Goal-seeking analysis* represents a "backward" solution approach. It attempts to calculate the value of the inputs necessary to achieve a desired level of output. For example, let's say that an initial BI analysis predicted a profit of $2 million. Management might want to know what sales volume would be necessary to generate a profit of $3 million. To find out, they would perform a goal-seeking analysis.

The managers, however, cannot simply press a button labeled "increase sales." Instead, the company will need to take certain actions to bring about the sales increase. Options include lowering prices, increasing funding for research and development, paying the sales force a higher commission rate, enhancing the advertising program, and, of course, implementing some combination of these actions. Whatever the action is, it will cost money, and the goal-seeking analysis must take this into account.

before you go on...

1. Describe multidimensional analysis.

2. What are the two basic operations of data mining?

3. What is the purpose of decision support systems?

Business Intelligence Applications for Presenting Results

12.4

The results of the types of data analyses you just learned about can be presented with dashboards and data visualization technologies. Today, users are increasingly relying on data that are real time or almost real time. Therefore, you also study real-time BI in this section.

Dashboards

Dashboards evolved from executive information systems, which were information systems designed specifically for the information needs of top executives. Today, however, many employees, business partners, and customers can access an organization's digital dashboards.

A dashboard provides easy access to timely information and direct access to management reports. It is user friendly, it is supported by graphics, and, most importantly, it enables managers to examine exception reports and drill down into detailed data. Table 12.1 summarizes the various capabilities common to many dashboards. Moreover, some of the capabilities discussed in this section have been incorporated into many BI products, as illustrated in Figure 12.3.

One outstanding example of a dashboard is the Bloomberg Terminal. Bloomberg LP (*www.bloomberg.com*), a privately held company, provides a subscription service that sells financial data, software to analyze these data, trading tools, and news (electronic, print, TV, and radio). All of this information is accessible through a color-coded Bloomberg keyboard that displays the desired information on a computer screen, either the user's screen or one that Bloomberg provides.

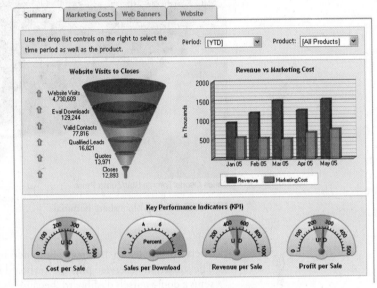

FIGURE 12.3 Sample performance dashboard. (*Source:* Dundas Software, demos1.dundas.com/Dundas Gauge/Marketing-Dashboard/Summary.aspx)

Capability	Description
Drill-down	The ability to go to details, at several levels; it can be done by a series of menus or by clicking on a drillable portion of the screen.
Critical success factors (CSFs)	The factors most critical for the success of business. These can be organizational, industry, departmental, or for individual workers.
Key performance indicators (KPIs)	The specific measures of CSFs.
Status access	The latest data available on KPI or some other metric, often in real time.
Trend analysis	Short-, medium-, and long-term trend of KPIs or metrics, which are projected using forecasting methods.
Exception reporting	Reports that highlight deviations larger than certain thresholds. Reports may include only deviations.

Table

12.1

The Capabilities of Dashboards

Carlos Osorio/Toronto Star/Zuma Press

FIGURE 12.4 A Bloomberg terminal.

Users can also set up their own computers to access the service without a Bloomberg keyboard. The subscription service plus the keyboard is called the Bloomberg Terminal. It literally represents a do-it-yourself dashboard, because users can customize their information feeds as well as the look and feel of those feeds (see Figure 12.4).

In another example, Figure 12.5 illustrates a human resources dashboard/scorecard developed by iDashboards, one of the leading BI software vendors. At a glance, users can see employee productivity, hours, team, department, and division performance in graphical, tabular, summary, and detailed form. The selector box to the left enables the user to easily change between specific analyses to compare their performance.

A unique and interesting application of dashboards to support the informational needs of executives is the Management Cockpit. Essentially, a Management Cockpit is a strategic management room containing an elaborate set of dashboards that enable top-level decision makers to pilot their businesses better. The goal is to create an environment that encourages more efficient management meetings and boosts team performance via effective communication. To help achieve this goal, the dashboard graphically displays key performance indicators and information relating to critical success factors on the walls of a meeting room called the *Management Cockpit Room* (see Figure 12.6). The cockpit-like arrangement of instrument panels and displays helps managers visualize how all of the different factors in the business interrelate.

Within the room, the four walls are designated by color: Black, Red, Blue, and White. The Black Wall displays the principal success factors and financial indicators. The Red Wall measures market performance. The Blue Wall projects the performance of internal processes and employees. Finally, the White Wall indicates the status of strategic projects. The Flight Deck, a six-screen, high-end PC, enables executives to drill down to detailed information. External information needed for competitive analyses can easily be imported into the room.

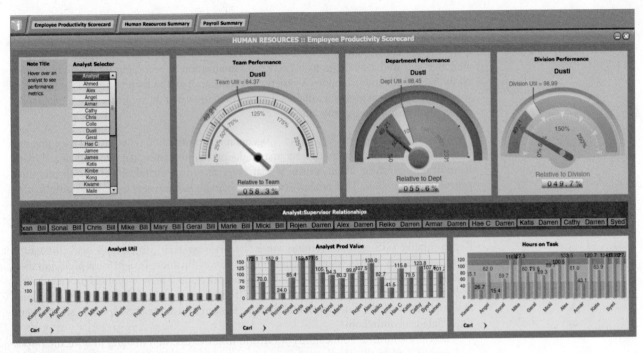

FIGURE 12.5 A human resources dashboard/scorecard. (*Source:* MicroStrategy.)

FIGURE 12.6 Management Cockpit.

The Management Cockpit is a registered trademark of SAP, created by Professor Patrick M Georges

Board members and other executives hold meetings in the Management Cockpit Room. Managers also meet there with the comptroller to discuss current business issues. The Management Cockpit can implement various what-if scenarios for this purpose. It also provides a common basis for information and communication. Finally, it supports efforts to translate a corporate strategy into concrete activities by identifying performance indicators.

Data Visualization Technologies

After data have been processed, they can be presented to users in visual formats such as text, graphics, and tables. This process, known as *data visualization*, makes IT applications more attractive and understandable to users. Data visualization is becoming increasingly popular on the Web for decision support. A variety of visualization methods and software packages that support decision making are available. Two particularly valuable applications are geographic information systems and reality mining.

Geographic Information Systems.   A **geographic information system (GIS)** is a computer-based system for capturing, integrating, manipulating, and displaying data using digitized maps. Its most distinguishing characteristic is that every record or digital object has an identified geographical location. This process, called *geocoding*, enables users to generate information for planning, problem solving, and decision making. In addition, the graphical format makes it easy for managers to visualize the data.

Today, relatively inexpensive, fully functional PC-based GIS packages are readily available. Representative GIS software vendors are ESRI (*www.esri.com*), Intergraph (*www.intergraph .com*), and Pitney Bowes MapInfo (now Pitney Bowes Business Insight *www.pbinsight.com/ welcome/mapinfo*). In addition, both government sources and private vendors provide diversified commercial GIS data. Some of these GIS packages are free; for example, downloadable material from the Environmental Systems Research Institute (ESRI; www.esri.com) and http://data.geocomm.com.

There are countless applications of GISs to improve decision making in both the public and private sectors. The following example shows how ESRI impacts a huge number of organizations.

Example

The mission of ESRI is to make it easier to turn complex data into understandable, insightful visual information, or to use geographic information systems to understand how things are changing and to describe these changes in maps. ESRI has had an impact on many organizations in areas such as land use, urban planning, disaster response, sustainable development, mining and oil exploration, wildlife preservation, planning for epidemics, and humanitarian relief.

ESRI recently adopted a policy of making its applications available to nonprofit organizations for free. As Jack Dangermond, ESRI's founder, explains, "Our world is evolving without consideration, and the result is a loss of biodiversity, energy issues, and congestion in cities. But geography, if used correctly, can be used to redesign sustainable and more livable cities."

Examples of nonprofit organizations using ESRI software abound. Residents of Glendale, California, for example, can text the location of potholes, trash, and graffiti to city officials via an online ESRI map. As another example, during the BP disaster in the Gulf of Mexico, ESRI created a Web site that combined data on wind and Gulf currents with Flickr photos and YouTube videos to map the spill and monitor the cleanup. BP and the Coast Guard used the site to set up booms and send in oil-skimming ships. In Also, in April 2013, the *Dallas Morning News* used ESRI technology to develop an interactive map depicting the people, infrastructure, and businesses affected by the fertilizer plant explosion in West, Texas.

Sources: Compiled from "Interactive Map: People, Infrastructure, and Businesses Affected by Explosion West, Texas," *The Dallas Morning News*, April 19, 2013; M. Bahree, "A Sense of Where You Are," *Forbes*, October 11, 2010; www.esri.com, accessed April 2, 2013.

Reality Mining.   One important emerging trend is the integration of GISs and global positioning systems (GPSs, discussed in Chapter 8). Using GISs and GPSs together can produce an interesting new type of technology called *reality mining*. **Reality mining** allows analysts to extract information from the usage patterns of mobile phones and other wireless devices. If you want to catch a cab in New York City, the next example will show you how.

Example

New York City.   Is there some kind of secret formula for finding a cab in New York City? The answer is, yes. The most popular corners to catch a yellow cab in Manhattan now can be pinpointed at any hour of any day of the week, thanks to a record 90 million actual taxi trips that have been tracked by the city.

Using the city's GPS data, Sense Networks (www.sensenetworks.com) examined the pickup point of every New York City cab ride taken over a six-month period. The result was a free mobile application called CabSense (www.cabsense.com). This app lets would-be taxi riders view a map of nearby street corners, ranked by the number of taxi hails they attract at that hour on that day of the week. The company uses an algorithm that takes into account parades, street construction, and other factors that could skew the results.

Here are two results from CabSense. The Upper East Side is more dependent on cabs than are its neighbors across Central Park. In one particular month, more than 2 million trips started on the Upper East Side, nearly twice as many as on the Upper West Side. Also, a neighborhood-by-neighborhood breakdown confirms what most New Yorkers already know: It is easier to get a cab below 96th Street in Manhattan, and much harder above 96th Street.

Singapore.   The idea of making it easier to find a cab has traveled to Singapore. Commuters who cannot find a cab use an app that points them to places where they are more likely to find one. The Agency for Science, Technology, and Research gathered sensor data from taxis on the road, including time, place, speed, and whether the taxis were occupied. Researchers developed a predictive mobile application that informs passengers where they are most likely to find empty cabs and cabbies where they are most likely to find fares. The app even tells train commuters where to get off the train so that they will have the best chance of finding a taxi.

Interestingly, taxi companies in Singapore are not pleased with the app. They do not want the app to bypass their own dispatch systems.

Other major cities.   Taxibeat (https://taxibeat.com), developed in Athens, Greece, helps users find taxis in major cities, including Paris, São Paulo, Rio de Janeiro, Bucharest, and Oslo. The app locates your position and contacts a cab near you. It indicates the taxi's location and the speed at which it is arriving. Significantly, it identifies both taxis and customers, which enhances both security and quality assurance. Quality assurance comes from the fact that customers and cab drivers can rate each other. In fact, one of Taxibeat's developers noted that when the app became popular in Athens, the city's taxi drivers became much more courteous. They actually got out of their cars to open doors for passengers, in hopes of receiving a higher rating.

Sources: Compiled from C. Tan, "Can't Find a Cab? New App Can Help," *The Straits Times*, March 12, 2013; "Taxibeat: A Greek Startup Makes Finding a Cab Easier and More Reliable," *Capgemini.com*, December 26, 2012; L. Dignan, "Meet CabSense: Now Your Apple iPhone and Android Device Will Hail a Cab for You," *ZDNet*, March 31, 2010; M. Grynbaum, "Need a Cab? New Analysis Shows Where to Find One," *The New York Times*, April 2, 2010; *www.sensenetworks.com*, *www .cabsense.com*, accessed April 7, 2011.

Real-Time BI

Until recently, BI focused on the use of historical data. This focus has changed with the emergence of technology for capturing, storing, and using real-time data. Real-time BI enables users to employ multidimensional analysis, data mining, and decision support systems to analyze data in real time. In addition, it helps organizations to make decisions and to interact with customers in new ways.

For example, 1-800 CONTACTS (www.1800contacts.com) is the world's largest contact lens store. Customers can place orders over the Internet, by mail, or by fax at Walmart, or by phone with nearly 300 customer service agents. 1-800 CONTACTS uses dashboards to monitor and motivate the customer service agents who handle sales calls. The company updates the dashboards every 15 minutes. The service agents and their supervisors can measure their performance based on key metrics and compare their performance to that of other operators. The operators' compensation is based in part on these performance measurements.

FIGURE 12.7 1-800 CONTACTS customer service agent dashboard.

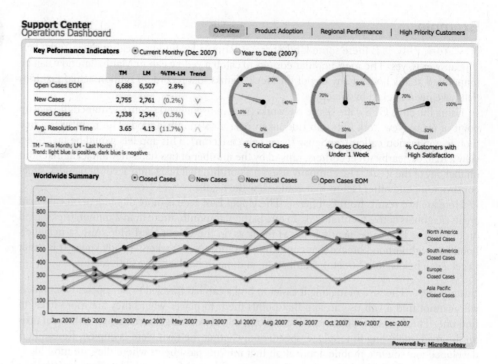

Figure 12.7 presents a typical operator's dashboard. The gauges on the left are for the current day, and they indicate how the operator is performing on three critical metrics: the closing ratio, average sale, and calls/hour. The bar charts to the right indicate how the agent is performing throughout the day. The straight line displays the agent's average performance for the month for the three metrics. You can see that the operator is exceeding his monthly average on closing ratio and average sale. However, he has scored higher on calls/hour only in the 1:00 PM hour. The ribbon at the bottom of the screen identifies the top five performers on various metrics.

In addition, the company calculates a Call Center Incentive (CCI) index for each operator, which it uses to determine the agents' monthly compensation. The CCI formula integrates a number of criteria: closing ratio index, average order size index, hours worked, bonus points for work such as setting up appointments, and a quality index based on audits of the quality of the operator's interactions with customers. Top agents receive bonuses.

The operators' dashboards are highly effective. After implementing the dashboards, the company's revenues increased by $50,000 per month, and the quality of the service calls remained high. Call center management attributed the increase to the dashboards. Significantly, the operators have responded well to the dashboards. They appreciate the ability to monitor their performance and to compare it to that of the other agents. Every 15 minutes the agents can see how far they have "moved the needle."

before you go on...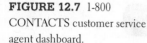

1. What is a dashboard? Why are dashboards so valuable to employees?

2. Explain the difference between geographic information systems and reality mining, and provide examples of how each of these technologies can be used by businesses and government agencies.

3. What is real-time BI, and why is this technology valuable to an organization's managers and executives?

Business Intelligence in Action: Corporate Performance Management

12.5

Corporate performance management (CPM) is involved with monitoring and managing an organization's performance according to *key performance indicators* (KPIs) such as revenue, return on investment (ROI), overhead, and operational costs. For online businesses, CPM includes additional factors such as the number of page views, server load, network traffic, and transactions per second. BI applications allow managers and analysts to analyze data to obtain valuable information and insights concerning the organization's KPIs. The following example demonstrates corporate performance management at the VAASAN Group.

Example

The VAASAN Group is one of the leading bakery operators in Northern Europe, producing fresh bakery goods for sale in retail chains, restaurants, and hotels. It is the largest thin crisp and the second-largest crisp bread producer in the world, exporting to more than 40 countries. With some 2,730 employees, the company's net sales exceeded $500 million (U.S.) in 2012.

Food manufacturers are always at risk of incurring inventory problems: either out-of-stock or excess inventory. Both conditions are costly. As a result, they constantly strive to prepare for fluctuations in order volume.

The VAASAN Group was experiencing exponential growth in its business operations, but it was unable to accurately forecast fluctuating sales orders. As a result, the company could not accurately plan its resources and production schedules. The firm's existing information systems lacked data integration and business analytics capabilities, which prevented it from acquiring the necessary insights to forecast customer demand.

To address this problem, the VAASAN Group implemented analytics software that identifies trends in customer demand and generates a rolling sales forecast. This software helped the company predict its production requirements and prepare for fluctuating customer orders. The system integrates near-real-time and historical customer data from the company's enterprise resource planning systems (discussed in Chapter 10) in a data warehouse (discussed in Chapter 5). The system then combines these data with sales order forecasts from its sales teams. The process helps VAASAN discover patterns in consumer purchasing behaviors at each customer retail location across its sales outlets.

For example, when the company won a large-volume account, its sales team employed near-real-time analysis to determine within minutes whether the company could fill the new order on time. Predictions generated by the system provided VAASAN with enough lead time to adjust its production schedules at its bakeries to deliver on its promise. The company now produces the correct amount of products to ship or to maintain in inventory, thereby improving its order fulfillment rates while reducing overstocks. Going further, it has reduced its business risk by aligning raw materials, human resources, and production schedules with customer demand.

Sources: Compiled from "The VAASAN Group," *IBM Customer Case Study*, April 15, 2013; G. Noseworthy, "Delivering On-Demand Analytics at the Speed of Thought," *The Big Data Hub (IBM)*, March 25, 2013; www.ibm.com, www.vaasan.com, accessed April 20, 2013.

before you go on...

1. What is corporate performance management?

2. How do BI applications contribute to corporate performance management?

What's In IT For Me?

For the Accounting Major

BI is used extensively in auditing to uncover irregularities. It also is used to uncover and prevent fraud. CPAs use BI for many of their duties, ranging from risk analysis to cost control.

For the Finance Major

People have been using computers for decades to solve financial problems. Innovative BI applications have been created for activities such as making stock market decisions, refinancing bonds, assessing debt risks, analyzing financial conditions, predicting business failures, forecasting financial trends, and investing in global markets.

For the Marketing Major

Marketing personnel utilize BI in many applications, from planning and executing marketing campaigns, to allocating advertising budgets, to evaluating alternative routings of salespeople. New marketing approaches such as targeted marketing and database marketing depend heavily on IT in general, and on data warehouses and business intelligence applications in particular.

For the Production/Operations Management Major

BI supports complex operations and production decisions from inventory control, to production planning, to supply chain integration.

For the Human Resources Management Major

Human resources personnel use BI for many of their activities. For example, BI applications can find resumes of applicants posted on the Web and sort them to match needed skills and to support management succession planning.

For the MIS Major

MIS provides the data infrastructure used in BI. MIS personnel are also involved in building, deploying, and supporting BI applications.

[Summary]

1. **Identify the phases in the decision-making process, and use a decision-support framework to demonstrate how technology supports managerial decision making.**

When making a decision, either organizational or personal, the decision maker goes through a three-step process: intelligence, design, and choice. When the choice is made, the decision is implemented.

Several information technologies have been successfully used to directly support managers. Collectively, they are referred to as *business intelligence information systems*. Figure 12.2 provides a matrix that shows how technology supports the various types of decisions that managers must make.

2. **Describe and provide examples of the three different ways in which organizations use business intelligence (BI).**

There are three major ways that organizations use BI:

- The development of one or a few related BI applications. This BI target often is a point solution for a departmental need, such as campaign management in marketing. A data mart usually is created to store necessary data.

- The development of infrastructure to support enterprisewide BI. This target supports current and future BI needs.
  A critical component is an enterprise data warehouse.
- Support for organizational transformation. With this target, BI is used to fundamentally change how a company competes in the marketplace. BI supports a new business model and enables the business strategy.

3. **Specify the BI applications available to users for data analysis, and provide examples of how each one might be used to solve a business problem at your university.**

Users have a variety of BI applications available to help them analyze data. These applications include multidimensional analysis, data mining, and decision support systems.

Multidimensional data analysis, also called *online analytical processing (OLAP)*, involves "slicing and dicing" data stored in a dimensional format, drilling down to greater data detail, and aggregating data. Data mining refers to the process of searching for valuable business information in a large database, data warehouse, or data mart. Decision support systems (DSS) combine models and data in an attempt to analyze semistructured and some unstructured problems with extensive user involvement. (We leave it to you to provide examples of using each application at your university.)

4. **Describe three BI applications that present the results of data analyses to users, and offer examples of how businesses and government agencies can use each of these technologies.**

A dashboard provides easy access to timely information and direct access to management reports. A geographic information system (GIS) is a computer-based system for capturing, integrating, manipulating, and displaying data using digitized maps. Reality mining analyzes information extracted from the usage patterns of mobile phones and other wireless devices. (Examples of how these technologies might be used by businesses and government agencies, we leave to you.)

5. **Describe corporate performance management, and provide an example of how your university could use CPM.**

Corporate performance management (CPM) is involved with monitoring and managing an organization's performance according to key performance indicators (KPIs) such as revenue, return on investment (ROI), overhead, and operational costs. (We leave it to you to supply an example of how your university might use CPM.)

[Chapter Glossary]

business intelligence (BI) A broad category of applications, technologies, and processes for gathering, storing, accessing, and analyzing data to help business users make better decisions.

corporate performance management (CPM) The area of business intelligence involved with monitoring and managing an organization's performance, according to key performance indicators (KPIs) such as revenue, return on investment (ROI), overhead, and operational costs.

dashboard A BI application that provides rapid access to timely information and direct access to management reports.

data mining The process of searching for valuable business information in a large database, data warehouse, or data mart.

decision A choice that individuals and groups make among two or more alternatives.

decision support systems (DSSs) Business intelligence systems that combine models and data in an attempt to solve semistructured and some unstructured problems with extensive user involvement.

geographic information system (GIS) A computer-based system for capturing, integrating, manipulating, and displaying data using digitized maps.

management A process by which organizational goals are achieved through the use of resources.

model (in decision making) A simplified representation, or abstraction, of reality.

multidimensional data analysis (see **online analytical processing (OLAP)**)

online analytical processing (OLAP) (or multidimensional data analysis) A set of capabilities for "slicing and dicing" data using dimensions and measures associated with the data.

productivity The ratio between the inputs to a process and the outputs from that process.

reality mining Allows analysts to extract information from the usage patterns of mobile phones and other wireless devices.

[Discussion Questions]

1. Your company is considering opening a new factory in China. List several typical activities involved in each phase of the decision (intelligence, design, and choice).

2. Recall that data mining found that young men tend to buy beer and diapers at the same time when they shop at convenience stores. Now that you know this relationship exists, can you provide a rationale for it?

3. American Can Company announced that it was interested in acquiring a company in the health maintenance

organization (HMO) field. Two decisions were involved in this act: (1) the decision to acquire an HMO, and (2) the decision of which HMO to acquire. How can the use of BI assist the company in this endeavor?

4. Discuss the strategic benefits of BI systems.

5. Will BI replace business analysts? (Hint: See W. McKnight, "Business Intelligence: Will Business Intelligence Replace the Business Analyst?" *DMReview*, February, 2005.)

[Problem-Solving Activities]

1. The city of London (U.K.) charges an entrance fee for automobiles and trucks into the central city district. About 1,000 digital cameras photograph the license plate of every vehicle passing by. Computers read the plate numbers and match them against records in a database of cars for which the fee has been paid for that day. If the computer does not find a match, the car owner receives a citation by mail. Examine the issues pertaining to how this process is accomplished, the mistakes it can make, and the consequences of those mistakes. Also, examine how well the system is working by checking press reports. Finally, relate the process to business intelligence.

2. Enter www.cognos.com, and visit the demos on the right side of the page. Prepare a report on the various features shown in each demo.

3. Enter www.fairisaac.com, and find products for fraud detection and risk analysis. Prepare a report.

4. Access www.ted.com/index.php/talks/view/id/92 to find the video of Hans Rosling's presentation. Comment on his data visualization techniques.

5. Enter www.visualmining.com. Explore the relationship between visualization and business intelligence. See how business intelligence is related to dashboards.

6. Access http://businessintelligence.ittoolbox.com. Identify all types of business intelligence software. Join a discussion group about topics discussed in this chapter. Prepare a report.

7. Visit the sites of some GIS vendors (such as www.mapinfo .com, www.esri.com, or www.autodesk.com). Download a demo. What are some of the most important capabilities and applications?

8. Analyze Microsoft® Bing Maps (www.microsoft.com/ maps) as a business intelligence tool. (Hint: Access www .microsoft.com/industry/government/products/bing_maps/ default.aspx.) What are the business intelligence features of this product?

[Team Assignments]

1. Using data mining, it is possible not only to capture information that has been buried in distant courthouses but also to manipulate and index it. This process can benefit law enforcement but invade privacy. In 1996, Lexis-Nexis, the online information service, was accused of permitting access to sensitive information on individuals. The company argued that it was unfairly targeted because it provided only basic residential data for lawyers and law enforcement personnel. Should Lexis-Nexis be prohibited from providing access to such information? Debate the issue.

2. Each group will use a search engine of their choice to find combined GIS/GPS applications as well as look at various vendor sites to find success stories. (For GPS vendors, look at http://biz.yahoo.com (directory) and Google.) Each group will make a presentation of five applications and their benefits.

3. Each group will access a leading business intelligence vendor's Web site (e.g., MicroStrategy, Oracle, Hyperion, Microsoft, SAS, SPSS, Cognos, and Business Objects). Each group will present a report on a vendor, highlighting each vendor's BI capabilities.

[Closing Case **Predictive Policing**]

The Problem

Cities today have to do more with fewer resources, and their police departments are no exception. For example, since 2001 the Santa Cruz Police Department (SCPD) of Santa Cruz, California, has had to lay off 10 of its 104 police officers, while the city population increased by 10 percent. Consequently, the SCPD needed to develop a strategy to maintain its performance levels despite its growing resource constraints.

The IT Solution

In July 2011, the SCPD implemented an analytics system called PredPol (www.predpol.com). This system provides intelligence to the police about when and where future crimes are most likely to occur. The SCPD can utilize this information to determine how it can best deploy its officers to prevent those crimes. The information system consists of a sophisticated algorithm that analyzes large sets of data. This approach is called *predictive policing*.

PredPol's algorithm (mathematical formula) is based on one used by seismologists to predict earthquakes. It targets property crime such as home burglaries, car break-ins, and vehicle thefts. Such crimes tend to cluster and spread in a way that is similar to the tremors that follow a large earthquake.

The algorithm identifies hot spots, which are 500- by-500-foot areas at the highest risk for property crimes. The SCPD then divides the city into five regions and makes certain that at least one car is on duty in each one. Officers pick up their hot spot maps at the roll call meeting that precedes each shift. Each map contains a hot spot. Above each map is a set of statistics: the probability that a crime will take place in that hot spot that day, the two hour-long windows when that potential crime is most likely to occur, and the likelihood that the crime will be a property crime.

Before the SCPD implemented the software, individual officers had to decide where and how to focus their patrol time based on their limited experience of the area. Since the implementation, officers can clearly identify hot spots based on the maps they receive and then patrol those areas more heavily.

The Results

The impacts of PredPol on crime in Santa Cruz are promising. By the end of July 2011, property crime was down 27 percent from the year before, an impressive drop, particularly given the 25 percent rise recorded during the first 6 months of that year. The city also experienced a 19 percent reduction in burglaries within one year after PredPol went into operation. Furthermore, seven criminals were discovered inside the hot spots.

For instance, one afternoon, two women were detained at a hot spot after they were caught looking into cars in a triple-decker parking garage. One of the women had an outstanding arrest warrant for possession of methamphetamines, and the other was caught in possession of meth at the site. At another hot spot, police officers stopped a man for suspicious behavior. When they searched him, they found stolen goods from a burglary that had taken place nearby a few days before. These arrests point to the effectiveness of the SCPD's new predictive policing system.

Predictive policing saves Santa Cruz money. Every time the police prevent a crime, they save the city the costs of processing and booking the perpetrators, detaining them if need be prior to trial, trying them in court, and housing them in correctional institutions after they have been convicted.

When Santa Cruz introduced predictive policing, some police officers dismissed it as "voodoo magic." Relying on mathematics and statistics to combat property crime ran counter to many officers' ideas of police work. Some officers took it as an affront to their skills. Others were concerned that it would involve extra work. However, many officers came around when they realized that driving through a 500-by-500-foot hot spot during an hour-long window requires very little effort in to generate quite a lot of result out. This favorable result-to-effort ratio perfectly exemplifies the impact of analytics systems on various organizations, businesses, and government operations. Small, directed efforts, guided and informed by analytics systems, can bring about great change.

When the city of Los Angeles tested PredPol, the LAPD found the system to be twice as proficient as human analysts at predicting where burglaries and car break-ins would happen. When police officers followed the system's advice and focused their patrols within the designated areas, those areas experienced a 25 percent drop in reported burglaries. Significantly, this drop was an anomaly compared to neighboring areas.

Sources: Compiled from R. Garrett, "Predict and Serve," *Law Enforcement Technology*, January 2013; J. Schectman, "Chicago Designing Predictive Software Platform to Identify Crime Patterns," *The Wall Street Journal*, November 6, 2012; H. Kelly, "Police Embracing Tech That Predicts Crimes," *CNN*, July 9, 2012; D. Talbott, "L.A. Cops Embrace Crime-Predicting Algorithm," *MIT Technology Review*, July 2, 2012; B. Orr, "LAPD Computer Program Prevents Crime By Predicting It," *CBS News*, April 11, 2012; B. Gourley, "Predictive Policing with Big Data," *Cloud Computing Journal*, February 26, 2012; L. Eldridge, "Predictive Policing Is Not 'Minority Report'... At Least Not Yet," *PoliceOne.com*, January 13, 2012; R. King, "IBM Analytics Help Memphis Cops Get 'Smart'," *Bloomberg BusinessWeek*, December 5, 2011; K. Thompson, "The Santa Cruz Experiment," *Popular Science*, November, 2011; L. Brokaw, "Predictive Policing: Working the Odds to Prevent Future Crimes," *Sloan Management Review*, September 12, 2011; J. Rubin, "Stopping Crime Before It Starts," *The Los Angeles Times*, August 21, 2011; E. Goode, "Sending the Police Before There's a Crime," *The New York Times*, August 15, 2011; www.cityofsantacruz.com, www.lacity.org, accessed February 26, 2013.

Questions

1. What are the advantages of predictive policing to the cities of Santa Cruz and Los Angeles? Provide specific examples.

2. What are potential disadvantages of predictive policing to the cities of Santa Cruz and Los Angeles? To the SCPD? To the LAPD? Provide specific examples.

3. Which of the following choices best describes predictive policing? (1) A way to catch criminals; (2) a way to prevent crimes from happening; or (3) both? Support your answer.

[Internship Activity]

Industry: Healthcare

Dashboards are a popular way to view business data. Because of this, many companies have developed "off-the-shelf" dashboards to allow companies to quickly and easily view their organizational health relative to a few key indicators. The problem is that no two companies are alike, and a dashboard is only helpful if it is showing you what you need to see.

Given that Anniston Orthopaedics recently migrated to a new Practice Management/Electronic Health Records system, they are now able to collect data in ways they couldn't before. But for Chad Prince, the Practice Administrator, he is having a tough time figuring out which measures are helpful. While it may be interesting to look at, if it isn't a good measure of the health of the organization then it is not serving its purpose.

Please visit the Book Companion Site to receive the full set of instructions on how you will help Chad develop criteria for determining which measures would be helpful in a Business Intelligence Dashboard.

Chapter 13

Acquiring Information Systems and Applications

What's In IT For Me?

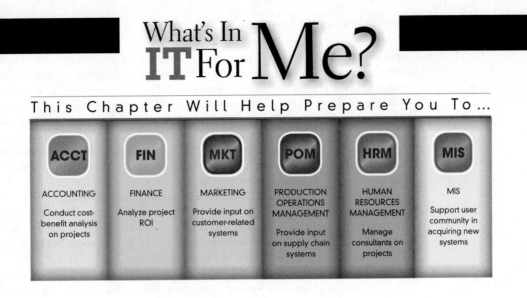

This Chapter Will Help Prepare You To...

ACCT	FIN	MKT	POM	HRM	MIS
ACCOUNTING	**FINANCE**	**MARKETING**	**PRODUCTION OPERATIONS MANAGEMENT**	**HUMAN RESOURCES MANAGEMENT**	**MIS**
Conduct cost-benefit analysis on projects	Analyze project ROI	Provide input on customer-related systems	Provide input on supply chain systems	Manage consultants on projects	Support user community in acquiring new systems

[**Tweak or Trash**]

The Problem

Chief Information Officers (CIOs) face a continuing dilemma: When the time comes to upgrade information technology equipment and systems, which is the better strategy: to repair what you already have by patching and tweaking systems and software to keep them operating, or to replace (a.k.a. trash) your old technology and start with an entirely new system?

The "tweak or trash" problem is extremely complicated. The main directive of every IT department is to ensure uptime and avoid downtime at all costs. This directive creates a bias toward risk avoidance, and therefore toward tweaking. Usually, tweaking seems to be far less risky than implementing an entirely new system. However, tweaking nurtures a growth of hybrid IT environments in which multiple systems coexist, making system documentation and qualified programmers hard to find. Additionally, tweaking often makes programmers feel that it is safer and cheaper to make tiny patches than to risk transformational change. This approach can limit a company's IT capability and create inefficiencies that cost the company time and money.

Consider the case of Accenture (www.accenture.com), a company that provides technology services and management consulting. When Accenture split with Arthur Andersen and became an independent company, it inherited legacy systems from its former parent company, and it needed to build separate technology capabilities. Accenture had ambitious growth strategies, and it realized that it needed appropriate IT infrastructure to support that growth.

The IT Solution

When Accenture started the process of revamping its IT infrastructure in the early 2000s, the company did not consciously pursue a policy of completely replacing its existing systems. However, the company's managers generally did not want to be encumbered by old technology. They understood that conflicts between different IT systems could seriously impair the company's performance. Therefore, they consistently eliminated old systems in favor of new ones. In other words, they chose to trash rather than to tweak.

Accenture kicked off the replacement process by establishing a coherent IT strategy and building its own independent IT capabilities. It then concentrated on operating the IT department just as it would any other business, with a focus on efficiency. To maximize its efficiency, Accenture centralized and standardized its IT function. The company reduced its total number of global applications from 600 to just 267, and it decreased its total number of local applications from 1,500 to 255. An example of this application-cutting process was Accenture's migration from multiple country-specific platforms to a single global enterprise resource planning (ERP) system from SAP (www.sap.com).

By the middle of the decade, Accenture had its IT function in order, and it began to address larger changes. These changes included a complete network transformation, which gave the company the bandwidth to construct one of the world's largest high-definition video conferencing networks and enabled it to introduce an entire suite of powerful collaboration tools. These tools reduced travel time for Accenture professionals, thereby saving the company money and time while providing enormous benefits for its employees' family life.

Accenture then shifted its focus to cloud computing (see Technology Guide 3). The company wanted to free its IT leadership from time-consuming, operational technology tasks so that they could focus on supporting Accenture's business strategy. It also wanted to provide additional technical capabilities, both internally and for its customers, but for less money. For all of these reasons it decided to utilize cloud computing.

The first application that Accenture migrated to the cloud was e-mail. Accenture had 250,000 knowledge workers located throughout the world, so creating and maintaining an effective communications system was mission-critical for the company. Therefore, the migration of e-mail to the cloud was a very high-risk venture. Fortunately, the strategy was successful, and the firm earned its investment back in one year. In fact, Accenture continues to save $10 million per year from its e-mail migration.

The Results

Between 2001 and 2012 Accenture invested approximately $1 billion in its IT infrastructure. These investments generated $3 billion in savings.

Each of the IT changes that Accenture achieved took time to implement and caused disruption to the business. For example, the company moved to its global SAP platform in a single "big-bang" implementation. The downside risks were huge, but so was the upside potential. When the company implemented SAP successfully, it was able to achieve a "single version of the truth" across its entire global enterprise more quickly than before. (A "single version of the truth" means that everyone in a company operates from the same data and information, at the same time.)

And the move to cloud computing? More than half of Accenture's applications now run on a combination of the company's private cloud and public clouds. Not only did this move save the company money, but it enabled its IT department to address the company's rapidly changing business needs more efficiently and productively.

Going further, Accenture's internal customers are pleased with the results of the IT transformation. The percentage of "satisfied sponsors" (sponsors being the pool of senior executives who work closely with the IT department on new initiatives) increased from 67 percent to 92 percent between 2001 and 2011.

In addition, Accenture's IT transformation led to a dramatic increase in operational efficiency. Total company expenditures on IT declined 22 percent over this period, and IT expense as a percentage of Accenture's net revenue decreased by almost 60 percent. Further, IT expense per employee decreased by 70 percent, even though Accenture had made massive IT investments throughout the decade to equip its professionals with the most advanced technology tools possible.

So, what was the final result of Accenture's decision to trash not tweak and then to employ cloud computing? Today, Accenture is a global company with more than 244,000 employees and revenues of more than $25 billion.

Sources: Compiled from "Capitalizing on the Cloud," *Accenture IT Report*, 2013; V. Byanna, "How Accenture's Cloud Migration of E-Mail and Team Collaboration Sites Boosted Cost Savings," *Accenture News*, February 5, 2013; D. Carr, "Accenture CIO Vision Emphasizes Social, Contextual IT," *InformationWeek*, February 27, 2012; F. Modruson, "Debate: Remaking IT at Accenture," *Baseline Magazine*, February 27, 2012; R. Perry, J. Pucciarelli, J. Bozman, and J. Scaramella, "The Cost of Retaining Aging IT Infrastructure," *IDC White Paper*, February 2012; S. Overby, "5 Things Accenture's CIO Has Learned About Cloud Computing," *CIO*, March 15, 2011; J. King, "The Grill: To Kishore Swaminathan, CIO Means 'Chief Intelligence Officer'," *Computerworld*, September 15, 2008; "CIO 100 2008 Winner Profile: Accenture," *CIO*, 2008; www.accenture.com, accessed February 28, 2013.

Questions

1. What are the risks associated with throwing out old information systems and replacing them with new information systems? Provide examples to support your answer.

2. Provide examples of a situation in which it would be better for an organization to tweak an existing information system rather than replace it with a new system.

What We Learned from This Case

As you learned from the Accenture case, competitive organizations move as quickly as they can to acquire new information technologies or modify existing ones when they need to improve efficiencies and gain strategic advantage. Today, however, acquisition goes beyond building new systems in-house, and IT resources involve far more than software and hardware. The old model in which firms built their own systems is being replaced with a broader perspective of IT resource acquisition that provides companies with a number of options. Thus, companies now must decide which IT tasks will remain in-house, and even whether the entire IT resource should be provided and managed by outside organizations. Regardless of which approach an organization chooses, however, it must be able to manage IT projects adeptly.

Even for a small business, information systems upgrades present a complex problem (see IT's About Business 13.1). Small organizations must select vendors based on a number of factors, particularly (1) the ability of the vendor's product(s) to meet the organization's current business needs, (2) the viability of the vendor as a whole (you do not want to sign a contract with someone who might go into bankruptcy), and (3) the relationship between the two companies. After the organization has selected a vendor, the two parties must agree on a contract and clear it with their lawyers. Finally, the organization must acquire the hardware to support the new software. Even for a small business, these decisions are critical because this investment will have a lasting impact on the company's well-being. Although the right information systems may not "make or break" the organization, they can significantly affect its performance and competitiveness.

In this chapter, you learn about the process of acquiring IT resources from a managerial perspective. This means from *your* perspective, because you will be closely involved in all aspects of acquiring information systems and applications in your organization. In fact, when we mention "users" in this chapter, we are talking about you. You will also study the available options for acquiring IT resources and how to evaluate those options. Finally, you will learn how organizations plan and justify the acquisition of new information systems.

IT's [about business]

13.1 Anniston Orthopedics and Greenway Medical Technologies

Anniston Orthopaedic Associates, P.A. (AOA) is a surgical group comprised of six physicians who provide services to the Calhoun County area of Alabama. As of mid-2012 the group had not updated its information systems for several years. When the federal government initiated a program to incentivize medical practices to migrate to electronic medical records (EMRs), the group's physicians realized that it was time to upgrade their systems.

To transition from paper to EMRs, AOA had to implement a system that would encompass hardware, software, and an upgraded network. After considering numerous vendors, AOA selected Greenway Medical Technologies' PrimeSuite product as the group's new information system. Arriving at this decision was only the beginning of the process, however.

To run the Greenway PrimeSuite software, AOA had to upgrade the group's IT infrastructure to match Greenway's requirements. To accomplish this task, AOA hired IT consultants to install new hardware and set up a new network. This network brought many needed upgrades, including interoffice e-mail and shared calendars. The staff adjusted well to these changes. One major challenge involved moving patient data that was typically recorded on paper charts, such as demographics and vital signs, into an electronic format. AOA selected third-party software solutions from ChartCapture, Phreesia, and MidMark to collect and format medical information so that physicians could review it electronically when they were meeting with their patients.

ChartCapture (www.chartcapture.com) captures data contained on paper charts for AOA. It then displays images of these documents in an intuitive format to provide the physicians with access to historical records. Phreesia (www.phreesia.com) is a check-in mobile kiosk system that collects demographic and payment information such as copays, conducts medical questionnaires on wireless touchscreen tablet devices, and enters all of this information into the Greenway PrimeSuite software. MidMark (www.midmark.com) provides machines that measure and record vital signs such as blood pressure, heart rate, and temperature and then enter these values into discrete fields within the Prime-Suite EMR. Physicians use speech recognition technology within PrimeSuite to complete their medical records for each patient visit.

In addition to upgrading their hardware and software to implement Greenway's Prime Suite software, AOA had to train their physicians and staff to use the new system. To speed this process along, Chad Prince, the group's business administrator, attended a week of intense training on PrimeSuite. He then presented this information to the practice. All of the training sessions and upgrades were conducted to prepare the physicians and staff for a phased implementation that would consist of two separate "go-lives." One "go-live" would involve the "practice" side of the office, which involved capturing patients' demographic and insurance information. The second go-live was directed toward the "chart" medical side of the practice. This second implementation would involve a full transition to EMR.

By mid-2012, AOA had organized all of its internal workflows around EMRs. The company is now in the process of training its staff. Two physicians will begin operating on the new system in April 2012. Two more physicians will join the system in June, and the final two in August. This gradual approach will give the AOA staff time to adjust to the changes. In addition, the trainers can work with fewer physicians during the training and go-live process. As you can see from this case, the process of acquiring new information systems can involve much more than a simple purchase decision.

Sources: Compiled from interviews with Chad Prince, www.greenwaymedical .com, http://annistonortho.com, accessed May 12, 2013.

Questions

1. Would acquiring a new information system for a small organization be a longer or a shorter process than acquiring one at a larger organization? Support your answer.
2. Why did AOA pick three separate vendors to help implement Greenway's PrimeSuite software application? What are the problems associated with managing four vendors to implement the group's switch to EMRs? Should AOA have purchased a software application from a company that would manage the entire process? Why or why not?

13.1 Planning for and Justifying IT Applications

Organizations must analyze the need for applications and then justify each purchase in terms of costs and benefits. The need for information systems is usually related to organizational planning and to the analysis of its performance vis-à-vis its competitors. The cost–benefit justification must consider the wisdom of investing in a specific IT application versus spending the funds on alternative projects. This chapter focuses on the formal processes of large organizations. Smaller organizations employ less formal processes, or no processes at all. It is important to note, however, that even if a small organization does not have a formal process for planning and justifying IT applications, the steps of a formal process exist for a reason, and they have value. At the very least, decision makers in small organizations should consider each step when they are planning changes in their information systems.

When a company examines its needs and performance, it generates a prioritized list of both existing and potential IT applications, called the **application portfolio**. These are the applications that have to be added, or modified if they already exist.

IT Planning

The planning process for new IT applications begins with an analysis of the *organizational strategic plan*, which is illustrated in Figure 13.1. The organization's strategic plan identifies the firm's overall mission, the goals that follow from that mission, and the broad steps required to reach these goals. The strategic planning process modifies the organization's objectives and resources to match its changing markets and opportunities.

The organizational strategic plan and the existing IT architecture provide the inputs in developing the IT strategic plan. The *IT architecture* delineates the way an organization should utilize its information resources to accomplish its mission. It encompasses both the technical and the managerial aspects of information resources. The technical aspects include hardware and operating systems, networking, data management systems, and applications software. The managerial aspects specify how the IT department will be managed, how the functional area managers will be involved, and how IT decisions will be made.

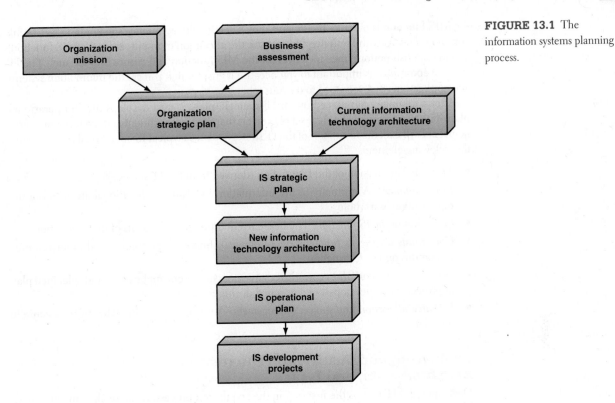

FIGURE 13.1 The information systems planning process.

The **IT strategic plan** is a set of long-range goals that describe the IT infrastructure and identify the major IT initiatives needed to achieve the organization's goals (see this chapter's Closing Case 2). The IT strategic plan must meet three objectives:

1. *It must be aligned with the organization's strategic plan.* This alignment is critical because the organization's information systems must support the organization's strategies. (Recall the discussion of organizational strategies and information systems in Chapter 2.)

    Consider the example of Nordstrom versus Walmart. An application that improves customer service at a small cost would be considered favorably at Nordstrom, but it would be rejected at Walmart. The reason is that the application would fit in favorably (i.e., align) with Nordstrom's service-at-any-cost strategy. However, it would not fit in well with Walmart's low-cost strategy. You see two department stores, same application, same cost and benefits—but different answers to the question "Should we develop the application?"

2. *It must provide for an IT architecture that seamlessly networks users, applications, and databases.*

3. *It must efficiently allocate IS development resources among competing projects so the projects can be completed on time and within budget and still have the required functionality.*

    The existing IT architecture is a necessary input into the IT strategic plan because it acts as a constraint on future development efforts. It is not an absolute constraint, however, because the organization can change to a new IT architecture. Companies prefer to avoid this strategy, however, because it is expensive and time-consuming.

    Consider this example. You have a Mac (Apple) system and you need a new software application. You search and find several such packages for both Mac and MS Windows. Unfortunately, the best package runs only on Windows. How much better would this package have to be for you to justify a switch to a new system?

    One critical component in developing and implementing the IT strategic plan is the **IT steering committee**. This committee, comprised of a group of managers and staff who represent the various organizational units, is created to establish IT priorities and to ensure that the MIS function is meeting the organization's needs. The committee's major tasks are to link corporate strategy with IT strategy, to approve the allocation of resources for the MIS function, and to establish performance measures for the MIS function and ensure they are met. The IT steering committee is important to you because it ensures that you get the information systems and applications that you need to do your job.

After a company has agreed on an IT strategic plan, it next develops the **IS operational plan**. This plan consists of a clear set of projects that the IS department and the functional area managers will execute in support of the IT strategic plan. A typical IS operational plan contains the following elements:

- *Mission:* The mission of the IS function (derived from the IT strategy)
- *IS environment:* A summary of the information needs of the functional areas and of the organization as a whole
- *Objectives of the IS function:* The best current estimate of the goals of the IS function
- *Constraints on the IS function:* Technological, financial, personnel, and other resource limitations on the IS function
- *The application portfolio:* A prioritized inventory of present applications and a detailed plan of projects to be developed or continued during the current year
- *Resource allocation and project management:* A listing of how and when who is going to do what

Evaluating and Justifying IT Investment: Benefits, Costs, and Issues

Developing an IT plan is the first step in the acquisition process. Because all companies have limited resources, they must justify investing resources in some areas, including IT, rather than in others. Essentially, justifying IT investment involves calculating the costs, assessing the benefits (values), and comparing the two. This comparison is frequently referred to as cost–benefit analysis. Cost–benefit analysis is not a simple task.

Assessing the Costs.   Calculating the dollar value of IT investments is not as simple as it may seem. One of the major challenges that companies face is to allocate fixed costs among different IT projects. *Fixed costs* are those costs that remain the same regardless of any change in the company's activity level. Fixed IT costs include infrastructure costs and the costs associated with IT services and IT management. For example, the salary of the IT director is fixed, and adding one more application will not change it.

Another complication is that the costs of a system do not end when the system is installed. Rather, costs for maintaining, debugging, and improving the system can accumulate over many years. This is a critical point because organizations sometimes fail to anticipate these costs when they make the investment.

A dramatic example of unanticipated expenses was the Year 2000 (Y2K) reprogramming projects, which cost organizations worldwide billions of dollars. In the 1960s, computer memory was very expensive. To save money, programmers coded the "year" in the date field 19_ _, instead of _ _ _ _. With the "1" and the "9" hard-coded in the computer program, only the last two digits varied, so computer programs needed less memory. However, this process meant that when the year 2000 rolled around, computers would display the year as 1900. This programming technique could have caused serious problems with financial applications, insurance applications, and countless other apps.

The Y2K example illustrates the point that database design choices tend to affect the organization for a long time. As the 21st century approached, no one still used hardware or software from the 1960s (other than a few legacy applications). Database design choices made in the 1960s, however, were often still in effect decades after the companies implemented them.

Assessing the Benefits.   Evaluating the benefits of IT projects is typically even more complex than calculating their costs. Benefits may be more difficult to quantify, especially because many of them are intangible—for example, improved customer or partner relations or improved decision making. As an employee, you will probably be asked for input about the intangible benefits that an IS provides for you.

The fact that organizations use IT for multiple purposes further complicates benefit analysis. In addition, to obtain a return from an IT investment, the company must implement the technology successfully. In reality, many systems are not implemented on time, within budget, or with all the features originally envisioned for them. Also, the proposed system may be "cutting edge." In these cases, there may be no basis for identifying the types of financial payback the company can expect.

Conducting the Cost–Benefit Analysis.   After a company has assessed the costs and benefits of IT investments, it must compare them. You have studied, or will study, cost–benefit analyses in more detail in your finance courses. The point is that real-world business problems do not come in neatly wrapped packages labeled "this is a finance problem" or "this is an IS problem." Rather, business problems span multiple functional areas.

There is no uniform strategy for conducting a cost–benefit analysis. Rather, an organization can perform this task in several ways. Here you see four common approaches: (1) net present value, (2) return on investment, (3) breakeven analysis, and (4) the business case approach.

- Analysts use the *net present value* (NPV) method to convert future values of benefits to their present-value equivalent by "discounting" them at the organization's cost of funds. They can then compare the present value of the future benefits to the cost required to achieve those benefits to determine whether the benefits exceed the costs.

- *Return on investment* (ROI) measures management's effectiveness in generating profits with its available assets. ROI is calculated by dividing the net income generated by a project by the average assets invested in the project. ROI is a percentage, and the higher the percentage return, the better.

- *Breakeven analysis* determines the point at which the cumulative dollar value of the benefits from a project equals the investment made in the project.

- In the *business case approach*, system developers write a business case to justify funding one or more specific applications or projects. IS professionals will be a major source of input when business cases are developed because these cases describe what you do, how you do it, and how a new system could better support you.

before you go on...

1. What are some problems associated with assessing the costs of IT?

2. What difficulties accompany the intangible benefits from IT?

3. Describe the NPV, ROI, breakeven analysis, and business case approaches.

Strategies for Acquiring IT Applications

13.2

After a company has justified an IT investment, it must then decide how to pursue it. As with cost–benefit analyses, there are several options for acquiring IT applications. To select the best option, companies must make a series of business decisions. The fundamental decisions are:

- *How much computer code does the company want to write?* A company can choose to use a totally prewritten application (to write no computer code), to customize a prewritten application (to write some computer code), or to custom-write an entire application (write all new computer code).

- *How will the company pay for the application?* Once the company has decided how much computer code to write, it must decide how to pay for it. With prewritten applications or customized prewritten applications, companies can buy them or lease them. With totally custom applications, companies use internal funding.

- *Where will the application run?* The next decision is whether to run the application on the company's platform or on someone else's platform. In other words, the company can employ either a software-as-a-service vendor or an application service provider. (You will examine these options later in this chapter.)
- *Where will the application originate?* Prewritten applications can be open-source software or they can come from a vendor. The company may choose to customize prewritten open-source applications or prewritten proprietary applications from vendors. Further, it may customize applications in-house or outsource the customization. Finally, it can write totally custom applications in-house or outsource this process.

In the following sections, you will find more detail on the variety of ways that companies can acquire applications. A good rule of thumb is that an organization should consider all feasible acquisition methods in light of its business requirements. You will learn about the following acquisition methods:

- Purchase a prewritten application.
- Customize a prewritten application.
- Lease the application.
- Use application service providers and software-as-a-service vendors.
- Use open-source software.
- Use outsourcing.
- Employ custom development.

Purchase a Prewritten Application

Many commercial software packages contain the standard features required by IT applications. Therefore, purchasing an existing package can be a cost-effective and time-saving strategy compared with custom-developing the application in-house. Nevertheless, a company should carefully consider and plan the buy option to ensure that the selected package contains all of the features necessary to address the company's current and future needs. Otherwise, these packages can quickly become obsolete. Before a company can perform this process, it must decide which features a suitable package must include.

In reality, a single software package can rarely satisfy all of an organization's needs. For this reason, a company sometimes must purchase multiple packages to fulfill different needs. It then must integrate these packages with one another as well as with its existing software. Table 13.1 summarizes the advantages and limitations of the buy option.

Customize a Prewritten Application

Customizing existing software is an especially attractive option if the software vendor allows the company to modify the application to meet its needs. However, this option may not be attractive in cases where customization is the *only* method of providing the necessary flexibility to address the company's needs. It also is not the best strategy when the software is either very expensive or is likely to become obsolete in a short time. Further, customizing a prewritten application can be extremely difficult, particularly for large, complex applications. IT's About Business 13.2 recounts a disastrous effort by Marin County, California, to implement an SAP system.

Lease the Application

Compared with the buy option and the option to develop applications in-house, the lease option can save a company both time and money. Of course, leased packages (like purchased packages) may not exactly fit the company's application requirements. However, as noted, vendor software generally includes the features that are most commonly needed by organizations in a given industry. Again, the company will decide which features are necessary.

Table
13.1
Advantages and Limitations of the Buy Option

Advantages

Many different types of off-the-shelf software are available.

Software can be tried out.

The company can save much time by buying rather than building.

The company can know what it is getting before it invests in the product.

The company is not the first and only user.

Purchased software may eliminate the need to hire personnel specifically dedicated to a project.

Disadvantages

Software may not exactly meet the company's needs.

Software may be difficult or impossible to modify, or it may require huge business process changes to implement.

The company will not have control over software improvements and new versions.

Purchased software can be difficult to integrate with existing systems.

Vendors may discontinue a product or go out of business.

Software is controlled by another company with its own priorities and business considerations.

Intimate knowledge in the purchasing company is lacking about how and why the software works as it does.

IT's [about business]

13.2 A Disastrous Development Project

In 2004, Marin County in California decided to replace its aging financial management, payroll, and human resources systems with a modern SAP enterprise resource planning system. The county solicited proposals from various companies to act as software consultants on the implementation. Thirteen companies, including Oracle, PeopleSoft, and SAP, submitted proposals. In April 2005 the county selected Deloitte Consulting based on the firm's representations concerning its in-depth knowledge of SAP systems and the extensive experience of its consultants.

From 2005 to 2009, Marin County paid increasing consulting fees to Deloitte as its staff grappled with serious fiscal problems. Essentially, the staff could not program the SAP system to perform even routine financial functions such as payroll and accounts receivable. A grand jury probe concluded that the system had cost taxpayers $28.6 million as of April 2009.

At that time, Marin County voted to stop the ongoing SAP project, implicitly acknowledging that it had wasted some $30 million on software and related implementation services from Deloitte. The Marin County Information Systems and Technology Group concluded that fixing the Deloitte-installed SAP system would cost nearly 25 percent more over a 10-year period than implementing a new system.

In 2010, Marin County filed a complaint alleging that Deloitte's representations were fraudulent. The complaint accused Deloitte of using the county's SAP project as a training ground to provide young consultants with public sector SAP experience, at the county's expense. It further charged that Deloitte intentionally failed to disclose its lack of SAP and public sector skills; withheld information about critical project risks; falsely represented to the county that the SAP system was ready to "go live" as originally planned; conducted inadequate testing; and concealed the fact that it had failed to perform necessary testing, thereby ensuring that system defects would remain hidden prior to the go-live date. Finally, the county maintained that, although it had paid substantial consulting fees to Deloitte, the system continued to have crippling problems.

Deloitte filed a counterclaim over the county's failure to pay more than $550,000 in fees and interest. The company maintained that it had fulfilled all of its obligations under the contract, as evidenced by the fact that all of Deloitte's work was approved by the county officials who were responsible for overseeing the project.

In December 2010, Marin County sued Deloitte and two SAP subsidiaries, alleging that Deloitte had "engaged in a pattern of racketeering activity designed to defraud the county of more than $20 million." The county's lawsuit also names as a defendant Ernest Culver, a former county employee who served as director on the SAP project. The county alleged that Culver interviewed for jobs at Deloitte and SAP, where he now works in SAP's Public Services division. It further claimed that during the SAP project,

Culver "was approving Deloitte's deficient work on the project, approving payments, and causing Marin County to enter into new contracts with Deloitte and SAP Public Services, Inc."

In late December 2011, a judge ruled that Marin County failed to allege sufficient facts to bring a racketeering claim against SAP under the terms of the federal Racketeer Influenced and Corrupt Organizations Act (RICO). However, he also ruled that Marin County could file an amended complaint. The judge further found that Marin County had alleged sufficient facts to bring a "plausible" bribery claim against SAP with respect to Culver. Finally, the judge denied SAP's motion to dismiss claims against its SAP America division.

In mid-January 2012, Marin County filed an amended complaint in federal court related to its actions against SAP, Deloitte Consulting, and Ernest Culver. The president of the Marin County Board of Supervisors stated that the board is committed to ensuring accountability for its taxpayers.

In early 2013, Marin County settled its lawsuit with Deloitte Consulting over the failed SAP project. The settlement followed the Court's dismissal of several of the county's claims as well as the county's conclusion, after a full investigation, that it should voluntarily dismiss its remaining fraud claims and its allegations of improper influence of a county employee (Culver) who managed the project. According to the *Marin Independent Journal*, the

county received $3.9 million from Deloitte, which is less than it paid in legal fees.

It is important to note that neither Marin County nor Deloitte placed any blame on the SAP software. The dynamics between the customer and the system integrator caused this failure.

Sources: Compiled from M. Krigsman, "Big Money: Marin County and Deloitte Settle ERP Lawsuit Under Gag Order," *ZDNet*, January 14, 2013; N. Johnson, "Marin County Cuts Its Losses, Settles Its Computer Lawsuit for $3.9 Million, " *Marin Independent Journal*, January 9, 2013; C. Kanaracus, "Judge Tosses Racketeering Claims in Marin County Lawsuit Against SAP," *PC World*, December 28, 2011; C. Kanaracus, "Marin County Alleges SAP, Deloitte Engaged in Racketeering," *Computerworld*, February 2, 2011; M. Krigsman, "Understanding Marin County's $30 Million ERP Failure," *ZDNet*, September 2, 2010; C. Kanaracus, "Marin County to Rip and Replace Ailing SAP System," *IDG News Service*, August 24, 2010; M. Krigsman, "Marin County Sues Deloitte: Alleges Fraud on SAP Project," *ZDNet*, June 3, 2010; J. Vijayan, "Deloitte Hit with $30M Lawsuit over ERP Project," *Computerworld*, June 3, 2010; T. Claburn, "Deloitte Sued Over Failed SAP Implementation," *InformationWeek*, June 1, 2010; www.co.marin.ca.us, www.deloitte.com, accessed March 14, 2013.

Questions

1. Debate the lawsuit from the point of view of Deloitte and SAP.
2. Debate the lawsuit from the point of view of Marin County.

Interested companies commonly apply the 80/20 rule when they evaluate vendor software. Put simply, if the software meets 80 percent of the company's needs, then the company should seriously consider modifying its business processes so it can utilize the remaining 20 percent. Many times this is a better long-term solution than modifying the vendor software. Otherwise, the company will have to customize the software every time the vendor releases an updated version.

Leasing can be especially attractive to small- to medium-size enterprises (SMEs) that cannot afford major investments in IT software. Large companies may also prefer to lease packages in order to test potential IT solutions before committing to major investments. In addition, a company that does not employ sufficient IT personnel with the appropriate skills for developing custom IT applications may choose to lease instead of developing software in-house. Even those companies that employ in-house experts may not be able to afford the long wait for strategic applications to be developed in-house. Therefore, they lease (or buy) applications from external resources to establish a quicker presence in the market.

Leasing can be executed in one of three ways. The first way is to lease the application from a software developer, install it, and run it on the company's platform. The vendor can assist with the installation and frequently will offer to contract for the support and maintenance of the system. Many conventional applications are leased this way.

The other two options involve leasing an application and running it on the vendor's platform. Organizations can accomplish this process by using an application service provider or a software-as-a-service vendor.

Application Service Providers and Software-as-a-Service Vendors

An **application service provider (ASP)** is an agent or a vendor who assembles the software needed by enterprises and then packages it with services such as development, operations, and maintenance. The customer then accesses these applications via the Internet. Figure 13.2 illustrates the operation of an ASP. Note that the ASP hosts both an application and a database for each customer.

Software-as-a-service (SaaS) is a method of delivering software in which a vendor hosts the applications and provides them as a service to customers over a network, typically the

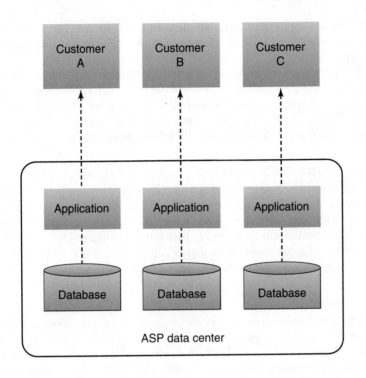

FIGURE 13.2 Operation of an application service provider (ASP).

Internet. Customers do not own the software; rather, they pay for using it. SaaS eliminates the need for customers to install and run the application on their own computers. Therefore, SaaS customers save the expense (money, time, IT staff) of buying, operating, and maintaining the software. For example, Salesforce (*www.salesforce.com*), a well-known SaaS provider for customer relationship management (CRM) software solutions, provides these advantages for its customers. Figure 13.3 displays the operation of a SaaS vendor. Note that

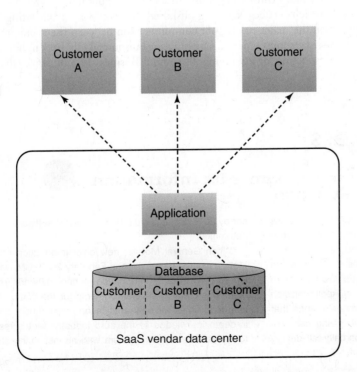

FIGURE 13.3 Operation of a Software-as-a-Service (SaaS) vendor.

the vendor hosts an application that multiple customers can use. The vendor also hosts a database that is partitioned for each customer to protect the privacy and security of each customer's data.

At this point, companies have made the first three decisions and must now decide where to obtain the application. Recall that in general, for prewritten applications, companies can use open-source software or obtain the software from a vendor. For customized prewritten applications, they can customize open-source software or customize vendor software. For totally custom applications, they can write the software in-house or outsource this process.

Use Open-Source Software

Organizations obtain a license to implement an open-source software product and either use it as is, customize it, or develop applications with it. Unless the company is one of the few that want to tinker with their source code, open-source applications are, basically, the same as a proprietary application except for licensing, payment, and support. Open-source is really an alternative source of applications rather than a conceptually different development option. (We discuss open-source software in Technology Guide 2.)

Outsourcing

Acquiring IT applications from outside contractors or external organizations is called **outsourcing**. Companies can utilize outsourcing in many situations. For example, they might want to experiment with new IT technologies without making a substantial up-front investment. They also might use outsourcing to gain access to outside experts. One disadvantage of outsourcing is that companies frequently must place their valuable corporate data under the control of the outsourcing vendor.

Several types of vendors offer services for creating and operating IT systems, including e-commerce applications. Many software companies, from IBM to Oracle, offer a range of outsourcing services for developing, operating, and maintaining IT applications. IT outsourcers, such as EDS, offer a variety of services. Also, the large CPA companies and management consultants—for example, Accenture—offer outsourcing services.

As the trend to outsource is on the rise, so is the trend to relocate these operations offshore, particularly in India and China. *Offshoring* can save money, but it includes risks as well. The risks depend on which services are being offshored. If a company is offshoring application development, then the major risk is poor communication between users and developers. In response to these risks, some companies are bringing outsourced jobs back in-house, a process called reverse outsourcing, or insourcing. IT's About Business 13.3 illustrates this process at General Motors.

IT's [about business]

13.3 General Motors Insources Its Information Technology Function

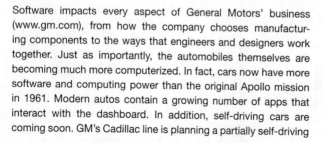

Software impacts every aspect of General Motors' business (www.gm.com), from how the company chooses manufacturing components to the ways that engineers and designers work together. Just as importantly, the automobiles themselves are becoming much more computerized. In fact, cars now have more software and computing power than the original Apollo mission in 1961. Modern autos contain a growing number of apps that interact with the dashboard. In addition, self-driving cars are coming soon. GM's Cadillac line is planning a partially self-driving

car by 2015. So, it is clear how important software is to the giant automaker.

When General Motors' new chief information officer, Randy Mott, assumed his position in February 2012, GM was outsourcing 90 percent of its information technology work. This arrangement was creating several problems for the company, including long lead times for new application development and a lack of in-depth knowledge of the auto industry. Mott's response was to replace the existing system with an insourcing strategy. This strategy includes hiring up to 10,000 employees and opening four software innovation centers in the U.S. GM feels that a much larger in-house IT staff, one that understands the automobile industry, could provide advantages to the automaker, including:

- Reducing the number of software applications. Mott estimates that GM has more than 4,000 applications throughout the world. Many are redundant and can be eliminated.

- Speeding up software application development to match the company's increased speed of new car and truck introductions.

- Replacing IT contractors who do not really understand the auto industry with in-house IT staff members who are familiar with the industry. GM believes that these individuals will possess the knowledge to develop superior, innovative software applications.

General Motors is consolidating the company's 23 data centers into 2 much larger, more efficient centers. It is also building a global data warehouse that will enable executives to analyze detailed internal market and sales data and incorporate external information sources, including social-media feedback, into their decision-making process. Finally, the company plans to hire additional IT professionals to staff the data centers and manage the data warehouse.

Sources: Compiled from J. Leber, "With Computerized Cars Ahead, GM Puts IT Outsourcing in the Rearview Mirror," *MIT Technology Review*, November 5, 2012; K. Flinders, "Could GM's Decision to Insource IT Start a Trend?" *Computer Weekly*, October 29, 2012; S. Overby, "GM Bets on Insourcing, Brings Back 10,000 IT Jobs," *CIO Magazine*, October 5, 2012; P. Thibodeau, "GM to Hire 10,000 IT Pros As It 'Insources' Work," *Computerworld*, September 7, 2012; C. Murphy, "General Motors Will Slash Outsourcing in IT Overhaul," *InformationWeek*, July 9, 2012; B. Howard, "Cadillac Promises Self-Driving Cars by 2015," *Extreme Tech*, April 23, 2012; K. Bullis, "GM Tests a Self-Driving Cadillac," *MIT Technology Review*, April 20, 2012; M. Pesce, "Software Takes on More Tasks in Today's Cars," *Wired*, April 25, 2011; www.gm.com, accessed March 19, 2013.

Questions

1. What are potential disadvantages of Mott's insourcing strategy?

2. What are the reasons why GM, with its outsourcing strategy, ended up with some 4,000 software applications?

Employ Custom Development

Companies may also decide to custom-build an application. They can either perform this operation in-house or outsource the process. Although custom development is usually more time-consuming and costly than buying or leasing, it often produces a better fit with the organization's specific requirements.

The development process starts when the IT steering committee (discussed previously in this chapter), having received suggestions for a new system, decides it is worth exploring. These suggestions come from users (who will be you in the near future). Understanding this process will help you obtain the systems that you need. Conversely, not understanding this process will reduce your chances, because other people who understand it better will make suggestions that use up available resources.

As the company goes through the development process, its mind-set changes. In systems investigation (the first stage of the traditional systems development life cycle), the organization is trying to decide whether to build something. Everyone knows it may or may not be built. In the later stages of the development process, the organization is committed to building the application. Although a project can be cancelled at any time, this change in attitude is still important.

The basic, backbone methodology for custom development is the systems development life cycle (SDLC), which you will read about in the next section. Section 13.4 examines the methodologies that complement the SDLC: prototyping, joint application development, integrated computer-assisted systems development tools, and rapid application development. You will also consider four other methodologies: agile development, end-user development, component-based development, and object-oriented development.

before you go on...

1. Describe the four fundamental business decisions that organizations must make when acquiring information systems.

2. Discuss each of the seven development methods in this section with regard to the four business decisions that organizations must make.

13.3   The Traditional Systems Development Life Cycle

The **systems development life cycle (SDLC)** is the traditional systems development method that organizations use for large-scale IT projects. The SDLC is a structured framework that consists of sequential processes by which information systems are developed. For our purposes (see Figure 13.4), we identify six processes, each of which consists of clearly defined tasks:

- Systems investigation
- Systems analysis
- Systems design
- Programming and testing
- Implementation
- Operation and maintenance

Alternative SDLC models contain more or fewer stages. The flow of tasks, however, remains largely the same. When problems occur in any phase of the SDLC, developers often must go back to previous phases.

Systems development projects produce desired results through team efforts. Development teams typically include users, systems analysts, programmers, and technical specialists. *Users* are employees from all functional areas and levels of the organization who interact with the system, either directly or indirectly. **Systems analysts** are IS professionals who specialize in analyzing and designing information systems. **Programmers** are IS professionals who either modify existing computer programs or write new programs to satisfy user requirements. **Technical specialists** are experts on a certain type of technology, such as databases or telecommunications. The **systems stakeholders** include everyone who is affected by changes in a company's information systems—for example, users and managers. All stakeholders are typically involved in systems development at various times and in varying degrees. IT's About Business 13.4 illustrates how Atlassian helps companies apply collaborative software development with large projects.

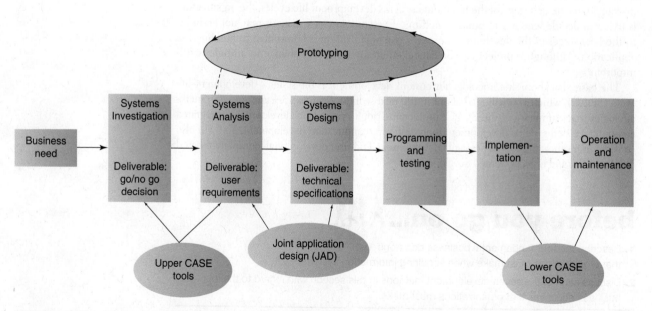

FIGURE 13.4 A six-stage systems development life cycle (SDLC) with supporting tools.

IT's [about business]

13.4 Atlassian Helps Manage Large Software Projects

In-house software development was once the sole responsibility of companies' IT departments. Today, the process is also of concern to business managers and executives. Business leaders are now involved in discussions about how well software projects are delivering. These discussions increasingly need to be open and global, as the work of development, implementation, bug fixes, and upgrades is increasingly scattered across different areas of expertise around the world. This process of cross-company discussion relating to software project development is called *collaborative software development*.

One example of a company that has successfully employed collaborative software development is Lancôme, a division of L'Oréal that owns brands such as YSL Beauty. In 2010, Lancôme decided to revamp its Web sites, electronic commerce, and online marketing efforts. To execute this task, the company had to devise a strategy to use software to manage its product development and production process. This task was rather daunting because it involved coordinating the work of in-house employees, freelance Web developers, and creative staff headquartered in such diverse locations as Chicago and India.

Rather than assign this task to its overworked IT staff, Lancôme turned to the software development company Atlassian (*www.atlassian.com*). Atlassian sells an online application called Jira, which can track and manage large software projects.

Jira helped speed up Lancôme's projects, and it made each step of the development process visible to everyone on the team. It also decreased the number of meetings and back-and-forth e-mails required for each project. These benefits translated into more sales on Lancôme's Web sites. After this successful experience, L'Oréal is considering implementing Jira in other divisions.

Another company that effectively utilized Jira is NYSE Euronext. NYSE Euronext wanted to speed up the development process of its software projects. The firm also wanted to revamp its Web site and its mobile and e-commerce data products. When NYSE Euronext deployed Atlassian, some employees who used to jealously guard their code did not like the openness and collaboration provided by the new tools. Significantly, these employees no longer work at NYSE Euronext. The company's CIO notes that the firm experienced a great deal of attrition among its developers, but he characterizes it as "good attrition." Productivity in software development improved from 30 to 50 percent in just the first 6 months after the company implemented Jira.

Research reveals that when a company uses one Atlassian product, it will often also end up using another one because Atlassian products work so well together. For example, a data management firm called Cloudera uses Jira to track bugs. Additionally, all 150 of Cloudera's employees use Atlassian's Confluence collaboration software to share information on sales, personnel issues, business development, and bug reports from Jira.

Atlassian devotes a great deal of attention to collaboration and transparency in how people work and how companies are run. It posts an unusually large amount of company information on an internal Web site for employees to view, including financials, sales performance, and pretty much everything except employee salaries.

Atlassian applies different community collaboration rules for different kinds of content. For example, it manages developer documentation in a wiki where anyone with an account can post or edit content. This process works well for generating code samples and usage examples. For the core product documentation, Atlassian gives editing abilities to some members of the community, but it requires those editors to first undergo a vetting process. Furthermore, the editors are required to sign an agreement that details their rights and responsibilities. Users who do not have editor rights can also post comments on the formal documentation. The editors are responsible for monitoring those comments to determine whether there are items that they need to add or change.

Once per quarter, Atlassian hosts its "FedEx Days," which are competitions in which employees compete to produce a product in 24 hours (typically fueled by pizza and beer). Atlassian uses a social event, rather than any promise of monetary reward, to spur innovation and creativity. FedEx the company has nothing to do with this competition, other than to be a source of inspiration. The name of the competition references FedEx's tradition of being the delivery company to choose "when it absolutely, positively has to be there overnight."

Atlassian adopted a policy of pricing Web software so inexpensively that small firms can afford to purchase their products. The company then grows virally through firms that adopt its software. Atlassian posts all of its prices on its Web site—typically $10 per month for up to 10 users for each product and up to $1,000 per month for up to 2,000 users per product. The firm invites customers to sign up with no negotiation necessary. This business model has proved its worth to Atlassian—the company now has 24,000 customers across 138 countries, including Microsoft, Oracle, Facebook, Twitter, LinkedIn, L'Oréal, and NYSE Euronext. This number continues to expand despite competition from IBM, Microsoft, MindTouch, and Jive.

Sources: Compiled from T. Geron, "We're All Coders," *Forbes*, March 12, 2012; D. Carr, "Atlassian Boosts JIRA Social Features, Social Integration," *InformationWeek*, February 22, 2012; D. Carr, "How Social Media Changes Technical Communication," *InformationWeek*, January 4, 2012; D. Carr, "How to Create a New Product in 24 Hours," *InformationWeek*, December 2, 2011; T. Taulli, "Atlassian: $100M Business With No Sales People?" *Forbes*, June 14, 2011; www.atlassian.com, accessed March 5, 2013.

Questions

1. Why are collaboration and transparency so important in the software development process?

2. What are potential problems that could arise when using Atlassian to manage software development? Provide specific examples to support your answer.

3. Provide an example of a software development project for which it would not be advisable to use Atlassian.

FIGURE 13.5 Comparison of user and developer involvement over the SDLC.

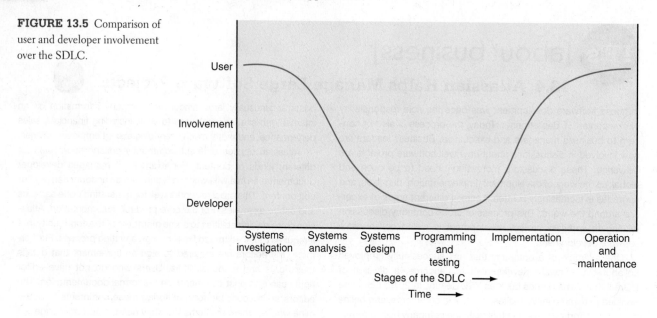

Figure 13.5 indicates that users have high involvement in the early stages of the SDLC, lower involvement in the programming and testing stage, and higher involvement in the later stages. Table 13.2 discusses the advantages and disadvantages of the SDLC.

Systems Investigation

The initial stage in a traditional SDLC is systems investigation. Systems development professionals agree that the more time they invest in (1) understanding the business problem to be solved, (2) specifying the technical options for the systems, and (3) anticipating the problems they are likely to encounter during development, the greater the chances of success. For these reasons, **systems investigation** addresses *the business problem* (or business opportunity) by means of the feasibility study.

The main task in the systems investigation stage is the **feasibility study**. Organizations have three basic solutions to any business problem relating to an information system: (1) do nothing and continue to use the existing system unchanged, (2) modify or enhance the existing system, and (3) develop a new system. The feasibility study analyzes which of these three solutions best fits the particular business problem. It also provides a rough assessment of the project's technical, economic, and behavioral feasibility, as explained below.

- *Technical feasibility* determines whether the company can develop and/or acquire the hardware, software, and communications components needed to solve the business problem. Technical feasibility also determines whether the organization can use its existing technology to achieve the project's performance objectives.
- *Economic feasibility* determines whether the project is an acceptable financial risk and, if so, whether the organization has the necessary time and money to successfully complete the project. You have already learned about the commonly used methods to determine economic feasibility: NPV, ROI, breakeven analysis, and the business case approach.
- *Behavioral feasibility* addresses the human issues of the systems development project. You will be heavily involved in this aspect of the feasibility study.

After the feasibility analysis is completed, a "go/no-go" decision is reached by the steering committee if there is one or by top management in the absence of a committee. The go/no-go decision does not depend solely on the feasibility analysis. Organizations often have more feasible projects than they can fund. Therefore, the firm must prioritize the feasible projects and pursue those with the highest priority. Unfunded feasible projects may not be presented to

Table **13.2**
Advantages and Disadvantages of System Acquisition Methods

Traditional Systems Development (SDLC)
Advantages

- Forces staff to systematically go through every step in a structured process.
- Enforces quality by maintaining standards.
- Has lower probability of missing important issues in collecting user requirements.

Disadvantages

- May produce excessive documentation.
- Users may be unwilling or unable to study the approved specifications.
- Takes too long to go from the original ideas to a working system.
- Users have trouble describing requirements for a proposed system.

Prototyping
Advantages

- Helps clarify user requirements.
- Helps verify the feasibility of the design.
- Promotes genuine user participation.
- Promotes close working relationship between systems developers and users.
- Works well for ill-defined problems.
- May produce part of the final system.

Disadvantages

- May encourage inadequate problem analysis.
- Not practical with large number of users.
- User may not give up the prototype when the system is completed.
- May generate confusion about whether the system is complete and maintainable.
- System may be built quickly, which may result in lower quality.

Joint Application Design
Advantages

- Involves many users in the development process.
- Saves time.
- Greater user support for new system.
- Improved quality of the new system.
- New system easier to implement.
- New system has lower training costs.

Disadvantages

- Difficult to get all users to attend JAD meeting.
- JAD approach has all the problems associated with any group meeting.

Integrated Computer-Assisted Software Engineering
Advantages

- Can produce systems with a longer effective operational life.
- Can produce systems that closely meet user requirements.
- Can speed up the development process.
- Can produce systems that are more flexible and adaptable to changing business conditions.
- Can produce excellent documentation.

Disadvantages

- Systems often more expensive to build and maintain.
- Require more extensive and accurate definition of user requirements.
- Difficult to customize.

Rapid Application Development
Advantages

- Can speed up systems development.
- Users intensively involved from the start.
- Improves the process of rewriting legacy applications.

Disadvantages

- Produces functional components of final systems, but not final systems.

End-User Development
Advantages

- Bypasses the IS department and avoids delays.
- User controls the application and can change it as needed.
- Directly meets user requirements.
- Increased user acceptance of new system.
- Frees up IT resources.
- May create lower-quality systems.

Disadvantages

- May eventually require maintenance from IS department.
- Documentation may be inadequate.
- Poor quality control.
- System may not have adequate interfaces to existing systems.

Object-Oriented Development
Advantages

- Objects model real-world entities.
- May be able to reuse some computer code.

Disadvantages

- Works best with systems of more limited scope (i.e., with systems that do not have huge numbers of objects).

the IT department at all. These projects therefore contribute to the *hidden backlog*, which are projects that the IT department is not aware of.

If the decision is no-go, then the project either is put on the shelf until conditions are more favorable or it is discarded. If the decision is go, then the project proceeds, and the systems analysis phase begins.

Systems Analysis

Once a development project has the necessary approvals from all participants, the systems analysis stage begins. **Systems analysis** is the process where systems analysts examine the business problem that the organization plans to solve with an information system.

The main purpose of the systems analysis stage is to gather information about the existing system in order to determine the requirements for an enhanced system or a new system. The end product of this stage, known as the *deliverable*, is a set of *system requirements*.

Arguably, the most difficult task in systems analysis is to identify the specific requirements that the system must satisfy. These requirements are often called *user requirements*, because users (meaning you) provide them. When the systems developers have accumulated the user requirements for the new system, they proceed to the systems design stage.

Systems Design

Systems design describes how the system will resolve the business problem. The deliverable of the systems design phase is the set of *technical system specifications*, which specify the following:

- System outputs, inputs, and user interfaces
- Hardware, software, databases, telecommunications, personnel, and procedures
- A blueprint of how these components are integrated

When the system specifications are approved by all participants, they are "frozen." That is, they should not be changed. Adding functions after the project has been initiated causes **scope creep**, which endangers the project's budget and schedule. Because scope creep is expensive, successful project managers place controls on changes requested by users. These controls help to prevent runaway projects.

Programming and Testing

If the organization decides to construct the software in-house, then programming begins. **Programming** involves translating the design specifications into computer code. This process can be lengthy and time-consuming, because writing computer code is as much an art as a science. Large-scale systems development projects can involve hundreds of computer programmers who are charged with creating hundreds of thousands of lines of computer code. These projects employ programming teams. The teams often include functional area users, who help the programmers focus on the business problem.

Thorough and continuous testing occurs throughout the programming stage. Testing is the process that assesses whether the computer code will produce the expected and desired results. It is also intended to detect errors, or bugs, in the computer code.

Implementation

Implementation (or *deployment*) is the process of converting from an old computer system to a new one. The conversion process involves organizational change. Only end users can manage organizational change, not the MIS department. The MIS department typically does not have enough credibility with the business users to manage the change process. Organizations use three major conversion strategies: direct, pilot, and phased.

In a **direct conversion**, the old system is cut off, and the new system is turned on at a certain point in time. This type of conversion is the least expensive. It is also the most risky because, if the new system does not work as planned, there is no support from the old system. Because of these risks, few systems are implemented using direct conversion. IT's About Business 13.5 demonstrates the risks of a direct conversion.

IT's [about business]

13.5 Virgin America Has Problems Converting to a New Reservation System

Reservation systems are the digital nervous systems of airlines. Among other things, reservation systems store, organize, and calculate flight schedules, prices, and passenger lists. To future growth, Virgin America (*www.virginamerica.com*) switched to a reservations system developed by Sabre Holdings Corporation (*www.sabre.com*). This system enables airlines to enter codeshare agreements, meaning that participating airlines can sell tickets for each other's flights.

Virgin America switched to its new reservations system on October 28, 2011. The airline had informed customers that its Web site would be down for 12 to 24 hours as it transferred 239,000 reservations and created 2 million new frequent-flier accounts. When the Web site went live again, however, it encountered widespread problems that persisted for several weeks. To compound this problem, these disruptions occurred during the airline's busy Thanksgiving travel period.

Most Virgin America customers were unable to modify their flights online, and many customers complained that they were overcharged or they could not book flights or check in online. Customers also complained that they could not select seats or book flights using frequent-flyer miles. Because customers could not perform these activities online, they did so in person at the airport. As a result, long lines developed at Virgin America ticket counters in airports across the country.

To further compound the issue, Web site error messages directed customers to call the airline, but phone lines were clogged with long waits, and some calls were disconnected altogether.

Virgin America call centers were overwhelmed, despite the fact that Virgin had temporarily doubled its call-center staff.

Fortunately, Virgin was able to fix almost all of its Web-related problems by December 1, 2011. The company placated its customer base by waiving certain fees and awarding free flights to about 56,000 affected fliers, at a total cost to the airline of more than $7 million.

Virgin reported a first quarter (2012) operating loss of $49 million. The airline attributed the loss partly to a revenue shortfall associated with the airline's transition to a new reservation system.

Sources: Compiled from J. Shillinglaw, "Virgin America Reports $49 Million First Quarter Operating Loss," *Travel Pulse*, July 3, 2012; "Virgin America Website Problems: Unable to Upgrade Online," *Travelsort.com*, February 13, 2012; P. Carr, "Virgin America's Broken Booking System," *Pandodaily.com*, January 24, 2012; B. Mutzabaugh, "Virgin America Dogged by Reservation Glitches," *USA Today*, December 22, 2011; J. Nicas, "Jet Lagged: Web Glitches Still Plague Virgin America," *The Wall Street Journal*, November 23, 2011; H. McCracken, "Virgin America's Web Site Meltdown: Four Weeks and Counting," *Technologizer*, November 22, 2011; www.virginamerica.com, www.sabre.com, accessed March 21, 2013.

Questions

1. What could Virgin America have done to reduce the risks associated with converting its reservation system? Provide several specific examples to support your answer.
2. What are the potential long-term problems for Virgin America that could result from its difficulties in converting to its new system?

A **pilot conversion** introduces the new system in one part of the organization, such as in one plant or one functional area. The new system runs for a period of time and is then assessed. If the assessment confirms that the system is working properly, then the system is implemented in other parts of the organization.

A **phased conversion** introduces components of the new system, such as individual modules, in stages. Each module is assessed. If it works properly, then other modules are introduced, until the entire new system is operational. Large organizations commonly combine the pilot and phased approaches. That is, they execute a phased conversion using a pilot group for each phase.

A fourth strategy is *parallel conversion*, in which the old and new systems operate simultaneously for a time. This strategy is seldom used today. One reason why is that parallel conversion is totally impractical when both the old and new systems are online. Imagine that you are completing an order on Amazon, only to be told, "Before your order can be entered here, you must provide all the same information again, in a different form, and on a different set of screens." The results would be disastrous for Amazon.

Operation and Maintenance

After the new system is implemented, it will operate for a period of time, until (like the old system it replaced) it no longer meets its objectives. Once the new system's operations are stabilized, the company performs audits to assess the system's capabilities and to determine if it is being utilized correctly.

Systems require several types of maintenance. The first type is *debugging* the program, a process that continues throughout the life of the system. The second type is *updating* the system to accommodate changes in business conditions. An example is adjusting to new governmental regulations, such as changes in tax rates. These corrections and upgrades usually do not add any new functions. Instead, they simply help the system to continue to achieve its objectives. In contrast, the third type of maintenance *adds new functions* to the existing system without disturbing its operation.

before you go on...

1. Describe the feasibility study.
2. What is the difference between systems analysis and systems design?
3. Describe structured programming.
4. What are the four conversion methods?

13.4 Alternative Methods and Tools for Systems Development

Alternative methods for systems development include joint application design, rapid application development, agile development, and end-user development.

Joint Application Design

Joint application design (JAD) is a group-based tool for collecting user requirements and creating system designs. It is most often used within the systems analysis and systems design stages of the SDLC. JAD involves a group meeting attended by the analysts and all of the users that can be conducted manually or via the computer. During this meeting, all users jointly define and agree on the systems requirements. This process saves a tremendous amount of time. Table 13.2 lists the advantages and disadvantages of the JAD process.

Rapid Application Development

Rapid application development (RAD) is a systems-development method that can combine JAD, prototyping, and integrated computer-assisted software engineering (ICASE) tools (discussed later in this section) to rapidly produce a high-quality system. In the first RAD stage, developers use JAD sessions to collect system requirements. This strategy ensures that users are intensively involved early on. The development process in RAD is iterative; that is, requirements, designs, and the system itself are developed and then undergo a series, or sequence, of improvements. RAD uses ICASE tools to quickly structure requirements and develop prototypes. As the prototypes are developed and refined, users review them in additional JAD sessions. RAD produces the functional components of a final system, rather than prototypes. To understand how RAD functions and how it differs from SDLC, see Figure 13.6. Table 13.2 highlights the advantages and disadvantages of the RAD process.

Agile Development

Agile development is a software-development methodology that delivers functionality in rapid iterations, which are usually measured in weeks. To be successful, this methodology requires frequent communication, development, testing, and delivery. Agile development focuses on

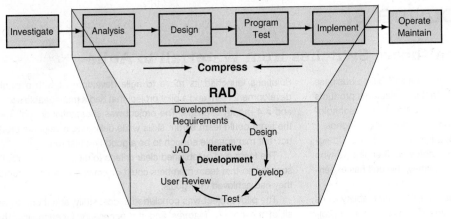

FIGURE 13.6 A rapid prototyping development process versus SDLC. (*Source:* datawarehouse-training.com/ Methodologies/rapidapplication-development.)

rapid development and frequent user contact to create software that addresses the needs of business users. This software does not have to include every possible feature the user will require. Rather, it must meet only the user's more important and immediate needs. It can be updated later to introduce additional functions as they become necessary. The core tenet of agile development is to do only what you have to do to be successful right now.

One type of agile development uses the *scrum approach*. A key principle of scrum is that during a project users can change their minds about what they want and need. Scrum acknowledges that a development problem cannot be fully understood or defined from the start. Therefore, scrum focuses on maximizing the development team's ability to deliver iterations quickly and to respond effectively to additional user requirements as they emerge.

Scrum contains sets of practices and predefined roles. The primary roles are these:

- The *Scrum Master*: maintains the processes (typically replaces a project manager)
- The *Product Owner*: represents the business users and any other stakeholders in the project
- The *Team*: a cross-functional group of about seven people who perform the actual analysis, design, coding, implementation, testing, and so on

Scrum works this way: During each *sprint*—typically a 2- to 4-week period—the team creates a potentially shippable product increment, such as working and tested software. The set of features that goes into each sprint comes from the product backlog, which is a prioritized set of high-level work requirements to be completed.

The sprint planning meeting determines which backlog items will be addressed during a sprint. During this meeting, the Product Owner informs the team of the items in the product backlog that he or she wants completed. The team members then determine how many of these projects they can commit to during the next sprint and they record this information in the sprint backlog.

During a sprint, no one is allowed to change the sprint backlog, which means that the requirements are frozen for the sprint. Each sprint must end on time. If the requirements are not completed for any reason, then they are left out and returned to the product backlog. After each sprint is completed, the team demonstrates how to use the software. IT's About Business 13.6 illustrates how GE Healthcare moved from the systems development life cycle to agile development.

End-User Development

End-user development is an approach in which the organization's end users develop their own applications with little or no formal assistance from the IT department. Table 13.2 lists the advantages and disadvantages of end-user development.

IT's [about business]

13.6 GE Healthcare Switches from Waterfall to Agile   MIS

GE Healthcare (www.gehealthcare.com) is a $17-billion business unit of General Electric (www.ge.com) that manufactures products designed to make clinicians more productive. These technologies, which range from high-definition CT scanners to diagnostic pharmaceutical devices, are developed by the company's Imaging Solutions unit. Imaging Solutions employs 375 engineers who support 18 high-tech products. Unfortunately, this unit has experienced several difficulties.

First, Imaging Solutions struggled with the predictability of its systems development project execution. The cycle time on projects was too long to begin with (from 12 to 24 months), and many projects experienced significant delays beyond this timeframe. These long cycle times frequently caused the business to add features beyond the initial user requirements, reflecting concerns that customers could not wait for a new system to provide these features. This process, in turn, often increased a project's scope, causing further delays and increasing the project cycle time even more. These longer cycle times increased the risk that the user requirements gathered at the beginning of the project would be out-of-date by the time the product reached the market.

Going further, Imaging Solutions' systems development process followed the systems development life cycle approach. In other words, it's the process that began with investigation, systems analysis, and systems design. After completing these steps, the unit then conducted a formal design review. After obtaining the various approvals for the design, the engineers began programming new systems.

Programming at Imaging Solutions typically took several months, after which the development team would release the new system into a test environment to collect user feedback. This point in the process was usually the first time that users came into contact with the new system. After the team accumulated and incorporated user input, it continued the testing effort prior to implementing the new system.

The problem with the SDLC approach was that the engineers could not incorporate user-requested modifications into the system until very late in the project cycle. As a result, any significant errors in the system could require the team to change the design completely—in effect, to start over. This approach wasted a great deal of time and effort, and it often caused significant delays in projects.

To address these issues, Imaging Solutions replaced its SDLC approach with an agile-based scrum initiative. Scrum focuses on maximizing the development team's ability to deliver iterations quickly and to respond effectively to additional user requirements as they emerge. In contrast to SDLC, agile development involves adding functionality in a series of phases and then testing the product after each phase has been completed. The Imaging Solutions unit particularly liked the idea of demonstrating each phase's functionality to users and then receiving immediate feedback. This approach was much more economical and efficient than not receiving feedback until the system was nearing completion. Imaging Solutions launched its move to agile development with a single development team and a pilot project that had a manageable scope and a 4-month deadline. The project was substantial enough that the team could learn scrum skills while delivering a valuable product, but manageable enough to be a good first test run.

The team also established clear criteria to measure the project's success so that team members could objectively evaluate whether they had achieved their goals.

The pilot project was concluded successfully, and it contained all of the correct features and the necessary functionality. The release, however, was one month past the desired roll-out date, so Imaging Solutions is still working on its predictability of delivery.

This pilot project revealed that Imaging Solutions could adopt agile development, but only with certain limitations. Specifically, the rigors of operating in a regulated industry required the company to deploy a hybrid development process that involved more initial planning and testing than would be practiced in other agile organizations.

Following the resolution of the pilot project, Imaging Solutions formed 10 scrum teams of 7 to 9 people each. Every two weeks, the teams met on Wednesday mornings to conduct increment reviews and on Wednesday afternoons to hold their planning meetings for the next increment. This process ensured that teams were sharing knowledge with their fellow team members and were aware of what was being done outside their particular team.

To obtain maximum benefits from the agile system, Imaging Solutions had to transform its culture somewhat by modifying the role of managers and individual contributors on scrum teams. For example, managers can no longer use a command-and-control style of management. Instead, they must concentrate on assembling empowered teams.

These cultural and process changes have generated positive results for Imaging Solutions. Obtaining user feedback early and often has enabled the company to prioritize features correctly. For instance, in one example, the new system helped a team identify a clinical workflow it previously was not aware of. Insights such as this one will continue to allow Imaging Solutions to develop products that will be successful in the market and to release those products in a timely manner, thereby increasing the company's profitability as well as its credibility.

Sources: Compiled from "Advanced Imaging Solutions for the Surgical Space," *GE Healthcare News*, November 30, 2012; S. Denning, "GE Healthcare Gets Agile," *Forbes*, June 1, 2012; R. King, "GE Becomes More Agile," *The Wall Street Journal*, May 30, 2012; K. Liang, "What Jobs Are Available for Software Engineers Who Want to Advance Medical Research?" *Forbes*, March 2, 2012; J. Hammond, "Customer-Centric Development: It's Now or Never for IT Shops," *InformationWeek*, April 26, 2011; S. Denning, "Six Common Mistakes That Salesforce.com Didn't Make," *Forbes*, April 18, 2011; A. Deitsch and R. Hughes, "GE Healthcare Goes Agile," *InformationWeek*, December 6, 2010; J. Vijayan, "The Grill: John Burke," *Computerworld*, September 13, 2010; J. Kobelius, "Agile Data Warehousing: Do You Scrum?" *InformationWeek*, July 21, 2010; www.ge.com, www.gehealthcare.com, www.rallydev.com, accessed March 17, 2013.

Questions

1. Why is it so important that Imaging Solutions become more responsive and flexible? How does your answer to this question relate to Imaging Solutions moving to agile development?

2. Search for the phrase *scope creep,* and relate your findings to systems development in the Imaging Systems unit of GE. How would this phenomenon cause a problem in the acquisition and implementation of information systems?

Tools for Systems Development

Several tools can be used with various systems development methods. These tools include prototyping, integrated computer-assisted software engineering (ICASE), component-based development, and object-oriented development.

Prototyping.   The **prototyping** approach defines an initial list of user requirements, builds a model of the system, and then refines the system in several iterations based on users' feedback. Developers do not try to obtain a complete set of user specifications for the system at the outset, and they do not plan to develop the system all at once. Instead, they quickly develop a smaller version of the system known as a **prototype**. A prototype can take two forms. In some cases, it contains only the components of the new system that are of most interest to the users. In other cases, it is a small-scale working model of the entire system.

Users make suggestions for improving the prototype, based on their experiences with it. The developers then review the prototype with the users and utilize their suggestions to refine the prototype. This process continues through several iterations either until the users approve the system or it becomes apparent that the system cannot meet the users' needs. If the system is viable, then the developers can use the prototype to build the full system. One typical use of prototyping is to develop screens that a user will see and interact with. Table 13.2 describes the advantages and disadvantages of the prototyping approach.

A practical problem with prototyping is that a prototype usually looks more complete than it is. That is, it may not use the real database, it usually does not have the necessary error checking, and it almost never includes the necessary security features. Users who review a prototype that resembles the finished system may not recognize these problems. Consequently, they might have unrealistic expectations about how close the actual system is to completion.

Integrated Computer-Assisted Software Engineering Tools.   **Computer-aided software engineering (CASE)** refers to a group of tools that automate many of the tasks in the SDLC. The tools that are used to automate the early stages of the SDLC (systems investigation, analysis, and design) are called **upper CASE tools**. The tools used to automate later stages in the SDLC (programming, testing, operation, and maintenance) are called **lower CASE tools**. CASE tools that provide links between upper CASE and lower CASE tools are called **integrated CASE (ICASE) tools**. Table 13.2 lists the advantages and disadvantages of ICASE tools.

Component-Based Development.   **Component-based development** uses standard components to build applications. Components are reusable applications that generally have one specific function, such as a shopping cart, user authentication, or a catalog. Compared with other approaches, component-based development generally involves less programming and more assembly. Component-based development is closely linked with the idea of Web services and service-oriented architectures, which you will study in Technology Guide 3.

Many startup companies are pursuing the idea of component-based application development. One example is Ning (www.ning.com), which allows organizations to create, customize, and share their own social network.

Object-Oriented Development.   **Object-oriented development** is based on a different view of computer systems than the perception that characterizes traditional development approaches. Traditional approaches can produce a system that performs the original task but may not be suited for handling other tasks. This limitation applies even when these other tasks involve the same real-world entities. For example, a billing system will handle billing, but it probably cannot be adapted to handle mailings for the marketing department or to generate leads for the sales force. This is true even though the billing, marketing, and sales functions all use similar data, including customer names, addresses, and purchases. In contrast, an *object-oriented (OO) system* begins not with the task to be performed, but with the aspects of the real world that must be modeled to perform that task. Therefore, in our example, if the firm has a good model of its customers and its interactions with them, then it can use this model equally well for billings, mailings, and sales leads.

The development process for an object-oriented system begins with a feasibility study and an analysis of the existing system. Systems developers identify the *objects* in the new system—the fundamental elements in OO analysis and design. Each object represents a tangible, real-world entity, such as a customer, bank account, student, or course. Objects have *properties*, or *data values*. For example, a customer has an identification number, a name, an address, an account number(s), and so on. Objects also contain the *operations* that can be performed on their properties. For example, operations that can be performed on the customer object may include obtain-account-balance, open-account, withdraw-funds, and so on. Operations are also referred to as *behaviors*.

This approach enables OO analysts to define all the relevant objects needed for the new system, including their properties and operations. The analysts then model how the objects interact to meet the objectives of the new system. In some cases, analysts can reuse existing objects from other applications (or from a library of objects) in the new system. This process saves the analysts the time they otherwise would spend coding these objects. In most cases, however, even with object reuse, some coding will be necessary to customize the objects and their interactions for the new system.

You have studied many methods that can be used to acquire new systems. Table 13.2 provides an overview of the advantages and disadvantages of each of these methods.

before you go on...

1. Describe the tools that augment the traditional SDLC.
2. Describe the alternate methods that can be used for systems development other than the SDLC.

What's In IT For Me?

ACCT

For the Accounting Major

Accounting personnel help perform the cost–benefit analyses on proposed projects. They may also monitor ongoing project costs to keep them within budget. Accounting personnel undoubtedly will find themselves involved with systems development at various points throughout their careers.

FIN

For the Finance Major

Finance personnel are frequently involved with the financial issues that accompany any large-scale systems development project (e.g., budgeting). They also are involved in cost–benefit and risk analyses. To perform these tasks they need to stay abreast of the emerging techniques used to determine project costs and ROI. Finally, because they must manage vast amounts of information, finance departments are also common recipients of new systems.

MKT

For the Marketing Major

In most organizations, marketing, like finance, involves massive amounts of data and information. Like finance, then, marketing is also a hotbed of systems development. Marketing personnel will increasingly find themselves participating on systems development teams. Such involvement increasingly means helping to develop systems, especially Web-based systems that reach out directly from the organization to its customers.

POM For the Production/Operations Management Major

Participation on development teams is also a common role for production/operations people. Manufacturing is becoming increasingly computerized and integrated with other allied systems, from design to logistics to customer support. Production systems interface frequently with marketing, finance, and human resources. In addition, they may be part of a larger, enterprisewide system. Also, many end users in POM either develop their own systems or collaborate with IT personnel on specific applications.

HRM For the Human Resources Management Major

The human resources department is closely involved with several aspects of the systems acquisitions process. Acquiring new systems may require hiring new employees, changing job descriptions, or terminating employees. Human resources staff performs all of these tasks. Further, if the organization hires consultants for the development project, or outsources it, the human resources department may handle the contracts with these suppliers.

MIS For the MIS Major

Regardless of the approach that the organization adopts for acquiring new systems, the MIS department spearheads it. If the organization chooses either to buy or to lease the application, the MIS department leads in examining the offerings of the various vendors and in negotiating with the vendors. If the organization chooses to develop the application in-house, then the process falls to the MIS department. MIS analysts work closely with users to develop their information requirements. MIS programmers then write the computer code, test it, and implement the new system.

[Summary]

1. **Discuss the different cost/benefit analyses that companies must take into account when formulating an IT strategic plan.**

   The four common approaches to cost–benefit analysis are these:

   - *The net present value* (NPV) method converts future values of benefits to their present-value equivalent by "discounting" them at the organization's cost of funds. They can then compare the present value of the future benefits to the cost required to achieve those benefits to determine whether the benefits exceed the costs.
   - *Return on investment* (ROI) measures management's effectiveness in generating profits with its available assets. ROI is calculated by dividing net income attributable to a project by the average assets invested in the project. ROI is a percentage, and the higher the percentage return, the better.
   - *Breakeven analysis* determines the point at which the cumulative dollar value of the benefits from a project equals the investment made in the project.
   - In the *business case approach*, system developers write a business case to justify funding one or more specific applications or projects.

2. **Discuss the four business decisions that companies must make when they acquire new applications.**

   - *How much computer code does the company want to write?* A company can choose to use a totally prewritten application (to write no computer code), to customize a prewritten application (to write some computer code), or to customize an entire application (write all new computer code).
   - *How will the company pay for the application?* Once the company has decided how much computer code to write, it must decide how to pay for it. With prewritten applications or customized prewritten applications, companies can buy them or lease them. With totally custom applications, companies use internal funding.
   - *Where will the application run?* Companies must now decide where to run the application. The company may run the application on its own platform or run the application on someone else's platform (use either a software-as-a-service vendor or an application service provider).
   - *Where will the application originate?* Prewritten applications can be open-source software or come from a vendor. Companies may choose to customize prewritten open-source applications or prewritten proprietary applications from vendors. Companies may customize applications in-house or outsource the customization. They also can write totally custom applications in-house or outsource this process.

3. **Enumerate the primary tasks and importance of each of the six processes involved in the systems development life cycle.**

   The six processes are these:

   - *Systems investigation:* Addresses the business problem (or business opportunity) by means of the feasibility study; main task in the systems investigation stage is the feasibility study.
   - *Systems analysis:* Examines the business problem that the organization plans to solve with an information system; main purpose is to gather information about the existing system in order to determine the requirements for the new system; end product of this stage, known as the "deliverable," is a set of system requirements.
   - *Systems design:* Describes how the system will resolve the business problem; deliverable is the set of technical system specifications.
   - *Programming and testing:* Programming translates the design specifications into computer code; testing checks to see if the computer code will produce the expected and desired results and detects errors, or bugs, in the computer code; deliverable is the new application.
   - *Implementation:* The process of converting from the old system to the new system via three major conversion strategies: direct, pilot, and phased; deliverable is properly working application.
   - *Operation and maintenance:* Types of maintenance include debugging, updating, and adding new functions when needed.

4. **Describe alternative development methods and tools that augment development methods.**

   These are the *alternative methods*:

   - *Joint application design* (JAD) is a group-based tool for collecting user requirements and creating system designs.
   - *Rapid application development* (RAD) is a systems development method that can combine JAD, prototyping, and ICASE tools to rapidly produce a high-quality system.
   - *Agile development* is a software development methodology that delivers functionality in rapid iterations, which are usually measured in weeks.
   - *End-user development* refers to an organization's end users developing their own applications with little or no formal assistance from the IT department.

These are the *tools*:

- The *prototyping* approach defines an initial list of user requirements, builds a model of the system, and then improves the system in several iterations based on users' feedback.
- *Integrated computer-aided software engineering (ICASE)* combines upper CASE tools (automate systems investigation, analysis, and design) and lower CASE tools (programming, testing, operation, and maintenance).
- *Component-based development* uses standard components to build applications. Components are reusable applications that generally have one specific function, such as a shopping cart, user authentication, or a catalog.
- *Object-oriented development* begins with the aspects of the real world that must be modeled to perform that task. Systems developers identify the *objects* in the new system. Each object represents a tangible, real-world entity, such as a customer, bank account, student, or course. Objects have *properties*, or *data values*. Objects also contain the *operations* that can be performed on their properties.

Table 13.2 shows advantages and disadvantages of alternative methods and tools.

5. **Analyze the process of vendor and software selection.**

The process of vendor and software selection is composed of six steps:

- Identify potential vendors.
- Determine evaluation criteria.
- Evaluate vendors and packages.
- Choose the vendor and package.
- Negotiate a contract.
- Establish service-level agreements.

[Chapter Glossary]

agile development A software development methodology that delivers functionality in rapid iterations, measured in weeks, requiring frequent communication, development, testing, and delivery.

application portfolio The set of recommended applications resulting from the planning and justification process in application development.

application service provider (ASP) An agent or vendor who assembles the software needed by enterprises and packages them with outsourced development, operations, maintenance, and other services.

component-based development A software development methodology that uses standard components to build applications.

computer-aided software engineering (CASE) Development approach that uses specialized tools to automate many of the tasks in the SDLC; upper CASE tools automate the early stages of the SDLC and lower CASE tools automate the later stages.

direct conversion Implementation process in which the old system is cut off and the new system is turned on at a certain point in time.

end-user development Approach in which the organization's end users develop their own applications with little or no formal assistance from the IT department.

feasibility study Investigation that gauges the probability of success of a proposed project and provides a rough assessment of the project's feasibility.

implementation The process of converting from an old computer system to a new one.

integrated CASE (ICASE) tools CASE tools that provide links between upper CASE and lower CASE tools.

IS operational plan Consists of a clear set of projects that the IS department and the functional area managers will execute in support of the IT strategic plan.

IT steering committee A committee, comprised of a group of managers and staff representing various organizational units, set up to establish IT priorities and to ensure that the MIS function is meeting the needs of the enterprise.

IT strategic plan A set of long-range goals that describe the IT infrastructure and major IT initiatives needed to achieve the goals of the organization.

joint application design (JAD) A group-based tool for collecting user requirements and creating system designs.

lower CASE tools Tools used to automate later stages in the SDLC (programming, testing, operation, and maintenance)

object-oriented development A systems development methodology that begins with aspects of the real world that must be modeled to perform a task.

outsourcing Use of outside contractors or external organizations to acquire IT services.

phased conversion Implementation process that introduces components of the new system in stages, until the entire new system is operational.

pilot conversion Implementation process that introduces the new system in one part of the organization on a trial basis; when the new system is working properly, it is introduced in other parts of the organization.

programmers IS professionals who modify existing computer programs or write new computer programs to satisfy user requirements.

programming The translation of a system's design specifications into computer code.

prototype A small-scale working model of an entire system or a model that contains only the components of the new system that are of most interest to the users.

prototyping An approach that defines an initial list of user requirements, builds a prototype system, and then improves the system in several iterations based on users' feedback.

rapid application development (RAD) A development method that uses special tools and an iterative approach to rapidly produce a high-quality system.

request for proposal (RFP) Document that is sent to potential vendors inviting them to submit a proposal describing their software package and how it would meet the company's needs.

scope creep Adding functions to an information system after the project has begun.

service-level agreements (SLAs) Formal agreements regarding the division of work between a company and its vendors.

software-as-a-service (SaaS) A method of delivering software in which a vendor hosts the applications and provides them as a service to customers over a network, typically the Internet.

systems analysis The examination of the business problem that the organization plans to solve with an information system.

systems analysts IS professionals who specialize in analyzing and designing information systems.

systems design Describes how the new system will resolve the business problem.

systems development life cycle (SDLC) Traditional structured framework, used for large IT projects, that consists of sequential processes by which information systems are developed.

systems investigation The initial stage in the traditional SDLC that addresses the business problem (or business opportunity) by means of the feasibility study.

systems stakeholders All people who are affected by changes in information systems.

technical specialists Experts on a certain type of technology, such as databases or telecommunications.

upper CASE tools Tools that are used to automate the early stages of the SDLC (systems investigation, analysis, and design).

[Discussion Questions]

1. Discuss the advantages of a lease option over a buy option.
2. Why is it important for all business managers to understand the issues of IT resource acquisition?
3. Why is it important for everyone in business organizations to have a basic understanding of the systems development process?
4. Should prototyping be used on every systems development project? Why or why not?
5. Discuss the various types of feasibility studies. Why are they all needed?
6. Discuss the issue of assessing intangible benefits and the proposed solutions.
7. Discuss the reasons why end-user-developed information systems can be of poor quality. What can be done to improve this situation?

[Problem-Solving Activities]

1. Access *www.ecommerce-guide.com*. Find the product review area. Read reviews of three software payment solutions. Assess them as possible components.
2. Use an Internet search engine to obtain information on CASE and ICASE tools. Select several vendors and compare and contrast their offerings.
3. Access *www.ning.com*. Observe how the site provides components for you to use to build applications. Build a small application at the site.
4. Enter *www-01.ibm.com/software*. Find its WebSphere product. Read recent customers' success stories. What makes this software so popular?
5. Enter the Web sites of the Gartner (*www.gartner.com*), the Yankee Group (*www.yankeegroup.com*), and CIO (*www .cio.com*). Search for recent material about ASPs and outsourcing, and prepare a report on your findings.
6. StoreFront (*www.storefront.net*) is a vendor of e-business software. At its site, the company provides demonstrations

illustrating the types of storefronts that it can create for shoppers. The site also provides demonstrations of how the company's software is used to create a store.

a. Run the StoreFront demonstration to see how this is done.

b. What features does StoreFront provide?

c. Does StoreFront support smaller or larger stores?

d. What other products does StoreFront offer for creating online stores? What types of stores do these products support?

Collaboration Exercise

Background

System acquisition and implementation is as important to the life of information system as is anything else. The right decision could be made about what is needed, but if the implementation of that system is not successful, the whole exercise is in vain. This chapter has covered many techniques for developing and implementing information systems, all of which apply to different needs and situations.

Activity

If you completed the Collaboration Exercise for Chapter 13, assemble that same group and complete this exercise. If you did not, please review the requirements for that activity. You will visit a local business and learn about its' supply chain management systems.

Once you have done this (no matter if it was for Chapter 13 or not), imagine that this company is going to develop and implement a new supply chain management system. The business has chosen to use the SDLC and has created a team of employees (your team) to layout the plan of attack. For this particular business situation, imagine how the SDLC would play out.

Ultimately, provide feedback as to whether or not the SDLC was the best pick for that business in that industry.

Deliverable

Work with your group to lay out the steps of the SDLC for the project implementation you have learned about. Submit your outline and your recommendation on acquisition methods to your professor.

[Closing Case **Putting It All Together**]   MIS

The Problem

With a net worth of $50 billion, Chubb Insurance (www.chubb.com) is the 11th largest property and casualty insurer in the United States. Rather than being guided by an overall vision, Chubb had, over the years, implemented its information systems on an ad hoc basis. Every business unit within the company had its own information systems and information systems plan. Chubb was therefore faced with the task of learning which information systems functioned most effectively at the corporate level and which ones performed best within the individual units.

The Solution

Chubb's senior corporate IT leadership determined that the company needed an overall strategic IT plan to make its information systems more effective. After meeting with IT leadership in each of the business units to hear different perspectives on how such a plan could be implemented, they selected a team to implement the overall strategic plan. The team was composed of leaders from IT and from the company's business units.

Team members spent a great deal of time with IT managers in the different business units, explaining why a federated architecture was so important to Chubb. A *federated architecture* is an IT strategic plan that clearly distinguishes the functional responsibilities of corporate information systems from those of the individual business ISs while promoting collaboration and information sharing among all of the systems.

Chubb based its federated architecture on The Open Group Architecture Framework (TOGAF). TOGAF is a framework for planning, designing, implementing, and governing an enterprise's information systems.

The team compared the overall plan for Chubb's portfolio of applications with a city plan. Applications are linked with "city blocks" that represent Chubb's business capabilities (e.g., marketing and sales, claims, etc.). All new information systems projects must obtain a "building permit" to ensure that they are following corporate standards and are not duplicating other IT efforts, either at the corporate level or in other business units. If an employee wants to use a technology that is nonstandard at Chubb, then he or she needs to request a "variance."

Business-unit review boards enforce corporate IT standards at Chubb for new applications within each unit. Each board scrutinizes new applications for certain characteristics, including efficiency, value, a focus on the needs of the business unit, and funding.

The Results

The strategic IT plan and federated architecture model have provided many benefits for Chubb. Because Chubb's plan and architecture demonstrate how data, technologies, applications, and business capabilities fit together, IT leaders in each line of the business can communicate with their non-IT business colleagues about where and how IT is investing in the capabilities they need. This process has increased IT's credibility because managers have confidence that Chubb is selecting the correct technologies to match their business needs.

The strategic IT plan also helps to identify opportunities to share common tools and processes across lines of business. For example, in only one year, Chubb saved $600,000 by redistributing unused site licenses for software. Using its strategic IT plan and federated architecture, Chubb is able to quickly make decisions about new products that result in large savings and quick launch-to-market time.

Sources: M. Weiss, "One Enterprise Architecture to Rule Them All," *Baseline Magazine*, March 1, 2012; Broderick, M. "Will TOGAF Guarantee Business Success?"

Articles Factory, November 15, 2011; M. Heller, "Making Enterprise Architecture Matter," *CIO*, April 27, 2011; www.chubb.com, accessed March 5, 2013.

Questions

1. Review the section in Chapter 1 on Managing Information Resources. Based on your review, which information systems capabilities should Chubb keep at the corporate level? Justify each one.

2. Based on your review, which information systems capabilities should Chubb keep in the business units? Justify each one.

[Internship Activity]

Manufacturing Industry

Interestingly enough, sometimes software is chosen (or not chosen rather) based on legal negotiations that fall apart. As you have seen in this chapter, both parties in the transaction of proprietary software must agree upon a Service Level Agreement (SLA). In personal software purchases, the software provider specifies the terms and conditions and the end user simply accepts them. For a business-to-business transaction, however, it is much more complicated.

Chad Prince, Practice Administrator of Anniston Orthopaedics, is facing serious legal issues negotiating the fine print with his chosen software vendor. In healthcare, patient information and privacy is of utmost importance. You can not be too careful when running someone else's software in a "cloud" hosted by another provider, all the while maintaining privacy of your patient data.

Please visit the Book Companion Site to receive the full set of instructions and learn how you can help Chad navigate this difficult situation.

Technology Guide ①

Hardware

[LEARNING OBJECTIVES]	[TECHNOLOGY GUIDE OUTLINE]	[WEB RESOURCES]
1. Identify the major hardware components of a computer system.	TG 1.1 Introduction	• Student PowerPoints for note taking
2. Discuss strategic issues that link hardware design to business strategy.	TG 1.2 Strategic Hardware Issues	**WileyPLUS**
3. Describe the hierarchy of computers according to power and their respective roles.	TG 1.3 Computer Hierarchy	• E-book
4. Differentiate the various types of input and output technologies and their uses.	TG 1.4 Input and Output Technologies	• Author video lecture for each chapter section
5. Describe the design and functioning of the central processing unit.	TG 1.5 The Central Processing Unit	• Practice quizzes
6. Discuss the relationships between microprocessor component designs and performance.		• Flash Cards for vocabulary review
7. Describe the main types of primary and secondary storage.		• Additional "IT's About Business" cases
8. Distinguish between primary and secondary storage along the dimensions of speed, cost, and capacity.		• Video interviews with managers
		• Lab Manuals for Microsoft Office 2010 and 2013

What's In IT For Me?

This Tech Guide Will Help Prepare You To...

ACCT	FIN	MKT	POM	HRM	MIS
ACCOUNTING	FINANCE	MARKETING	PRODUCTION OPERATIONS MANAGEMENT	HUMAN RESOURCES MANAGEMENT	MIS

As you begin this Technology Guide, you might be wondering, why do I have to know anything about hardware? There are several reasons why you will benefit from understanding the basics of hardware. First, regardless of your major (and future functional area in an organization), you will be using different types of hardware throughout your career. Second, you will have input concerning the hardware you will use. In this capacity you will be required to answer many questions, such as "Is my hardware performing adequately for my needs? If not, what types of problems am I experiencing?" Third, you will also have input into decisions when your functional area or organization upgrades or replaces its hardware. MIS employees will act as advisors, but you will provide important input into such decisions. Finally, in some organizations, the budget for hardware is allocated to functional areas or departments. In such cases, you might be making hardware decisions (at least locally) yourself.

This Technology Guide will help you better understand the hardware decisions your organization must make as well as your personal computing decisions. Many of the design principles presented here apply to systems of all sizes, from an enterprisewide system to your home computer system. In addition, the dynamics of innovation and cost that you will read about can affect personal as well as corporate hardware decisions.

Introduction to Hardware

TG 1.1

Recall from Chapter 1 that the term hardware refers to the physical equipment used for the input, processing, output, and storage activities of a computer system. Decisions about hardware focus on three interrelated factors: appropriateness for the task, speed, and cost. The incredibly rapid rate of innovation in the computer industry complicates hardware decisions because computer technologies become obsolete more quickly than other organizational technologies.

The overall trends in hardware are that it becomes smaller, faster, cheaper, and more powerful over time. In fact, these trends are so rapid that they make it difficult to know when to purchase (or upgrade) hardware. This difficulty lies in the fact that companies that delay hardware purchases will, more than likely, be able to buy more powerful hardware for the same amount of money in the future. It is important to note that buying more powerful hardware for the same amount of money in the future is a trade-off. An organization that delays purchasing computer hardware gives up the benefits of whatever it could buy today until the future purchase date arrives.

Hardware consists of the following:

- *Central processing unit (CPU).* Manipulates the data and controls the tasks performed by the other components.
- *Primary storage.* Temporarily stores data and program instructions during processing.
- *Secondary storage.* Stores data and programs for future use.
- *Input technologies.* Accept data and instructions and convert them to a form that the computer can understand.
- *Output technologies.* Present data and information in a form people can understand.
- *Communication technologies.* Provide for the flow of data from external computer networks (e.g., the Internet and intranets) to the CPU, and from the CPU to computer networks.

TG 1.2 Strategic Hardware Issues

For most businesspeople the most important issues are what the hardware enables, how it is advancing, and how rapidly it is advancing. In many industries, exploiting computer hardware is a key to achieving competitive advantage. Successful hardware exploitation comes from thoughtful consideration of the following questions:

- How do organizations keep up with the rapid price reductions and performance advancements in hardware? For example, how often should an organization upgrade its computers and storage systems? Will upgrades increase personal and organizational productivity? How can organizations measure such increases?
- How should organizations determine the need for the new hardware infrastructures, such as server farms, virtualization, grid computing, and utility computing? (We discuss these technologies in Technology Guide 3.)
- Portable computers and advanced communications technologies have enabled employees to work from home or from anywhere. Will these new work styles benefit employees and the organization? How do organizations manage such new work styles?

TG 1.3 Computer Hierarchy

The traditional standard for comparing classes of computers is their processing power. This section presents each class of computers, from the most powerful to the least powerful. It describes both the computers and their roles in modern organizations.

Supercomputers

The term **supercomputer** does not refer to a specific technology. Rather, it indicates the fastest computers available at any given time. At the time of this writing (mid-2013), the fastest supercomputers had speeds exceeding 1 petaflop (1 petaflop is 1,000 trillion floating point operations per second). A floating point operation is an arithmetic operation that involves decimals.

Because supercomputers are costly as well as very fast, they are generally used by large organizations to execute computationally demanding tasks involving very large data sets. In contrast to mainframes, which specialize in transaction processing and business applications, supercomputers typically run military and scientific applications. Although they cost millions of dollars, they are also being used for commercial applications where huge amounts of data must be analyzed. For example, large banks use supercomputers to calculate the risks and returns of various investment strategies, and healthcare organizations use them to analyze giant databases of patient data to determine optimal treatments for various diseases.

Mainframe Computers

Although mainframe computers are increasingly viewed as just another type of server, albeit at the high end of the performance and reliability scales, they remain a distinct class of systems differentiated by hardware and software features. **Mainframes** remain popular in large enterprises for extensive computing applications that are accessed by thousands of users at one time. Examples of mainframe applications are airline reservation systems, corporate payroll programs, Web site transaction processing systems (e.g., Amazon and eBay), and student grade calculation and reporting.

Today's mainframes perform at teraflop (trillions of floating point operations per second) speeds and can handle millions of transactions per day. In addition, mainframes provide a secure, robust environment in which to run strategic, mission-critical applications.

Midrange Computers

Larger midrange computers, called **minicomputers**, are relatively small, inexpensive, and compact computers that perform the same functions as mainframe computers, but to a more limited extent. In fact, the lines between minicomputers and mainframes have blurred in both price and performance. Minicomputers are a type of server—that is, a computer that supports computer networks and enables users to share files, software, peripheral devices, and other resources. Mainframes are a type of server as well because they provide support for entire enterprise networks.

Microcomputers

Microcomputers—also called micros, personal computers, or PCs—are the smallest and least expensive category of general-purpose computers. It is important to point out that people frequently define a PC as a computer that utilizes the Microsoft Windows operating system. In fact, a variety of PCs are available, and many of them do not use Windows. One well-known example is Apple Macs, which use the Mac OS X operating system (discussed in Technology Guide 2). The major categories of microcomputers are desktops, thin clients, notebooks and laptops, netbooks, and tablets.

Desktop PCs The desktop personal computer is the familiar microcomputer system that has become a standard tool for business and the home. A desktop generally includes a central processing unit (CPU)—which you will learn about later—and a separate but connected monitor and keyboard. Modern desktop computers have gigabytes of primary storage, a rewriteable CD-ROM drive and a DVD drive, and up to several terabytes of secondary storage. Today, desktops are being replaced with portable devices such as laptops, netbooks, and tablets.

Thin-Client Systems Before you address thin-client systems, recall that servers are computers that provide a variety of services for clients, including running networks, processing Web sites, processing e-mail, and many other functions. Clients are typically computers on which users perform their tasks, such as word processing, spreadsheets, and others.

Thin-client systems are desktop computer systems that do not offer the full functionality of a PC. Compared to PCs, or **fat clients**, thin clients are less complex, particularly because they do not have locally installed software. When thin clients need to run an application, they access it from a server over a network instead of from a local disk drive.

For example, a thin client would not have Microsoft Office installed on it. Thus, thin clients are easier and less expensive to operate and support than PCs. The benefits of thin clients include fast application deployment, centralized management, lower cost of ownership, and

FIGURE TG 1.1 Laptop, notebook, and tablet computers.

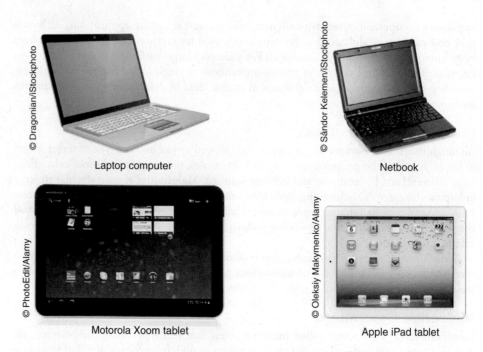

Laptop computer

Netbook

Motorola Xoom tablet

Apple iPad tablet

easier installation, management, maintenance, and support. The main disadvantage of thin clients is that if the network fails, then users can do very little on their computers. In contrast, if users have fat clients and the network fails, they can still perform some functions because they have software, such as Microsoft Office, installed on their computers.

Laptop and Notebook Computers **Laptop computers** (or **notebook computers**) are small, easily transportable, lightweight microcomputers that fit comfortably into a briefcase (Figure TG 1.1). Notebooks and laptops are designed to be as convenient and easy to transport as possible. Just as important, they also provide users with access to processing power and data outside an office environment. However, they cost more than desktops for similar functionality.

Netbooks A **netbook** is a very small, lightweight, low-cost, energy-efficient, portable computer. Netbooks are generally optimized for Internet-based services such as Web browsing and e-mail.

Tablet Computers A **tablet computer** (or **tablet**) is a complete computer contained entirely in a flat touch screen that users operate via a stylus, digital pen, or fingertip instead of a keyboard or mouse. Examples of tablets are the Apple iPad 3 (www.apple.com/ipad), the HP Slate 2 (www.hp.com), the Toshiba Thrive (www.toshiba.com), and the Motorola Xoom 2 (www.motorola.com).

Wearable Computers

Wearable computers are miniature computers that people wear under, with, or on top of their clothing. Key features of wearable computers are that there is constant interaction between the computer and the users and that the users can multitask, meaning they do not have to stop what they are doing to utilize the device. Examples of wearable computers are the iPod Nano (www.apple.com/ipod-nano) with a wristwatch attachment, the Sony SmartWatch (www.sony.com/SmartWatch), the Apple iWatch (planned for release in mid-to-late 2013), Google Glass, and Vuzix (www.vuzix.com) M100Smart Glasses (a Google Glass competitor). For a closer look at Google Glass (www.google.com/glass/start), see IT's About Business 3.3.

Google Glass is an excellent example of a device that provides augmented reality. **Augmented reality** is a live, direct or indirect, view of a physical, real-world environment whose elements are augmented, or enhanced, by computer-generated sensory input such as sound, video, graphics, or GPS data. That is, augmented reality enhances the user's perception of reality. Note that in contrast, virtual reality replaces the real world with a simulated world.

As an example of augmented reality with Google Glass, let's say that you are looking for a destination in an unfamiliar city. You ask Google Glass for directions, and the device will overlay your vision with a graphic display of a street map, with the route to your destination highlighted.

IT's Personal: Purchasing a Computer

One day you will purchase a computer for yourself or your job. When that day comes, it will be important for you to know what to look for. Buying a computer can be very confusing if you just read the box. This Technology Guide has explained the major hardware components of a computer. There are more things you need to consider, however, when you purchase a computer: what you plan to do with it, where you plan to use it, and how long you need service from it. Let's look at each question more closely.

- What do you plan to do with your computer? Consider that when you buy a vehicle, your plans for using the vehicle determine the type of vehicle you will purchase. The same rules apply to purchasing a computer. You need to consider what you currently do with a computer and what you may do before you replace the one under consideration. Although many people simply buy as much as they can afford, they may overpay because they do not consider what they need the computer for.

- Where do you plan to use your computer? If you only plan to use it at home at your desk, then a desktop model will be fine. In general, you can get more computer for your money in a desktop model as opposed to a laptop (i.e., you pay extra for mobility). However, if you think you may want to take the computer with you, then you will need some type of a laptop or tablet computer. When portability is a requirement, you will want to reconsider what you plan to use the computer for because as computers become more portable (smaller), their functionality changes, and you want to make sure the computer will meet your needs.

- How long do you need service from this computer? Today, we anticipate that most of the devices we purchase will become outdated and need to be replaced in a few years. Therefore, the length of service is really more about warranty and the availability of repair services. In some cases, you should base your purchase decision on these issues rather than speed because they can extend the life of your computer.

Input and Output Technologies

TG 1.4

Input technologies allow people and other technologies to enter data into a computer. The two main types of input devices are human data-entry devices and source-data automation devices. As their name implies, human data-entry devices require a certain amount of human effort to input data. Examples are keyboard, mouse, pointing stick, trackball, joystick, touch screen, stylus, and voice recognition.

In contrast, source-data automation devices input data with minimal human intervention. These technologies speed up data collection, reduce errors, and gather data at the source of a transaction or other event. Bar code readers are an example of source-data automation. Table TG 1.1 describes the various input devices.

The output generated by a computer can be transmitted to the user via several output devices and media. These devices include monitors, printers, plotters, and voice. Table TG 1.2 describes the various output devices.

Multimedia technology is the computer-based integration of text, sound, still images, animation, and digitized motion video. It usually consists of a collection of various input and output technologies. Multimedia merges the capabilities of computers with televisions, CD players, DVD players, video and audio recording equipment, and music and gaming technologies. High-quality multimedia processing requires powerful microprocessors and extensive memory capacity, including both primary and secondary storage.

Table TG 1.1
Input Devices

Input Device	Description
Human Data-Entry Devices	
Keyboards	Most common input device (for text and numerical data).
Mouse	Handheld device used to point the cursor at a point on screen, such as an icon; the user clicks a button on the mouse, instructing the computer to take some action.
Optical mouse	The mouse is not connected to computer by a cable; rather, it uses camera chip to take images of surface it passes over, comparing successive images to determine its position.
Trackball	User rotates a ball built into top of device to move the cursor (rather than moving an entire device such as a mouse).
Pointing stick	Small button-like device; the cursor moves in the direction of the pressure the user places on the stick. Located between the keys near the center of the keyboard.
Touchpad	User moves the cursor by sliding a finger across a sensitized pad and then can tap the pad when the cursor is in (also called a trackpad) the desired position to instruct the computer to take action (also called *glide-and-tap pad*).
Graphics tablet	A device that can be used in place of, or in conjunction with, a mouse or trackball; it has a flat surface for drawing and a pen or stylus that is programmed to work with the tablet.
Joystick	The joystick moves the cursor to the desired place on the screen; commonly used in video games and in workstations that display dynamic graphics.
Touch screen	Users instruct computer to take some action by touching a particular part of the screen; commonly used in information kiosks such as ATM machines. Touch screens now have gesture controls for browsing through photographs, moving objects around on a screen, flicking to turn the page of a book, and playing video games. For example, see the Apple iPhone.
Stylus	Pen-style device that allows user either to touch parts of a predetermined menu of options or to handwrite information into the computer (as with some PDAs); works with touch-sensitive screens.
Digital pen	Mobile device that digitally captures everything you write; built-in screen confirms that what you write has been saved; also captures sketches, figures, and so on with on-board flash memory.
Web camera (Webcam)	A real-time video camera whose images can be accessed via the Web or instant messaging.
Voice-recognition	Microphone converts analog voice sounds into digital input for a computer; critical technology for physically challenged people who cannot use other input devices.

Table **TG 1.1** (Continued)

Input Device	Description
Gesture-Based Input	

Gesture recognition refers to technologies that enable computers to interpret human gestures. These technologies would be the first step in designing computers that can understand human body language. This process creates a richer interaction between machines and humans than has been possible via keyboards, graphical user interfaces, and the mouse. Gesture recognition enables humans to interact naturally with a computer without any intervening mechanical devices. With gesture-based technologies, the user can move the cursor by pointing a finger at a computer screen. These technologies could make conventional input devices (the mouse, keyboards, and touch screens) redundant. Examples of gesture-based input devices are the Nintendo Wii (www.nintendo.com/wii), the Microsoft Kinect (www.xbox.com/kinect), and the Leap Motion controller (www.leapmotion.com).

Input Device	Description
Wii	A video game console produced by Nintendo. A distinguishing feature of the Wii is its wireless controller, which can be used as a handheld pointing device and can detect movement in three dimensions.
Microsoft Kinect	A device that enables users to control and interact with the Xbox 360 through a natural interface using gestures and spoken commands. Kinect eliminates the need for a game controller.
Leap Motion Controller	A motion-sensing, matchbox-sized device placed on a physical desktop. Using two cameras, the device "observes" an area up to a distance of about three feet. It precisely tracks fingers or items such as a pen that cross into the observed area. The Leap can perform tasks such as navigating a Web site, using pinch-to-zoom gestures on maps, performing high-precision drawing, and manipulating complex three-dimensional visualizations. The smaller observation area and higher resolution of the device differentiates it from the Microsoft Kinect, which is more suitable for whole-body tracking in a space the size of a living room.
Source-Data Automation Input Devices	
Automated teller machine (ATM)	A device that includes source-data automation input in the form of a magnetic stripe reader; human input via a keyboard; and output via a monitor, printer, and cash dispenser.
Magnetic stripe reader	A device that reads data from a magnetic stripe, usually on the back of a plastic card (e.g., credit and debit cards).
Point-of-sale terminals	Computerized cash registers that also may incorporate touch screen technology and bar code scanners to input data such as item sold and price.
Barcode scanners	Devices that scan black-and-white bar code lines printed on merchandise labels.
Optical mark reader	Scanner for detecting the presence of dark marks on a predetermined grid, such as multiple-choice test answer sheets.
Magnetic ink character reader	A device that reads magnetic ink printed on checks that identify the bank, checking account, and check number.
Optical character recognition	Software that converts text into digital form for input into computer.
Sensors	Devices that collect data directly from the environment and input data directly into computer; examples are vehicle airbag activation sensors and radio-frequency identification (RFID) tags.
Cameras	Digital cameras capture images and convert them into digital files.
Radio Frequency) Identification (RFID)	Uses technology that uses active or passive tags (transmitters) to wirelessly transmit product information to electronic readers. (We discuss RFID in detail in Chapter 8.

Table **TG 1.2**
Output Devices

Output Device	Description
Monitors	
Cathode ray tubes	Video screens on which an electron beam illuminates pixels on a display screen.
Liquid crystal display (LCDs)	Flat displays that have liquid crystals between two polarizers to form characters and images on a backlit screen.
Flexible displays	Thin, plastic, bendable computer screens.
Organic light-emitting diodes (OLEDs)	Displays that are brighter, thinner, lighter, cheaper, faster, and take less power to run displays than LCDs.
Retinal scanning displays	Project image directly onto a viewer's retina; used in medicine, air traffic control, and controlling industrial machines.
Heads-up displays	Any transparent display that presents data without requiring the user to look away from his or her usual viewpoint; for example, see Microvision (www.microvision.com).
Printers	
Laser	Use laser beams to write information on photosensitive drums; produce high-resolution text and graphics.
Inkjet	Shoot fine streams of colored ink onto paper; usually less expensive to buy than laser printers but can be more expensive to operate; can offer resolution quality equal to laser printers.
Thermal	Produces a printed image by selectively heating coated thermal paper; when the paper passes over the thermal print head, the coating turns black in the areas where it is heated, producing an image.
Plotters	Use computer-directed pens for creating high-quality images, blueprints, schematics, drawing of new products, and so on.
Voice Output	A speaker/headset that can output sounds of any type; voice output is a software function that uses this equipment.
Electronic Book Reader	A wireless, portable reading device with access to books, blogs, newspapers, and magazines. On-board storage holds hundreds of books (e.g., Amazon Kindle, Sony Reader, Barnes and Noble Nook).
Pocket Projector	A projector in a handheld device that provides an alternative display method to alleviate the problem of tiny display screens in handheld devices. Pocket projectors will project digital images onto any viewing surface (e.g., see the Pico Projector).

TG 1.5 The Central Processing Unit

The **central processing unit (CPU)** performs the actual computation or "number crunching" inside any computer. The CPU is a **microprocessor** (e.g., Intel's Core i3, i5, and i7 chips with more to come) made up of millions of microscopic transistors embedded in a circuit on a silicon wafer or chip. For this reason, microprocessors are commonly referred to as chips.

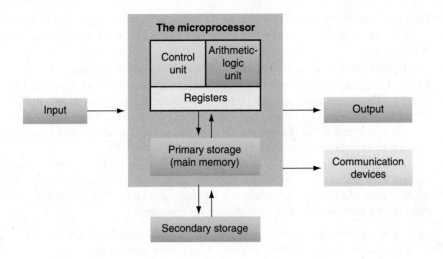

FIGURE TG 1.2 Parts of a microprocessor.

As shown in Figure TG 1.2, the microprocessor has different parts, which perform different functions. The **control unit** sequentially accesses program instructions, decodes them, and controls the flow of data to and from the arithmetic-logic unit, the registers, the caches, primary storage, secondary storage, and various output devices. The **arithmetic-logic unit (ALU)** performs the mathematic calculations and makes logical comparisons. The **registers** are high-speed storage areas that store very small amounts of data and instructions for short periods.

How the CPU Works

In the CPU, inputs enter and are stored until they are needed. At that point, they are retrieved and processed, and the output is stored and then delivered somewhere. Figure TG 1.3 illustrates this process, which works as follows:

- The inputs consist of data and brief instructions about what to do with the data. These instructions come into the CPU from random access memory (RAM). Data might be entered by the user through the keyboard, for example, or read from a data file in another part of the computer. The inputs are stored in registers until they are sent to the next step in the processing.

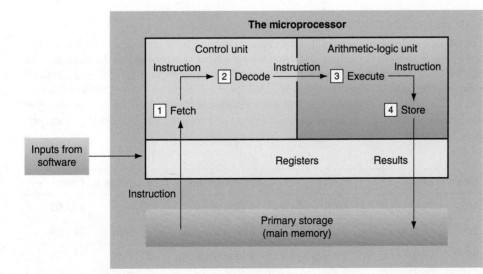

FIGURE TG 1.3 How the CPU works.

- Data and instructions travel in the chip via electrical pathways called *buses*. The size of the bus—analogous to the width of a highway—determines how much information can flow at any time.
- The control unit directs the flow of data and instructions within the chip.
- The ALU receives the data and instructions from the registers and makes the desired computation. These data and instructions have been translated into **binary form**—that is, only 0s and 1s. A "0" or a "1" is called a **bit**. The CPU can process only binary data. All types of data, such as letters, decimal numbers, photographs, music, and so on, can be converted to a binary representation, which can then be processed by the CPU.
- The data in their original form and the instructions are sent to storage registers and then are sent back to a storage place outside the chip, such as the computer's hard drive. Meanwhile, the transformed data go to another register and then on to other parts of the computer (to the monitor for display or to storage, for example).

Intel offers excellent demonstrations of how CPUs work: Search the web for "Intel" with "Explore the Curriculum" to find their demos. This cycle of processing, known as a machine instruction cycle, occurs billions of times per second.

Advances in Microprocessor Design

Innovations in chip designs are coming at a faster and faster rate, as described by **Moore's law**. In 1965, Gordon Moore, a cofounder of Intel Corporation, predicted that microprocessor complexity would double approximately every 2 years. His prediction has been amazingly accurate.

The advances predicted from Moore's law arise mainly from the following changes:

- Producing increasingly miniaturized transistors.
- Placing multiple processors on a single chip. Chips with more than one processor are called *multicore* chips. For example, the Cell chip, produced by a consortium of Sony, Toshiba, and IBM, contains nine processors. Computers using the Cell chip display very rich graphics. The chip is also used in TV sets and home theaters that can download and show large numbers of high-definition programs. Intel (www.intel.com) and AMD (www.amd.com) offer multicore chips.
- In April 2012, Intel launched its next-generation chips, which employ a three-dimensional (3D) design. The 3D chips require less power than Intel's current chips while improving performance. These chips enhance the performance of all computers. However, they are particularly valuable in handheld devices, because they extend the device's battery life.

In addition to increased speeds and performance, Moore's law has had an impact on costs, as you can see in Table TG 1.3.

Computer Memory

The amount and type of memory that a computer possesses has a great deal to do with its general utility. A computer's memory also determines the types of programs that the computer can run, the work it can perform, its speed, and its cost. There are two basic categories of computer memory. The first is *primary storage*. It is called "primary" because it stores small amounts of data and information that the CPU will use immediately. The second category is *secondary storage*, which stores much larger amounts of data and information (an entire software program, for example) for extended periods.

Table

TG 1.3

Comparison of Personal Computer Components and Cost over Time

Year	Chip	RAM	Hard Drive	Monitor	Cost
1997	Pentium II	64 megabytes	4 gigabytes	17-inch	$4,000
2007	Dual-core	1 gigabyte	250 gigabytes	19-inch	$1,700
2013	Quad-core	16 gigabytes	2 terabytes	27-inch	$1,700

Memory Capacity As you have seen, CPUs process only binary units—0s and 1s—which are translated through computer languages into bits. A particular combination of bits represents a certain alphanumeric character or a simple mathematical operation. Eight bits are needed to represent any one of these characters. This 8-bit string is known as a **byte**. The storage capacity of a computer is measured in bytes. Bits typically are used as units of measure only for telecommunications capacity, as in how many million bits per second can be sent through a particular medium.

The hierarchy of terms used to describe memory capacity is as follows:

- *Kilobyte.* Kilo means "one thousand," so a kilobyte (KB) is approximately 1,000 bytes. Actually, a kilobyte is 1,024 bytes. Computer designers find it convenient to work with powers of 2: 1,024 is 2 to the 10th power, and 1,024 is close enough to 1,000 that for *kilobyte* people use the standard prefix *kilo*, which means exactly 1,000 in familiar units such as the kilogram or kilometer.
- *Megabyte.* Mega means "one million," so a megabyte (MB) is approximately 1 million bytes. Most personal computers have hundreds of megabytes of RAM memory.
- *Gigabyte.* Giga means "one billion," so a gigabyte (GB) is approximately 1 billion bytes.
- *Terabyte.* A terabyte is approximately 1 trillion bytes. The storage capacity of modern personal computers can be several terabytes.
- *Petabyte.* A petabyte is approximately 1,000 terabytes.
- *Exabyte.* An exabyte is approximately 1,000 petabytes.
- *Zettabyte.* A zettabyte is approximately 1,000 exabytes.

To get a feel for these amounts, consider the following example: If your computer has one terabyte of storage capacity on its hard drive (a type of secondary storage), it can store approximately 1 trillion bytes of data. If the average page of text contains about 2,000 bytes, then your hard drive could store approximately 10 percent of all the print collections of the Library of Congress. That same terabyte can store 70 hours of standard-definition compressed video.

Primary Storage. **Primary storage**, or **main memory**, as it is sometimes called, stores three types of information for very brief periods of time: (1) data to be processed by the CPU, (2) instructions for the CPU as to how to process the data, and (3) operating system programs that manage various aspects of the computer's operation. Primary storage takes place in chips mounted on the computer's main circuit board, called the *motherboard*. These chips are located as close as physically possible to the CPU chip. As with the CPU, all the data and instructions in primary storage have been translated into binary code.

The four main types of primary storage are (1) register, (2) cache memory, (3) random access memory (RAM), and (4) read-only memory (ROM). You learn about each type of primary storage next.

Registers are part of the CPU. They have the least capacity, storing extremely limited amounts of instructions and data only immediately before and after processing.

Cache memory is a type of high-speed memory that enables the computer to temporarily store blocks of data that are used more often and that a processor can access more rapidly than main memory (RAM). Cache memory is physically located closer to the CPU than RAM. Blocks that are used less often remain in RAM until they are transferred to cache; blocks used infrequently remain in secondary storage. Cache memory is faster than RAM because the instructions travel a shorter distance to the CPU.

Random access memory (RAM) is the part of primary storage that holds a software program and small amounts of data for processing. When you start most software programs (such as Microsoft Word) on your computer, the entire program is brought from secondary storage into RAM. As you use the program, small parts of the program's instructions and data are sent into the registers and then to the CPU. Compared with the registers, RAM stores more information and is located farther away from the CPU. However, compared with secondary storage, RAM stores less information and is much closer to the CPU.

RAM is temporary and, in most cases, *volatile*—that is, RAM chips lose their contents if the current is lost or turned off, as from a power surge, brownout, or electrical noise generated by lightning or nearby machines.

FIGURE TG 1.4 Primary memory compared to secondary storage.

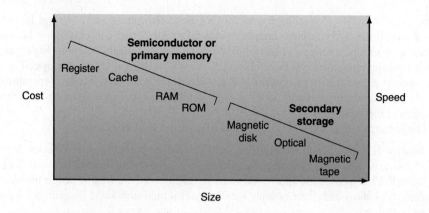

Most of us have lost data at one time or another due to a computer "crash" or a power failure. What is usually lost is whatever is in RAM, cache, or the registers at the time, because these types of memory are volatile. Therefore, you need greater security when you are storing certain types of critical data or instructions. Cautious computer users frequently save data to nonvolatile memory (secondary storage). In addition, most modern software applications have autosave functions. Programs stored in secondary storage, even though they are temporarily copied into RAM when they are being used, remain intact because only the copy is lost, not the original.

Read-only memory (ROM) is the place—actually, a type of chip—where certain critical instructions are safeguarded. ROM is nonvolatile, so it retains these instructions when the power to the computer is turned off. The read-only designation means that these instructions can only be read by the computer and cannot be changed by the user. An example of ROM is the instructions needed to start or "boot" the computer after it has been shut off.

Secondary Storage. **Secondary storage** is designed to store very large amounts of data for extended periods. Secondary storage has the following characteristics:

• It is nonvolatile.
• It takes more time to retrieve data from it than from RAM.
• It is cheaper than primary storage (see Figure TG 1.4).
• It can utilize a variety of media, each with its own technology, as you see next.

One secondary storage medium, **magnetic tape**, is kept on a large open reel or in a smaller cartridge or cassette. Although this is an old technology, it remains popular because it is the cheapest storage medium, and it can handle enormous amounts of data. As a result, many organizations (e.g., the U.S. government Social Security Administration) use magnetic tape for archival storage. The downside is that it is the slowest method for retrieving data because all the data are placed on the tape sequentially. **Sequential access** means that the system might have to run through the majority of the tape before it comes to the desired piece of data.

Magnetic disks (or **hard drives** or **fixed disk drives**) are the most commonly used mass storage devices because of their low cost, high speed, and large storage capacity. Hard disk drives read from, and write to, stacks of rotating (at up to 15,000 rpm) magnetic disk platters mounted in rigid enclosures and sealed against environmental and atmospheric contamination (see Figure TG 1.5). These disks are permanently mounted in a unit that may be internal or external to the computer.

Solid state drives (SSDs) are data storage devices that serve the same purpose as a hard drive and store data in memory chips. Where hard drives have moving parts, SSDs do not. SSDs use the same interface with the computer's CPU as hard drives and are therefore a seamless replacement for hard drives. SSDs offer many advantages over hard drives. They use less power, are silent and faster, and produce about one-third the heat of a hard drive. The major disadvantage of SSDs is that they cost more than hard drives.

Unlike magnetic media, **optical storage devices** do not store data via magnetism. Rather, a laser reads the surface of a reflective plastic platter. Optical disk drives are slower than magnetic hard drives, but they are less fragile and less susceptible to damage from contamination.

Homiel / iStockphoto   © Krzysztof Krzyscin/iStockphoto

FIGURE TG 1.5 Traditional hard drives are less expensive, but solid state drives are faster and are more reliable.

In addition, optical disks can store a great deal of information, both on a routine basis and when combined into storage systems. Types of optical disks include compact disk read-only memory and digital video disk.

Compact disk read-only memory (*CD-ROM*) storage devices feature high capacity, low cost, and high durability. However, because a CD-ROM is a read-only medium, it cannot be written on. *CD-R* can be written to, but once this is done, what was written on it cannot be changed later. That is, CD-R is writeable, which CD-ROM is not, but it is not rewriteable, which *CD-RW* (compact disk, rewritable) is. There are applications where not being rewriteable is a plus, because it prevents some types of accidental data destruction. CD-RW adds rewritability to the recordable compact disk market.

The digital video disk (*DVD*) is a 5-inch disk with the capacity to store about 135 minutes of digital video. DVDs can also perform as computer storage disks, providing storage capabilities of 17 gigabytes. DVD players can read current CD-ROMs, but current CD-ROM players cannot read DVDs. The access speed of a DVD drive is faster than that of a typical CD-ROM drive.

A dual-layer *Blu-ray disc* can store 50 gigabytes, almost 3 times the capacity of a dual-layer DVD. Development of Blu-ray technology is ongoing, with 3-layered and 4-layered Blu-ray discs available.

Flash memory devices (or *memory cards*) are nonvolatile electronic storage devices that contain no moving parts and use 30 times less battery power than hard drives. Flash devices are also smaller and more durable than hard drives. The trade-offs are that flash devices store less data than hard drives. Flash devices are used with digital cameras, handheld and laptop computers, telephones, music players, and video game consoles.

One popular flash memory device is the **thumb drive** (also called *memory stick, jump drive,* or *flash drive*). These devices fit into Universal Serial Bus (USB) ports on personal computers and other devices, and they can store many gigabytes. Thumb drives have replaced magnetic floppy disks for portable storage.

before you go on...

1. Decisions about hardware focus on what three factors?

2. What are the overall trends in hardware?

3. Define hardware and list the major hardware components.

4. Describe the computer hierarchy from the largest to the smallest computers.

5. Distinguish between human data-input devices and source-data automation.

6. Briefly describe how a microprocessor functions.

7. Distinguish between primary storage and secondary storage.

For All Business Majors

The design of computer hardware has profound impacts for businesspeople. Personal and organizational success can depend on an understanding of hardware design and a commitment to knowing where it is going and what opportunities and challenges hardware innovations will bring. Because these innovations are occurring so rapidly, hardware decisions at both the individual level and at the organizational level are difficult.

At the individual level, most people who have a home or office computer system and want to upgrade it, or people who are contemplating their first computer purchase, are faced with the decision of when to buy as much as what to buy and at what cost. At the organizational level, these same issues plague IS professionals. However, they are more complex and more costly. Most organizations have many different computer systems in place at the same time. Innovations may come to different classes of computers at different times or rates. Therefore, managers must decide when old hardware legacy systems still have a productive role in the organization and when they should be replaced. A legacy system is an old computer system or application that continues to be used, typically because it still functions for the users' needs, even though newer technology is available.

[Summary]

1. **Identify the major hardware components of a computer system.**

   Modern computer systems have six major components: the central processing unit (CPU), primary storage, secondary storage, input technologies, output technologies, and communications technologies.

2. **Discuss the strategic issues that link hardware design to business strategy.**

   Strategic issues linking hardware design to business strategy include: How do organizations keep up with the rapid price/performance advancements in hardware? How often should an organization upgrade its computers and storage systems? How can organizations measure benefits gained from price/performance improvements in hardware?

3. **Describe the hierarchy of computers according to power and their respective roles.**

   Supercomputers are the most powerful computers, designed to handle the maximum computational demands of science and the military. Mainframes, although not as powerful as supercomputers, are powerful enough for large organizations to use for centralized data processing and large databases. Minicomputers are smaller and less-powerful versions of mainframes that are often devoted to managing specific subsystems. Desktop personal computers (PCs) are the common, well-known personal and business computers. Laptop or notebook computers are small, easily transportable PCs. Tablet computers (or tablets) are complete computers contained entirely in a flat touch screen that uses a stylus, digital pen, or fingertip as an input device instead of a keyboard or mouse.

4. **Differentiate the various types of input and output technologies and their uses.**

   Principal human data-entry input technologies include the keyboard, mouse, optical mouse, trackball, touchpad, joystick, touch screen, stylus, and voice-recognition systems. Principal source-data automation input devices are ATMs, POS terminals, barcode scanners, optical mark readers, magnetic ink character readers, optical character readers, sensors, cameras, radio frequency identification, and retinal scanning displays. Common output technologies include various types of monitors, impact and nonimpact printers, plotters, and voice output.

5. **Describe the design and functioning of the central processing unit.**

The CPU is made up of the arithmetic-logic unit (ALU), which performs the calculations; the registers, which store minute amounts of data and instructions immediately before and after processing; and the control unit, which controls the flow of information on the microprocessor chip. After processing, the data in their original form and the instructions are sent back to a storage place outside the chip.

6. **Discuss the relationships between microprocessor component designs and performance.**

Microprocessor designs aim to increase processing speed by minimizing the physical distance that the data (as electrical impulses) must travel, increasing the number of transistors on the chip, increasing the number of CPUs on the chip, and using three-dimensional chip architecture.

7. **Describe the main types of primary and secondary storage.**

There are four types of primary storage: registers, cache memory, random access memory (RAM), and read-only memory (ROM). Secondary storage includes magnetic media (tapes; hard drives; and thumb, or flash, drives) and optical media (CD-ROM, DVD, and Blu-ray disks).

8. **Distinguish between primary and secondary storage along the dimensions of speed, cost, and capacity.**

Primary storage has much less capacity than secondary storage, and it is faster and more expensive per byte stored. It is also located much closer to the CPU. Sequential-access secondary storage media such as magnetic tape are much slower and less expensive than hard drives and optical media.

[Chapter Glossary]

arithmetic-logic unit (ALU) Portion of the CPU that performs the mathematic calculations and makes logical comparisons.

augmented reality A live, direct or indirect, view of a physical, real-world environment whose elements are enhanced by computer-generated sensory input such as sound, video, graphics, or GPS data.

binary form The form in which data and instructions can be read by the CPU—only 0s and 1s.

bit Short for binary digit (0s and 1s), the only data that a CPU can process.

byte An 8-bit string of data, needed to represent any one alphanumeric character or simple mathematical operation.

cache memory A type of high-speed memory that enables the computer to temporarily store blocks of data that are used more often and that a processor can access more rapidly than main memory (RAM).

central processing unit (CPU) Hardware that performs the actual computation or "number crunching" inside any computer.

control unit Portion of the CPU that controls the flow of information.

fat clients Desktop computer systems that offer full functionality.

flash memory devices Nonvolatile electronic storage devices that are compact, are portable, require little power, and contain no moving parts.

gesture recognition an input method that interprets human gestures, in an attempt for computers to begin to understand human body language.

laptop computers (notebook computers) Small, easily transportable, lightweight microcomputers.

magnetic disks (or hard drives or fixed disk drives) A form of secondary storage on a magnetized disk divided into tracks and sectors that provide addresses for various pieces of data.

magnetic tape A secondary storage medium on a large open reel or in a smaller cartridge or cassette.

mainframes Relatively large computers used in large enterprises for extensive computing applications that are accessed by thousands of users.

microcomputers The smallest and least expensive category of general-purpose computers; also called micros, personal computers, or PCs.

microprocessor The CPU, made up of millions of transistors embedded in a circuit on a silicon wafer or chip.

minicomputers Relatively small, inexpensive, and compact midrange computers that perform the same functions as mainframe computers, but to a more limited extent.

Moore's law Prediction by Gordon Moore, an Intel cofounder, that microprocessor complexity would double approximately every 2 years.

multimedia technology Computer-based integration of text, sound, still images, animation, and digitized full-motion video.

netbook A very small, lightweight, low-cost, energy-efficient, portable computer, typically optimized for Internet-based services such as Web browsing and e-mailing.

notebook computer (see computer)

optical storage devices A form of secondary storage in which a laser reads the surface of a reflective plastic platter.

primary storage (also called main memory) High-speed storage located directly on the motherboard that stores data to be processed by the CPU, instructions telling the CPU how to process the data, and operating systems programs.

random access memory (RAM) The part of primary storage that holds a software program and small amounts of data when they are brought from secondary storage.

read-only memory (ROM) Type of primary storage where certain critical instructions are safeguarded; the storage is nonvolatile and retains the instructions when the power to the computer is turned off.

registers High-speed storage areas in the CPU that store very small amounts of data and instructions for short periods.

secondary storage Technology that can store very large amounts of data for extended periods.

sequential access Data access in which the computer system must run through data in sequence to locate a particular piece.

server Smaller midrange computers that support networks, enabling users to share files, software, and other network devices.

solid state drives (SSDs) Data storage devices that serve the same purpose as a hard drive and store data in memory chips.

supercomputer Computers with the most processing power available; used primarily in scientific and military work for computationally demanding tasks on very large data sets.

tablet computer (or tablet) A complete computer contained entirely in a flat touch screen that uses a stylus, digital pen, or fingertip as an input device instead of a keyboard or mouse.

thin-client systems Desktop computer systems that do not offer the full functionality of a PC.

thumb drive Storage device that fits into the USB port of a personal computer and is used for portable storage.

wearable computer A miniature computer worn by a person allowing the user to multitask.

[Discussion Questions]

1. What factors affect the speed of a microprocessor?
2. If you were the CIO of a firm, what factors would you consider when selecting secondary storage media for your company's records (files)?
3. Given that Moore's law has proved itself over the past two decades, speculate on what chip capabilities will be in 10 years. What might your desktop PC be able to do?
4. If you were the CIO of a firm, how would you explain the workings, benefits, and limitations of using thin clients as opposed to fat clients?
5. Where might you find embedded computers at home, at school, and/or at work?

[Problem-Solving Activities]

1. Access the Web sites of the major chip manufacturers—for example, Intel (www.intel.com), Motorola (www.motorola.com), and Advanced Micro Devices (www.amd.com)—and obtain the latest information regarding new and planned chips. Compare performance and costs across these vendors. Be sure to take a close look at the various multicore chips.

2. Access "The Journey Inside" on Intel's Web site at http://www.intel.com/content/www/us/en/education/k12/the-journey-inside.html. Prepare a presentation of each step in the machine instruction cycle.

[Internship Activity]

Retail Industry

It seems that everyone wants a tablet these days. PCs are on the decline and smart phones and tablets are gaining market share every quarter...in the consumer market. The business market has been slightly slower to move to these mobile devices. For businesses, hardware is not a toy; it is a tool that must serve a purpose to justify the expense!

In the retail industry, tablets allow the sales force to carry product and customer information with them on a call and have much quicker access to information. For Dave Herring of Northwestern Financial, it seems that moving to a tablet would be an easy decision. However, there are many options of lightweight devices (even laptops) that are viable options to tablets.

Please visit the Book Companion Site to receive the full set of instructions and learn how you can help Dave research the options and help him with some decision-making guidance on laptops, tablets, and other mobile devices.

Technology Guide 2

Software

[LEARNING OBJECTIVES]	[TECHNOLOGY GUIDE OUTLINE]	[WEB RESOURCES]
1. Discuss the major software issues that confront modern organizations.	TG 2.1 Introduction to Software	• Student PowerPoints for note taking
2. Analyze the advantages and disadvantages of open-source software.	TG 2.2 Software Issues	**WileyPLUS**
3. Differentiate between the two major types of software.	TG 2.3 Systems Software	• E-book
4. Describe the general functions of the operating system.	TG 2.4 Application Software	• Author video lecture for each chapter section
5. Identify the major types of application software.		• Practice quizzes
		• Flash Cards for vocabulary review
		• Additional "IT's About Business" cases
		• Video interviews with managers
		• Lab Manuals for Microsoft Office 2010 and 2013

What's In IT For Me?

This Tech Guide Will Help Prepare You To ...

ACCT ACCOUNTING

FIN FINANCE

MKT MARKETING

POM PRODUCTION OPERATIONS MANAGEMENT

HRM HUMAN RESOURCES MANAGEMENT

MIS MIS

As you begin this Technology Guide, you might be wondering, "Why do I have to know anything about software?" There are several reasons why you need to know the basics of software. First, regardless of your major (and the functional area in which you will work), you will use different types of software throughout your career. Second, you will provide input concerning the software you will use. In this capacity, you will be required to answer many questions, such as "Does my software help me do my job?" "Is this software easy to use?" "Do I need more functionality and, if so, what functionality would be most helpful to me?" Third, you will also provide input when your functional area or organization upgrades or replaces its software. Finally, some organizations allocate the software budget to functional areas or departments. In such cases, you might be responsible for making software decisions (at least locally) yourself.

Introduction to Software

TG 2.1

Computer hardware is only as effective as the instructions you give it. Those instructions are contained in **software**. The importance of computer software cannot be overestimated. The first software applications for computers in business were developed in the early 1950s. At that time, software was less costly. Today, software comprises a much larger percentage of the cost of modern computer systems because the price of hardware has dramatically decreased, while both the complexity and the price of software have dramatically increased.

The ever-increasing complexity of software has also increased the potential for errors, or *bugs*. Large applications today may contain millions of lines of computer code, written by hundreds of people over the course of several years. Thus, the potential for errors is huge, and testing and debugging software is expensive and time consuming.

In spite of these overall trends—increasing complexity, cost, and numbers of defects—software has become an everyday feature of our business and personal lives. Your examination of software begins with definitions of some fundamental concepts. Software consists of **computer programs**, which are sequences of instructions for the computer. The process of writing or coding programs is called **programming**. Individuals who perform this task are called *programmers*.

Computer programs include **documentation**, which is a written description of the program's functions. Documentation helps the user operate the computer system, and it helps other programmers understand what the program does and how it accomplishes its purpose. Documentation is vital to the business organization. Without it, the departure of a key

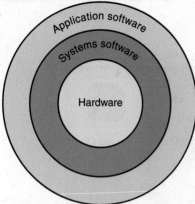

FIGURE TG 2.1 Systems software serves as an intermediary between hardware and functional applications.

programmer or user could deprive the organization of the knowledge of how the program is designed and functions.

The computer can do nothing until it is instructed by software. Computer hardware, by design, is general purpose. Software enables the user to instruct the hardware to perform specific functions that provide business value. There are two major types of software: systems software and application software. Figure TG 2.1 illustrates the relationship among hardware, systems software, and application software.

Systems software is a set of instructions that serves primarily as an intermediary between computer hardware and application programs. Systems software enables computer systems to perform self-regulatory functions by loading itself when the computer is first turned on and providing commonly used sets of instructions for all applications. Systems programming refers to both the creation and the maintenance of systems software.

Application software is a set of computer instructions that provide more specific functionality to a user. This functionality may be broad, such as general word processing, or narrow, such as an organization's payroll program. Essentially, an application program applies a computer to a certain need. *Application programming* refers to the creation, modification, and improvement of application software. Application software may be proprietary or off-the-shelf. As you will see, modern organizations use many different software applications.

before you go on...

1. What is documentation and why is documentation so important to organizations?

2. Differentiate between system software and application software.

TG 2.2 Software Issues

The importance of software in computer systems has brought new issues to the forefront for organizational managers. These issues include software defects (bugs), licensing, open systems, and open-source software.

Software Defects

All too often, computer program code is inefficient, poorly designed, and riddled with errors. The Software Engineering Institute (SEI) at Carnegie Mellon University in Pittsburgh defines good software as usable, reliable, defect free, cost effective, and maintainable. As our dependence on computers and networks increases, the risks associated with software defects are becoming more serious.

The SEI maintains that, on average, professional programmers make between 100 and 150 errors in every 1,000 lines of code they write. Fortunately, the software industry recognizes this problem. Unfortunately, however, the problem is enormous, and the industry is taking only initial steps to resolve it. One critical step is better design and planning at the beginning of the development process (discussed in Chapter 13).

Software Licensing

Many people routinely copy proprietary software. However, making copies without the manufacturer's explicit permission—a practice known as *piracy*—is illegal. The Business Software Alliance (BSA) (*www.bsa.org*), a nonprofit trade association dedicated to promoting a safe and legal digital world, collects, investigates, and acts on software piracy tips. The BSA has calculated that piracy costs software vendors around the world billions of dollars annually. Most of the tips the BSA receives come from current and past employees of offending companies.

To protect their investment, software vendors must prevent their products from being copied and distributed by individuals and other software companies. A company can copyright its software, which means that the U.S. Copyright Office grants the company the exclusive legal right to reproduce, publish, and sell that software.

The number of computing devices in organizations continues to grow, and businesses continue to decentralize, so IS managers are finding it increasingly difficult to supervise their software assets. In fact, the majority of chief information officers (CIOs) are not confident that their companies were in compliance with software licensing agreements. For example, one medium-size company was fined $10,000 for unknowingly using Microsoft® Exchange mailbox licenses that had not been purchased. Worse, the company was also fined $100,000 for not having the necessary licenses for Autodesk, Inc.'s AutoCAD® design software.

To help companies manage their software licenses, new firms have arisen that specialize in tracking software licenses for a fee. For example, Express Metrix (www.expressmetrix.com) will track and manage a company's software licenses to ensure they are in compliance with U.S. copyright laws.

Open Systems

The **open systems** concept refers to a group of computing products that work together. In an open system, the same operating system with compatible software is installed on all computers that interact within an organization. A complementary approach is to employ application software that will run across all computer platforms. Where hardware, operating systems, and application software are all designed as open systems, users can purchase the best software, called *best of breed*, for a job without worrying whether it will run on particular hardware.

Open-source Software

Organizations today are increasingly selecting open-source software rather than proprietary software. **Proprietary software** is purchased software that has restrictions on its use, copying, and modification. Companies that develop proprietary software spend money and time developing their products, which they then sell in the marketplace. This software is labeled *proprietary* because the developer keeps the source code—the actual computer instructions—private (just as Coca-Cola does with its formula). Therefore, companies that purchase the software can utilize it in their operations, but they cannot change the source code themselves.

In contrast, the source code for **open-source software** is available at no cost to both developers and users. This software is distributed with license terms that ensure that its source code will always be available.

Open-source software is produced by worldwide "communities" of developers who write and maintain the code. Inside each community, however, only a small group of developers, called *core developers*, is allowed to modify the code directly. All the other developers must submit their suggested changes to the core developers.

There are advantages to implementing open-source software in an organization. According to OpenSource (www.opensource.org), open-source development produces high-quality, reliable, low-cost software. This software is also flexible, meaning that the code can be changed to meet users' needs. In many cases, open-source software can be more reliable than proprietary software. Because the code is available to many developers, more bugs are discovered early and quickly, and they are fixed immediately. Technical support for open-source software is also available from firms that offer products derived from the software. An example is Red Hat (www.redhat.com), a major Linux vendor that supplies solutions to problems associated with open-source technology. Specifically Red Hat provides education, training, and technical support, for a fee.

Open-source software also has disadvantages, however. The major drawback is that companies that use open-source software depend on the continued good will of an army of volunteers for enhancements, bug fixes, and so on, even if they have signed a contract that includes support. Some companies will not accept this risk, although as a practical matter the support community for Linux, Apache, and Firefox is not likely to disappear. Further, organizations that do not have in-house technical experts will have to purchase maintenance-support contracts from a third party. In addition, open-source software poses questions concerning ease of use, the time and expense needed to train users, and compatibility with existing systems either within or outside the organization.

There are many examples of open-source software, including the GNU (GNU's Not UNIX) suite of software (www.gnu.org) developed by the Free Software Foundation (www.fsf.org); the Linux operating system (see www.linux-hq.com); Apache Web server (www.apache.org); sendmail SMTP (Send Mail Transport Protocol) e-mail server (www.sendmail.org); the Perl programming language (www.perl.org); the Firefox browser from Mozilla (www.mozilla.com); and Sun's StarOffice applications suite (www.sun.com/software/star/staroffice/index.jsp). In fact, more than 150,000 open-source projects are under way at SourceForge (www.sourceforge. net), the popular open-source hosting site.

Open-source software is moving to the mainstream, as you see by the many major companies that use this type of software. For example, Japan's Shinsei Bank (www.shinseibank.com) uses Linux on its servers; SugarCRM (www.sugarcrm.com) for certain customer relationship management tasks; and MySQL (www.mysql.com) open-source database management software. Further, the *Los Angeles Times* uses Alfresco (www.alfresco.com) to manage some of the images and video for its Web site.

before you go on... 👤👤👤👤

1. Why is software licensing so important to organizations?

2. Differentiate between open systems and open source software.

3. Describe the advantages and disadvantages of open source software.

TG 2.3 Systems Software

As you saw earlier, the programs contained in systems software control and support the computer system and its information-processing activities. Systems software also helps users and IT personnel program, test, and debug their own computer programs. Systems software programs support application software by directing the computer's basic functions. For example, when the computer is turned on, the initialization program (a systems program) prepares and readies all devices for processing. The major type of systems software with which we are concerned is the operating system.

The **operating system (OS)** is the "director" of your computer system's operations. It supervises the overall operation of the computer by monitoring the computer's status, scheduling operations, and managing input and output processes. Well-known desktop operating systems include Microsoft® Windows (www.microsoft.com), Apple Mac OS X (www.apple.com), Linux (www.linuxhq.com), and Google Chrome (www.google.com/chrome). When a new version with new features is released, the developers often give the new version a new designation. For example, in mid-2013, the latest version of Windows was Windows 8, and the latest version of OS X was Mountain Lion or OS X 10.8.

The operating system also provides an interface between the user and the hardware. This user interface hides the complexity of the hardware from the user. That is, you do not have to know how the hardware actually operates; you simply have to know what the hardware will do and what you need to do to obtain the desired results.

The ease or difficulty of the interaction between the user and the computer is determined to a large extent by the **graphical user interface (GUI)**. The GUI allows users to directly control the hardware by manipulating visible objects (such as icons) and actions that replace complex commands. Microsoft® Windows provides a widely recognized GUI.

In mid-2013, GUI technology incorporates features such as virtual reality, head-mounted displays, speech input (user commands) and output, pen and gesture recognition, animation, multimedia, artificial intelligence, and cellular/wireless communication capabilities. These new interfaces, called *natural user interfaces* (NUIs), will combine social, haptic, and touch-enabled gesture-control interfaces. (A *haptic interface* provides tactile feedback through the sense of touch by applying forces, vibrations, or motions to the user.)

A **social interface** guides the user through computer applications by using cartoonlike characters, graphics, animation, and voice commands. The cartoonlike characters can be puppets, narrators, guides, inhabitants, or *avatars* (computer-generated humanlike figures). Social interfaces are hard to create without being corny. For example, the assistant "Clippy" was so annoying to users of Microsoft® Office 97 that it was eliminated from Office 2003 and all subsequent versions.

Motion control gaming consoles are another type of interface. Three major players currently offer this interface: the Xbox 360 Kinect, the PS3 PlayStation Move, and the Nintendo Wii.

- Kinect tracks your movements without a physical controller, has voice recognition, and accommodates multiple players.
- The PlayStation Move uses a physical controller with motion-sensing electronics, making it the technological "cross" between Kinect and Wii. Move requires each player to use a wand.
- Wii uses a physical controller. Compared to Kinect and Move, Wii has been on the market longer, it has the biggest library of motion-sensing games, and it is the least expensive. On the negative side, Wii has the least accurate motion sensing of the three systems, and, unlike Kinect and Move, it is not available in high-definition.

Touch-enabled gesture-control interfaces enable users to browse through photos, "toss" objects around a screen, "flick" to turn the pages of a book, play video games, and watch movies. Examples of this type of interface are Microsoft® Surface and the Apple iPhone. Microsoft® Surface is used in casinos such as Harrah's iBar in Las Vegas and in some AT&T stores. A very visible use of Surface was the touch wall used by the major television networks during their coverage of the 2012 presidential election.

before you go on...

1. Describe the functions of the operating system.

2. What is a social interface?

Application Software

TG 2.4

As you saw earlier, application software consists of instructions that direct a computer system to perform specific information-processing activities and also to provide functionality for users. Because there are so many different uses for computers, the number of application software programs is correspondingly large.

Application software may be developed in-house by the organization's information systems personnel, or it may be commissioned from a software vendor. Alternatively, the software can be purchased, leased, or rented from a vendor that develops applications and sells them to many organizations. This "off-the-shelf" software may be a standard package, or it may be customizable. Special-purpose programs or "packages" can be tailored for a specific purpose, such as inventory control and payroll. A **package**, or **software suite**, is a group of programs with integrated functions that has been developed by a vendor and is available for purchase in a prepackaged form. Microsoft® Office is a well-known example of a package, or software suite.

General-purpose, off-the-shelf application programs designed to help individual users increase their productivity are referred to as **personal application software**. Table TG 2.1 lists some of the major types of personal application software.

Speech-recognition software, also called *voice recognition*, is an input technology, rather than strictly an application, that enables users to provide input to systems software and application software. As the name suggests, this software recognizes and interprets human speech, either one

Table TG 2.1
Personal Application Software

Category of Personal Application Software	Major Functions	Examples
Spreadsheets	Use rows and columns to manipulate primarily numerical data; useful for analyzing financial information and for what-if and goal-seeking analyses.	Microsoft® Excel Corel Quattro Pro Apple iWork Numbers
Word Processing	Allow users to manipulate primarily text with many writing and editing features.	Microsoft® Word Apple iWork Pages
Desktop Publishing	Extend word processing software to allow production of finished, camera-ready documents, which may contain photographs, diagrams, and other images combined with text in different fonts.	Microsoft® Publisher QuarkXPress
Data Management	Allows users to store, retrieve, and manipulate related data.	Microsoft® Access FileMaker Pro
Presentation	Allows users to create and edit graphically rich information to appear on electronic slides.	Microsoft® PowerPoint Apple iWork Keynote
Graphics	Allows users to create, store, and display or print charts, graphs, maps, and drawings.	Adobe® PhotoShop Corel DRAW
Personal Information Management	Allows users to create and maintain calendars, appointments, to-do lists, and business contacts.	IBM Lotus Notes Microsoft® Outlook
Personal Finance	Allows users to maintain checkbooks, track investments, monitor credit cards, and bank and pay bills electronically.	Quicken Microsoft® Money
Web Authoring	Allows users to design Web sites and publish them on the Web.	Microsoft® FrontPage Macromedia Dreamweaver
Communications	Allows users to communicate with other people over any distance.	Novell Groupwise

word at a time (*discrete speech*) or in a conversational stream (*continuous speech*). Advances in processing power, new software algorithms, and better microphones have enabled developers to design extremely accurate speech-recognition software. Experts predict that, in the near future, voice recognition systems will be built into almost every device, appliance, and machine that people use. Applications for voice recognition technology abound. Consider these examples:

- Call centers are using this technology. The average call costs $5 if it is handled by an employee, but only 50 cents with a self-service, speech-enabled system. The online brokerage firm E-Trade Financial uses Microsoft's Tellme (www.microsoft.com/en-us/tellme) to field about 50,000 calls per day, thereby saving at least $30 million annually.

- Apple's Macintosh OS X and Microsoft's Windows 8 operating systems come with built-in voice technology.

- Nuance's Dragon NaturallySpeaking (www.nuance.com) enables accurate voice-to-text and e-mail dictation.

- Vocera Communications (www.vocera.com) has developed a communicator badge that combines voice recognition with wireless technologies. Among its first customers were medical workers, who used the badge to search hospital directories for the appropriate person to manage a patient problem or to find medical records.

- Vox-Tec's (www.voxtec.com) Phraselator, a handheld device about the size of a checkbook, listens to requests for a phrase and then translates it into any of 41 specified languages. U.S. troops in Iraq and Afghanistan are using it to provide translations in Arabic and Pashto, respectively.

before you go on...

1. Describe the major types of application software.
2. Why is speech-recognition software becoming a vital interface between humans and computers?

For the Accounting Major

Accounting application software performs the organization's accounting functions, which are repetitive and performed in high volumes. Each business transaction (e.g., a person hired, a paycheck produced, an item sold) produces data that must be captured. Accounting applications capture these data and then manipulate them as necessary. Accounting applications adhere to relatively standardized procedures, handle detailed data, and have a historical focus (i.e., what happened in the past).

For the Finance Major

Financial application software provides information about the firm's financial status to persons and groups inside and outside the firm. Financial applications include forecasting, funds management, and control applications. Forecasting applications predict and project the firm's future activity in the economic environment. Funds management applications use cash flow models to analyze expected cash flows. Control applications enable managers to monitor their financial performance, typically by providing information about the budgeting process and performance ratios.

For the Marketing Major

Marketing application software helps management solve problems that involve marketing the firm's products. Marketing software includes marketing research and marketing intelligence applications. Marketing applications provide information about the firm's products and competitors, its distribution system, its advertising and personal selling activities, and its pricing strategies. Overall, marketing applications help managers develop strategies that combine the four major elements of marketing: product, promotion, place, and price.

For the Production/Operations Management Major

Managers use production/operations management (POM) applications software for production planning and as part of the physical production system. POM applications include production, inventory, quality, and cost software. These applications help management operate manufacturing facilities and logistics. Materials requirements planning (MRP) software also is widely used in manufacturing. This software identifies which materials will be needed, how much will be needed, and the dates on which they will be needed. This information enables managers to be proactive.

For the Human Resources Management Major

Human resources management application software provides information concerning recruiting and hiring, education and training, maintaining the employee database, termination, and administering benefits. HRM applications include workforce planning, recruiting, workforce management, compensation, benefits, and environmental reporting subsystems (e.g., equal employment opportunity records and analysis, union enrollment, toxic substances, and grievances).

For the MIS Major

If your company decides to develop its own software, the MIS function is responsible for managing this activity. If the company decides to buy software, the MIS function deals with software vendors in analyzing their products. The MIS function also is responsible for upgrading software as vendors release new versions.

[Summary]

1. **Discuss the major software issues that confront modern organizations.**

   Computer program code often contains errors. The industry recognizes the enormous problem of software defects, but only initial steps are being taken to resolve it. Software licensing is yet another issue for organizations and individuals. Copying proprietary software is illegal. Software vendors copyright their software to protect it from being copied. As a result, companies must license vendor-developed software to use it.

2. **Analyze the advantages and disadvantages of open-source software.**

   The advantages of open-source software include high quality, reliability, flexibility (code can be changed to meet users' needs), and low cost. Open-source software can be more reliable than commercial software. Because the code is available to many developers, more bugs are discovered early and quickly and are fixed immediately. Disadvantages include the cost of maintenance support contracts, ease of use, the time and expense needed to train users, and the lack of compatibility with existing systems both inside and outside the organization.

3. **Differentiate between the two major types of software.**

   Software consists of computer programs (coded instructions) that control the functions of computer hardware. There are two main categories of software: systems software and application software. Systems software manages the hardware resources of the computer system; it functions between the hardware and the application software. The major type of systems software is the operating system. Application software enables users to perform specific tasks and information-processing activities. Application software may be proprietary or off-the-shelf.

4. **Describe the general functions of the operating system.**

   Operating systems manage the actual computer resources (i.e., the hardware). They schedule and process applications (jobs); manage and protect memory; manage the input and output functions and hardware; manage data and files; and provide security, fault tolerance, graphical user interfaces, and windowing.

5. **Identify the major types of application software.**

   The major types of application software are spreadsheet, data management, word processing, desktop publishing, graphics, multimedia, communications, speech recognition, and groupware. Software suites combine several types of application software (e.g., word processing, spreadsheet, and data management) into an integrated package.

[Chapter Glossary]

application software The class of computer instructions that directs a computer system to perform specific processing activities and provide functionality for users.

computer programs The sequences of instructions for the computer, which comprise software.

documentation Written description of the functions of a software program.

graphical user interface (GUI) System software that allows users to have direct control of the hardware by manipulating visible objects (such as icons) and actions, which replace command syntax.

open-source software Software made available in source-code form at no cost to developers.

open systems Computing products that work together by using the same operating system with compatible software on all the computers that interact in an organization.

operating system (OS) The main system control program, which supervises the overall operations of the computer, allocates CPU time and main memory to programs, and provides an interface between the user and the hardware.

package Common term for an integrated group of computer programs developed by a vendor and available for purchase in prepackaged form.

personal application software General-purpose, off-the-shelf application programs that support general types of processing, rather than being linked to any specific business function.

programming The process of writing or coding programs.

proprietary software Software that has been developed by a company and has restrictions on its use, copying, and modification.

social interface A user interface that guides the user through computer applications by using cartoonlike characters, graphics, animation, and voice commands.

software A set of computer programs that enable the hardware to process data.

software suite (see **package**)

speech-recognition software Software that recognizes and interprets human speech, either one word at a time (discrete speech) or in a stream (continuous speech).

systems software The class of computer instructions that serve primarily as an intermediary between computer hardware and application programs; provides important self-regulatory functions for computer systems.

[Discussion Question]

1. You are the CIO of your company, and you have to develop an application of strategic importance to your firm. What are the advantages and disadvantages of using open-source software?

2. What does this statement mean: "Hardware is useless without software."

[Problem-Solving Activities]

1. A great deal of free software is available over the Internet. Go to http://www.pcmag.com/article2/0,2817,2381528,00.asp, and observe all the software available for free. Choose a software program, and download it to your computer. Prepare a brief discussion about the software for your class.

2. Enter the IBM Web site (www.ibm.com), and perform a search on the term "software." Click on the drop box for Products, and notice how many software products IBM produces. Is IBM only a hardware company?

3. Compare the following proprietary software packages with their open-source software counterparts. Prepare your comparison for the class.

Proprietary	Open Source
Microsoft® Office	Google Docs, OpenOffice
Adobe® Photoshop	Picnik.com, Google Picasa

4. Compare the Microsoft® Surface interface with Oblong Industries' (www.oblong.com) g-speak spatial operating environment. Demonstrate examples of both interfaces to the class. What are the advantages and disadvantages of each one?

[Internship Activity]

Banking Industry

Computers are only as useful as the software that tells them what to do. When you see a need in the realm of business processes, it seems that it should only be a matter of finding someone to write a program to do what you need. In reality, it is much more complicated than that.

Jeremy Farr of Noble Bank wants to better use the data they have access to in their bank. They want to use software to keep network logs that they can use to prevent security threats. There are some available for free under different open source licenses. Others are proprietary (for sale by companies that specialize in writing this type of software). Your task will be to help Jeremy understand the advantages/disadvantages of using open source software or proprietary software.

Please visit the Book Companion Site to receive the full set of instructions.

Technology Guide ③

Cloud Computing

[LEARNING OBJECTIVES]	[TECHNOLOGY GUIDE OUTLINE]	[WEB RESOURCES]

[LEARNING OBJECTIVES]

1. Describe the problems that modern information technology departments face.

2. Describe the key characteristics and advantages of cloud computing.

3. Identify a use-case-scenario for each of the four types of clouds.

4. Explain the operational model of each of the three types of cloud services.

5. Identify the key benefits of cloud computing.

6. Discuss the concerns and risks associated with cloud computing.

7. Explain the role of Web services in building a firm's IT applications, providing examples.

[TECHNOLOGY GUIDE OUTLINE]

TG 3.1 Introduction

TG 3.2 What Is Cloud Computing?

TG 3.3 Different Types of Clouds

TG 3.4 Cloud Computing Services

TG 3.5 The Benefits of Cloud Computing

TG 3.6 Concerns and Risks with Cloud Computing

[WEB RESOURCES]

- Student PowerPoints for note taking

WileyPLUS

- E-book

- Author video lecture for each chapter section

- Practice quizzes

- Flash Cards for vocabulary review

- Additional "IT's About Business" cases

- Video interviews with managers

- Lab Manuals for Microsoft Office 2010 and 2013

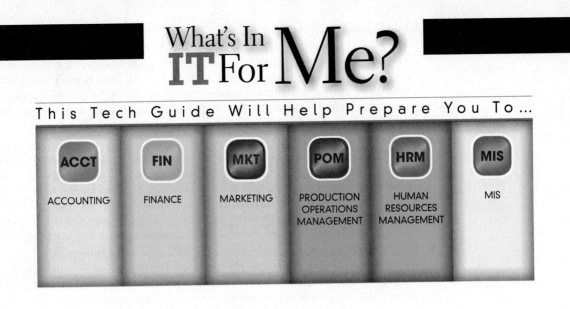

What's In IT For Me?

This Tech Guide Will Help Prepare You To...

ACCT	FIN	MKT	POM	HRM	MIS
ACCOUNTING	FINANCE	MARKETING	PRODUCTION OPERATIONS MANAGEMENT	HUMAN RESOURCES MANAGEMENT	MIS

Because the overall goal of this book is for you to be an informed user of information technology, we devote this Technology Guide to a vital and cutting-edge topic: cloud computing. A working knowledge of cloud computing will enhance your appreciation of what technology can and cannot do for a business. In addition, it will enable you to make an immediate contribution by analyzing how your organization manages its information technology assets.

Going further, you will be using these computing resources in your career, and you will have input into decisions about how your department and organization can best utilize them. Additionally, cloud computing can be extremely valuable if you decide to start your own business.

This Technology Guide defines **cloud computing** as a type of computing that delivers convenient, on-demand, pay-as-you-go access for multiple customers to a shared pool of configurable computing resources (e.g., servers, networks, storage, applications, and services) that can be rapidly and easily accessed over the Internet. Cloud computing allows customers to acquire resources at any time and then delete them the instant they are no longer needed. We present many examples of how the cloud can be used for business purposes. In addition, the cloud provides you with personal applications. Therefore, this guide can help you plan for your own use of the cloud. For a more detailed discussion of how you can utilize the cloud, see the section titled IT's Personal: "The Cloud."

TG 3.1

Introduction

You were introduced to the concept of IT infrastructure in Chapter 1. Recall that an organization's *IT infrastructure* consists of IT components—hardware, software, networks, and databases—and IT services—developing information systems, managing security and risk, and managing data. (It is helpful to review Figure 1.3 here.) The organization's IT infrastructure is the foundation for all of the information systems that the organization uses.

Modern IT infrastructure has evolved through several stages since the early 1950s, when firms first began to apply information technology to business applications. These stages are as follows:

- *Stand-alone mainframes.* Organizations initially used mainframe computers in their engineering and accounting departments. The mainframe was typically housed in a secure area and only MIS personnel had access to it.

- *Mainframe and dumb terminals.* Forcing users to go to wherever the mainframe was located was time-consuming and inefficient. As a result, firms began placing so-called dumb terminals—essentially electronic typewriters with little processing power—in user departments. This arrangement enabled users to input computer programs into the mainframe from their departments, a process called *remote job entry*.

- *Stand-alone personal computers.* In the late 1970s, the first personal computers appeared. The IBM PC's debut in 1981 legitimized the entire personal computer market. Users began bringing personal computers to the workplace to improve their productivity—for example, by using spreadsheet and word processing applications. These computers were not initially supported by the firm's MIS department. However, as the number of personal computers increased dramatically, organizations decided to support personal computers, and they established policies as to which personal computers and software they would support.

- *Local area networks (client/server computing).* When personal computers are networked, individual productivity is substantially increased. For this reason, organizations began to connect personal computers into local area networks (LANs) and then connect these LANs to the mainframe, a type of processing known as *client/server computing*.

- *Enterprise computing.* In the early 1990s, organizations began to use networking standards to integrate different kinds of networks throughout the firm, thereby creating enterprise computing. As the Internet became widespread after 1995, organizations began using the TCP/IP networking protocol to integrate different types of networks. All types of hardware were networked, from mainframes to personal computers to smartphones. Software applications and data could now flow seamlessly throughout the enterprise and between and among organizations.

- *Cloud computing and mobile computing.* Today, organizations and individuals can use the power of cloud computing. As you will see in this Technology Guide, cloud computing provides access to a shared pool of computing resources, including computers, storage, applications, and services, over a network, typically the Internet.

Keep in mind that the computing resources in each stage can be cumulative. For instance, most large firms still use mainframe computers (in addition to all the other types of computing resources) as large servers to manage operations that involve millions of transactions per day.

As you have seen from the evolution of IT infrastructures, the world is experiencing a digital and mobile transformation, with more information becoming available more quickly from more sources than ever before. As a result, businesspeople need IT-enabled services to help them handle this transformation and envision new opportunities.

To appreciate the transformation effects of cloud computing, you first need to understand traditional IT departments in organizations and the problems they face. Today, most companies own IT infrastructure (their software, hardware, networks, and data management) and maintain them "on premise" in their data centers. On-premise software, then, is the traditional model of the IT function in organizations.

Traditional IT departments spend huge amounts on both IT infrastructure and the expert staffs they need to build and maintain complex IT systems. These expenses include software licenses, hardware, and staff training and salaries. Despite all of this spending, however, organizations typically do not use their infrastructure to its full capacity. The majority of these expenses are typically applied to maintaining the existing IT infrastructure, with the remainder being allocated to developing new systems. In addition, companies are being buried under vast amounts of data (which you learned about in Chapter 5). Traditional IT departments are struggling to capture, store, manage, and analyze all of these data. As a result of these problems, traditional IT infrastructures can actually inhibit an organization's ability to respond quickly and appropriately to today's rapidly changing business environments.

Large organizations can afford comprehensive enterprise software and top IT talent. These companies can buy or build software and install these systems in their data centers. They can enable their applications to be used on different devices—desktops, laptops, tablets, and smartphones—and make them accessible to employees regardless of their location. These companies can also make their applications available to people outside the organization, such as consultants, contractors, suppliers, customers, and other business partners. These capabilities, however, come with huge costs. In addition, the companies' IT departments are often overtaxed and unable to execute all of these functions effectively. This problem is even more acute for smaller organizations, which typically do not have the resources required to execute these functions.

As you will see in the next section, cloud computing can help organizations manage the problems that traditional IT departments face. The next section defines cloud computing and describes its essential characteristics.

What Is Cloud Computing?

TG 3.2

Information technology departments have always been tasked to deliver useful IT applications to business users. For a variety of reasons, today's IT departments are facing increased challenges in delivering useful applications. As you learn about cloud computing, you will see how it can help organizations manage the problems that occur in traditional IT departments. You will also see why so many organizations are utilizing cloud computing. A 2012 survey conducted by the Open Data Center Alliance—which includes companies such as Lockheed Martin, BMW, Deutsche Bank, China Unicom, and Terremark—found that organizations are utilizing cloud computing at a faster rate than was previously forecast. In fact, more than half of the survey respondents expect to run 40 percent half of their IT operations in private clouds by 2015.

Cloud Computing Characteristics

The cloud computing phenomenon has several important characteristics. We take a closer look at them in this section.

Cloud Computing Provides On-Demand Self-Service. A customer can access needed computing resources automatically.

Cloud Computing Encompasses the Characteristics of Grid Computing. Grid computing pools various hardware and software components to create a single IT environment with shared resources. Grid computing shares the processing resources of many geographically dispersed computers across a network.

- Grid computing enables organizations to utilize their computing resources more efficiently.
- Grid computing provides fault tolerance and redundancy, meaning that there is no single point of failure, so the failure of one computer will not stop an application from executing.
- Grid computing makes it easy to *scale up*—that is, to access increased computing resources—to meet the processing demands of complex applications.
- Grid computing makes it easy to *scale down* (remove computers) if extensive processing is not needed.

Consider Dell Computing (www.dell.com). After years of database proliferation, Dell began to run out of physical space in its data center for its databases. The company deployed each new database on its own server. It ended up with roughly 10,000 databases, each of which ran on individual servers and spread across multiple data centers. In addition to occupying physical space, this system resulted in high costs for power, cooling, and management. Further, it was taking Dell as long as two to three months to launch a new database project. The company needed to speed up the process so that it could be more responsive to changes in its business environment.

Dell chose a grid computing solution to its problem. The solution reduced the physical database environment by 30 percent, accelerated new database project launches to less than five days, and saved the company more than $20 million.

Cloud Computing Encompasses the Characteristics of Utility Computing. In **utility computing**, a service provider makes computing resources and infrastructure management available to a customer as needed. The provider then charges the customer for its specific

FIGURE TG 3.1 A server farm. Notice the ventilation in the racks and ceiling.

Media Bakery

usage rather than a flat rate. Utility computing enables companies to efficiently meet fluctuating demands for computing power by lowering the costs of owning the hardware infrastructure.

Cloud Computing Utilizes Broad Network Access. The cloud provider's computing resources are available over a network, accessed with a Web browser, and they are configured so they can be used with any computing device.

Cloud Computing Pools Computing Resources. The provider's computing resources are available to serve multiple customers. These resources are dynamically assigned and reassigned according to customer demand.

Cloud Computing Often Occurs on Virtualized Servers. Cloud computing providers have placed hundreds or thousands of networked servers inside massive data centers called **server farms** (see Figure TG 3.1). Recall that a *server* is a computer that supports networks, thus enabling users to share files, software, and other network devices. Server farms require massive amounts of electrical power, air-conditioning, backup generators, and security. They also need to be located fairly closely to fiber-optic communications links (see Figure TG 3.2).

Going further, Gartner estimates that typical utilization rates on servers are very low, generally from 5 to 10 percent. That is, most of the time, organizations are using only a small percentage of their total computing capacity. CIOs tolerate this inefficiency to make certain that they can supply sufficient computing resources to users in case demand should spike. To alleviate with this underutilization problem, companies and cloud computing providers are turning to virtualization.

Server virtualization uses software-based partitions to create multiple virtual servers— called *virtual machines*—on a single physical server. The major benefit of this system is that each server no longer has to be dedicated to a particular task. Instead, multiple applications can run on a single physical server, with each application running within its own software environment. As a result, virtualization enables companies to increase server utilization. In addition, companies realize cost savings in two areas. First, they do not have to buy additional servers to meet peak demand. Second, they reduce their utility costs because they are using less energy. The following example illustrates the benefits of virtualization for MaximumASP.

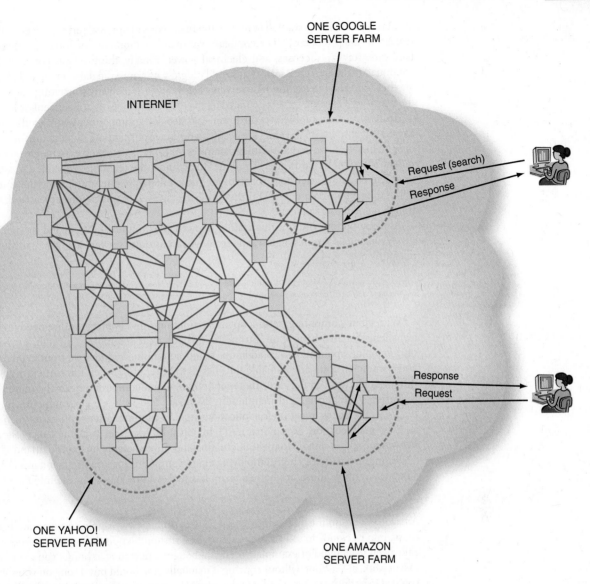

FIGURE TG 3.2 Organizational server farms in relation to the Internet.

Example

MaximumASP is a Web-hosting company based in Louisville, Kentucky. Its 35 employees host more than 48,000 domains for customers located in more than 60 countries. MaximumASP prides itself on its innovative offerings and its outstanding customer service. Unfortunately, the company's rapid expansion resulted in a proliferation of servers that required increasing amounts of resources to manage. This situation adversely affected the company's bottom line. Furthermore, servers, the company pulled staff away from researching new services, which diminished the company's agility and innovation.

Web hosting has become extremely competitive and even commoditized in many parts of the world. The company's CIO noted that there is tremendous market pressure to develop new products. To accomplish this task, MaximumASP had to add new servers, which increased the company's costs. MaximumASP added hundreds of new servers every year, each of which took roughly 4 hours to deploy. The company spent so much time deploying new servers that it could not respond as quickly to its customers' needs or its competitors' moves as it had in the past.

MaximumASP also wanted to reduce the rising costs of physical servers as well as the related real estate and power costs. The company was spending thousands of dollars every year on new hardware, software licenses, and electrical power. Finally, the firm was concerned that if it continued to deploy more servers, it would outgrow its Louisville data center and have to build another one. Having to fund new servers each year was especially frustrating because most of the company's existing servers operated at a very low capacity, often 5 percent or less.

To resolve these problems, MaximumASP decided to implement Microsoft's server virtualization technology. Thus far, the results have been outstanding. The company was able to operate between five and ten virtual machines on each physical server, which generated a savings of $350,000 in hardware costs alone. In addition, the technology enabled MaximumASP to utilize its data center floor space much more efficiently, thereby sparing the firm the cost of building a new data center. Furthermore, average server utilization increased dramatically from 5 percent to 65 percent.

And the bottom line? Virtualization allowed MaximumASP to expand its product offerings, enhance its business agility, and improve its customer service, while actually lowering its operating costs.

Sources: "MaximumASP," *Microsoft Virtualization Case Study*, 2011; J. Hoover, "Microsoft Ramps Up Virtualization Management, Management Services," *InformationWeek*, April 28, 2009; www.maximumasp.com, accessed March 19, 2013.

With cloud computing, setting up and maintaining an IT infrastructure need no longer be a challenge for an organization. Businesses do not have to scramble to meet the evolving needs of developing applications. In addition, cloud computing reduces up-front capital expenses and operational costs, and it enables businesses to better utilize their infrastructure and to share it from one project to the next. In general, then, cloud computing eases the difficult tasks of procuring, configuring, and maintaining hardware and software environments. In addition, it allows enterprises to get their applications up and running faster, with easier manageability and less maintenance. It also enables IT to adjust IT resources (such as servers, storage, and networking) more rapidly to meet fluctuating and unpredictable business demand.

Businesses are increasingly employing cloud computing for important and innovative work. The next example illustrates how Amazon has successfully "moved music into the cloud."

Example

Amazon, whose online music store competes with Apple's (www.apple.com/icloud), has "moved music into its cloud" to solve two problems. The first problem is that music libraries have typically been scattered. For example, when you bought a new song at home, you could not listen to it at work, at least not without copying it manually. You could buy a song on your phone, but you had to perform a sync in order to download it onto your computer. Moreover, if your music library was large, then you could fit only a portion of it onto your phone. The second problem is that Amazon wants more people to buy music from its proprietary store instead of from iTunes.

In March 2011, Amazon released a package of software and services that solved both of these problems. The fundamental idea behind the new package is that your music collection will reside in the cloud. That way, you can conveniently listen to it from any computer—at home, at work, at a friend's home—by logging into a special Web page called the Amazon Cloud Player (www.amazon.com/clouddrive).

You can also listen to any of the songs in your music collection on an Android phone without having to copy or sync the music. All your songs are always available everywhere, and they do not take up any storage space on your phone itself.

In addition to being accessible from anywhere, the Cloud Player has some other notable perks. It contains a list of your songs, which you can sort and search. You can also drag songs into playlists and play back a song, an album, or a playlist. Plus, you can download songs to your computer. Amazon also provides a free Uploader app that lets you send your existing music files to your online library so your music is available anywhere.

The Cloud Player is almost free. To attract new customers, Amazon offers everyone 5 gigabytes of free space online—enough room for about 1,200 MP3 songs. You can buy additional storage for the price of $1 per gigabyte per year. Although this price might seem insignificant, the service can become expensive if you have a huge music collection—enough to make sites like Rhapsody that offer "pay $15 per month for unlimited music" look appealing.

In addition to these special deals, Amazon is also offering incentives. For example, if you buy an album from Amazon's music store, your Cloud Player storage is increased to 20 gigabytes for the year at no charge. In addition, any songs you buy from Amazon do not count against your storage limit.

Despite these aggressive marketing efforts, Amazon's Cloud Player faces tough competition. Many other companies offer similar systems. Apple (www.apple.com/icloud) and Google (http://music.google.com) offer similar services. Also, Rdio (www.rdio.com), Audio Galaxy (www.audiogalaxy.com), Spotify (www.spotify.com), and GrooveShark (www.grooveshark. com) all offer some elements of the Amazon concept for less money.

Sources: Compiled from D. Sung, "Apple iCloud vs. Google vs. Amazon Cloud Drive vs. Dropbox vs. Microsoft SkyDrive," *Pocket Lint*, April 26, 2012; A. Kingsley-Hughes, "The Dangerous Side of Apple's iCloud," *Forbes*, August 4, 2012; L. Bedigian, "What Apple, Google Need to Beat Amazon's Cloud Drive," *Forbes*, April 1, 2011; E. Bott, "How Amazon Has Outsmarted the Music Industry (and Apple)," *ZDNet*, March 30, 2011; D. Pogue, "The Cloud That Rains Music," *New York Times*, March 30, 2011; www.amazon.com/clouddrive, www.apple.com/icloud, http://music.google.com, accessed April 1, 2013.

In the next section, you learn about the various ways in which customers (individuals and organizations) can implement cloud computing. Specifically, you will read about public clouds, private clouds, hybrid clouds, and vertical clouds.

Different Types of Clouds

TG 3.3

There are three major types of cloud computing that companies provide to customers or groups of customers: public clouds, private clouds, and hybrid clouds. A fourth type of cloud computing is called vertical clouds (see Figure TG 3.3).

Public Cloud

Public clouds are shared, easily accessible, multicustomer IT infrastructures that are available nonexclusively to any entity in the general public (individuals, groups, and/or organizations). Public cloud vendors provide applications, storage, and other computing resources as services over the Internet. These services may be free or offered on a pay-per-usage model.

Movirtu, a private technology company, is an example of a public cloud. Significantly, it is playing a major role in addressing a widespread global problem. In the developing world, people commonly share their mobile phones. They frequently use their own SIM card, which they switch in and out when they borrow a mobile device. This practice can compromise privacy, however. In addition, SIM cards are easy to lose.

FIGURE TG 3.3

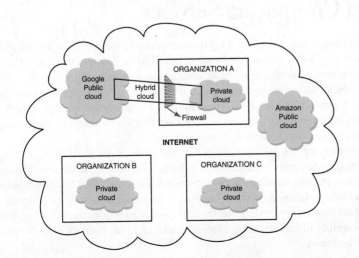

Now, millions of impoverished citizens in Africa and Asia will receive mobile phone numbers under a plan developed by the United Nations. Movirtu (*www.movirtu.com*) is a cloud-based phone service that allows people to manage their own mobile network accounts—phone number, voice mail, texting, etc.—without ever owning a phone or a SIM card. Movirtu prices its service with lower-income users in mind, and it shares its profits with the mobile network carriers.

Under the UN plan, Movirtu will supply low-cost mobile phone numbers to participants, who can use any mobile device to log in with their own number to make and receive calls and to access information and services. The primary beneficiaries will be women in rural communities in South Asia and sub-Saharan Africa, because they are far less likely than men to own their own phones.

Movirtu will bring this technology to 12 or more markets in the selected regions by early 2013, thereby improving the lives and expanding the earning potential of at least 50 million people. The company selected Madagascar, an island nation off Africa's east coast, as a starting point. The country has an extensive network, but many of its citizens cannot afford their own phone. The service became available throughout the island via a local carrier in August 2011.

Private Cloud

Private clouds (also known as *internal clouds* or *corporate clouds*) are IT infrastructures that can be accessed only by a single entity or by an exclusive group of related entities that share the same purpose and requirements, such as all of the business units within a single organization. Private clouds provide IT activities and applications as a service over an intranet within an enterprise. Enterprises adopt private clouds to ensure system and data security. For this reason these systems are implemented behind the corporate firewall.

Hybrid Cloud

Hybrid clouds are composed of public and private clouds that remain unique entities but are nevertheless bound together, thereby offering users the benefits of multiple deployment models. Hybrid clouds deliver services based on security requirements, the mission-critical nature of applications, and other company-established policies. For example, customers may need to keep some of their data in a private cloud for security and privacy reasons while storing other, less-sensitive data in a public cloud because it is less expensive.

Vertical Clouds

It is now possible to build cloud infrastructure and applications for different businesses—the construction, finance, or insurance businesses, for example—thus building vertical clouds (see *www.vertical-cloud.com*).

TG 3.4 Cloud Computing Services

Cloud computing services are based on three models: infrastructure-as-a-service (IaaS), platform-as-a-service (PaaS), and software-as-a-service (SaaS). These models represent the three types of computing generally required by consumers: infrastructure to run software and store data (IaaS), platforms to develop applications (PaaS), and software applications to process their data (SaaS). Figure TG 3.4 illustrates the differences between the three models.

As you examine the figure from left to right, note that the customer manages the service less and less, and the vendor manages it more and more.

Although each model has its distinctive features, all three share certain characteristics. First, customers rent them instead of buying them. This arrangement shifts IT from a capital expense to an operating expense. Second, vendors are responsible for maintenance, administration, capacity planning, troubleshooting, and backups. Finally, obtaining additional computing resources (i.e., scale from the cloud—for example, more storage from an IaaS vendor, the ability to handle more PaaS projects, or more users of a SaaS application) is usually fast and easy.

ON-PREMISE SOFTWARE	INFRASTRUCTURE-AS-A-SERVICE	PLATFORM-AS-A-SERVICE	SOFTWARE-AS-A-SERVICE
CUSTOMER MANAGES: Applications, Data, Operating system, Servers, Virtualization, Storage, Networking	CUSTOMER MANAGES: Applications, Data, Operating system. VENDOR MANAGES: Servers, Virtualization, Storage, Networking	CUSTOMER MANAGES: Applications, Data. VENDOR MANAGES: Operating system, Servers, Virtualization, Storage, Networking	VENDOR MANAGES: Applications, Data, Operating system, Servers, Virtualization, Storage, Networking
Examples	Amazon, IBM, Google, Microsoft, Rackspace	Mircosoft Windows Azure, Google App Engine, Force.com	Salesforce.com, Google Apps, Dropbox, Apple iCloud, Box.net

FIGURE TG 3.4 Comparison of On-premise software, Infrastructure-as-a-Service, Platform-as-a-Service, and Software-as-a-Service.

Infrastructure as a Service (IaaS)

With the **infrastructure-as-a-service** (IaaS) model, cloud computing providers offer remotely accessible servers, networks, and storage capacity. They supply these resources on demand from their large pools of such resources, which are located in their data centers.

IaaS customers are often technology companies with IT expertise. They want access to computing power, but they do not want to be responsible for installing or maintaining it. Companies use the infrastructure to run software or simply to store data.

To deploy their applications, IaaS users install their operating system and their application software on the cloud computing provider's computers. They can deploy any software on this infrastructure, including different operating systems, applications, and development platforms. Each user is responsible for maintaining their operating system and application software. Cloud providers typically bill IaaS services on a utility computing basis—that is, the cost reflects the amount of resources the user consumes.

Amazon is a well-known IaaS provider. The company sells the spare capacity of its vast IT infrastructure to its customers in a cloud environment. These services include its Simple Storage Service (S3) for storing customers' data and its Elastic Compute Cloud (EC2) service for operating their customers' applications. Customers pay only for the amount of storage and computing they use.

Platform as a Service (PaaS)

In the **platform-as-a-service** (PaaS) model, customers rent servers, operating systems, storage, a database, software development technologies such as Java and .NET, and network capacity over the Internet. The PaaS model allows the customer both to run existing applications and to develop and test new applications.

PaaS offers customers several advantages, which include the following:

- Application developers can develop and run their software solutions on a cloud platform without the cost and complexity of buying and managing the underlying hardware and software layers.
- Underlying computing and storage resources automatically scale to match application demand.
- Operating system features can be upgraded frequently.

- Geographically distributed development teams can work together on software development projects.
- PaaS services can be provided by diverse sources located throughout the world.
- Initial and ongoing costs can be reduced by the use of infrastructure services from a single vendor rather than maintaining multiple hardware facilities that often perform duplicate functions or suffer from incompatibility problems.

As an example of an entity that employed PaaS to improve its performance, consider the city of Miami (*www.miamigov.com*). Miami has created a service that monitors nonemergency 311 requests. City officials and local residents can access a Web site that pulls up a map of the city with pins in every spot that is tied to a 311 complaint. Before cloud computing became available, the city would have needed three months to develop the concept, buy new hardware (including backups in case of a hurricane), hire a team to install the necessary software, and then build the application. In contrast, by utilizing cloud computing, Miami created a working prototype within 8 days, and it deployed the application shortly thereafter.

Software as a Service (SaaS)

With the **software-as-a-service** (**SaaS**) delivery model, cloud computing vendors provide software that is specific to their customers' requirements. SaaS is the most widely utilized service model, and it provides a broad range of software applications. SaaS providers typically charge their customers a monthly or yearly subscription fee.

SaaS applications reside in the cloud instead of on a user's hard drive or in a data center. The host manages the software and the infrastructure that runs this software and stores data. The customers do not control either the software, beyond the usual configuration settings, or the infrastructure, beyond changing the resources they use, such as the amount of disk space required for their data. This process eliminates the need to install and run the application on the user's computers, thereby simplifying maintenance and support.

What differentiates SaaS applications from other applications is its ability to scale. As a result, applications can run on as many servers as is necessary to meet changing demands. This process is transparent to the user.

To reduce the risk of an infrastructure outage, SaaS providers regularly back up all of their customers' data. In addition, customers can back up their data on their storage hardware.

To understand how SaaS operates, consider the case of Flextronics (*www.flextronics.com*), the Singapore-based manufacturer of such devices as Research in Motion's BlackBerry handsets and Microsoft's motion-sensing Kinect add-on for the Xbox 360 gaming console. Flextronics utilizes SaaS from Workday (*www.workday.com*), an outside provider, for some of its human resources management function. Workday handles Flextronics's human resources processes from tracking employee compensation and benefits to hiring for open positions. By outsourcing to Workday rather than handling HR computing in-house with on-premise IT infrastructure, Flextronics was able to save $100 million in 3 years. These expense reductions were extremely important because Flextronics has an operating margin of only 2.9 percent.

As we previously discussed, a major concern related to cloud computing is security. In the case of Flextronics, the company's CIO realized he was taking risks as he handed over the human resources computing tasks for his 200,000-employee company to Workday. What would happen, for example, if Workday lost sensitive employee data? Fortunately for Flextronics, the company's employee information remained secure.

A subset of SaaS is the *Desktop-as-a-Service* (DaaS) model, also known as a *cloud desktop* or *desktop in the cloud*. In this model, a SaaS provider hosts a software environment for a desktop personal computer, including productivity and collaboration software—spreadsheets, word processing programs, and so on—such as Google Apps, Microsoft 365, and other products. Significantly, in DaaS only a thin client (discussed in Technology Guide 1) can access all the required software. The DaaS model can be financially advantageous for the consumer because they do have to necessarily buy a fully-configured personal computer, or fat client (discussed in Technology Guide 1). In addition, it makes the PC environment simpler to deploy and administer.

IT's Personal: "The Cloud"

This Technology Guide defines the cloud as distributed computing services, and it presents many examples of how the cloud can be used for both personal and business purposes. This IT's Personal is intended to help you differentiate between the business and personal applications of the cloud and to help you plan for your own use of the cloud.

First, you need to understand that there is no single "cloud." Rather, almost all businesses refer to their Internet-based services as "cloud services." Basically, anything you do over the Internet that you used to do on a local computer is a form of cloud computing. When you store files on Dropbox, type a document with Google Docs, use iCloud to store purchases or sync documents, or use OnLive on your iPad, you are using cloud-based services that are intended for personal use.

Infrastructure-as-a-service is an important application of the cloud for personal purposes. Dropbox is one of the most prominent companies in this area. In the past, users had to carry around a USB drive, a CD, an external hard drive, or (way back in the day) floppy discs to store their personal information. At the time of this writing, a free Dropbox account offered 2 GB of online storage. Not only does Dropbox offer you a place to store your files (eliminating the need for a personal infrastructure of removable storage), but it provides synchronization across computers and access from mobile devices!

Virtualization is gaining ground. If you have an iPad, you should look up the app called "OnLive" and give it a test run. OnLive allows you to log into a virtual computer that is running Windows 7. Here, your iPad is simply providing the input/output, and the server is "serving up" a virtual operating system. It is very likely that one day your home computer will be virtual as well.

Software-as-a-service has been a popular option for quite some time. For example, Google Docs offers Internet-based word processing, spreadsheet, presentation, forms, and drawing tools. Recently, Microsoft has moved into the game with their Microsoft Office 365 product. Basically, each of these services allows you to use a computer program without having to install it on your computer or mobile device. You simply access the entire program (and your saved files) over the Internet.

Google recently combined a couple of these cloud services with Google Drive, a service that offers the same services as Dropbox in addition to Google Docs' online editing and file-sharing capabilities. This also crosses over with software-as-a-service because of the added benefit of Google Docs. It is very likely that one day Google will merge virtualization, infrastructure, and software into a single cloud-based service. If this technology becomes available, then all you will need as a consumer is an Internet-connected device, and you will be able to store, access, edit, and share your files from the cloud. You will also be able to choose apps to run on your "virtual machine" much the way that today you go through a vendor-approved store to purchase applications for your mobile devices.

So, what is the point? Simply, cloud-based services are here to stay. The rise of ubiquitous Internet access has engendered a new world of possibilities.

A word of caution, however. Along with its seemingly endless possibilities, cloud computing raises many critical security and privacy issues. Because your files, apps, and editing capability will no longer be stored on a local machine, they are only as safe as the company to which you have entrusted them makes them. So, when you select a cloud provider, make sure you choose wisely!

The Benefits of Cloud Computing   TG 3.5

Cloud computing offers benefits for both individuals and groups. It allows companies to increase the scale and power of their IT and the speed at which it can be deployed and accessed. It eliminates administrative headaches, and it works across locations, devices, and organizational boundaries.

Cloud computing has transformed both business and everyday life—from consumers who use it to access their favorite music to companies that harness its powerful resources. When cloud computing capabilities are utilized effectively, they offer numerous opportunities to businesses to drive innovation. Organizations are exploiting cloud computing to transform both product and service development as well as to strengthen customer relationships.

Organizations of all sizes, across geographies, and in virtually every industry are using cloud computing to reduce the complexity and costs associated with traditional IT approaches. Nearly half of the respondents in a recent CIO Economic Impact survey indicated that they evaluate cloud computing options first—over traditional IT approaches—before making any new IT investments.

Organizations are relying on cloud computing not only to enhance internal efficiencies, but also to target more strategic business capabilities. IBM predicts that the global cloud computing market will grow 22 percent annually to $241 billion by 2020. Below we examine seven major benefits that cloud computing provides to individuals and organizations.

Benefit 1: Making Individuals More Productive

Cloud computing can enable companies to provide their employees with access to all the information they need no matter where they are, what device they are using, or whom they are working with.

Cloud computing provides a mechanism for organizations to "hide" some of the complexity of their operations from end users, which can help attract a broader range of consumers. By hiding complexity from the end user, a company can expand its product and service sophistication without requiring its users to substantially increase their knowledge in order to utilize or maintain the product or service.

For example, Chicago-based law firm Segal McCambridge Singer & Mahoney (www.smsm.com) operates offices in seven states. Its attorneys need to access documents and data on a constant, year-round basis. Since 2000, the firm's data had expanded dramatically from 30 gigabytes to more than 40 terabytes. All of these data must be stored and accessed securely. To manage and protect this vast amount of data, the firm needed more flexibility and scalability than it was able to obtain from its existing IT infrastructure.

To address this problem, the firm turned to cloud computing for data storage, offsite disaster recovery, and global multisite access within a highly secure public cloud. Rather than maintaining a massive inventory of extra storage as required by its old IT infrastructure, the firm can now increase storage capacity on demand. The cloud provides perpetual access via encrypted communications channels for attorneys. Further, the cloud helps distributed teams of attorneys collaborate, thereby increasing their overall productivity.

In the past, to place huge amounts of case-relevant information on the computers, attorneys often had to manually copy data onto external hard drives and USB devices. Alternatively, the firm had to physically ship hard drives to them. These processes were inherently non-secure. At times, attorneys had to submit a request for information to the firm's Chicago headquarters and wait for someone there to process it and send them the necessary information. Today, an attorney can conduct database queries over the company's cloud network, and offices and attorneys can share documents in near real time.

The firm's cloud environment has made its attorneys much more efficient. As a result, the firm's IT expenses have declined by 60 percent.

Benefit 2: Facilitating Collaboration

Cloud computing enables groups and communities to work together in ways that were previously not possible. For example, it enhances a company's ability to collaborate with its partners and customers, a process that can lead to greater productivity and increased innovation. Cloud-based platforms can bring together disparate groups of people who can collaborate and share resources, information, and processes.

For example, to improve knowledge capture and sharing among its 90,000 employees, Computer Systems Corporation (CSC; www.csc.com) is using Jive's cloud-based collaboration software. CSC's first step was an experiment to determine whether people would be receptive to working with the software. The company made Jive available to all of its employees, an approach that would have been prohibitively expensive if it had to buy all the hardware and software licenses itself. Employees could use Jive to perform a number of diverse tasks such as posing a question to the entire company, visiting and contributing to digital forums like "Where Have We Done This Before?" and "Excel Power Tips," and setting up new communities as needed.

During the initial 20-week experiment, more than 25,000 employees voluntarily registered for the new cloud-based resource, called C3. They created more than 2,100 groups and logged as many as 150,000 activities per month. Those results persuaded CSC to make C3 permanent.

The company's CIO characterized the results as "stunning." C3 is now the standard for how CSC collaborates.

Benefit 3: Mining Insights from Data

Analytics is one of the most popular cloud computing applications. Companies today gather massive amounts of data, and cloud providers are providing hardware and software algorithms to help businesses perform sophisticated analyses of these data.

For example, restaurant owners can utilize a cloud-based service from Radiant Systems to reduce shrinkage. Shrinkage, a polite term for employee theft, is a serious problem in the food service industry. It is also a difficult problem to solve, because there is no easy way for restaurant owners to closely monitor servers and bartenders in their busy work environments.

Enter Radiant Systems (www.radiantsystems.com), a company that supplies the Aloha point-of-sale system to thousands of restaurants and also maintains their data. Radiant possesses the capability to analyze the huge amounts of transaction data that it keeps for each customer for suspicious patterns, such as a significantly greater-than-average volume of large tips for bartenders on a Friday night. This pattern often indicates that the bartender is not charging people for drinks in hopes of getting a big tip.

Using data from all of its customers, Radiant developed a set of algorithms to detect many types of shrinkage. It then bundled them into a product called Aloha Restaurant Guard (ARG). ARG generates a weekly set of reports on suspicious activity by site and by employee. It sends these reports to restaurant owners and managers, who use them to take corrective action. The results can be surprising and dramatic. According to Radiant, one casual dining restaurant experienced a profit increase of $20,000 to $40,000 per year after using ARG to detect employee theft. Significantly, the restaurant owner did not have to buy or install any new software, hire IT people, or alter his IT infrastructure in any way.

Benefit 4: Reduce Costs

Cloud computing can help an organization reduce fixed IT costs by enabling them to shift from capital expenses to operational expenses—or from fixed to variable. IT *capital expenses*—which typically include enterprise software licenses, servers and networking equipment, and other costs—tend to be more expensive than routine IT *operating expenses*. Cloud computing applications eliminate the need to purchase hardware, build and install software, and pay software licensing fees. The organization pays only for the computing resources it needs, and then only when it needs them. This pay-for-use model provides greater flexibility, and it eliminates the need for significant capital expenditures.

Consider State Street Bank (www.statestreet.com) in Boston. The bank writes its own highly customized software to manage its assets. In fact, 20 to 25 percent of the bank's annual IT budget has gone to software development. As is true of many other large companies, the State Street data center contains a broad array of best-of-breed systems. Integrating these systems, a job that State Street traditionally has performed done in-house, is quite expensive.

Consequently, State Street is moving to a private cloud to achieve cost savings from more-efficient software development and increased efficiency in its data center. The bank expects to realize $600 million in savings by the end of 2014. The savings in software development are due to the fact that the developers are writing software for the same cloud-based development platform, making code sharing much easier. Therefore, the bank will have to write dramatically less code.

The cloud environment simplifies and standardizes State Street's data center systems. This process reduces the company's expenses by making it easier to maintain the system and to modify it when necessary.

Over time, the economics of building and operating an IT infrastructure will favor cloud computing. Cloud providers purchase massive amounts of technology infrastructure (e.g., hardware and bandwidth) because they can obtain better prices by buying in bulk. They also buy technology on a continuous basis. As a result, they can take advantage of the declines in computing cost predicted by Moore's law (discussed in Technology Guide 1). For example, the Amazon cloud, known as Amazon Web Services, reduced its prices a dozen times between 2008 and 2012.

Benefit 5: Expand the Scope of Business Operations

Cloud computing allows organizations to use the amount of computing resources they need. Therefore, companies utilizing cloud computing are able to increase the scope of their business operations.

Consider College Hunks Hauling Junk (CHHJ; www.collegehunkshaulingjunk.com), a moving and junk removal company with 43 franchises around the country. CHHJ was experiencing numerous issues with the proprietary software system it was using to run its scheduling and franchising operations. When CHHJ first deployed this system, it was exclusively a junk removal company. Over time, however, it had added new and more complex businesses, such as moving customers' goods. The original system did not easily support these new lines of business. In addition, CHHJ needed a system that could collect different types of data and produce necessary reports based on an analysis of those data. Essentially, CHHJ needed a system for all of its service lines and to provide flexibility for continued growth, both in new areas of business and in new franchises.

CHHJ turned to Waterstreet Technology Group (www.waterstreet.net) to develop an entirely new system from the ground up. Waterstreet developed the software and housed it on its own servers. CHHJ uses the software as a software-as-a-service product. The software supports CHHJ's junk removal and moving businesses as well as its franchise operations and call center.

The new software provides vastly improved reporting on data gathered from customers and franchisees. This capability enables CHHJ to provide better customer service and to support its growing franchise business more effectively. In addition, the software enables CHHJ to expand its lines of business and its franchises.

Benefit 6: Respond Quickly to Market Changes

The ability to quickly respond to rapidly changing customer needs is a critical strategic goal for organizations. Therefore, companies are continuously seeking ways to improve their agility in adjusting to market demands. Cloud computing enables businesses to rapidly adjust their processes, products, and services to meet the changing needs of the market. Furthermore, cloud computing facilitates rapid prototyping and innovation, and it speeds time to market for new products.

For example, ActiveVideo (www.activevideo.com) recognized cloud computing's potential to enhance their market adaptability when they created CloudTV, a cloud-based platform that unifies all forms of content—Web, television, mobile, social, video-on-demand, etc.—onto any video screen. Content and applications from Web content creators, television networks, advertisers, and other media entities can be quickly developed for CloudTV using standard Web tools. CloudTV leverages content stored and processed in the cloud to significantly expand the reach and availability of Web-based user experiences. It also enables operators to quickly deploy a consistent user interface across diverse set top boxes and connected devices. A set top box is a device that enables a TV set to become a user interface to the Internet and also enables a TV set to receive and decode digital television broadcasts. The CloudTV approach of placing the intelligence in the network, rather than in the device, enables content creators, service providers, and consumer electronics manufacturers to create new television experiences for their viewers.

Benefit 7: Customize Products and Services

Because of its expanded computing power and capacity, cloud computing can store massive amounts of information about user preferences. Companies can then utilize this information to customize their products and services. This context-driven variability allows businesses to offer personal experiences to users by adapting the service or product to subtle changes in the user-defined context. Customers are more likely to enjoy their personally customized experience and are therefore more likely to become return customers.

A good example of a product that has effectively made use of cloud computing's user preference storage is Siri, the Apple iPhone 4S cloud-based natural language "intelligent assistant." Siri allows users to send messages, schedule meetings, place phone calls, locate restaurants, and much more. Whereas other phones have some voice recognition features, Siri effectively "learns your voice." It uses artificial intelligence and a growing base of knowledge about the user, including his or her location and frequent contacts, to understand not only what users say, but what they actually mean. Siri leverages cloud computing to enable individualized, context-relevant customer experiences.

Concerns and Risks with Cloud Computing   TG 3.6

Gartner predicts that cloud computing will grow at an annual rate of 19 percent through the year 2015. Even if this prediction is accurate, however, cloud computing will still account for less than 5 percent of total worldwide IT spending that year. Why is this percentage so low? The reason is that there are serious concerns with cloud computing. These concerns fall into five categories: legacy IT systems, reliability, privacy, security, and regulations.

Concern 1: Legacy IT Systems

Historically, organizational IT systems have accumulated a diversity of hardware, operating systems, and applications. When bundled together, these systems are called "legacy spaghetti." These systems cannot easily be transferred to the cloud because they must first be untangled and simplified. Furthermore, many IT professionals have vested interests in various legacy systems, and they resist efforts to exchange these systems for cloud computing.

Concern 2: Reliability

Many skeptics contend that cloud computing is not as reliable as a well-managed, on-premise IT infrastructure. The cloud's reliability was called into question in April 2011 when large parts of Amazon's Web Services infrastructure went down for as long as three days (see the example below). This outage created serious problems for many companies that used the service. Although the outage was serious, however, it affected only one of Amazon's U.S. data centers. Amazon had also explicitly advised its customers to design their IT architectures to withstand a service interruption. Other cloud companies have learned from Amazon's experience, and they are improving the redundancy and reliability of their offerings.

Example

Amazon Web Services (AWS; http://aws.amazon.com) is designed with backups to the backups' backups to prevent its hosted Web sites and applications from failing. Despite all of these safety measures, however, in April 2011 Amazon's cloud crashed, taking with it Reddit (www.reddit.com), Quora (www.quora.com), FourSquare (www.foursquare.com), ProPublica (www.propublica.org), parts of the *New York Times* (www.nytimes.com), and about 70 other Web sites. The massive outage raised questions about the reliability of Amazon Web Services and about the cloud itself.

Thousands of companies use Amazon Web Services (AWS) to run their Web sites through a service called Elastic Compute Cloud (EC2). Rather than hosting their sites on their own servers, these customers essentially rent some of Amazon's unused server capacity. EC2 is hosted in five regions: Virginia, California, Ireland, Tokyo, and Singapore. Within each region are multiple "availability zones," and within each availability zone are multiple "locations" or data centers.

Amazon assured its customers that its method of linking together many different data centers would protect its customers from isolated failures. It promised to keep customers' sites up and running 99.95 percent of the year, or it would reduce their monthly bills by 10 percent. Based on these claims, customers could be down a maximum of just 4.4 hours in a year. In fact, during the outage, some customers' Web sites were down for days.

The crash occurred at Amazon's Virginia data center, located in one of the company's East Coast availability zones. Amazon claimed that a "networking event" caused a domino effect across other availability zones in that region, which in turn caused many of its storage volumes to create backups of themselves. That process filled up Amazon's available storage capacity, and it prevented some Web sites from accessing their data. Amazon did not reveal what the "networking event" was.

Web sites like Quora and Reddit were able to come back online in "read-only" mode, but users were not able to post new content for many hours. Many experts blamed Amazon's customers themselves, asserting that their Web sites should have spread out their processing among multiple geographical regions to take full advantage of Amazon's backup systems. In fact, sites like Reddit were simply following the instructions that Amazon provided in its service agreement. The agreement states that hosting in a single region should be sufficient. Furthermore, some smaller companies could not afford the resources needed to duplicate their infrastructure in data centers all over the world.

One company that experienced an Amazon outage was able to put a dollar figure on the resulting damage. Amazon outages completely took down the online date site WhatsYourPrice (www.whatsyourprice.com). Men and women create profiles on the site, featuring the basic information one would find on most dating sites. However, women also include the amount of money they would accept from someone to go on a date with him. Men browse the profiles and make offers to women who "catch their eye." Once an offer is made, the woman checks the man's profile and can choose to accept the offer, reject it, or come up with a different price.

During a two-hour outage, staff at the Web site fielded nearly 1,000 complaints from users who were trying to make a date. The outage did more than simply tarnish the reputation of WhatsYourPrice.com and leave its customers without dates. The company claims that in the two hours it was unable to operate it lost almost $8,000 from lost commissions.

Sources: Compiled from M. Boisvert, "Still Single? Blame the Recent Amazon EC2 Outages," *SearchCloudComputing.com*, July 13, 2012; S. Johnston, "Cloud Outage Report of 13 Providers Reveals Downtime Costs," *SearchCloudComputing.com*, June 22, 2012; S. Johnston, "Will Amazon's Outage Cause Would-Be Cloud Adopters to Run Screaming?" *SearchCloudComputing.com*, June 20, 2012; C. Brooks, "A Crack in the Cloud: Why the Amazon Outage Caught So Many by Surprise," *SearchCloudComputing.com*, April 27, 2011; D. Goldman, "Why Amazon's Cloud Titanic Went Down," *CNN Money*, April 22, 2011; J. Brodkin, "Amazon EC2 Outage Calls 'Availability Zones' into Question," *CIO*, April 21, 2011; http://aws.amazon.com, accessed March 19, 2013.

Concern 3: Privacy

Privacy advocates have criticized cloud computing for posing a major threat to privacy because the providers control, and thus lawfully or unlawfully monitor, the data and communication stored between the user and the host company. For example, AT&T and Verizon collaborated with NSA to use cloud computing to record more than 10 million phone calls between American citizens. In addition, providers could accidentally or deliberately alter or even delete some information.

Using a cloud computing provider also complicates data privacy because of the extent to which cloud processing and cloud storage are used to implement cloud services. The point is that customer data may not remain on the same system or in the same data center. This situation can lead to legal concerns over jurisdiction.

There have been efforts to address this problem by integrating the legal environment. One example is the US–EU Safe Harbor, a streamlined process for U.S. companies to comply with the European Union directive on the protection of personal data.

Concern 4: Security

Critics also question how secure cloud computing really is. Because the characteristics of cloud computing can differ widely from those of traditional IT architectures, providers need to reconsider the effectiveness and efficiency of traditional security mechanisms. Security issues include access to sensitive data, data segregation (among customers), privacy, error exploitation, recovery, accountability, malicious insiders, and account control.

The security of cloud computing services is a contentious issue that may be delaying the adoption of this technology. Security issues arise primarily from the unease of both the private and public sectors with the external management of security-based services. The fact that providers manage these services provides great incentive for them to prioritize building and maintaining strong security services.

Another security issue involves the control over who is able to access and utilize the information stored in the cloud. (Recall our discussion of least privilege in Chapter 4.) Many organizations exercise least privilege controls effectively with their on-premise IT infrastructures. Some cloud computing environments, in contrast, cannot exercise least privilege controls effectively. This problem occurs because cloud computing environments were originally designed for individuals or groups, not for hierarchical organizations in which some people have both the right and the responsibility to exercise control over other people's private information. To address this problem, cloud computing vendors are working to incorporate administrative, least-privilege functionality into their products. In fact, many have already done so.

Security experts note that the best strategies to achieve excellent security are to constantly monitor the threat landscape, to buy or build the best technologies to protect devices and networks, and to hire and retain top digital security specialists. Cloud computing vendors are better able to do these things than all but the very largest and most security-conscious organizations.

Concern 5: The Regulatory and Legal Environment

There are numerous legal and regulatory barriers to cloud computing, many of which involve data access and transport. For example, the European Union prohibits consumers' data from being transferred to nonmember countries without the consumers' prior consent and approval. Companies located outside the EU can overcome this restriction by demonstrating that they provide a "safe harbor" for the data. Some countries, such as Germany, have enacted even more restrictive data export laws. It is not clear (as of mid-2013) if the safe harbor process will satisfy them. Cloud computing vendors are aware of these regulations and laws, and they are working to modify their offerings so that they can assure customers and regulators that data entrusted to them are secure enough to meet all of them.

In order to obtain compliance with regulations such as the Federal Information Security Management Act (FISMA), the Health Insurance Portability and Accountability Act (HIPAA), and the Sarbanes-Oxley Act (SOX) in the United States, the Data Protection Directive in the European Union, and the credit card industry's Payment Card Industry's Data Security Standard (PCI DSS), cloud computing customers may have to adopt hybrid deployment modes that are typically more expensive and may offer restricted benefits. This process is how, for example, Google is able to "manage and meet additional government policy requirements beyond FISMA," and Rackspace (*www.rackspace.com*) is able to claim PCI compliance. FISMA requires each federal agency to develop, document, and implement a program to provide information security for the information and information systems that support the operations of the agency, including those provided by contractors. PCI DSS is a set of requirements designed to ensure that all companies that process, store, or transmit credit card information maintain a secure environment.

For All Business Majors

As with hardware (Technology Guide 1), the design of enterprise IT architectures has profound impacts for businesspeople. Personal and organizational success can depend on an understanding of cloud computing and a commitment to knowing the opportunities and challenges they will bring.

At the organizational level, cloud computing has the potential to make the organization function more efficiently and effectively, while saving the organization money. Web services and SOA make the organization more flexible when deploying new IT applications.

At the individual level, you might utilize cloud computing yourself if you start your own business. Remember that cloud computing provides start-up companies with world-class IT capabilities at a very low cost.

What's In **IT** For **Me?**

[Summary]

1. **Describe the problems that modern information technology departments face.**

   Traditional IT departments face many problems:

   - They spend huge amounts on IT infrastructure and expert staffs to build and maintain complex IT systems. These expenses include software licenses, hardware, and staff training and salaries.
   - They must manage an infrastructure that often is not used to its full capacity.
   - They spend the majority of their budgets on maintaining existing IT infrastructure, with the remainder being spent on developing new systems.
   - They have difficulty capturing, storing, managing, and analyzing all this data.
   - They can actually inhibit an organization's ability to respond quickly and appropriately to rapidly changing dynamic environments.
   - They are expensive.

2. **Describe the key characteristics and advantages of cloud computing.**

   Cloud computing is a type of computing that delivers convenient, on-demand, pay-as-you-go access for multiple customers to a shared pool of configurable computing resources (e.g., servers, networks, storage, applications, and services) that can be rapidly and easily accessed over the Internet. The essential *characteristics* of cloud computing include the following:

   - Cloud computing provides on-demand self-service.
   - Cloud computing includes the characteristics of grid computing.
   - Cloud computing includes the characteristics of utility computing.
   - Cloud computing utilizes broad network access.
   - Cloud computing pools computing resources.
   - Cloud computing typically occurs on virtualized servers.

3. **Identify a use-case-scenario for each of the four types of clouds.**

   Public clouds are shared, easily accessible, multi-customer IT infrastructures that are available non-exclusively to any entity in the public (individuals, groups, and/or organizations). *Private clouds* (also known as *internal clouds* or *corporate clouds*) are IT infrastructures that are accessible only by a single entity, or by an exclusive group of related entities that share the same purpose and requirements, such as all the business units within a single organization. *Hybrid clouds* are composed of public and private clouds that remain unique entities but are bound together, offering the benefits of multiple deployment models. *Vertical clouds* serve specific industries.

4. **Explain the operational model of each of the three types of cloud services.**

   With the *Infrastructure-as-a-Service* (IaaS) model, cloud computing providers offer remotely accessible servers, networks, and storage capacity. In the *Platform-as-a-Service* (PaaS) model, customers rent servers, operating systems, storage, a database, software development technologies such as Java and .NET, and network capacity over the Internet. With the *software-as-a-service* (SaaS) delivery model, cloud computing vendors provide software that is specific to their customers' requirements.

5. **Identify the key benefits of cloud computing.**

   The benefits of cloud computing include making individuals more productive; facilitating collaboration; mining insights from data; developing and hosting applications; cost flexibility; business scalability; improved utilization of hardware; market adaptability; and product and service customization.

6. **Discuss the concerns and risks associated with cloud computing.**

   Cloud computing does raise concerns and have risks, which include legacy spaghetti, cost, reliability, privacy, security, and the regulatory and legal environment.

7. **Explain the role of Web services in building a firm's IT applications, providing examples.**

   Web services are applications delivered over the Internet that MIS professionals can select and combine through almost any device, from personal computers to mobile phones. A *service-oriented architecture* makes it possible to for MIS professionals to construct business applications using Web services.

[Chapter Glossary]

cloud computing A technology in which tasks are performed by computers physically removed from the user and accessed over a network, in particular the Internet.

Extensible markup language (XML) A computer language that makes it easier to exchange data among a variety of applications and to validate and interpret these data.

grid computing A technology that applies the unused processing resources of many geographically dispersed computers in a network to form a virtual supercomputer.

Hybrid clouds Clouds composed of public and private clouds that remain unique entities but are bound together, offering the benefits of multiple deployment models.

HTML5 A page-description language that makes it possible to embed images, audio, and video directly into a document without add-ons. Also makes it easier for Web pages to function across different display devices, including mobile devices as well as desktops. Supports the storage of data offline.

hypertext markup language (HTML) A page-description language for specifying how text, graphics, video, and sound are placed on a Web page document.

infrastructure-as-a-service (IaaS) model Cloud computing providers offer remotely accessible servers, networks, and storage capacity.

platform-as-a-service (PaaS) model Customers rent servers, operating systems, storage, a database, software development technologies such as Java and .NET, and network capacity over the Internet.

Private clouds (also known as *internal clouds* or *corporate clouds*) IT infrastructures that are accessible only by a single entity or by an exclusive group of related entities that share the same purpose and requirements, such as all the business units within a single organization.

Public clouds Shared, easily accessible, multicustomer IT infrastructures that are available nonexclusively to any entity in the general public (individuals, groups, and/or organizations).

server farms Massive data centers, which may contain hundreds of thousands of networked computer servers.

server virtualization A technology that uses software-based partitions to create multiple virtual servers (called *virtual machines*) on a single physical server.

service-oriented architecture An IT architecture that makes it possible to construct business applications using Web services.

software-as-a-service (SaaS) delivery model Cloud computing vendors provide software that is specific to their customers' requirements.

utility computing A technology whereby a service provider makes computing resources and infrastructure management available to a customer as needed.

Web services Applications delivered over the Internet that IT developers can select and combine through almost any device, from personal computers to mobile phones.

[Discussion Questions]

1. What is the value of server farms and virtualization to any large organization?
2. If you were the chief information officer (CIO) of a firm, how would you explain the workings, benefits, and limitations of cloud computing?
3. What is the value of cloud computing to a small organization?
4. What is the value of cloud computing to an entrepreneur who is starting a business?

[Problem-Solving Activities]

1. Investigate the status of cloud computing by researching the offerings of the following leading vendors. Note any inhibitors to cloud computing.

   - Dell (see, e.g., *http://www.wiley.com/go/rainer/problem solving*)
   - Oracle (see, e.g., *http://www.wiley.com/go/rainer/problem solving*)
   - IBM (see, e.g., *http://www.wiley.com/go/rainer/problem solving*)
   - Amazon (see, e.g., *http://www.wiley.com/go/rainer/problem solving*)
   - Microsoft (see, e.g., *http://www.wiley.com/go/rainer/problemsolving*)
   - Google (see, e.g., *http://www.wiley.com/go/rainer/problem solving*)

[Internship Activity]

Industry: Healthcare

In an earlier activity (Chapter 6) you helped Chad Prince and Anniston Orthopaedics determine criteria for measuring latency in the cloud. Again, related to the cloud, they have a need to determine how they can print from the cloud. When printing is done on a local network there is a print server and it is physically connected to each of the computers and printers available. Software then is programmed to manage the printing in the office.

But what if your data is all in the cloud? How will the cloud-based print servers interact with the local print servers? While this may sound trivial, in a health-care related industry, the ability to print records quickly and easily is vital!

Please visit the Book Companion Site to receive the full set of instructions on how you will help Chad research the interaction between cloud and local print servers.

Technology Guide 4

Intelligent Systems

[LEARNING OBJECTIVES]	[TECHNOLOGY GUIDE OUTLINE]	[WEB RESOURCES]
1. Explain the potential value and the potential limitations of artificial intelligence.	TG 4.1 Introduction to Intelligent Systems	• Student PowerPoints for note taking
2. Provide examples of the benefits, applications, and limitations of expert systems.	TG 4.2 Expert Systems	**WileyPLUS**
3. Provide examples of the use of neural networks.	TG 4.3 Neural Networks	• E-book
4. Provide examples of the use of fuzzy logic.	TG 4.4 Fuzzy Logic	• Author video lecture for each chapter section
5. Describe the situations in which genetic algorithms would be most useful.	TG 4.5 Genetic Algorithms	• Practice quizzes
6. Describe the use case for several major types of intelligent agents.	TG 4.6 Intelligent Agents	• Flash Cards for vocabulary review
		• Additional "IT's About Business" cases
		• Video interviews with managers
		• Lab Manuals for Microsoft Office 2010 and 2013

What's In IT For Me?

This Tech Guide Will Help Prepare You To...

ACCT	**FIN**	**MKT**	**POM**	**HRM**	**MIS**
ACCOUNTING	FINANCE	MARKETING	PRODUCTION OPERATIONS MANAGEMENT	HUMAN RESOURCES MANAGEMENT	MIS

Introduction to Intelligent Systems

TG 4.1

This technology guide focuses on information systems that can make decisions by themselves. These systems are called **intelligent systems**. The major categories of intelligent systems are expert systems, neural networks, fuzzy logic, genetic algorithms, and intelligent agents. You will learn about each of these systems in the following sections.

The term *intelligent systems* describes the various commercial applications of artificial intelligence. **Artificial intelligence (AI)** is a subfield of computer science that studies the thought processes of humans and re-creates the effects of those processes via machines, such as computers and robots.

One well-publicized definition of AI is "behavior by a machine that, if performed by a human being, would be considered intelligent." This definition raises the question, "What is *intelligent behavior?*" The following capabilities are considered to be signs of intelligence: learning or understanding from experience, making sense of ambiguous or contradictory messages, and responding quickly and successfully to new situations.

The ultimate goal of AI is to build machines that mimic human intelligence. A widely used test to determine whether a computer exhibits intelligent behavior was designed by Alan Turing, a British AI pioneer. The **Turing test** proposes a scenario in which a man and a computer both pretend to be women or men, and a human interviewer has to identify which is the real human. Based on this standard, the intelligent systems exemplified in commercial AI products are far from exhibiting any significant intelligence.

We can better understand the potential value of AI by contrasting it with *natural (human) intelligence*. AI has several important commercial advantages over natural intelligence, but it also displays some limitations, as outlined in Table TG 4.1.

Intelligent systems show up in a number of places, some of them surprising, as the following examples illustrate:

- A good session player is hard to find, but ujam (*www.ujam.com*) is always ready to rock. This Web app doubles as a studio band and a recording studio. It analyzes a melody and then produces sophisticated harmonies, bass lines, drum tracks, horn parts, and more.

  Before ujam can produce accompaniment, the app must figure out which notes the user is singing or playing. Once ujam recognizes these notes, its algorithms (an **algorithm**

Table **TG 4.1**

Comparison of the Capabilities of Natural vs. Artificial Intelligence

Capabilities	Natural Intelligence	Artificial Intelligence
Preservation of knowledge	Perishable from an organizational point of view	Permanent
Duplication and dissemination of knowledge	Difficult, expensive, takes time	Easy, fast, and inexpensive once in a computer
Total cost of knowledge	Can be erratic and inconsistent, incomplete at times	Consistent and thorough
Documentability of process and knowledge	Difficult, expensive	Fairly easy, inexpensive
Creativity	Can be very high	Low, uninspired
Use of sensory experiences	Direct and rich in possibilities	Must be interpreted first; limited
Recognizing patterns and relationships	Fast, easy to explain	Machine learning still not as good as people in most cases, but in some cases better than people
Reasoning	Making use of wide context of experiences	Good only in narrow, focused, and stable domains

is a problem-solving method expressed as a finite sequence of steps) use a mix of statistical techniques and programmed musical rules to search for chords to match the tune.

- To the human eye, an x-ray is a murky puzzle. But to a machine, an x-ray—or a CT scan or MRI scan—is a dense data field that can be assessed down to the pixel level. AI techniques currently are being applied aggressively in the field of medical imaging.

  New software gathers high-resolution image data from multiple sources—x-rays, MRI scans, ultrasounds, CT scans—and then groups together biological structures that share hard-to-detect similarities. For instance, the software can examine several images of the same breast to measure tissue density. The software then color-codes tissues of similar densities so humans can observe the pattern as well.

  The software finds and indexes pixels that share certain properties, even pixels that are far apart in one image or in a different image altogether. This process enables medical personnel to identify hidden features of diffuse structures as well as features within a region of tissue.

- The human brain receives visual information from two eyes. Google's AI system receives visual information from billions of smartphone camera lenses. The company collects these images from users of Google Goggles (*www.google.com/mobile/goggles*), a mobile service that lets users run Web searches by taking pictures. Snap a barcode, and Goggles will shop for the item's best price. Take a picture of a book, and users will be linked to, for instance, a Wikipedia page about the book's author. Photograph the Eiffel Tower, and Goggles will give you historical background on the landmark.

  The software behind Goggles coordinates the efforts of multiple object-specific recognition databases. There is a database for text, one for landmarks, one for corporate logos, and so on. When an image arrives, Goggles transmits it to each of these databases, which in turn use a variety of visual-recognition techniques to identify potential matches and compute confidence scores (measures of how definitive the match is). Goggles then applies its own algorithm to decide which result(s), if any, go back to the user. Goggles' next category? Identifying plants.

- Building a model to run a major railroad is a complex task. One of the nation's largest freight carriers, Norfolk Southern (*www.nscorp.com*), uses an intelligent system, the Princeton Locomotive and Shop Management System (PLASMA), to manage its huge operation. PLASMA uses algorithms to analyze the railroad's operations by tracking thousands of variables to predict the impact of changes in fleet size, maintenance policies, transit time, and other factors. The key breakthrough was refining PLASMA so that it could mimic the complex behavior of the company's dispatch center in Atlanta, Georgia. PLASMA examines vast amounts of historical data contained in the railroad's databases. It then uses this analysis to model the dispatch center's collective human decision making and suggest improvements.

before you go on...

1. What is artificial intelligence?

2. Differentiate between artificial and human intelligence.

Expert Systems

TG 4.2

When an organization has to make a complex decision or solve a problem, it often turns to experts for advice. These experts possess specific knowledge and experience in the problem area. They can offer alternative solutions and predict whether the proposed solutions will succeed. At the same time, they can calculate the costs that the organization may incur if it doesn't resolve the problem. Companies engage experts for advice on such matters as mergers and acquisitions, advertising strategy, and purchasing equipment. The more unstructured the situation, the more specialized and expensive is the advice.

Expertise refers to the extensive, task-specific knowledge acquired from training, reading, and experience. This knowledge enables experts to make better and faster decisions than nonexperts in solving complex problems. Expertise takes a long time (often many years) to acquire, and it is distributed unevenly across organizations.

Expert systems (ESs) are computer systems that attempt to mimic human experts by applying expertise in a specific domain. Expert systems can either *support* decision makers or completely *replace* them. Expert systems are the most widely applied and commercially successful intelligent systems. A fascinating example of an expert system is IBM's Watson (see the closing case of Chapter 2).

Human resources management uses expert systems to analyze applicants for available positions. These systems assign "scores" to candidates, lessening the workload for HR managers in the hiring process. Human HR managers still make the final decision, but the expert system provides useful information and recommendations.

An ES typically is decision-making software that can perform at a level comparable to a human expert in certain specialized problem areas. Essentially, an ES transfers expertise from a domain expert (or other source) to the computer. This knowledge is then stored in the computer, which users can call on for specific advice as needed. The computer can make inferences and arrive at conclusions. Then, like a human expert, it offers advice or recommendations. In addition, it can explain the logic behind the advice. Because ESs can integrate and manipulate enormous amounts of data, they sometimes perform better than any single expert can.

An often overlooked benefit of expert systems is that they can be embedded in larger systems. For example, credit card issuers use expert systems to process credit card applications.

The transfer of expertise from an expert to a computer and then to the user involves four activities:

1. *Knowledge acquisition.* Knowledge is acquired from domain experts or from documented sources.

2. *Knowledge representation.* Acquired knowledge is organized as rules or frames (object-oriented) and stored electronically in a knowledge base.
3. *Knowledge inferencing.* The computer is programmed so that it can make inferences based on the stored knowledge.
4. *Knowledge transfer.* The inferenced expertise is transferred to the user in the form of a recommendation.

The above examples demonstrate the usefulness of expert systems in a relatively narrow domain. Overall, however, expert systems may not be as useful as users would like. Consider the Microsoft® Windows troubleshooting software located in the Help section in the task-bar menu. Microsoft has designed this expert system to provide solutions, advice, and suggestions for common errors that users encounter in the operating system. We have all found however, that in some cases the Help section does not provide particularly useful advice.

The Components of Expert Systems

An expert system contains the following components: knowledge base, inference engine, user interface, blackboard (workplace), and explanation subsystem (justifier). In the future, ESs will include a knowledge-refining component as well. You will learn about all these components below. In addition, Figure TG 4.1 diagrams the relationships among these components.

The *knowledge base* contains knowledge necessary for understanding, formulating, and solving problems. It comprises two basic elements: (1) *facts*, such as the problem situation, and (2) *rules* that direct the use of knowledge to solve specific problems in a particular domain.

The *inference engine* is essentially a computer program that provides a methodology for reasoning and formulating conclusions. It enables the system to make inferences based on the stored knowledge. The inference engine is considered the "brain" of the ES.

Here is an example of the inference engine for a medical expert system for lung cancer treatment:

IF lung capacity is high
AND X-ray results are positive

FIGURE TG 4.1 Structure and process of an expert system.

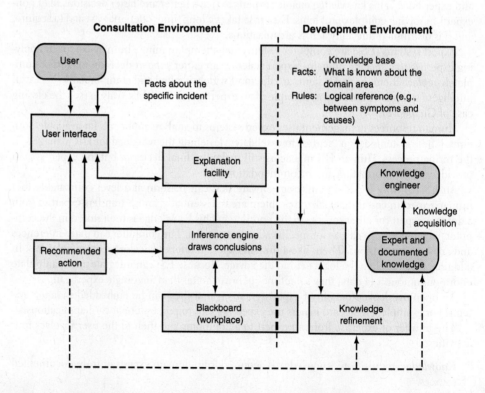

AND patient has fever
AND patient has coughing
THEN surgery is necessary.
IF tumor has spread
OR contraindications to surgery exist
THEN surgery cannot be performed.

The *user interface* enables users to communicate with the computer. The communication is carried out in a natural language, usually a question-and-answer format, and in some cases is supplemented by graphics. The dialogue between the user and the computer triggers the inference engine to match the problem symptoms with the knowledge contained in the knowledge base and then generate advice.

The *blackboard* is an area of working memory set aside for the description of a current problem, as specified by the input data. Thus, it is a kind of database.

Unique to an ES is its ability to *explain* its recommendations. This function is performed in a subsystem called the *explanation subsystem* or *justifier*. The explanation subsystem interactively answers questions such as the following: *Why* did the ES ask a certain question? *How* did the ES reach a particular conclusion? *What* is the plan to reach the solution?

Human experts have a *knowledge-refining* system; that is, they can analyze their own performance, learn from it, and improve it for future consultations. This type of evaluation is necessary in computerized learning as well so that the program can be improved by analyzing the reasons for its success or failure. Unfortunately, such a component is not available in commercial expert systems at the moment; however, it is being developed in experimental systems.

Applications, Benefits, and Limitations of Expert Systems

Today, expert systems are found in all types of organizations. They are especially useful in the ten generic categories shown in Table TG 4.2.

During the past few years, thousands of organizations worldwide have successfully applied ES technology to problems ranging from researching AIDS to analyzing dust in mines. Why have ESs become so popular? The answer is, because they provide such a large number of capabilities and benefits. Table TG 4.3 lists the major benefits of ESs.

Category	Problem Addressed
Interpretation	Inferring situation descriptions from observations
Prediction	Inferring likely consequences of given situations
Diagnosis	Inferring system malfunctions from observations
Design	Configuring objects under constraints
Planning	Developing plans to achieve goal(s)
Monitoring	Comparing observations to plans, flagging exceptions
Debugging	Prescribing remedies for malfunctions
Repair	Executing a plan to administer a prescribed remedy
Instruction	Diagnosing, debugging, and correcting student performance
Control	Interpreting, predicting, repairing, and monitoring systems behavior

Table

TG 4.2
Ten Generic Categories of Expert Systems

Table
TG 4.3
Benefits of Expert Systems

Benefit	Description
Increased output and productivity	ESs can configure components for each custom order, increasing production capabilities.
Increased quality	ESs can provide consistent advice and reduce error rates.
Capture and dissemination of scarce expertise	Expertise from anywhere in the world can be obtained and used.
Operation in hazardous environments	Sensors can collect information that an ES interprets, enabling human workers to avoid hot, humid, or toxic environments.
Accessibility to knowledge and help desks	ESs can increase the productivity of help-desk employees, or even automate this function.
Reliability	ESs do not become tired or bored, call in sick, or go on strike. They consistently pay attention to details.
Ability to work with incomplete or uncertain information	Even with an answer of "don't know," an ES can produce an answer, although it may not be a definite one.
Provision of training	The explanation facility of an ES can serve as a teaching device and a knowledge base for novices.
Enhancement of decision-making and problem-solving capabilities	ESs allow the integration of expert judgment into analysis (e.g., diagnosis of machine malfunction and even medical diagnosis).
Decreased decision-making time	ESs usually can make faster decisions than humans working alone.
Reduced downtime	ESs can quickly diagnose machine malfunctions and prescribe repairs.

Despite all of these benefits, expert systems present some problems as well. The difficulties involved with using expert systems include the following:

- Transferring domain expertise from human experts to the expert system can be difficult because people cannot always explain *how* they know what they know. Often they are not aware of their complete reasoning process.

- Even if the domain experts can explain their entire reasoning process, automating that process may not be possible. The process might be either too complex or too vague, or it might require too many rules.

- In some contexts, there is a potential liability from the use of expert systems. Humans make errors occasionally, but they are generally "let off the hook" if they took reasonable care and applied generally accepted methods. An organization that uses an expert system, however, may lack this legal protection if problems arise later. The usual example of this issue is medical treatment, but it can also arise if a business decision driven by an expert system harms someone financially.

In the case of medical treatment, consider a physician who consults with a medical expert system when treating a patient. If the patient's care goes poorly, then the question arises, who is liable? The physician? The expert system? The vendor of the expert system?

before you go on...

1. What is an expert system?

2. Describe the benefits and limitations of using expert systems.

TG 4.3

Neural Networks

A **neural network** is a system of programs and data structures that simulates the underlying functions of the biological brain. A neural network usually involves a large number of processors operating in parallel, each with its own small sphere of knowledge and access to data in its local memory (see Figure TG 4.2). Typically, a neural network is initially "trained" or fed large amounts of data and rules about data relationships.

Neural networks are particularly adept at recognizing subtle, hidden, and newly emerging patterns within complex data, as well as interpreting incomplete inputs. Neural networks can help users solve a wide range of problems, from airline security to infectious disease control. They are the standard for combating fraud in the credit card, healthcare, and telecom industries, and they are becoming increasingly important in today's stepped-up international efforts to prevent money laundering.

Neural networks are used in a variety of ways, as illustrated by the following examples.

- The Bruce nuclear facility in Ontario, Canada, has eight nuclear reactors, making it the largest facility in North America and the second largest in the world. The plant uses a neural network in its checkpoint x-ray screening system to detect weapons concealed in personal belongings. The system also identifies biologically dangerous liquids.
- Neural networks are used in research into diseases like Alzheimer's, Parkinson's, and epilepsy. Researchers build robots with simulated rat brains that mimic the rats' neural activity. The researchers then can study the brain's function and its reaction to stimuli.
- Investors employ neural networks to forecast the performance of stock index futures, currencies, natural gas and oil stocks, T-bond futures, gold stocks, and other major investments.
- In banking systems, neural networks help detect fraud in credit card transactions and insurance claims, fight crime, and gauge customer satisfaction.

Figure TG 4.2 illustrates how a neural network might process a typical mortgage application. Note that the network has three levels of interconnected nodes (similar to the human brain): an input layer; a middle, or hidden, layer; and an output layer. When the neural network is

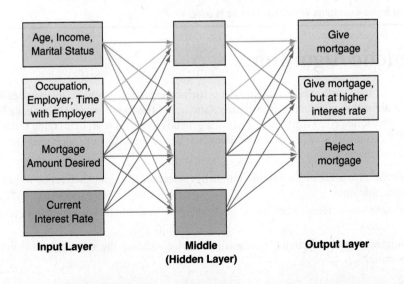

Input Layer

Middle (Hidden Layer)

Output Layer

FIGURE TG 4.2 Neural network.

trained, the strengths, or *weights*, of its connections change. In our example, the input nodes are age, income, occupation, marital status, employer, length of time with that employer, the desired amount of the mortgage, and the current interest rate. The neural network has already been trained with data input from many mortgage applications, successful and unsuccessful. That is, the neural network has established a pattern as to which input variables are necessary for a successful mortgage application. Interestingly, the neural network can adjust as both mortgage amounts and interest rates increase or decrease.

before you go on...

1. What are neural networks?
2. Describe how neural networks function.

TG 4.4 Fuzzy Logic

Fuzzy logic is a branch of mathematics that deals with uncertainties by simulating the processes of human reasoning. The rationale behind fuzzy logic is that decision making is not always a matter of black or white, or true or false. Rather, it frequently involves gray areas where the term *maybe* is more appropriate.

A computer programmed to use fuzzy logic precisely defines subjective concepts that humans do not define precisely. For example, for the concept "income," descriptive terms such as "high" and "moderate" are subjective and imprecise. Using fuzzy logic, however, a computer could define "high" incomes as those exceeding $200,000 per year, and "moderate" incomes as those ranging from $150,000 to $200,000 per year. A loan officer at a bank might then use these values when considering a loan application.

Fuzzy logic has also been used in financial analysis and Internet searches. In accounting and finance, fuzzy logic allows you to analyze assets expressed in imprecise values (e.g., intangible ones like goodwill). As an example, Google uses fuzzy logic to locate answers to your search terms, based on your perception of the topic as reflected in how you phrase your query, which determines the relevance of the Web pages that Google delivers to you.

before you go on...

1. What is fuzzy logic?
2. Give some examples where fuzzy logic is used.

TG 4.5 Genetic Algorithms

Recall that an algorithm is a problem-solving method expressed as a finite sequence of steps. A **genetic algorithm** mimics the evolutionary, "survival-of-the-fittest" process to generate increasingly better solutions to a problem. That is, a genetic algorithm is an optimizing method that finds the combination of inputs that produces the best outputs. Genetic algorithms have three functional characteristics:

- Selection (survival of the fittest): The key to selection is to give preference to better and better outcomes.
- Crossover: Combining portions of good outcomes in the hope of creating an even better outcome.
- Mutation: Randomly trying combinations and evaluating the success (or failure) of an outcome.

Genetic algorithms are best suited to decision-making environments in which thousands or millions of solutions are possible. Genetic algorithms can find and evaluate solutions intelligently, and they can process many more possibilities more thoroughly and quickly than a human can. (Users do have to tell the genetic algorithm what constitutes a "good" solution, which could be low cost or high return, or any number of other results.) Let's look at some examples:

- Boeing uses genetic algorithms to design aircraft parts such as the fan blades on its 777 jet. Rolls Royce and Honda also use genetic algorithms in their design processes.

- Retailers such as Marks and Spencer, a British chain with 320 stores, use genetic algorithms to manage their inventories more effectively and to optimize their store displays.

- Air Liquide, a producer of industrial gases, uses genetic algorithms to find optimal production schedules and distribution points in its supply chain. The company, which has 40 plants and 8,000 client sites, must consider factors such as power prices and projections of customer demand, as well as the power costs and efficiency of each plant.

before you go on...

1. What is a genetic algorithm?

2. Give examples of the use of genetic algorithms.

Intelligent Agents

TG 4.6

An **intelligent agent** is a software program that assists you, or acts on your behalf, in performing repetitive computer-related tasks. Intelligent agents often use expert systems and fuzzy logic behind the scenes to create their seemingly intelligent behavior.

You may be familiar with an early type of intelligent agent—the paper clip ("Clippy") that popped up in early versions of Microsoft® Word. For example, if your document appeared as though it was going to be a business letter—that is, if you typed in a date, name, and address—the animated paper clip would offer helpful suggestions on how to proceed. Users objected so strenuously to this primitive intelligent agent that Microsoft eliminated it from subsequent versions.

There are many intelligent agents (also called *bots*), used for a wide variety of tasks. You can view the many different types of available agents by visiting BotSpot (*www.botspot.com*) and SmartBot (*www.smartbot.com*). The following sections examine three types of agents: information agents, monitoring-and-surveillance agents, and user or personal agents.

Information Agents

Information agents search for information and display it to users. The best known information agents are buyer agents. A **buyer agent**, also called a **shopping bot**, helps customers find the products and services they need on a Web site. There are many examples of information agents. We present a few illustrative cases below.

- The information agents for Amazon.com display lists of books and other products that customers might like, based on past purchases.

- Google and Ask.com use information agents to find information, and not just when you request it. Google, for example, sends out Googlebots to surf all the Web sites in Google's index. These bots copy individual pages to Google's repository, where Google's software indexes them. Therefore, whenever you perform a Google search, the search engine builds a list of all the pages that have the keywords you specify, and it presents them to you in PageRank order. Google's PageRank algorithm sorts Web pages based on the number of links on the Web that point to each page. That is, the more Web links that point to a particular page, the higher that page will be on the list.

- The Federal Electronic Research and Review Extraction Tool, or FERRET, was developed jointly by the Census Bureau and the Bureau of Labor Statistics. You can use FERRET to find information on employment, healthcare, education, race and ethnicity, health insurance, housing, income and poverty, aging, and marriage and the family.

Monitoring-and-Surveillance Agents

Monitoring-and-surveillance agents, also called **predictive agents**, constantly observe and report on some item of interest. There are many examples of predictive agents. Consider the following:

- Allstate uses monitoring-and-surveillance agents to manage its large computer networks 24/7/365. Every 5 seconds, the agent measures 1,200 data points. It can predict a system crash 45 minutes before it happens. The agent also watches to detect electronic attacks early so that they can be prevented.
- Monitoring-and-surveillance agents can watch your competitors and notify you of price changes and special offers.
- Predictive agents can monitor Internet sites, discussion groups, and mailing lists for stock manipulations, insider trading, and rumors that might affect stock prices.
- These agents can search Web sites for updated information on topics of your choice, such as price changes on desired products (e.g., airline tickets).

User Agents

User agents, also called **personal agents**, take action on your behalf. Let's look at what these agents can do (or will be able to do shortly).

- Check your e-mail, sort it according to your priority rules, and alert you when high-value e-mails appear in your in-box.
- Automatically fill out forms on the Web for you. They also will store your information for future use.

before you go on...

1. Define intelligent agents, information agents, monitoring-and-surveillance agents, and user agents.

2. Explain the uses of each type of intelligent agent.

What's In IT For Me?

For the Accounting Major
ACCT
Intelligent systems are used extensively in auditing to uncover irregularities. They also are used to uncover and prevent fraud. Today's CPAs use intelligent systems for many of their duties, ranging from risk analysis to cost control. Accounting personnel also use intelligent agents for mundane tasks such as managing accounts and monitoring employees' Internet use.

For the Finance Major
FIN
People have been using computers for decades to solve financial problems. Innovative intelligent applications have been developed for activities such as making stock market decisions, refinancing bonds, assessing debt risks, analyzing financial conditions, predicting business failures, forecasting financial trends, and investing in global markets. Often, intelligent systems can facilitate the use of spreadsheets and other computerized systems used in finance. Finally, intelligent systems can help reduce fraud in credit cards, stocks, and other financial services.

For the Marketing Major

Marketing personnel use intelligent systems in many applications, from allocating advertising budgets to evaluating alternative routings of salespeople. New marketing approaches such as targeted marketing and marketing transaction databases are heavily dependent on IT in general and on intelligent systems in particular. Intelligent systems are especially useful for mining customer databases and predicting customer behavior. Successful applications appear in almost every area of marketing and sales, from analyzing the success of one-to-one advertising to supporting customer help desks. With customer service becoming increasingly important, the use of intelligent agents is critical for providing fast response.

For the Production/Operations Management Major

Intelligent systems support complex operations and production decisions, from inventory to production planning. Many of the early expert systems in the production/operations management field were developed for tasks ranging from diagnosing machine failures and prescribing repairs to complex production scheduling and inventory control. Some companies, such as DuPont and Kodak, have deployed hundreds of ESs in the planning, organizing, and control of their operational systems.

For the Human Resources Management Major

Human resources personnel employ intelligent systems for many applications. For example, recruiters use these systems to find applicants' resumes on the Web and sort them to match needed skills. Expert systems are also used in evaluating candidates (tests, interviews). HR personnel use intelligent systems to train and support employees in managing their fringe benefits. In addition, they use neural networks to predict employee job performance and future labor needs.

For the MIS Major

The MIS function develops (or acquires) and maintains the organization's various intelligent systems, as well as the data and models that these systems use. In addition, MIS staffers sometimes interact with subject-area experts to capture the expertise used in expert systems.

[Summary]

1. **Explain the potential value and the potential limitations of artificial intelligence.**

   Table TG 4.1 differentiates between artificial and human intelligence on a number of characteristics.

2. **Provide examples of the benefits, applications, and limitations of expert systems.**

   Expert systems are computer systems that attempt to mimic human experts by applying expertise in a specific domain. Tables TG 4.2 and TG 4.3 offer examples of expert systems.

3. **Provide examples of the use of neural networks.**

   A neural network is a system of programs and data structures that simulate the underlying concepts of the human brain. Neural networks are used to detect weapons concealed in personal belongings, in research on various diseases, for financial forecasting, to detect fraud in credit card transactions, to fight crime, and many other applications.

4. **Provide examples of the use of fuzzy logic.**

   Fuzzy logic is a branch of mathematics that deals with uncertainties by simulating the process of human reasoning. Fuzzy logic is used in financial analysis, the manufacture of antilock brakes, measuring intangible assets like goodwill, and finding responses to search terms in Google.

5. **Describe the situations in which genetic algorithms would be most useful.**

A genetic algorithm is an intelligent system that mimics the evolutionary, survival-of-the-fittest process to generate increasingly better solutions to a problem. Genetic algorithms are used to design aircraft parts such as fan blades, to manage inventories more effectively, to optimize store displays, and to find optimal production schedules and distribution points.

6. **Describe the use case for several major types of intelligent agents.**

An intelligent agent is a software program that assists you, or acts on your behalf, in performing repetitive, computer-related tasks. Intelligent agents are used to display lists of books or other products that customers might like, based on past purchases; to find information; to manage and monitor large computer networks 24/7/365; to detect electronic attacks early so they can be stopped; to watch competitors and send notices of price changes and special offers; to monitor Internet sites, discussion groups, and mailing lists for stock manipulations, insider trading, and rumors that might impact stock prices; to check e-mail, sort it according to established priority rules, and alert recipients when high-value e-mails appear in their inbox; and to automatically fill out forms on the Web.

[Chapter Glossary]

algorithm A problem-solving method expressed as a finite sequence of steps.

artificial intelligence (AI) A subfield of computer science that is concerned with studying the thought processes of humans and re-creating the effects of those processes via machines, such as computers.

buyer agent (or shopping bot) An intelligent agent on a Web site that helps customers find products and services that they need.

expert systems (ESs) Computer systems that attempt to mimic human experts by applying expertise in a specific domain.

fuzzy logic A branch of mathematics that deals with uncertainties by simulating the processes of human reasoning.

genetic algorithm An approach that mimics the evolutionary, "survival-of-the-fittest" process to generate increasingly better solutions to a problem.

information agent A type of intelligent agent that searches for information and displays it to users.

intelligent agent A software program that assists you, or acts on your behalf, in performing repetitive, computer-related tasks.

intelligent systems A term that describes the various commercial applications of artificial intelligence.

monitoring-and-surveillance agents (or predictive agents) Intelligent agents that constantly observe and report on some item of interest.

neural network A system of programs and data structures that simulates the underlying concepts of the human brain.

personal agents (see **user agents**)

predictive agents (see **monitoring-and-surveillance agents**)

shopping bot (see **buyer agent**)

Turing test A test in which a man and a computer both pretend to be women (or men), and the human interviewer has to decide which is the real human.

user agents (or personal agents) Intelligent agents that take action on your behalf.

[Discussion Questions]

1. Explain how your university could employ an expert system in its admission process. Could it use a neural network?

   What might happen if a student were denied admission to the university and his parents discovered that an expert system was involved in the admissions process?

2. One difference between a conventional business intelligence system and an expert system is that the former can explain *how* questions, whereas the latter can explain both *how* and *why* questions. Discuss the implications of this statement.

[Problem-Solving Activities]

1. You have decided to purchase a new video camcorder. To purchase it as inexpensively as possible and still get the features you want, you use a shopping bot. Visit several of the shopping bot Web sites that perform price comparisons for you. Begin with MySimon (*www.mysimon.com*), BizRate. com (*www.bizrate.com*), and Google Product Search.

   Compare these shopping bots in terms of ease of use, number of product offerings, speed in obtaining information, thoroughness of information offered about products and sellers, and price selection. Which site or sites would you use, and why? Which camcorder would you select and buy? How helpful were these sites in making your decision?

2. Access the MyMajors Web site (*www.mymajors.com*). This site contains a rule-based expert system to help students find majors. The expert system has more than 300 rules and 15,000 possible conclusions. The site ranks majors according to the likelihood that a student will succeed in them, and it provides six possible majors from among 60 alternative majors that a student might consider.

   Take the quiz, and see if you are in the "right major" as defined by the expert system. You must register to take the quiz.

3. Access Exsys (*www.exsys.com*), and click on the Corvid Demo (*www.exsyssoftware.com/CORVID52/corvidsr?KBNAME=../ Download2/DownloadForm.cvR*). Provide your e-mail address, and click on the link for "Student—Needed for Class." Try the various demos, and report your results to the class.

[Internship Activity]

Retail Industry

Amazon has huge advantage over bricks and mortar retailers with the intelligent systems they employ. All you have to do is get somewhere close to a product category and their intelligent systems will provide links to products other customers shopped for or bought after they viewed that particular item. Often, in a few clicks you have found a top rated product that you were not aware of a few minutes earlier.

For Harrison Kirby (owner of the golf shop from the Internship Activity from Chapter 7) this causes a real problem. He has a tough time competing with online golf stores because he is not able to carry their amount of inventory nor does he have the amount of data necessary to create these intelligent systems. Harrison is interested in creating a system that would allow his customers to tap into the intelligent systems that are available online but keep his customers in his store for purchases.

Please visit the Book Companion Site to receive the full set of instructions and learn how you can help Harrison develop a plan that would help him compete in such a highly competitive market.

Index

Page numbers in **bold** indicate end of chapter glossary terms.
Page number in *italics* indicate figures.